F L I G H T
V O L U M E   S E V E N

Villard Trade Paperbacks • New York

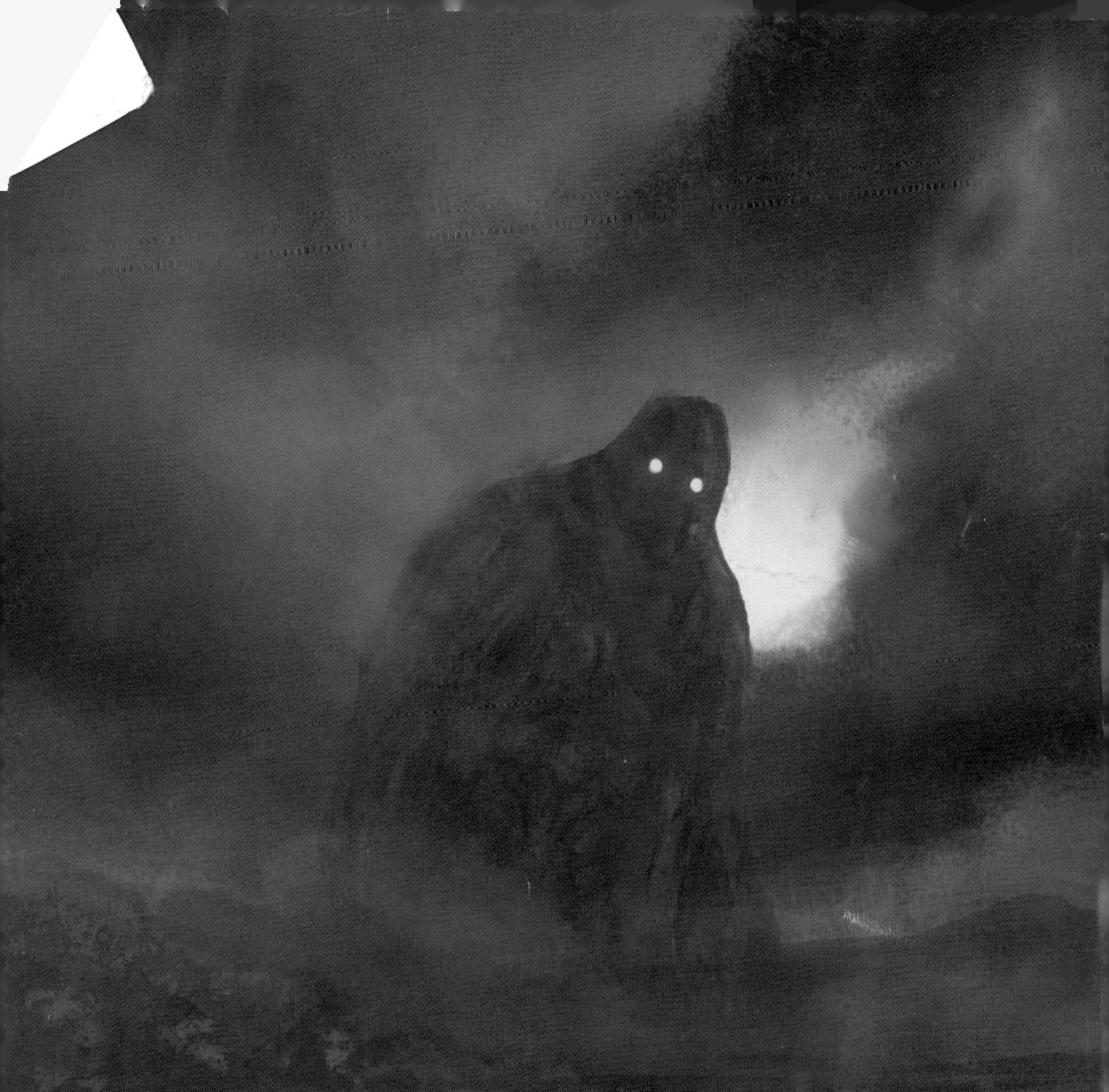

A Villard Books Trade Paperback Original

Published in the United States by Villard Books, an imprint of The Random House Publishing Group, a division of Random House, Inc., New York.

Published by arrangement with Flight Comics LLC.

ISBN 978-0-345-51737-1

Printed in China

www.villardbooks.com

9 8 7 6 5 4 3

Illustration on pages ii–iii by Jason Caffoe
Illustration on page 283 by Phil Craven

Editor/Art Director: Kazu Kibuishi
Assistant Editors: Kean Soo, Phil Craven, and Jason Caffoe
Our Editor at Villard: Chris Schluep

CONTENTS

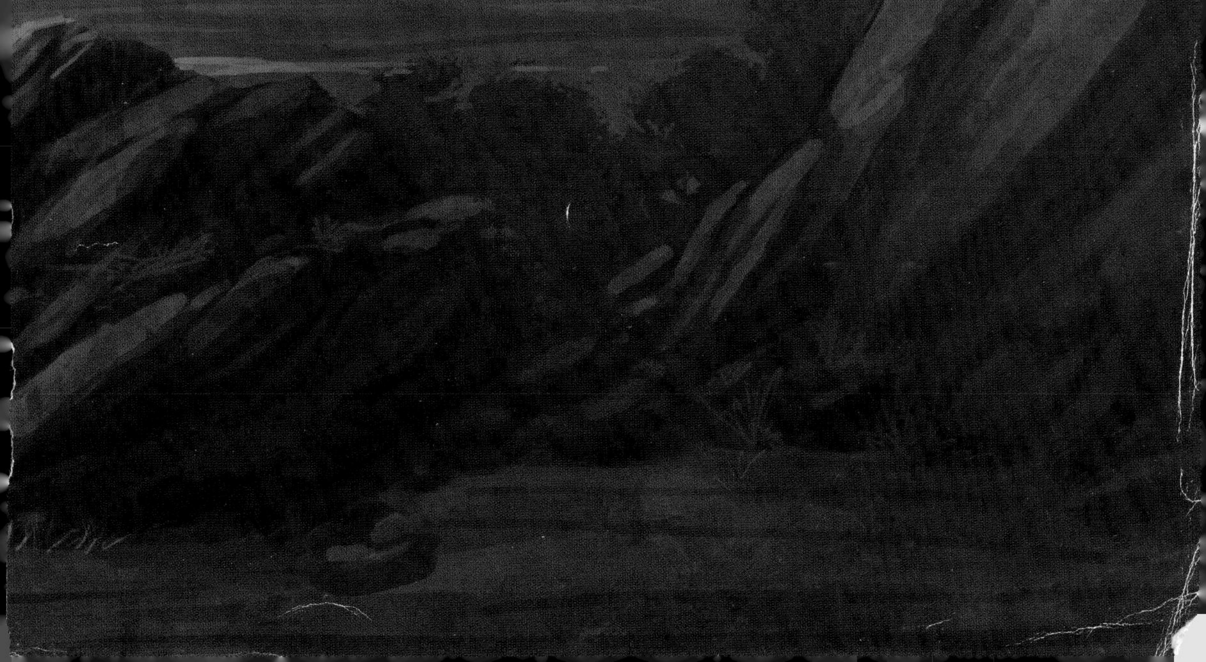

FLIGHT

VOLUME SEVEN

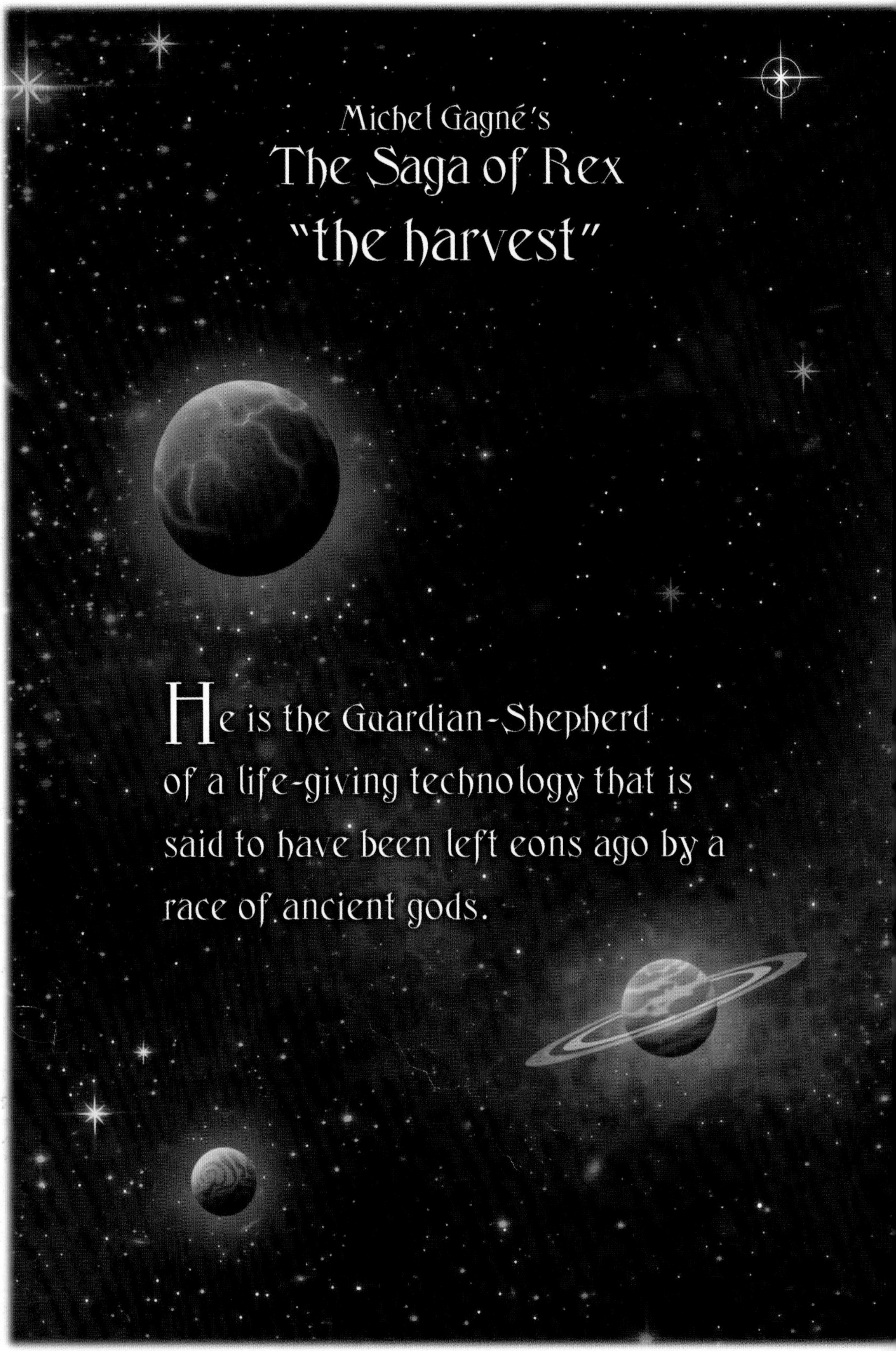
Michel Gagné's
The Saga of Rex
"the harvest"
He is the Guardian-Shepherd of a life-giving technology that is said to have been left eons ago by a race of ancient gods.

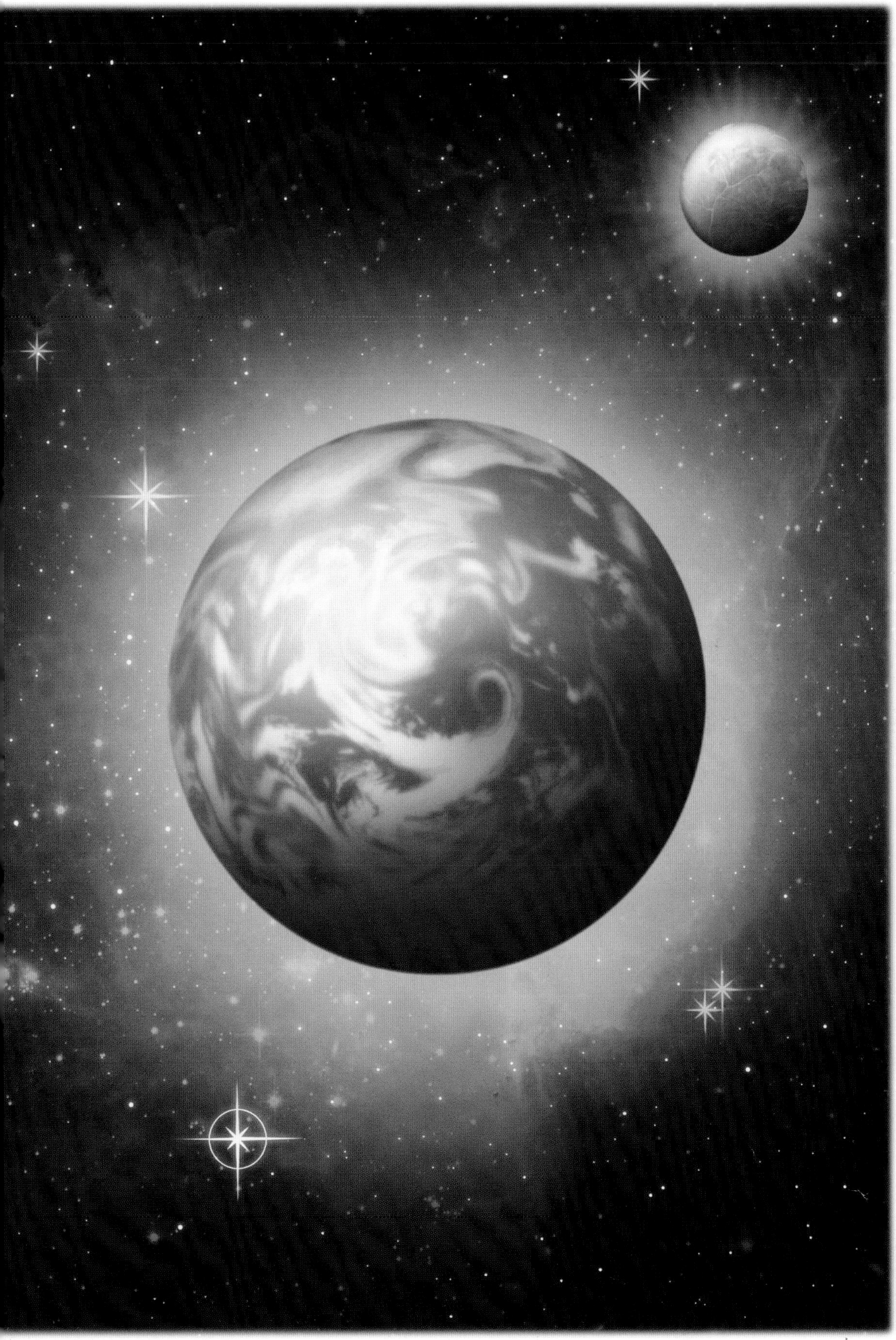

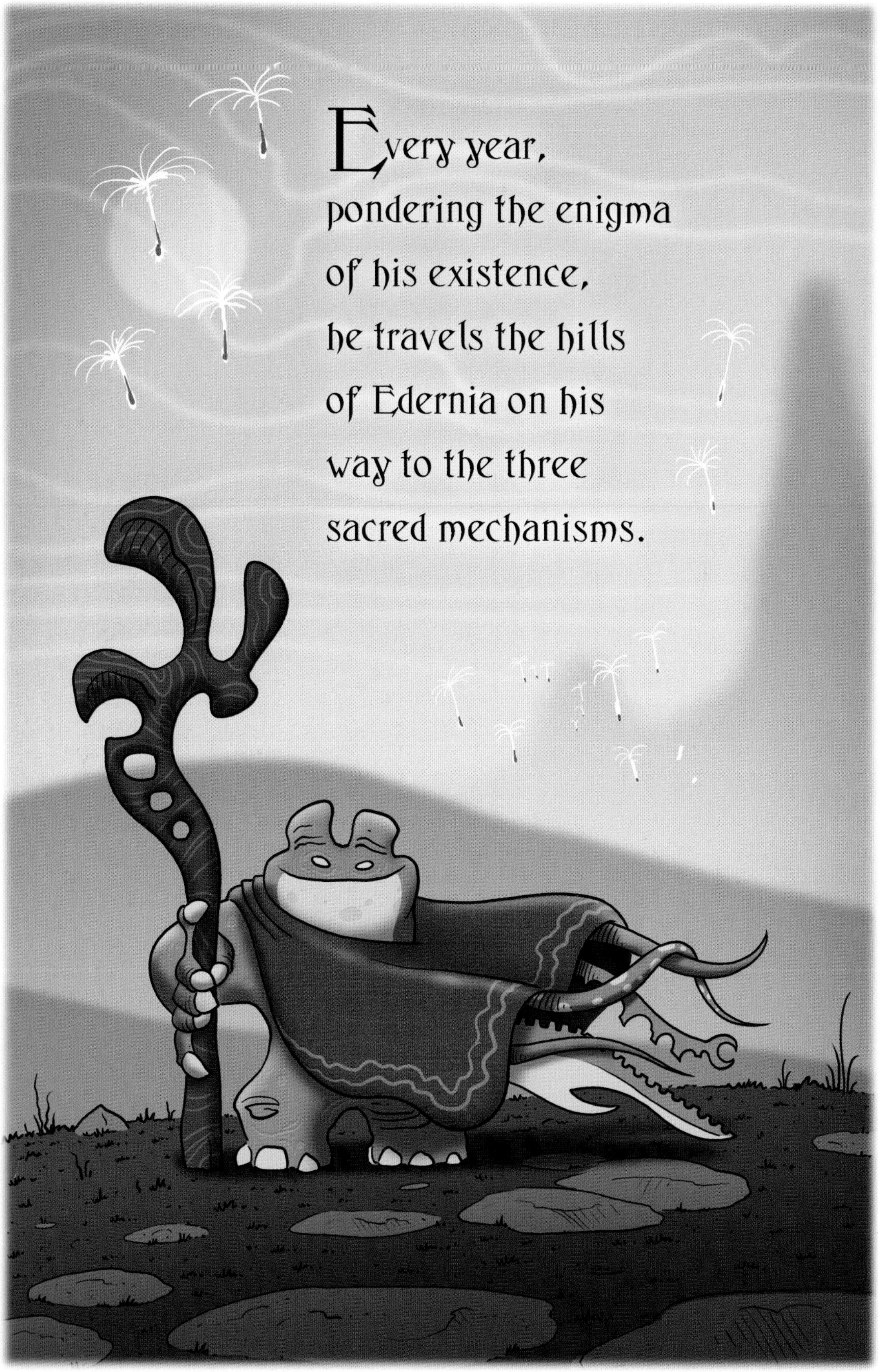

Every year,
pondering the enigma
of his existence,
he travels the hills
of Edernia on his
way to the three
sacred mechanisms.

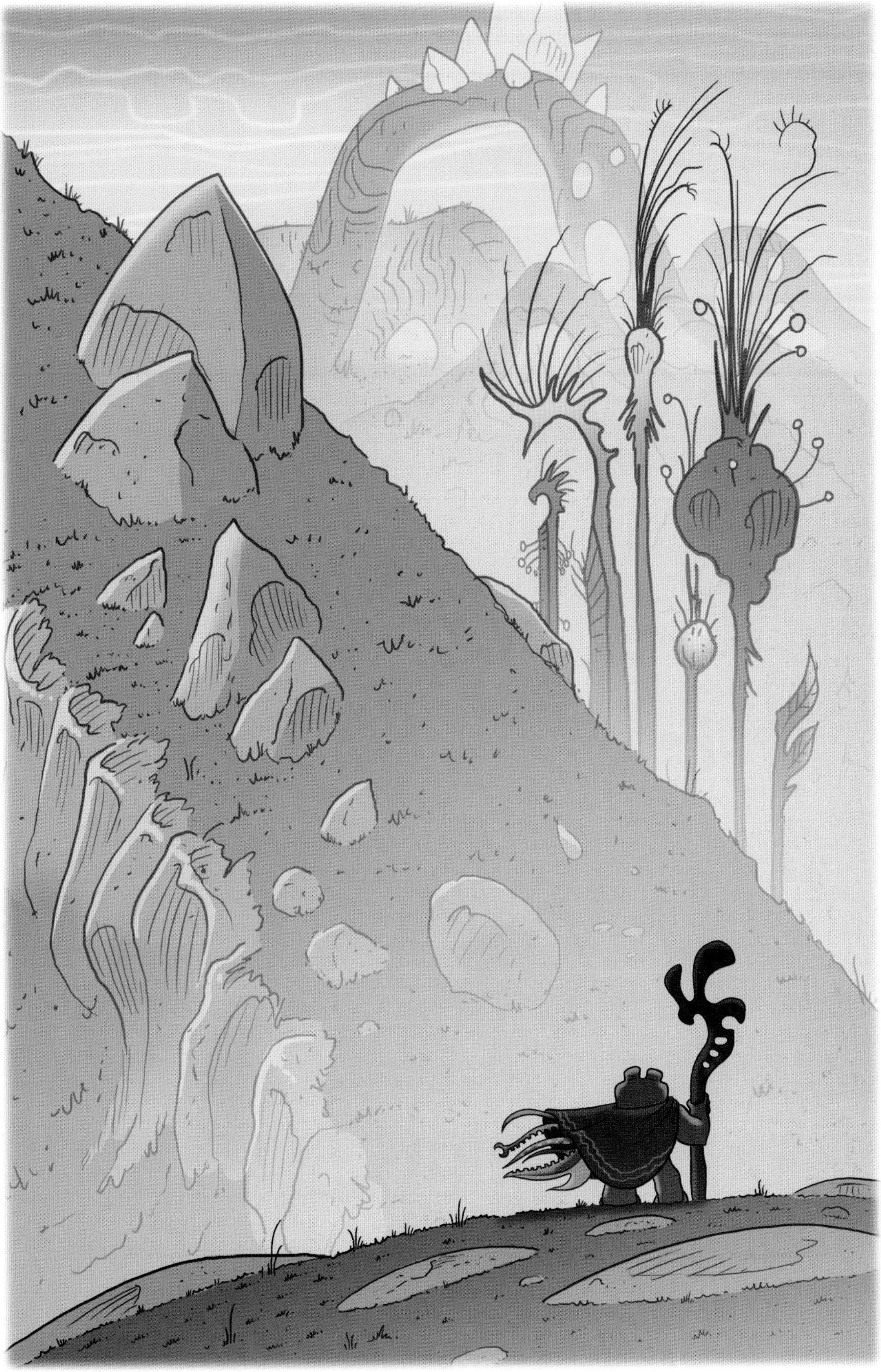

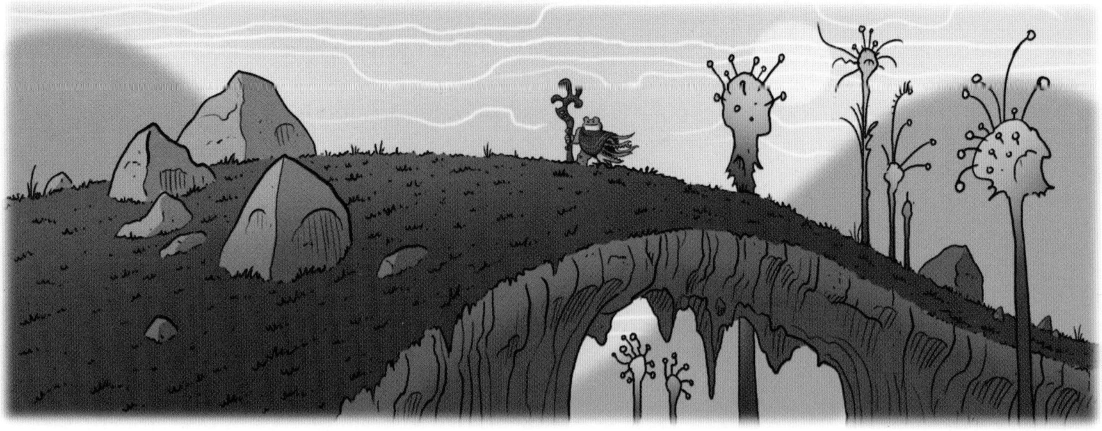

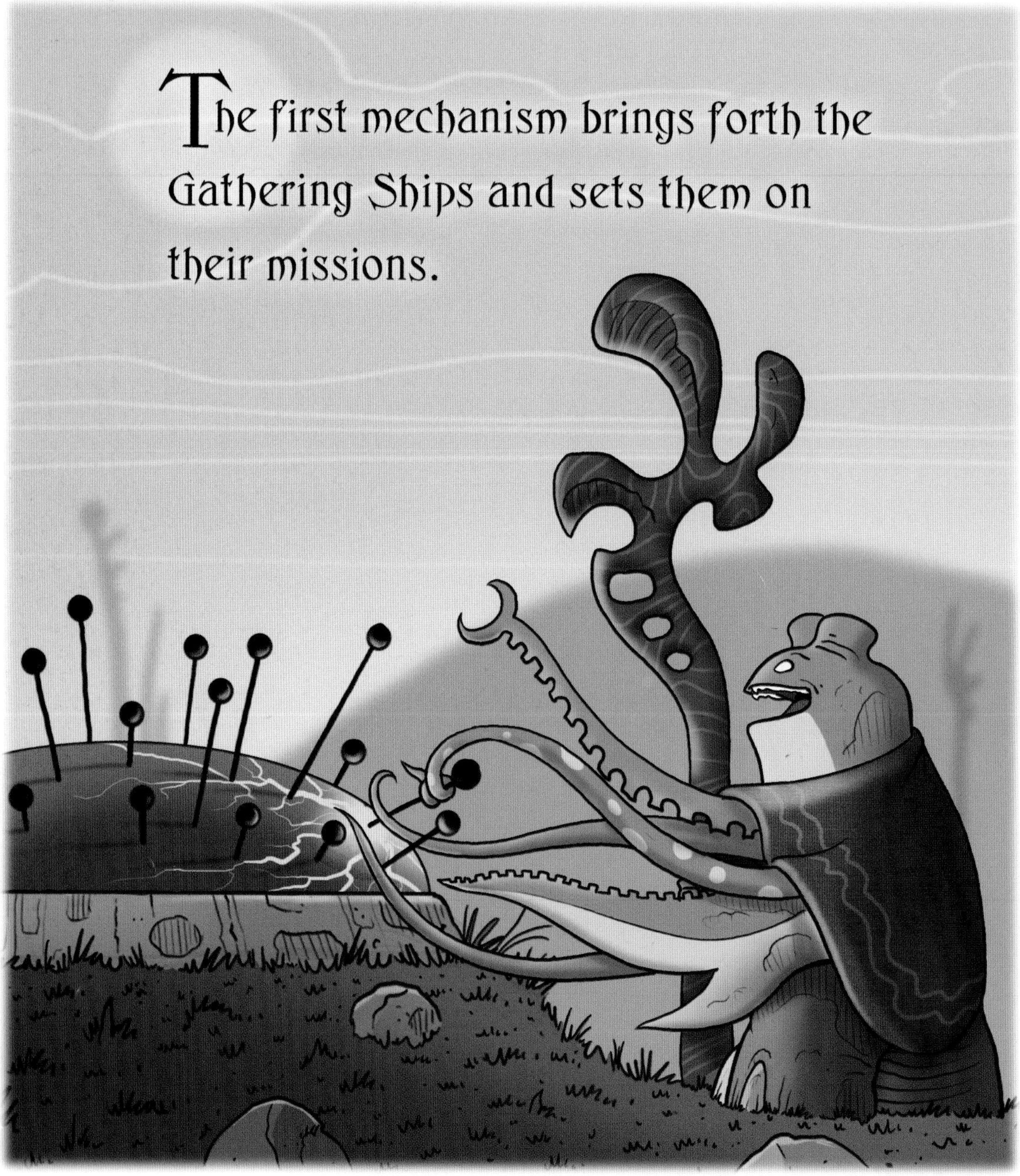

The first mechanism brings forth the Gathering Ships and sets them on their missions.

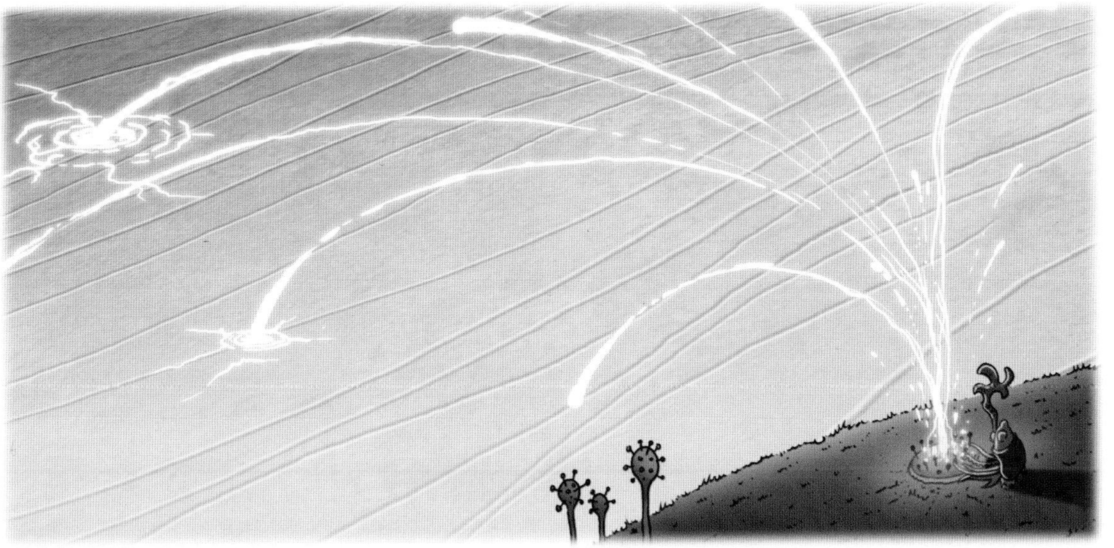

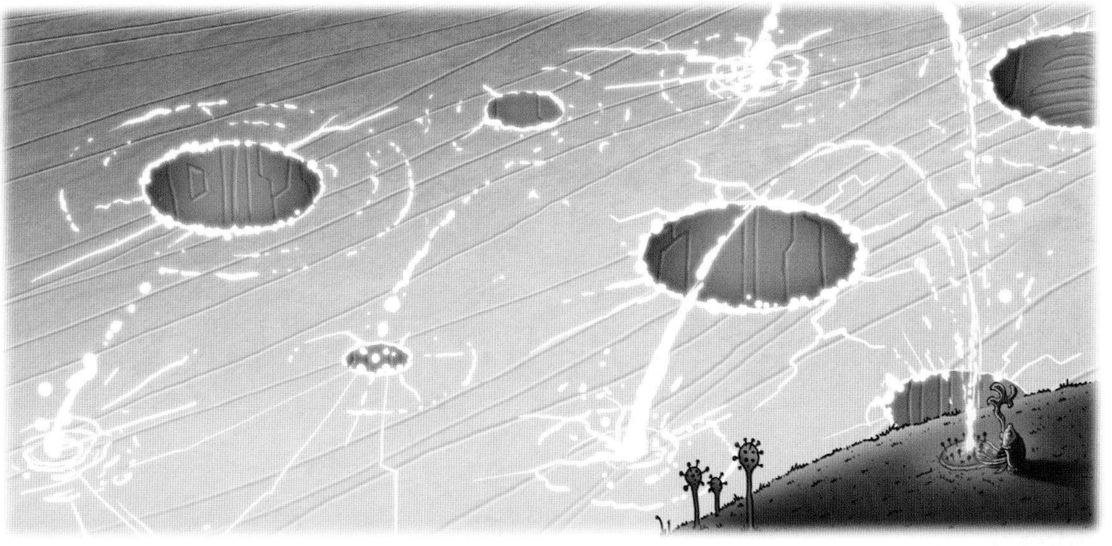

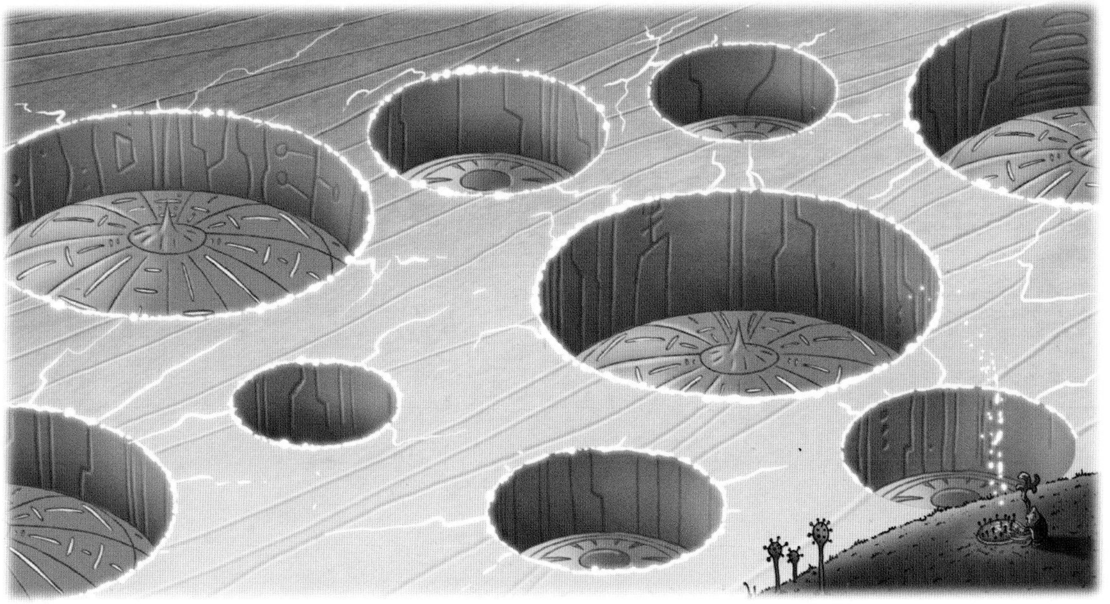

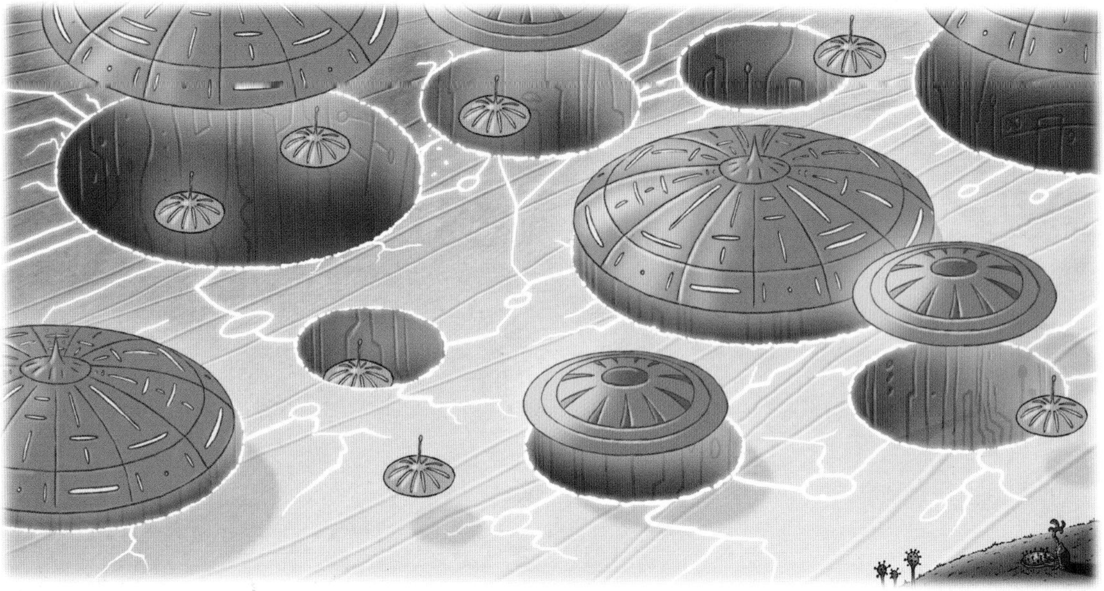

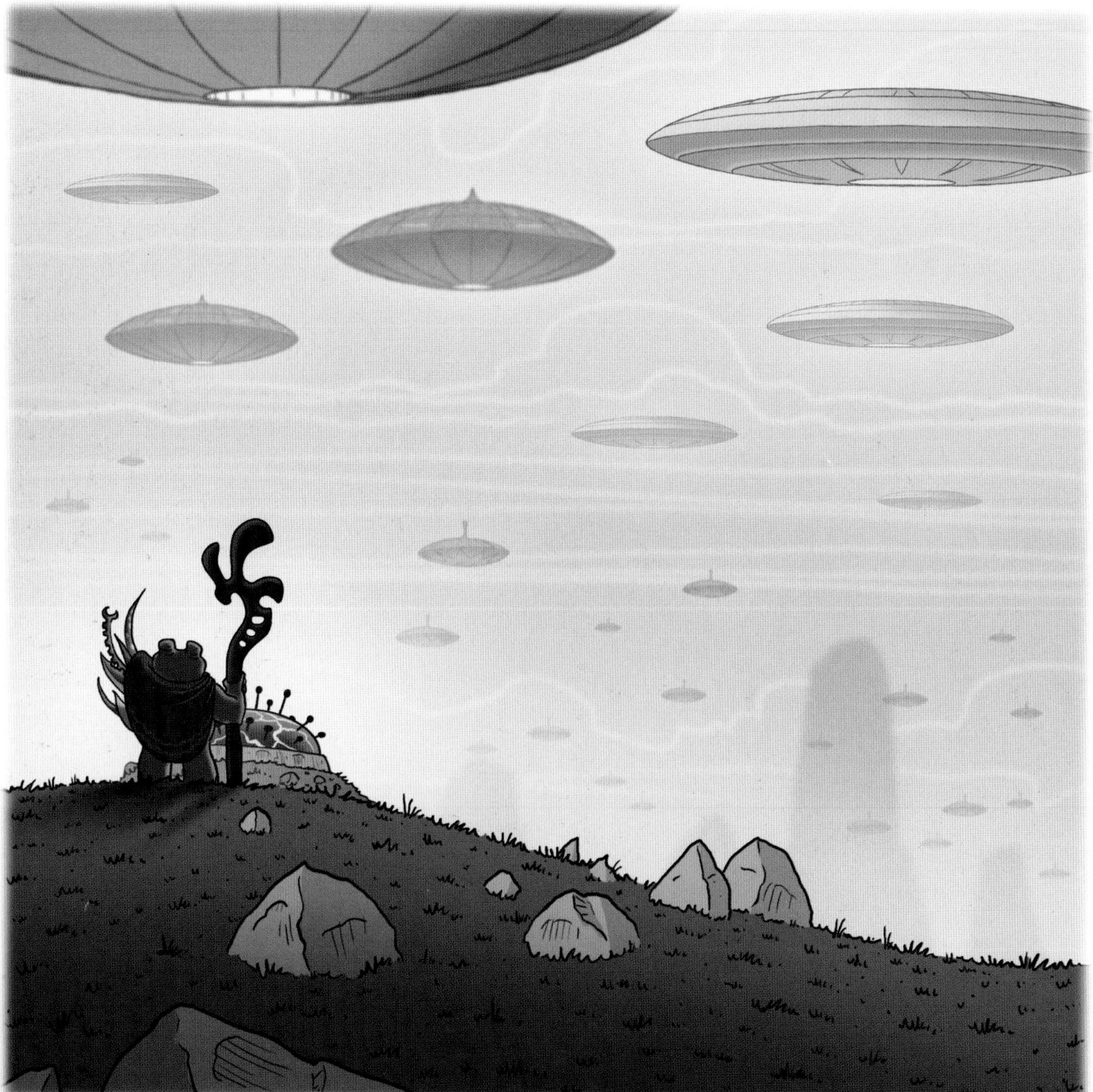

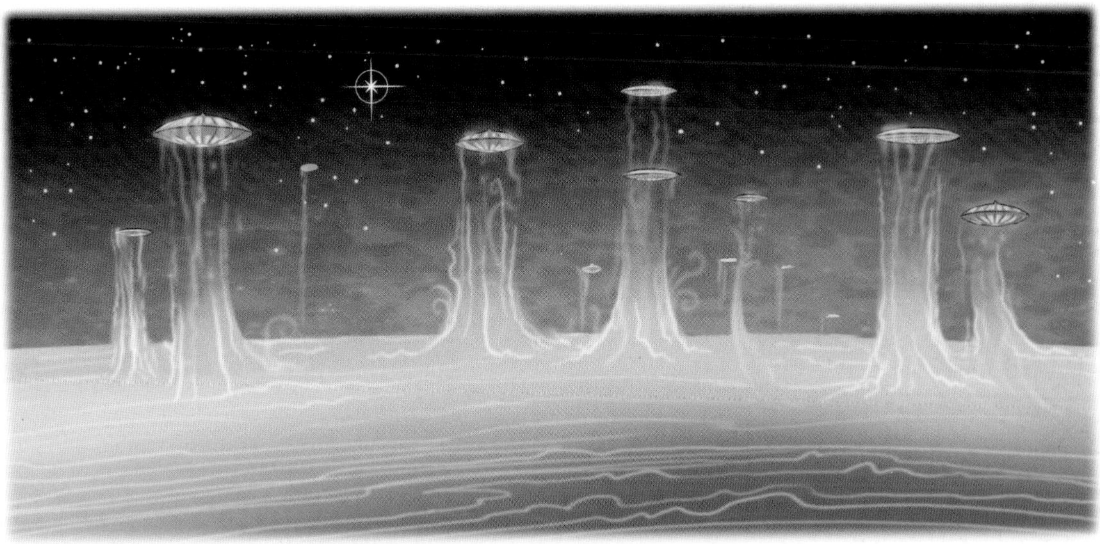

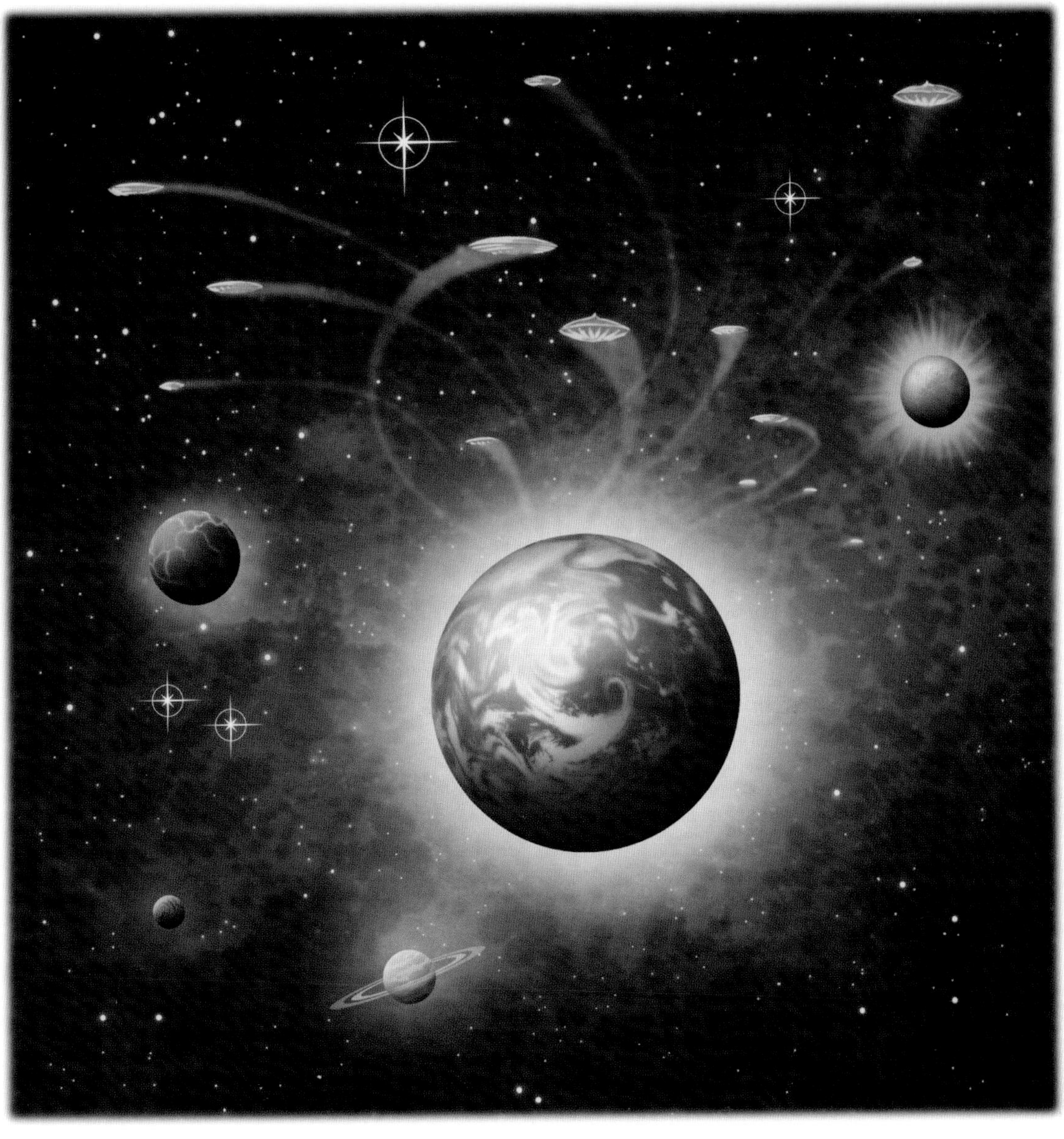

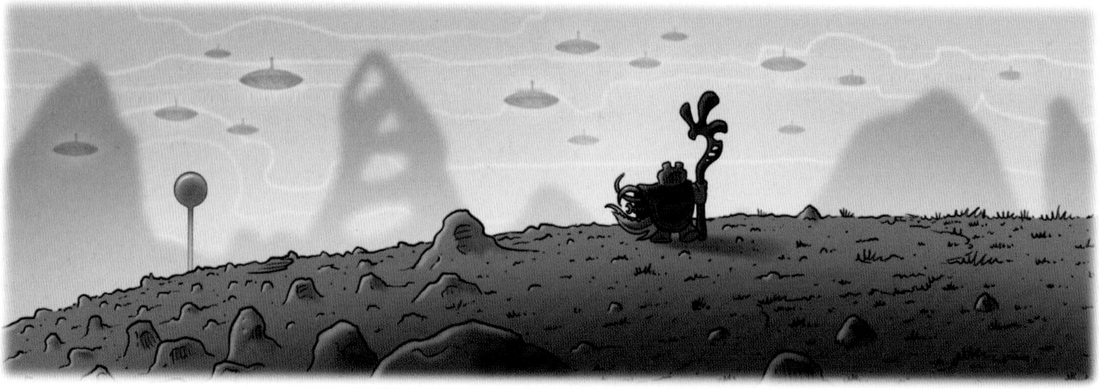

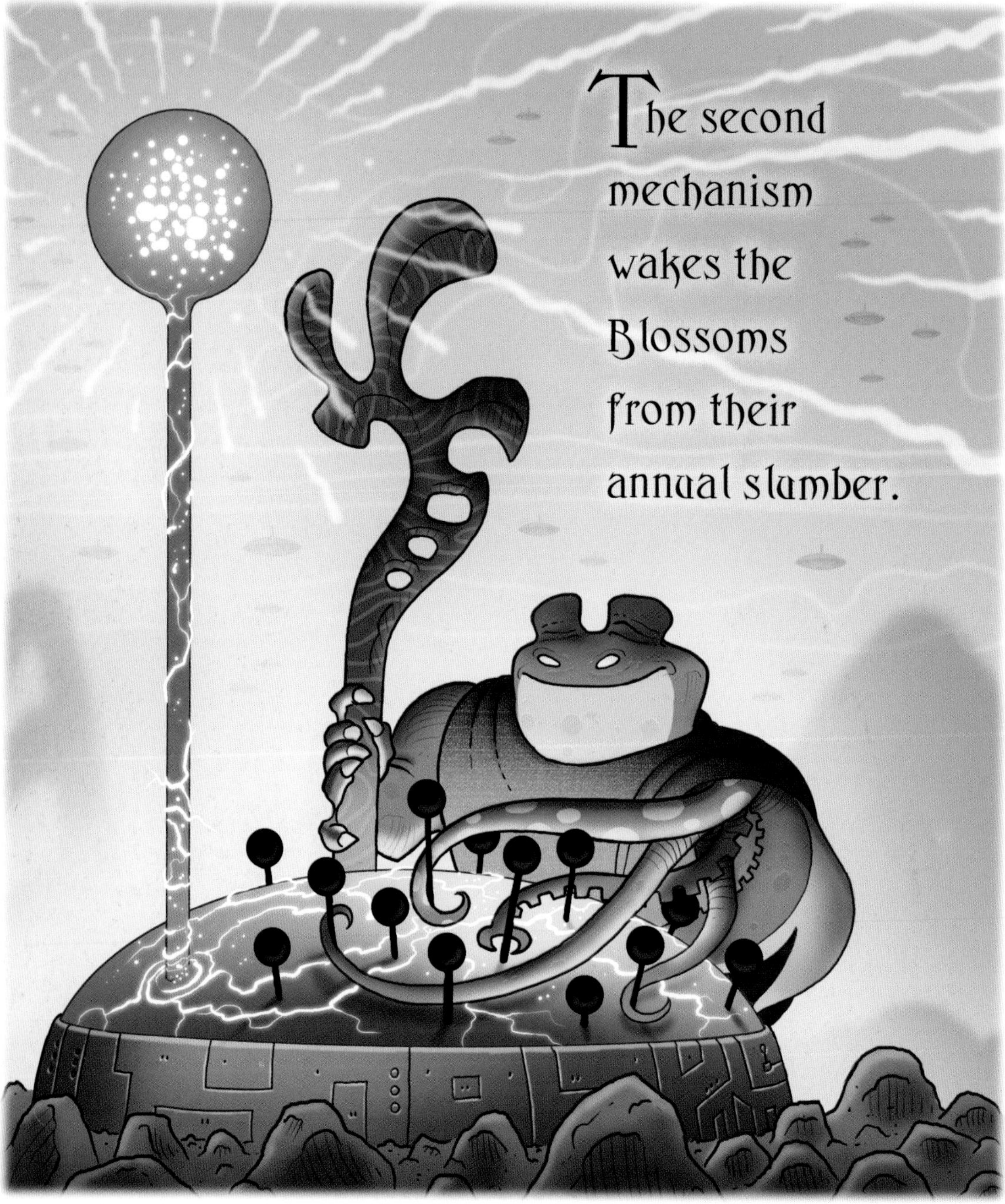
The second mechanism wakes the Blossoms from their annual slumber.

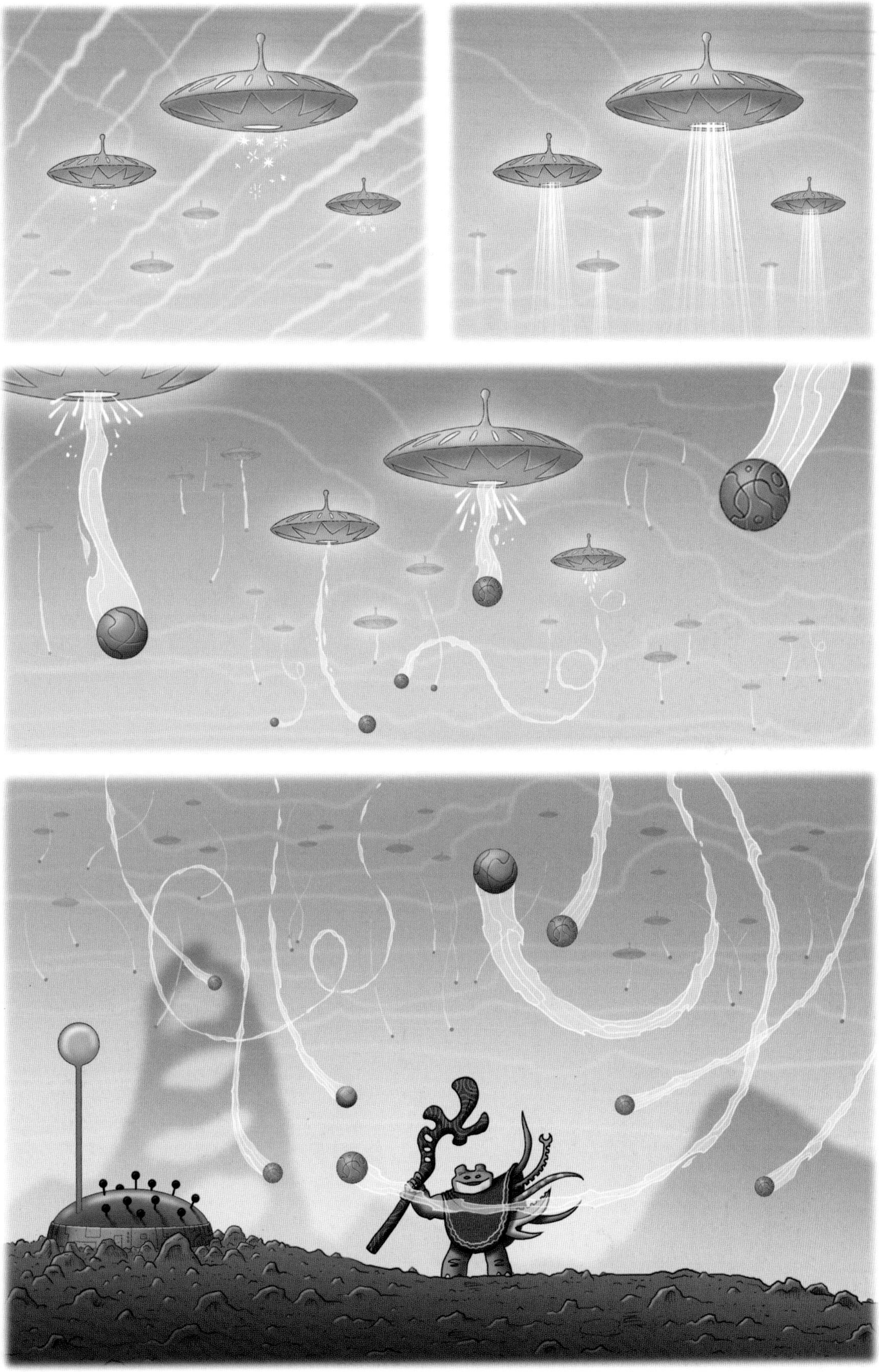

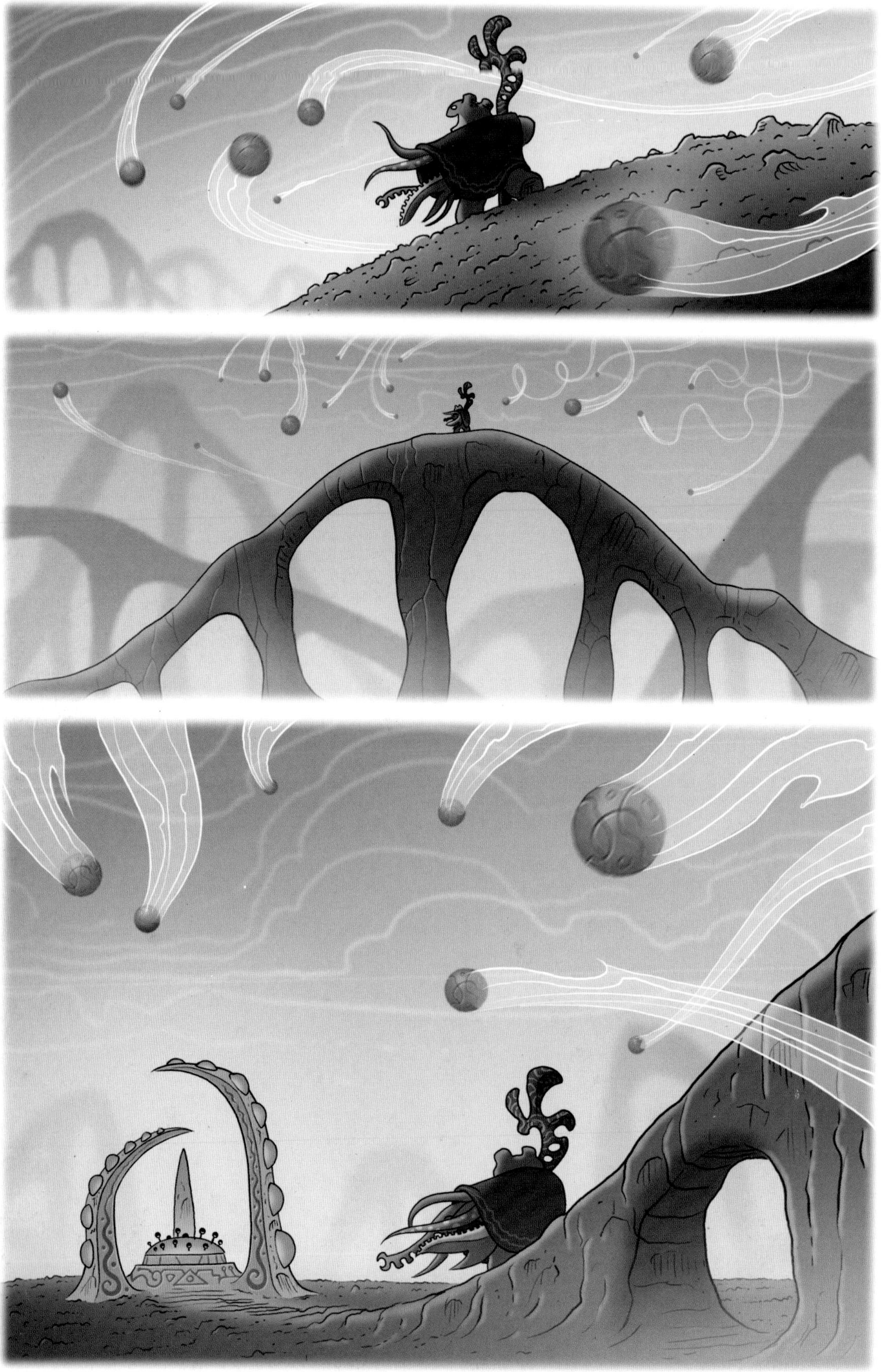

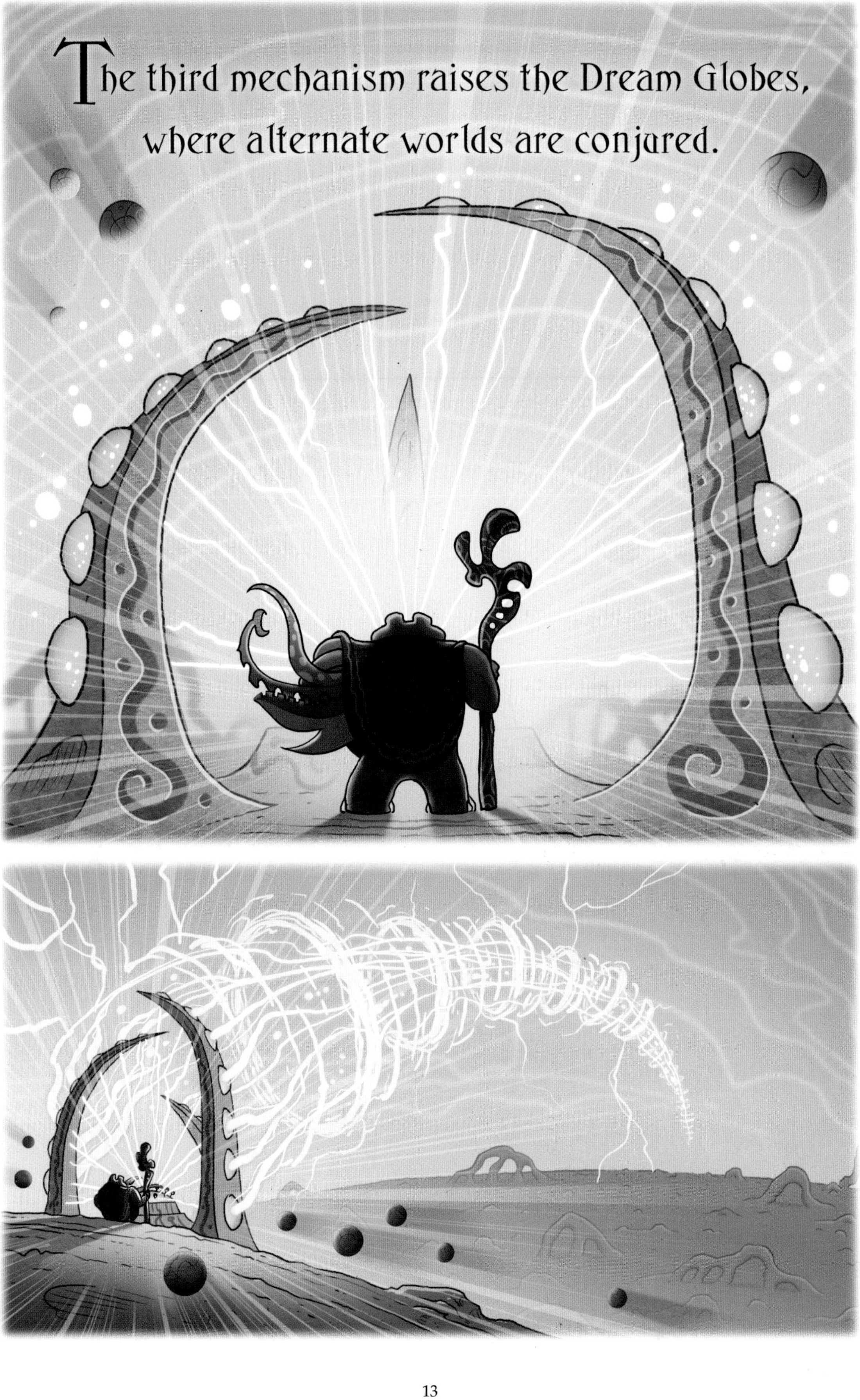
The third mechanism raises the Dream Globes, where alternate worlds are conjured.

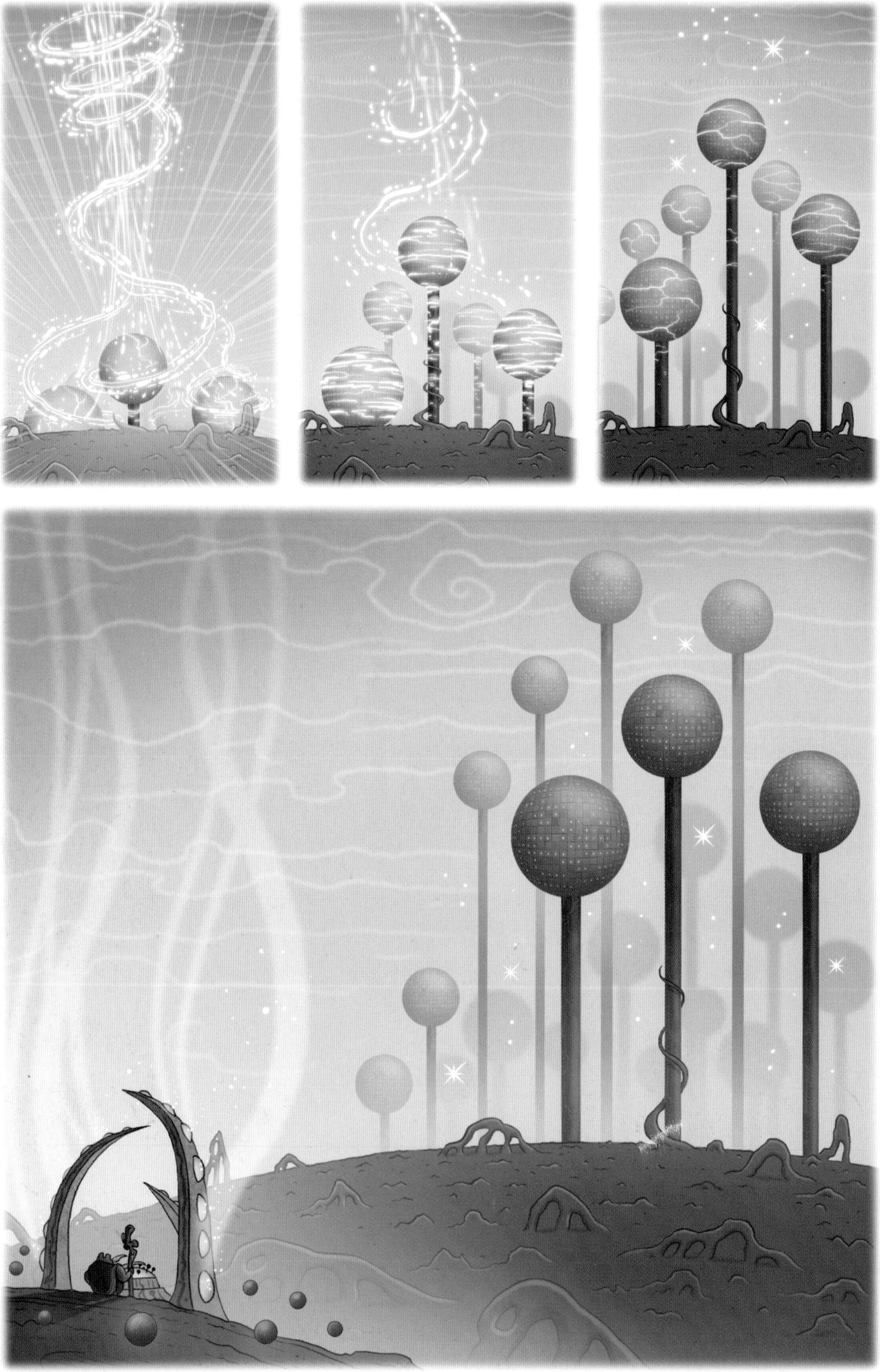

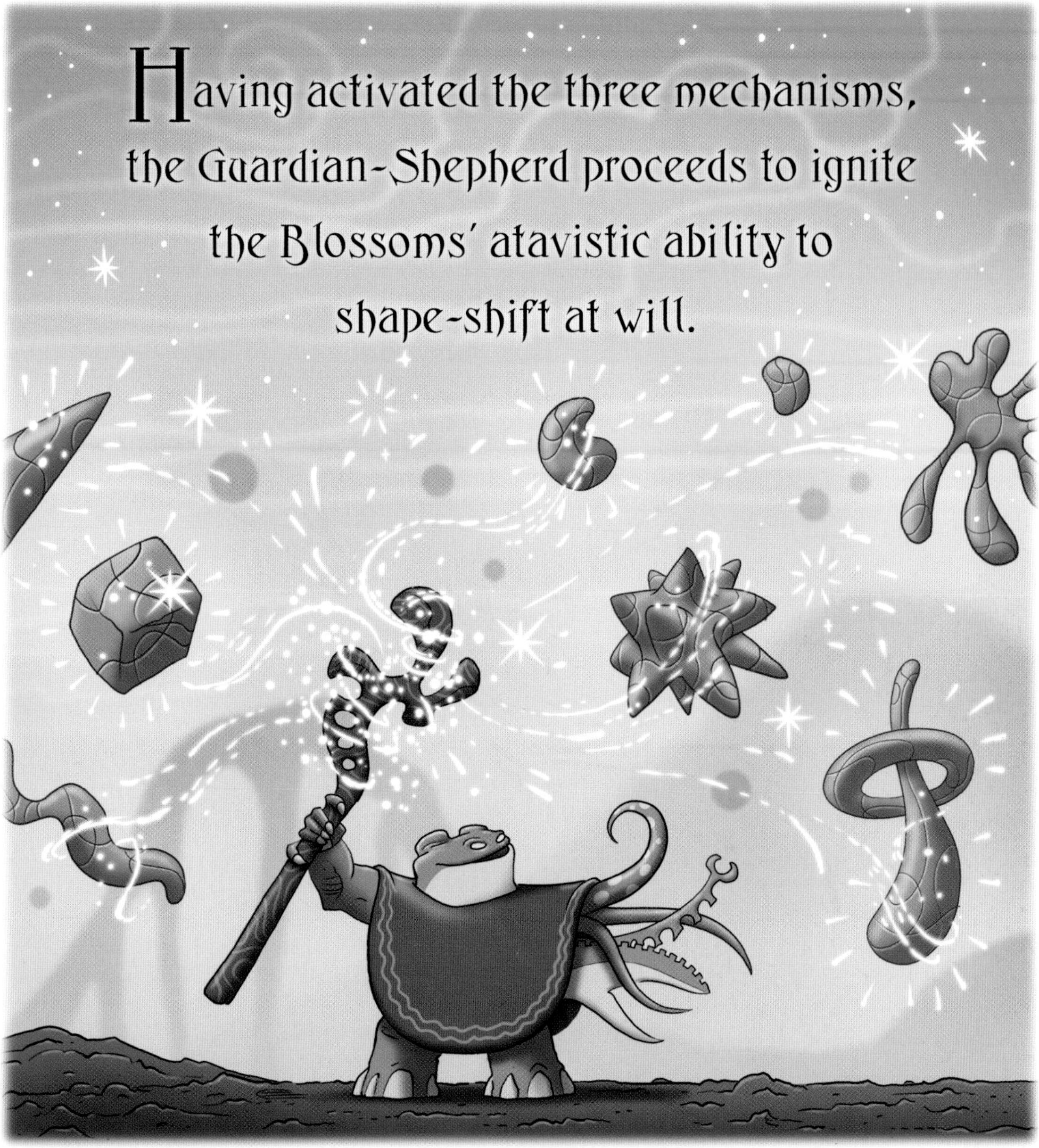
Having activated the three mechanisms,
the Guardian-Shepherd proceeds to ignite
the Blossoms' atavistic ability to
shape-shift at will.

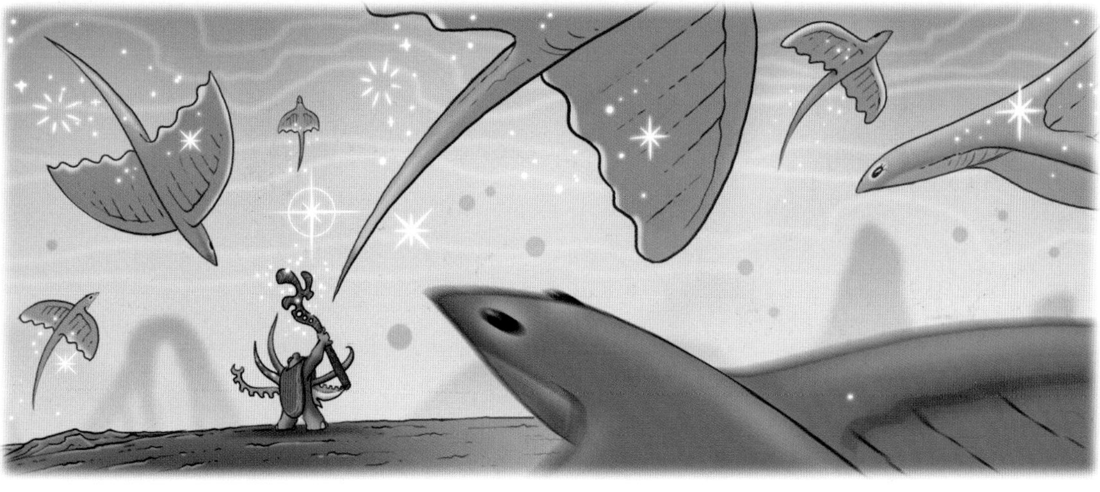

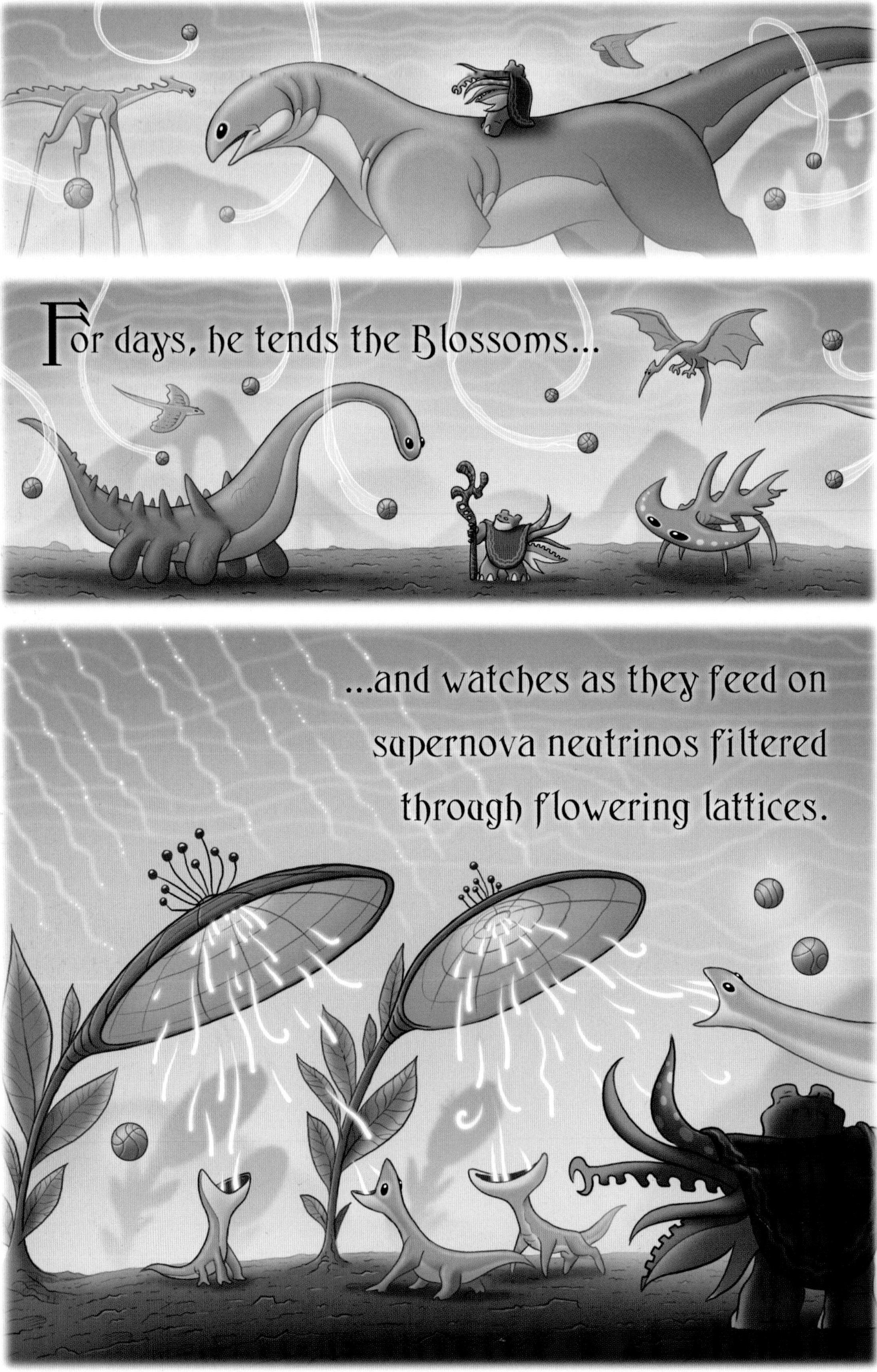
For days, he tends the Blossoms...
...and watches as they feed on supernova neutrinos filtered through flowering lattices.

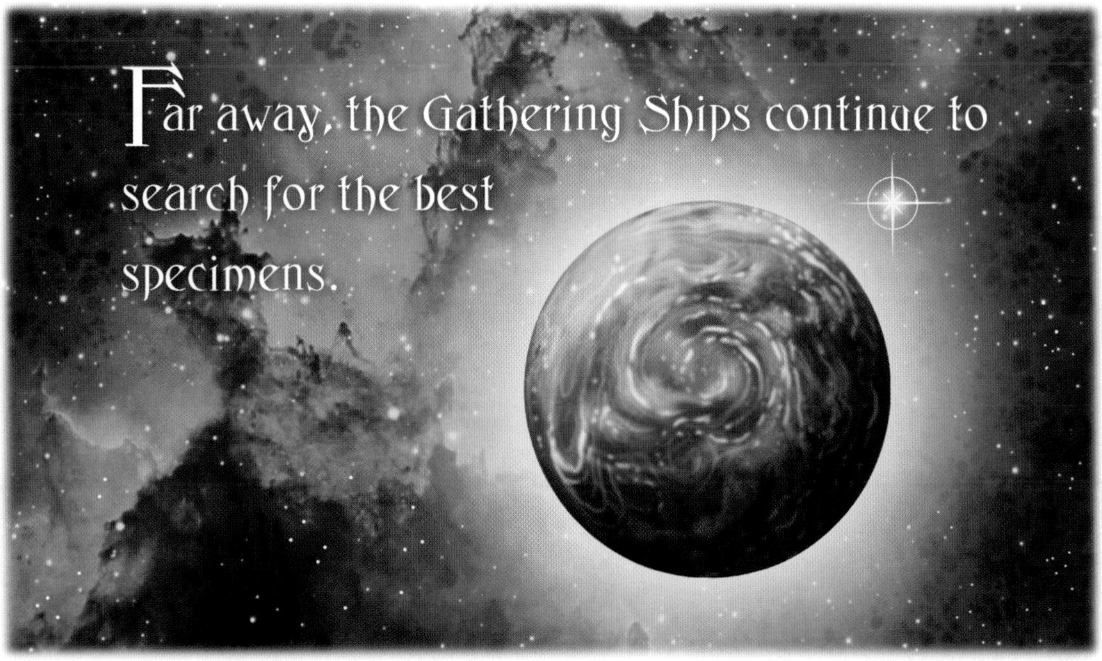
Far away, the Gathering Ships continue to search for the best specimens.

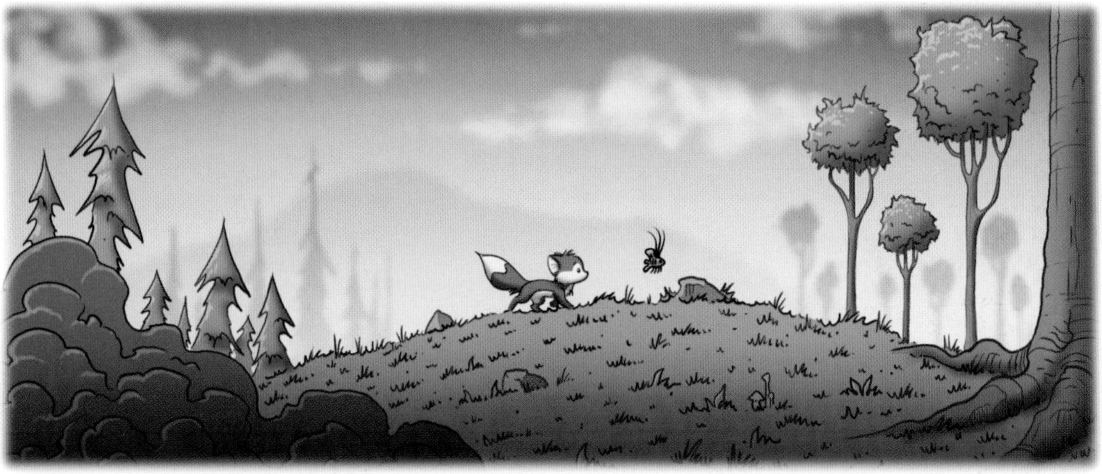

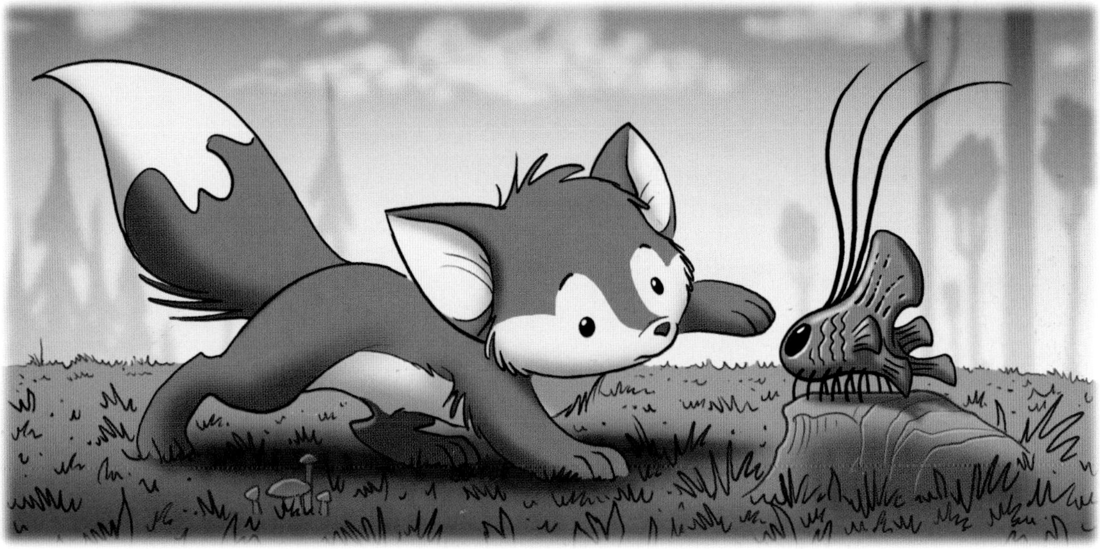

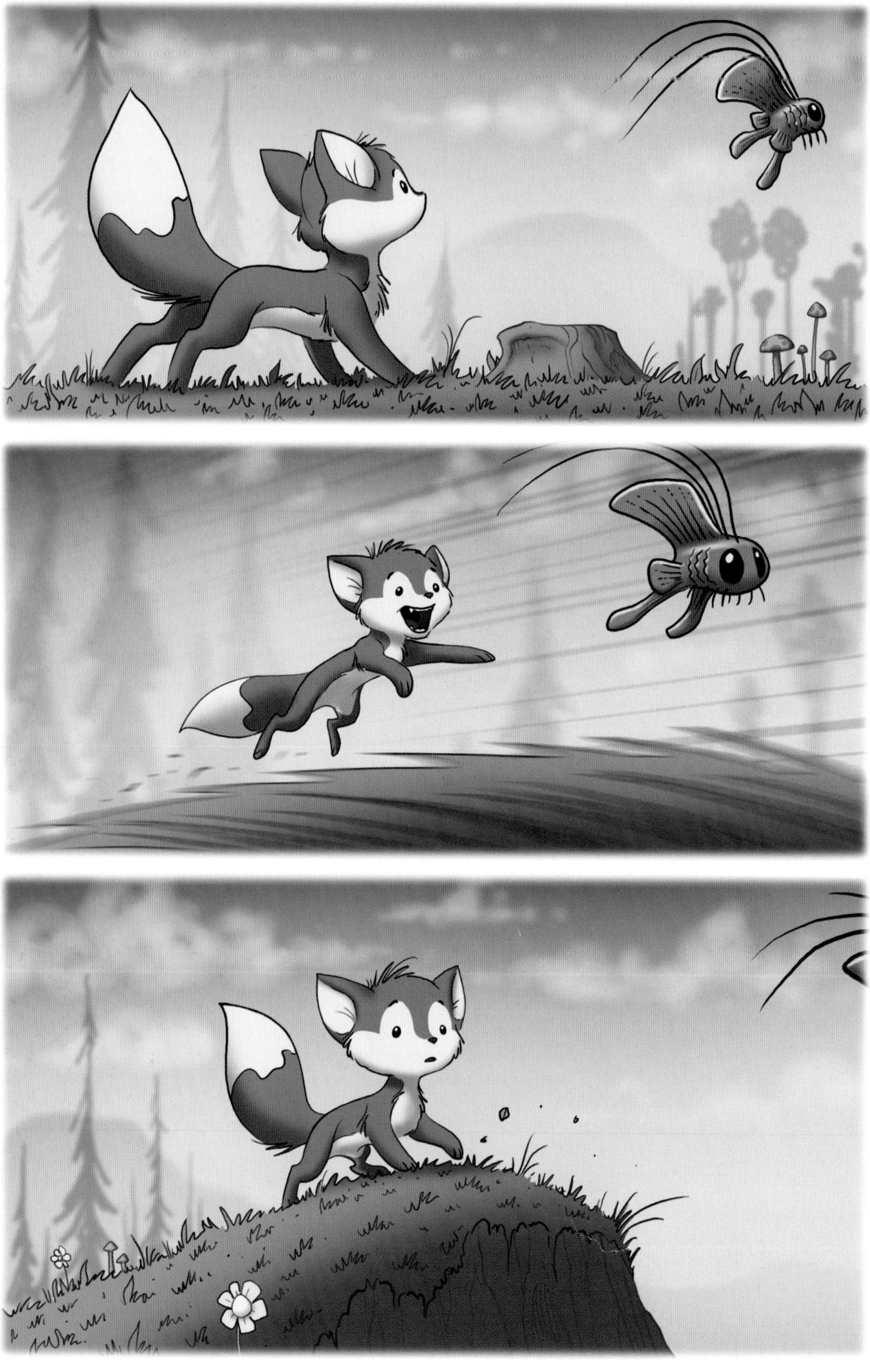

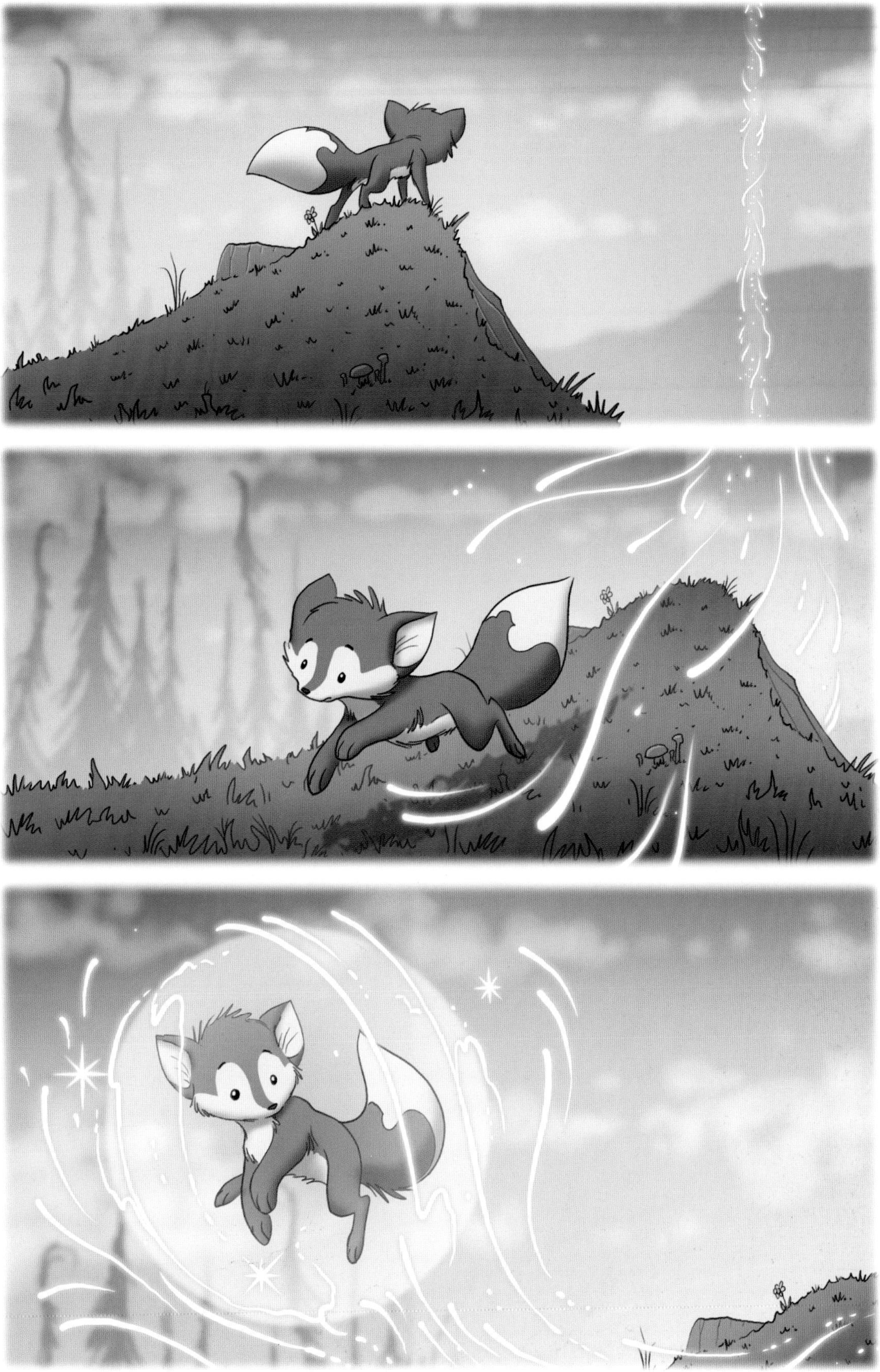

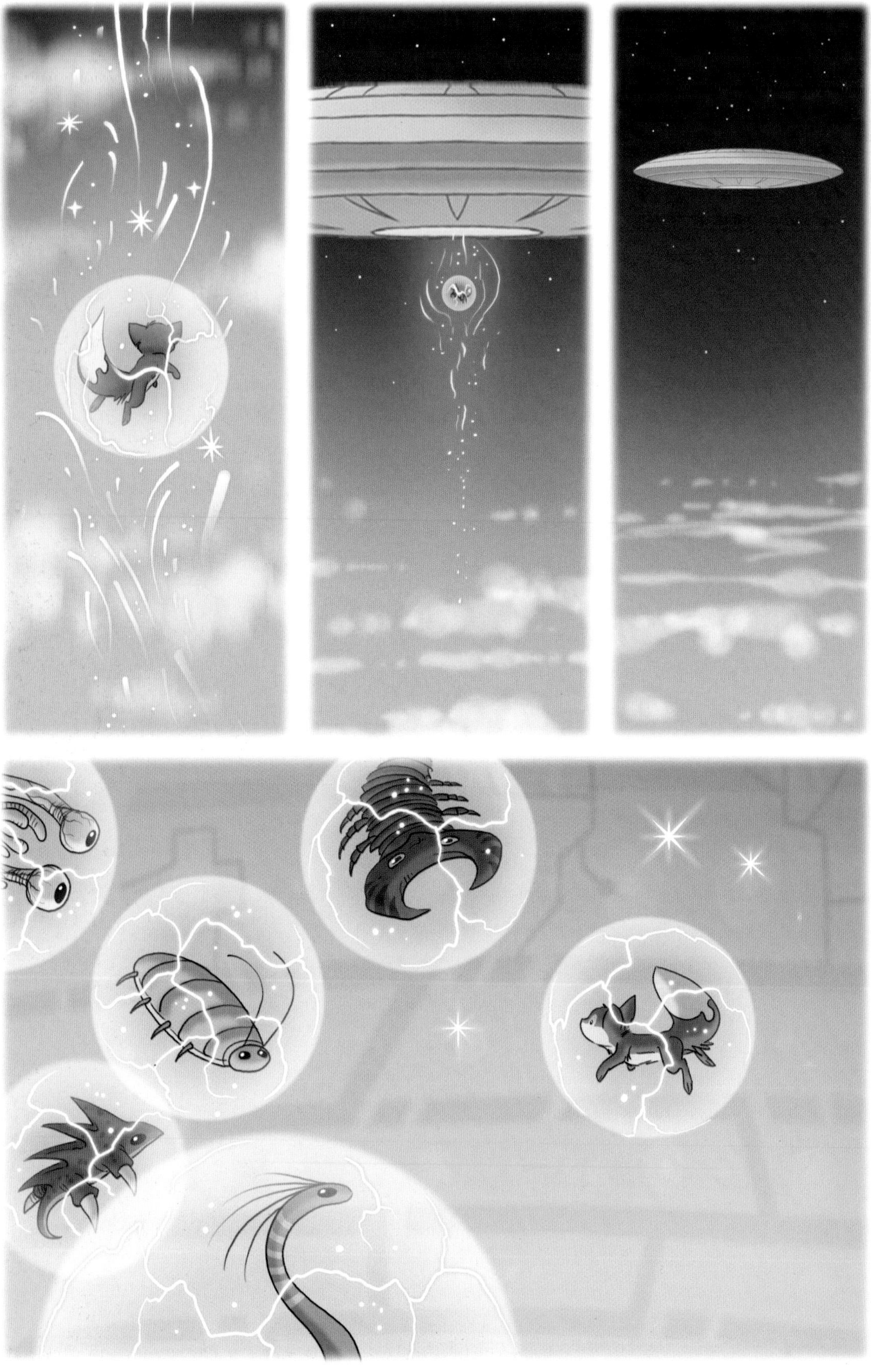

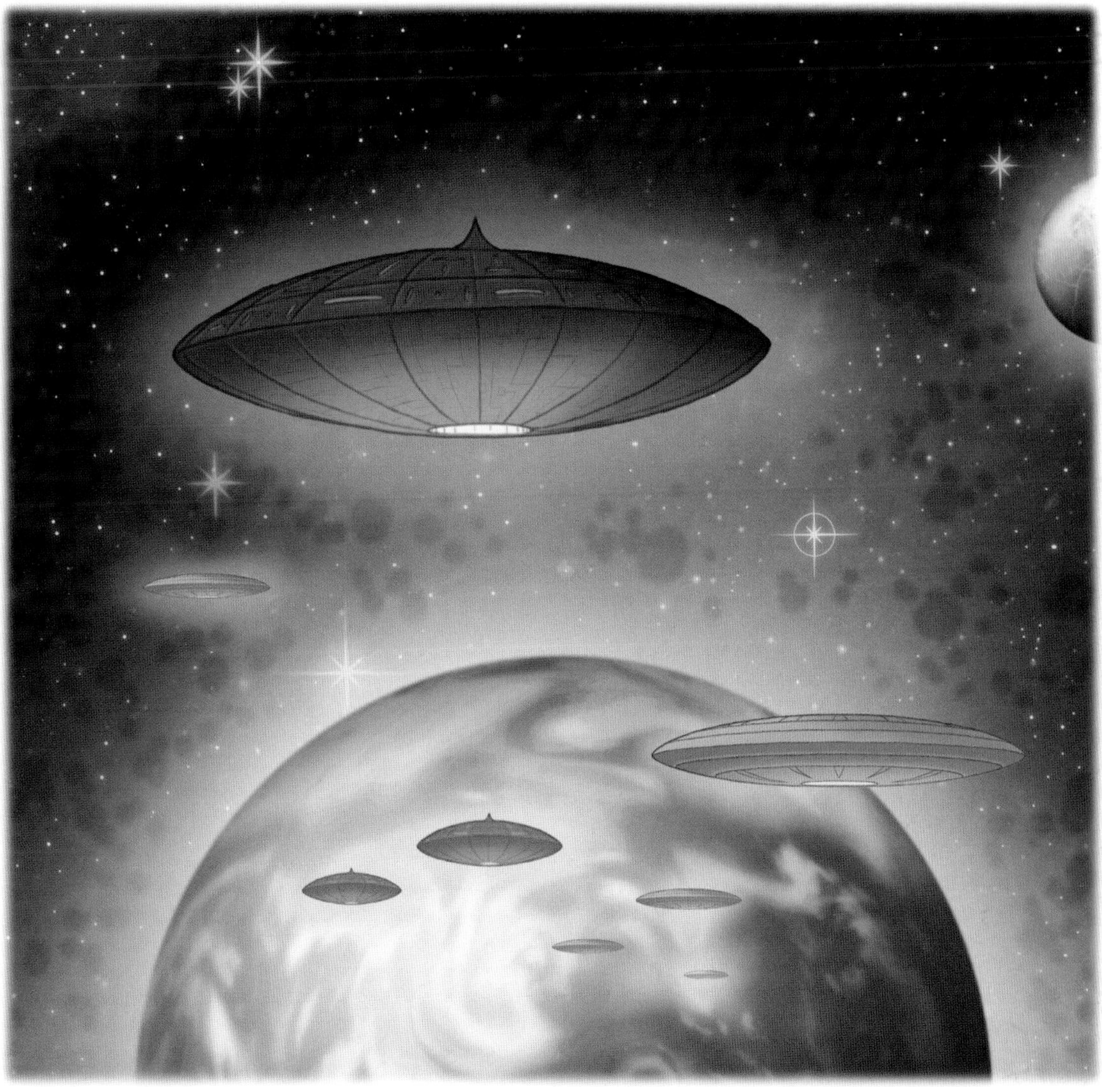
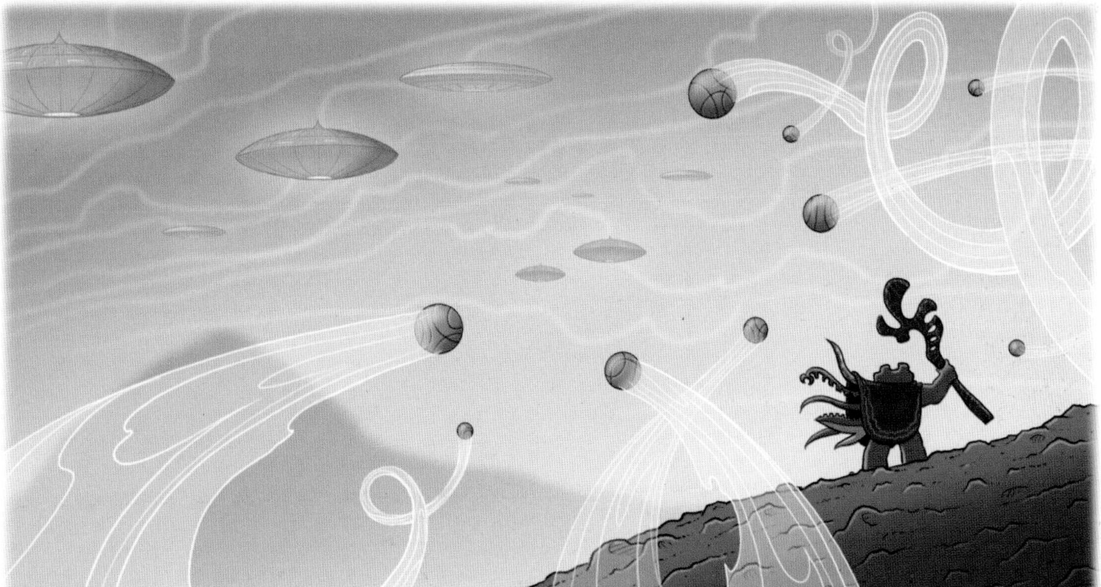

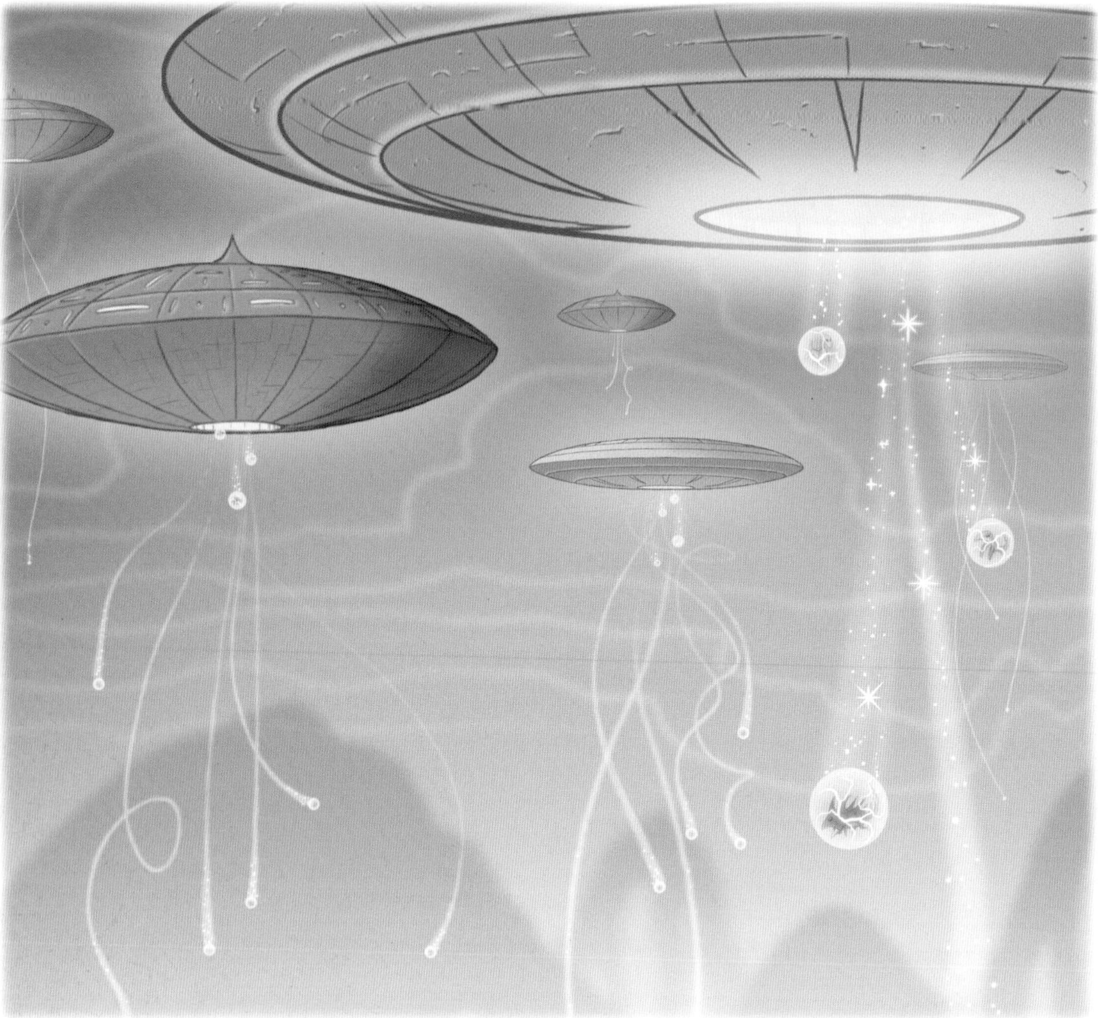

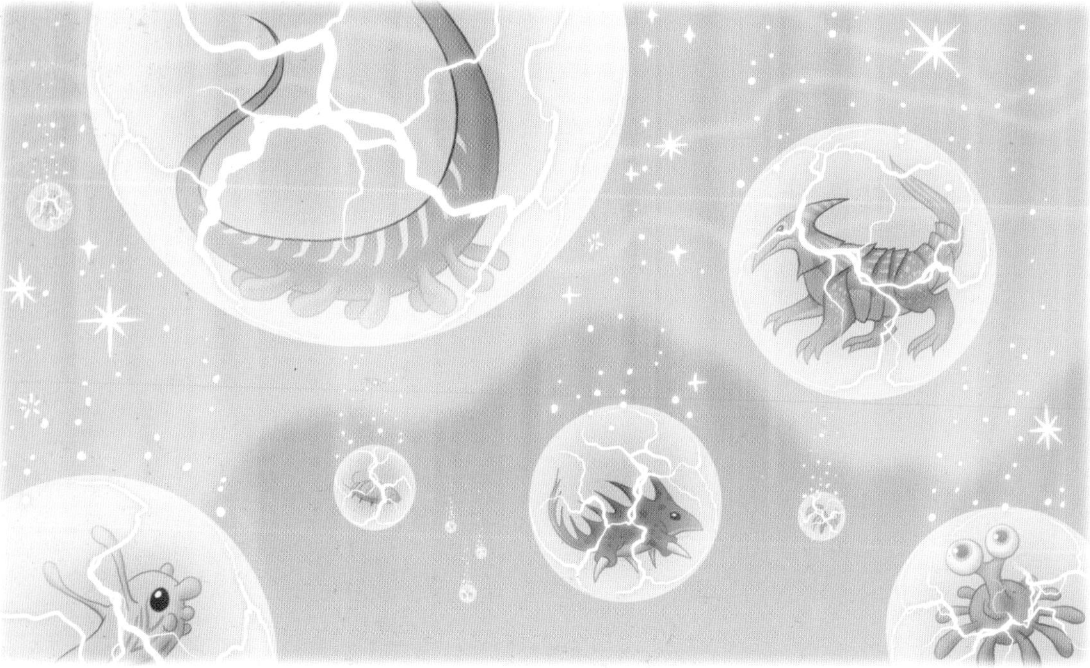

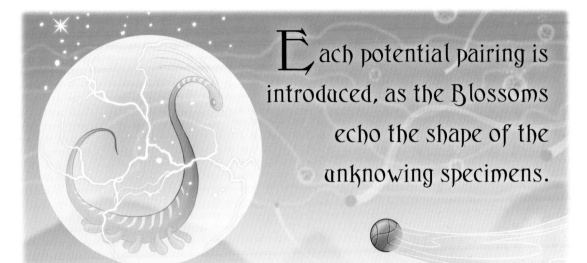

Each potential pairing is introduced, as the Blossoms echo the shape of the unknowing specimens.

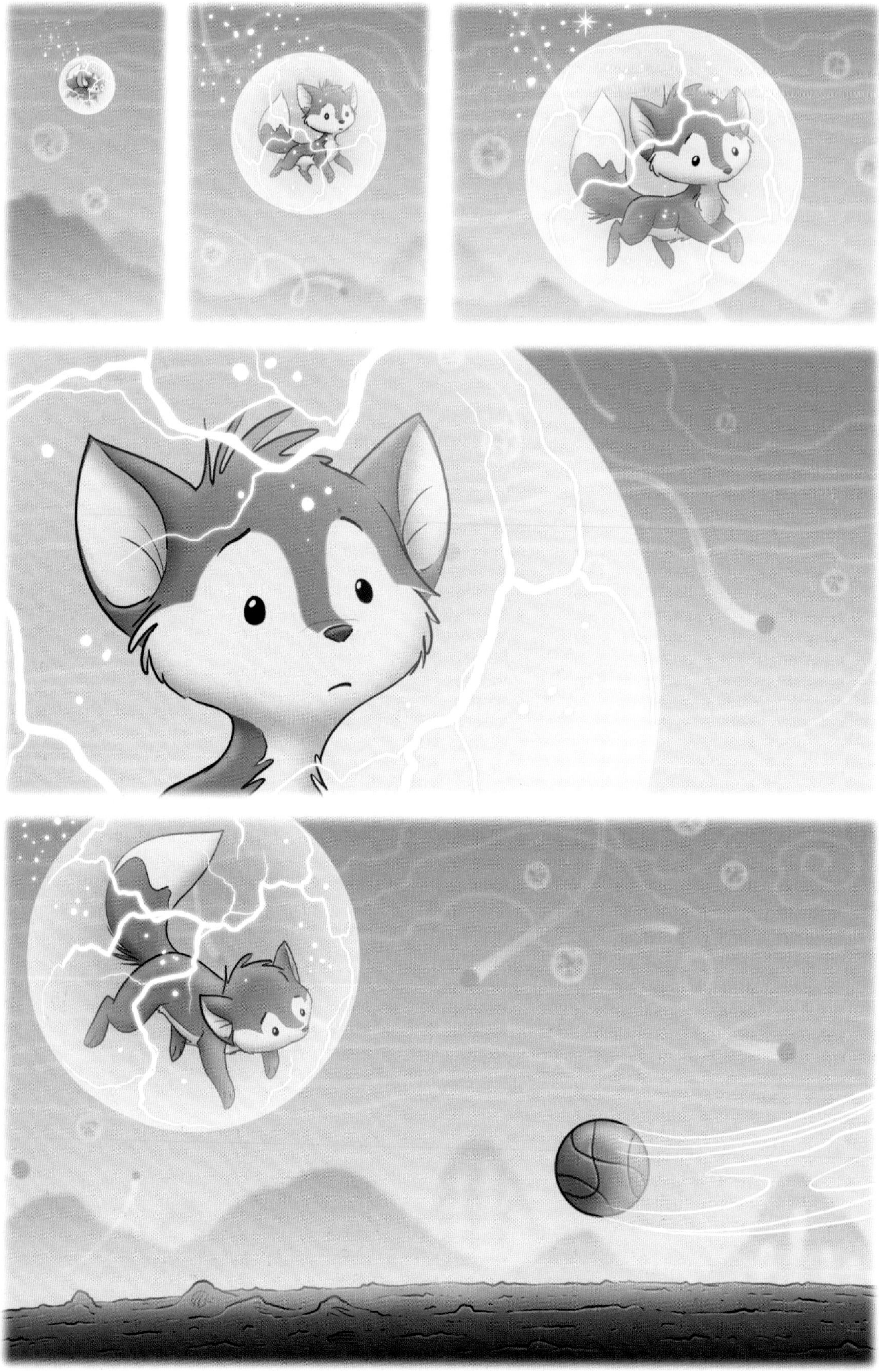

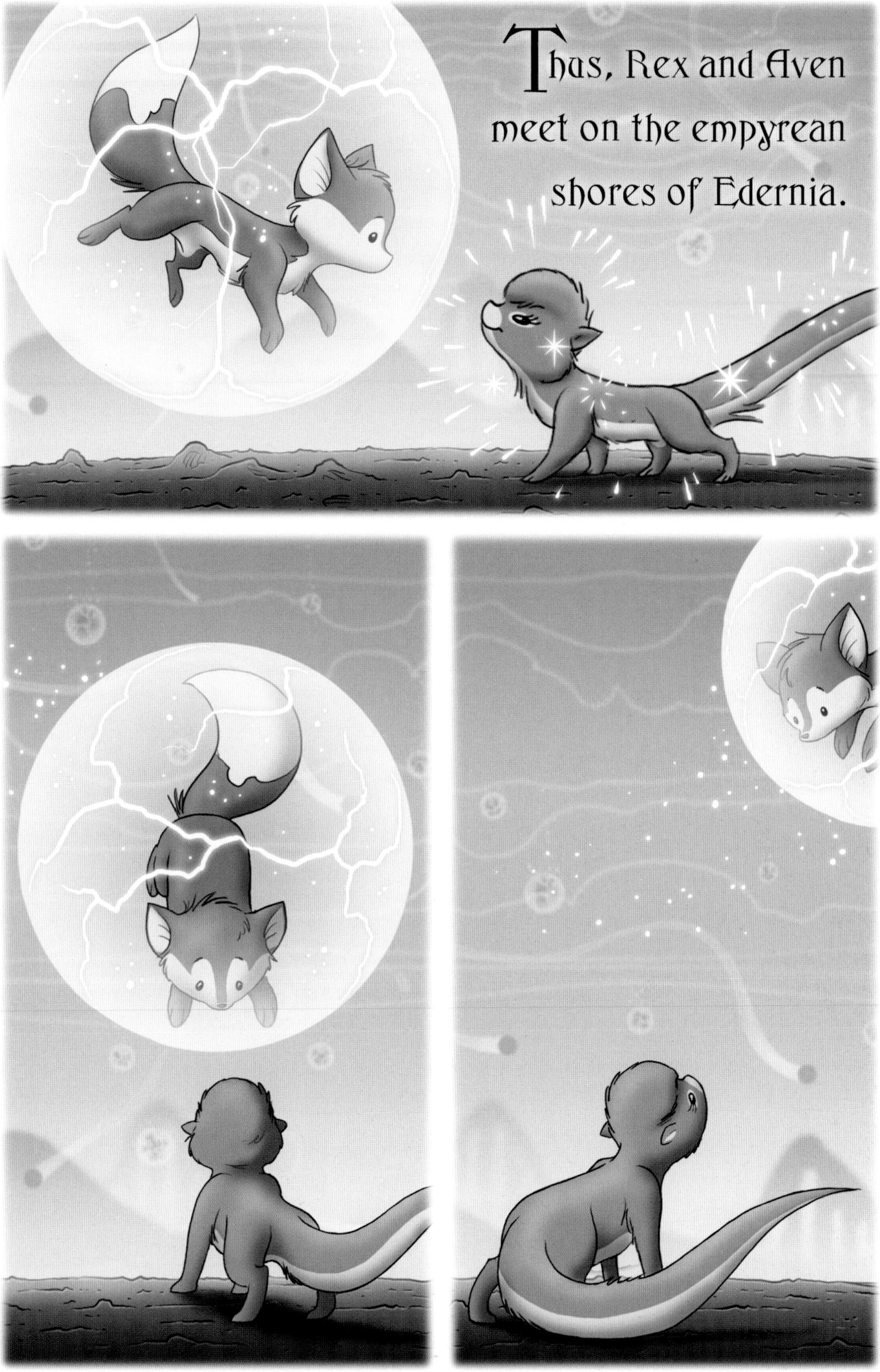
Thus, Rex and Aven meet on the empyrean shores of Edernia.

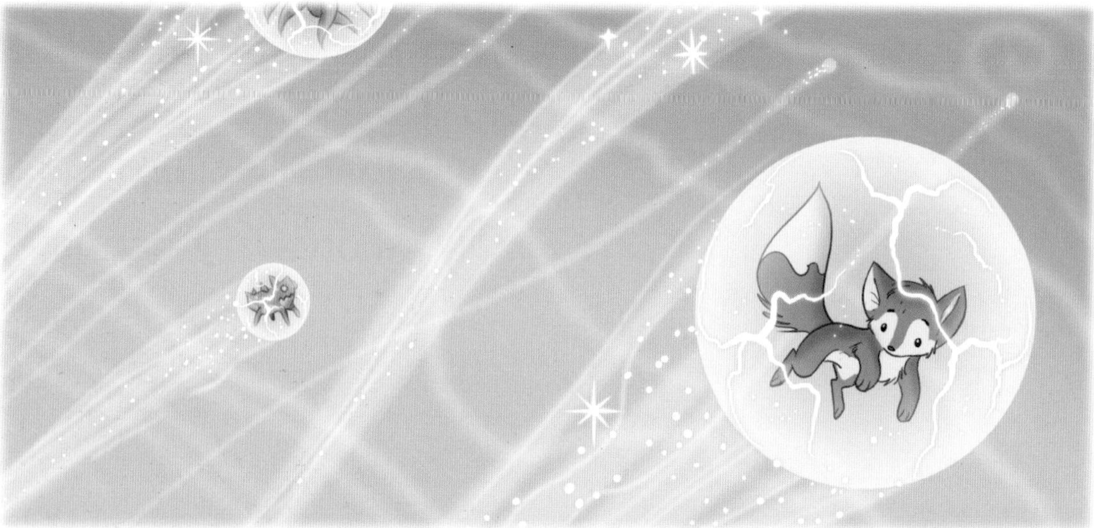

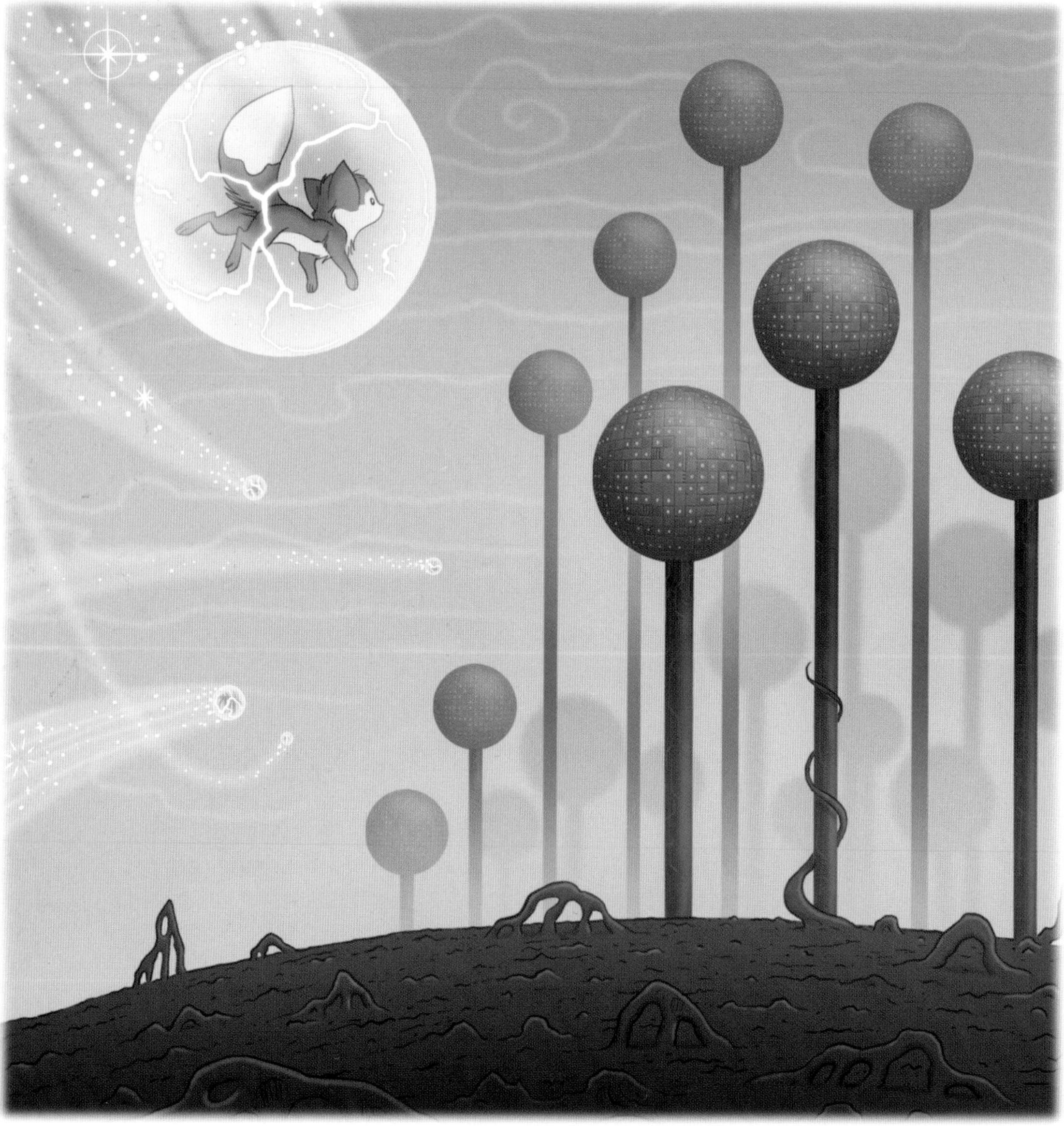

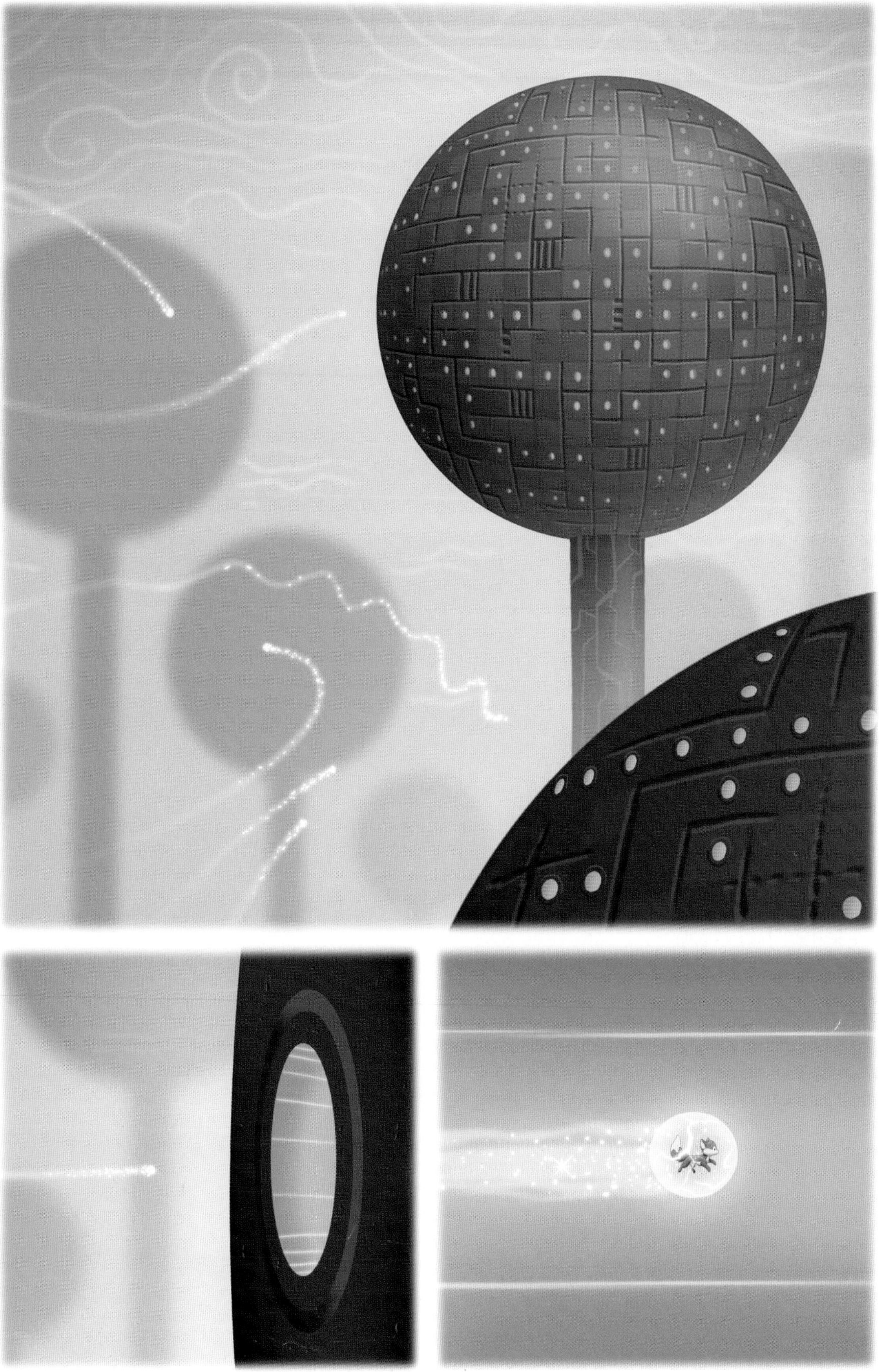

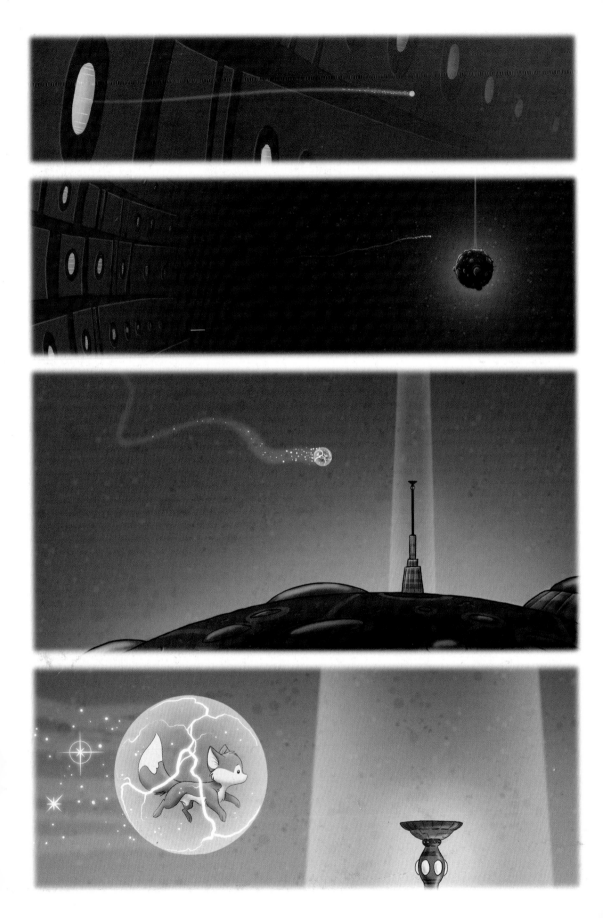

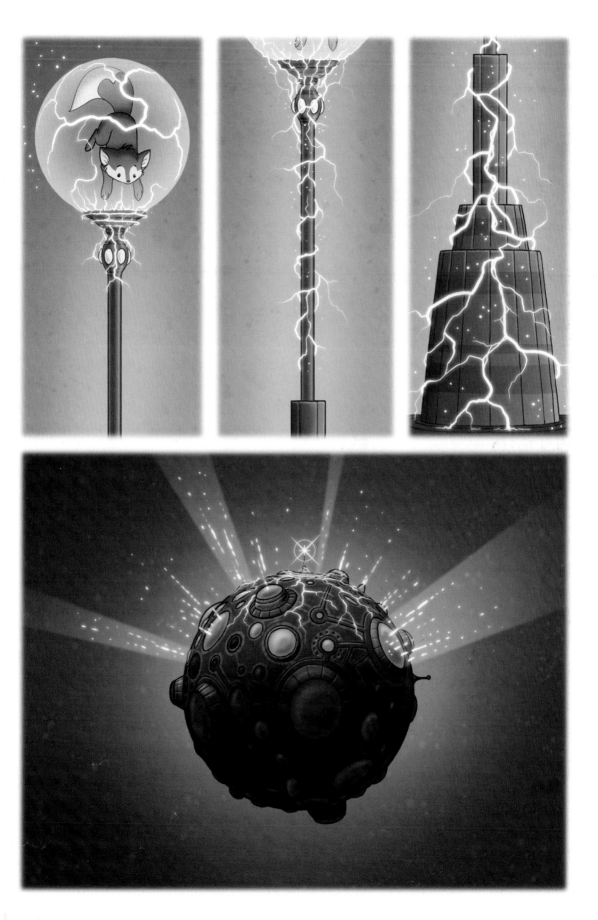

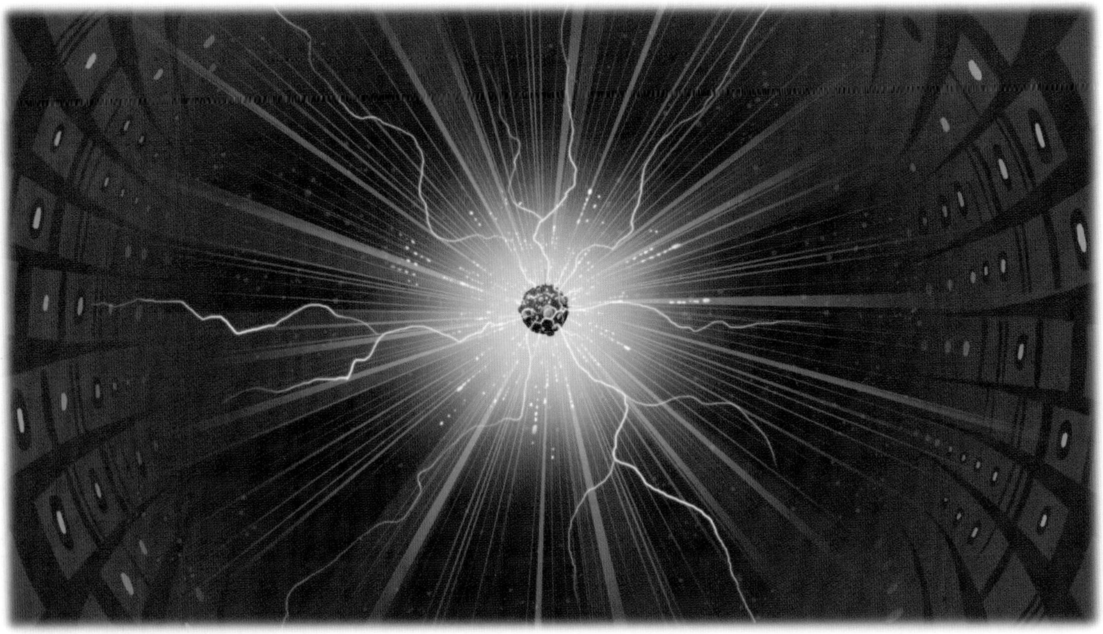

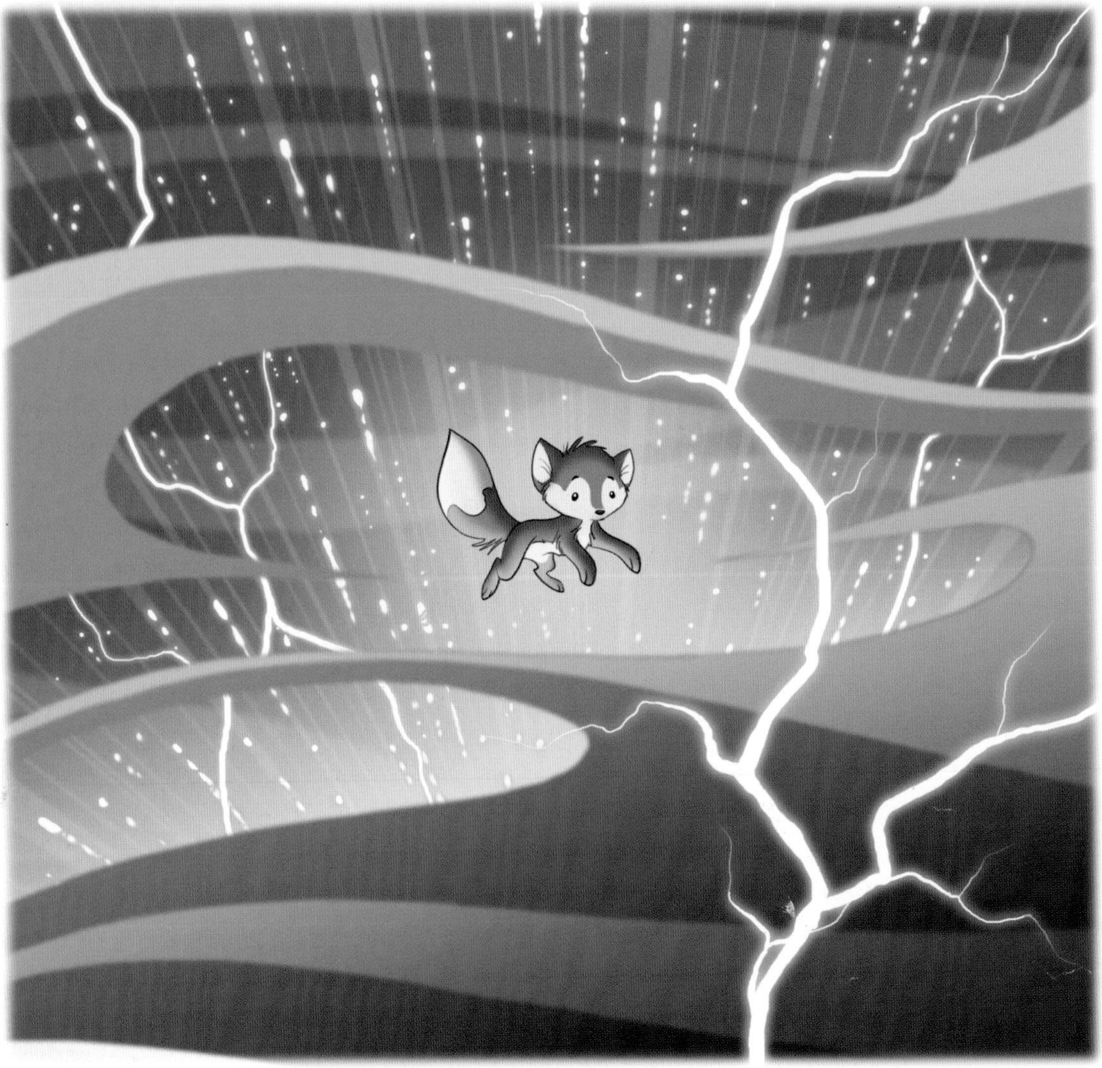

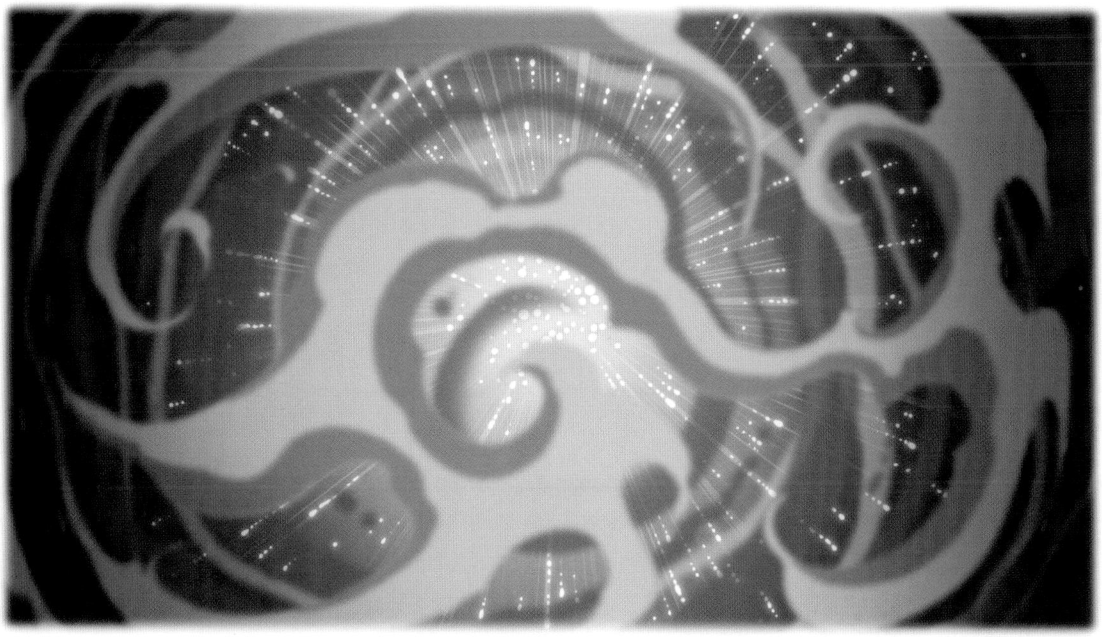

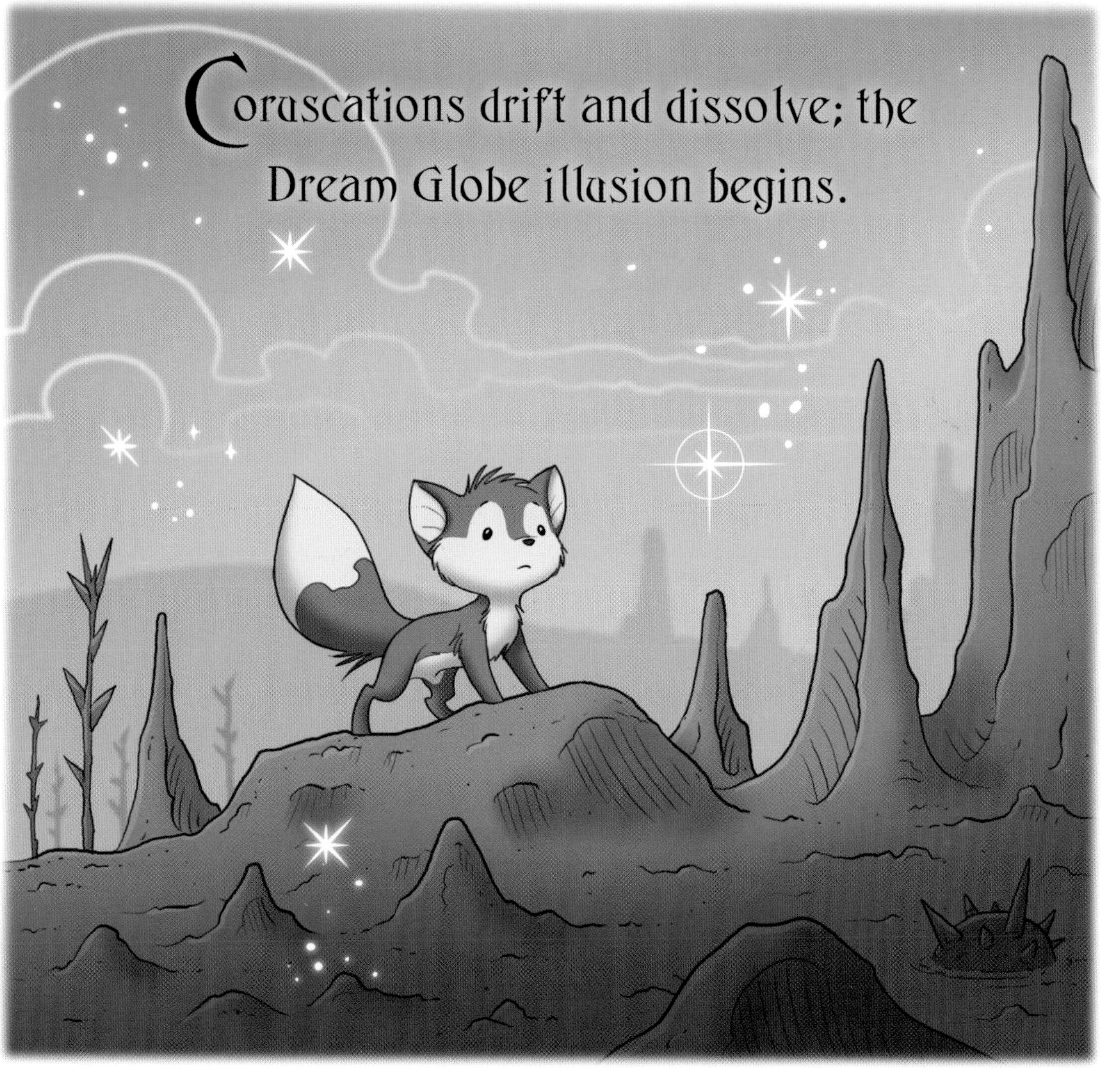
Coruscations drift and dissolve; the
Dream Globe illusion begins.

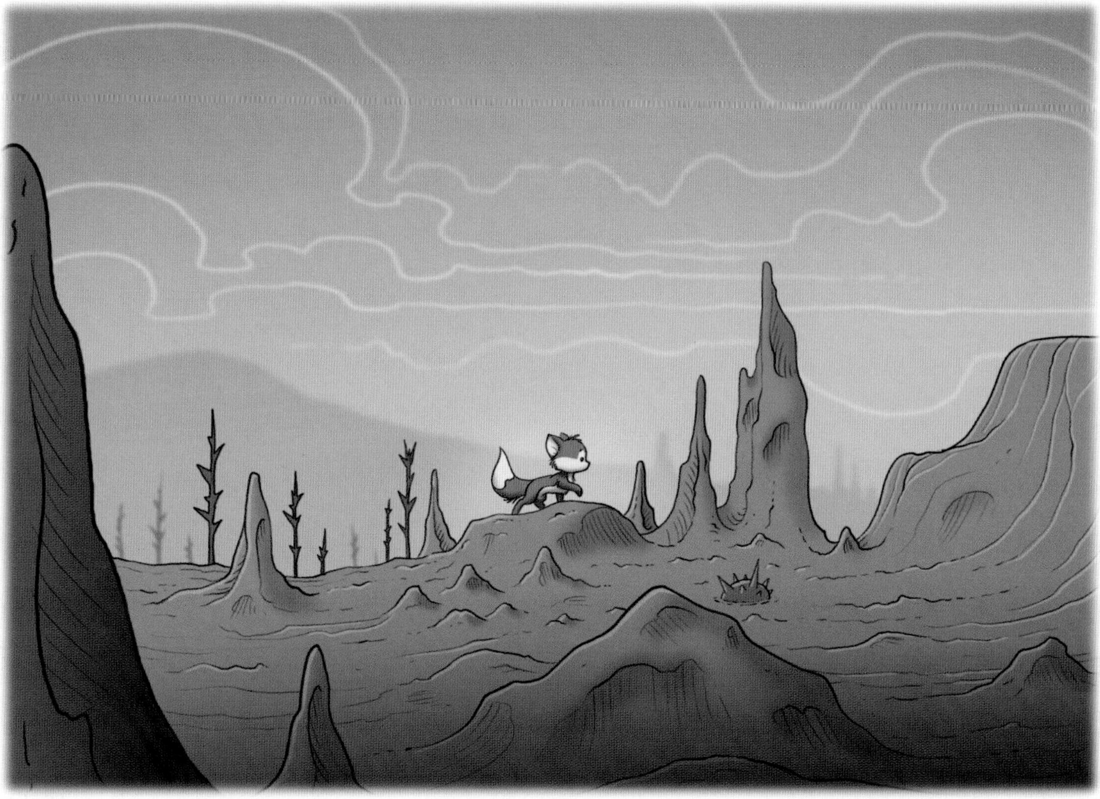

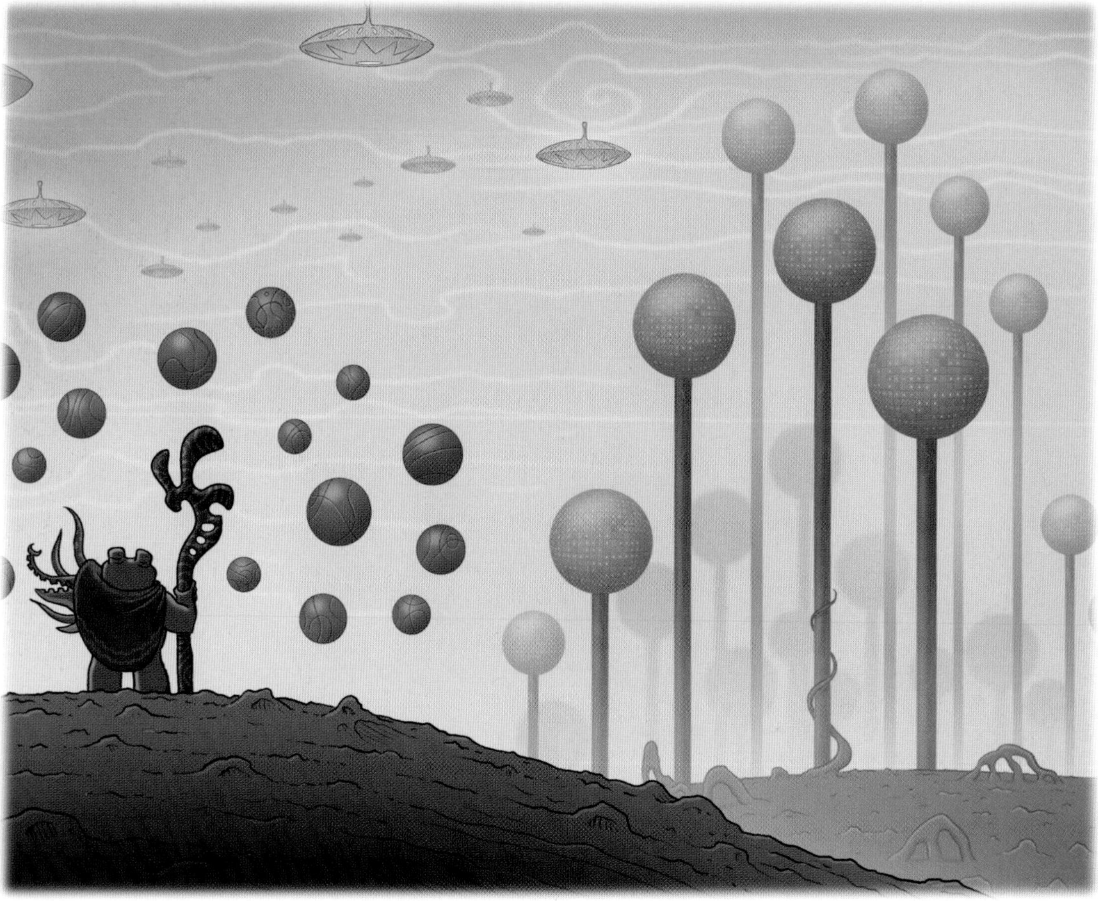

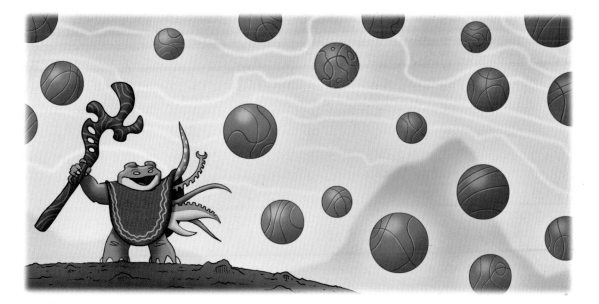

After receiving a final blessing from the Guardian-Shepherd, the Blossoms flow to their vessels with eagerness. Soon they will join their chosen consorts within the Dream Globes.

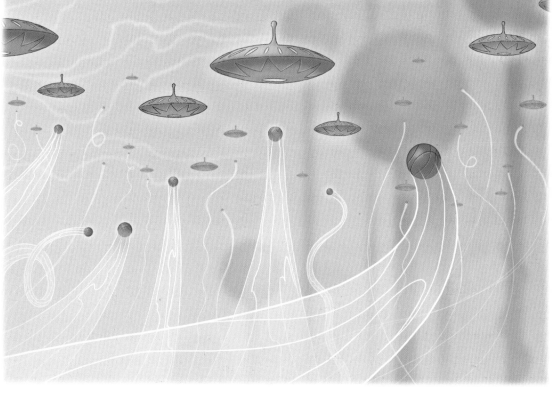

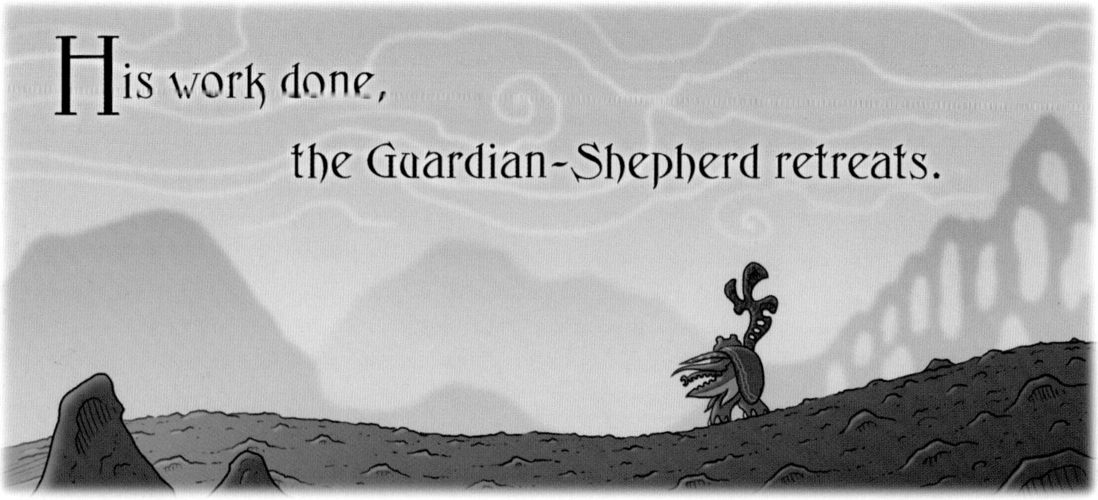
His work done,
the Guardian-Shepherd retreats.

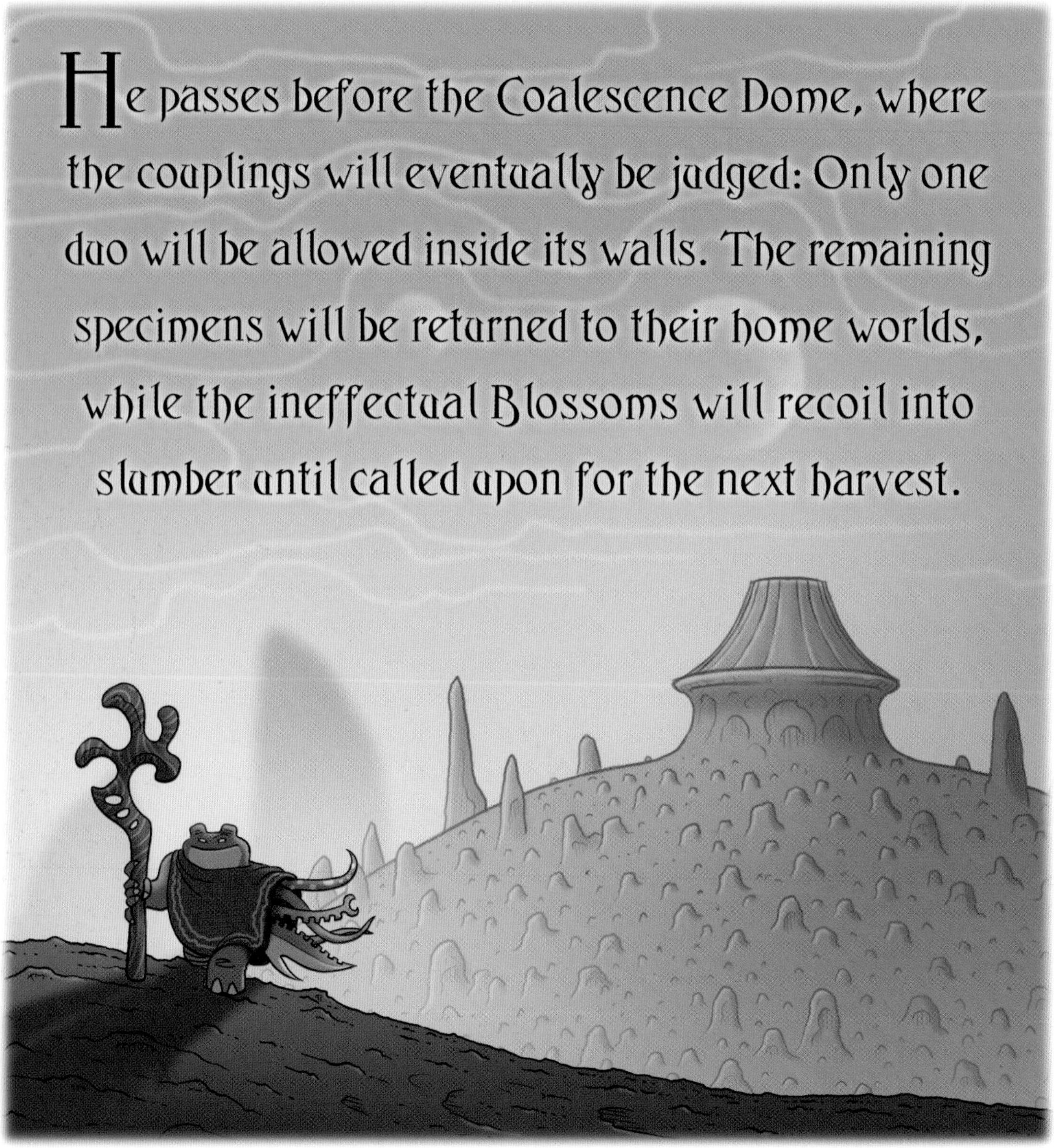
He passes before the Coalescence Dome, where the couplings will eventually be judged: Only one duo will be allowed inside its walls. The remaining specimens will be returned to their home worlds, while the ineffectual Blossoms will recoil into slumber until called upon for the next harvest.

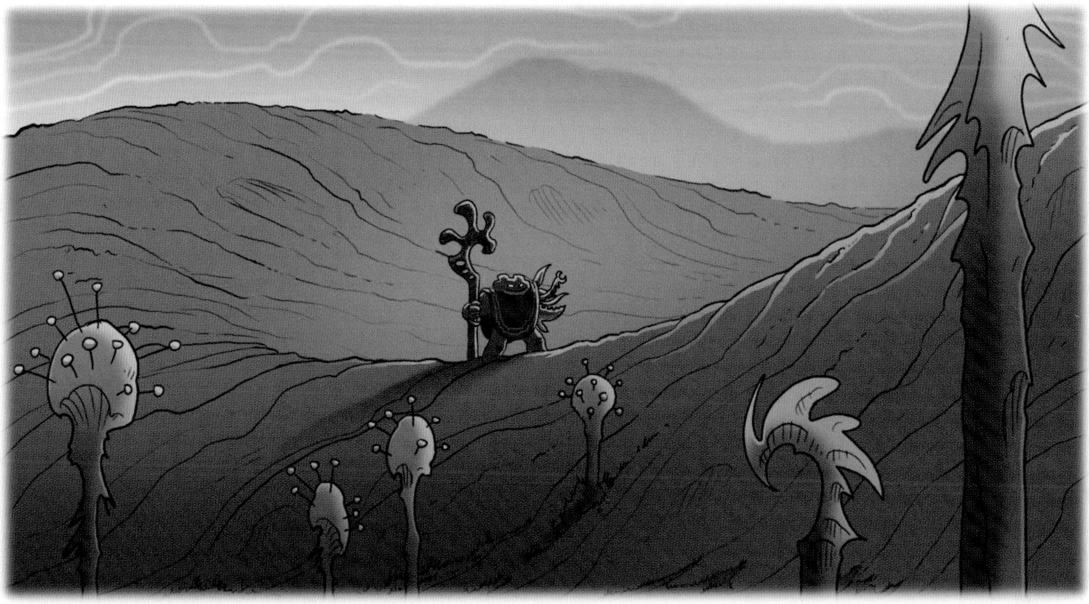

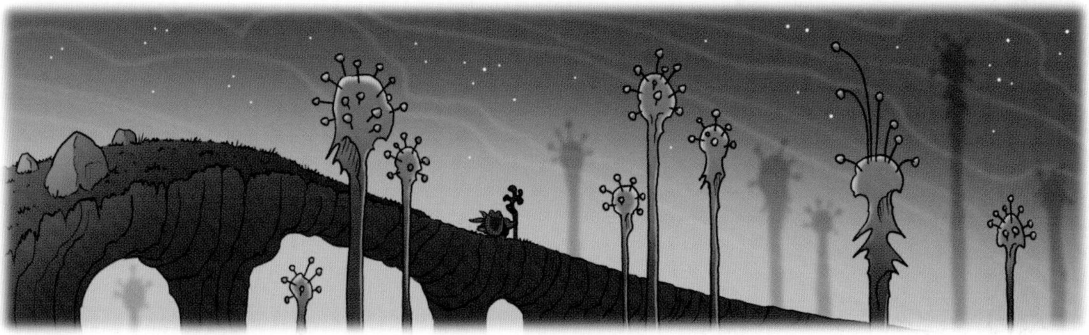

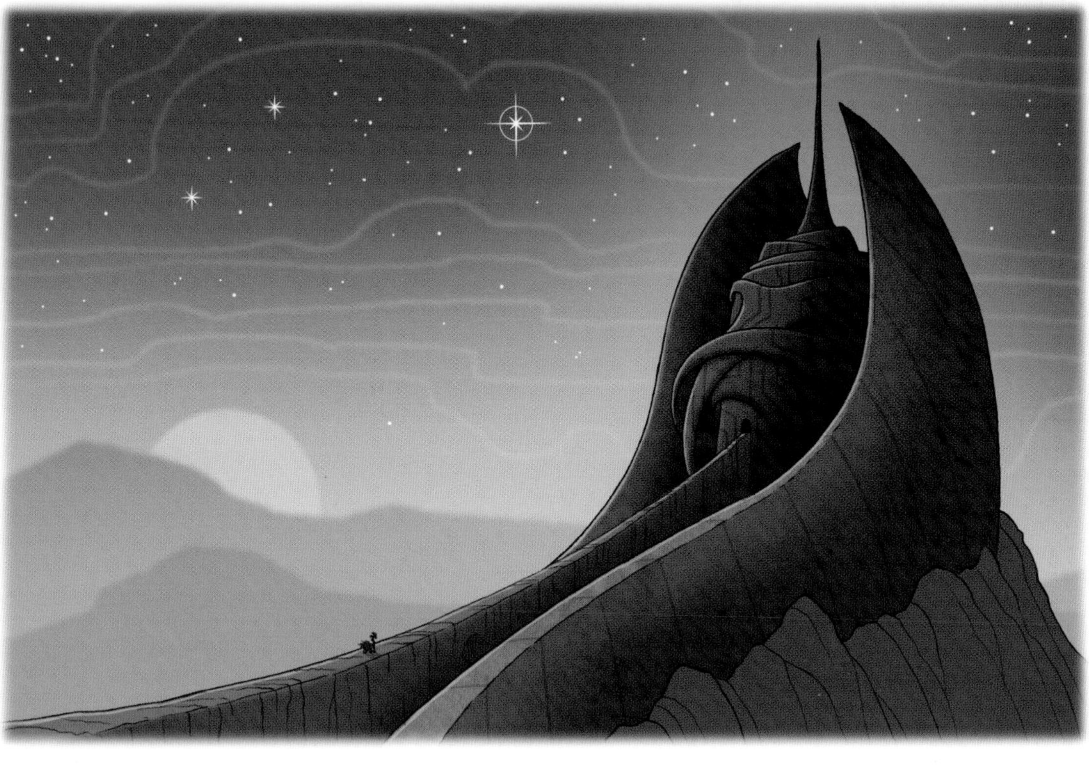

No one knows when the first ritual took place, nor how the Guardian-Shepherd came into being. Those secrets have long been lost in the catacombs of time.

But legends persist that Edernia continues to be visited by mischievious deities who indulge in the mad experiment they set in motion so long ago—celestial beings in search of amusement, who behold the event year after year with curiosity and silent glee.

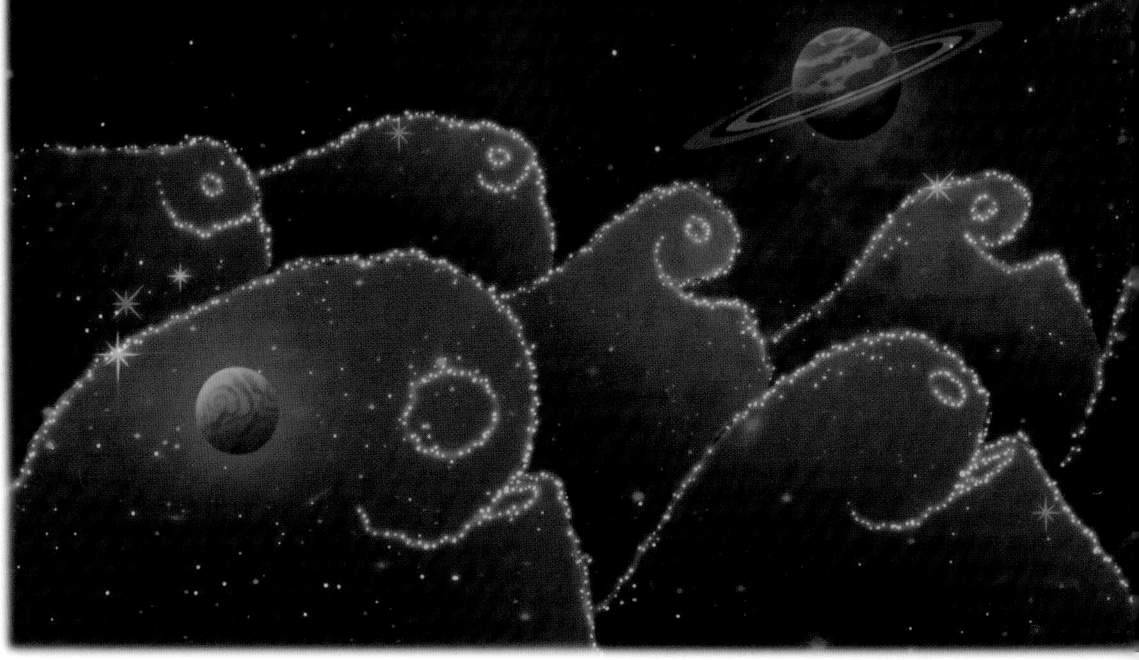

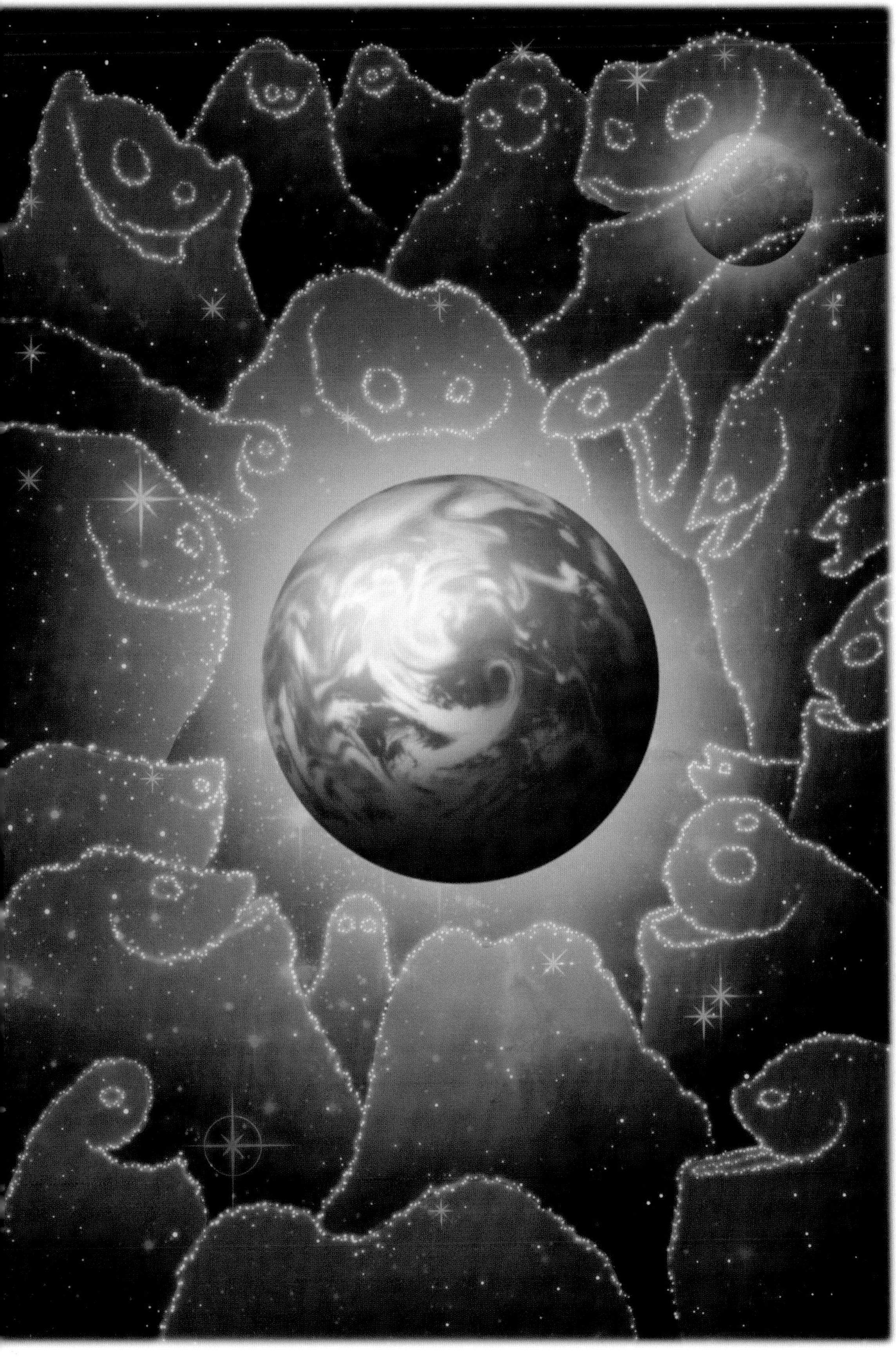

Continued in *Flight:* Volume 2

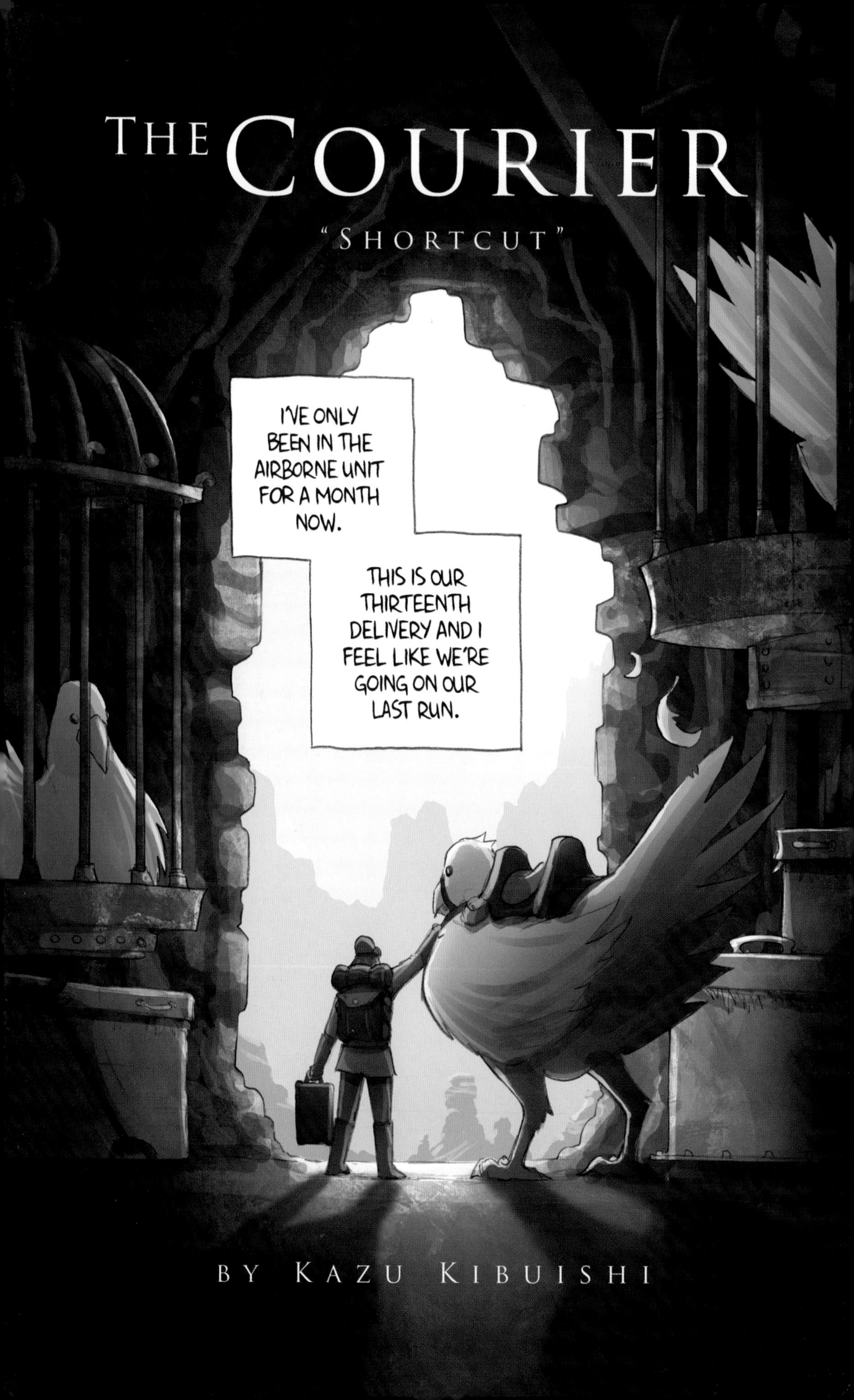
THE COURIER
"SHORTCUT"
I'VE ONLY BEEN IN THE AIRBORNE UNIT FOR A MONTH NOW.
THIS IS OUR THIRTEENTH DELIVERY AND I FEEL LIKE WE'RE GOING ON OUR LAST RUN.
BY KAZU KIBUISHI

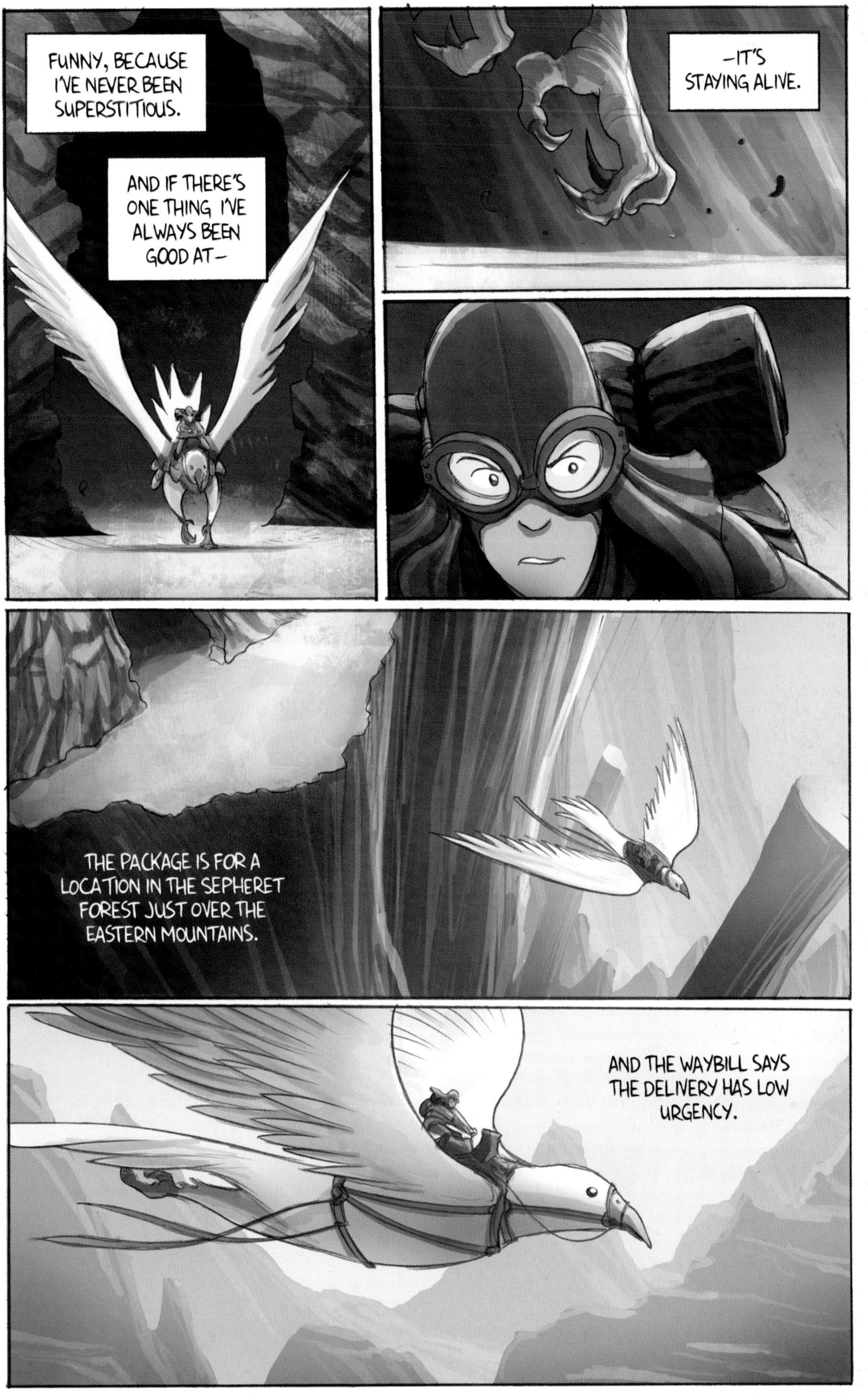

FUNNY, BECAUSE I'VE NEVER BEEN SUPERSTITIOUS.
AND IF THERE'S ONE THING I'VE ALWAYS BEEN GOOD AT—
—IT'S STAYING ALIVE.
THE PACKAGE IS FOR A LOCATION IN THE SEPHERET FOREST JUST OVER THE EASTERN MOUNTAINS.
AND THE WAYBILL SAYS THE DELIVERY HAS LOW URGENCY.

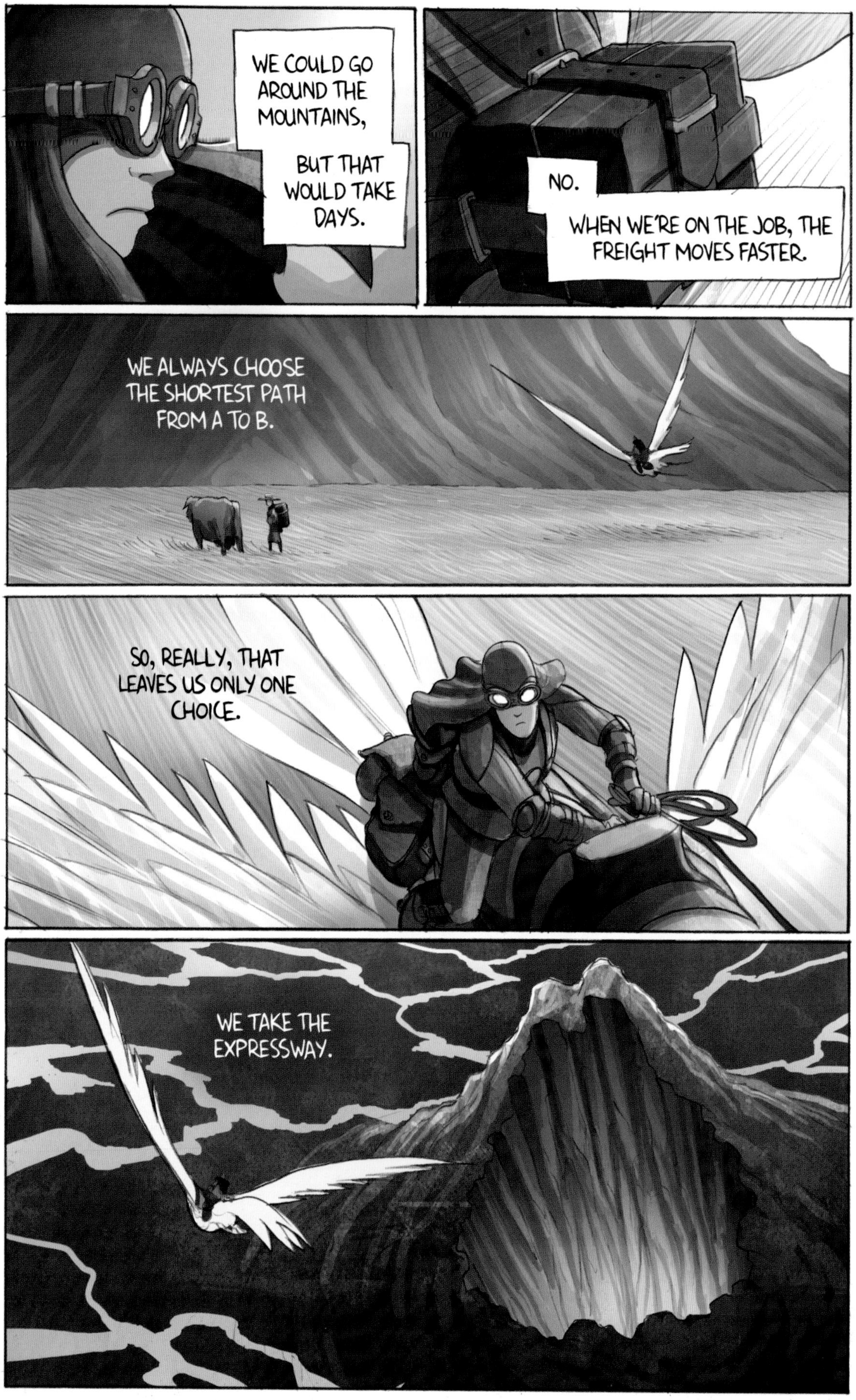
WE COULD GO AROUND THE MOUNTAINS,
BUT THAT WOULD TAKE DAYS.
NO.
WHEN WE'RE ON THE JOB, THE FREIGHT MOVES FASTER.
WE ALWAYS CHOOSE THE SHORTEST PATH FROM A TO B.
SO, REALLY, THAT LEAVES US ONLY ONE CHOICE.
WE TAKE THE EXPRESSWAY.

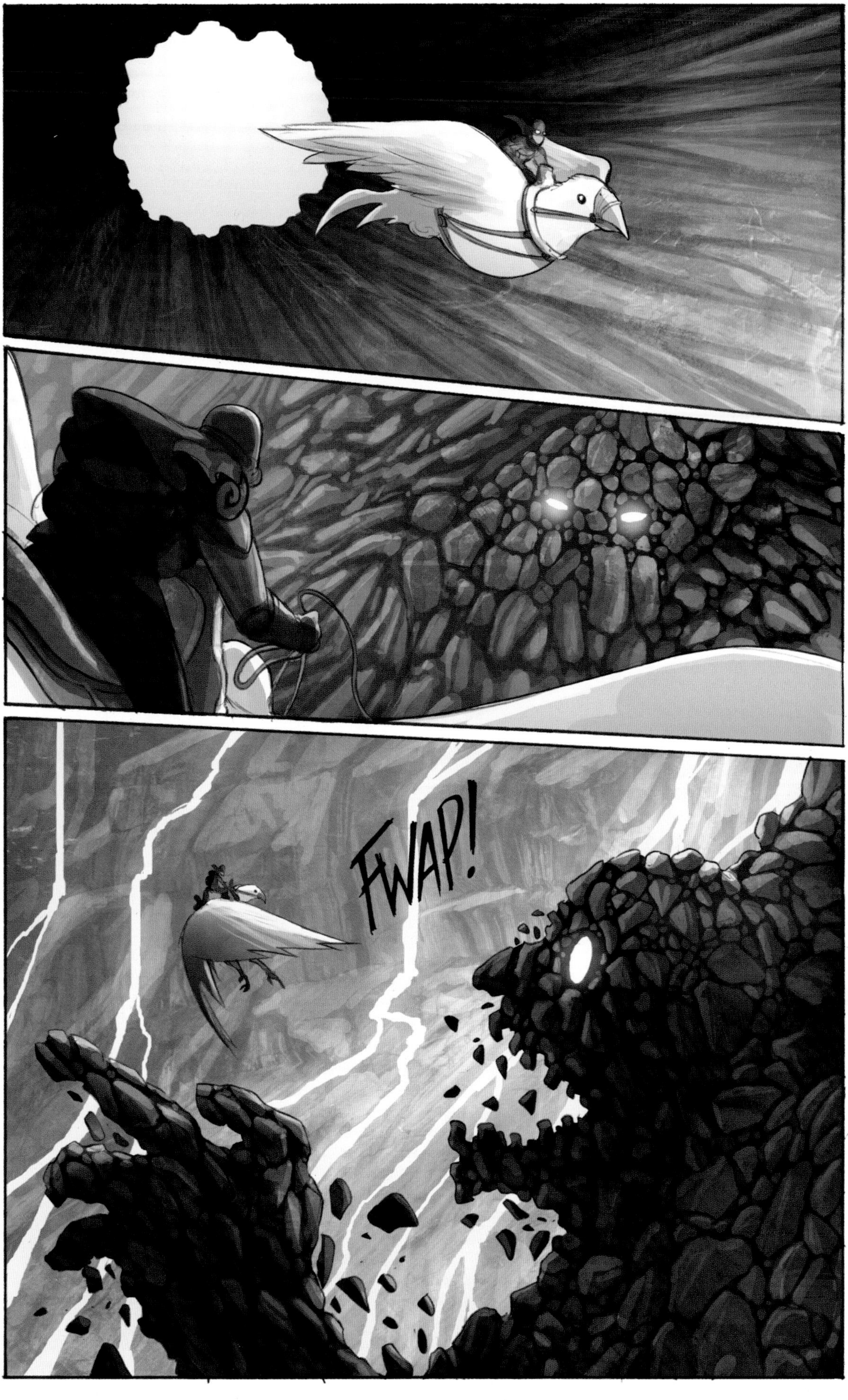
FWAP!

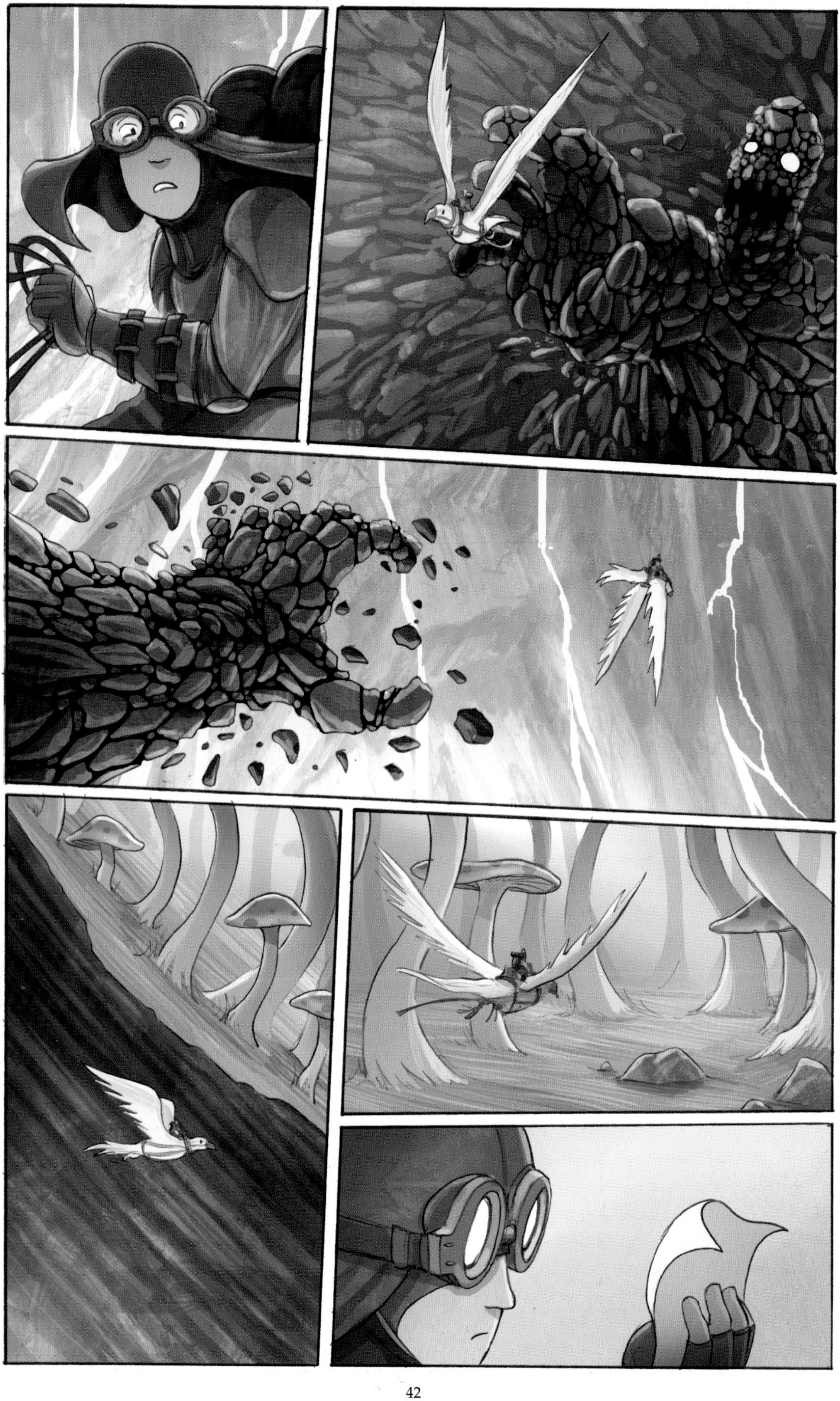

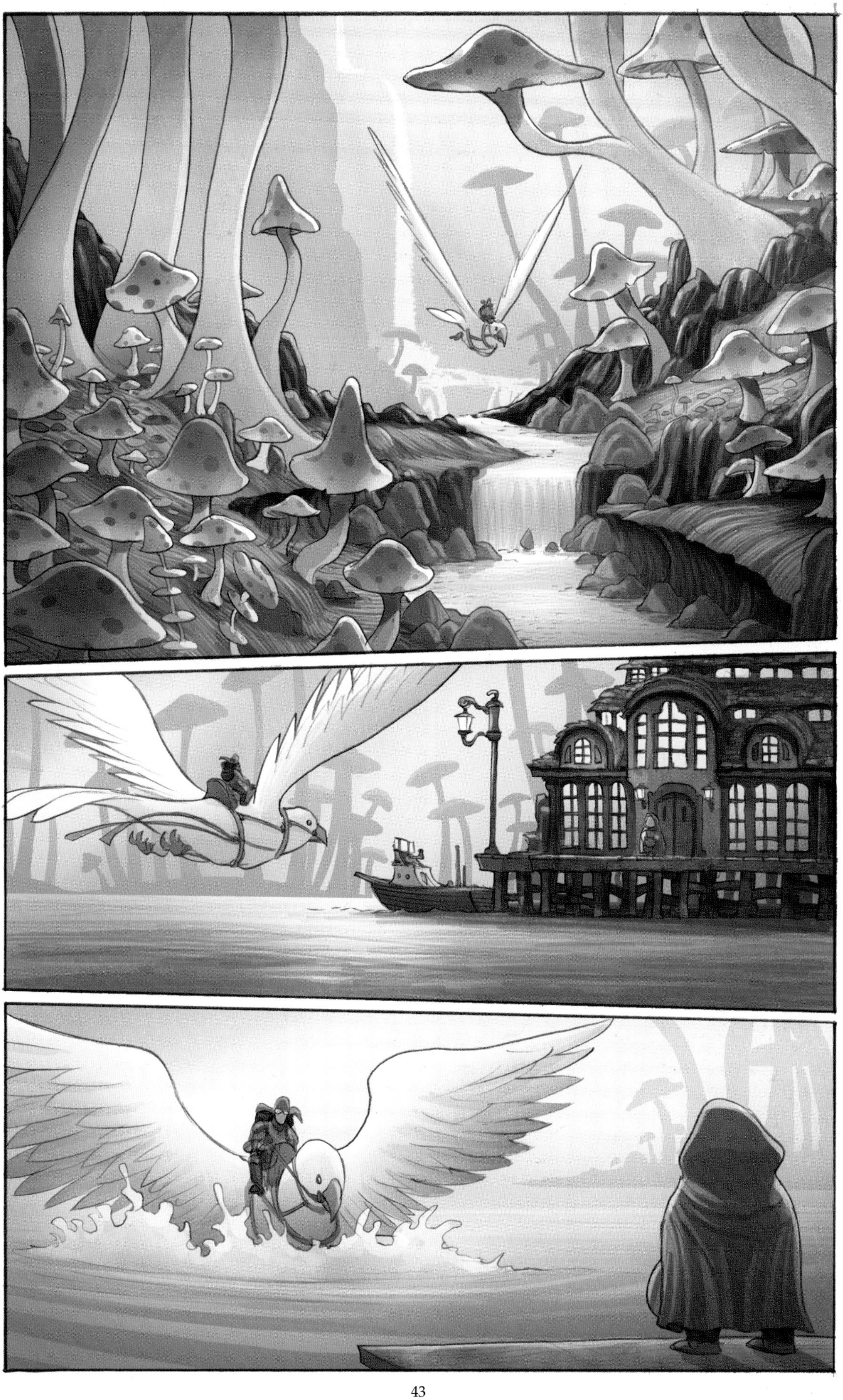

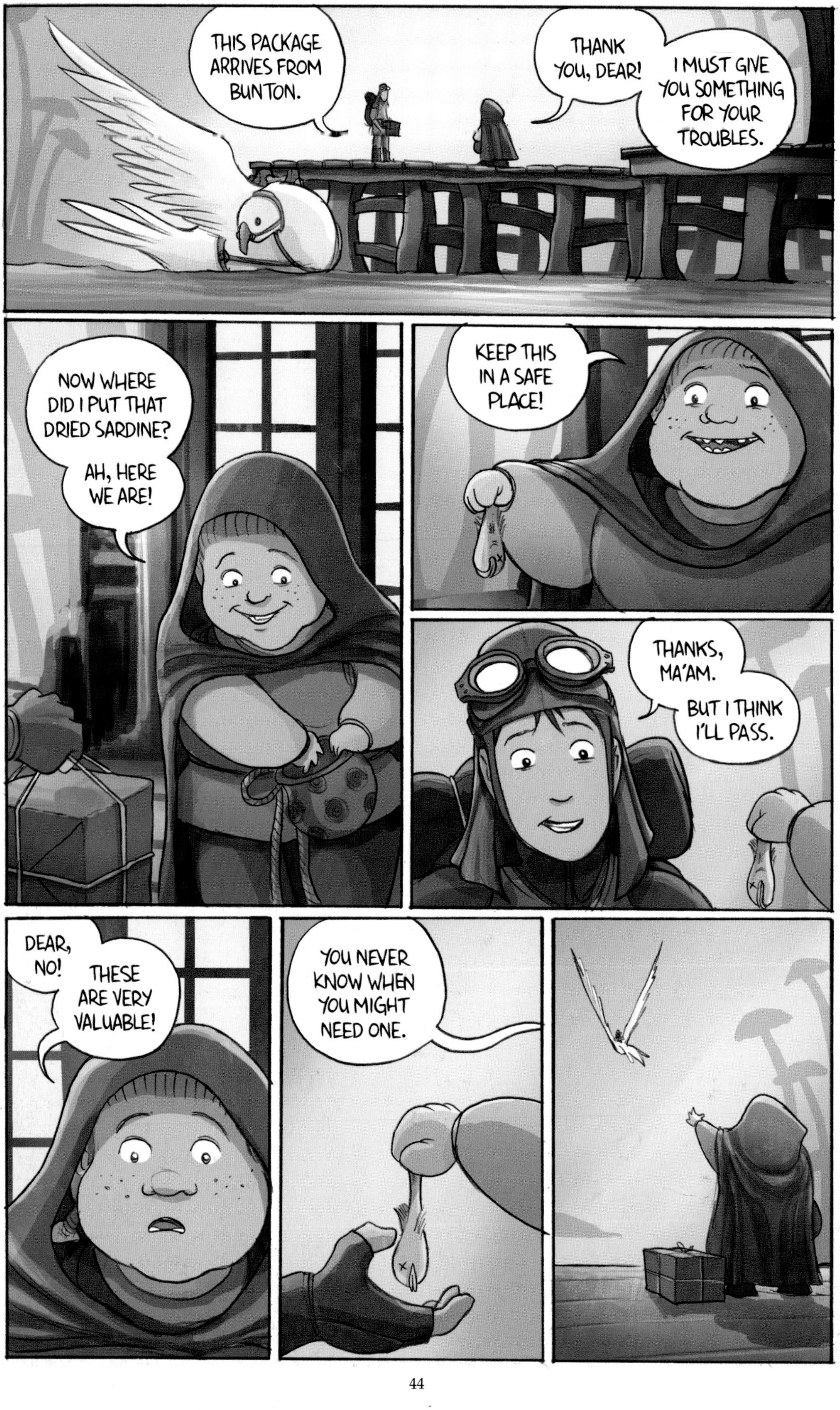
THIS PACKAGE ARRIVES FROM BUNTON.
THANK YOU, DEAR!
I MUST GIVE YOU SOMETHING FOR YOUR TROUBLES.
NOW WHERE DID I PUT THAT DRIED SARDINE?
AH, HERE WE ARE!
KEEP THIS IN A SAFE PLACE!
THANKS, MA'AM.
BUT I THINK I'LL PASS.
DEAR, NO!
THESE ARE VERY VALUABLE!
YOU NEVER KNOW WHEN YOU MIGHT NEED ONE.

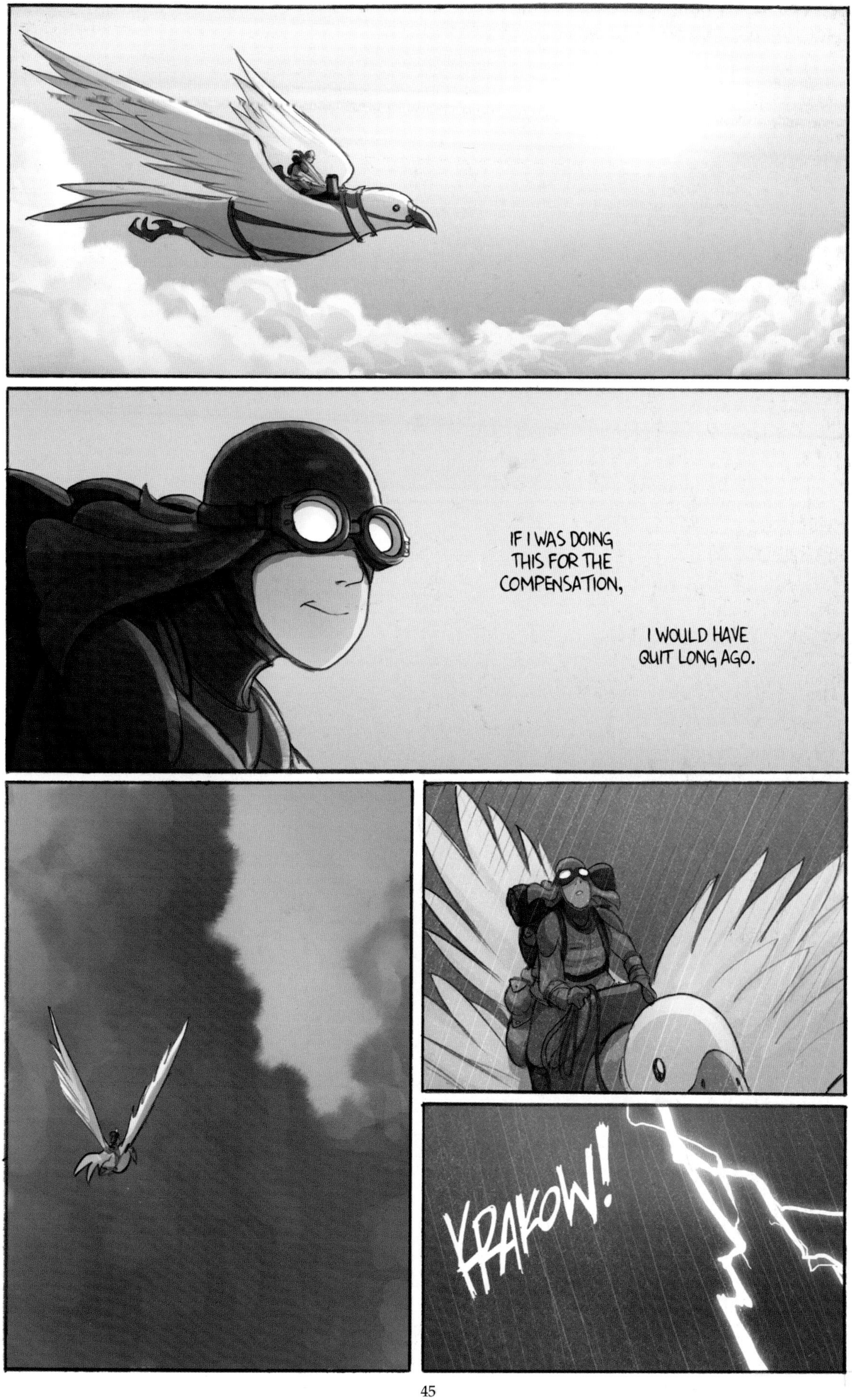
IF I WAS DOING THIS FOR THE COMPENSATION,
I WOULD HAVE QUIT LONG AGO.
KRAKOW!

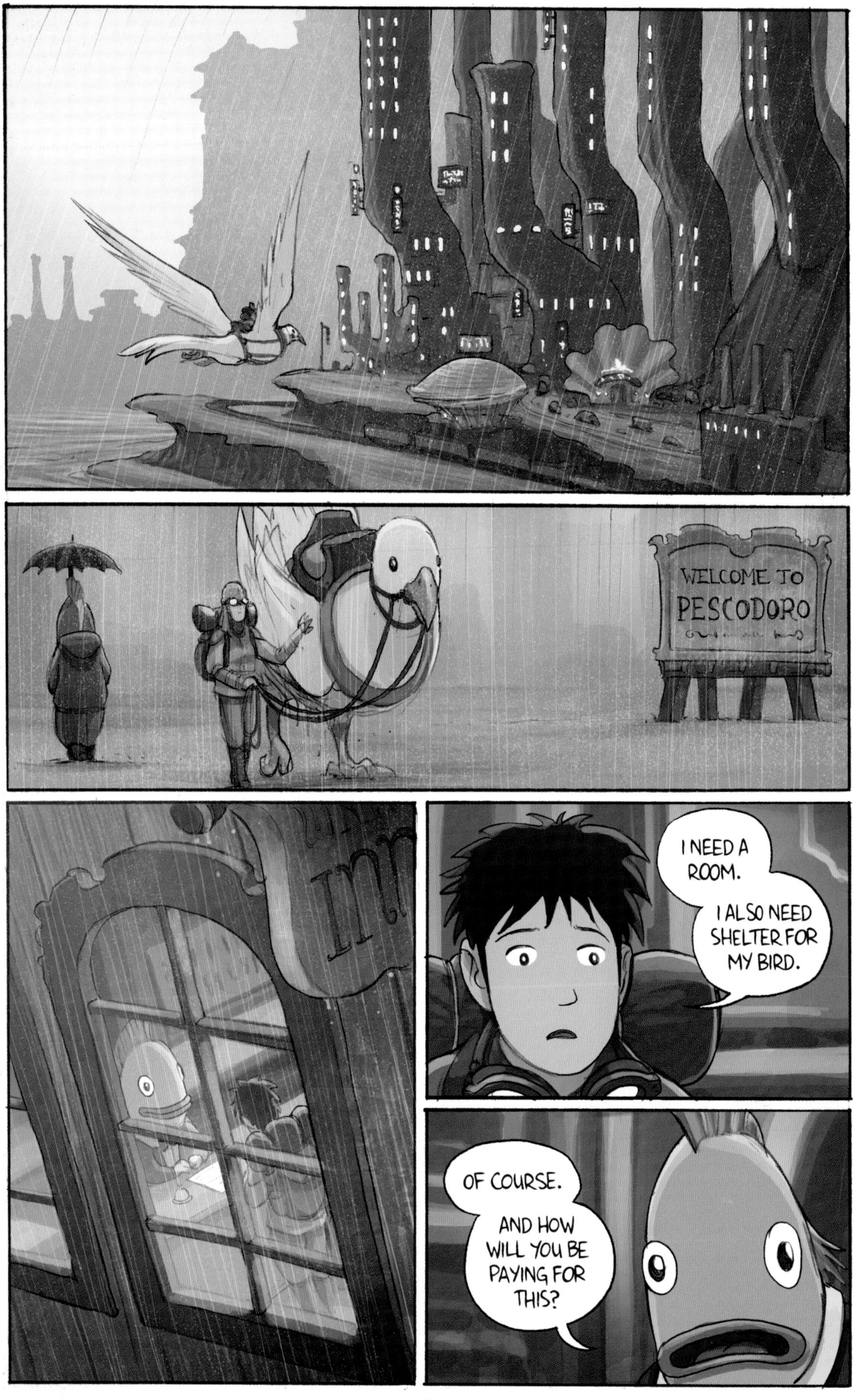
WELCOME TO
PESCODORO
INN
I NEED A ROOM.
I ALSO NEED SHELTER FOR MY BIRD.
OF COURSE.
AND HOW WILL YOU BE PAYING FOR THIS?

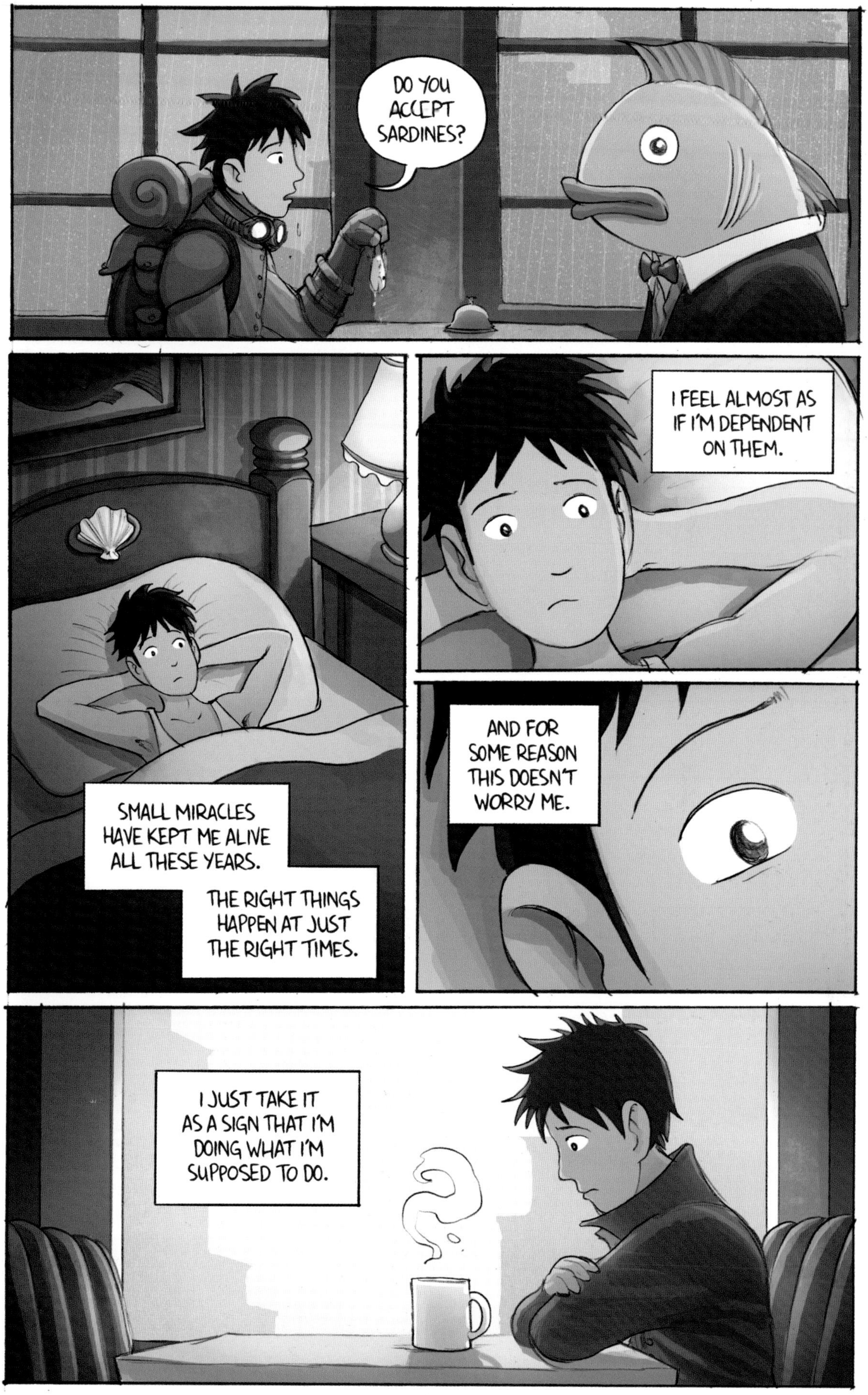
DO YOU ACCEPT SARDINES?
I FEEL ALMOST AS IF I'M DEPENDENT ON THEM.
SMALL MIRACLES HAVE KEPT ME ALIVE ALL THESE YEARS.
THE RIGHT THINGS HAPPEN AT JUST THE RIGHT TIMES.
AND FOR SOME REASON THIS DOESN'T WORRY ME.
I JUST TAKE IT AS A SIGN THAT I'M DOING WHAT I'M SUPPOSED TO DO.

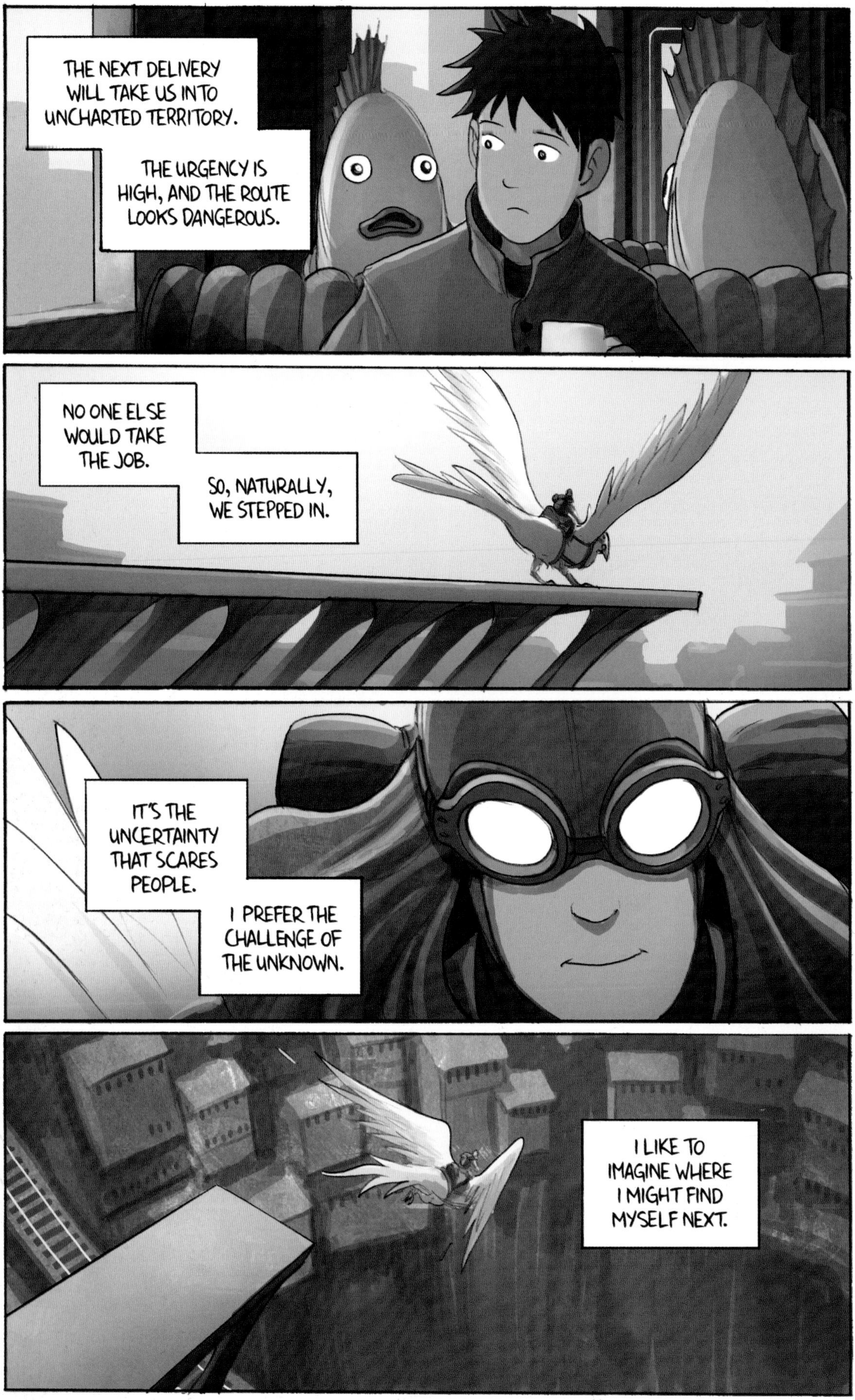
THE NEXT DELIVERY WILL TAKE US INTO UNCHARTED TERRITORY.
THE URGENCY IS HIGH, AND THE ROUTE LOOKS DANGEROUS.
NO ONE ELSE WOULD TAKE THE JOB.
SO, NATURALLY, WE STEPPED IN.
IT'S THE UNCERTAINTY THAT SCARES PEOPLE.
I PREFER THE CHALLENGE OF THE UNKNOWN.
I LIKE TO IMAGINE WHERE I MIGHT FIND MYSELF NEXT.

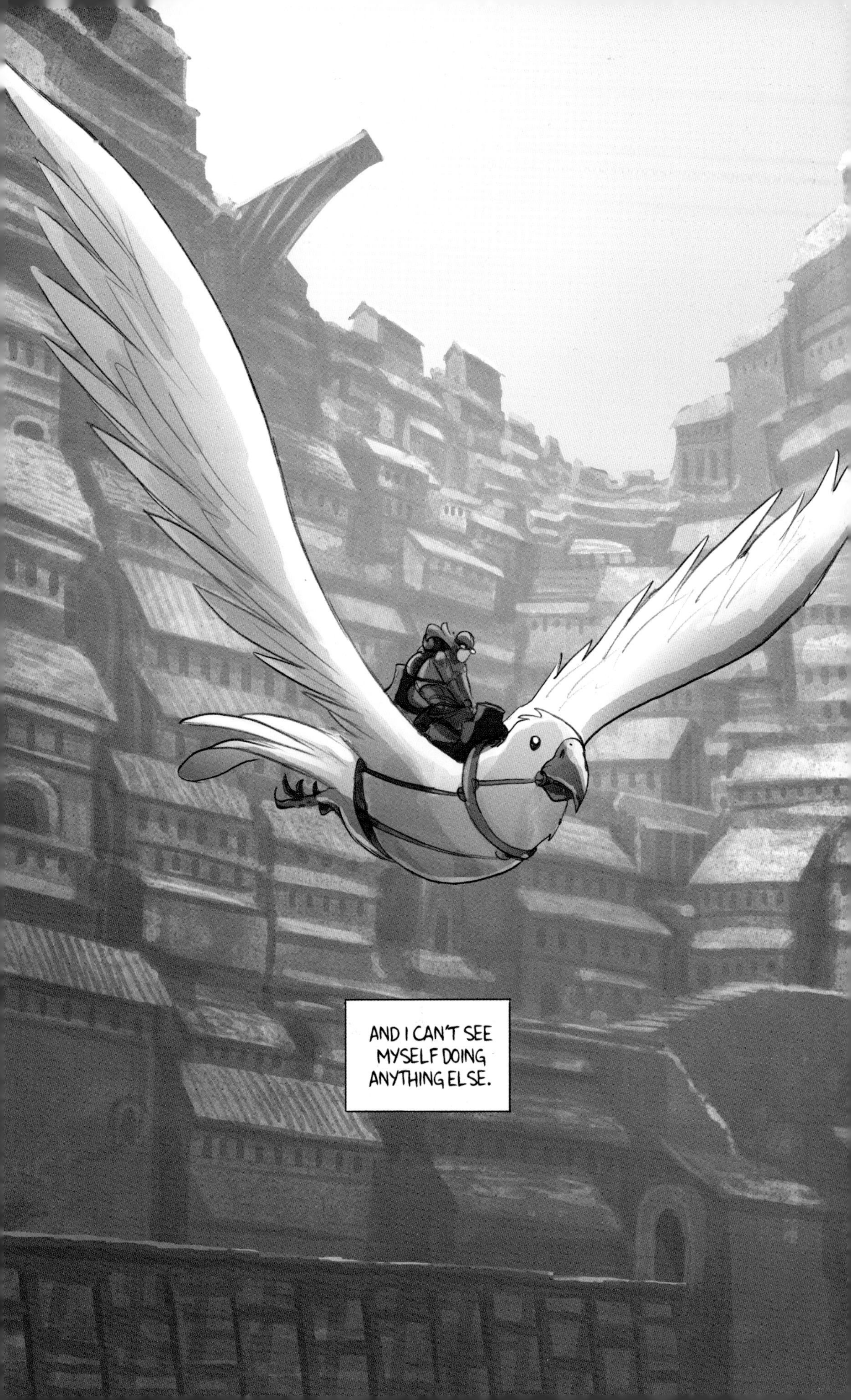
AND I CAN'T SEE MYSELF DOING ANYTHING ELSE.

LIVE BAIT

BY JUSTIN GERARD

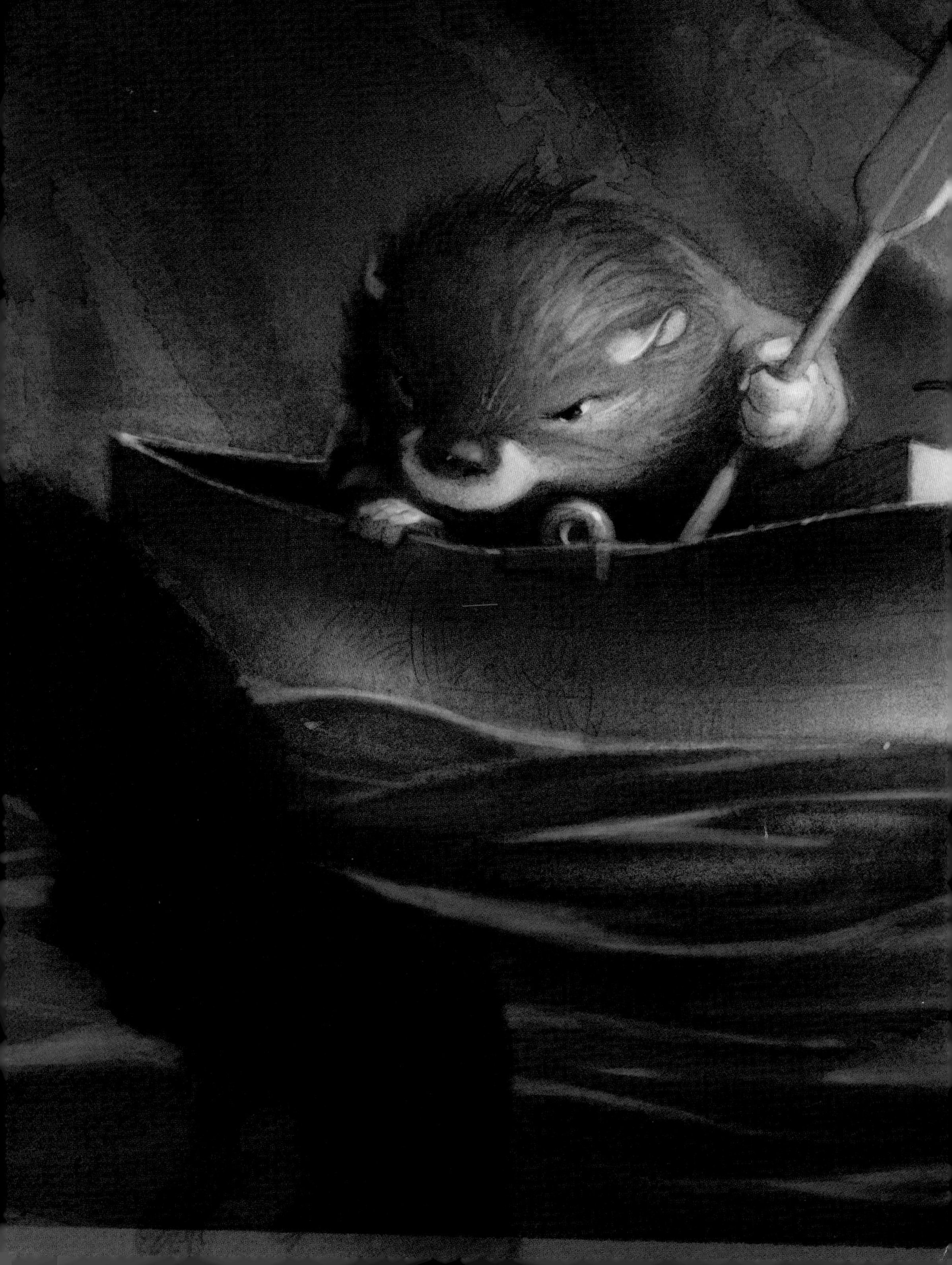

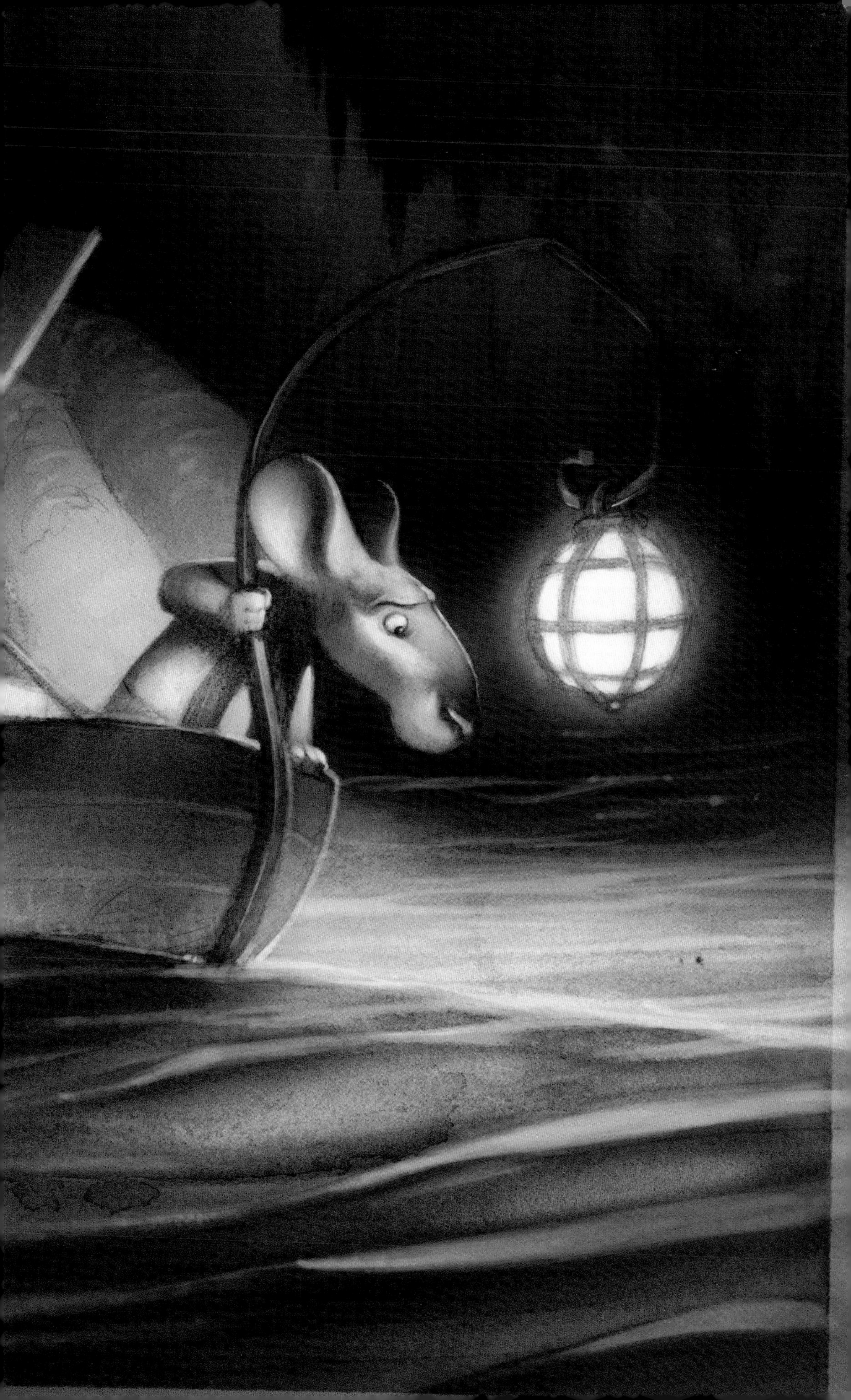

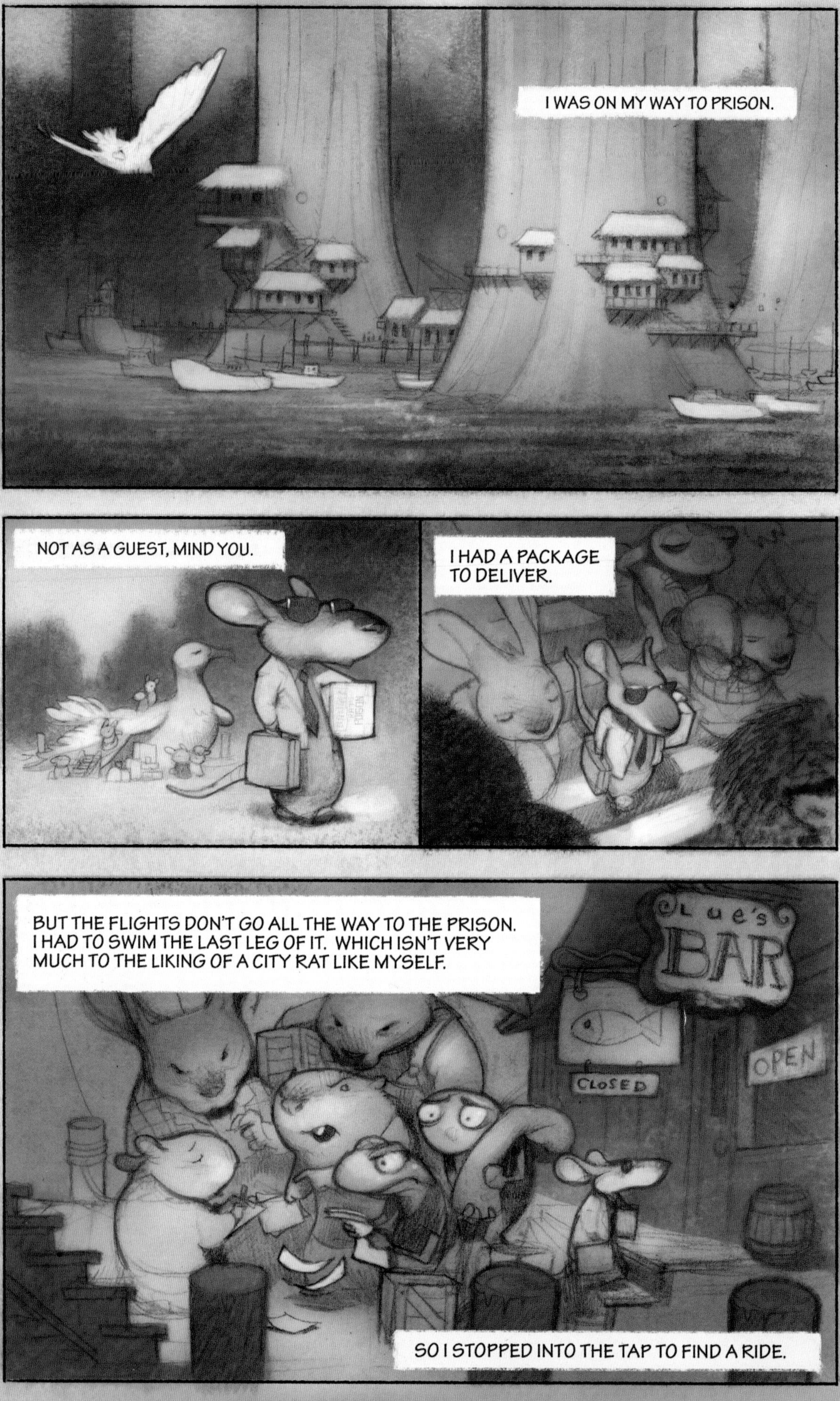
I WAS ON MY WAY TO PRISON.
NOT AS A GUEST, MIND YOU.
I HAD A PACKAGE TO DELIVER.
BUT THE FLIGHTS DON'T GO ALL THE WAY TO THE PRISON. I HAD TO SWIM THE LAST LEG OF IT. WHICH ISN'T VERY MUCH TO THE LIKING OF A CITY RAT LIKE MYSELF.
Lue's
BAR
OPEN
CLOSED
SO I STOPPED INTO THE TAP TO FIND A RIDE.

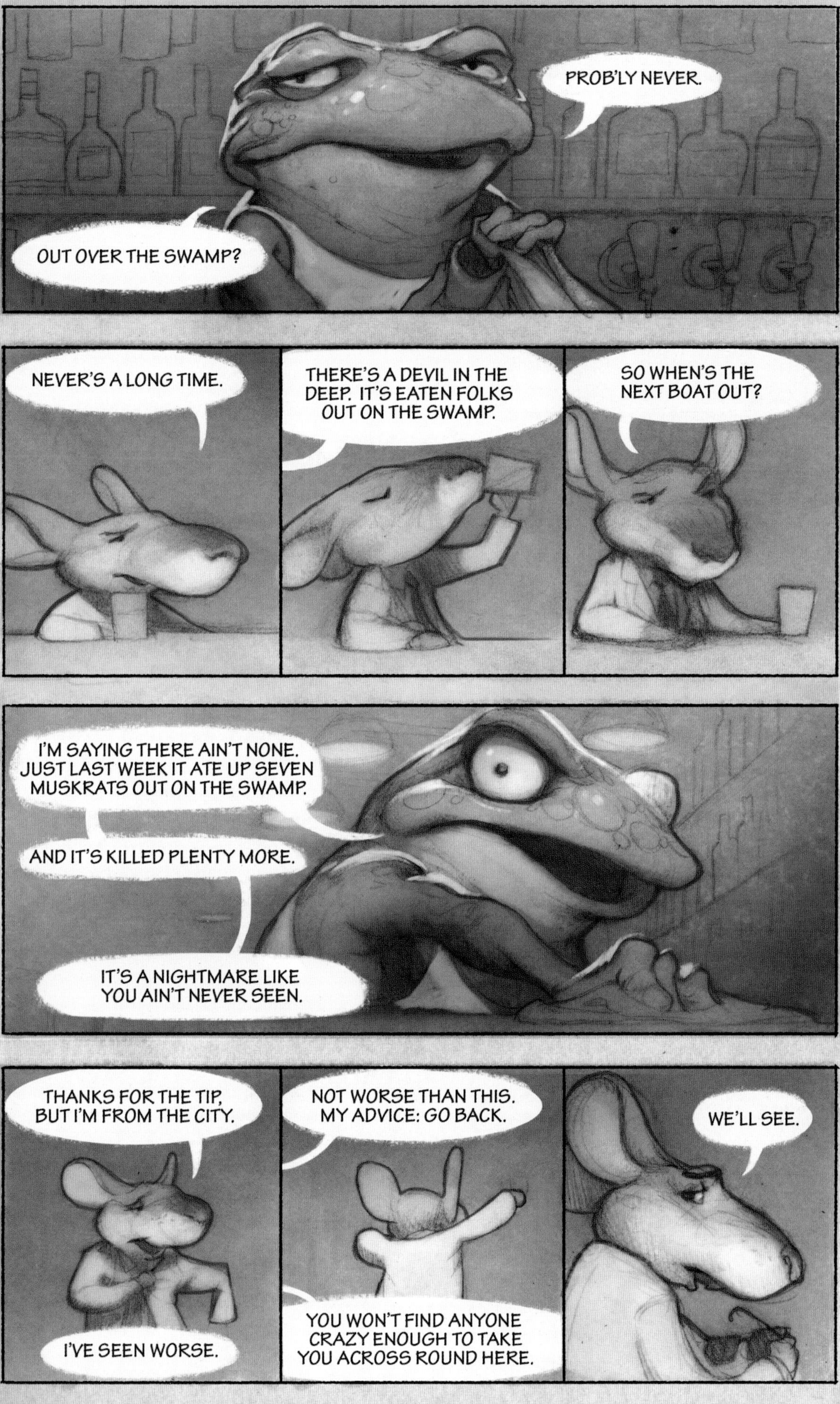
PROB'LY NEVER.
OUT OVER THE SWAMP?
NEVER'S A LONG TIME.
THERE'S A DEVIL IN THE DEEP. IT'S EATEN FOLKS OUT ON THE SWAMP.
SO WHEN'S THE NEXT BOAT OUT?
I'M SAYING THERE AIN'T NONE. JUST LAST WEEK IT ATE UP SEVEN MUSKRATS OUT ON THE SWAMP.
AND IT'S KILLED PLENTY MORE.
IT'S A NIGHTMARE LIKE YOU AIN'T NEVER SEEN.
THANKS FOR THE TIP, BUT I'M FROM THE CITY.
I'VE SEEN WORSE.
NOT WORSE THAN THIS. MY ADVICE: GO BACK.
YOU WON'T FIND ANYONE CRAZY ENOUGH TO TAKE YOU ACROSS ROUND HERE.
WE'LL SEE.

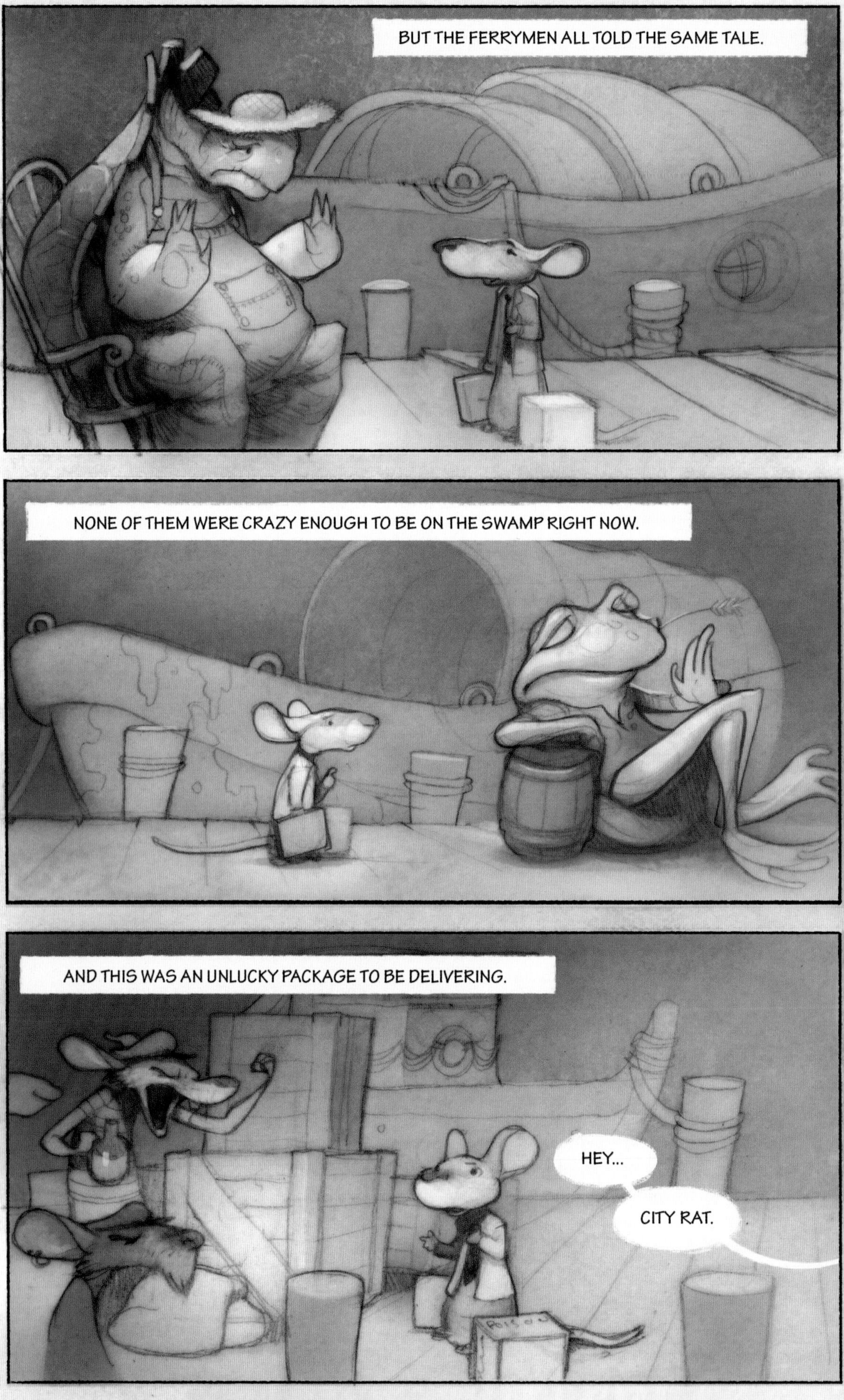
BUT THE FERRYMEN ALL TOLD THE SAME TALE.
NONE OF THEM WERE CRAZY ENOUGH TO BE ON THE SWAMP RIGHT NOW.
AND THIS WAS AN UNLUCKY PACKAGE TO BE DELIVERING.
HEY...
CITY RAT.

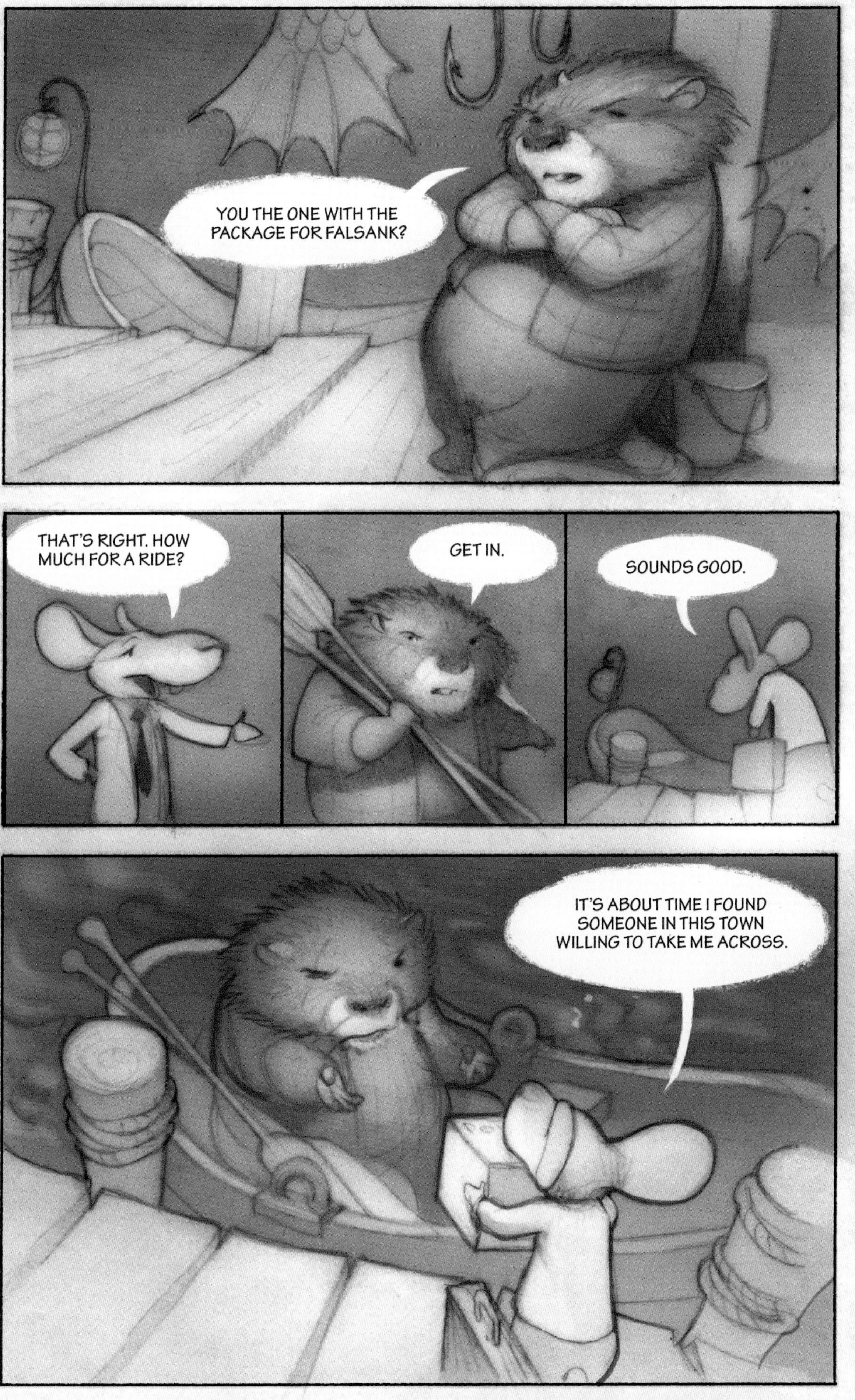
YOU THE ONE WITH THE PACKAGE FOR FALSANK?
THAT'S RIGHT. HOW MUCH FOR A RIDE?
GET IN.
SOUNDS GOOD.
IT'S ABOUT TIME I FOUND SOMEONE IN THIS TOWN WILLING TO TAKE ME ACROSS.

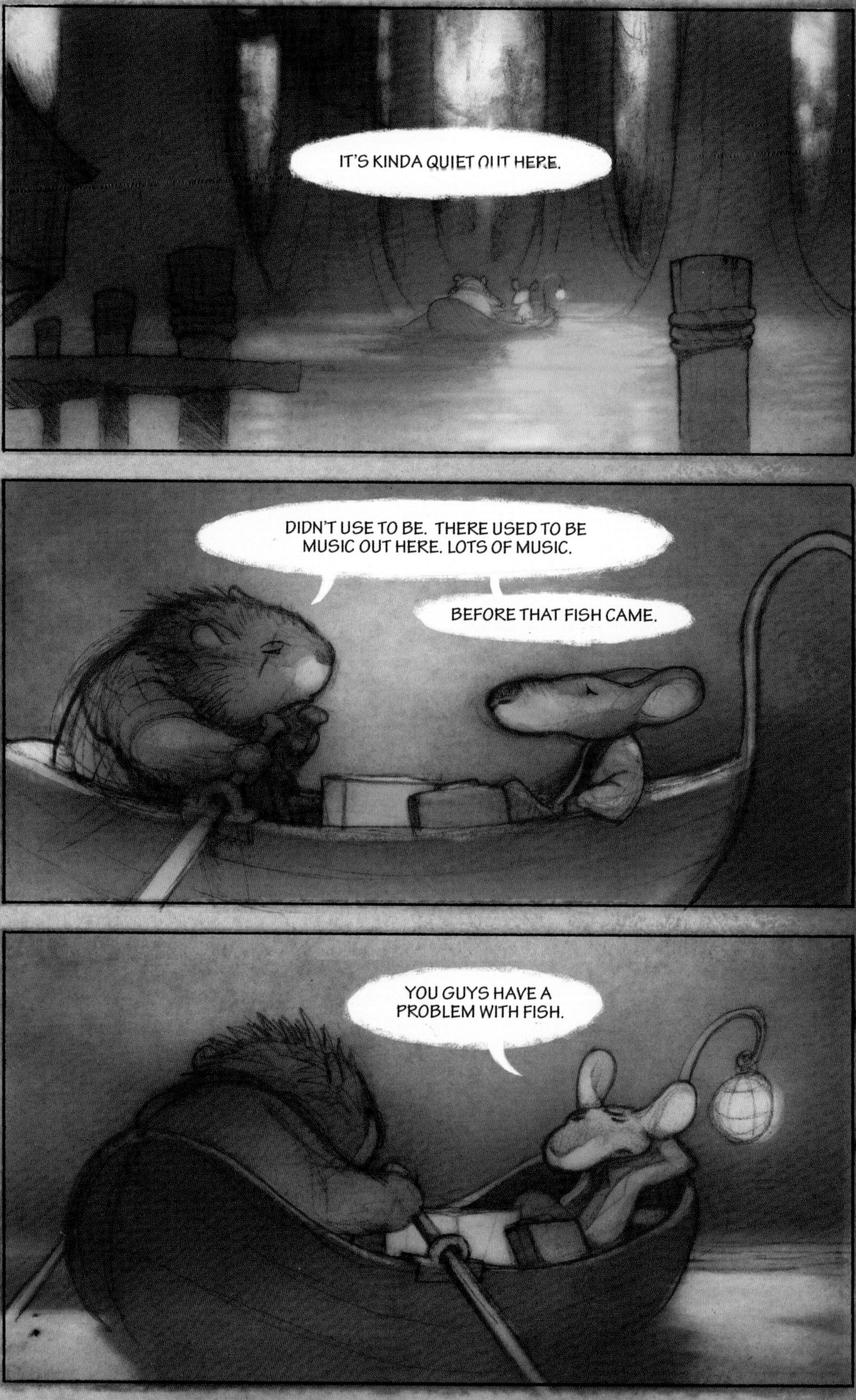
IT'S KINDA QUIET OUT HERE.
DIDN'T USE TO BE. THERE USED TO BE MUSIC OUT HERE. LOTS OF MUSIC.
BEFORE THAT FISH CAME.
YOU GUYS HAVE A PROBLEM WITH FISH.

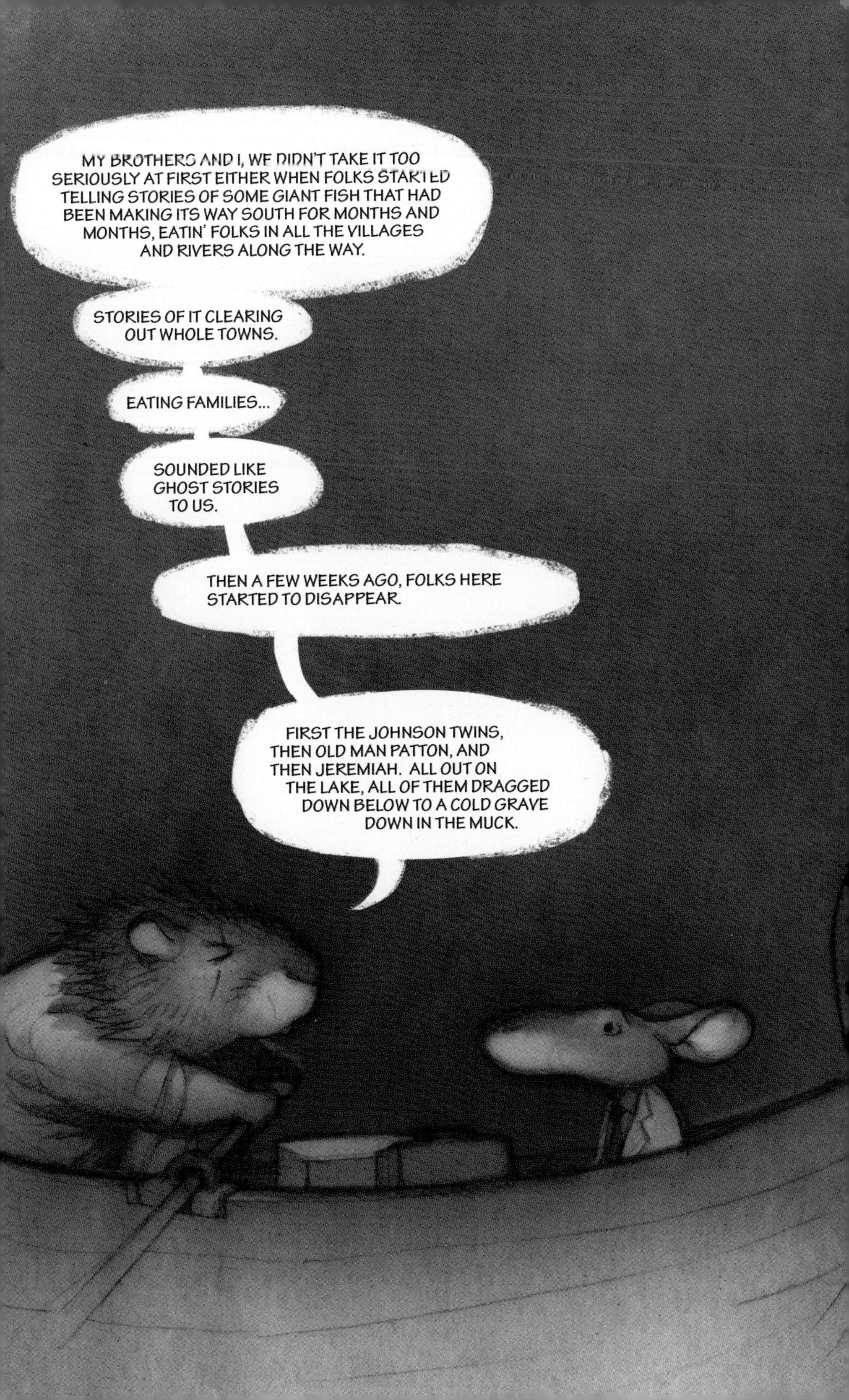
MY BROTHERS AND I, WE DIDN'T TAKE IT TOO SERIOUSLY AT FIRST EITHER WHEN FOLKS STARTED TELLING STORIES OF SOME GIANT FISH THAT HAD BEEN MAKING ITS WAY SOUTH FOR MONTHS AND MONTHS, EATIN' FOLKS IN ALL THE VILLAGES AND RIVERS ALONG THE WAY.
STORIES OF IT CLEARING OUT WHOLE TOWNS.
EATING FAMILIES...
SOUNDED LIKE GHOST STORIES TO US.
THEN A FEW WEEKS AGO, FOLKS HERE STARTED TO DISAPPEAR.
FIRST THE JOHNSON TWINS, THEN OLD MAN PATTON, AND THEN JEREMIAH. ALL OUT ON THE LAKE, ALL OF THEM DRAGGED DOWN BELOW TO A COLD GRAVE DOWN IN THE MUCK.

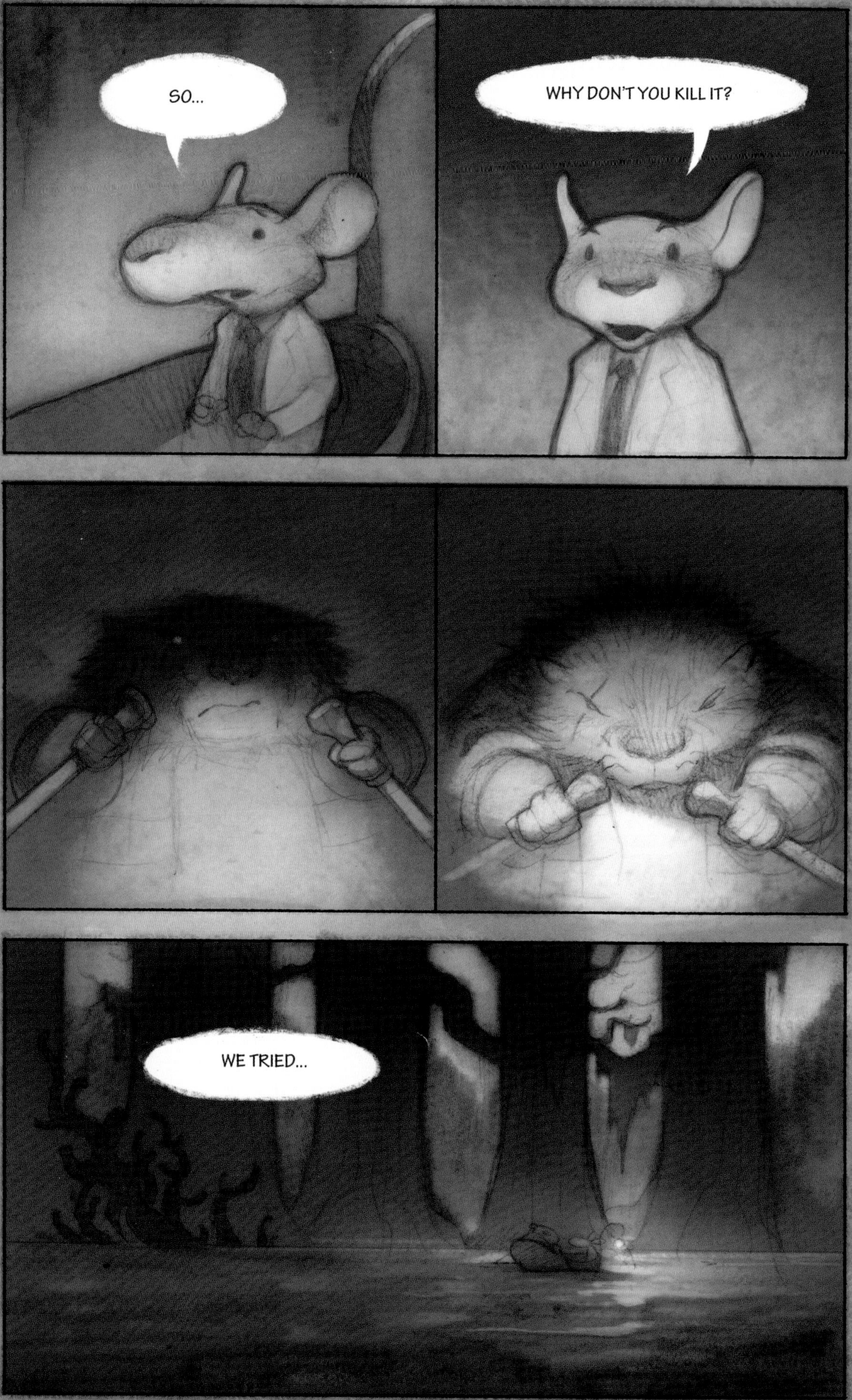
SO...
WHY DON'T YOU KILL IT?
WE TRIED...

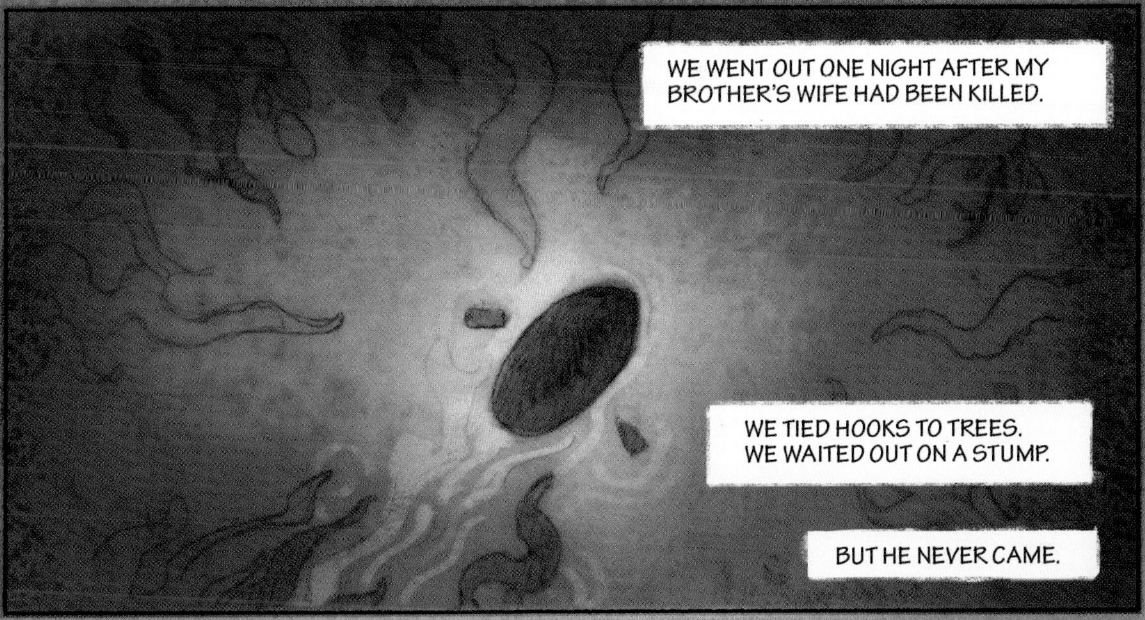
WE WENT OUT ONE NIGHT AFTER MY BROTHER'S WIFE HAD BEEN KILLED.
WE TIED HOOKS TO TREES. WE WAITED OUT ON A STUMP.
BUT HE NEVER CAME.

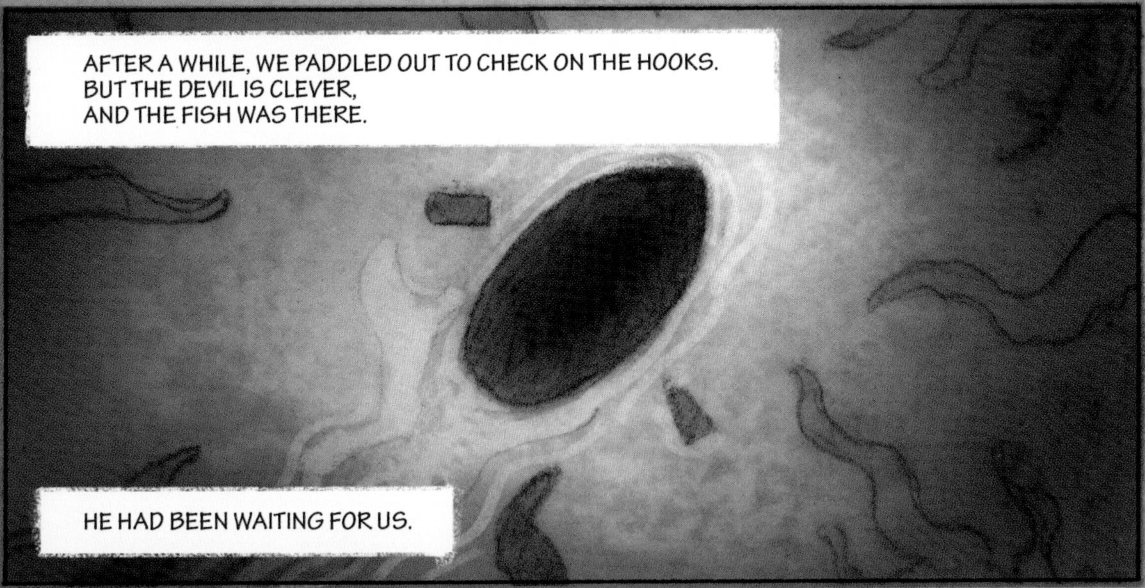
AFTER A WHILE, WE PADDLED OUT TO CHECK ON THE HOOKS. BUT THE DEVIL IS CLEVER, AND THE FISH WAS THERE.
HE HAD BEEN WAITING FOR US.

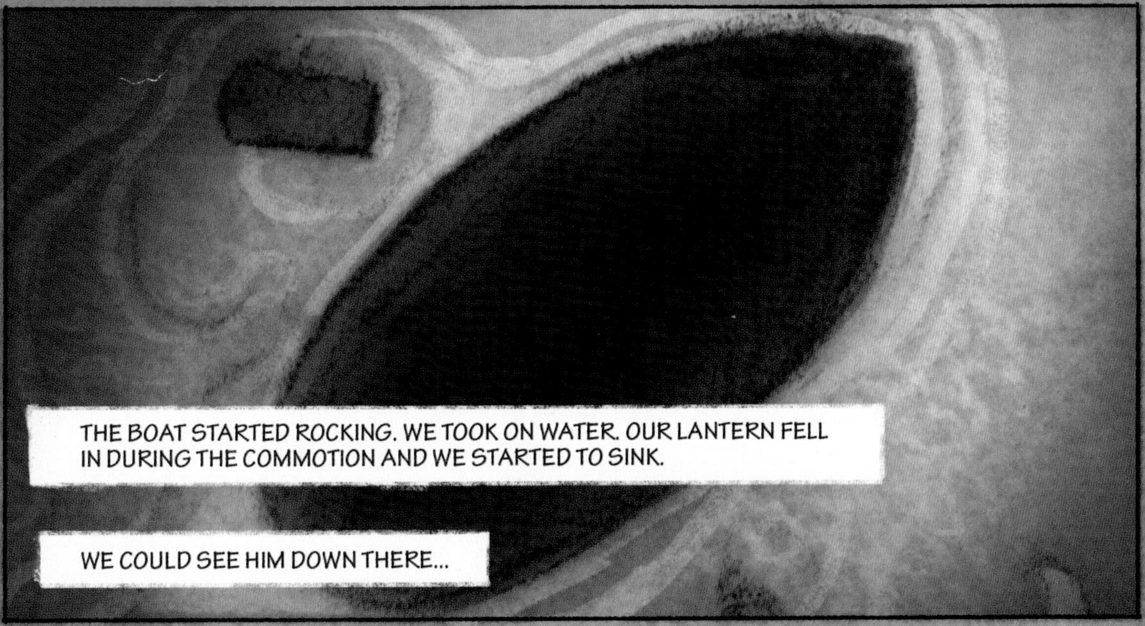
THE BOAT STARTED ROCKING. WE TOOK ON WATER. OUR LANTERN FELL IN DURING THE COMMOTION AND WE STARTED TO SINK.
WE COULD SEE HIM DOWN THERE...

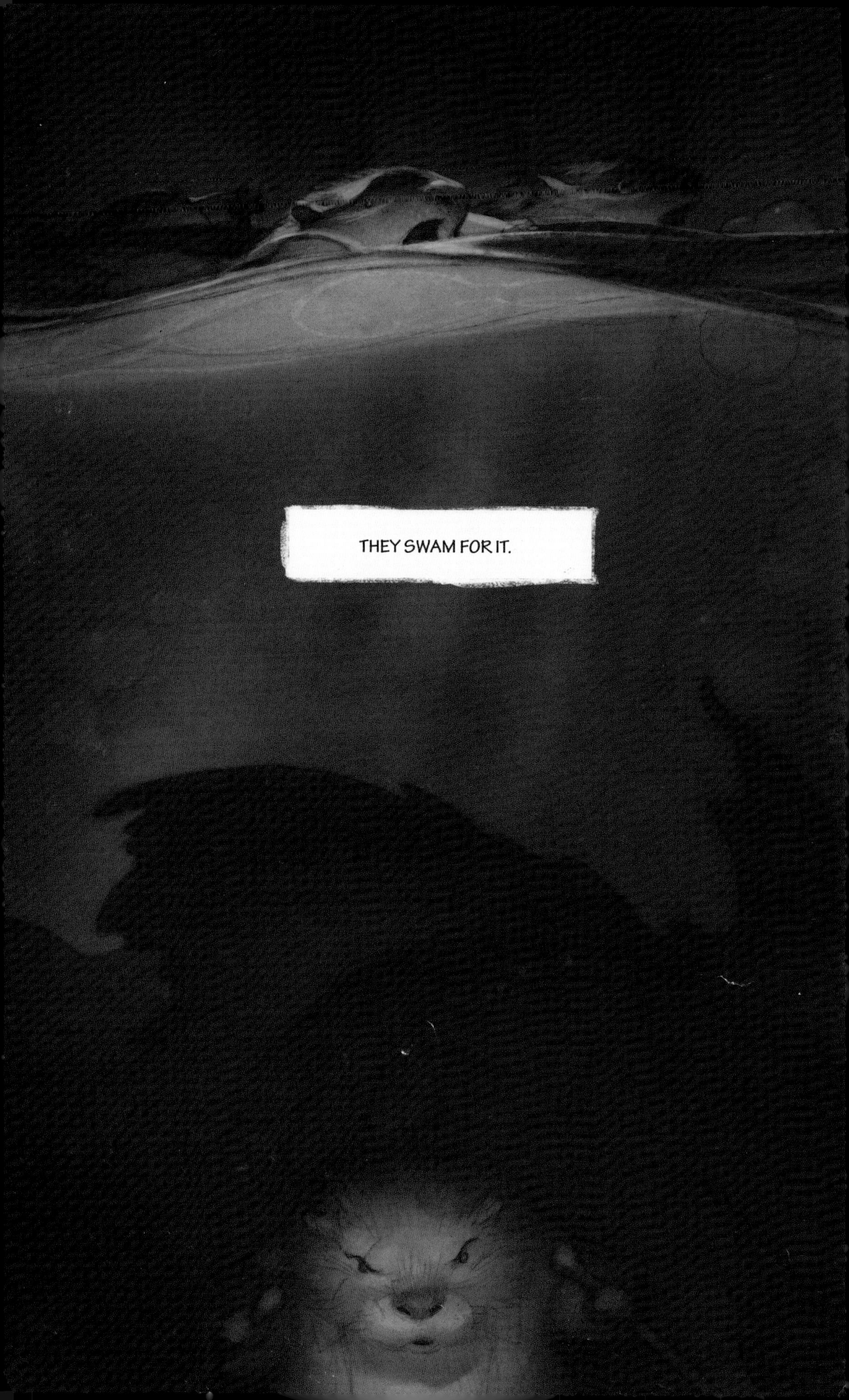
THEY SWAM FOR IT.

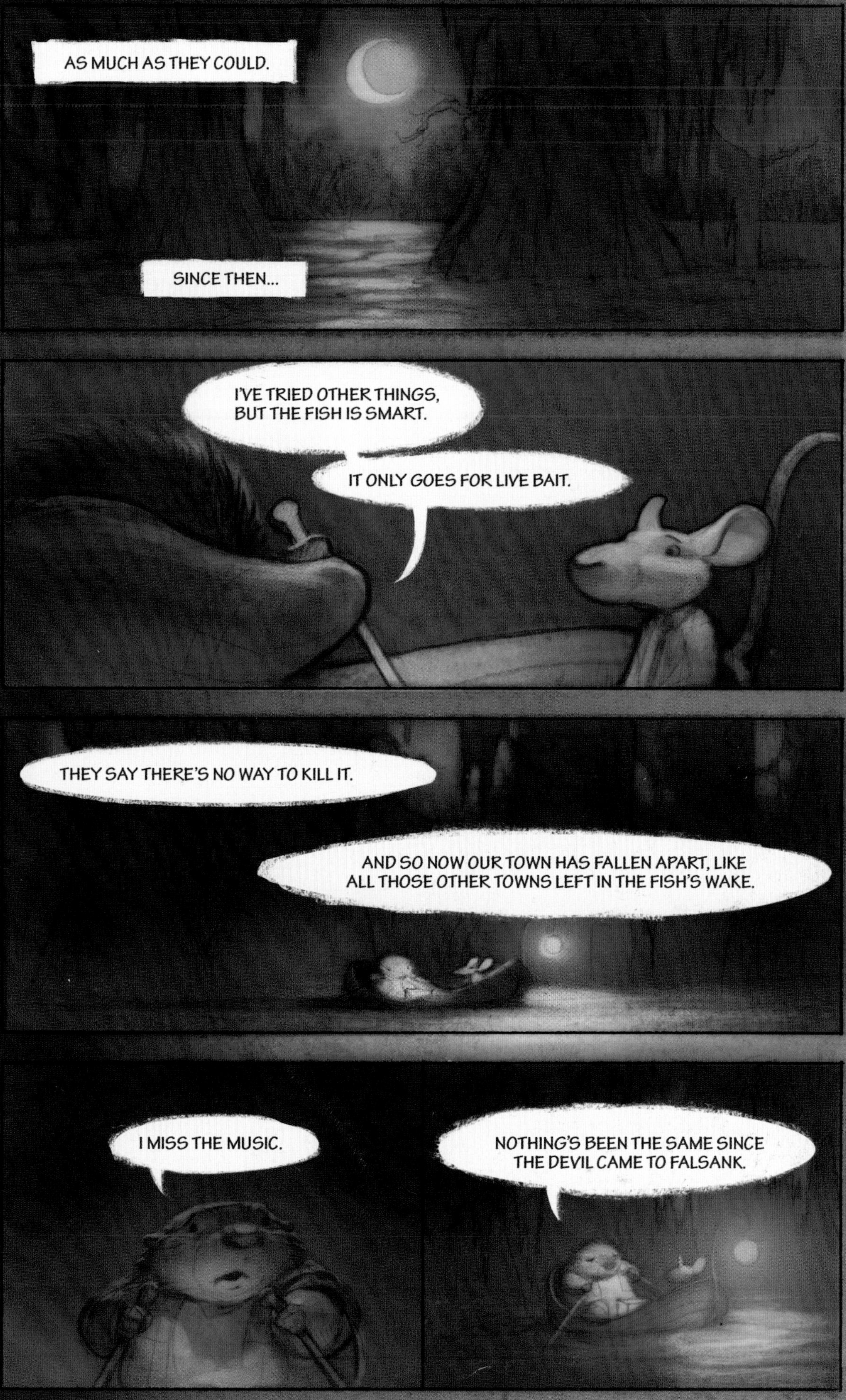
AS MUCH AS THEY COULD.
SINCE THEN...
I'VE TRIED OTHER THINGS, BUT THE FISH IS SMART.
IT ONLY GOES FOR LIVE BAIT.
THEY SAY THERE'S NO WAY TO KILL IT.
AND SO NOW OUR TOWN HAS FALLEN APART, LIKE ALL THOSE OTHER TOWNS LEFT IN THE FISH'S WAKE.
I MISS THE MUSIC.
NOTHING'S BEEN THE SAME SINCE THE DEVIL CAME TO FALSANK.

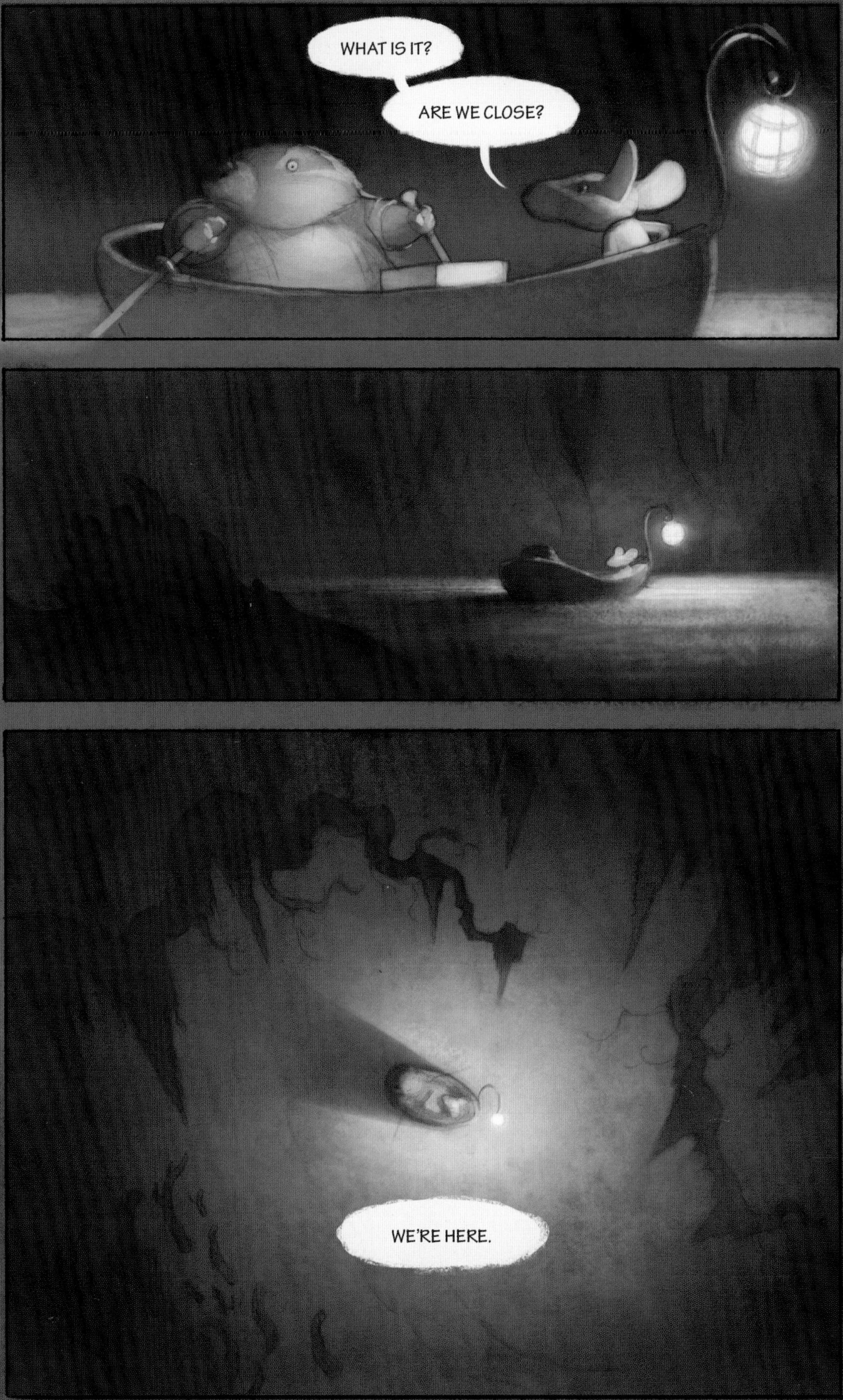
WHAT IS IT?
ARE WE CLOSE?
WE'RE HERE.

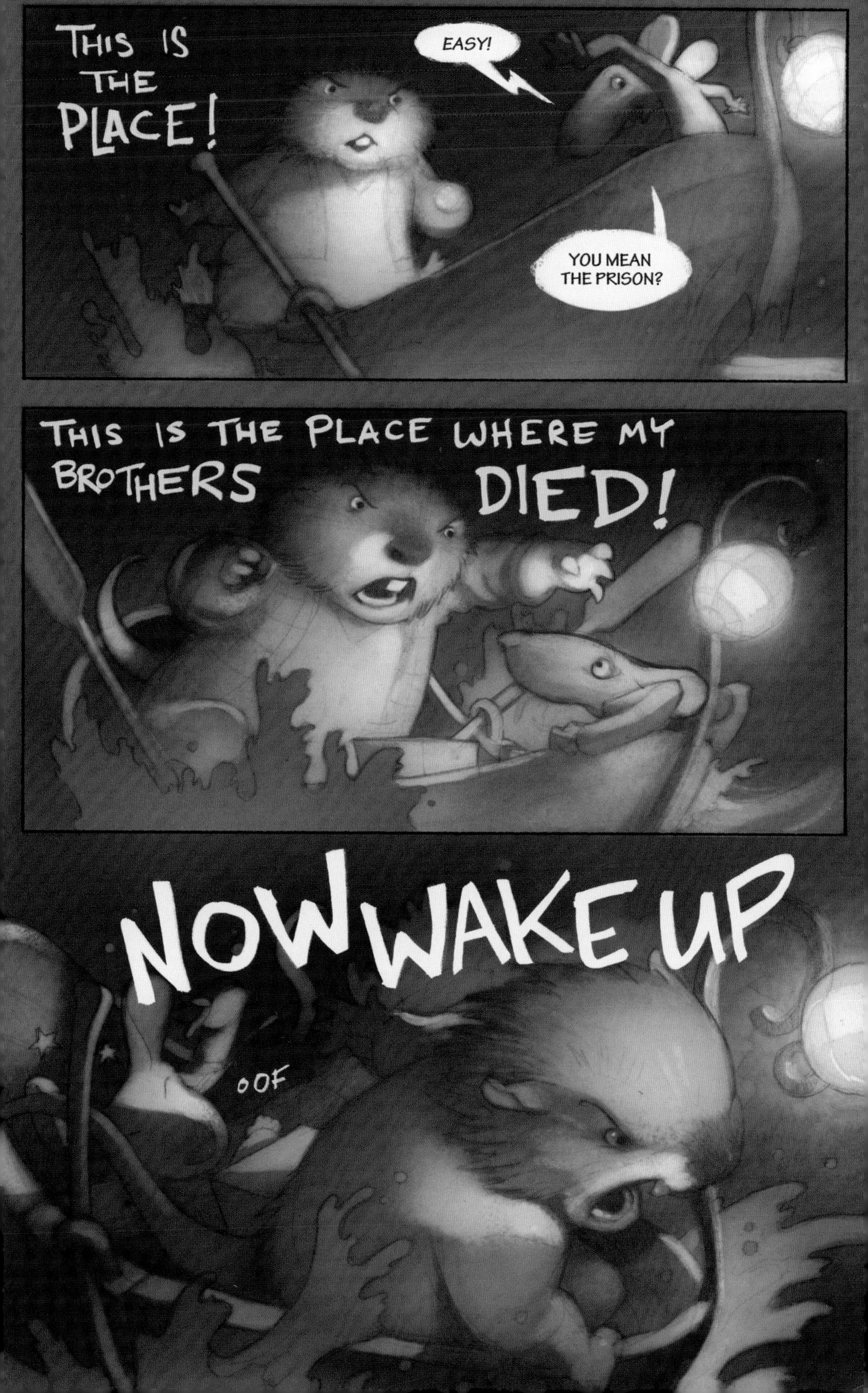
THIS IS THE PLACE!
EASY!
YOU MEAN THE PRISON?
THIS IS THE PLACE WHERE MY BROTHERS DIED!
NOW WAKE UP
OOF

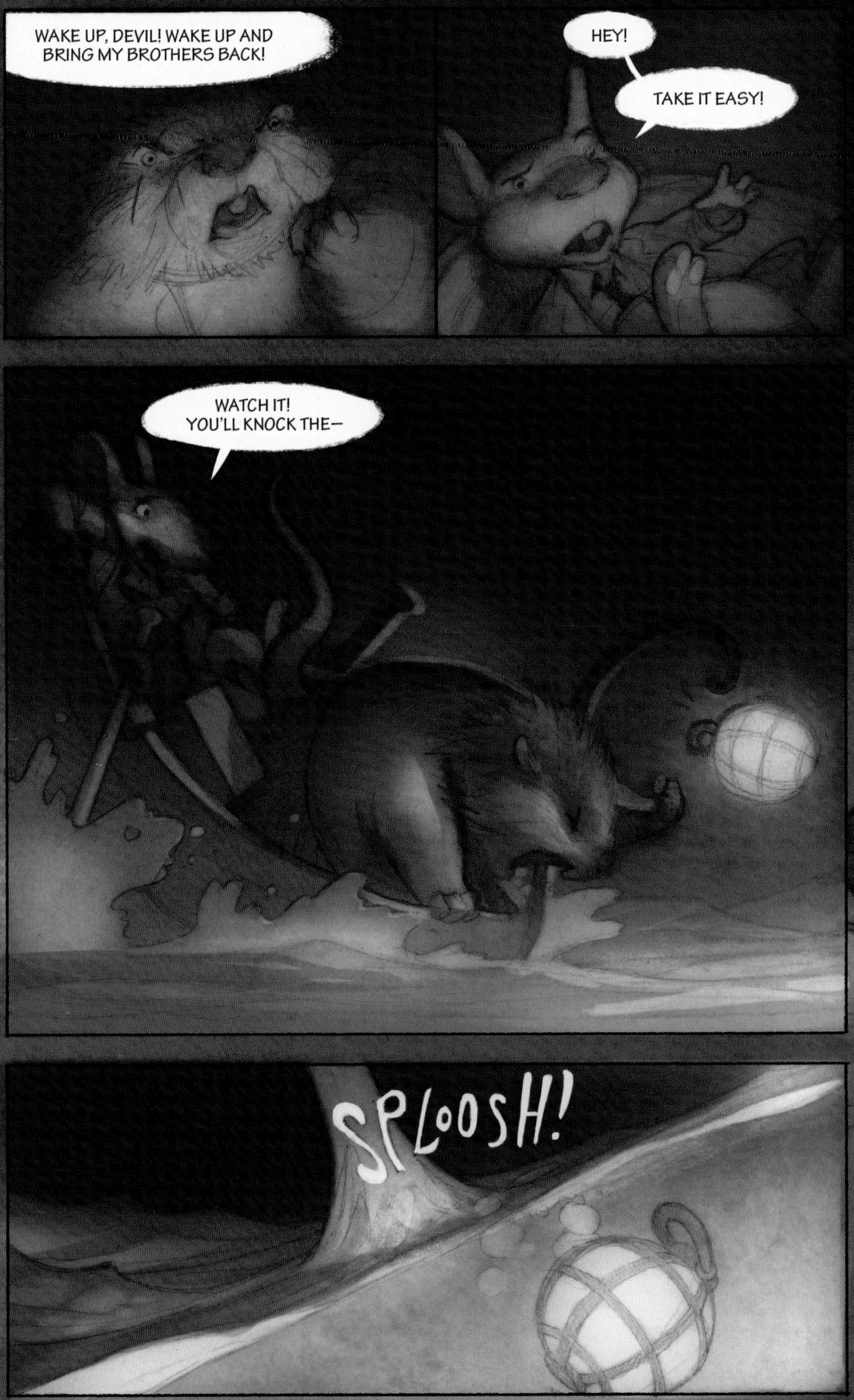
WAKE UP, DEVIL! WAKE UP AND BRING MY BROTHERS BACK!
HEY!
TAKE IT EASY!
WATCH IT! YOU'LL KNOCK THE—
SPLOOSH!

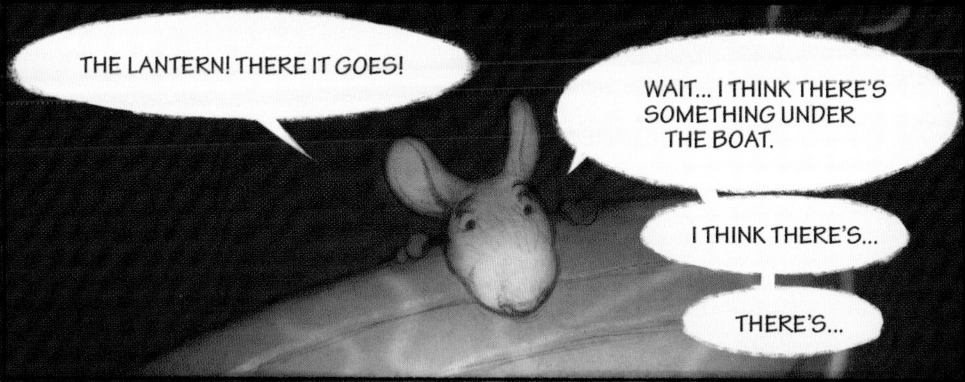
THE LANTERN! THERE IT GOES!
WAIT... I THINK THERE'S SOMETHING UNDER THE BOAT.
I THINK THERE'S...
THERE'S...

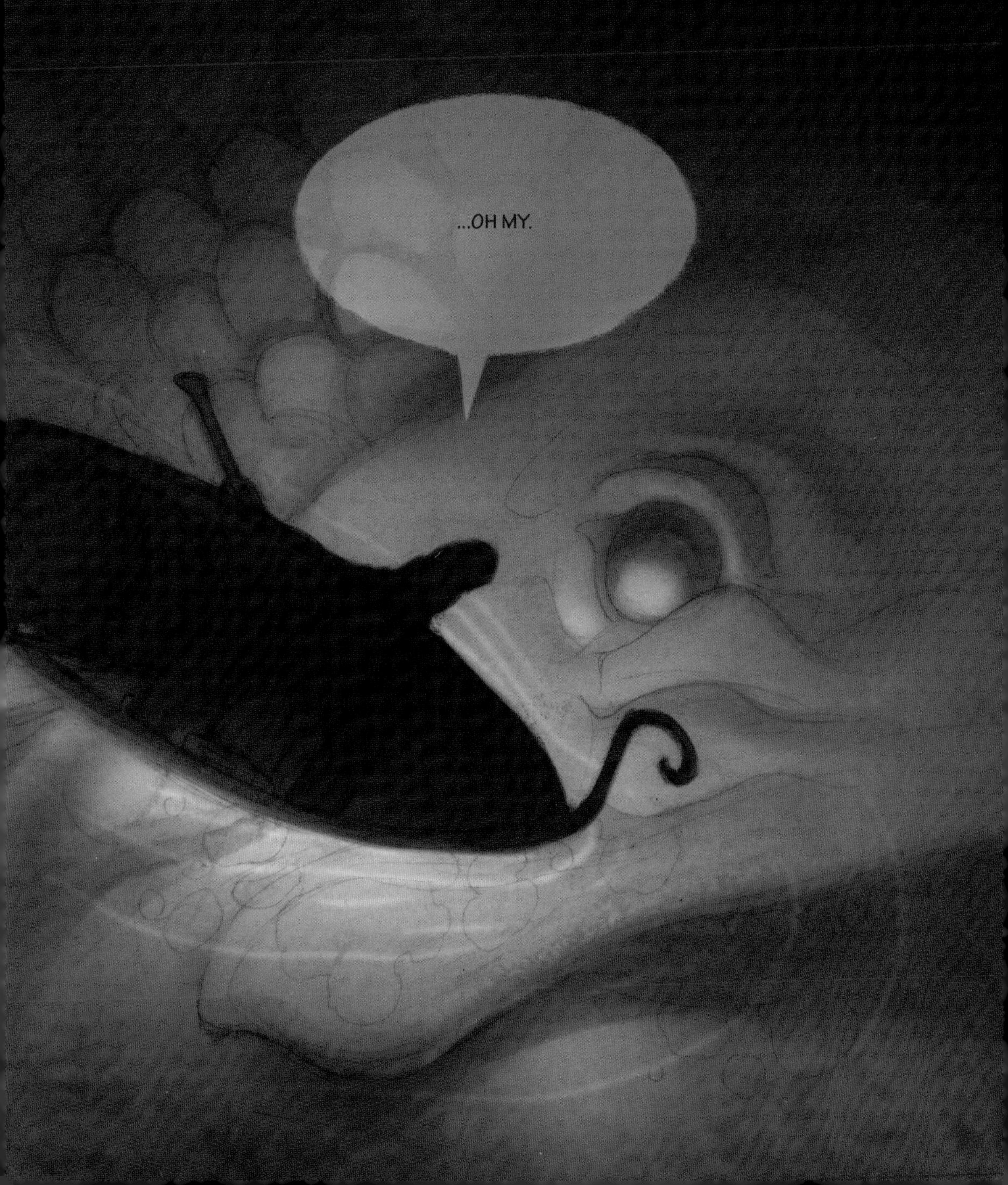
...OH MY.

WE WEREN'T GOING TO THE PRISON, WERE WE?
WHAT ARE WE—
THANKS FOR YOUR HELP, CITY RAT!
CRACK
I SHOULD HAVE KNOWN THE RAT WAS CRAZY,
WHEN HE DIDN'T TAKE THE MONEY.

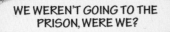

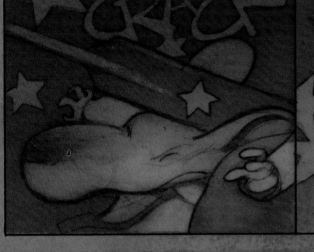

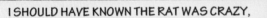

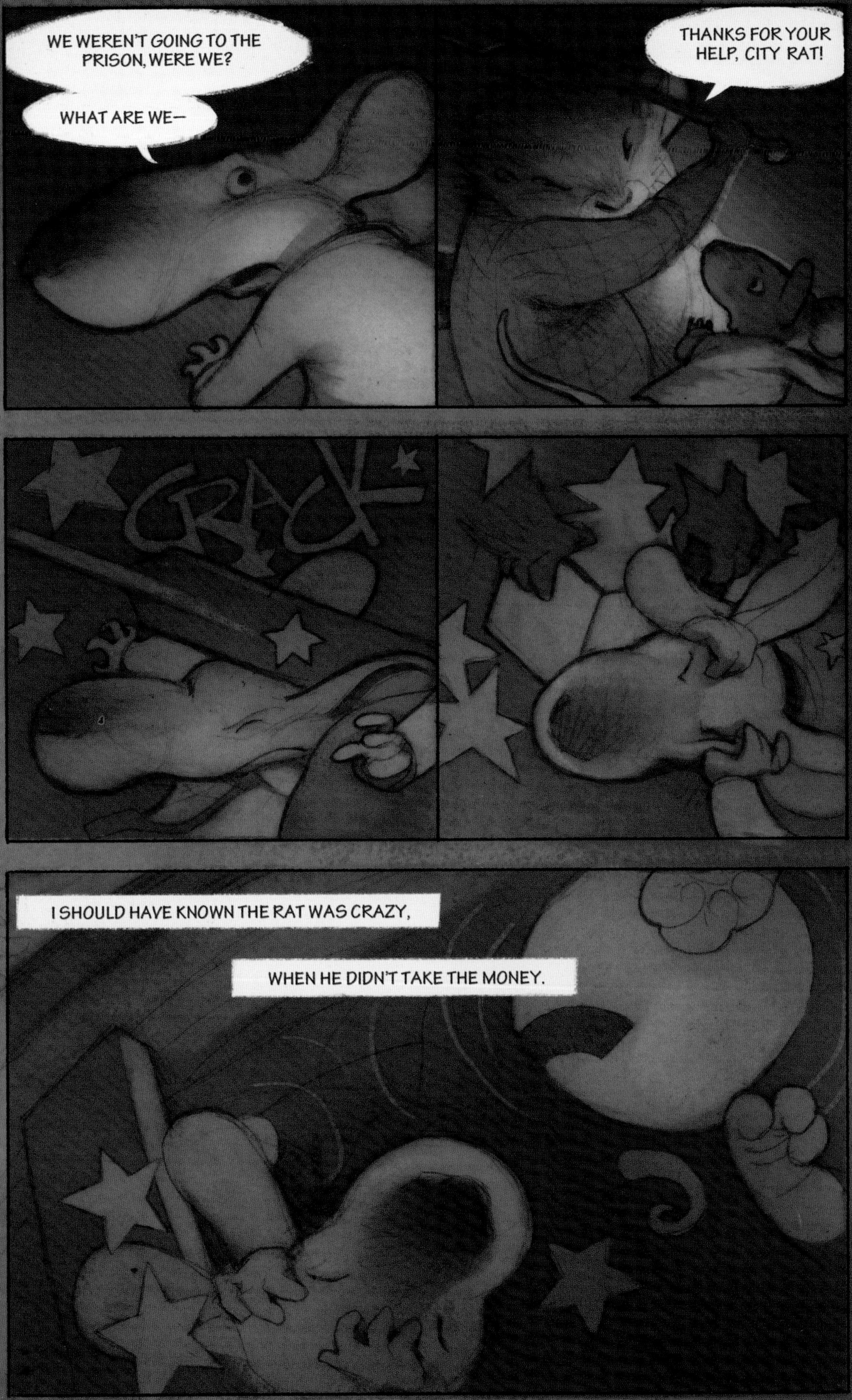

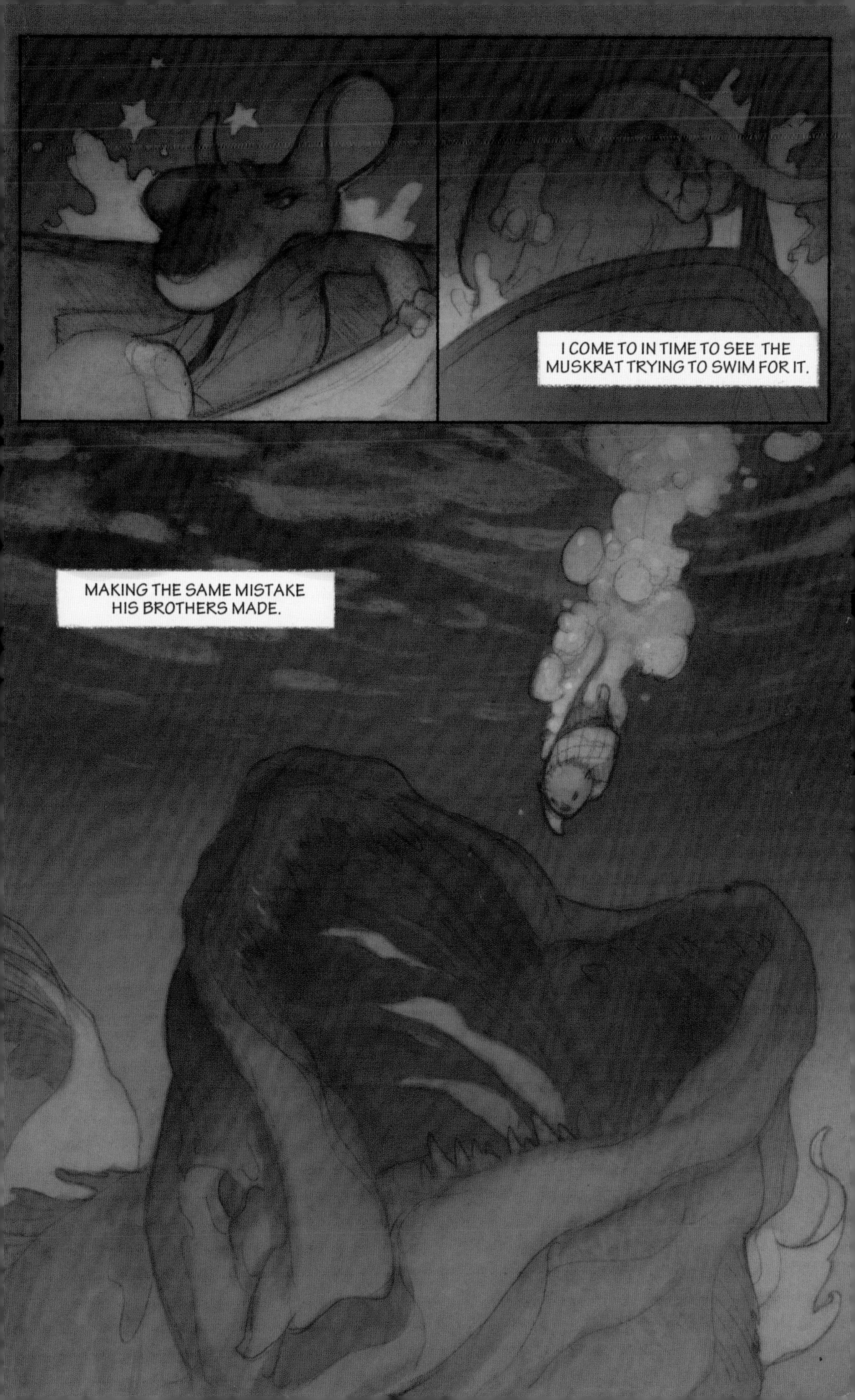
I COME TO IN TIME TO SEE THE MUSKRAT TRYING TO SWIM FOR IT.
MAKING THE SAME MISTAKE HIS BROTHERS MADE.

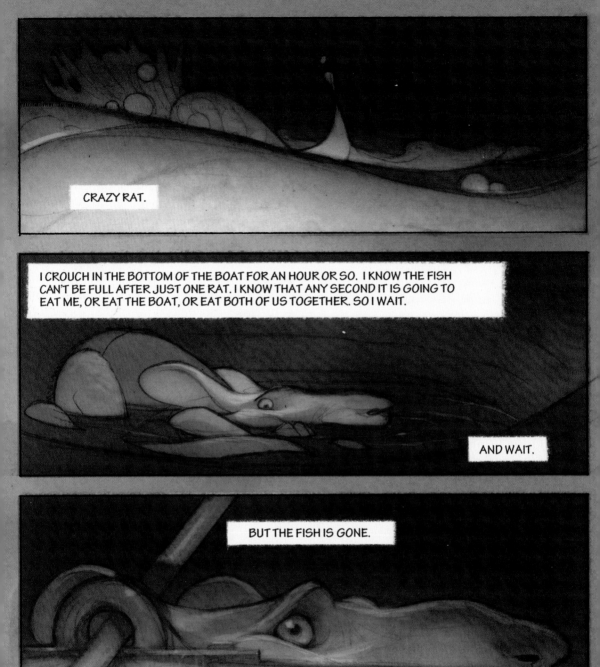

CRAZY RAT.

I CROUCH IN THE BOTTOM OF THE BOAT FOR AN HOUR OR SO. I KNOW THE FISH CAN'T BE FULL AFTER JUST ONE RAT. I KNOW THAT ANY SECOND IT IS GOING TO EAT ME, OR EAT THE BOAT, OR EAT BOTH OF US TOGETHER. SO I WAIT.

AND WAIT.

BUT THE FISH IS GONE.

I BAIL OUT THE REST AND PADDLE AS FAST AS I CAN AWAY FROM THERE.

BACK TOWARD TOWN. BACK TO TELL THEM THAT THE CRAZY OLD MUSKRAT WON'T BE COMING HOME.

AND BACK TO FIND ANOTHER WAY ACROSS THIS SWAMP TO DELIVER THE PACKAGE...

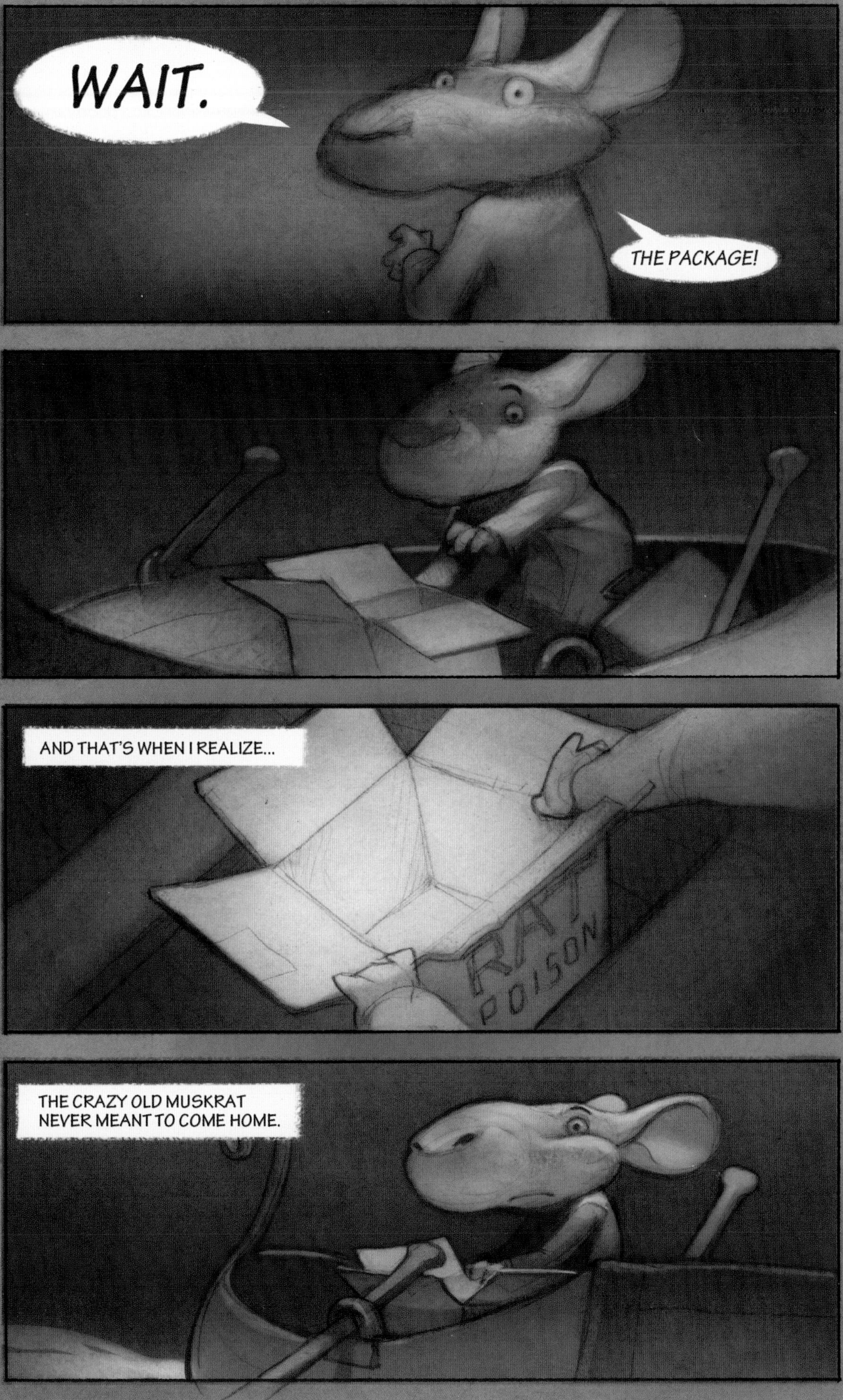
WAIT.
THE PACKAGE!
AND THAT'S WHEN I REALIZE...
RAT POISON
THE CRAZY OLD MUSKRAT NEVER MEANT TO COME HOME.

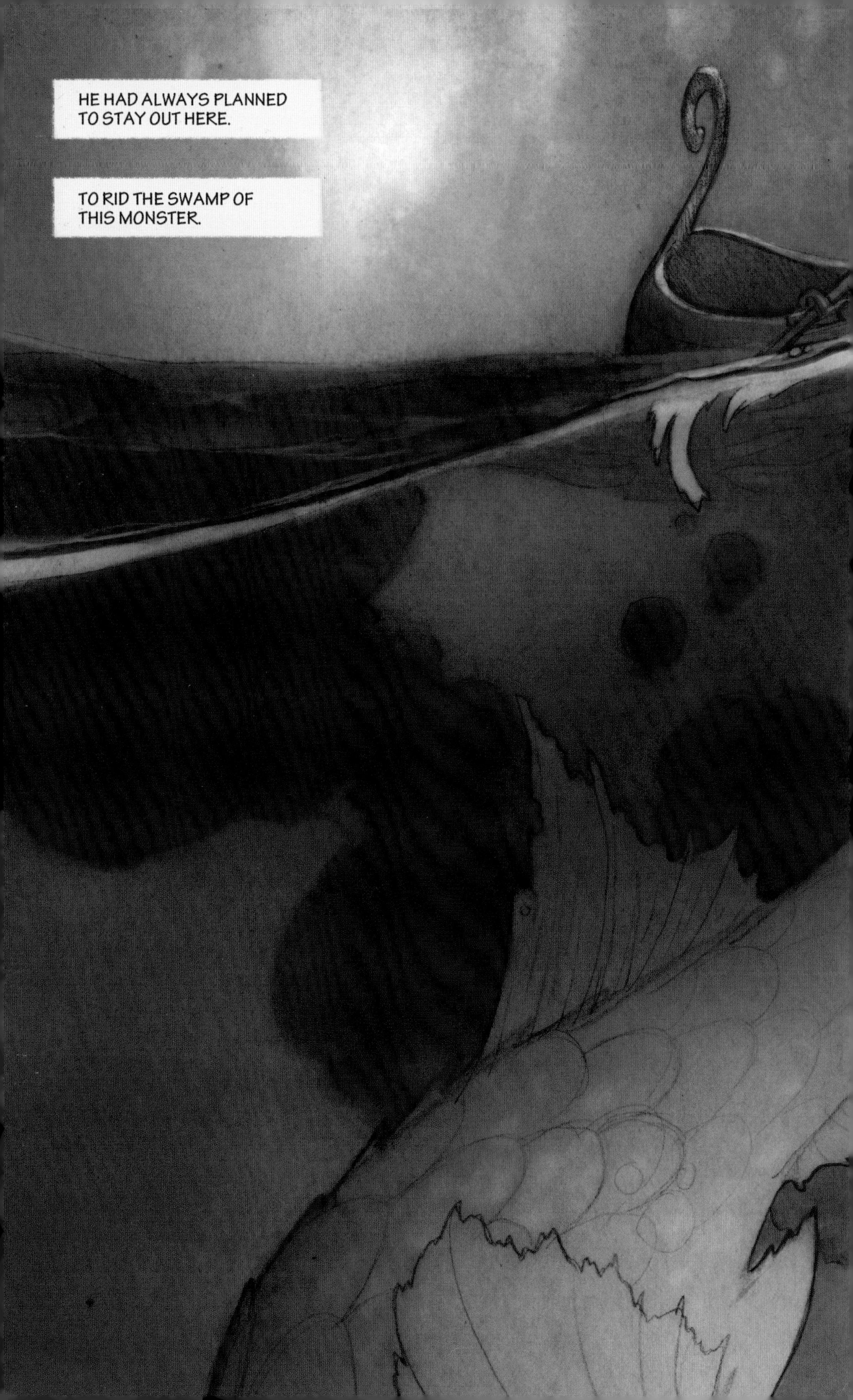
HE HAD ALWAYS PLANNED TO STAY OUT HERE.
TO RID THE SWAMP OF THIS MONSTER.

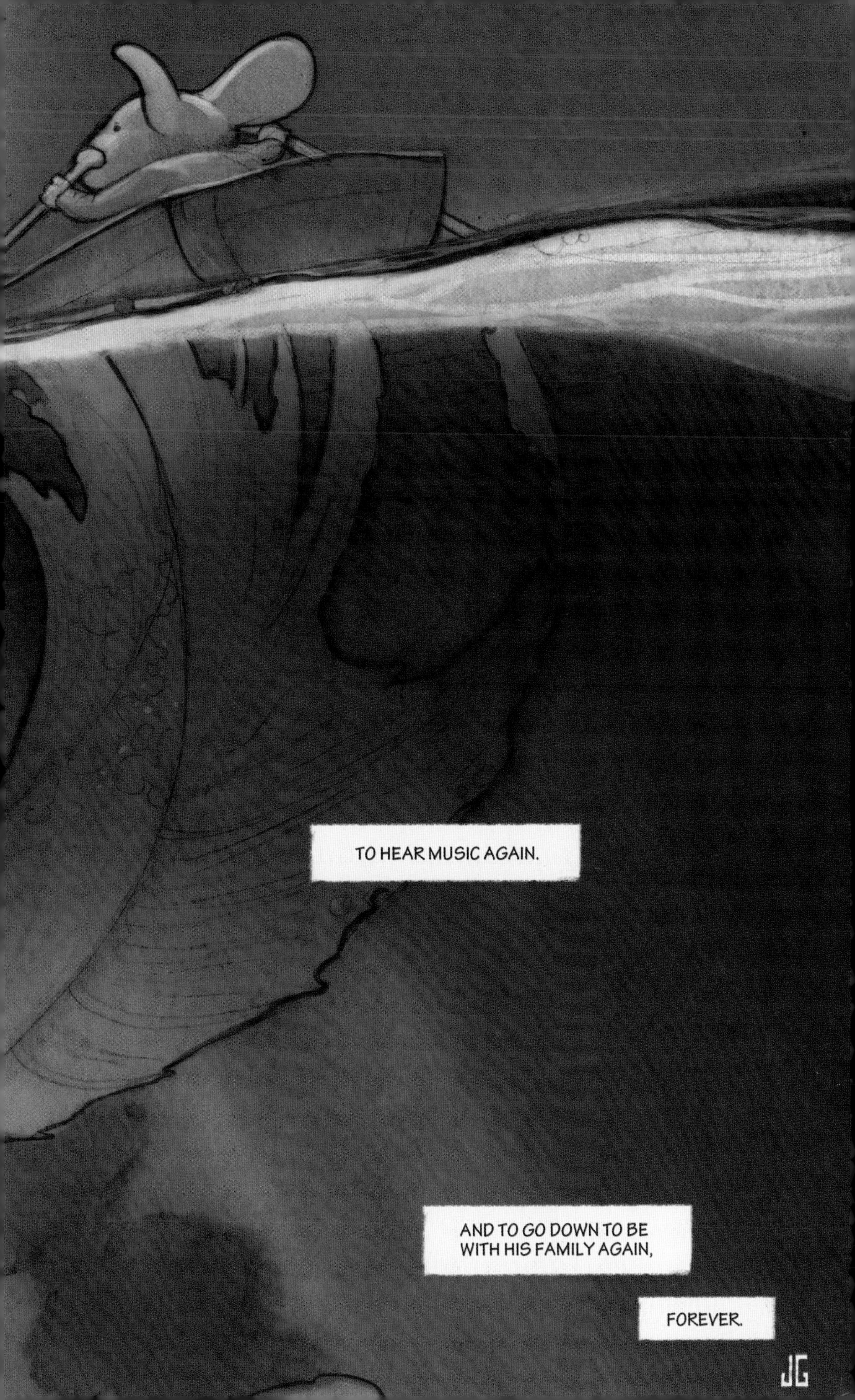
TO HEAR MUSIC AGAIN.
AND TO GO DOWN TO BE WITH HIS FAMILY AGAIN,
FOREVER.
JG

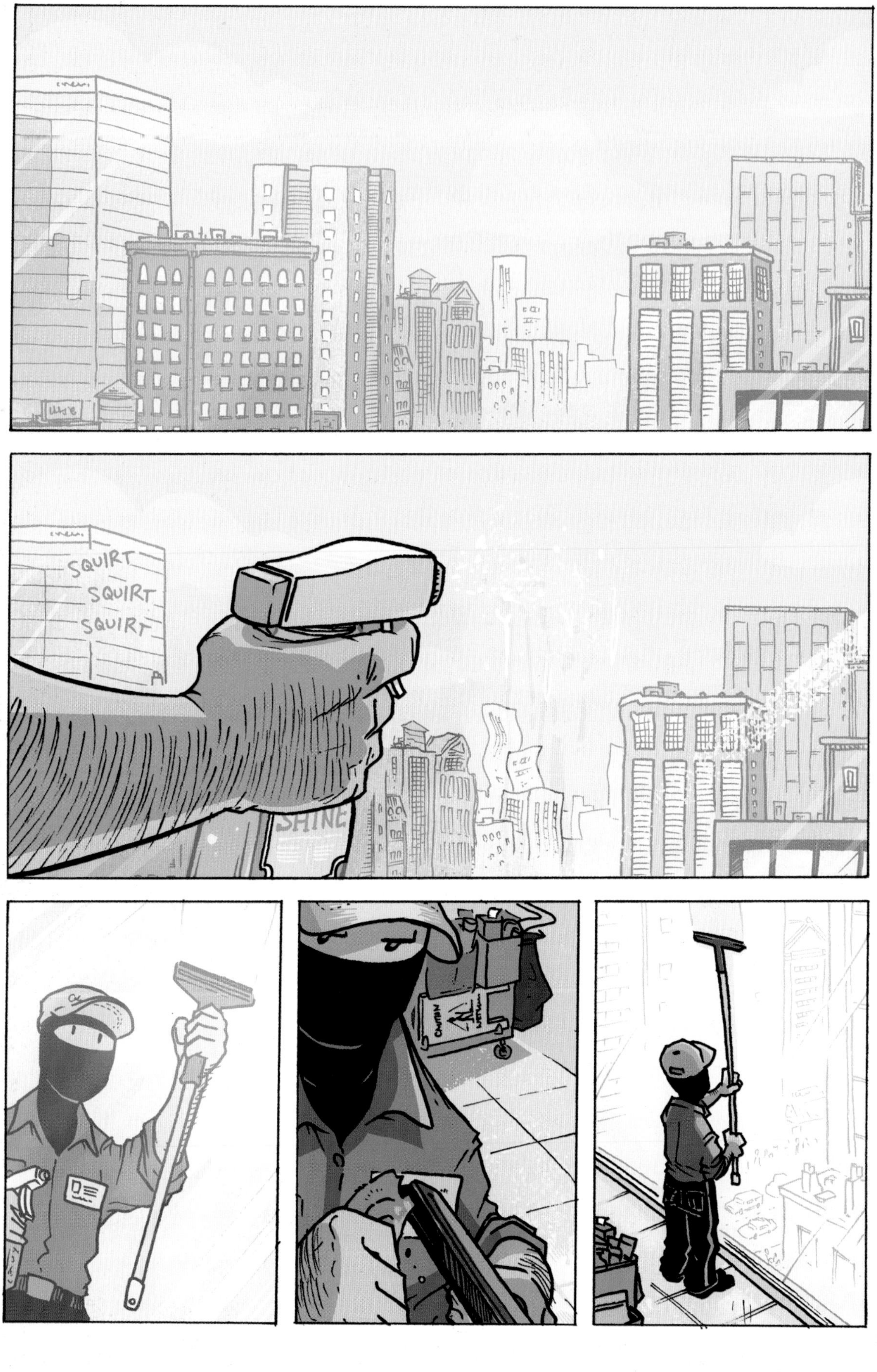
SQUIRT
SQUIRT
SQUIRT
SHINE

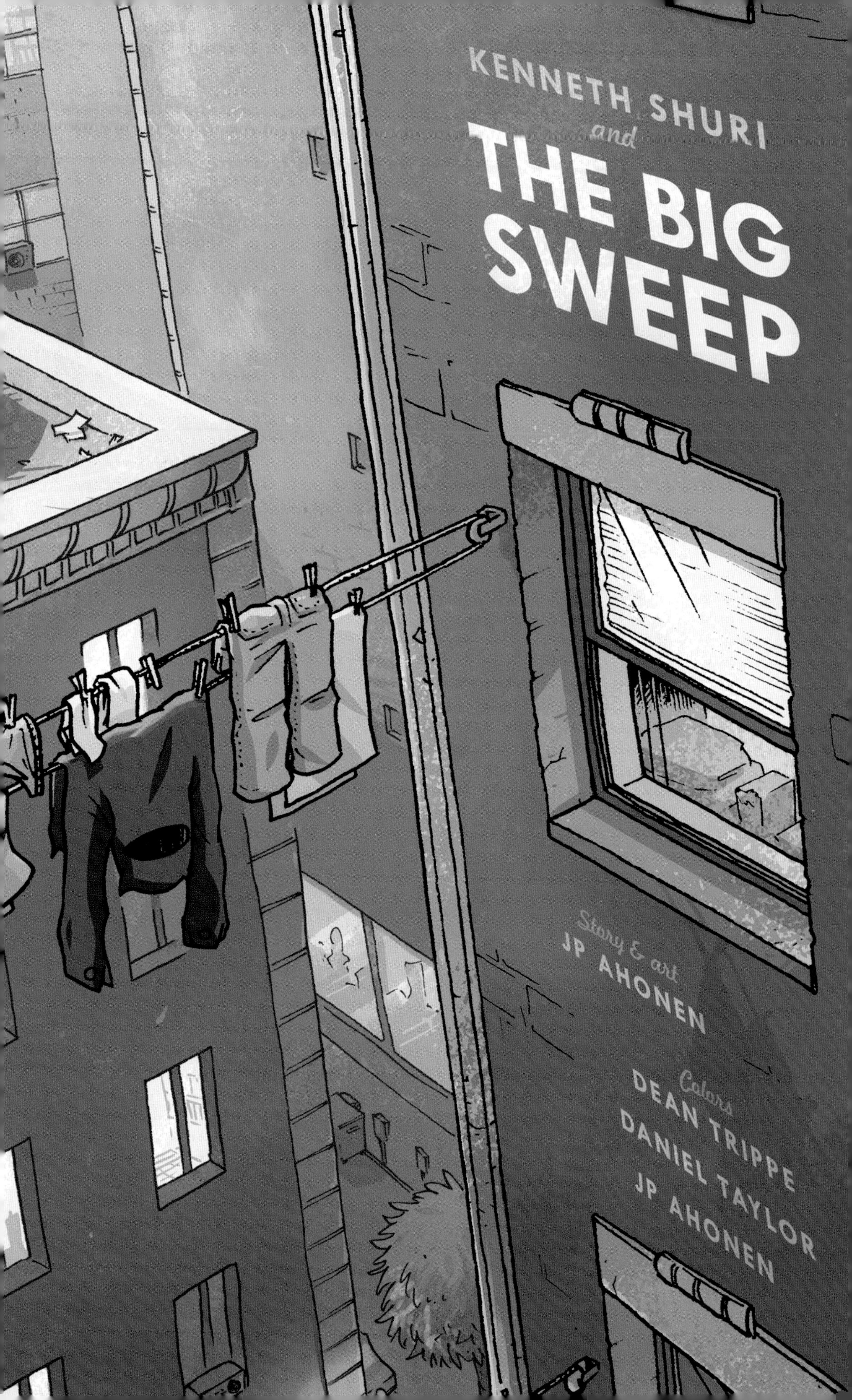
KENNETH SHURI
and
THE BIG SWEEP
Story & art
JP AHONEN
Colors
DEAN TRIPPE
DANIEL TAYLOR
JP AHONEN

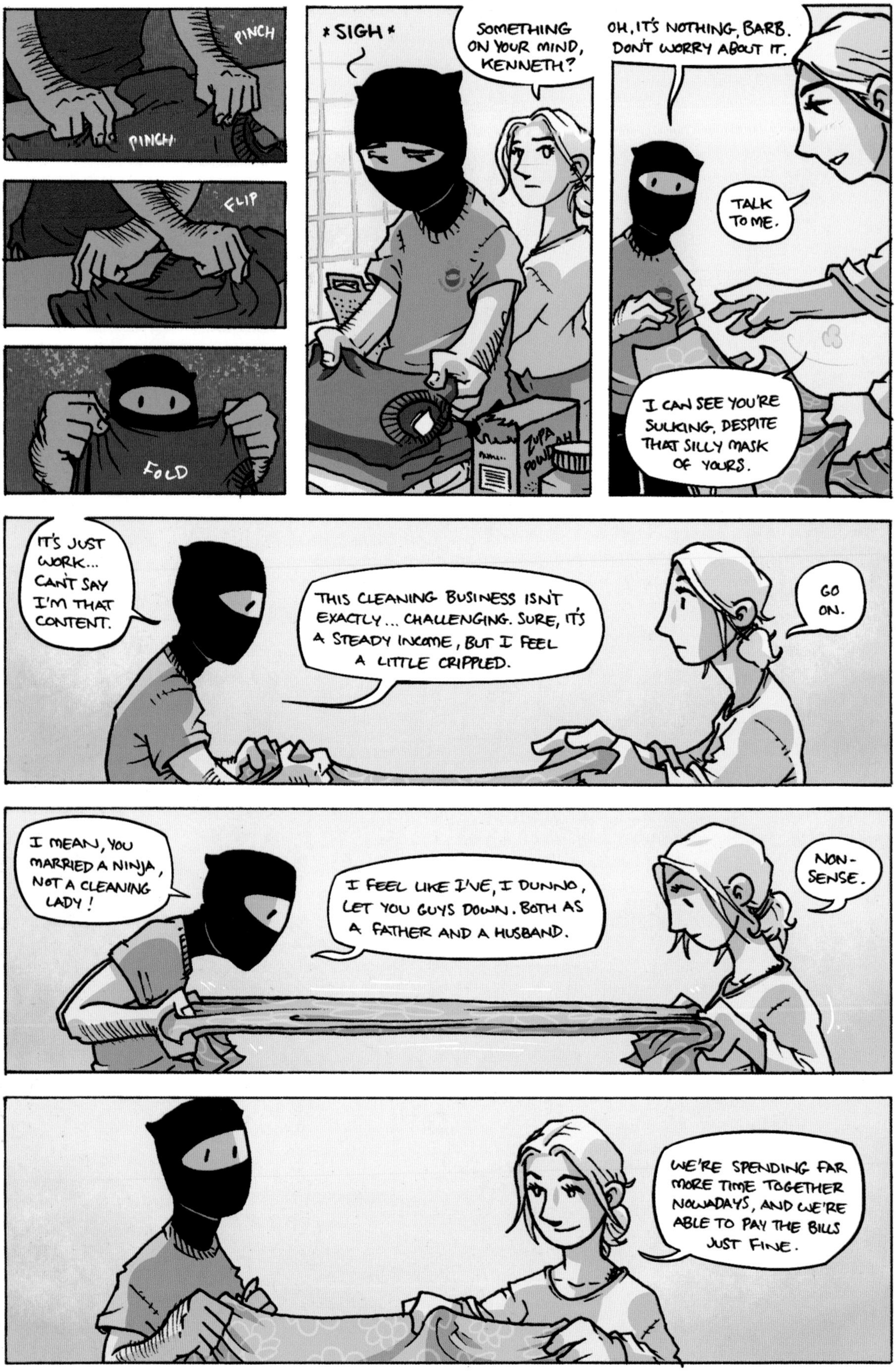
PINCH
PINCH
FLIP
FOLD
SIGH
SOMETHING ON YOUR MIND, KENNETH?
OH, IT'S NOTHING, BARB. DON'T WORRY ABOUT IT.
TALK TO ME.
I CAN SEE YOU'RE SULKING, DESPITE THAT SILLY MASK OF YOURS.
ZUPA POWDAH
IT'S JUST WORK... CAN'T SAY I'M THAT CONTENT.
THIS CLEANING BUSINESS ISN'T EXACTLY... CHALLENGING. SURE, IT'S A STEADY INCOME, BUT I FEEL A LITTLE CRIPPLED.
GO ON.
I MEAN, YOU MARRIED A NINJA, NOT A CLEANING LADY!
I FEEL LIKE I'VE, I DUNNO, LET YOU GUYS DOWN. BOTH AS A FATHER AND A HUSBAND.
NON-SENSE.
WE'RE SPENDING FAR MORE TIME TOGETHER NOWADAYS, AND WE'RE ABLE TO PAY THE BILLS JUST FINE.

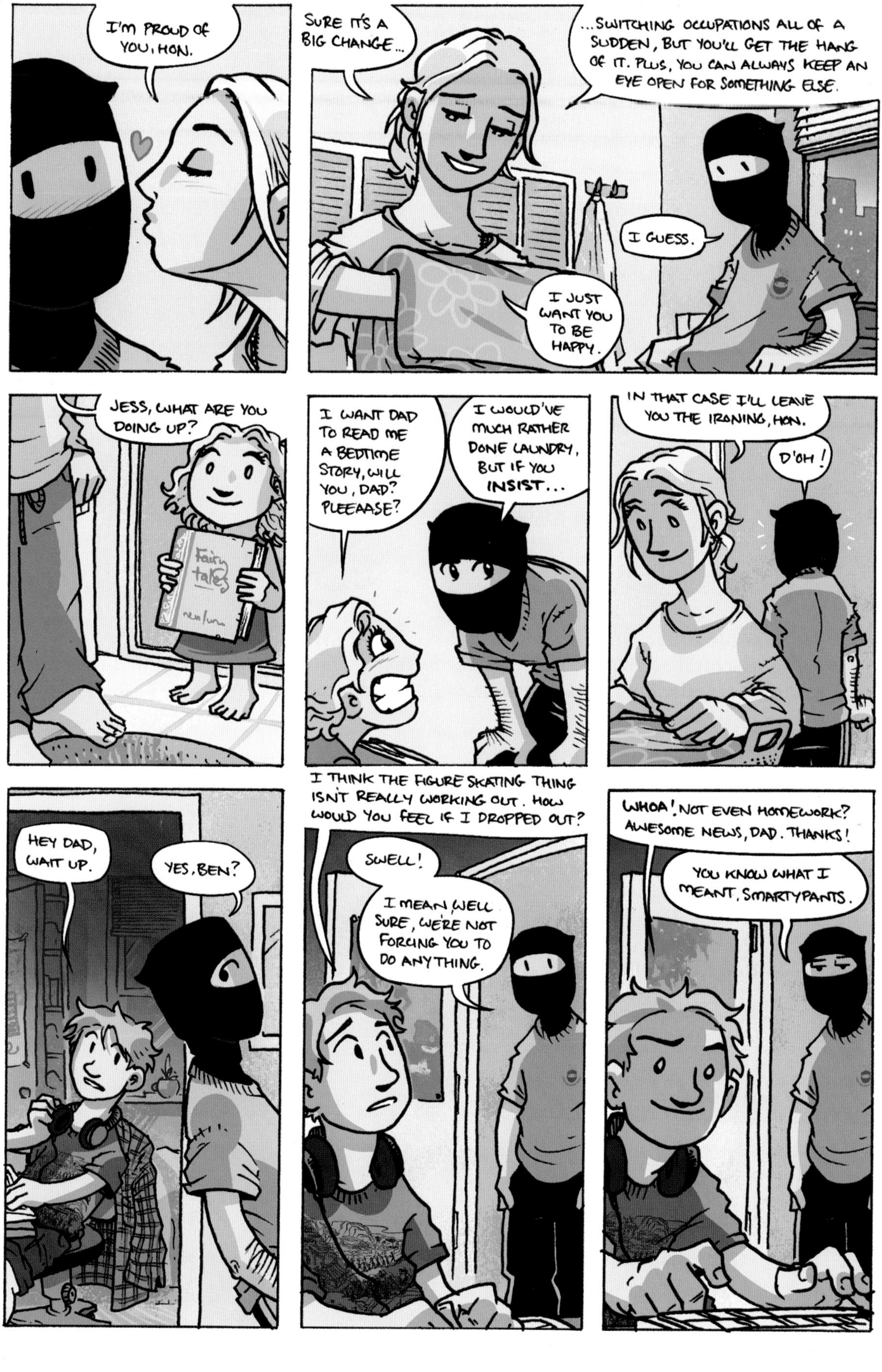
I'M PROUD OF YOU, HON.
SURE IT'S A BIG CHANGE...
...SWITCHING OCCUPATIONS ALL OF A SUDDEN, BUT YOU'LL GET THE HANG OF IT. PLUS, YOU CAN ALWAYS KEEP AN EYE OPEN FOR SOMETHING ELSE.
I GUESS.
I JUST WANT YOU TO BE HAPPY.
JESS, WHAT ARE YOU DOING UP?
Fairy tales
I WANT DAD TO READ ME A BEDTIME STORY, WILL YOU, DAD? PLEEAASE?
I WOULD'VE MUCH RATHER DONE LAUNDRY, BUT IF YOU INSIST...
IN THAT CASE I'LL LEAVE YOU THE IRONING, HON.
D'OH!
HEY DAD, WAIT UP.
YES, BEN?
I THINK THE FIGURE SKATING THING ISN'T REALLY WORKING OUT. HOW WOULD YOU FEEL IF I DROPPED OUT?
SWELL!
I MEAN, WELL SURE, WE'RE NOT FORCING YOU TO DO ANYTHING.
WHOA! NOT EVEN HOMEWORK? AWESOME NEWS, DAD. THANKS!
YOU KNOW WHAT I MEANT, SMARTYPANTS.

"But Grandmother! What big ears you have," said Little Red Riding Hood, staring at Grandma's pointed, furry ears.

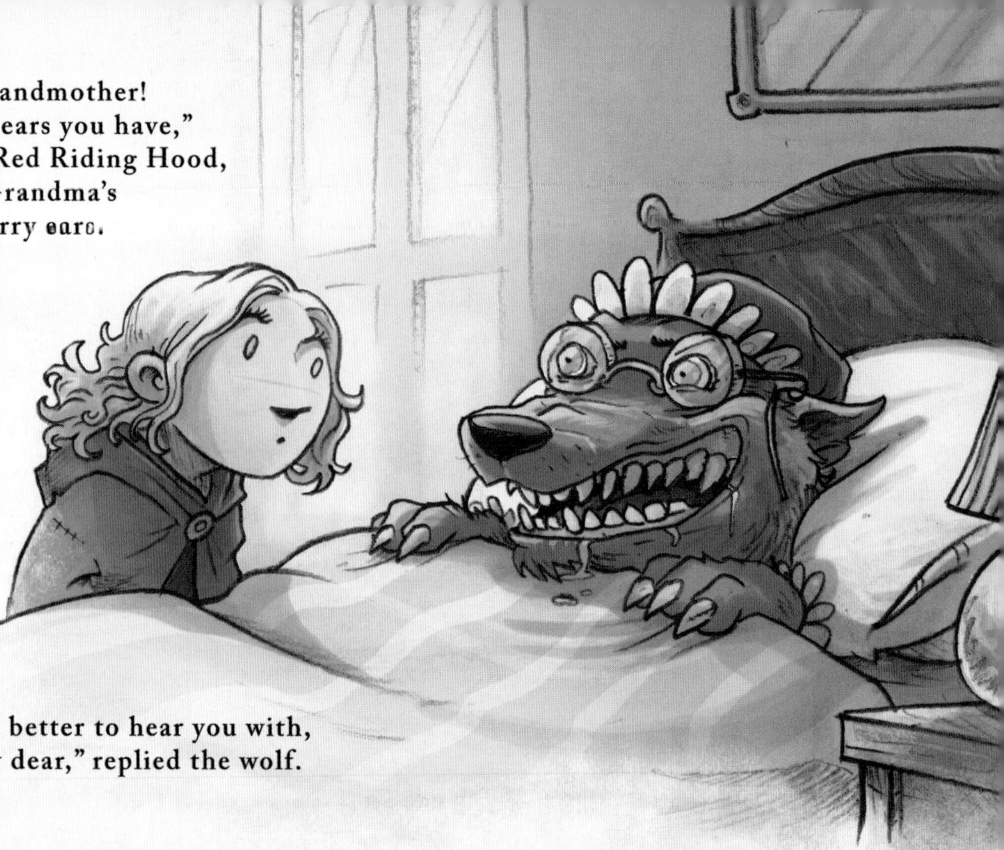

"The better to hear you with, my dear," replied the wolf.

"But Grandmother, what big eyes you have," said Little Red Riding Hood, now edging closer to the bed. "The better to see you with, my dear," replied the wolf, faking an elderly, high-pitched voice as best as he could.

"Must be the menopause," thought the girl to herself.

"But Grandmother! What big teeth you have," said Little Red Riding Hood her voice slightly quivering.

"The better to eat you up with!" snarled the wolf and jumped up from the bed.

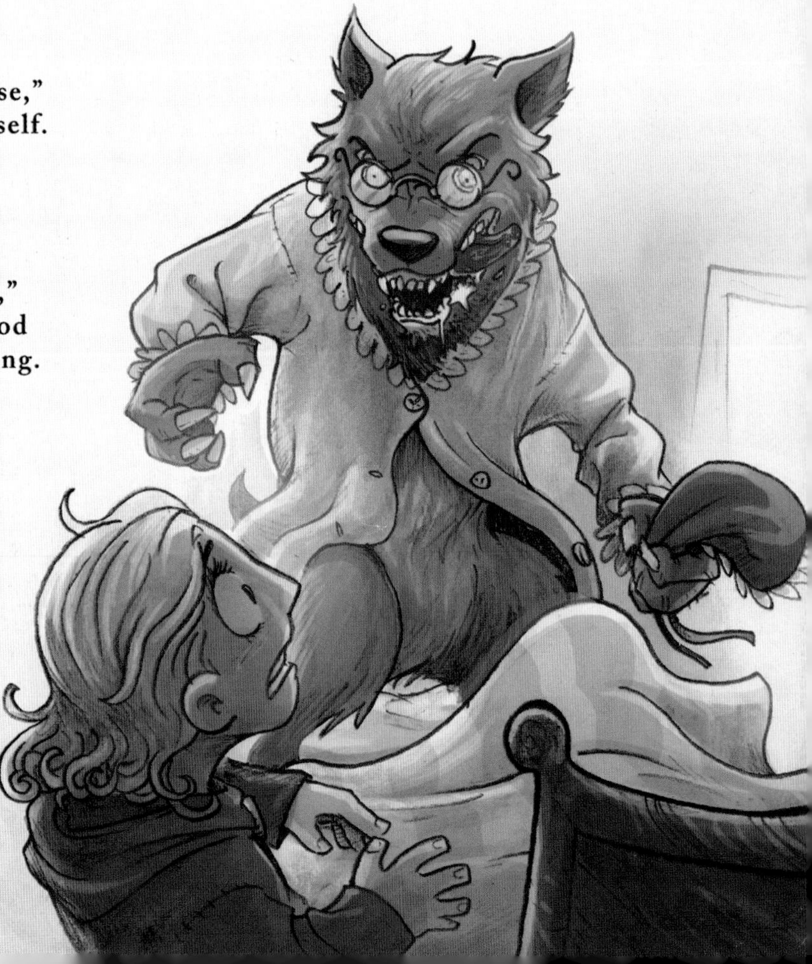

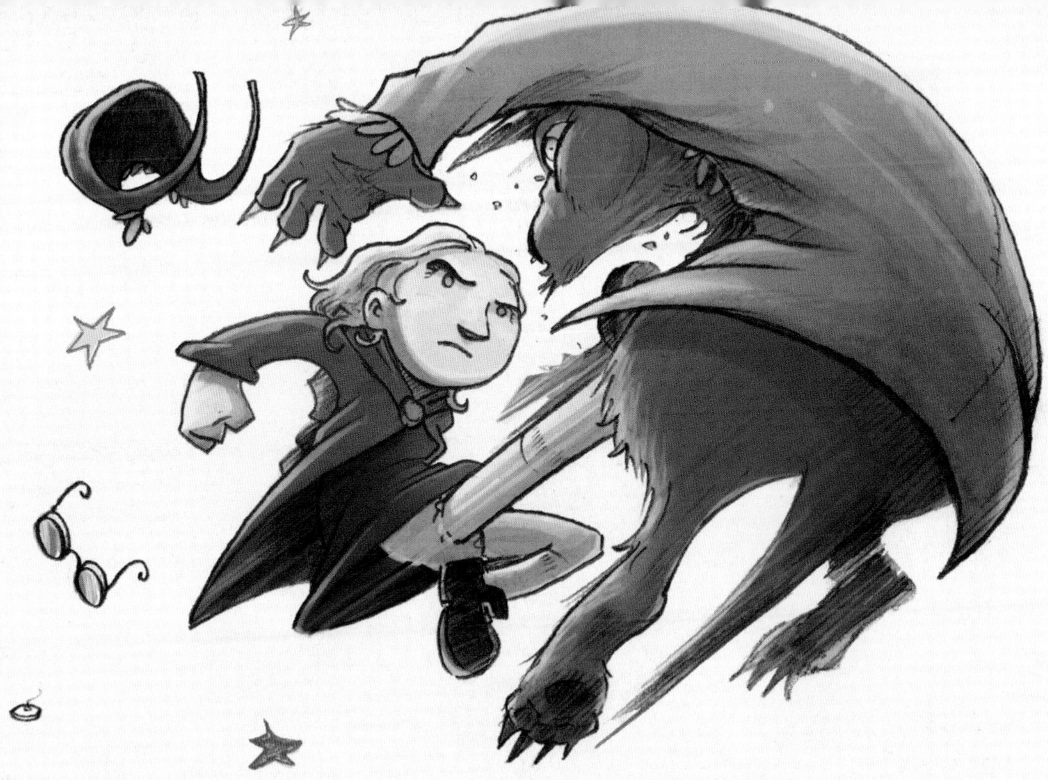

It was a reflex, a spontaneous reaction. Without further brainstorming, Little Red Riding Hood leaped forward, gut-kicking the wind out of the cross-dressing wolf.

With another swift move, Little Red Riding Hood spun around, reached for the wolf's tongue, and threw the beast flat on his hairy back.

Then, while still dazed, the—

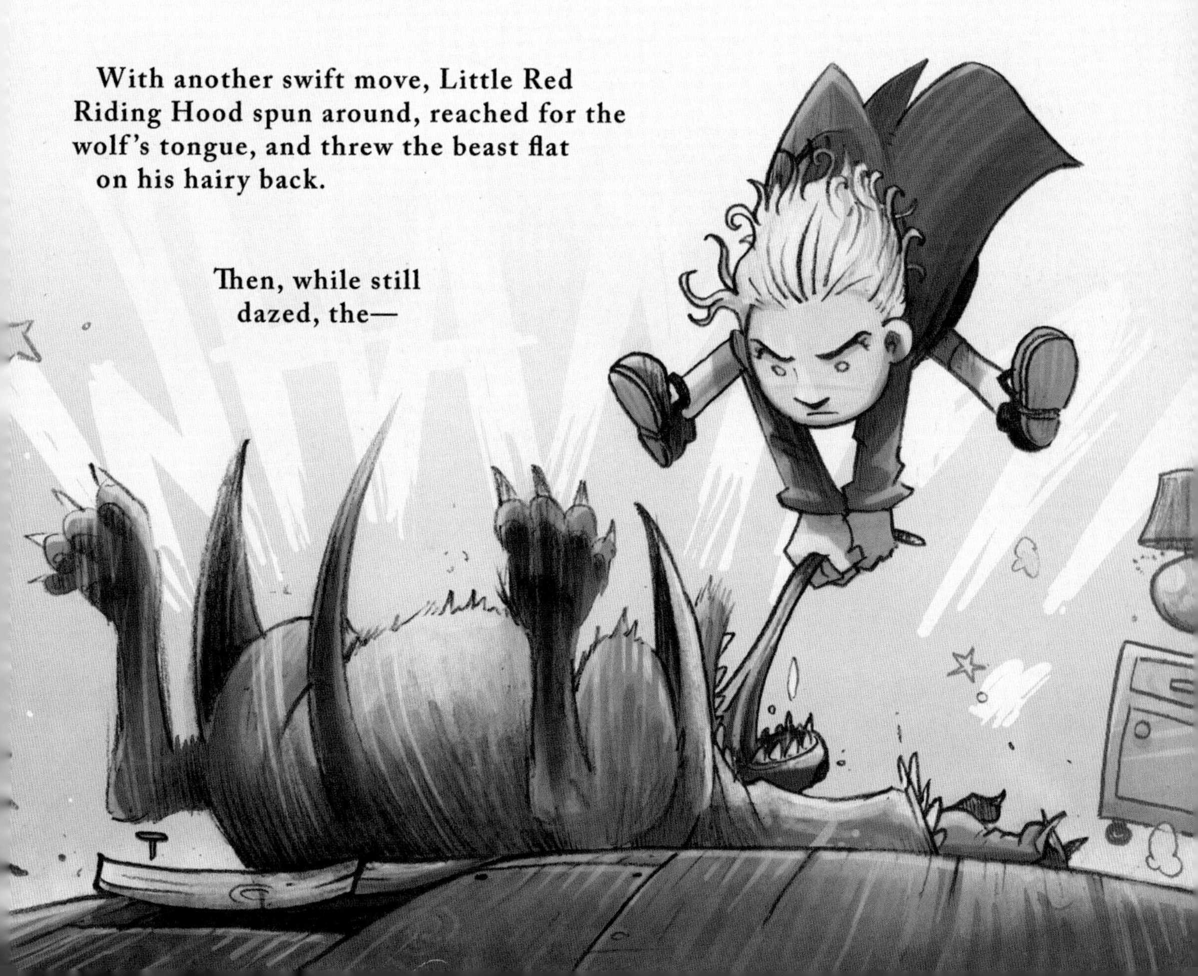

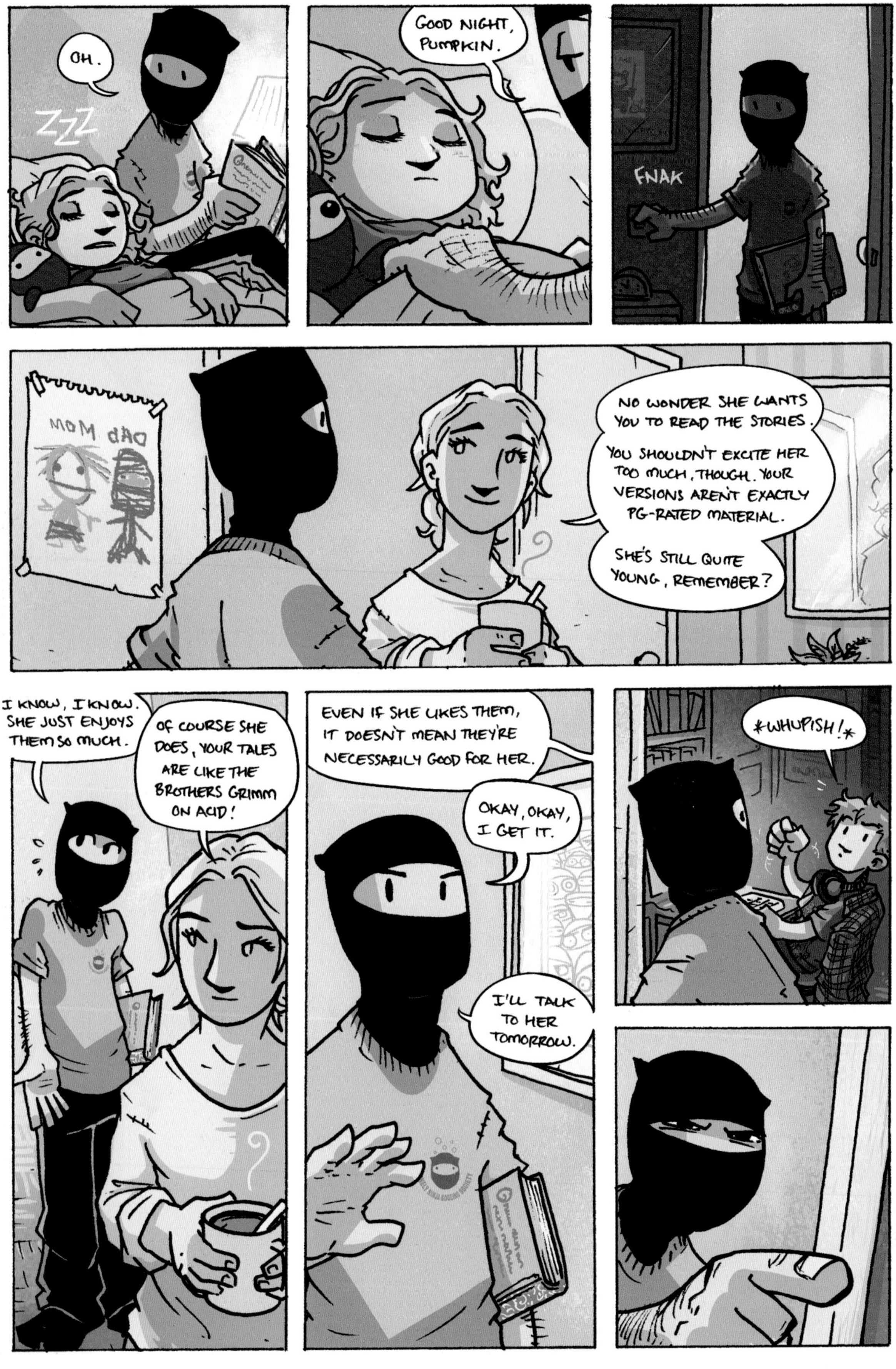
OH.
ZZZ
GOOD NIGHT, PUMPKIN.
FNAK
MOM DAD
NO WONDER SHE WANTS YOU TO READ THE STORIES.
YOU SHOULDN'T EXCITE HER TOO MUCH, THOUGH. YOUR VERSIONS AREN'T EXACTLY PG-RATED MATERIAL.
SHE'S STILL QUITE YOUNG, REMEMBER?
I KNOW, I KNOW. SHE JUST ENJOYS THEM SO MUCH.
OF COURSE SHE DOES, YOUR TALES ARE LIKE THE BROTHERS GRIMM ON ACID!
EVEN IF SHE LIKES THEM, IT DOESN'T MEAN THEY'RE NECESSARILY GOOD FOR HER.
OKAY, OKAY, I GET IT.
I'LL TALK TO HER TOMORROW.
WHUPISH!

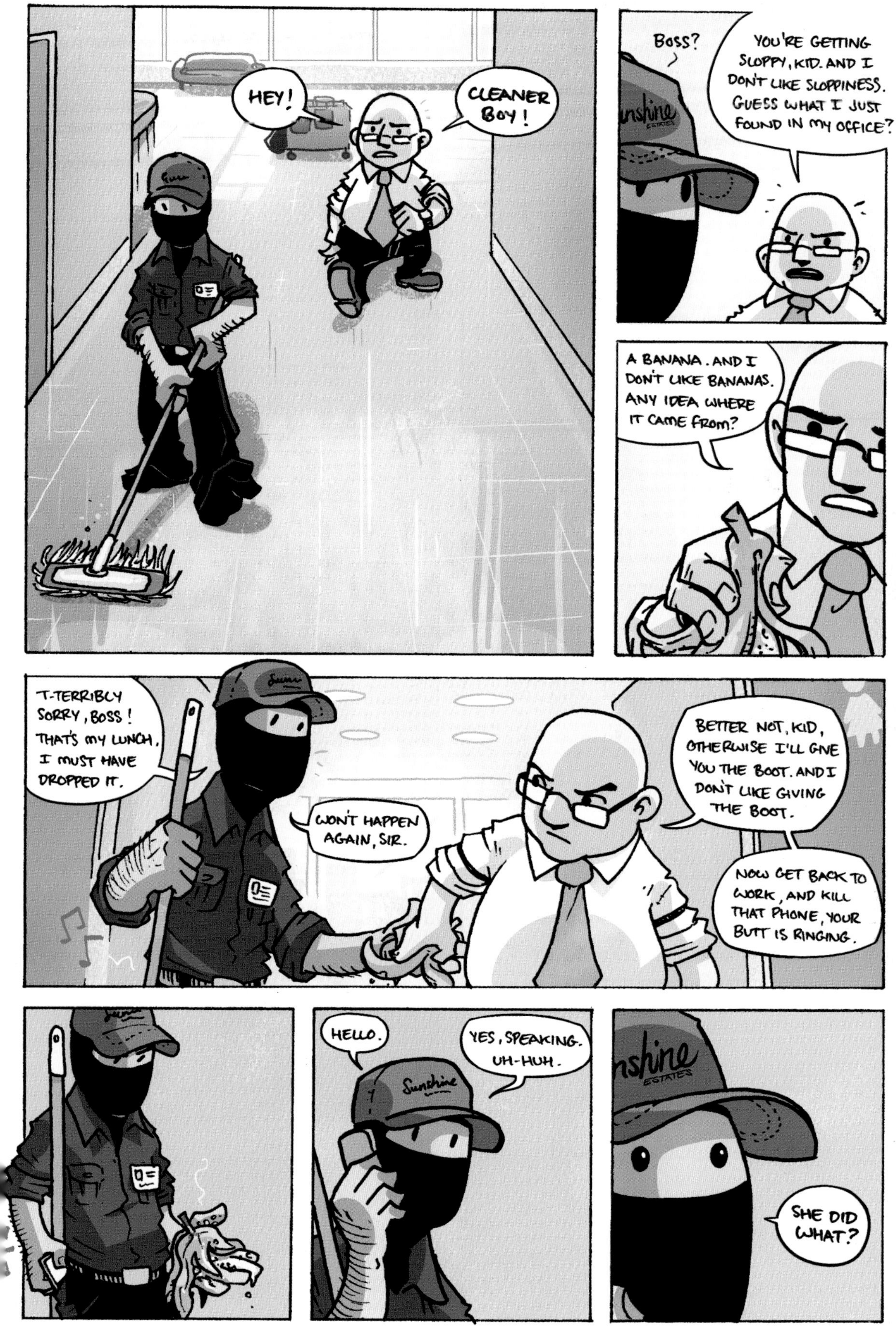
HEY!
CLEANER BOY!
BOSS?
YOU'RE GETTING SLOPPY, KID. AND I DON'T LIKE SLOPPINESS. GUESS WHAT I JUST FOUND IN MY OFFICE?
A BANANA. AND I DON'T LIKE BANANAS. ANY IDEA WHERE IT CAME FROM?
T-TERRIBLY SORRY, BOSS! THAT'S MY LUNCH. I MUST HAVE DROPPED IT.
WON'T HAPPEN AGAIN, SIR.
BETTER NOT, KID, OTHERWISE I'LL GIVE YOU THE BOOT. AND I DON'T LIKE GIVING THE BOOT.
NOW GET BACK TO WORK, AND KILL THAT PHONE, YOUR BUTT IS RINGING.
HELLO.
YES, SPEAKING. UH-HUH.
SHE DID WHAT?

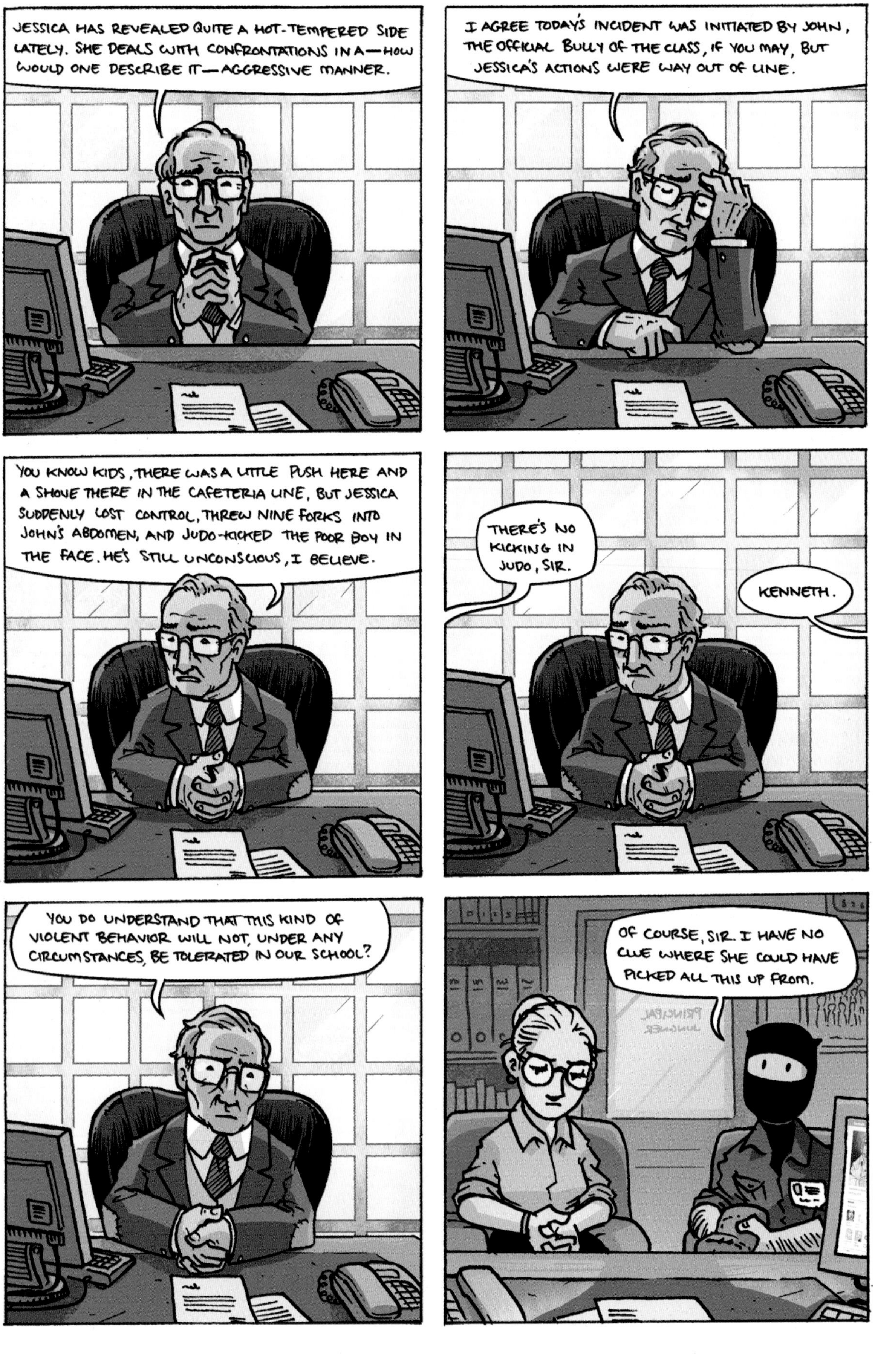
JESSICA HAS REVEALED QUITE A HOT-TEMPERED SIDE LATELY. SHE DEALS WITH CONFRONTATIONS IN A—HOW WOULD ONE DESCRIBE IT—AGGRESSIVE MANNER.
I AGREE TODAY'S INCIDENT WAS INITIATED BY JOHN, THE OFFICIAL BULLY OF THE CLASS, IF YOU MAY, BUT JESSICA'S ACTIONS WERE WAY OUT OF LINE.
YOU KNOW KIDS, THERE WAS A LITTLE PUSH HERE AND A SHOVE THERE IN THE CAFETERIA LINE, BUT JESSICA SUDDENLY LOST CONTROL, THREW NINE FORKS INTO JOHN'S ABDOMEN, AND JUDO-KICKED THE POOR BOY IN THE FACE. HE'S STILL UNCONSCIOUS, I BELIEVE.
THERE'S NO KICKING IN JUDO, SIR.
KENNETH.
YOU DO UNDERSTAND THAT THIS KIND OF VIOLENT BEHAVIOR WILL NOT, UNDER ANY CIRCUMSTANCES, BE TOLERATED IN OUR SCHOOL?
OF COURSE, SIR. I HAVE NO CLUE WHERE SHE COULD HAVE PICKED ALL THIS UP FROM.

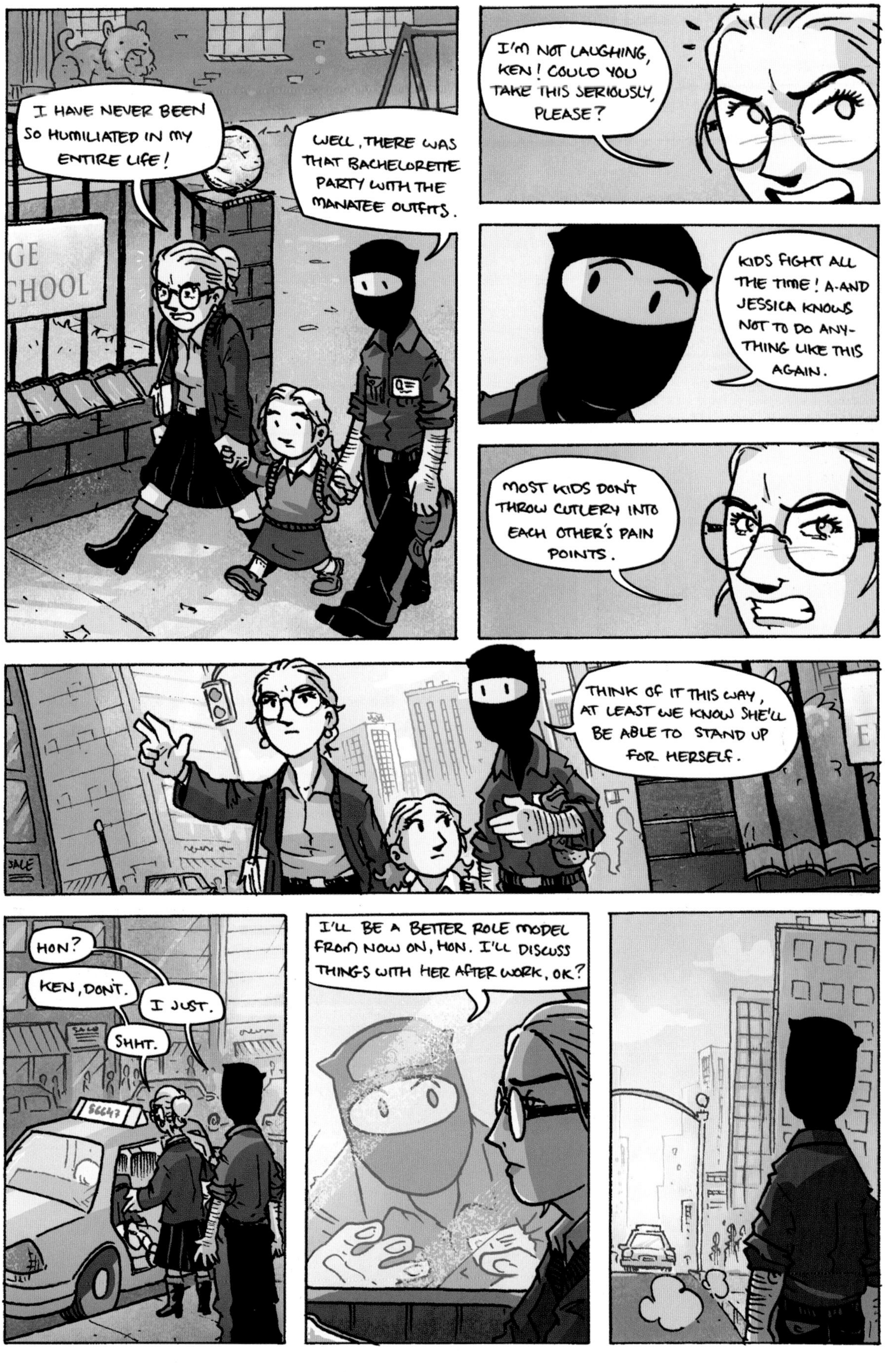
GE
SCHOOL
I HAVE NEVER BEEN SO HUMILIATED IN MY ENTIRE LIFE!
WELL, THERE WAS THAT BACHELORETTE PARTY WITH THE MANATEE OUTFITS.
I'M NOT LAUGHING, KEN! COULD YOU TAKE THIS SERIOUSLY, PLEASE?
KIDS FIGHT ALL THE TIME! A-AND JESSICA KNOWS NOT TO DO ANYTHING LIKE THIS AGAIN.
MOST KIDS DON'T THROW CUTLERY INTO EACH OTHER'S PAIN POINTS.
THINK OF IT THIS WAY, AT LEAST WE KNOW SHE'LL BE ABLE TO STAND UP FOR HERSELF.
SALE
HON?
KEN, DON'T.
I JUST.
SHHT.
86647
I'LL BE A BETTER ROLE MODEL FROM NOW ON, HON. I'LL DISCUSS THINGS WITH HER AFTER WORK, OK?

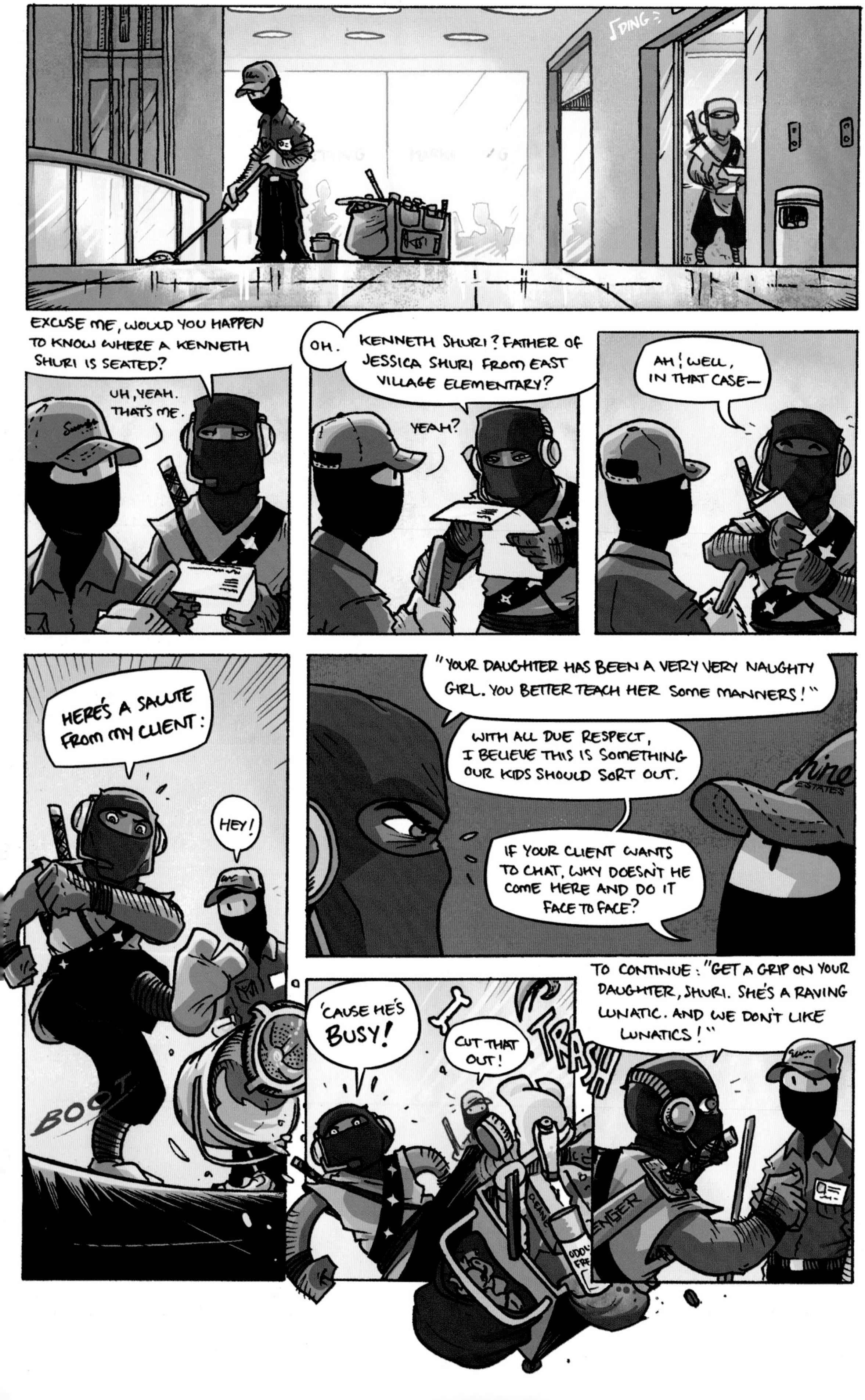
DING
EXCUSE ME, WOULD YOU HAPPEN TO KNOW WHERE A KENNETH SHURI IS SEATED?
UH, YEAH. THAT'S ME.
OH.
KENNETH SHURI? FATHER OF JESSICA SHURI FROM EAST VILLAGE ELEMENTARY?
YEAH?
AH! WELL, IN THAT CASE—
HERE'S A SALUTE FROM MY CLIENT:
HEY!
BOOT
"YOUR DAUGHTER HAS BEEN A VERY VERY NAUGHTY GIRL. YOU BETTER TEACH HER SOME MANNERS!"
WITH ALL DUE RESPECT, I BELIEVE THIS IS SOMETHING OUR KIDS SHOULD SORT OUT.
IF YOUR CLIENT WANTS TO CHAT, WHY DOESN'T HE COME HERE AND DO IT FACE TO FACE?
'CAUSE HE'S BUSY!
CUT THAT OUT!
TRASH
TO CONTINUE: "GET A GRIP ON YOUR DAUGHTER, SHURI. SHE'S A RAVING LUNATIC. AND WE DON'T LIKE LUNATICS!"

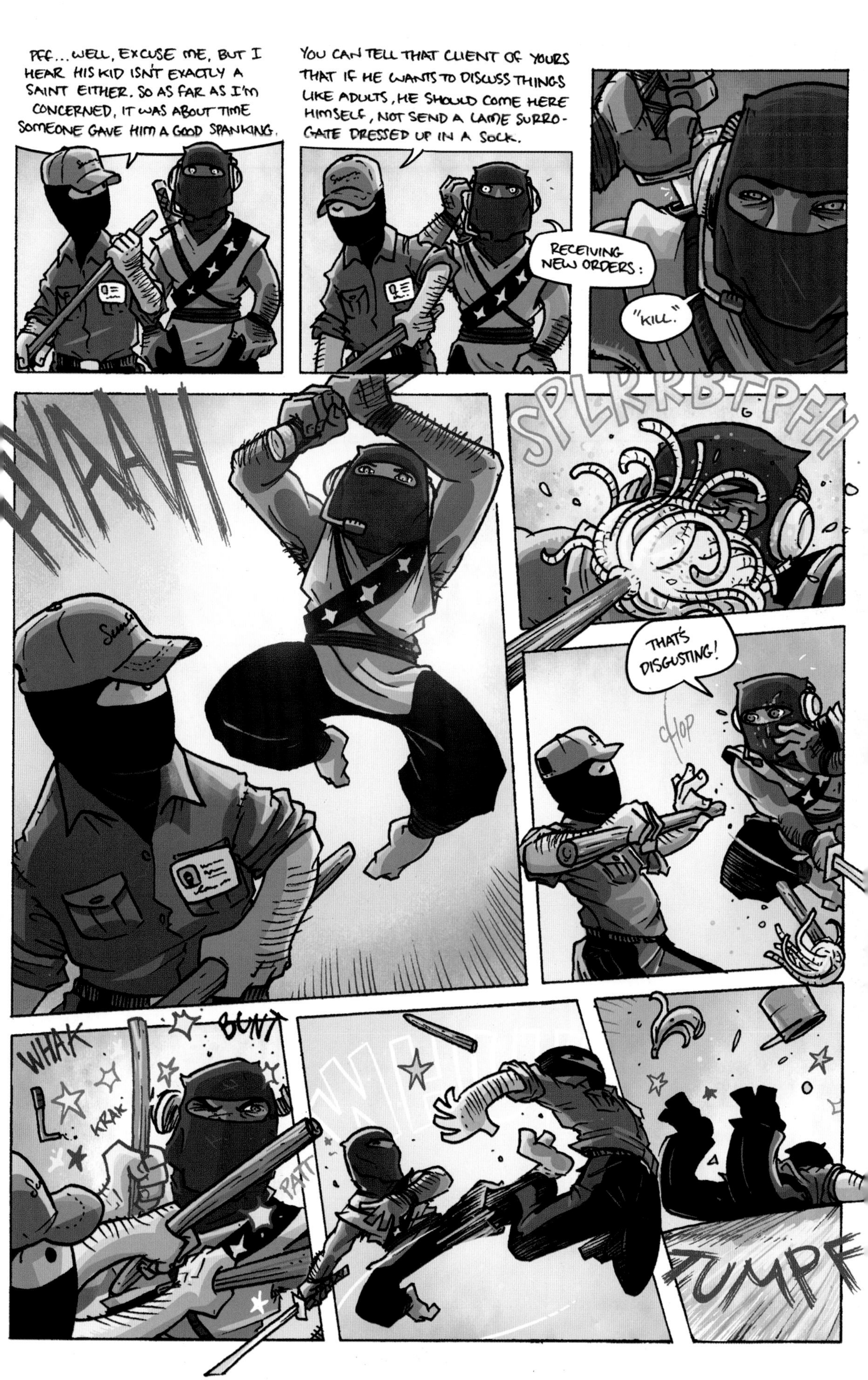

PFF... WELL, EXCUSE ME, BUT I HEAR HIS KID ISN'T EXACTLY A SAINT EITHER. SO AS FAR AS I'M CONCERNED, IT WAS ABOUT TIME SOMEONE GAVE HIM A GOOD SPANKING.
YOU CAN TELL THAT CLIENT OF YOURS THAT IF HE WANTS TO DISCUSS THINGS LIKE ADULTS, HE SHOULD COME HERE HIMSELF, NOT SEND A LAME SURROGATE DRESSED UP IN A SOCK.
RECEIVING NEW ORDERS:
"KILL."
HYAAH
SPLRRBTPFH
THAT'S DISGUSTING!
CHOP
WHAK
BUNT
KRAK
JUMPF

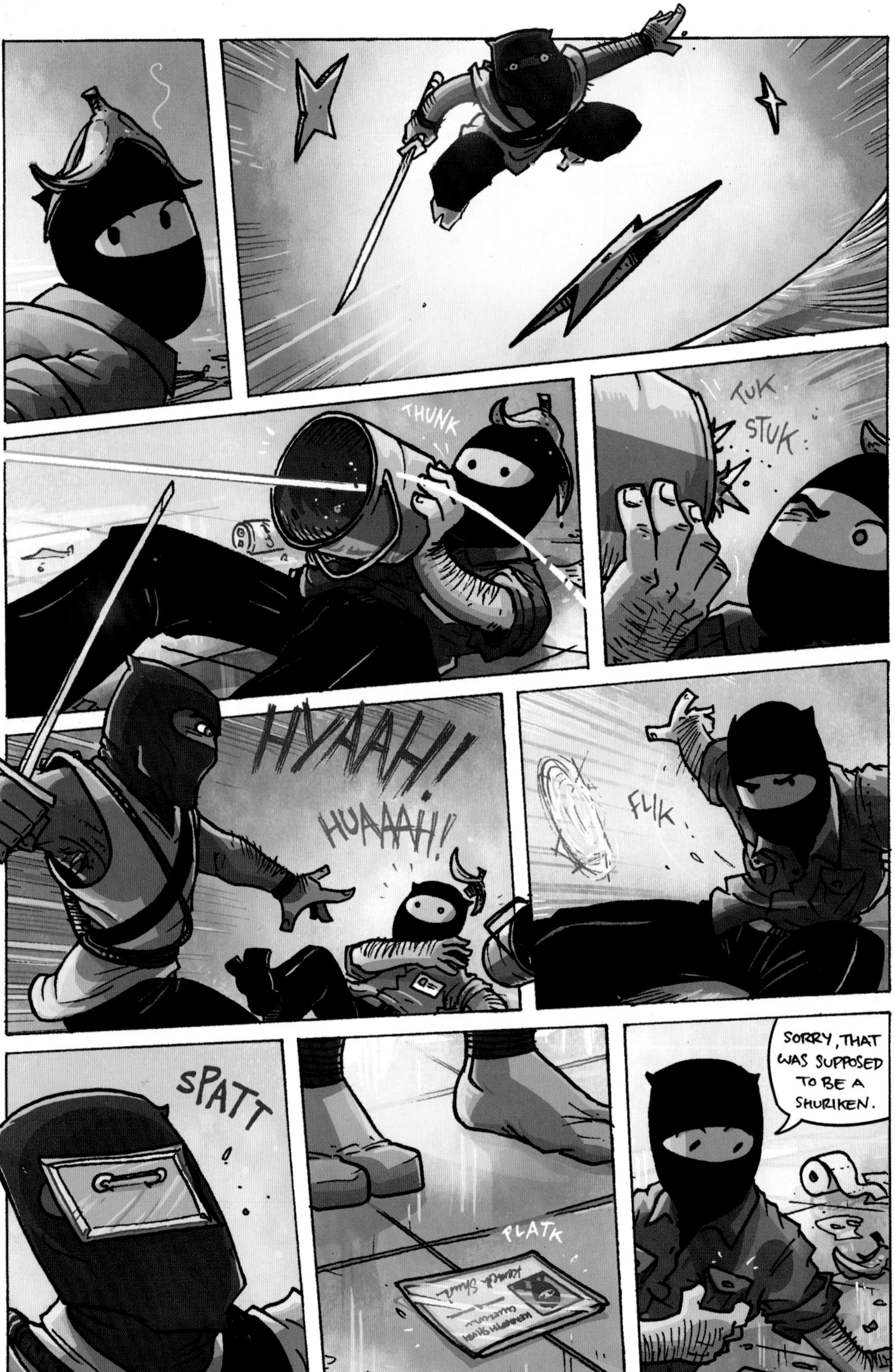
THUNK
TUK
STUK
HYAAAH!
HUAAAH!
FLIK
SPATT
PLATK
SORRY, THAT WAS SUPPOSED TO BE A SHURIKEN.

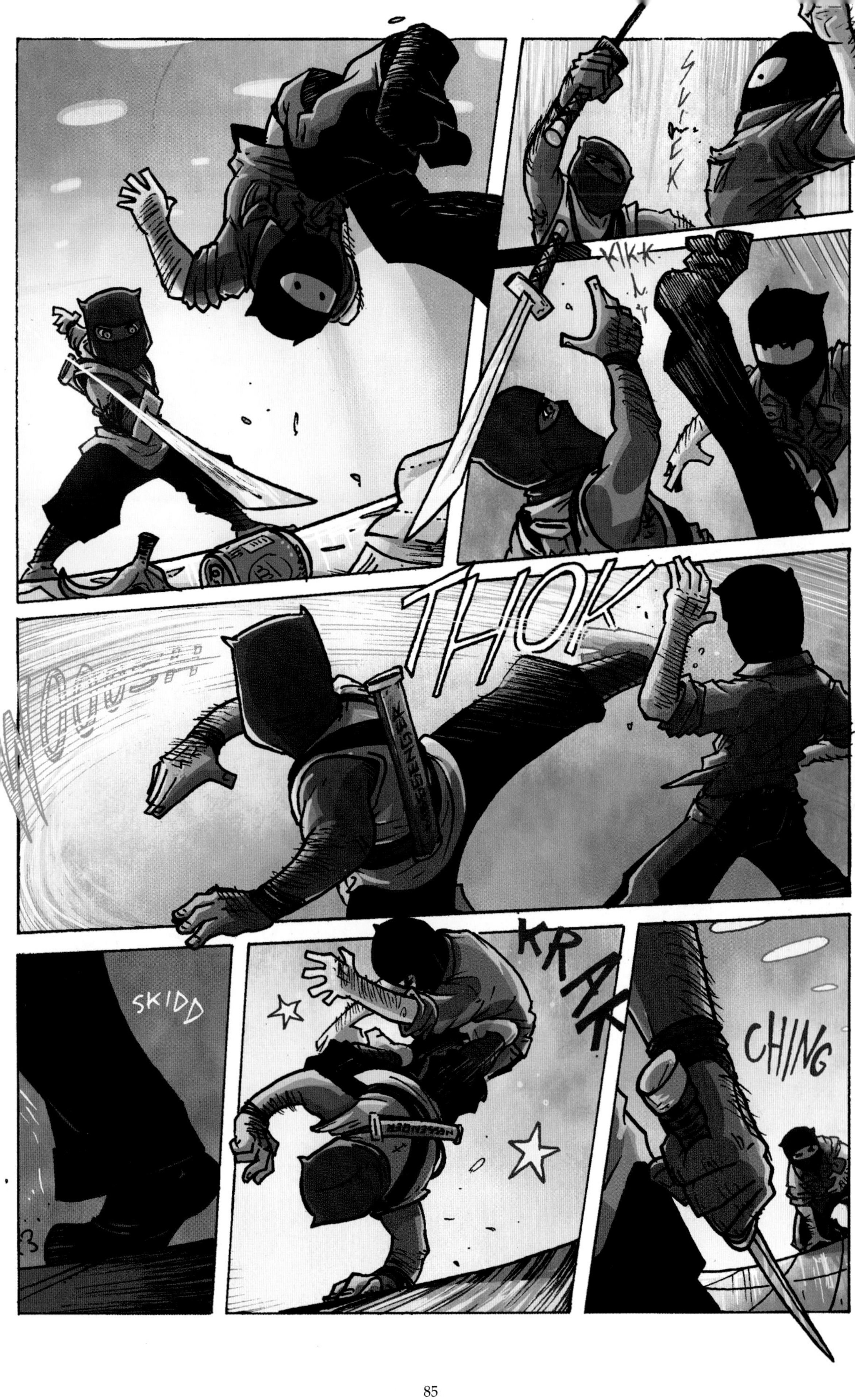
KIKK
WOOOSH!!
THOK
SKIDD
KRAK
CHING

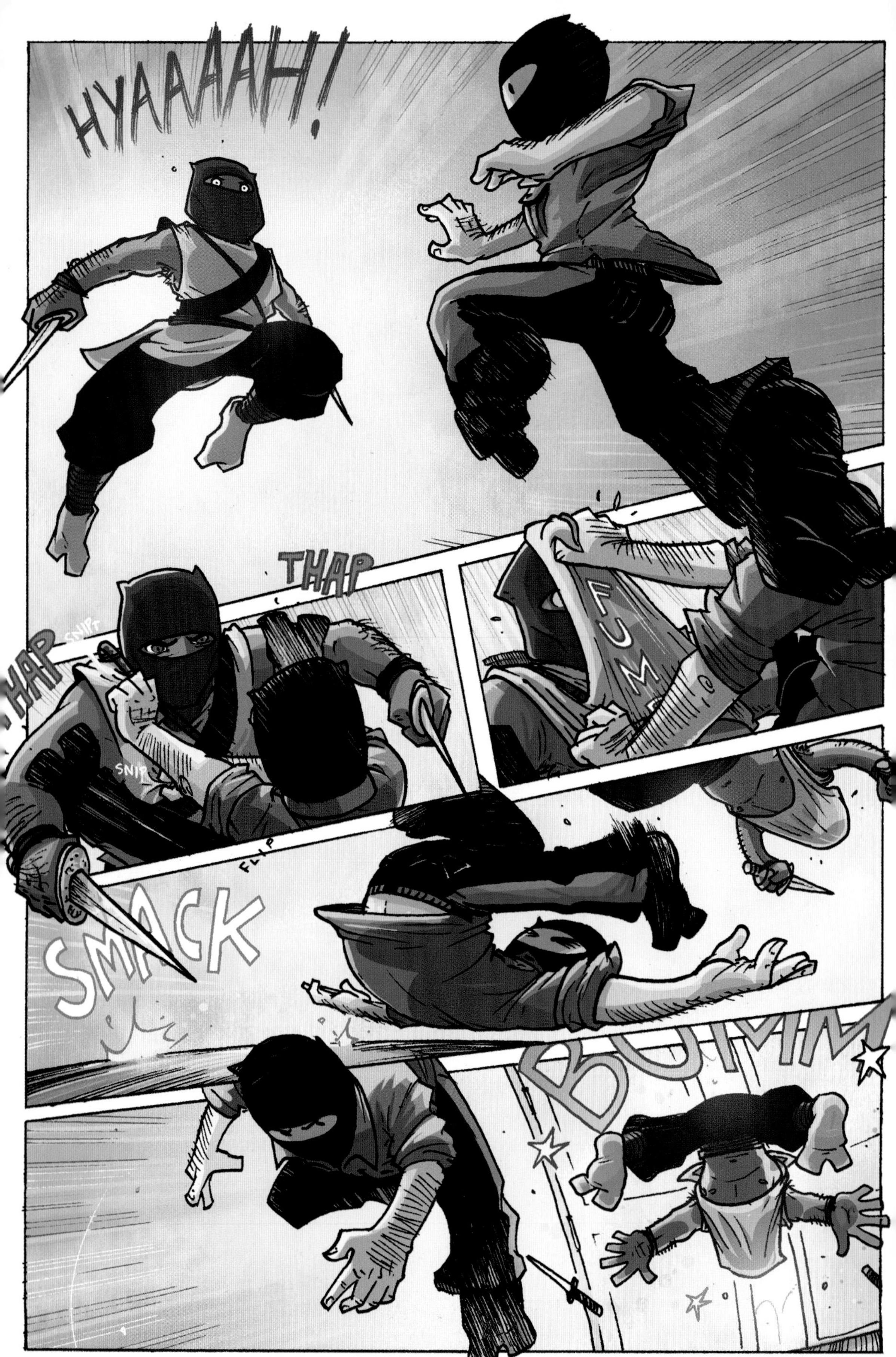
HYAAAAH!
THAP
HAP
SNIPT
SNIP
FUM
FLIP
SMACK
BUMM

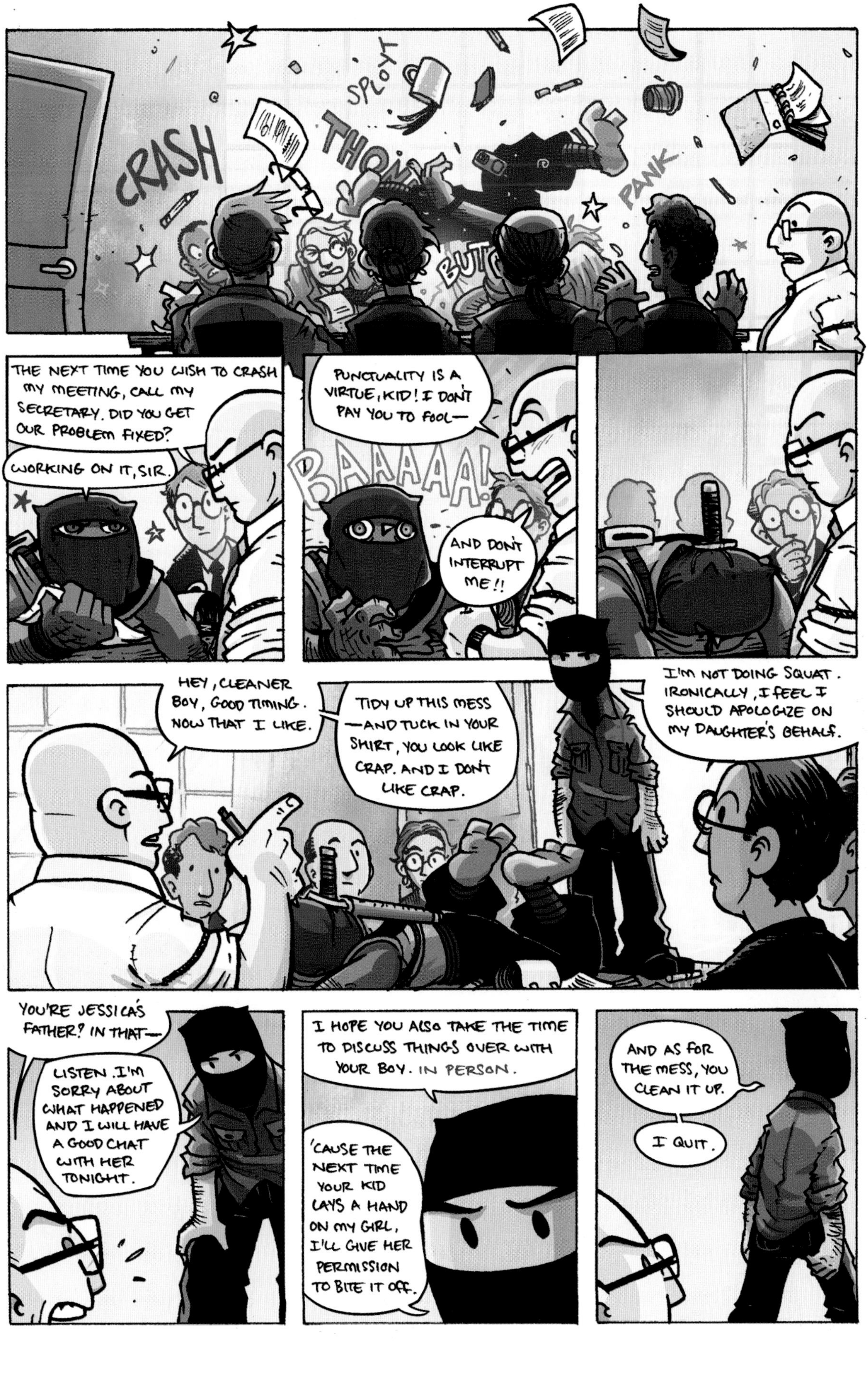
SPLOYT
CRASH
THONK
PANK
BUT
THE NEXT TIME YOU WISH TO CRASH MY MEETING, CALL MY SECRETARY. DID YOU GET OUR PROBLEM FIXED?
WORKING ON IT, SIR.
PUNCTUALITY IS A VIRTUE, KID! I DON'T PAY YOU TO FOOL—
BAAAAA!
AND DON'T INTERRUPT ME!!
HEY, CLEANER BOY, GOOD TIMING. NOW THAT I LIKE.
TIDY UP THIS MESS —AND TUCK IN YOUR SHIRT, YOU LOOK LIKE CRAP. AND I DON'T LIKE CRAP.
I'M NOT DOING SQUAT. IRONICALLY, I FEEL I SHOULD APOLOGIZE ON MY DAUGHTER'S BEHALF.
YOU'RE JESSICA'S FATHER? IN THAT—
LISTEN. I'M SORRY ABOUT WHAT HAPPENED AND I WILL HAVE A GOOD CHAT WITH HER TONIGHT.
I HOPE YOU ALSO TAKE THE TIME TO DISCUSS THINGS OVER WITH YOUR BOY. IN PERSON.
'CAUSE THE NEXT TIME YOUR KID LAYS A HAND ON MY GIRL, I'LL GIVE HER PERMISSION TO BITE IT OFF.
AND AS FOR THE MESS, YOU CLEAN IT UP.
I QUIT.

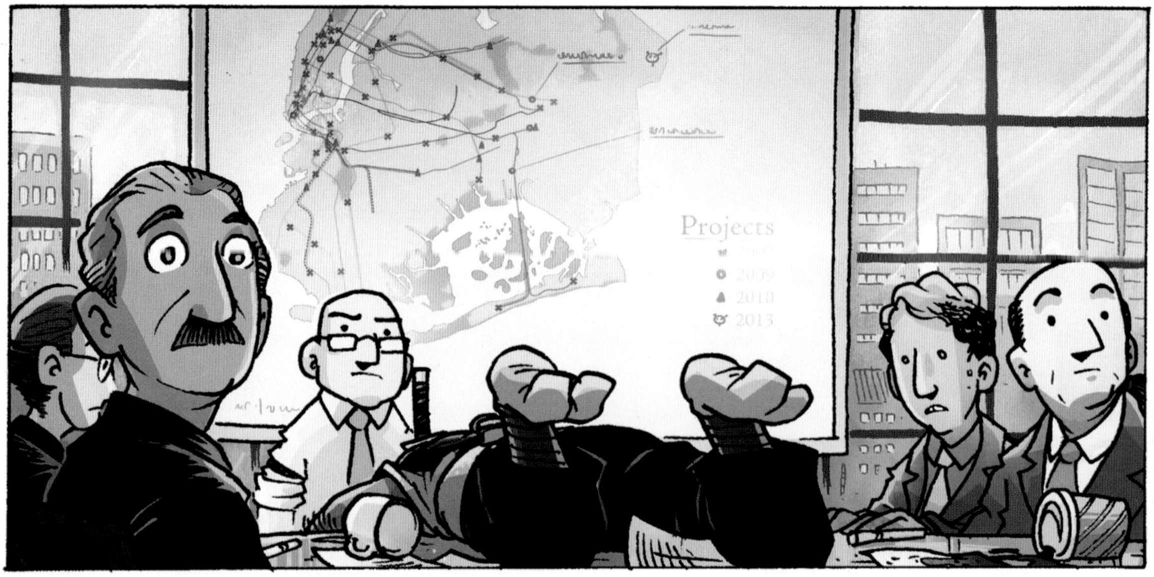
Projects
2009
2010
2013

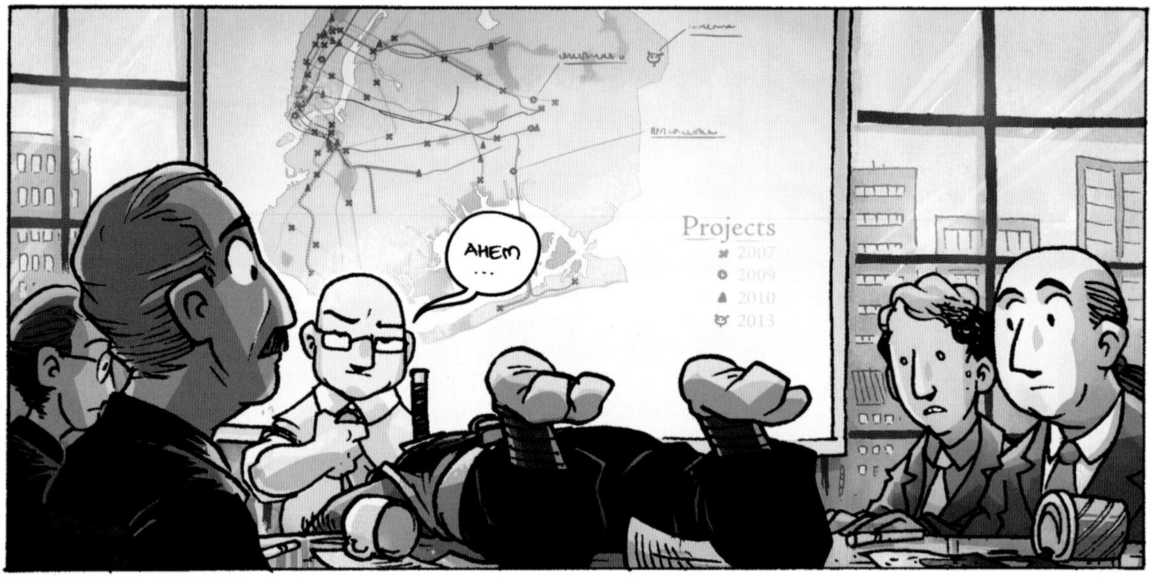
Projects
2007
2009
2010
2013
AHEM ...

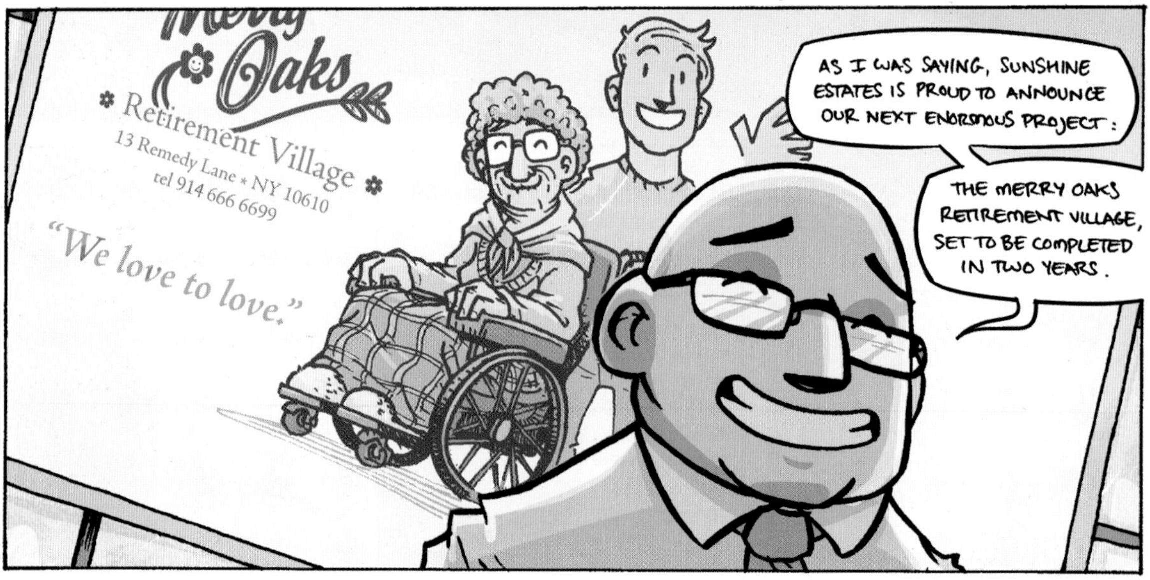
Oaks
Retirement Village
13 Remedy Lane * NY 10610
tel 914 666 6699
"We love to love."
AS I WAS SAYING, SUNSHINE ESTATES IS PROUD TO ANNOUNCE OUR NEXT ENORMOUS PROJECT:
THE MERRY OAKS RETIREMENT VILLAGE, SET TO BE COMPLETED IN TWO YEARS.

BUT HE PUSHED ME FIRST!

I KNOW, AND WHAT HE DID WAS WRONG.

BUT VIOLENCE IS NEVER THE ANSWER.

IT SIMPLY BREEDS MORE VIOLENCE.

LITTLE RED RIDING HOOD WOULD'VE BEEN EATEN ALIVE IF SHE HADN'T FOUGHT BACK.

NOT TRUE, HON. REMEMBER THE REAL ENDING? WITH THE WOODSMAN?

NO.

AHA—I'LL READ IT TO YOU THEN, BUT ONLY IF YOU PROMISE TO BEHAVE.

YOU KNOW I CAN'T POSSIBLY GUARANTEE ANYTHING.

I...I WILL SETTLE FOR THAT.

SO...

"THE WOLF RECOVERED QUICKLY AND SPRUNG UP ON HIS FEET AGAIN."

Once upon a time there were storytellers such as the Brothers Grimm and H.C. Andersen and others, who inspired the likes of Kaori Koiwichi and other flight artists. This collection of ...

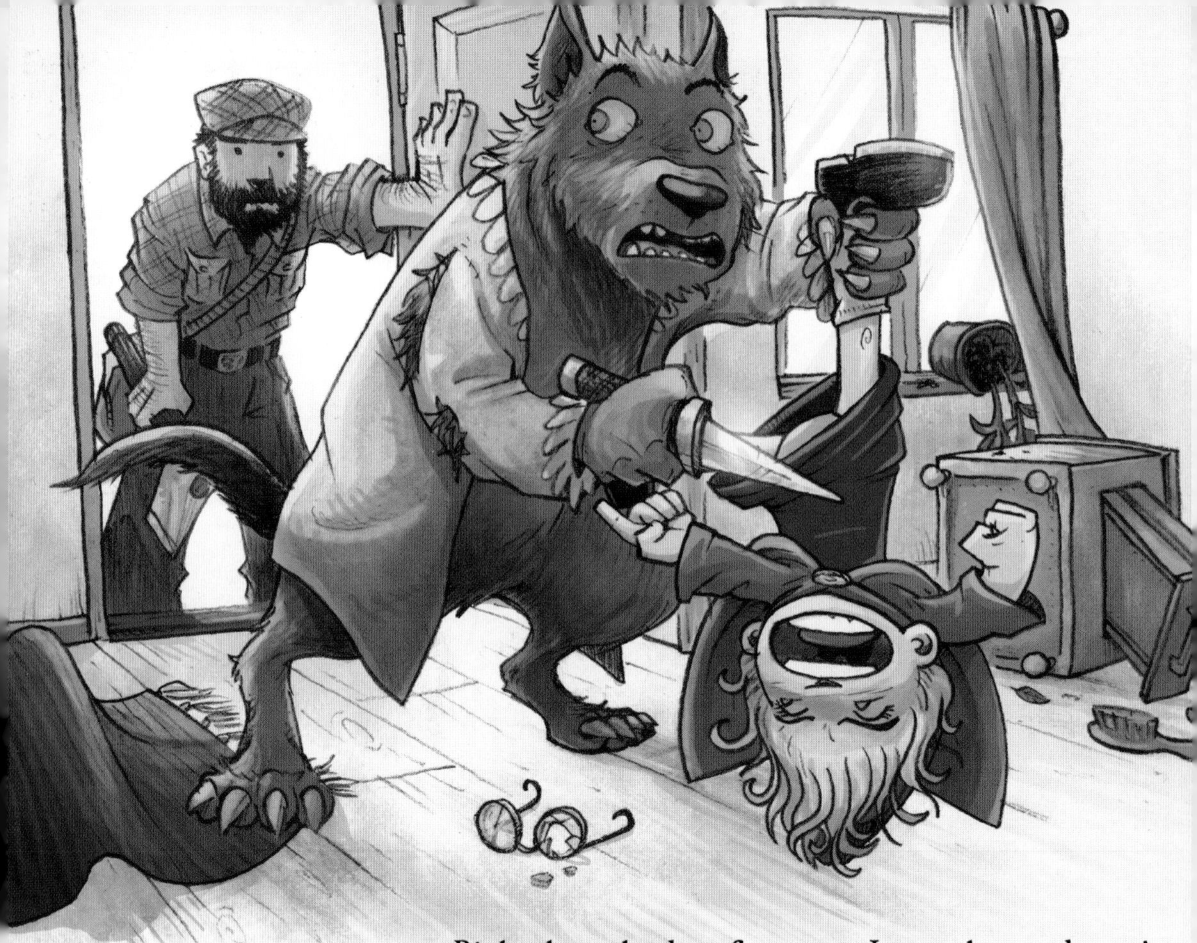

Right then, the door flew open. It was the woodsman! "Help me!" screamed the little girl. "Chop his head off with your ax!"

But the woodsman didn't approve of such actions. He was very disappointed to find the two quarreling, so he gave them a good lecture. The wolf and Little Red Riding Hood felt ashamed...

"I will not tolerate such reckless behavior," said the woodsman. "Let's wash away that anger of yours."

The little girl and the wolf were terrified.

The woodsman gave them horrible chores all around Grandma's house, just to teach them some manners...

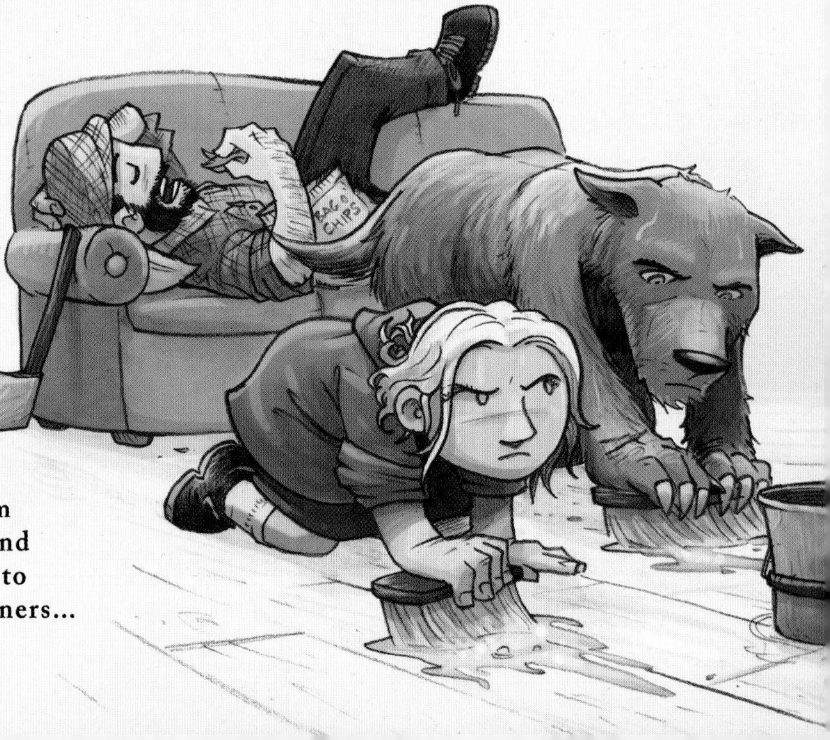
BAG O CHIPS

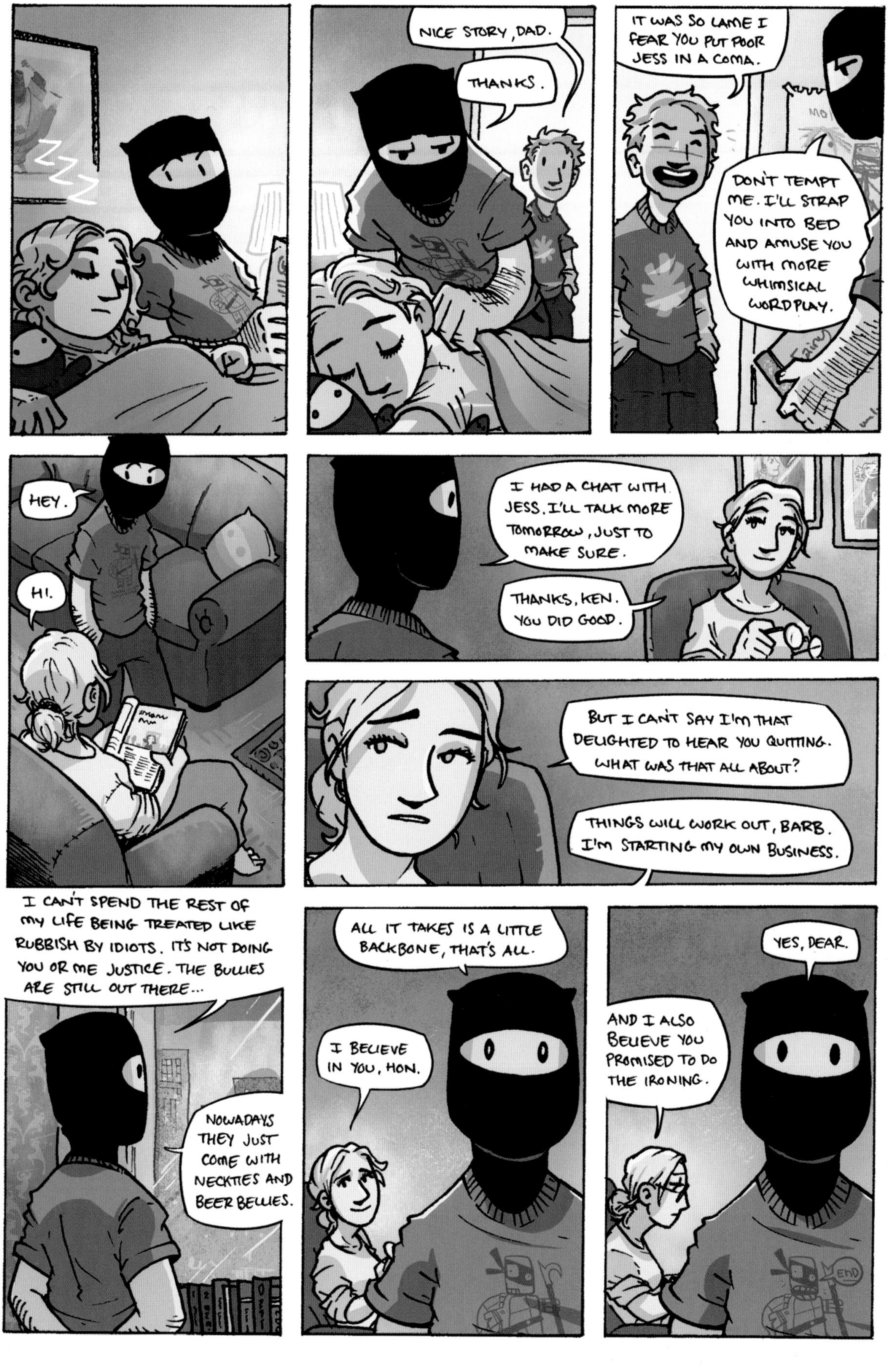
ZZZ
NICE STORY, DAD.
THANKS.
IT WAS SO LAME I FEAR YOU PUT POOR JESS IN A COMA.
DON'T TEMPT ME. I'LL STRAP YOU INTO BED AND AMUSE YOU WITH MORE WHIMSICAL WORDPLAY.
HEY.
HI.
I HAD A CHAT WITH JESS. I'LL TALK MORE TOMORROW, JUST TO MAKE SURE.
THANKS, KEN. YOU DID GOOD.
BUT I CAN'T SAY I'M THAT DELIGHTED TO HEAR YOU QUITTING. WHAT WAS THAT ALL ABOUT?
THINGS WILL WORK OUT, BARB. I'M STARTING MY OWN BUSINESS.
I CAN'T SPEND THE REST OF MY LIFE BEING TREATED LIKE RUBBISH BY IDIOTS. IT'S NOT DOING YOU OR ME JUSTICE. THE BULLIES ARE STILL OUT THERE...
NOWADAYS THEY JUST COME WITH NECKTIES AND BEER BELLIES.
ALL IT TAKES IS A LITTLE BACKBONE, THAT'S ALL.
I BELIEVE IN YOU, HON.
YES, DEAR.
AND I ALSO BELIEVE YOU PROMISED TO DO THE IRONING.
END

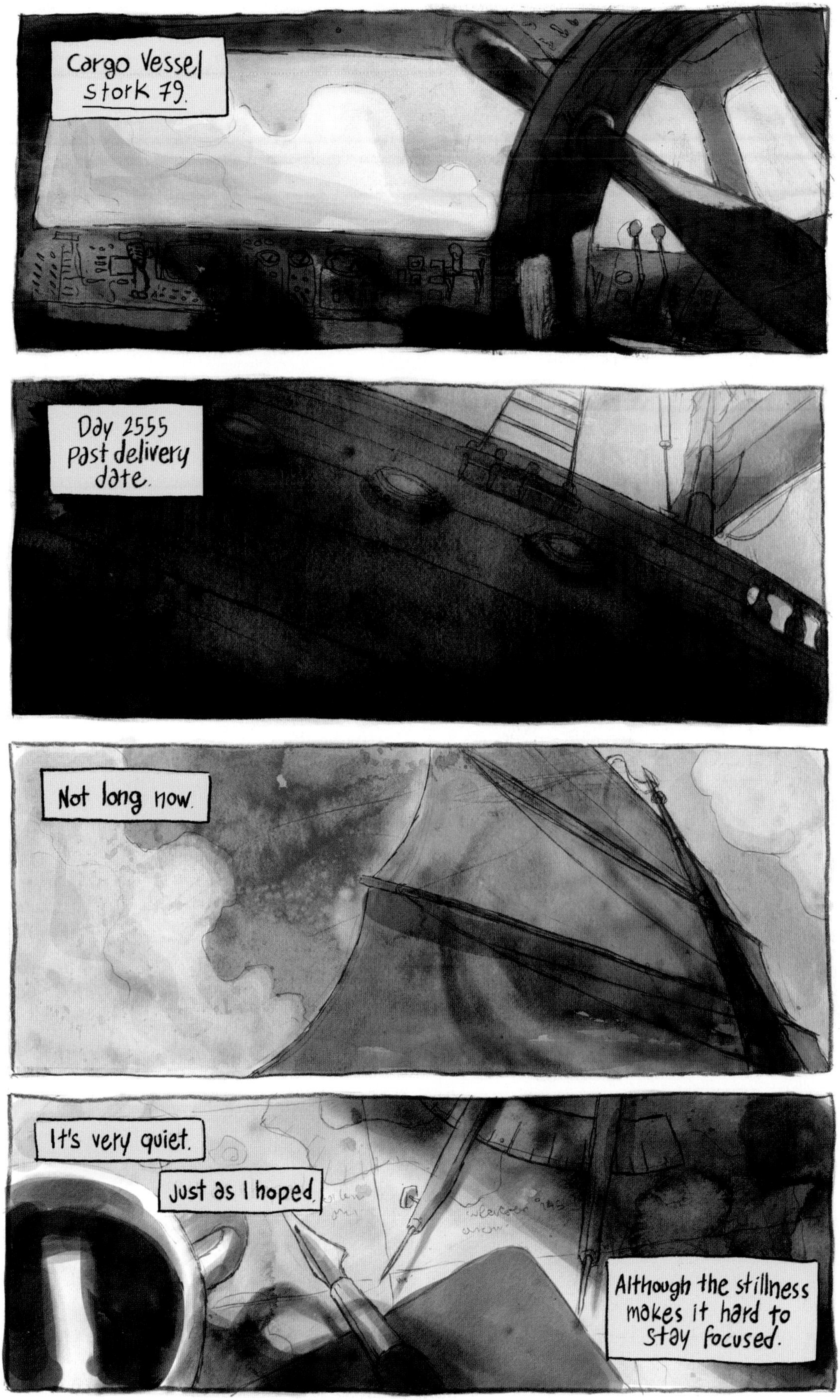
Cargo Vessel stork 79.
Day 2555 past delivery date.
Not long now.
It's very quiet.
Just as I hoped.
Although the stillness makes it hard to stay focused.

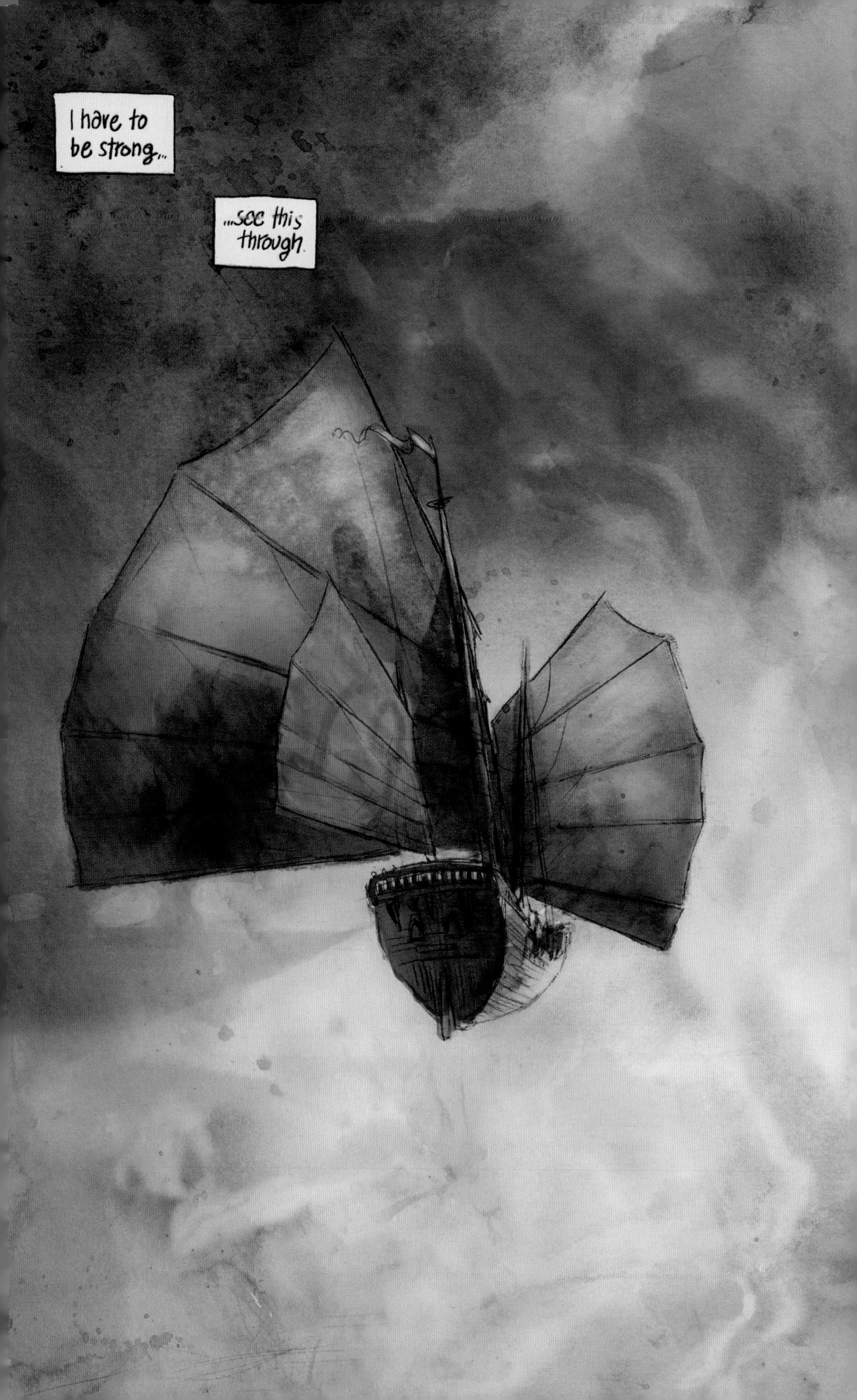
I have to be strong...
...see this through.

Premium
Cargo

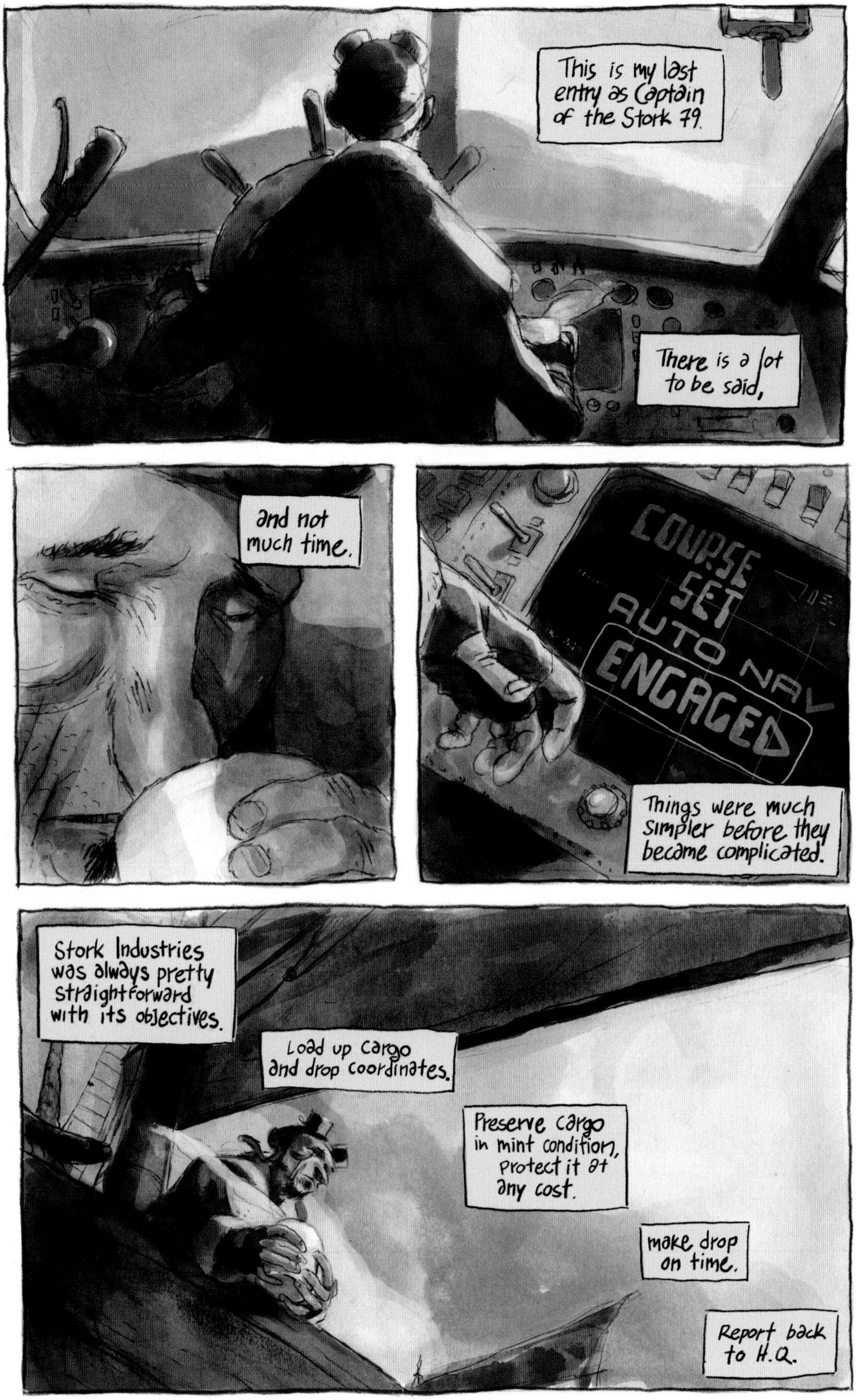
This is my last entry as Captain of the Stork 79.
There is a lot to be said,
and not much time.
COURSE SET
AUTO NAV
ENGAGED
Things were much simpler before they became complicated.
Stork Industries was always pretty straightforward with its objectives.
Load up cargo and drop coordinates.
Preserve cargo in mint condition, protect it at any cost.
make drop on time.
Report back to H.Q.

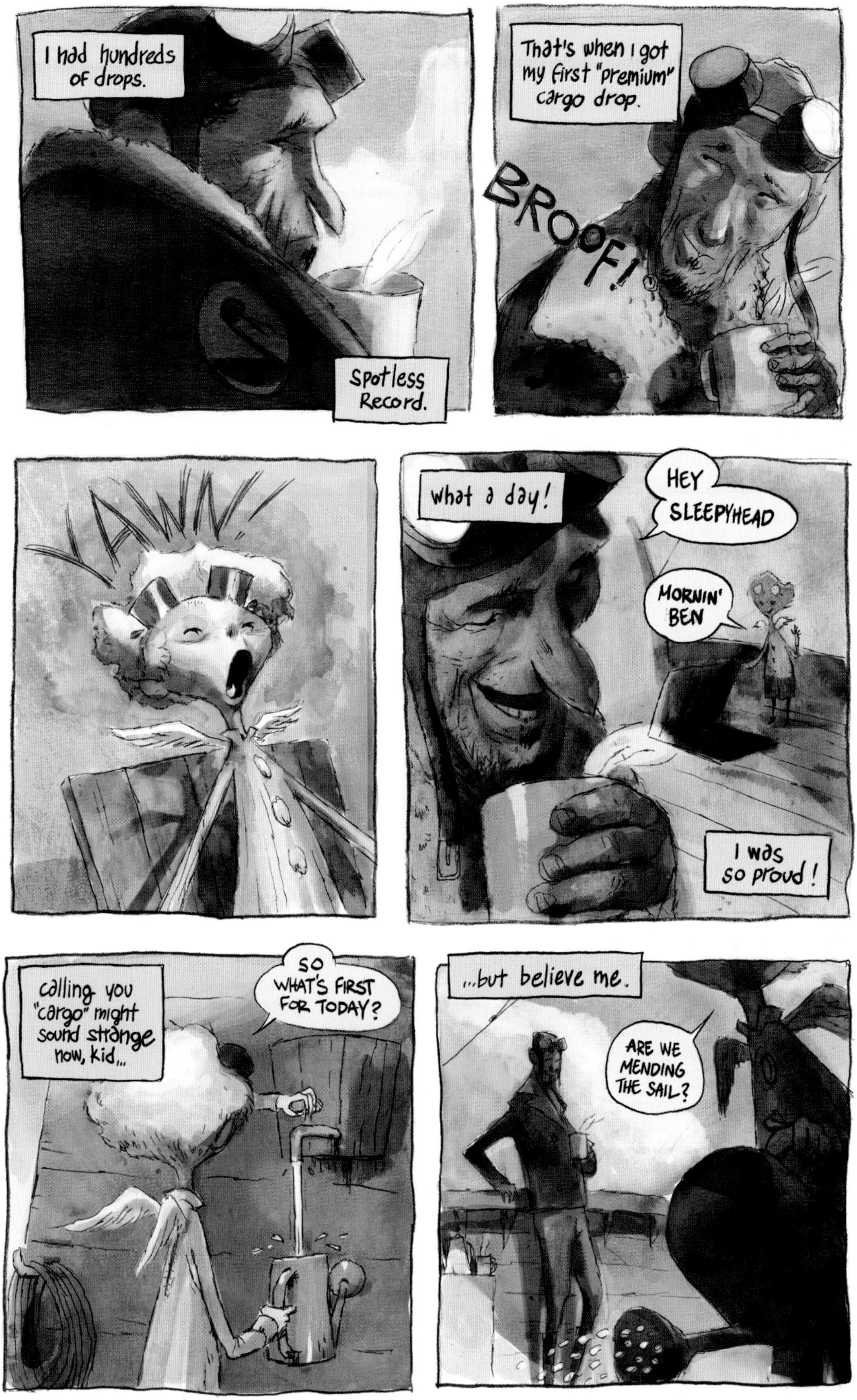
I had hundreds of drops.
Spotless Record.
That's when I got my first "premium" cargo drop.
BROOF!
YAWN!
what a day!
HEY SLEEPYHEAD
MORNIN' BEN
I was so proud!
calling you "cargo" might sound strange now, kid...
SO WHAT'S FIRST FOR TODAY?
...but believe me.
ARE WE MENDING THE SAIL?

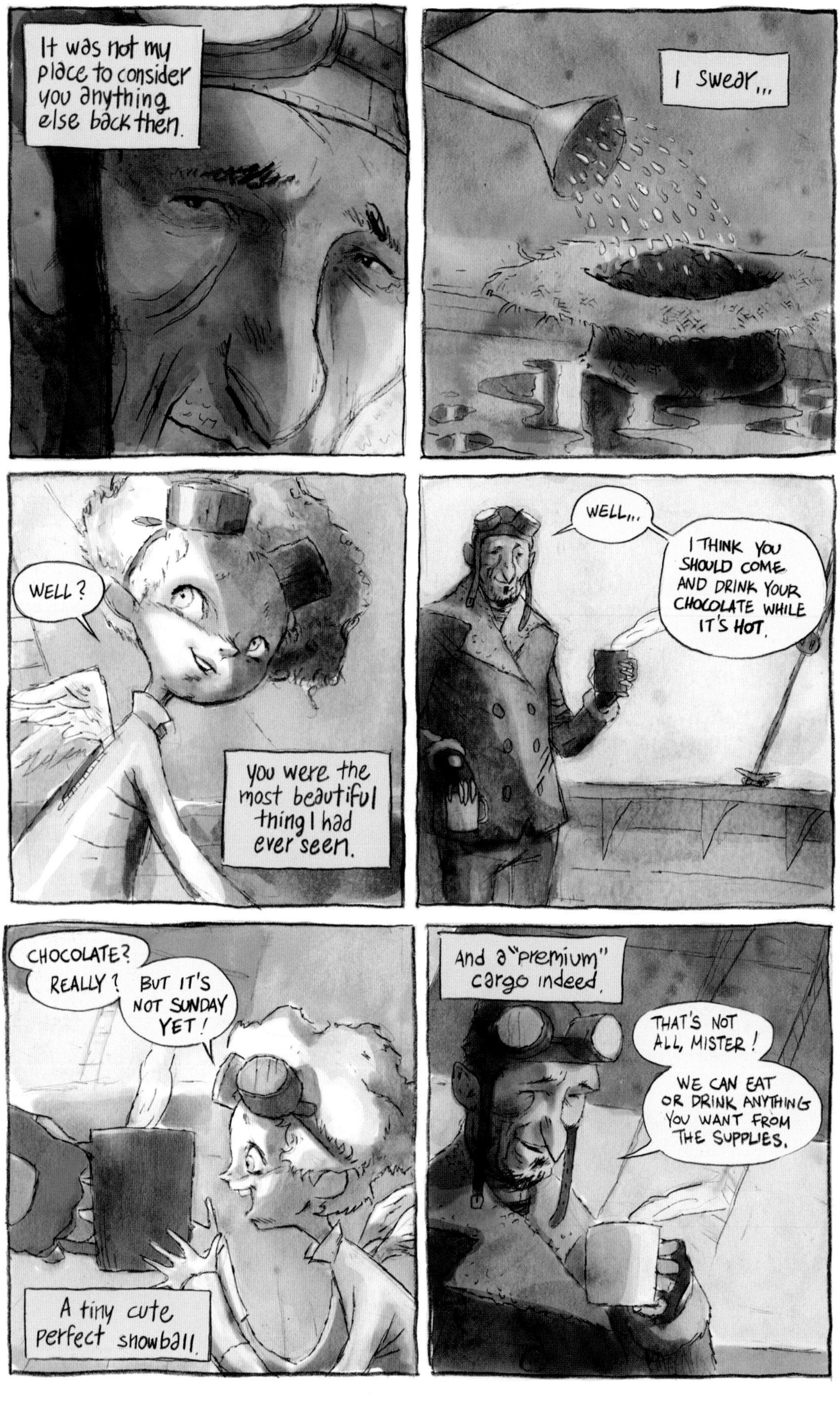

It was not my place to consider you anything else back then.
I swear...
WELL?
you were the most beautiful thing I had ever seen.
WELL...
I THINK YOU SHOULD COME AND DRINK YOUR CHOCOLATE WHILE IT'S HOT.
CHOCOLATE? REALLY?
BUT IT'S NOT SUNDAY YET!
A tiny cute perfect snowball.
And a "premium" cargo indeed.
THAT'S NOT ALL, MISTER!
WE CAN EAT OR DRINK ANYTHING YOU WANT FROM THE SUPPLIES.

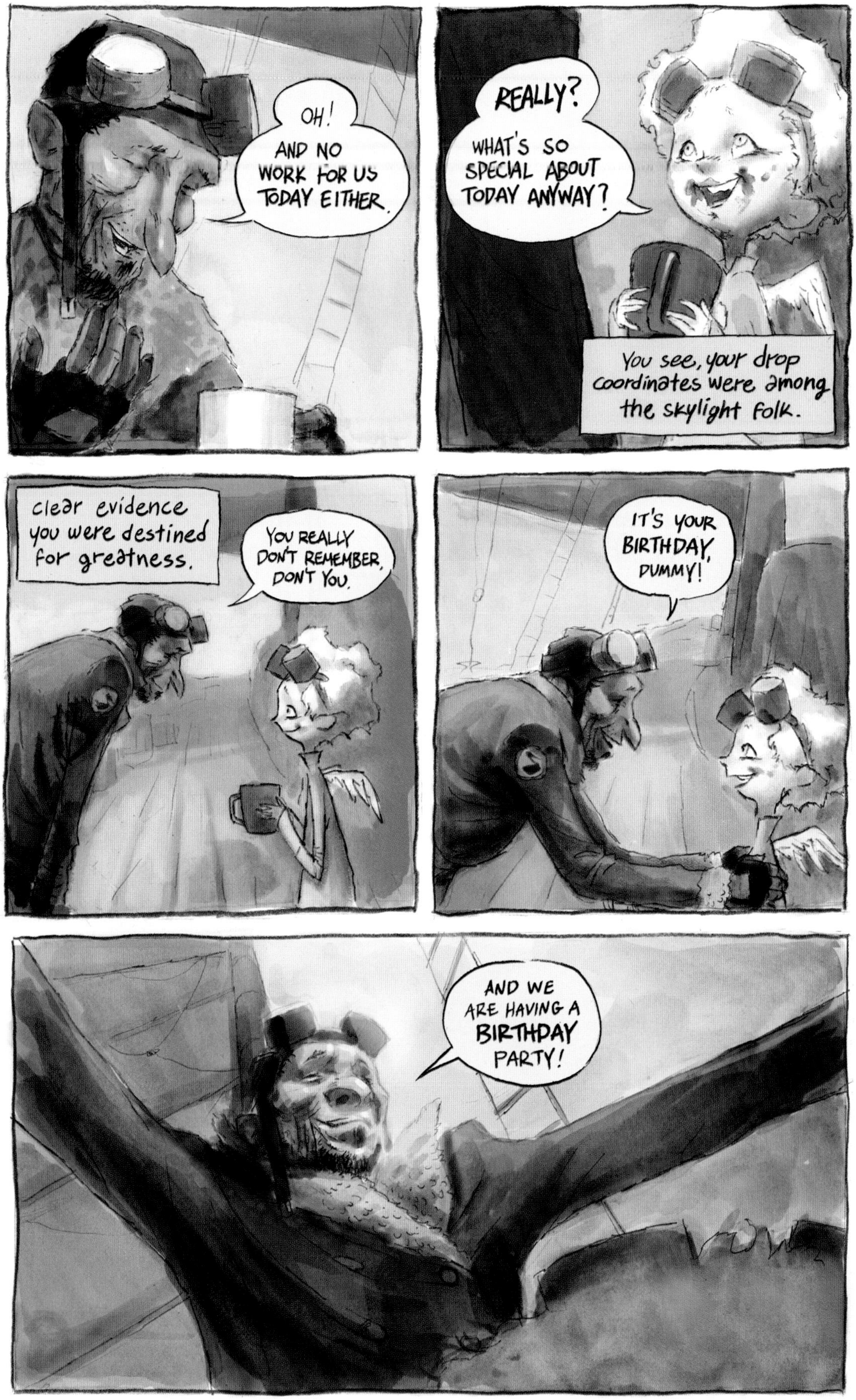
OH!
AND NO WORK FOR US TODAY EITHER.
REALLY?
WHAT'S SO SPECIAL ABOUT TODAY ANYWAY?
You see, your drop coordinates were among the skylight folk.
clear evidence you were destined for greatness.
YOU REALLY DON'T REMEMBER, DON'T YOU.
IT'S YOUR BIRTHDAY, DUMMY!
AND WE ARE HAVING A BIRTHDAY PARTY!

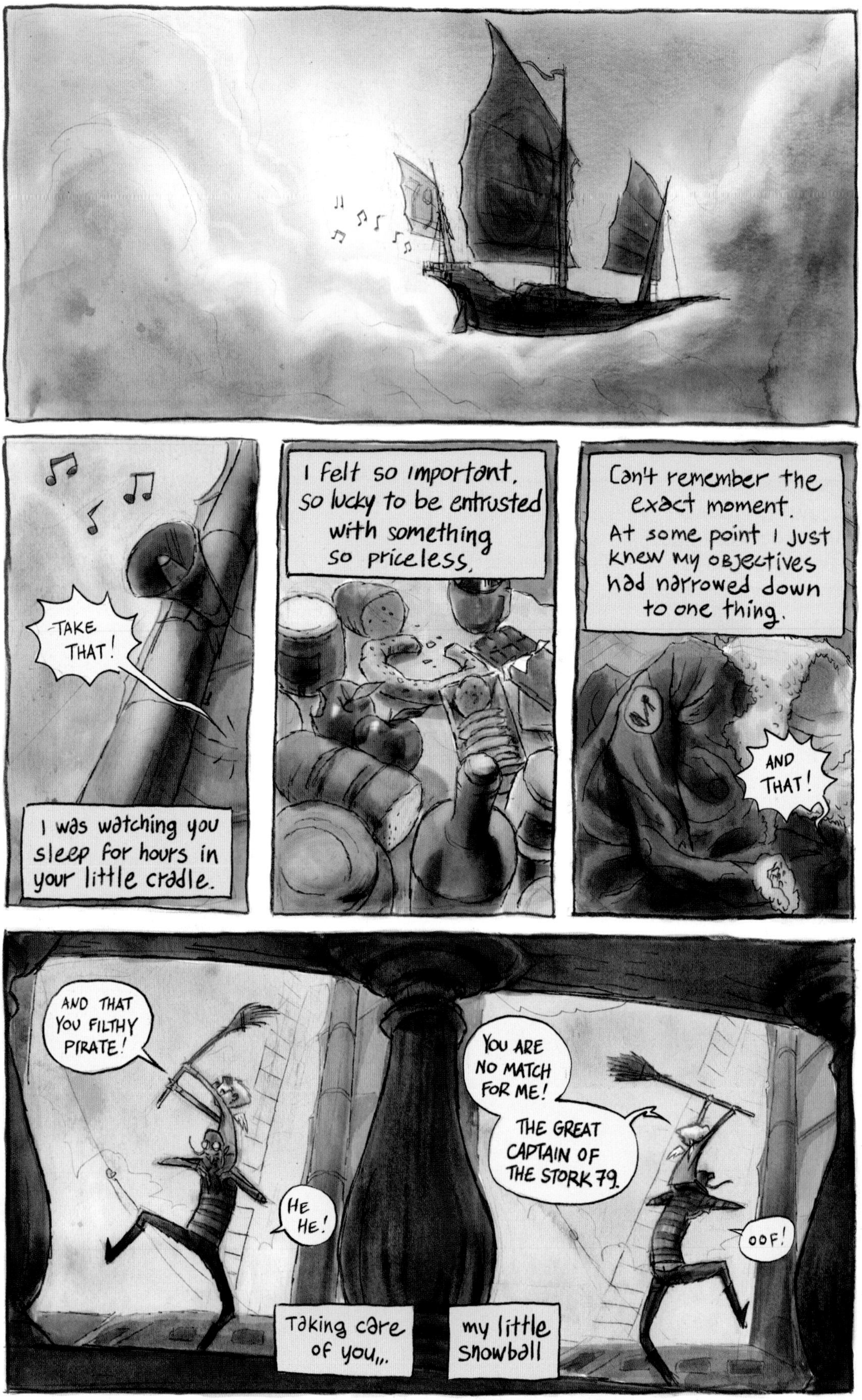

TAKE THAT!
I was watching you sleep for hours in your little cradle.
I felt so important, so lucky to be entrusted with something so priceless.
Can't remember the exact moment. At some point I just knew my objectives had narrowed down to one thing.
AND THAT!
AND THAT YOU FILTHY PIRATE!
HE HE!
YOU ARE NO MATCH FOR ME!
THE GREAT CAPTAIN OF THE STORK 79.
OOF!
Taking care of you,,.
my little snowball

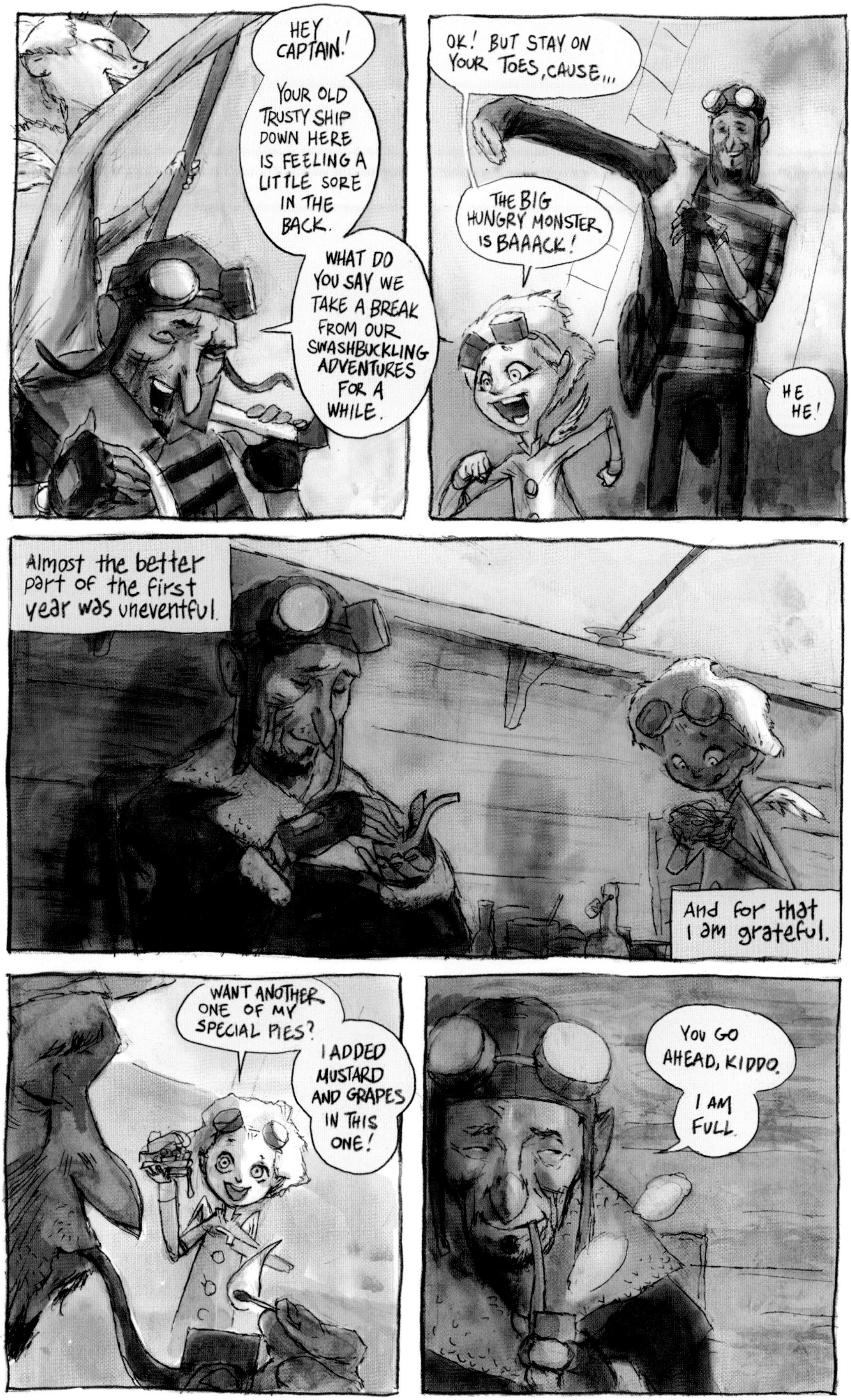
HEY CAPTAIN!
YOUR OLD TRUSTY SHIP DOWN HERE IS FEELING A LITTLE SORE IN THE BACK.
WHAT DO YOU SAY WE TAKE A BREAK FROM OUR SWASHBUCKLING ADVENTURES FOR A WHILE.
OK! BUT STAY ON YOUR TOES, CAUSE...
THE BIG HUNGRY MONSTER IS BAAACK!
HE HE!
Almost the better part of the first year was uneventful.
And for that I am grateful.
WANT ANOTHER ONE OF MY SPECIAL PIES?
I ADDED MUSTARD AND GRAPES IN THIS ONE!
You GO AHEAD, KIDDO.
I AM FULL.

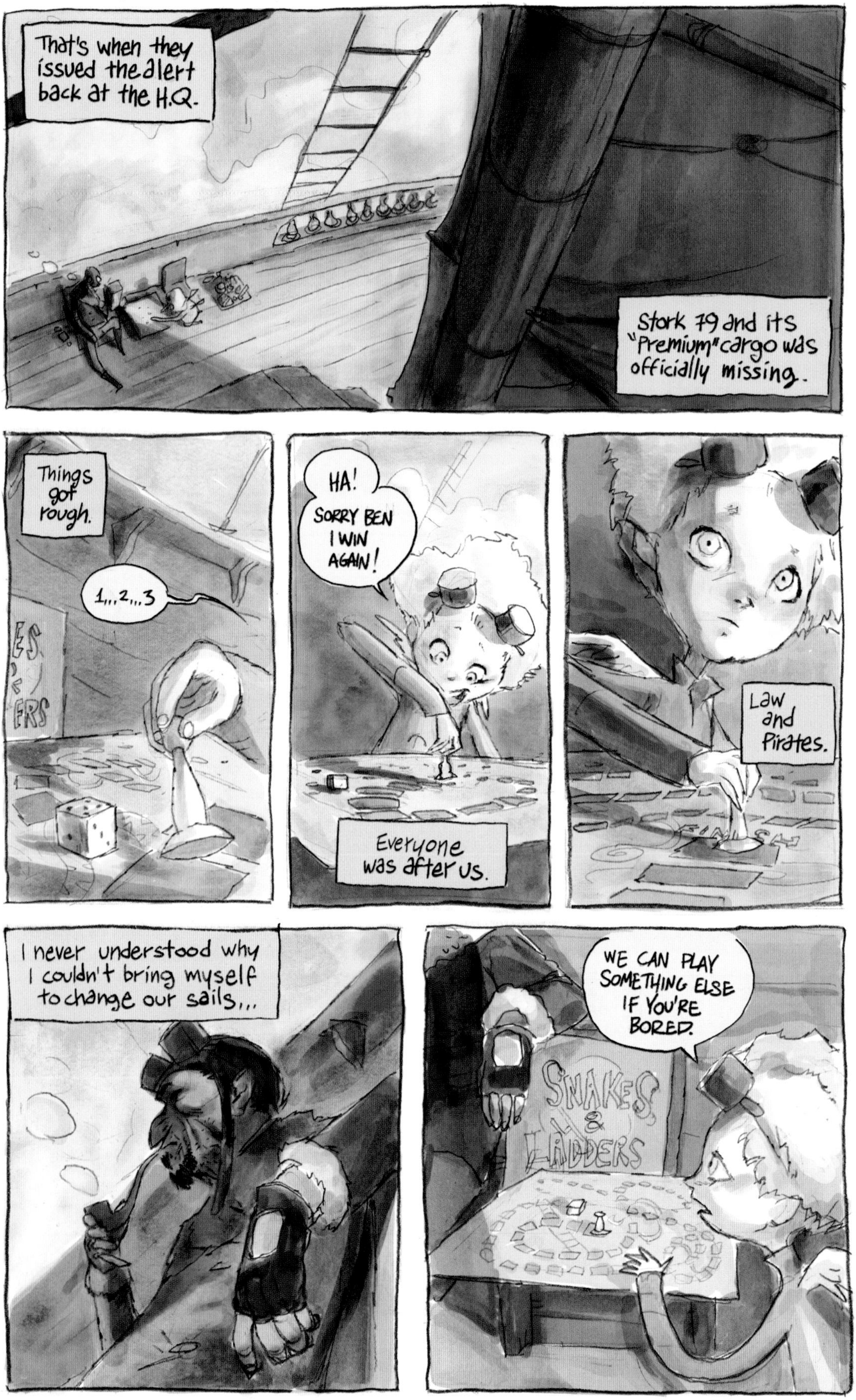
That's when they issued the alert back at the H.Q.
Stork 79 and its "Premium" cargo was officially missing.
Things got rough.
1,,,2,,,3
HA!
SORRY BEN I WIN AGAIN!
Everyone was after us.
Law and Pirates.
I never understood why I couldn't bring myself to change our sails,,,
WE CAN PLAY SOMETHING ELSE IF YOU'RE BORED.
SNAKES & LADDERS

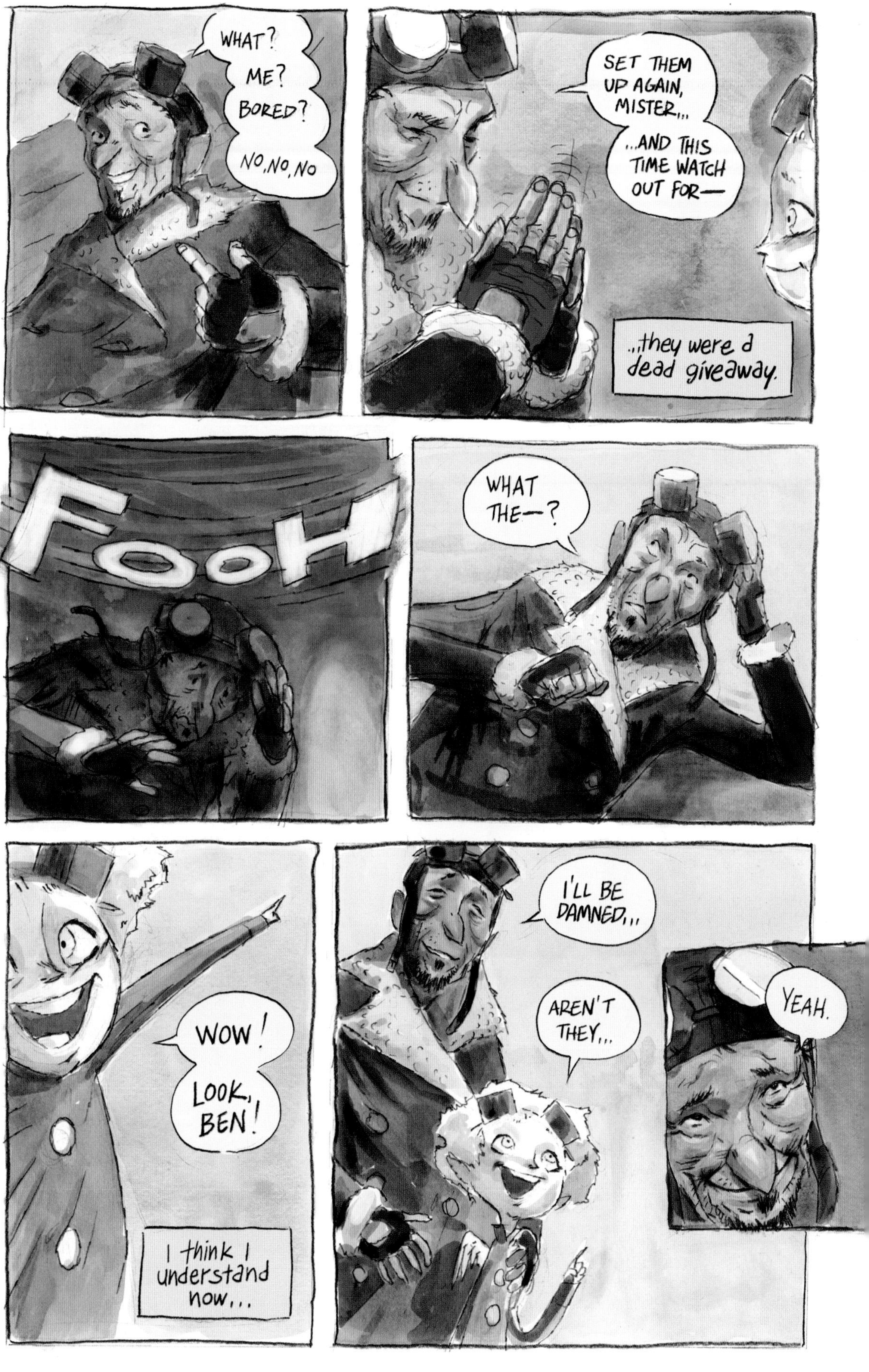
WHAT?
ME?
BORED?
NO, NO, NO
SET THEM UP AGAIN, MISTER...
...AND THIS TIME WATCH OUT FOR—
...they were a dead giveaway.
FOOH
WHAT THE—?
WOW!
LOOK, BEN!
I think I understand now...
I'LL BE DAMNED...
AREN'T THEY...
YEAH.

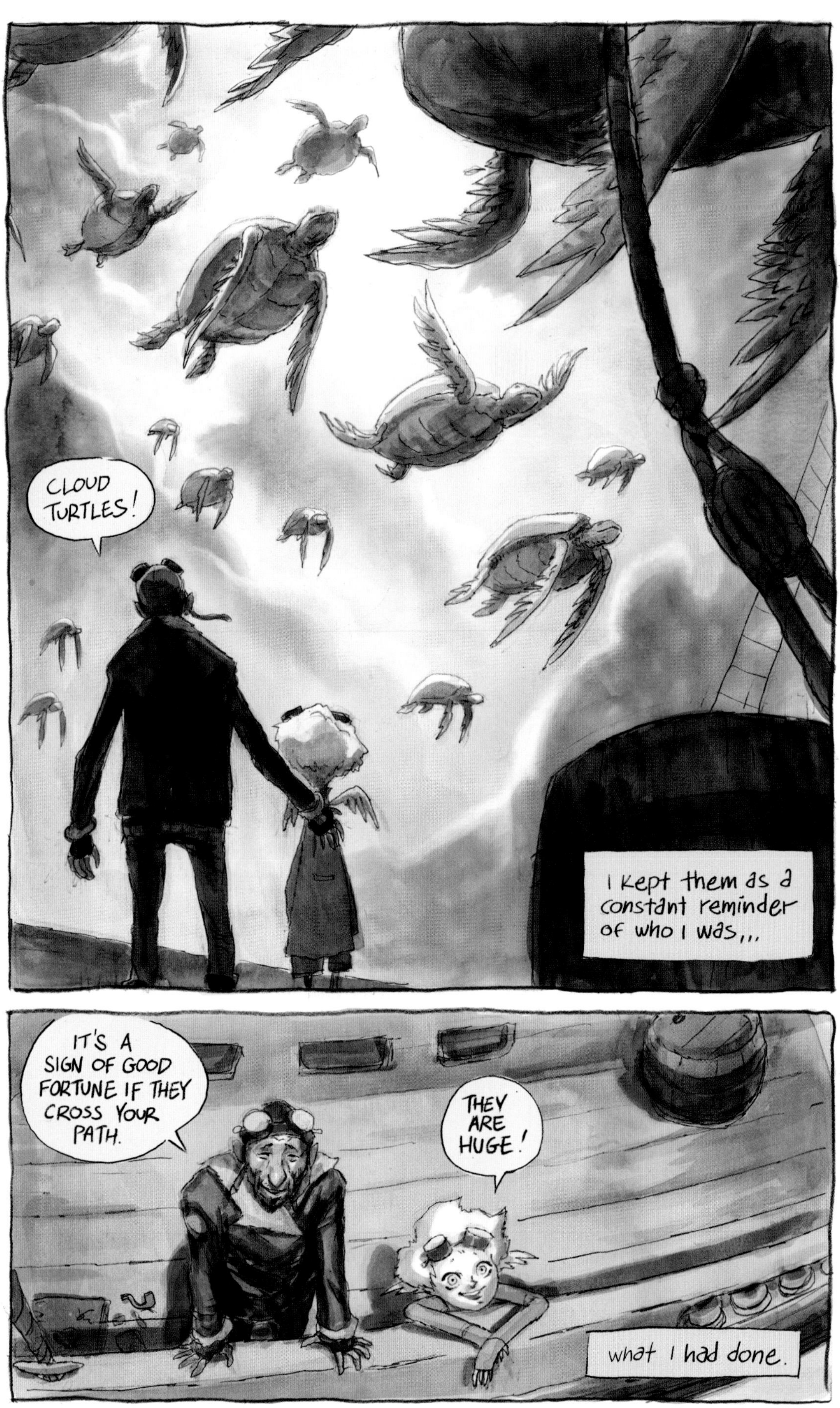
CLOUD TURTLES!
I kept them as a constant reminder of who I was,,,
IT'S A SIGN OF GOOD FORTUNE IF THEY CROSS YOUR PATH.
THEY ARE HUGE!
what I had done.

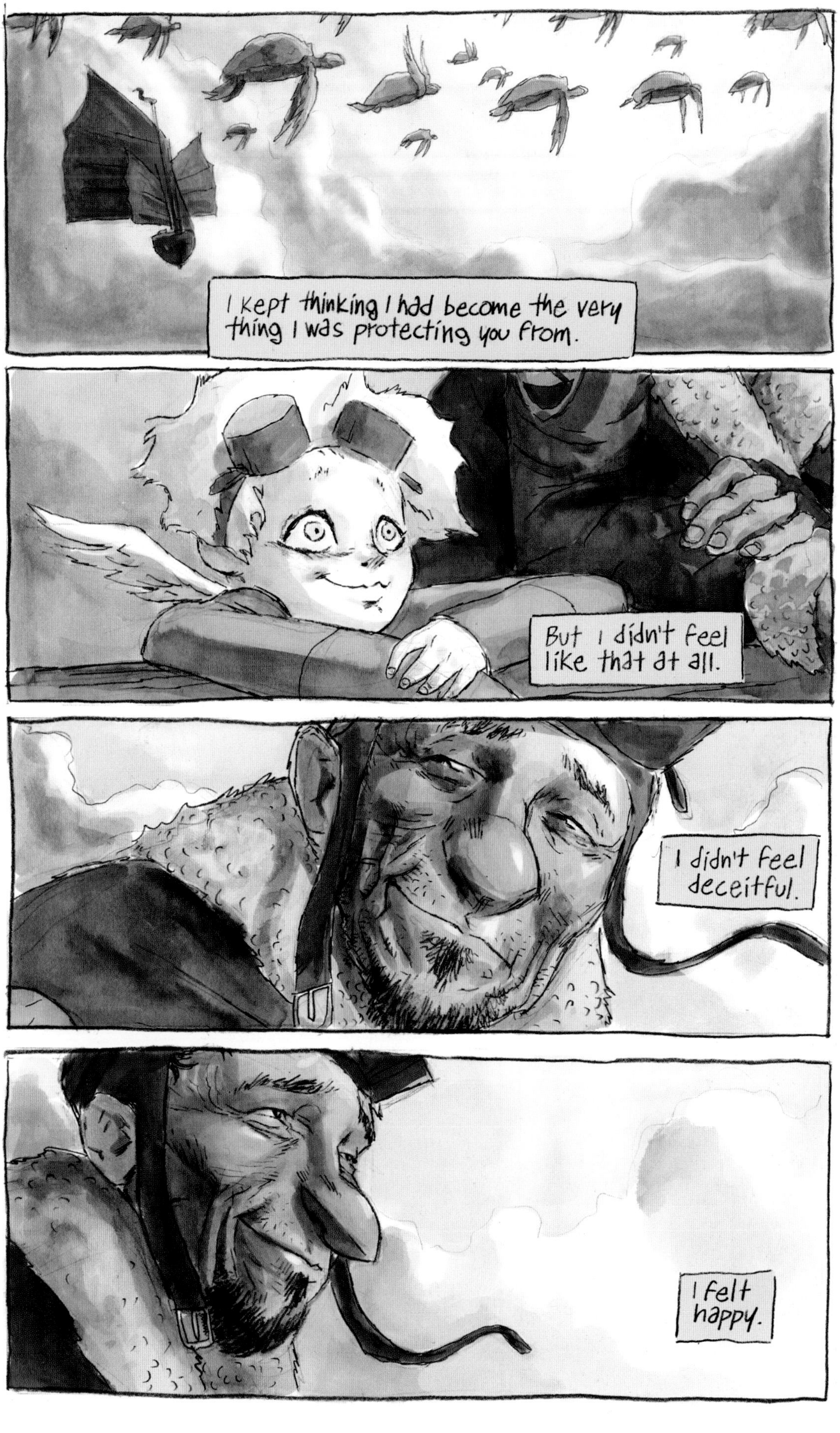

I kept thinking I had become the very thing I was protecting you from.
But I didn't feel like that at all.
I didn't feel deceitful.
I felt happy.

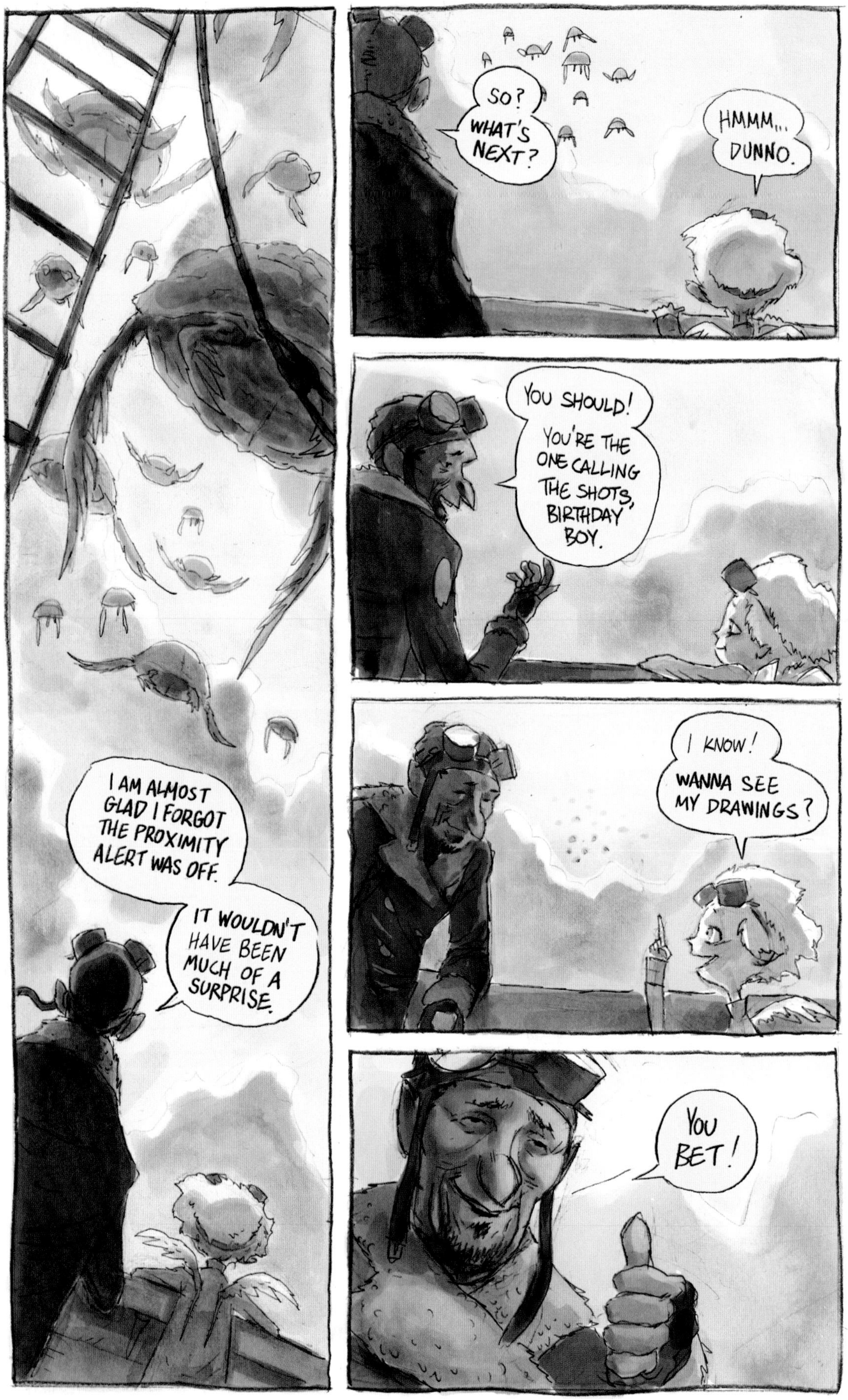
I AM ALMOST GLAD I FORGOT THE PROXIMITY ALERT WAS OFF.
IT WOULDN'T HAVE BEEN MUCH OF A SURPRISE.
SO? WHAT'S NEXT?
HMMM... DUNNO.
YOU SHOULD! YOU'RE THE ONE CALLING THE SHOTS, BIRTHDAY BOY.
I KNOW! WANNA SEE MY DRAWINGS?
YOU BET!

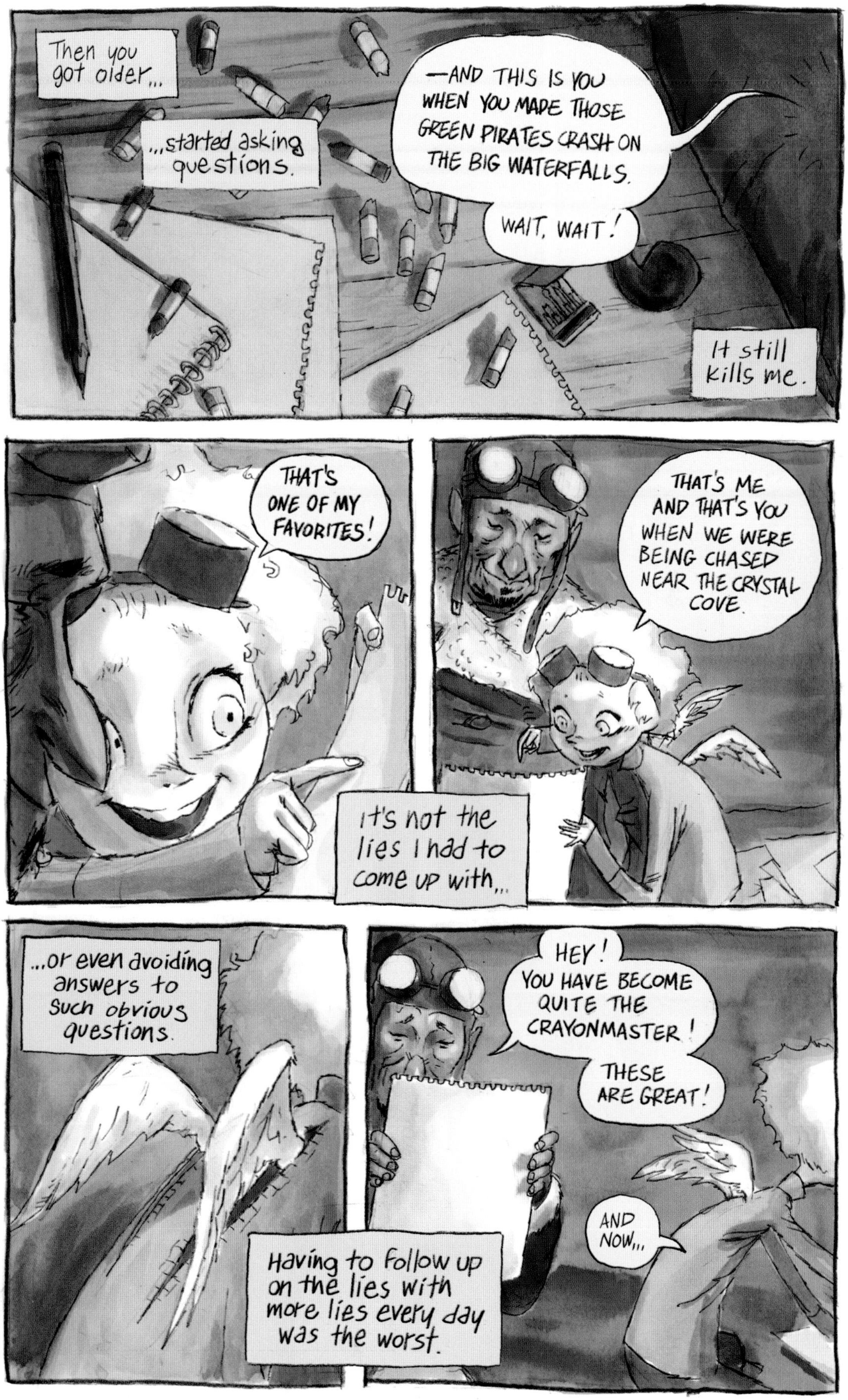
Then you got older...
...started asking questions.
—AND THIS IS YOU WHEN YOU MADE THOSE GREEN PIRATES CRASH ON THE BIG WATERFALLS.
WAIT, WAIT!
It still kills me.
THAT'S ONE OF MY FAVORITES!
THAT'S ME AND THAT'S YOU WHEN WE WERE BEING CHASED NEAR THE CRYSTAL COVE.
It's not the lies I had to come up with...
...or even avoiding answers to such obvious questions.
HEY! YOU HAVE BECOME QUITE THE CRAYONMASTER!
THESE ARE GREAT!
AND NOW...
Having to follow up on the lies with more lies every day was the worst.

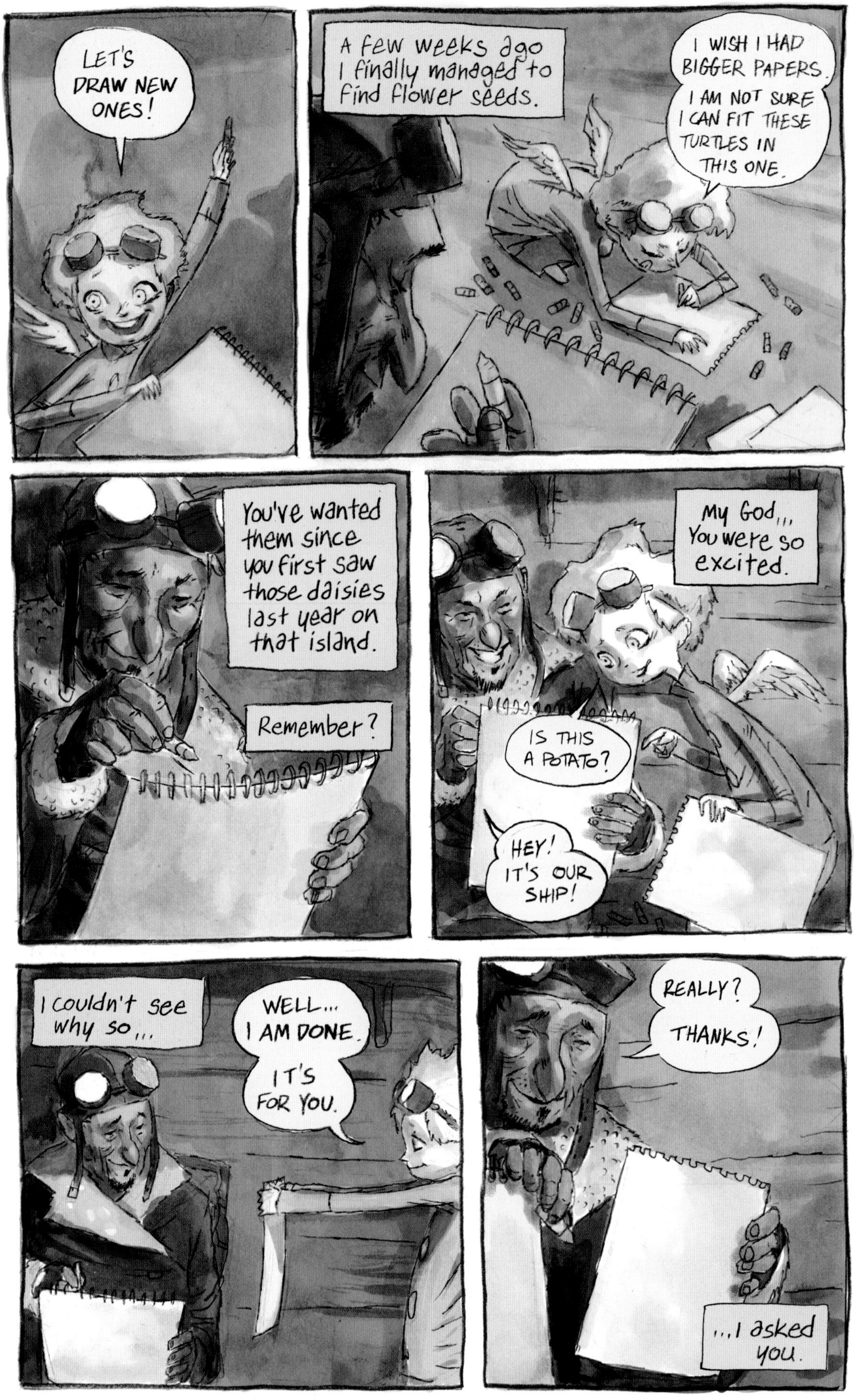
LET'S DRAW NEW ONES!
A few weeks ago I finally managed to find flower seeds.
I WISH I HAD BIGGER PAPERS.
I AM NOT SURE I CAN FIT THESE TURTLES IN THIS ONE.
You've wanted them since you first saw those daisies last year on that island.
Remember?
My God... You were so excited.
IS THIS A POTATO?
HEY! IT'S OUR SHIP!
I couldn't see why so...
WELL... I AM DONE.
IT'S FOR YOU.
REALLY?
THANKS!
...I asked you.

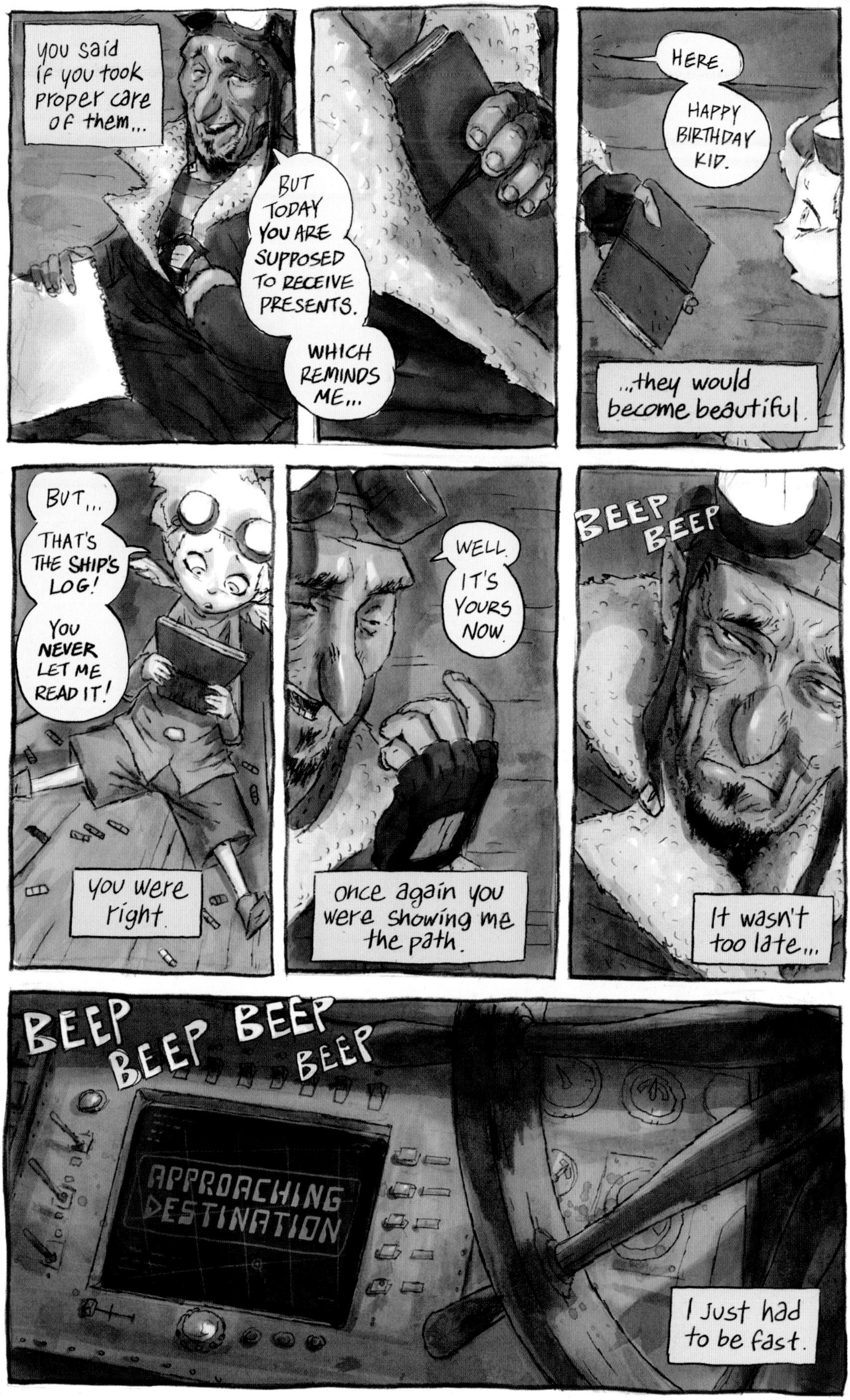
you said if you took proper care of them...
BUT TODAY YOU ARE SUPPOSED TO RECEIVE PRESENTS.
WHICH REMINDS ME...
HERE.
HAPPY BIRTHDAY KID.
...they would become beautiful.
BUT...
THAT'S THE SHIP'S LOG!
YOU NEVER LET ME READ IT!
you were right.
WELL. IT'S YOURS NOW.
once again you were showing me the path.
BEEP BEEP
It wasn't too late...
BEEP BEEP BEEP BEEP
APPROACHING DESTINATION
I just had to be fast.

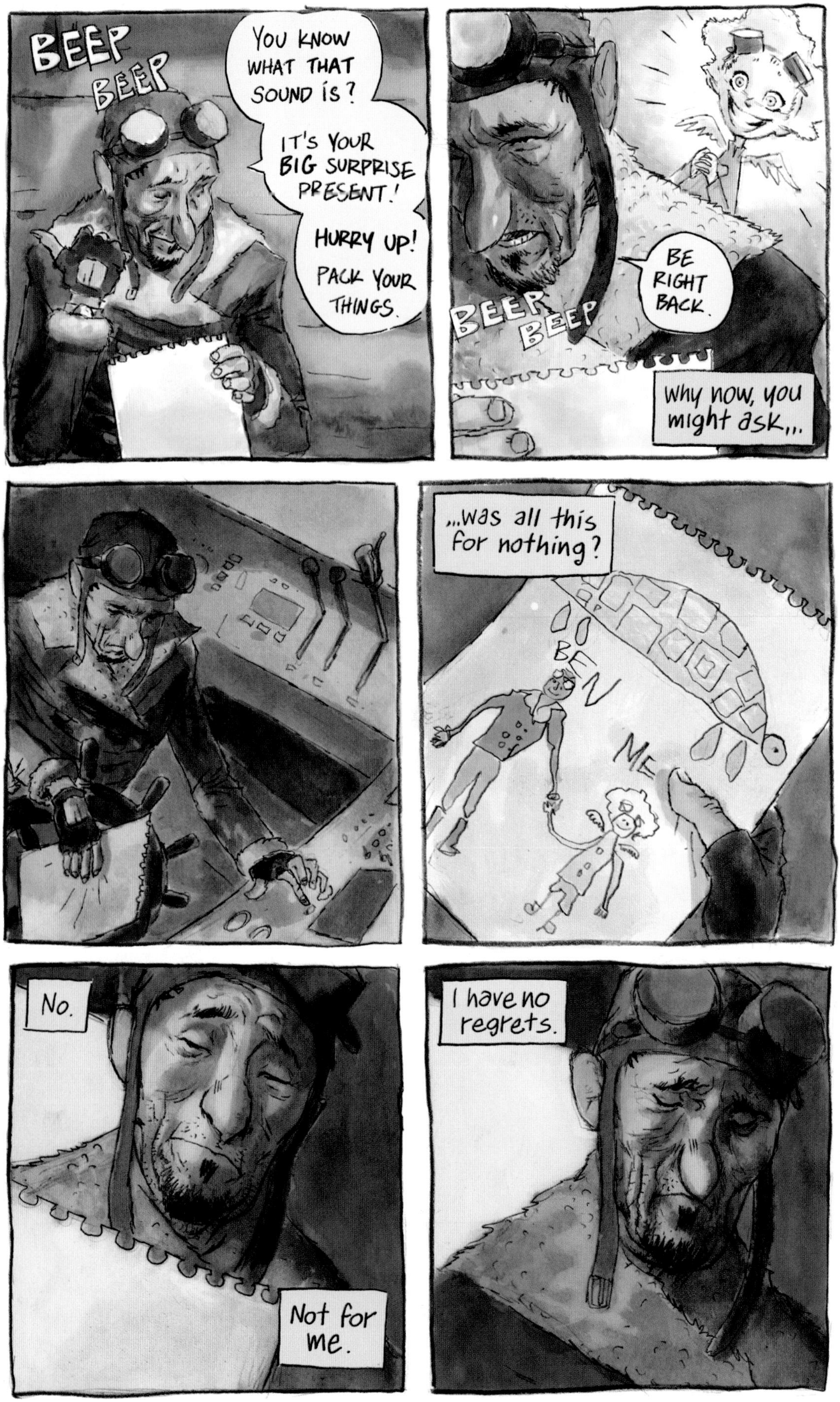
BEEP
BEEP
YOU KNOW WHAT THAT SOUND IS?
IT'S YOUR BIG SURPRISE PRESENT!
HURRY UP! PACK YOUR THINGS.
BE RIGHT BACK.
BEEP
BEEP
why now, you might ask,,,
,,,was all this for nothing?
BEN
ME
No.
Not for me.
I have no regrets.

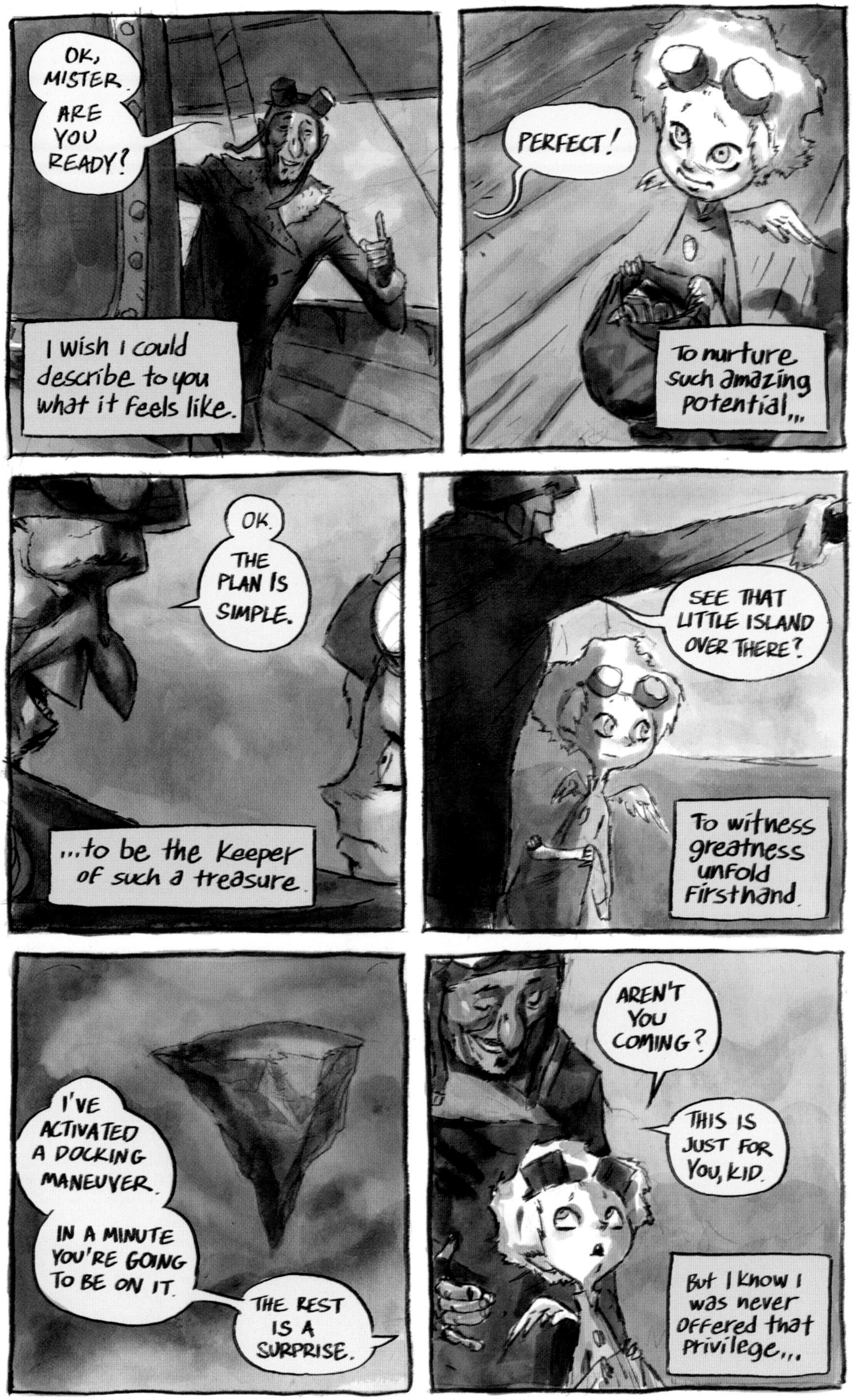
OK, MISTER.
ARE YOU READY?
I wish I could describe to you what it feels like.
PERFECT!
To nurture such amazing potential...
OK.
THE PLAN IS SIMPLE.
...to be the keeper of such a treasure.
SEE THAT LITTLE ISLAND OVER THERE?
To witness greatness unfold firsthand.
I'VE ACTIVATED A DOCKING MANEUVER.
IN A MINUTE YOU'RE GOING TO BE ON IT.
THE REST IS A SURPRISE.
AREN'T YOU COMING?
THIS IS JUST FOR YOU, KID.
But I know I was never offered that privilege...

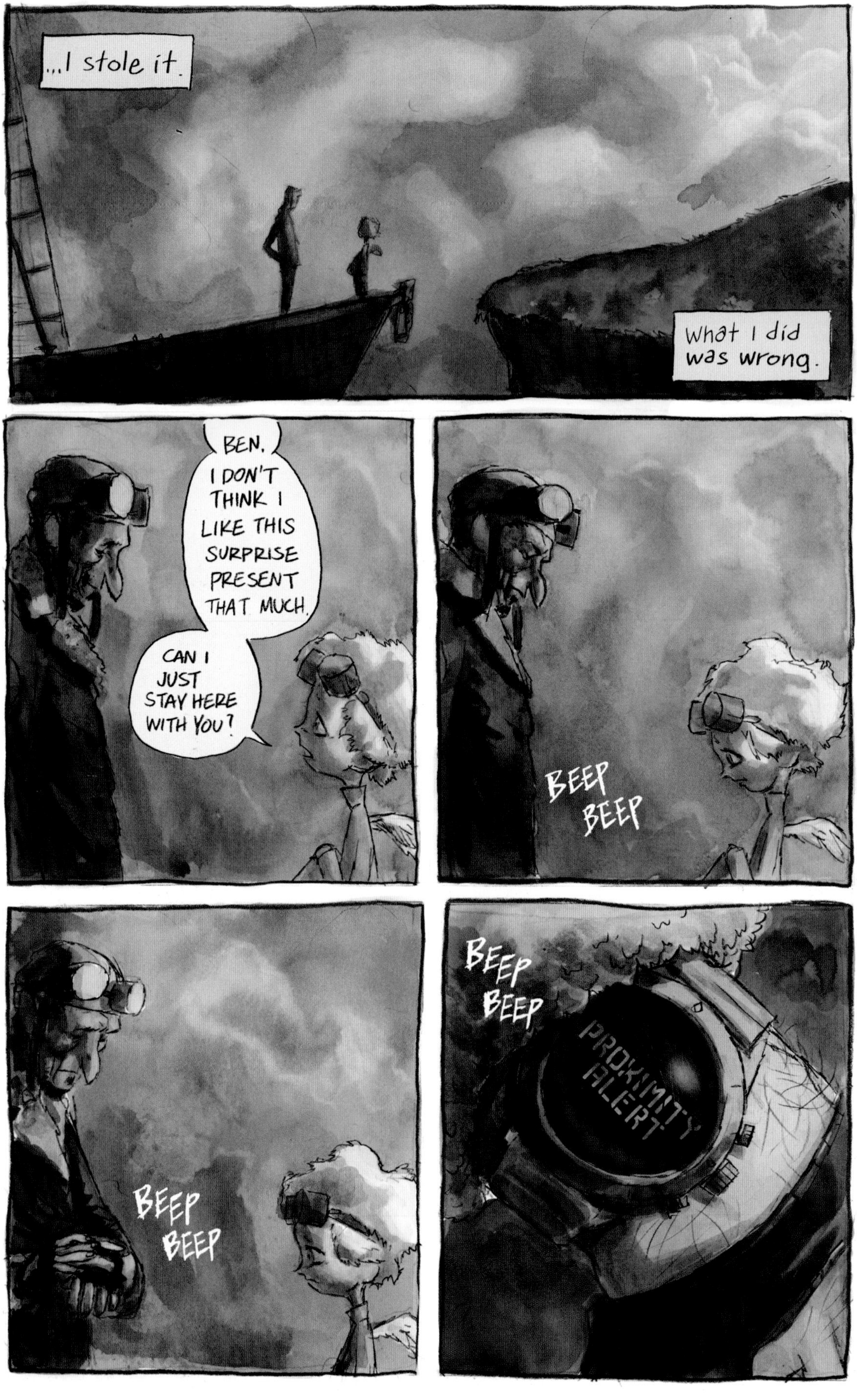
...I stole it.
What I did was wrong.
BEN. I DON'T THINK I LIKE THIS SURPRISE PRESENT THAT MUCH.
CAN I JUST STAY HERE WITH YOU?
BEEP BEEP
BEEP BEEP
BEEP BEEP
PROXIMITY ALERT

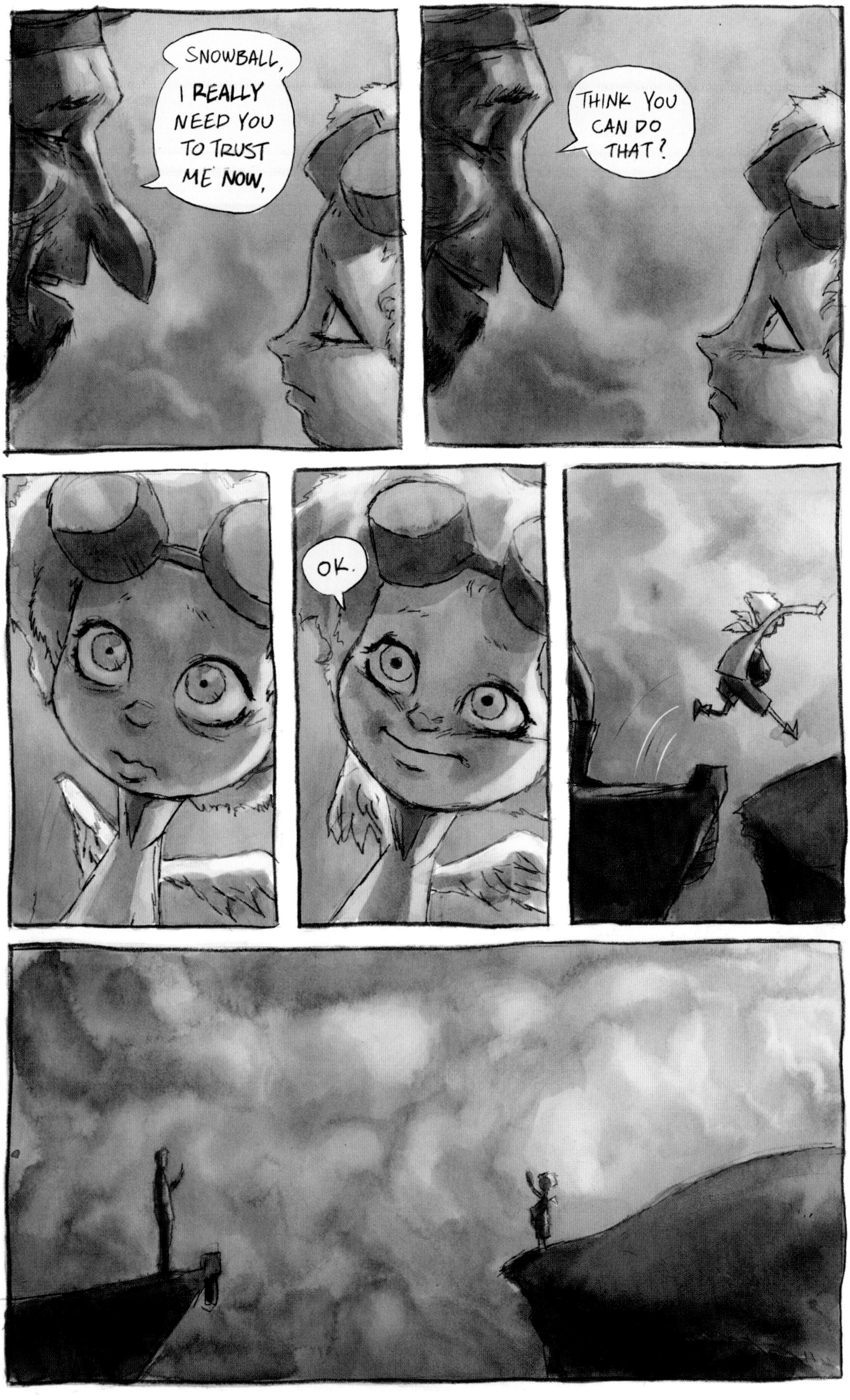
SNOWBALL, I REALLY NEED YOU TO TRUST ME NOW,
THINK YOU CAN DO THAT?
OK.

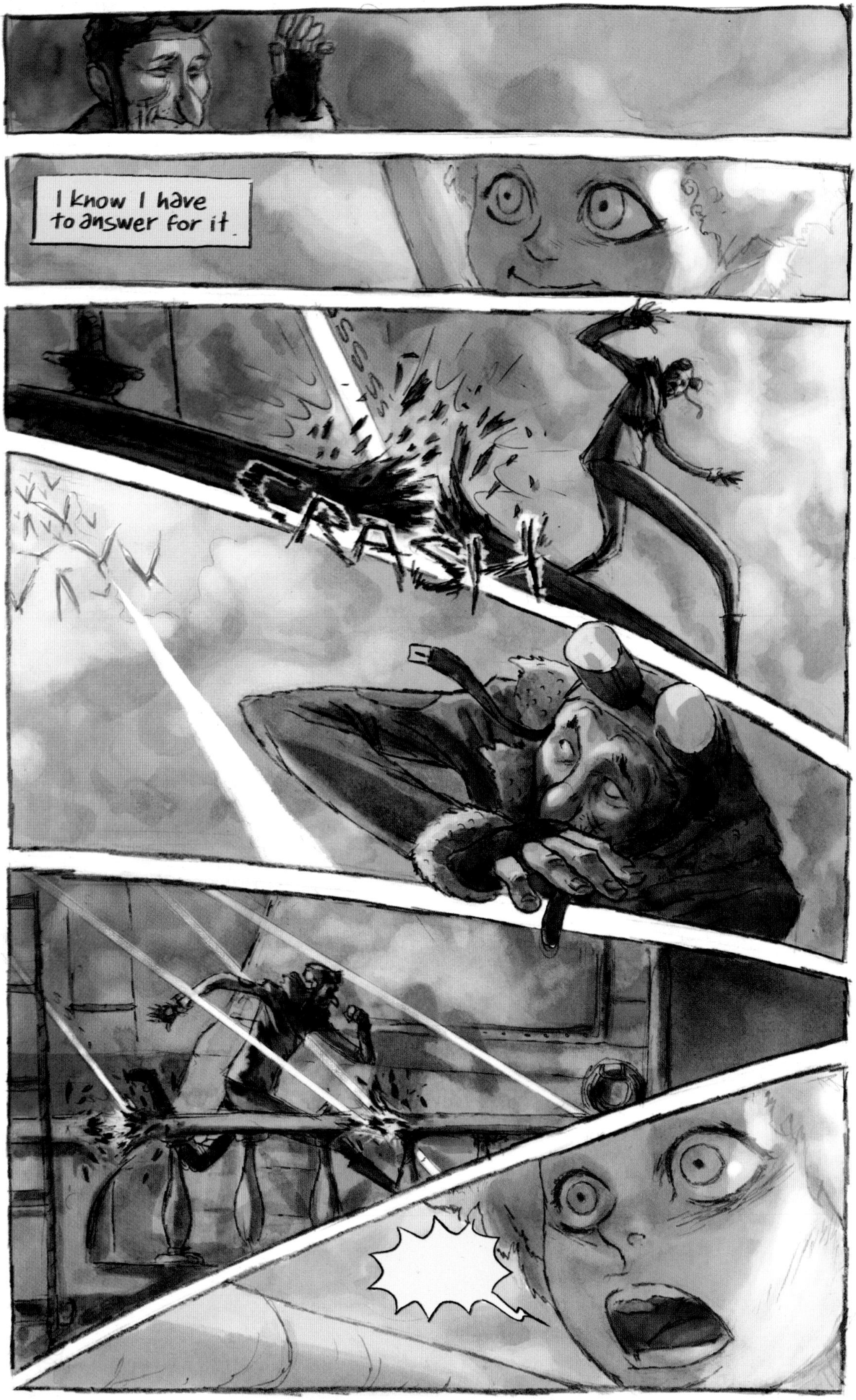
I know I have to answer for it.
SSSSSS
CRASH!

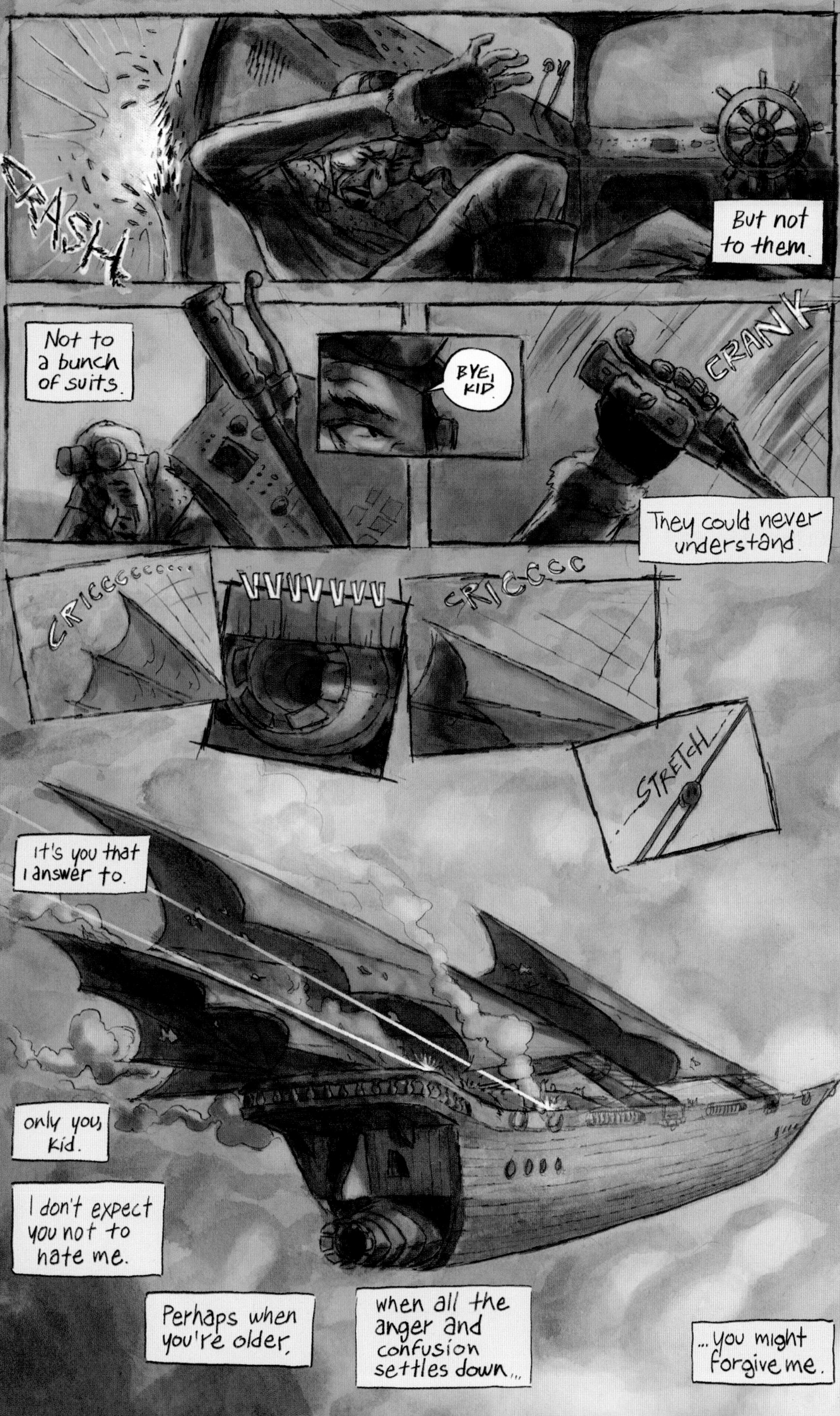
CRASH
But not to them.
Not to a bunch of suits.
BYE, KID.
CRANK
They could never understand.
CRICCCCCCC...
VVVVVVVV
CRICCCC
STRETCH
It's you that I answer to.
only you, kid.
I don't expect you not to hate me.
Perhaps when you're older,
when all the anger and confusion settles down...
...you might forgive me.

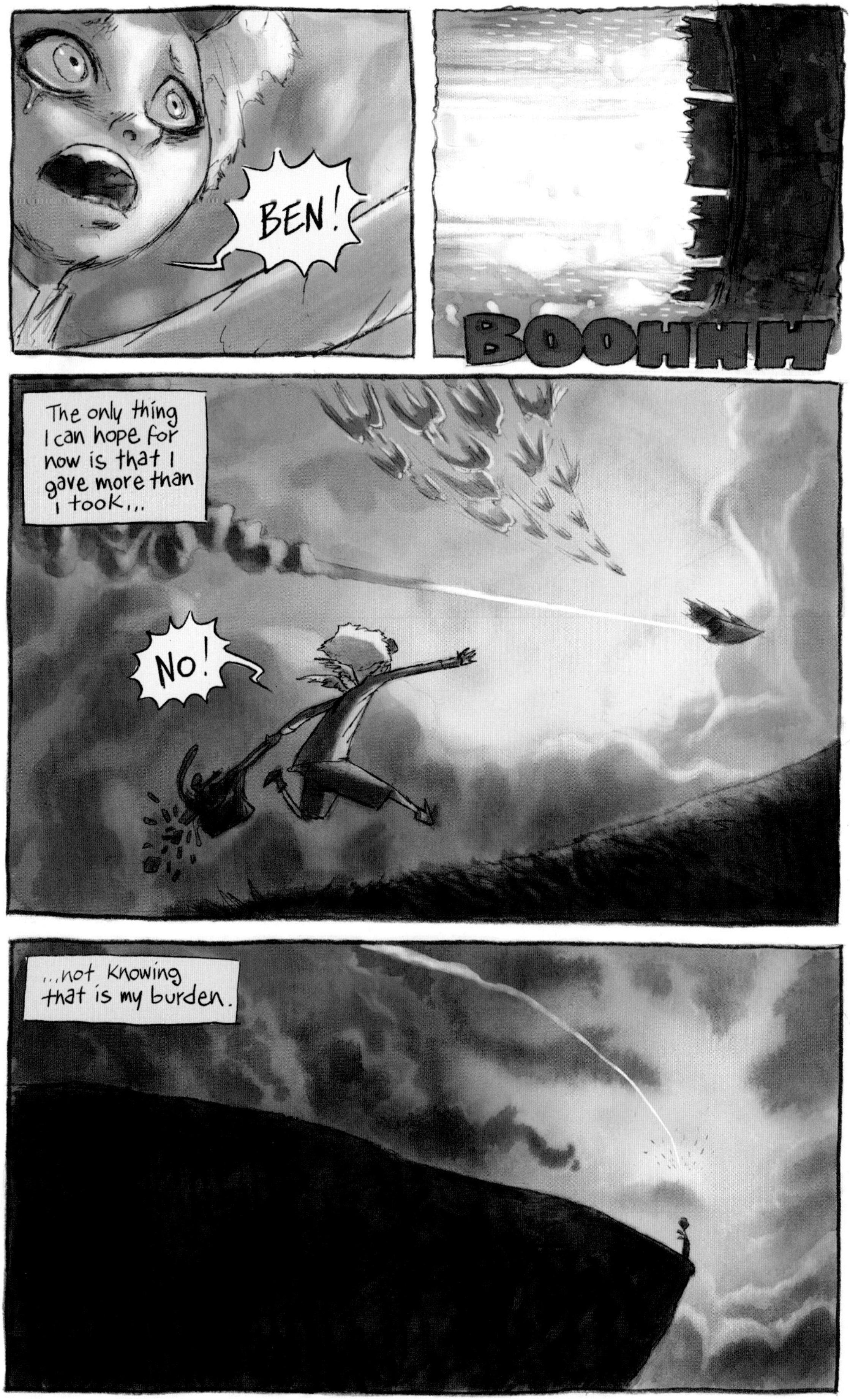
BEN!
BOOHHH
The only thing I can hope for now is that I gave more than I took...
No!
...not knowing that is my burden.

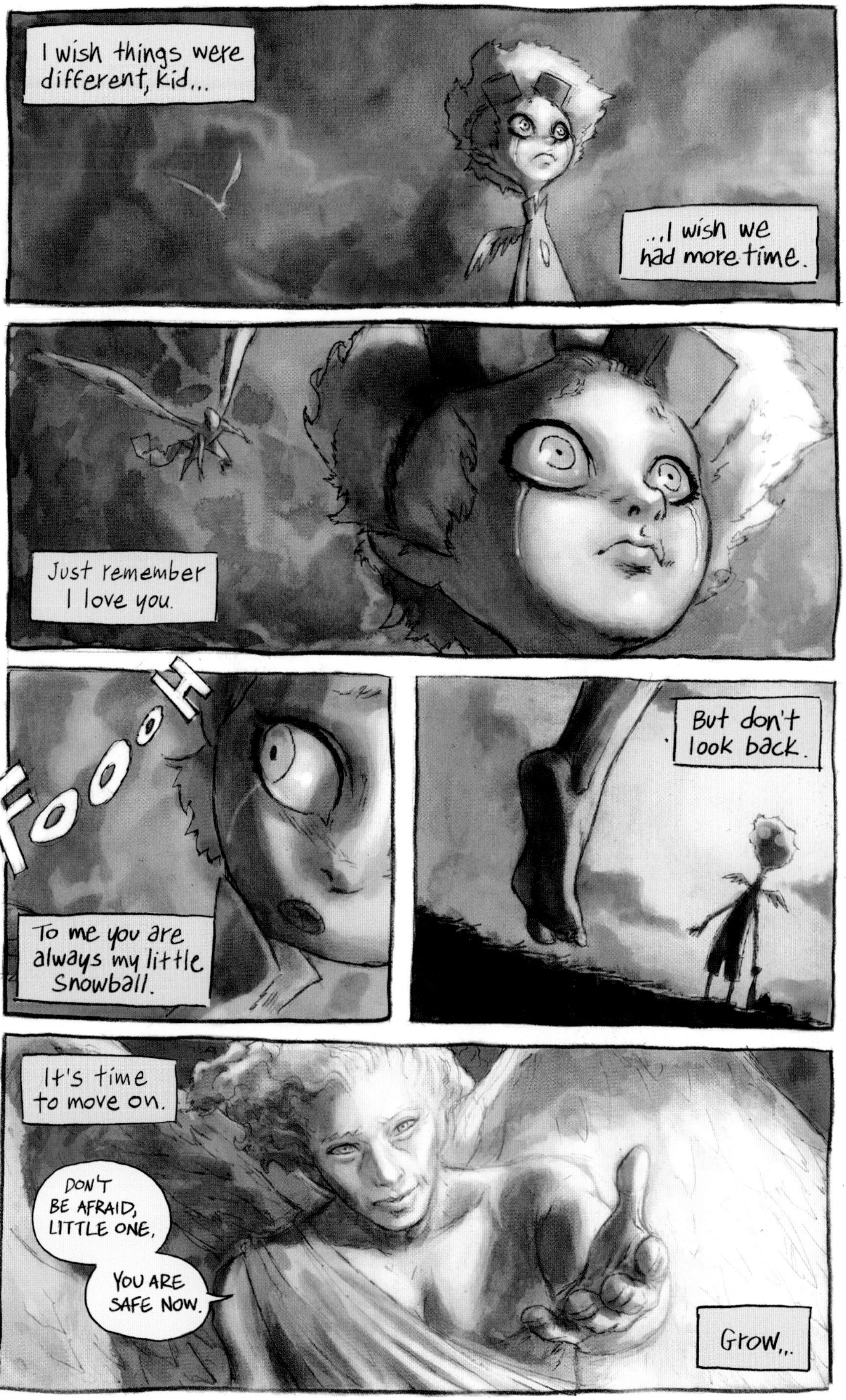
I wish things were different, kid...
...I wish we had more time.
Just remember I love you.
FOOOOH
To me you are always my little Snowball.
But don't look back.
It's time to move on.
DON'T BE AFRAID, LITTLE ONE,
YOU ARE SAFE NOW.
Grow...

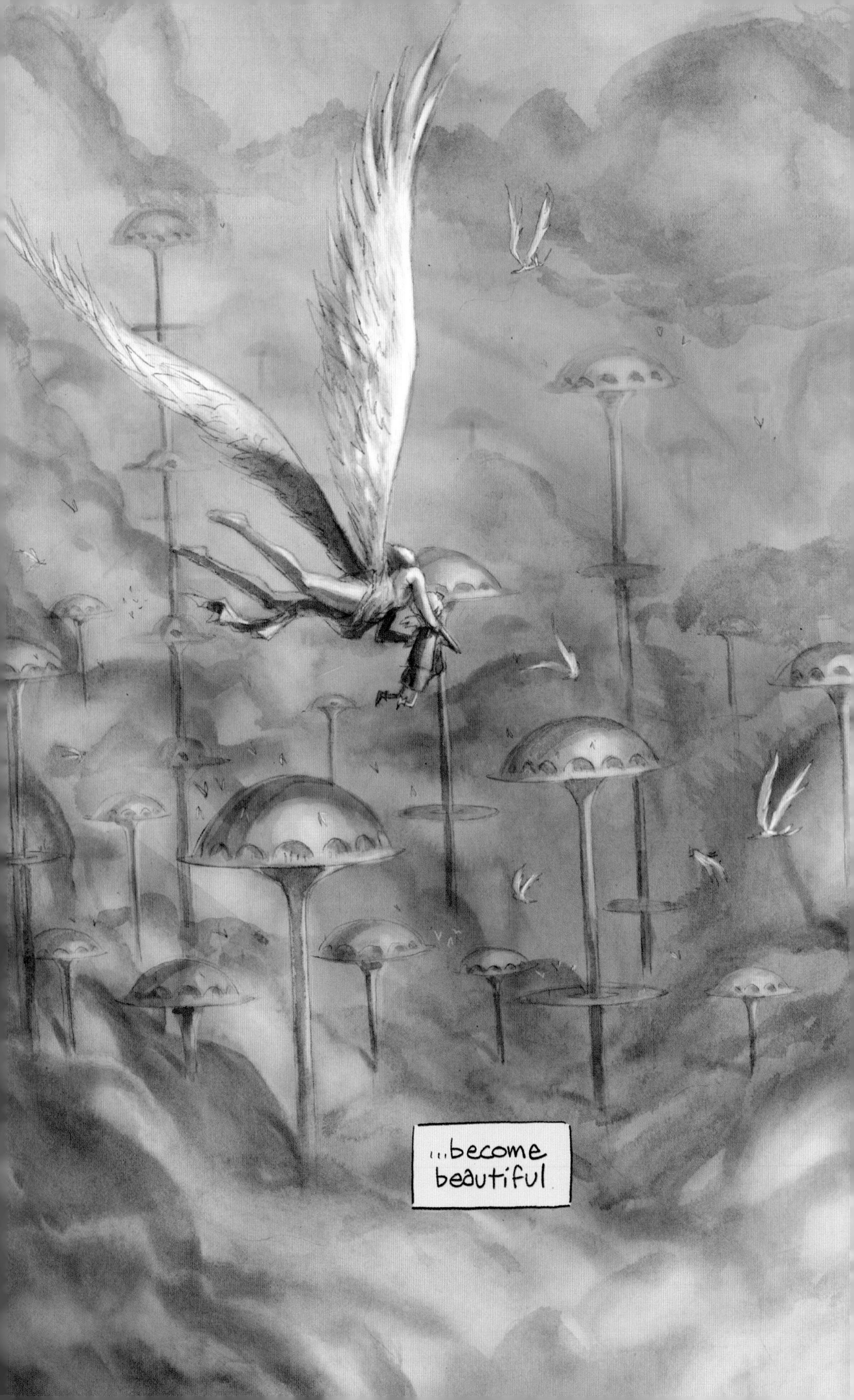
...become
beautiful

by
Kostas
Kiriakakis

Sustain
This Song

Leland Myrick

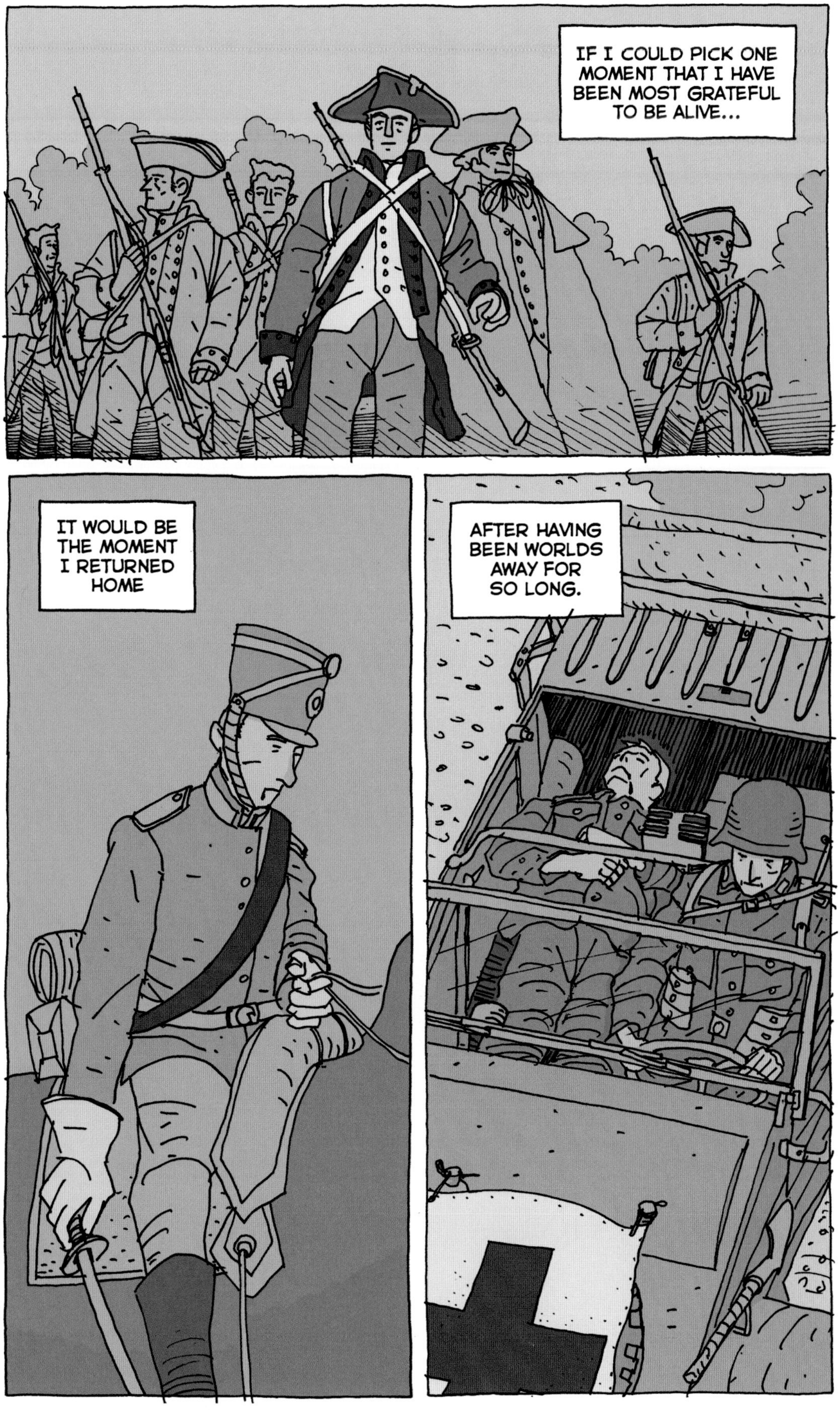
IF I COULD PICK ONE MOMENT THAT I HAVE BEEN MOST GRATEFUL TO BE ALIVE...
IT WOULD BE THE MOMENT I RETURNED HOME
AFTER HAVING BEEN WORLDS AWAY FOR SO LONG.

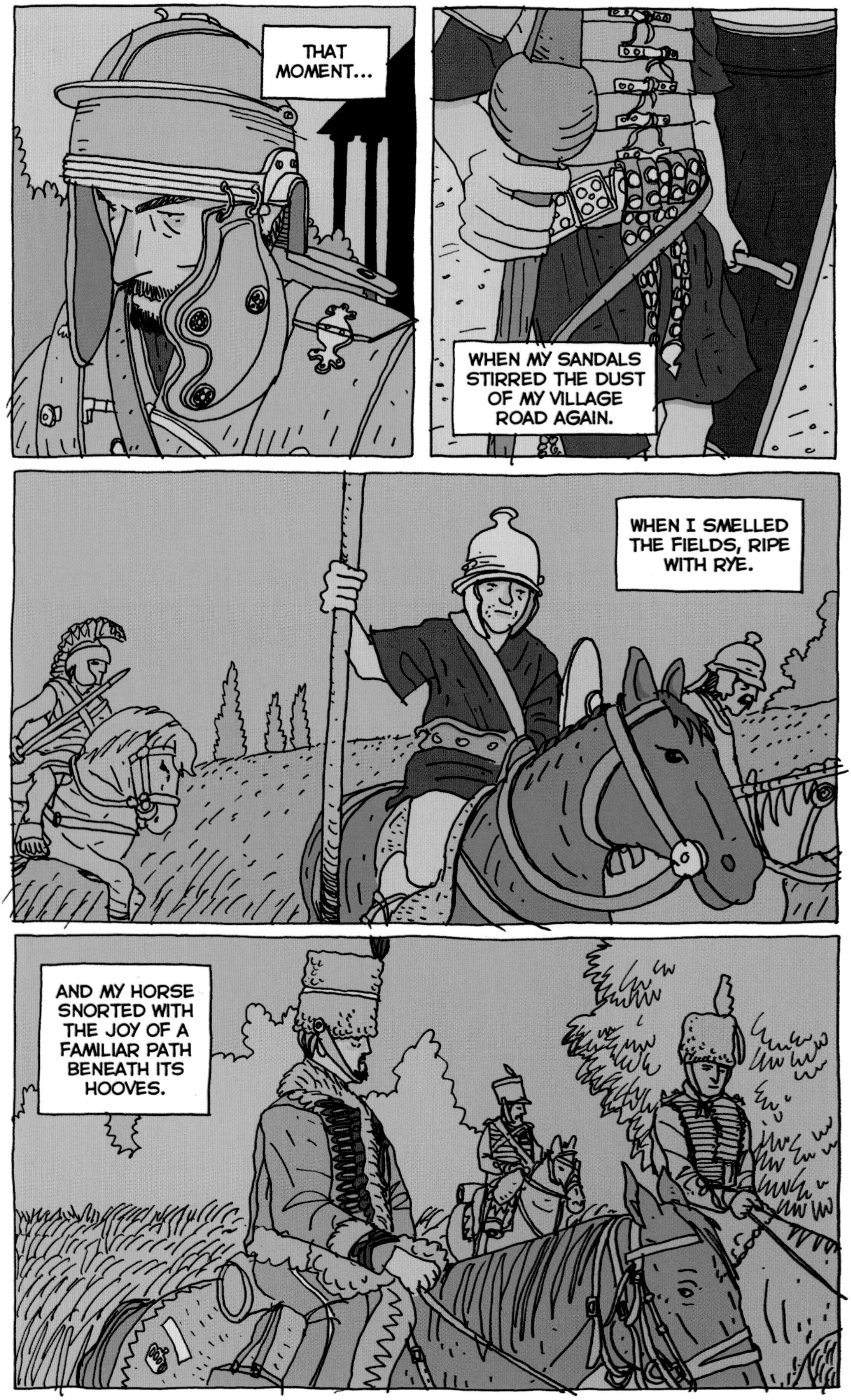
THAT MOMENT...
WHEN MY SANDALS STIRRED THE DUST OF MY VILLAGE ROAD AGAIN.
WHEN I SMELLED THE FIELDS, RIPE WITH RYE.
AND MY HORSE SNORTED WITH THE JOY OF A FAMILIAR PATH BENEATH ITS HOOVES.

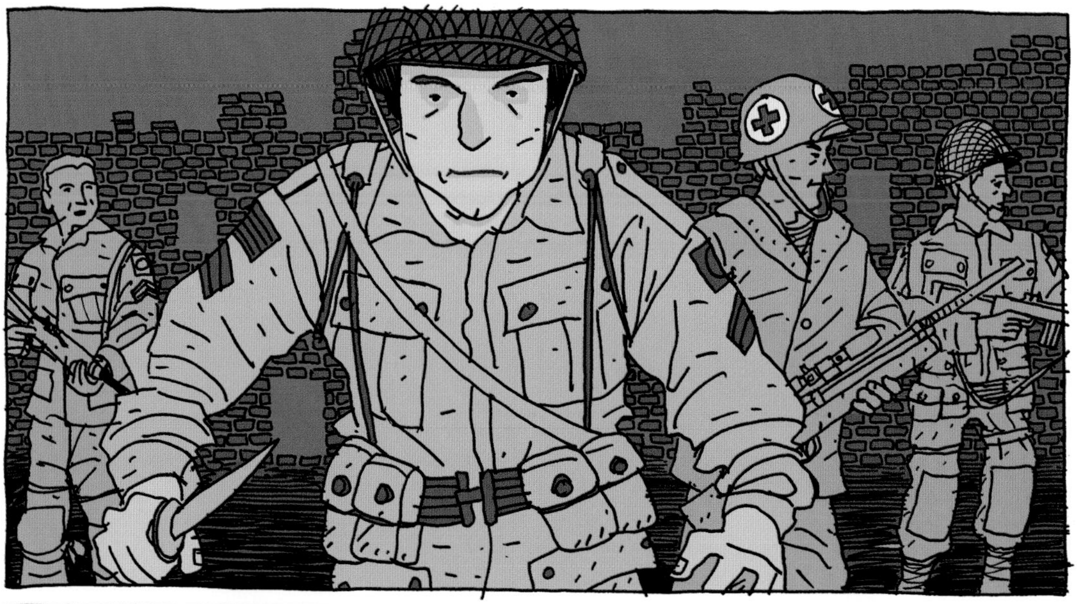

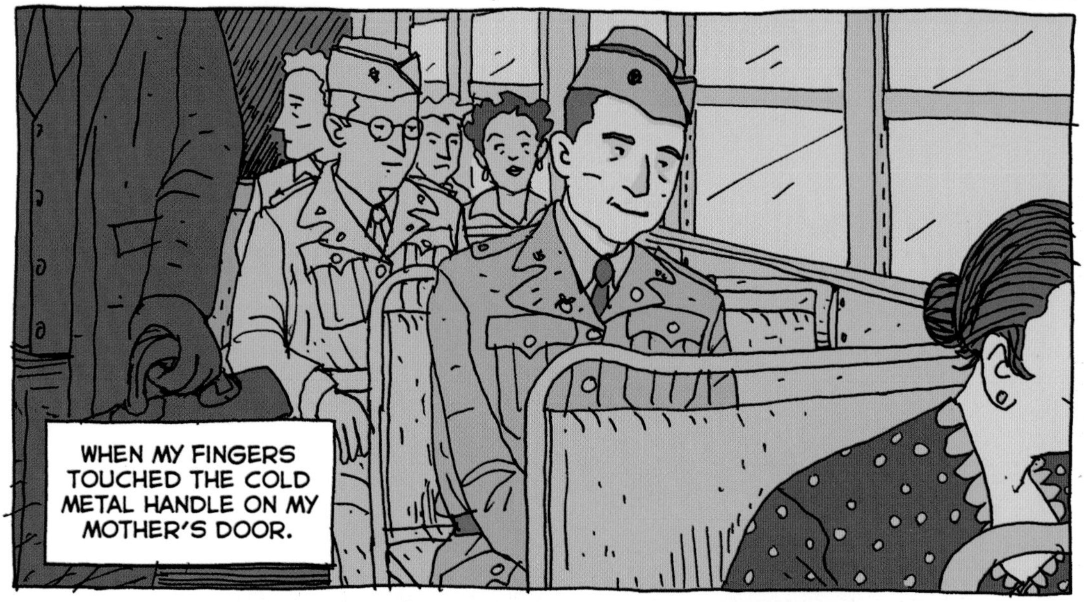
WHEN MY FINGERS TOUCHED THE COLD METAL HANDLE ON MY MOTHER'S DOOR.

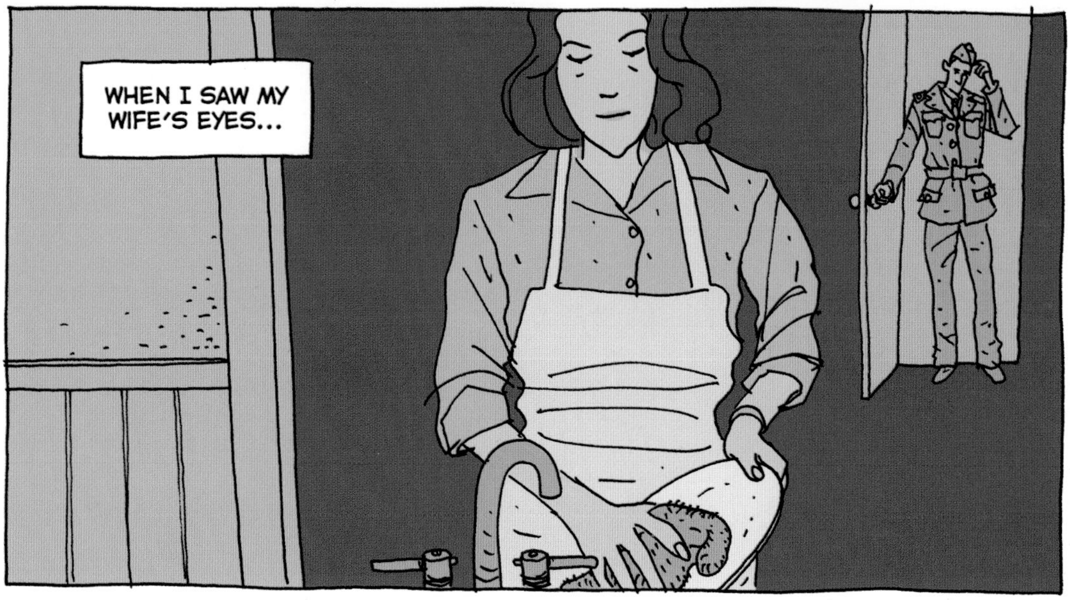
WHEN I SAW MY WIFE'S EYES...

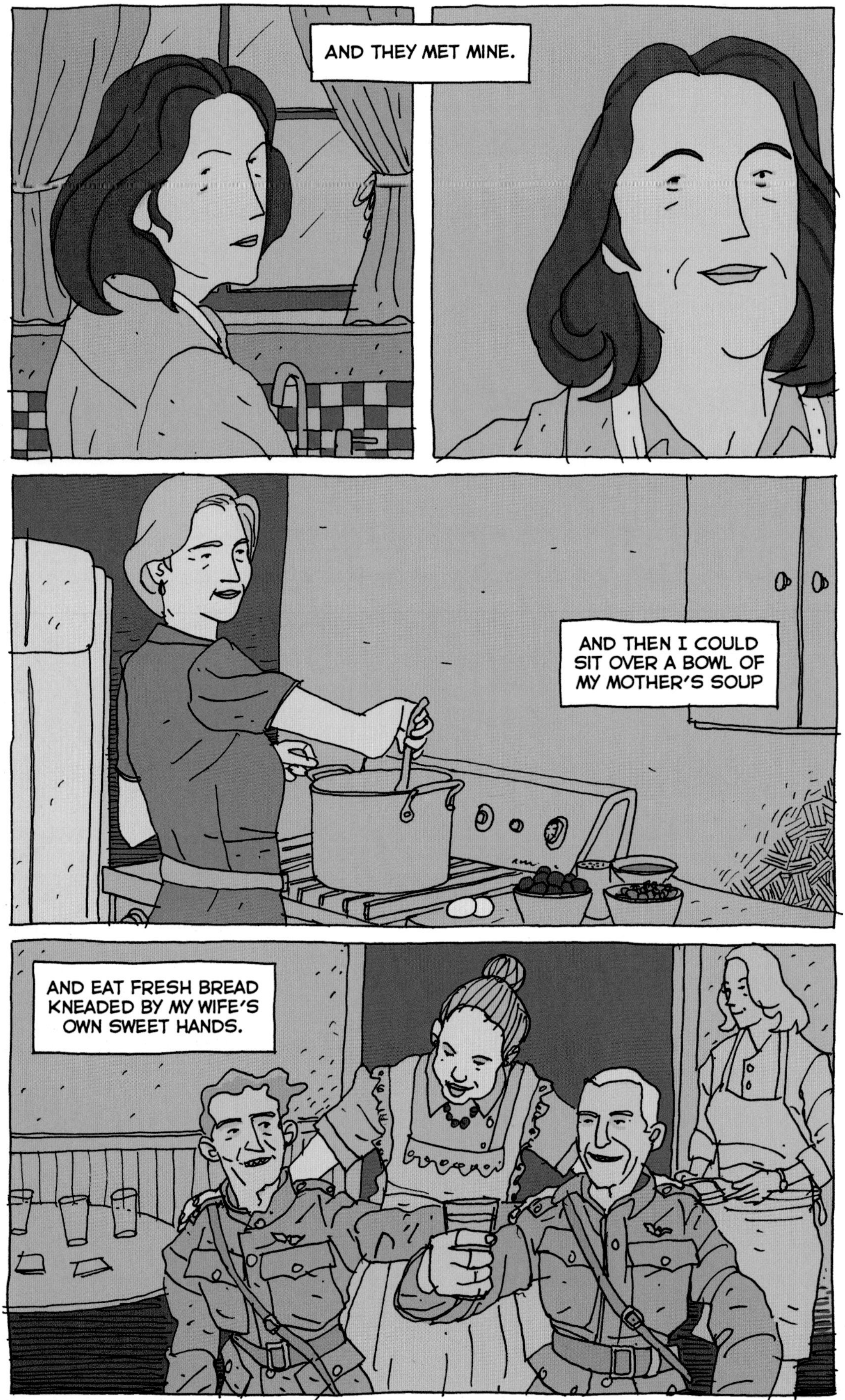
AND THEY MET MINE.
AND THEN I COULD SIT OVER A BOWL OF MY MOTHER'S SOUP
AND EAT FRESH BREAD KNEADED BY MY WIFE'S OWN SWEET HANDS.

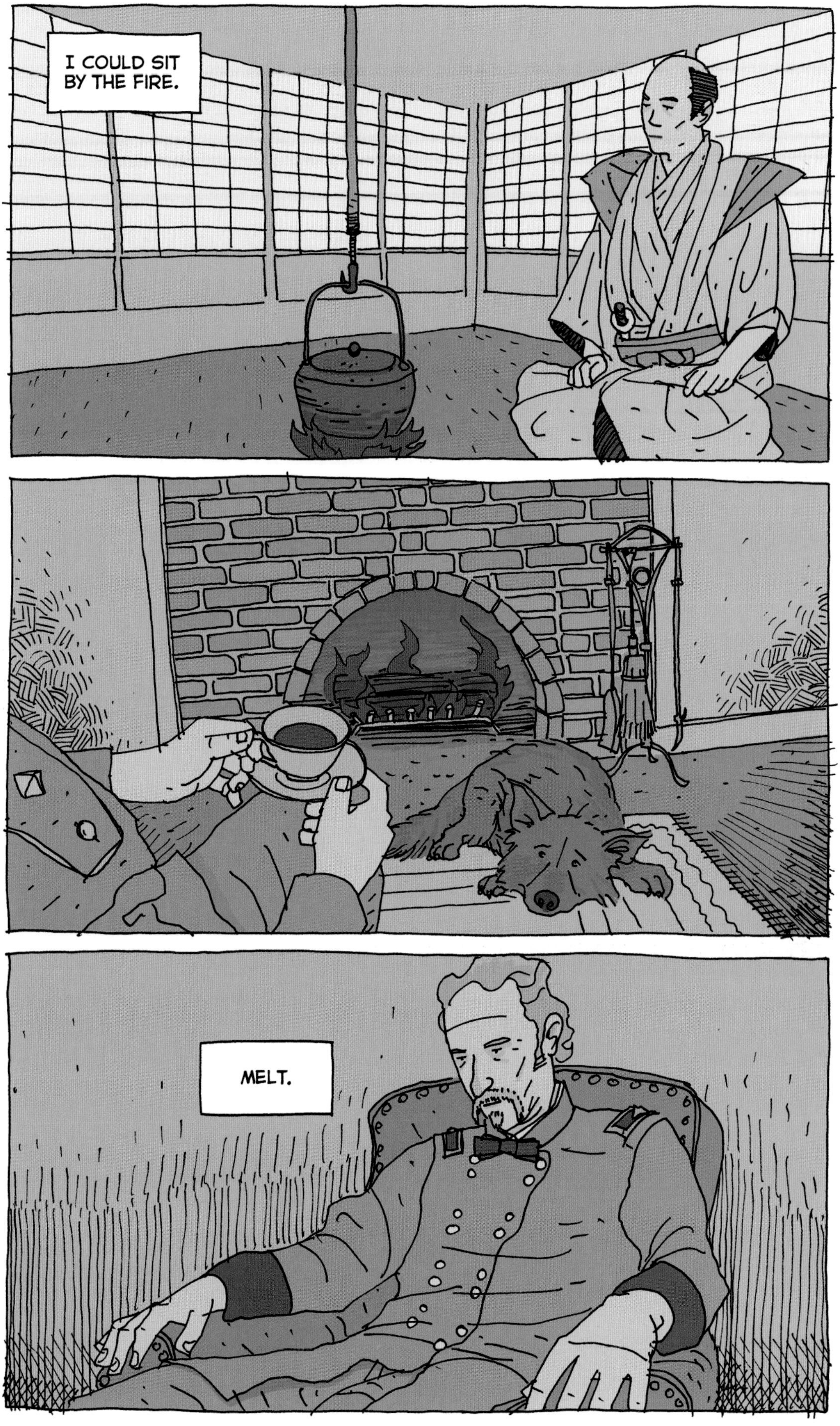
I COULD SIT BY THE FIRE.
MELT.

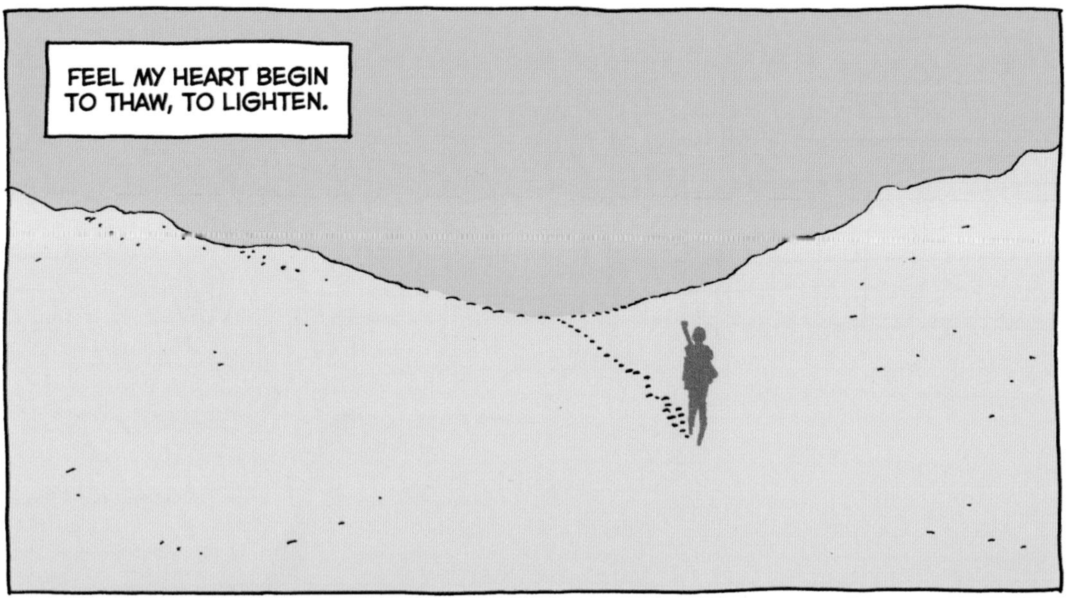
FEEL MY HEART BEGIN
TO THAW, TO LIGHTEN.

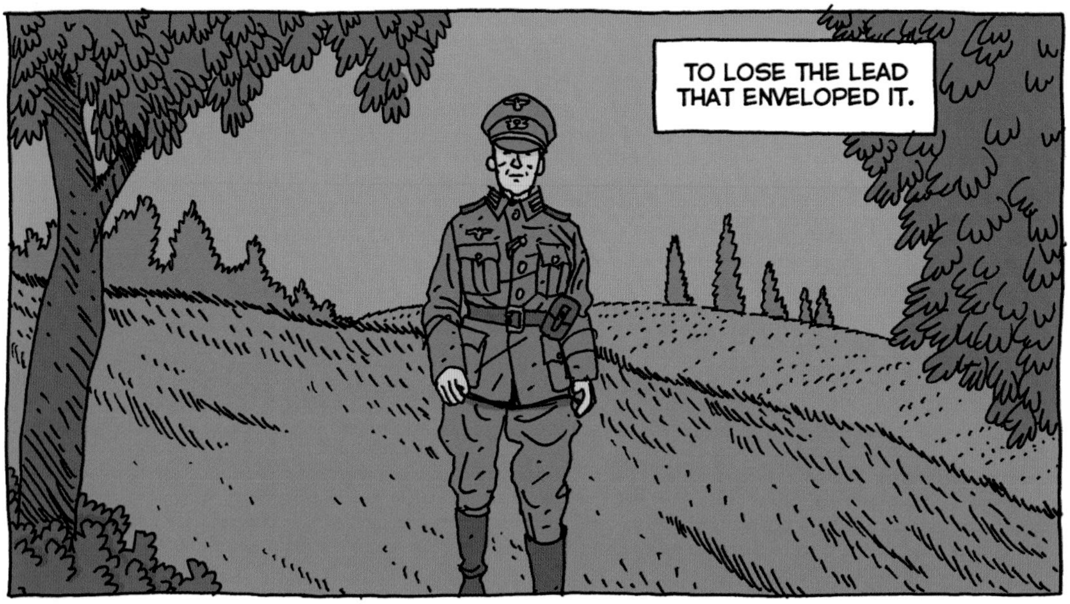
TO LOSE THE LEAD
THAT ENVELOPED IT.

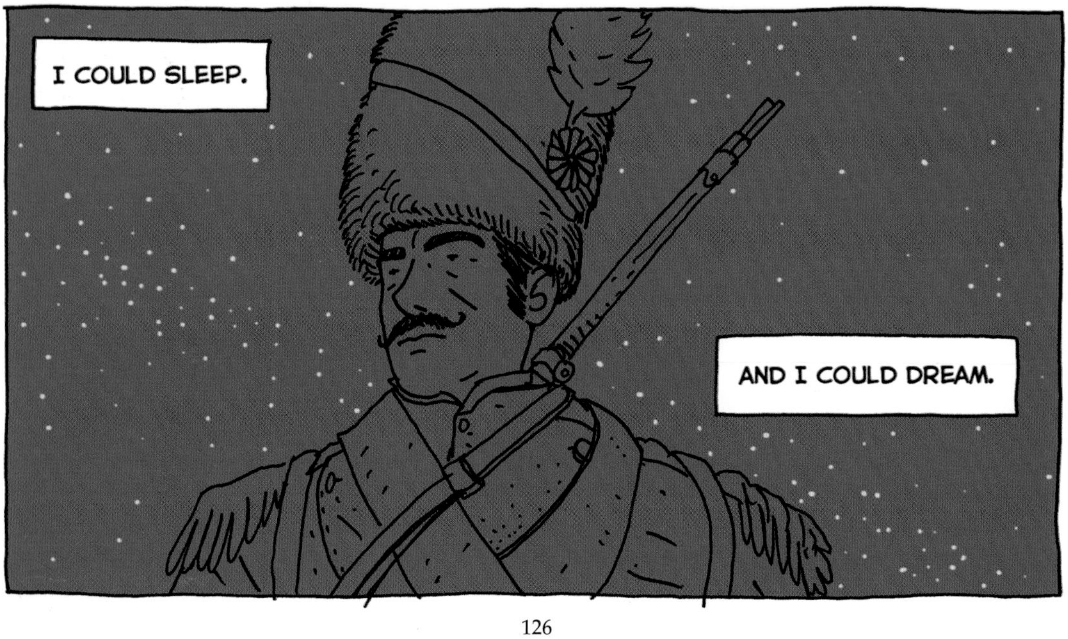
I COULD SLEEP.
AND I COULD DREAM.

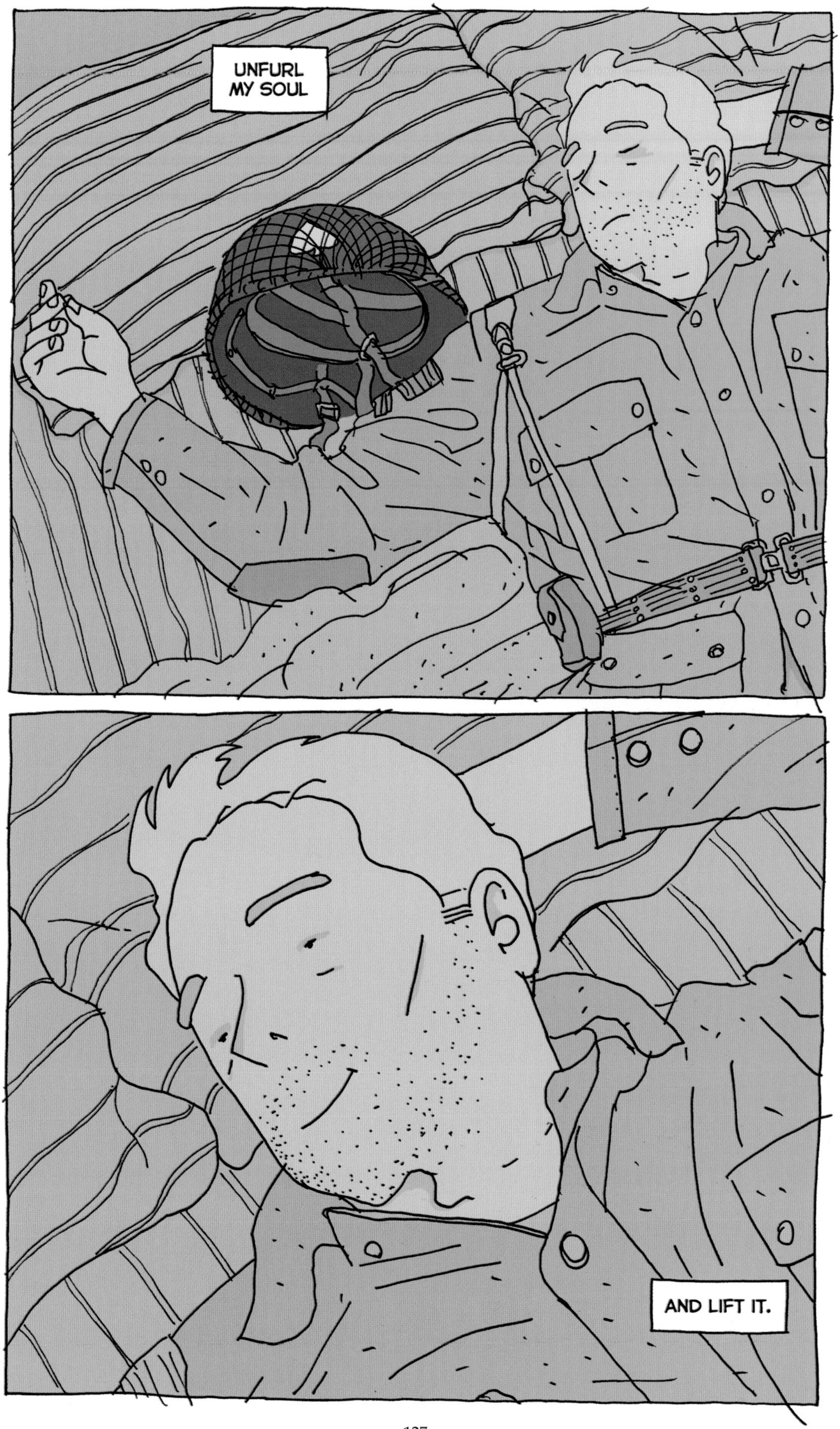
UNFURL
MY SOUL
AND LIFT IT.

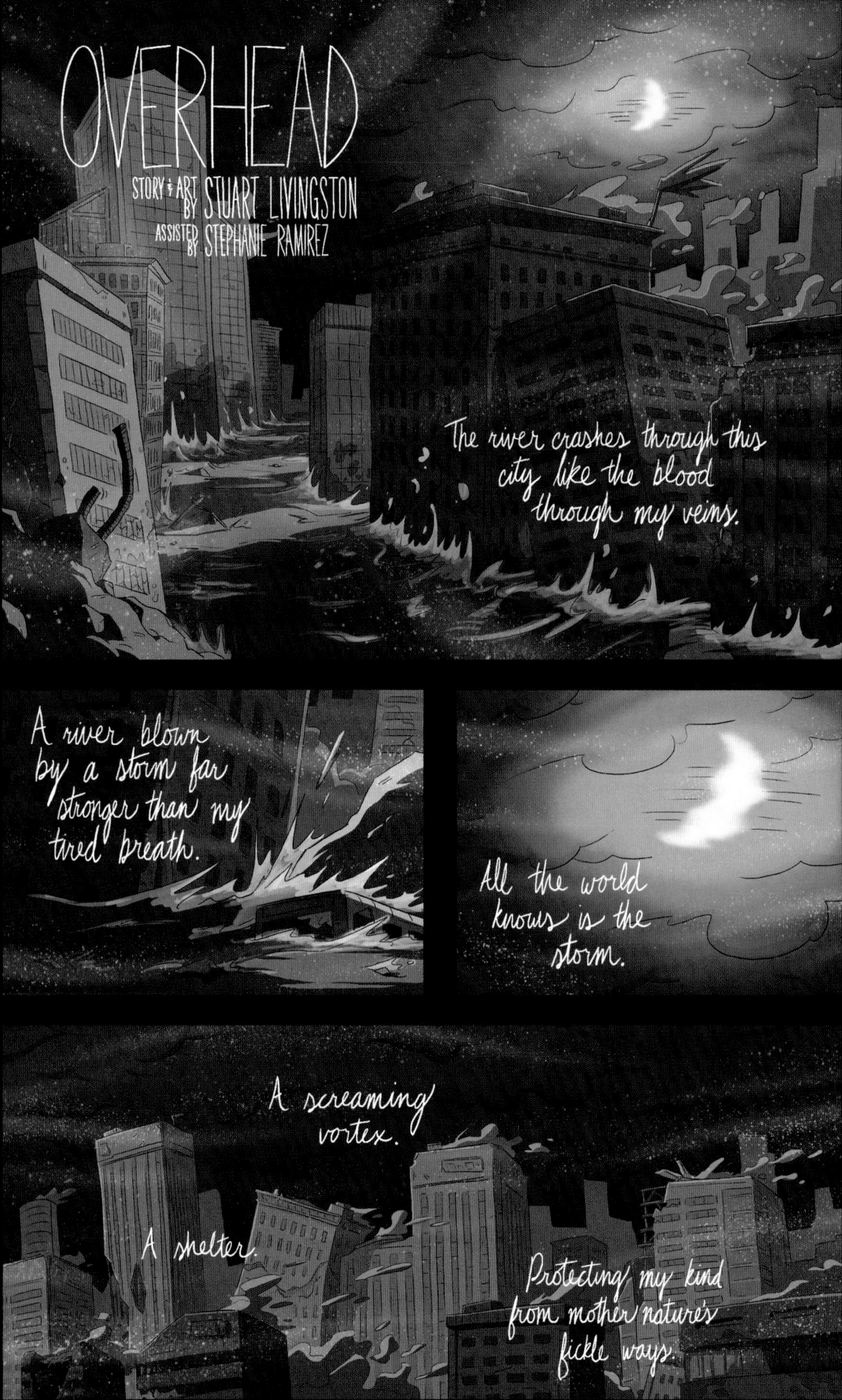

OVERHEAD
STORY & ART BY STUART LIVINGSTON
ASSISTED BY STEPHANIE RAMIREZ
The river crashes through this city like the blood through my veins.
A river blown by a storm far stronger than my tired breath.
All the world knows is the storm.
A screaming vortex.
A shelter.
Protecting my kind from mother nature's fickle ways.

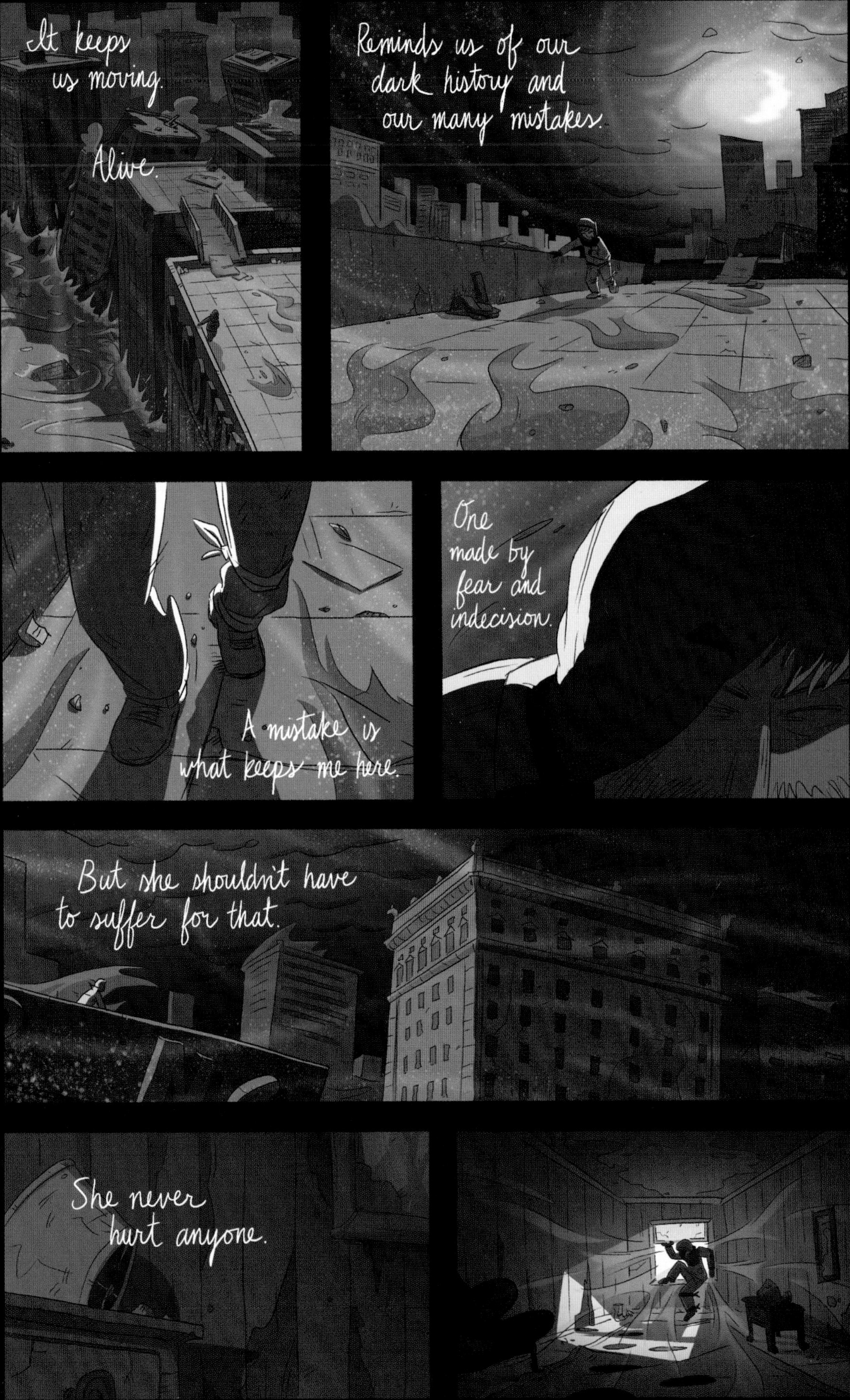
It keeps us moving.
Alive.
Reminds us of our dark history and our many mistakes.
A mistake is what keeps me here.
One made by fear and indecision.
But she shouldn't have to suffer for that.
She never hurt anyone.

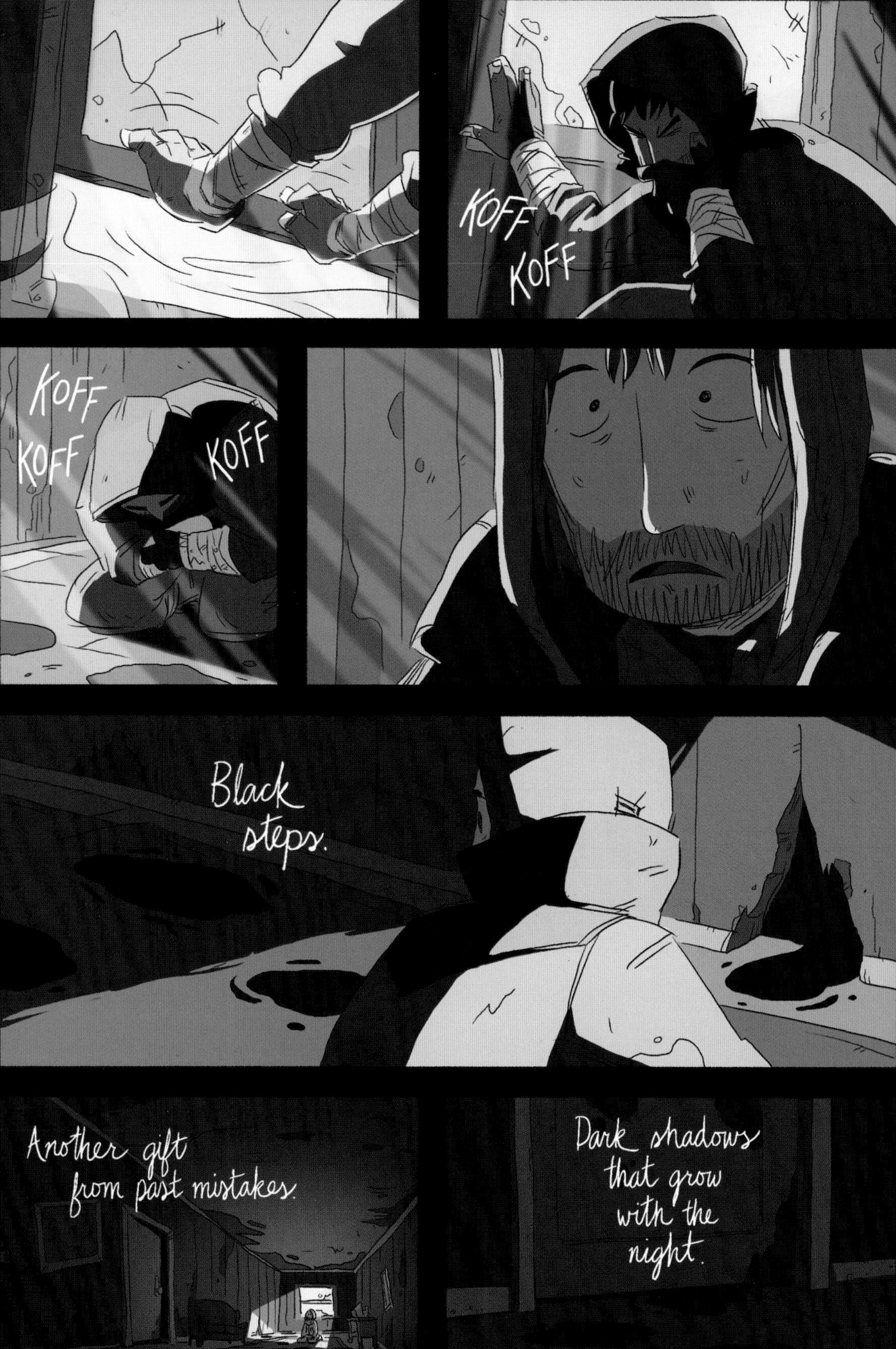
KOFF
KOFF
KOFF
KOFF
KOFF
Black steps.
Another gift from past mistakes.
Dark shadows that grow with the night.

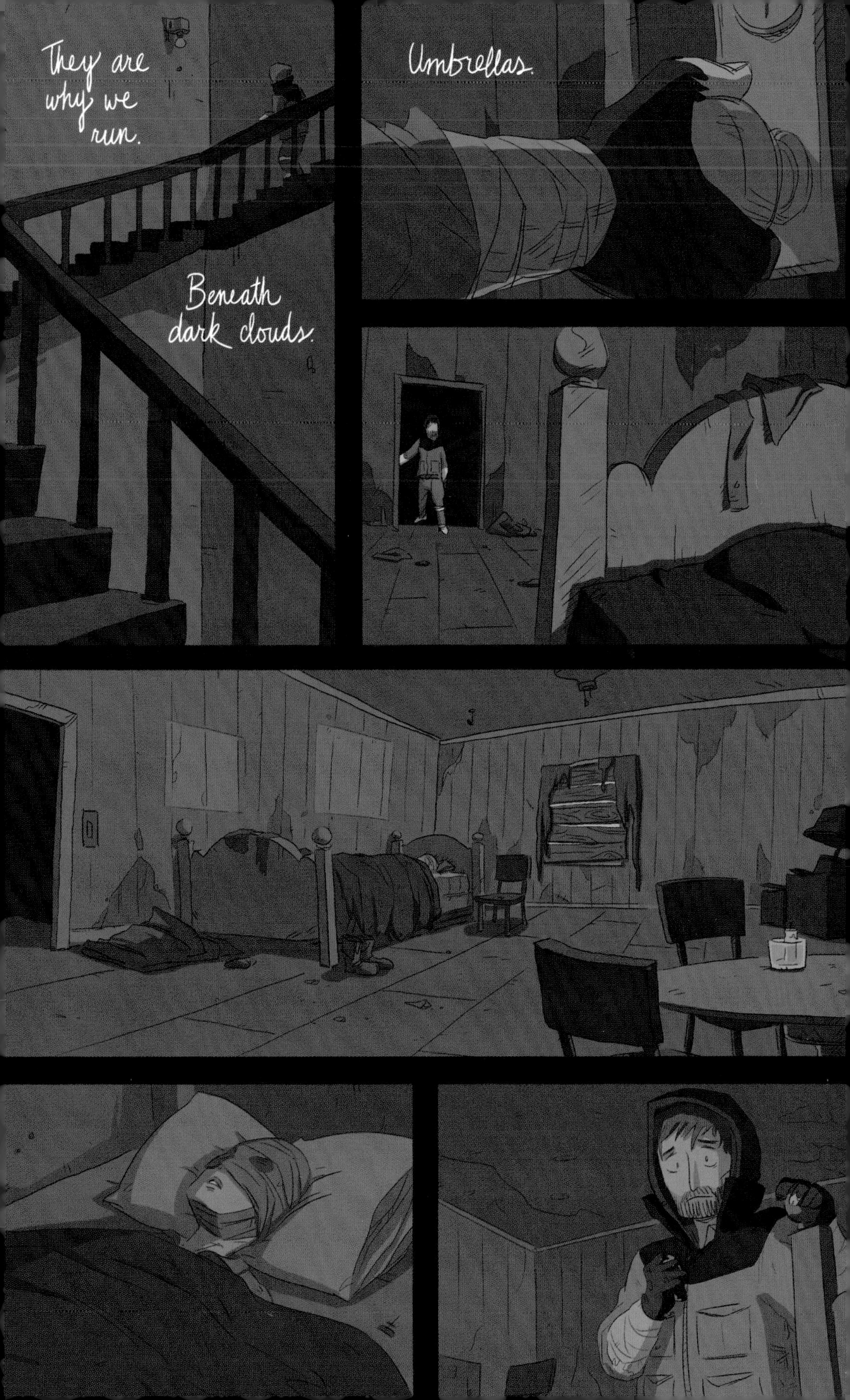
They are why we run.
Umbrellas.
Beneath dark clouds.

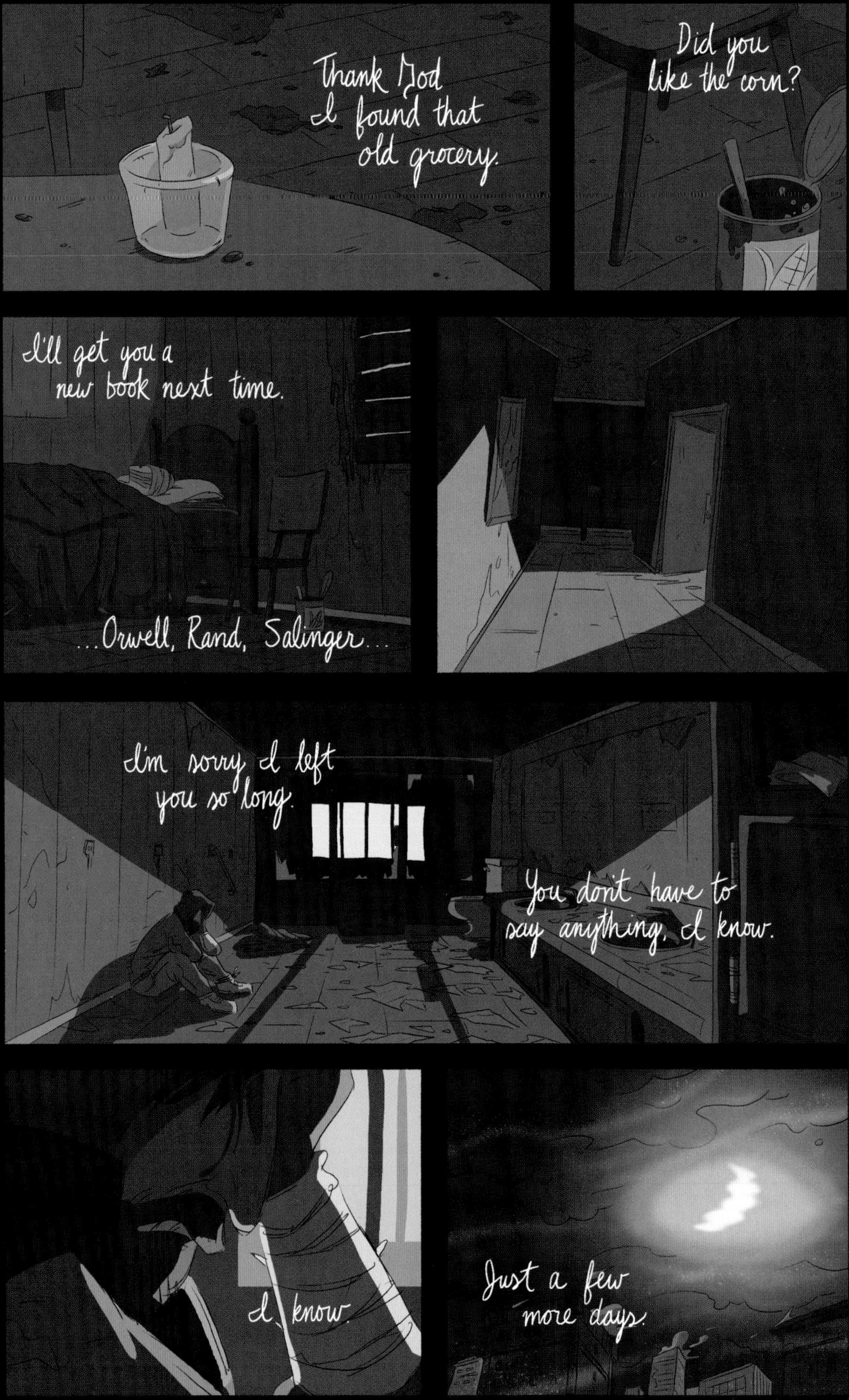
Thank God
I found that
old grocery.
Did you
like the corn?
I'll get you a
new book next time.
...Orwell, Rand, Salinger...
I'm sorry I left
you so long.
You don't have to
say anything. I know.
I know.
Just a few
more days.

PM
705

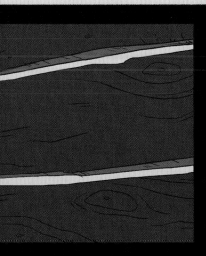

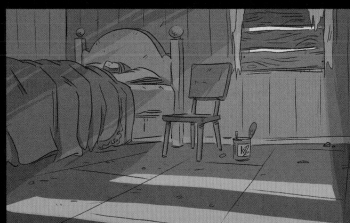

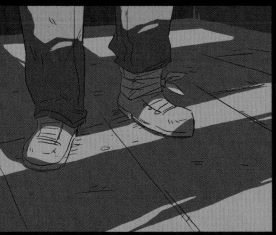

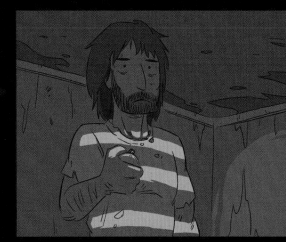

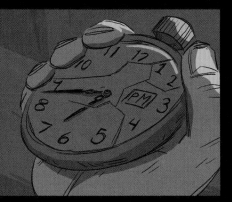

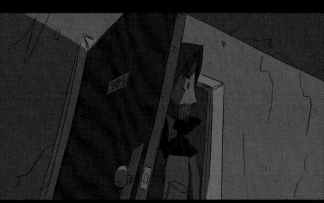

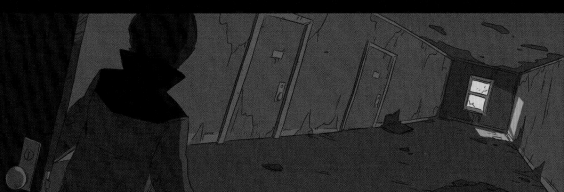

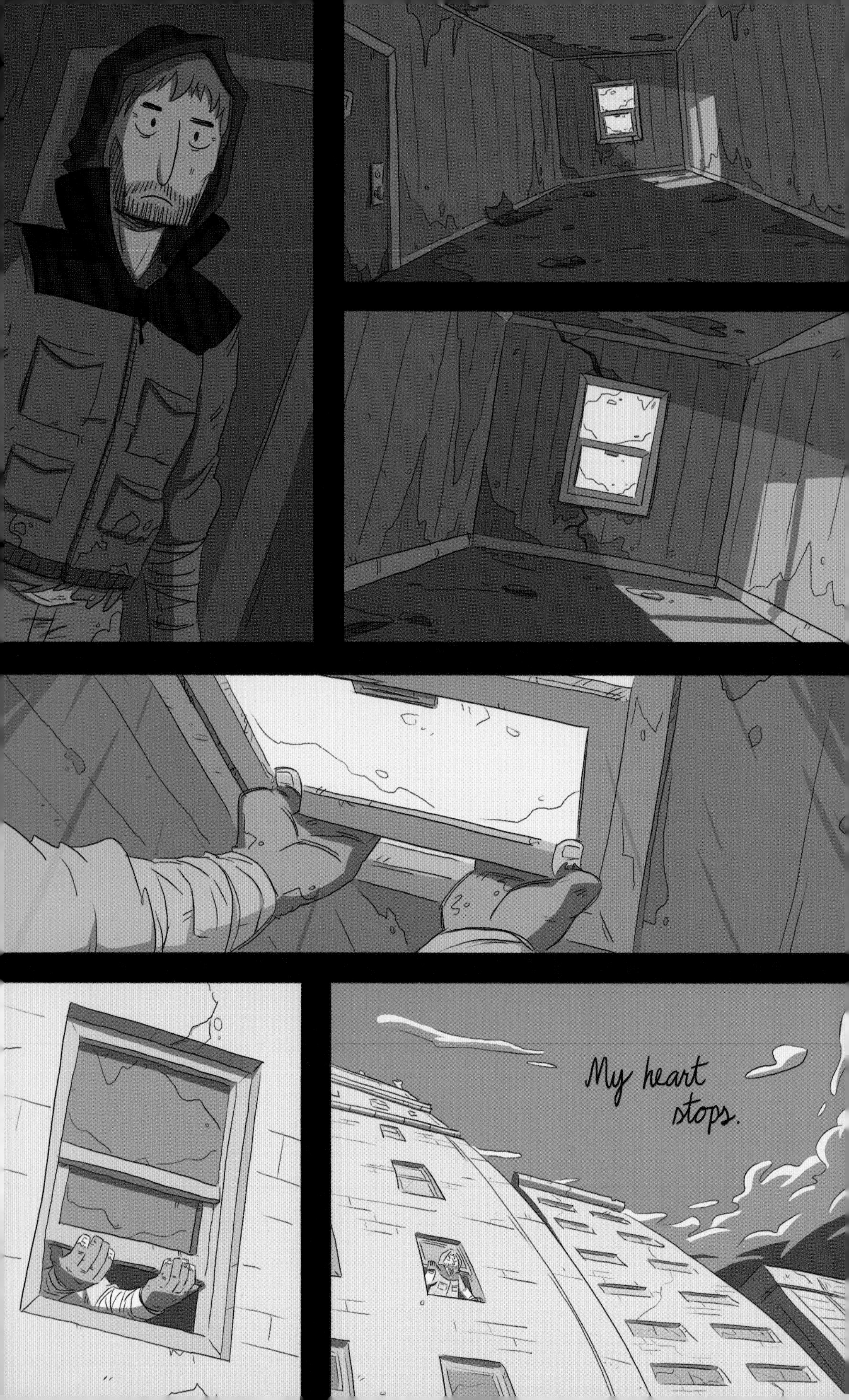
My heart stops.

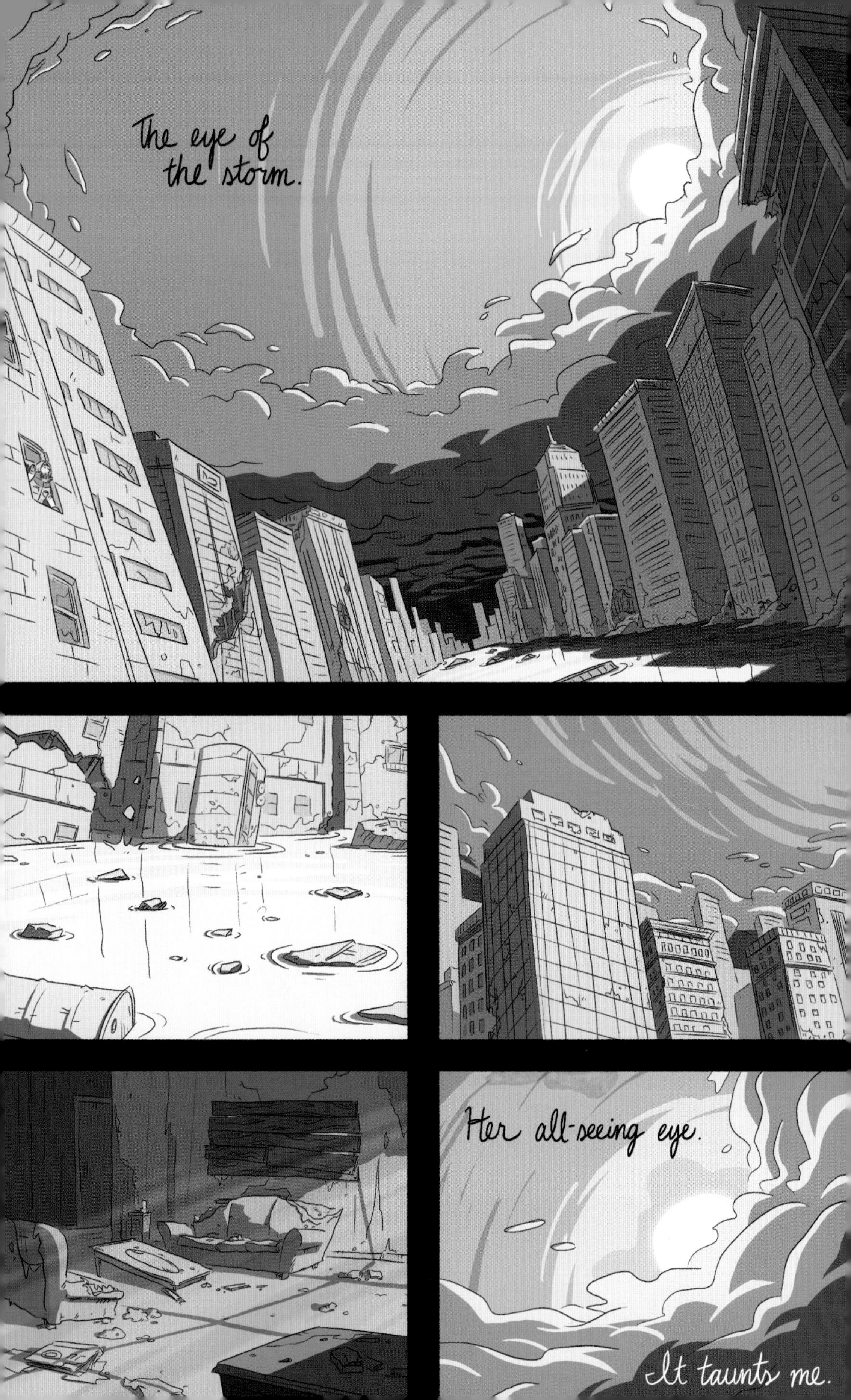
The eye of the storm.
Her all-seeing eye.
It taunts me.

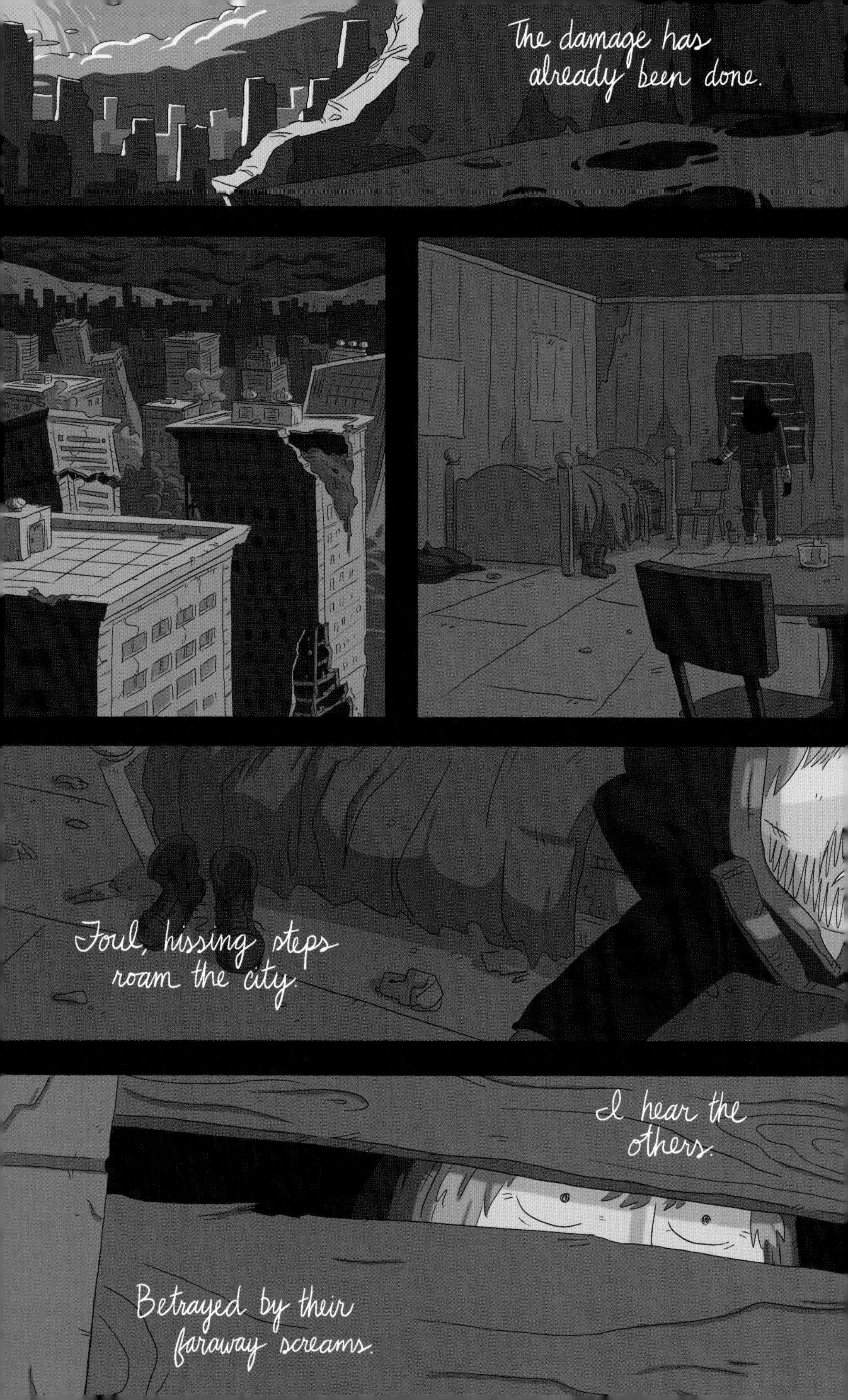
The damage has already been done.
Foul, hissing steps roam the city.
I hear the others.
Betrayed by their faraway screams.

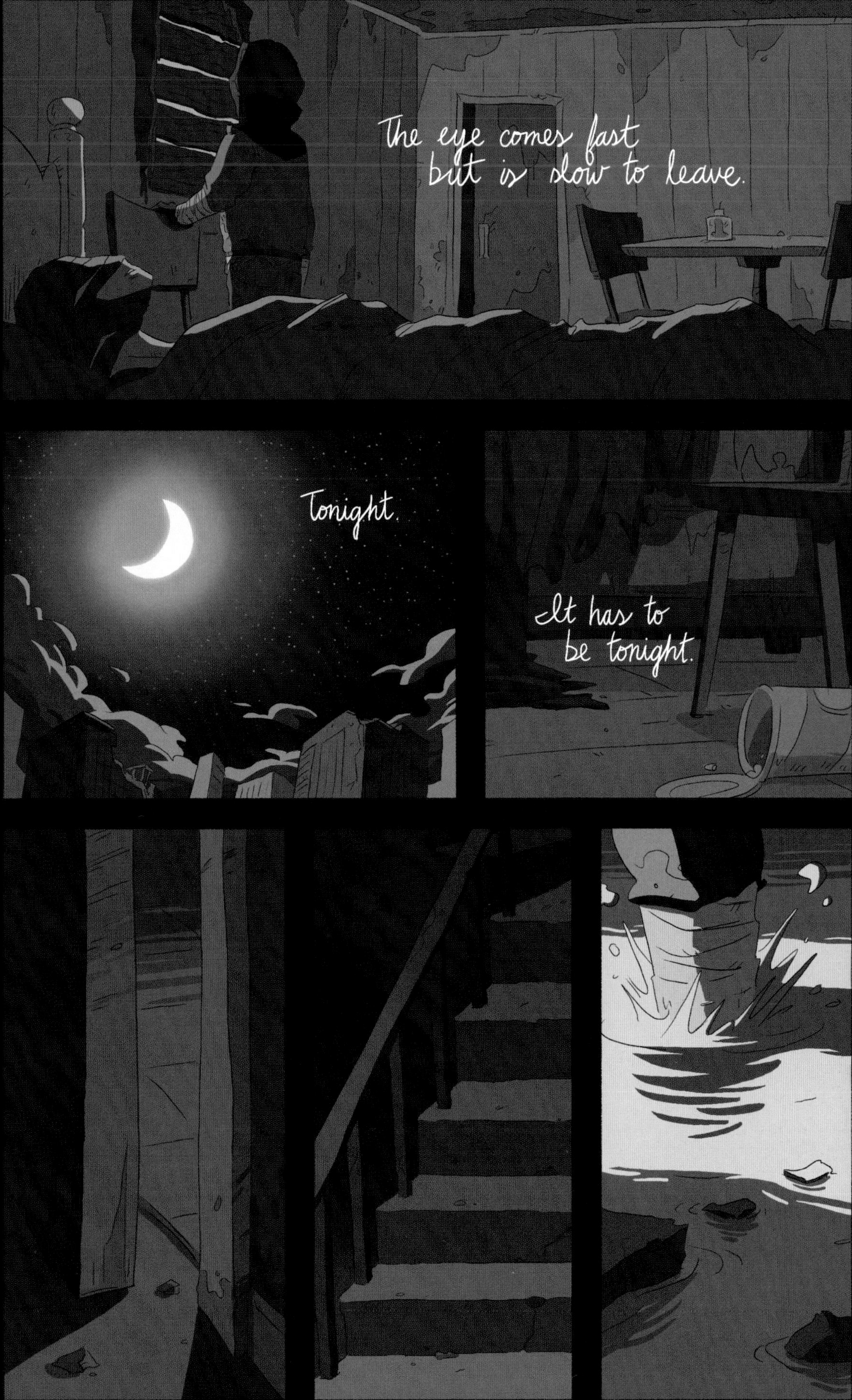
The eye comes fast
but is slow to leave.
Tonight.
It has to
be tonight.

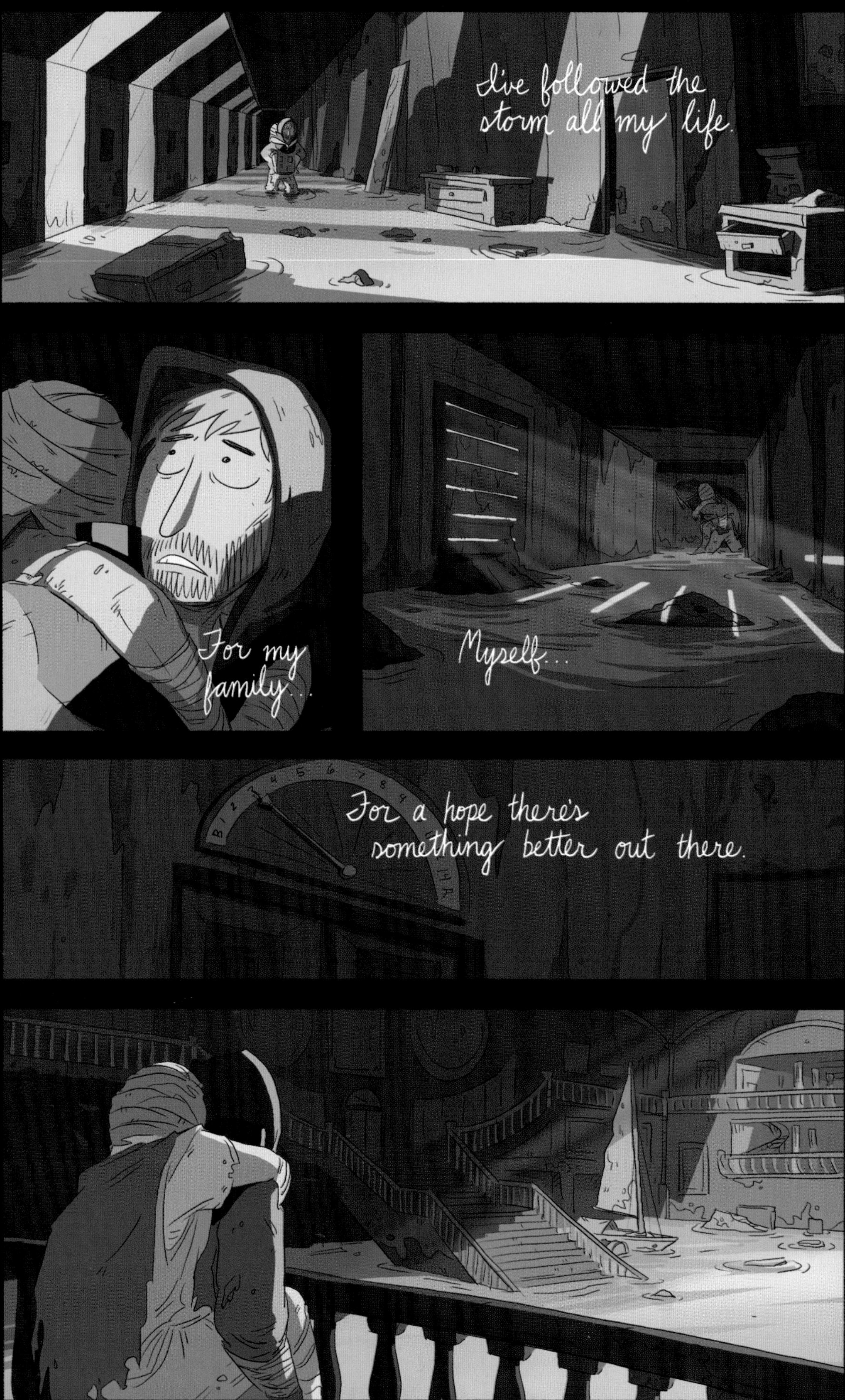
I've followed the storm all my life.
For my family...
Myself...
For a hope there's something better out there.

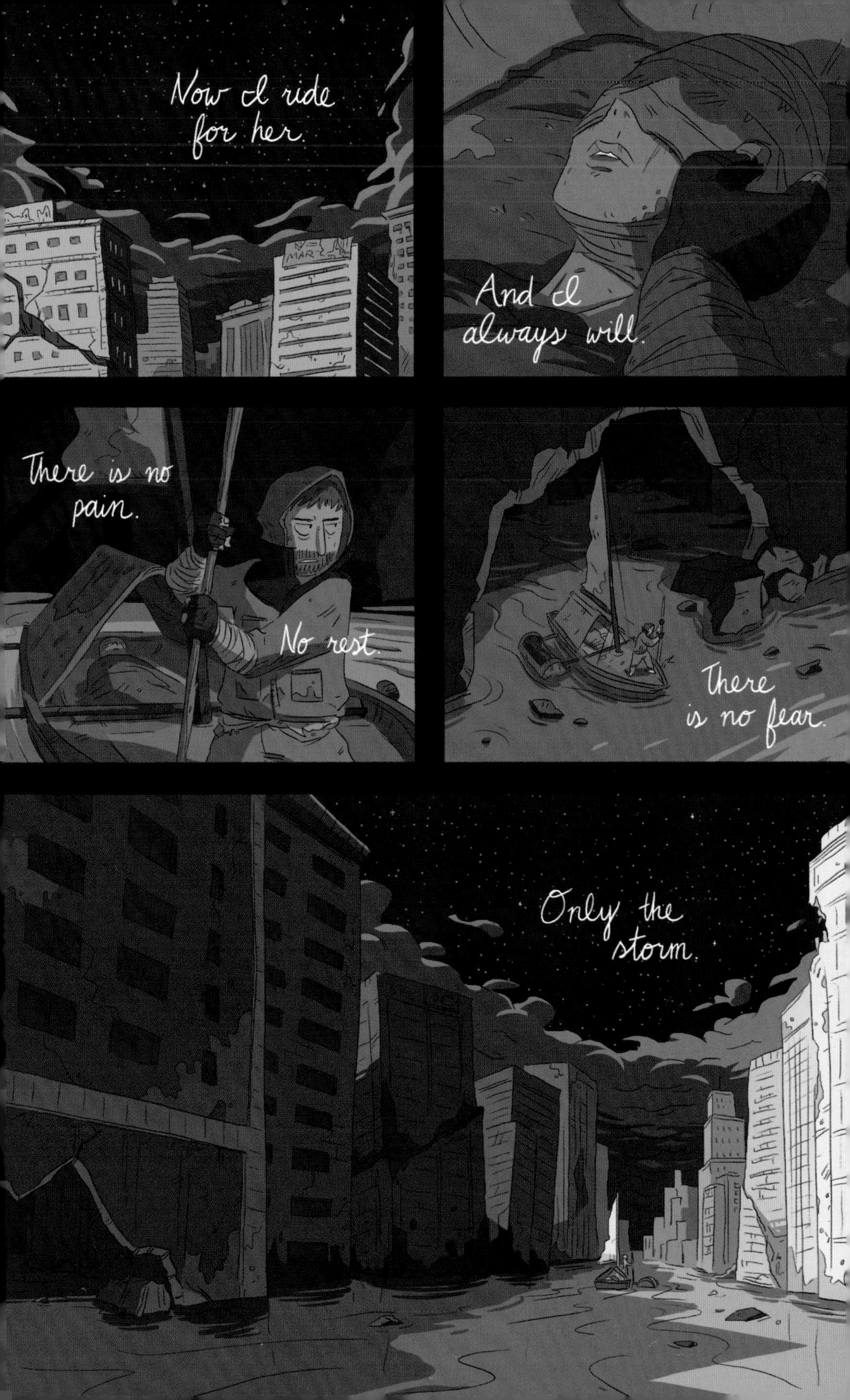
Now I ride for her.
MAR
And I always will.
There is no pain.
No rest.
There is no fear.
Only the storm.

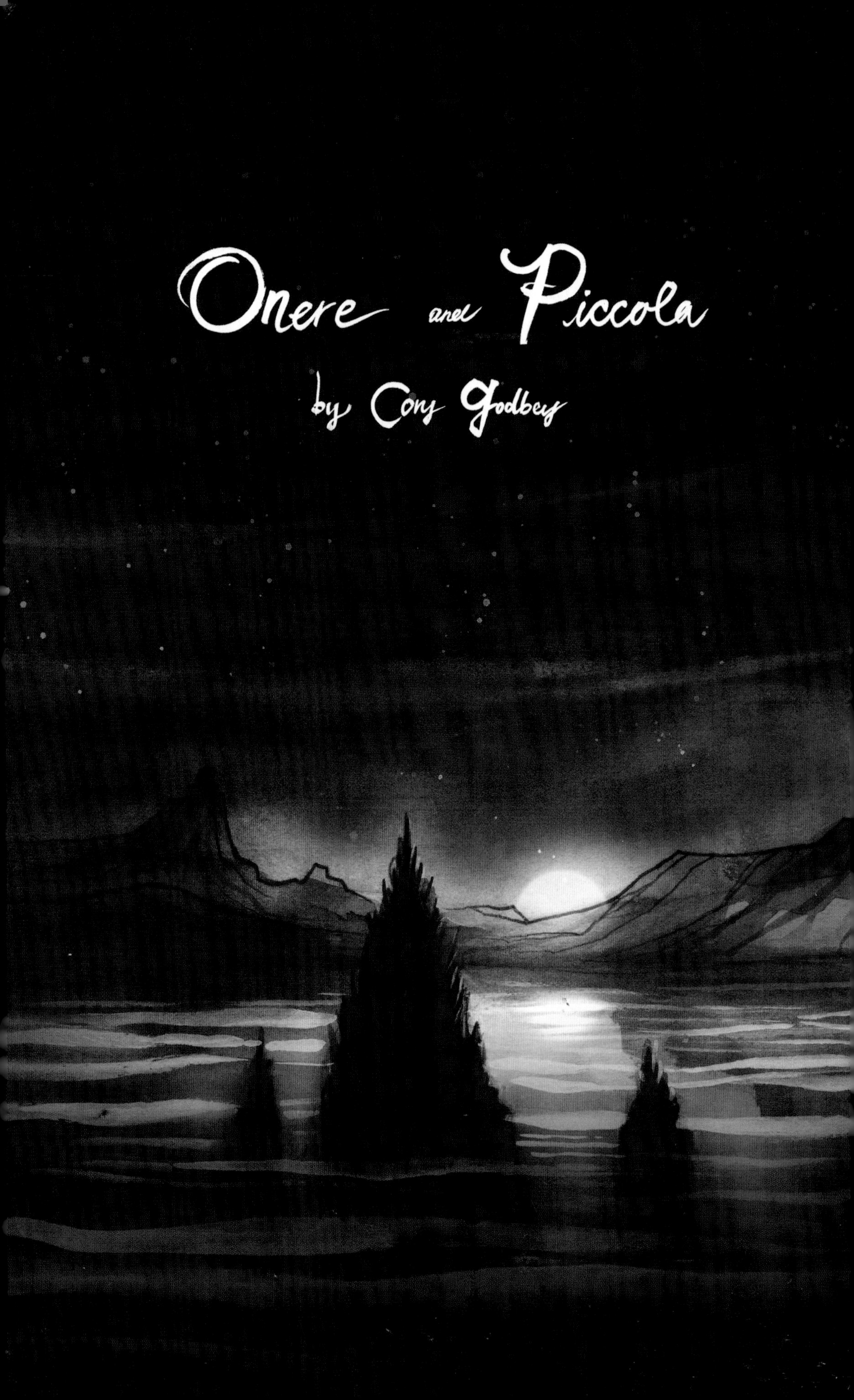
Onere and Piccola
by Cory Godbey

One day, many years ago, the gods discovered
that the earth was sinking into the ocean.

The waters rose and flooded fields.
They covered mountains and soon even the
birds of the air would have no rest,
so great was the excess.

At last, the gods determined that
someone must go down under the earth
and hold it up, but none of the gods
or heroes would step forward.

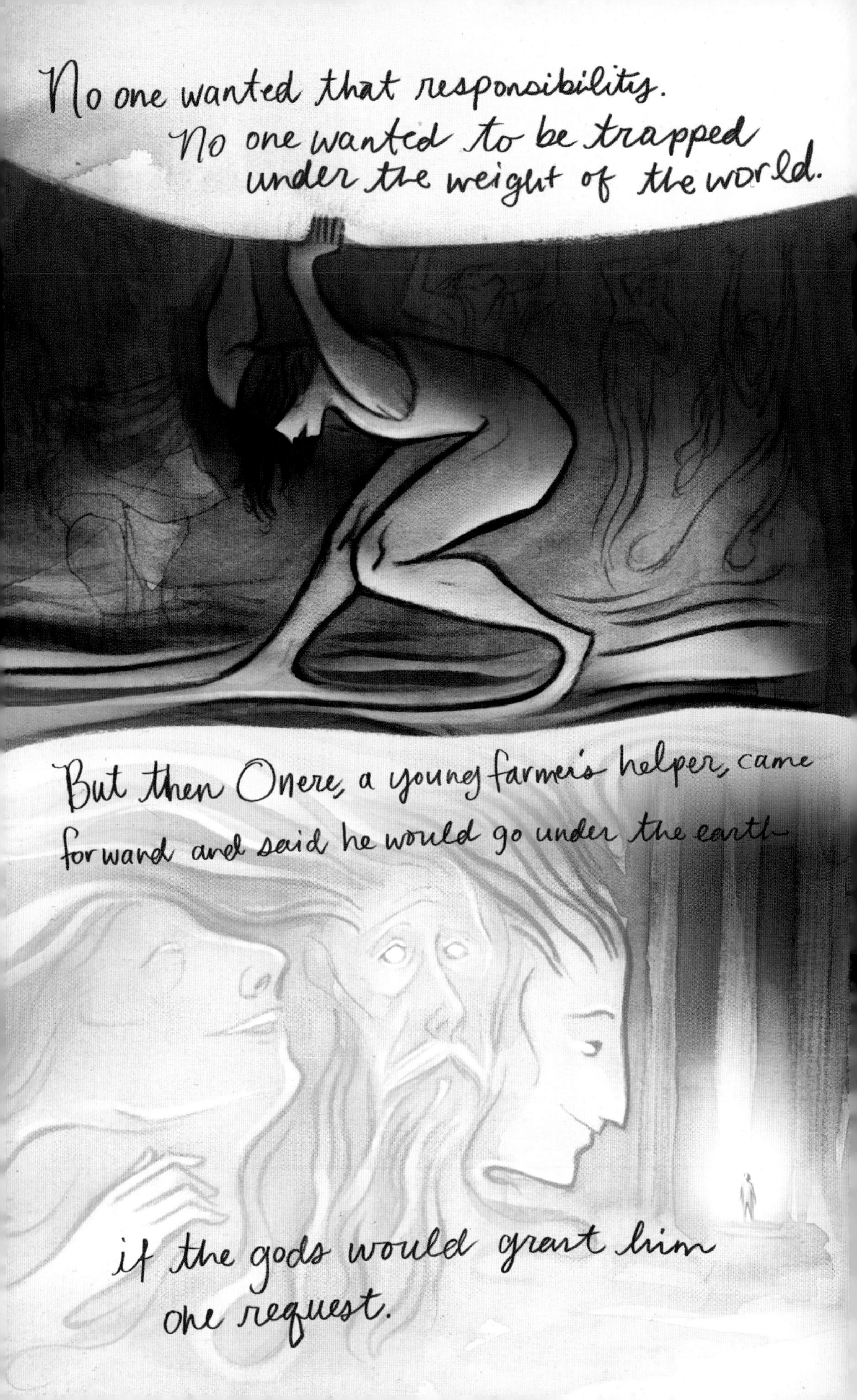
No one wanted that responsibility.
No one wanted to be trapped under the weight of the world.
But then Onere, a young farmer's helper, came forward and said he would go under the earth—
if the gods would grant him one request.

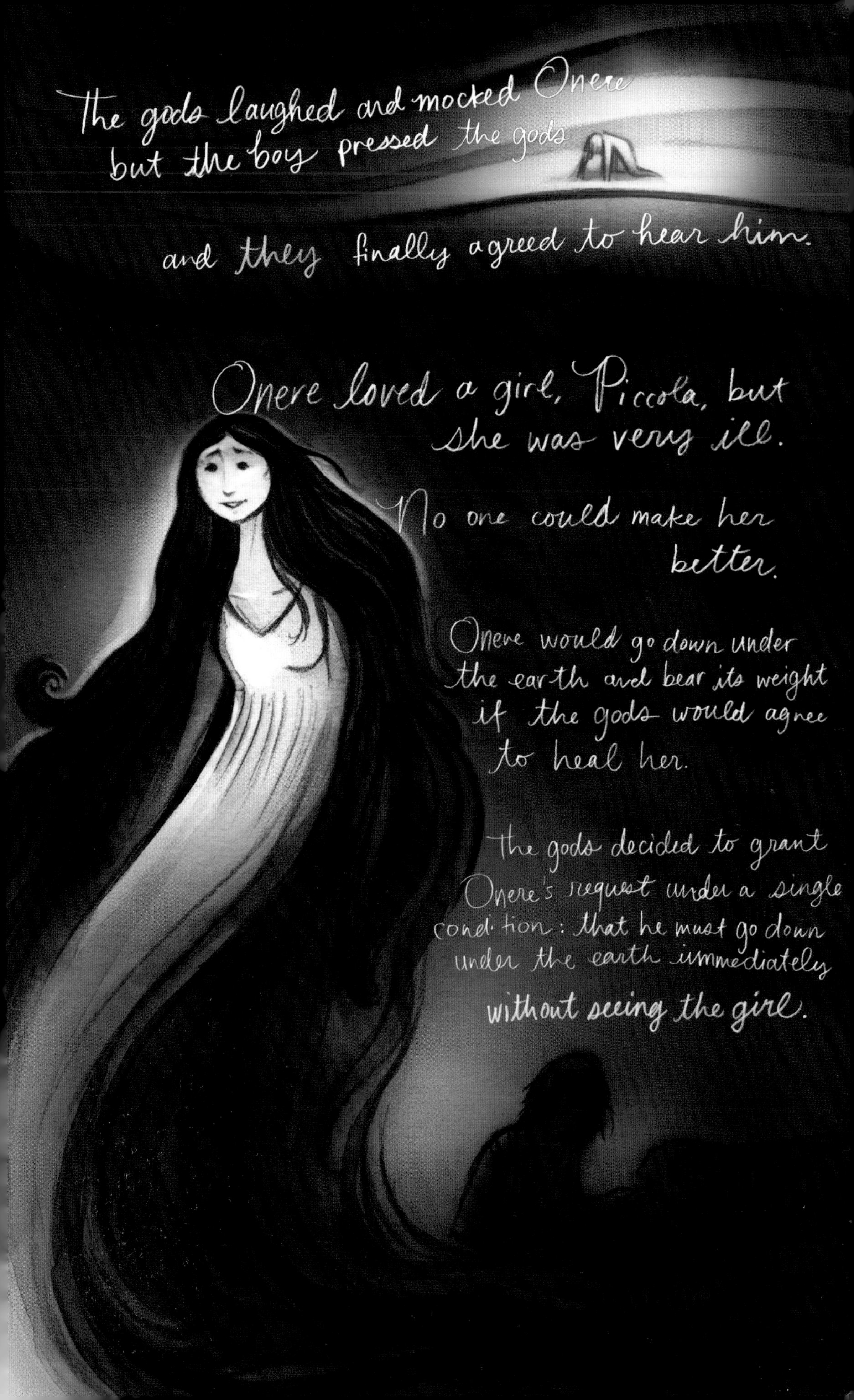
The gods laughed and mocked Onere
but the boy pressed the gods
and they finally agreed to hear him.
Onere loved a girl, Piccola, but
she was very ill.
No one could make her
better.
Onere would go down under
the earth and bear its weight
if the gods would agree
to heal her.
The gods decided to grant
Onere's request under a single
condition: that he must go down
under the earth immediately
without seeing the girl.

Onere agreed to the promise of the gods and traveled down under the foundations of the earth.

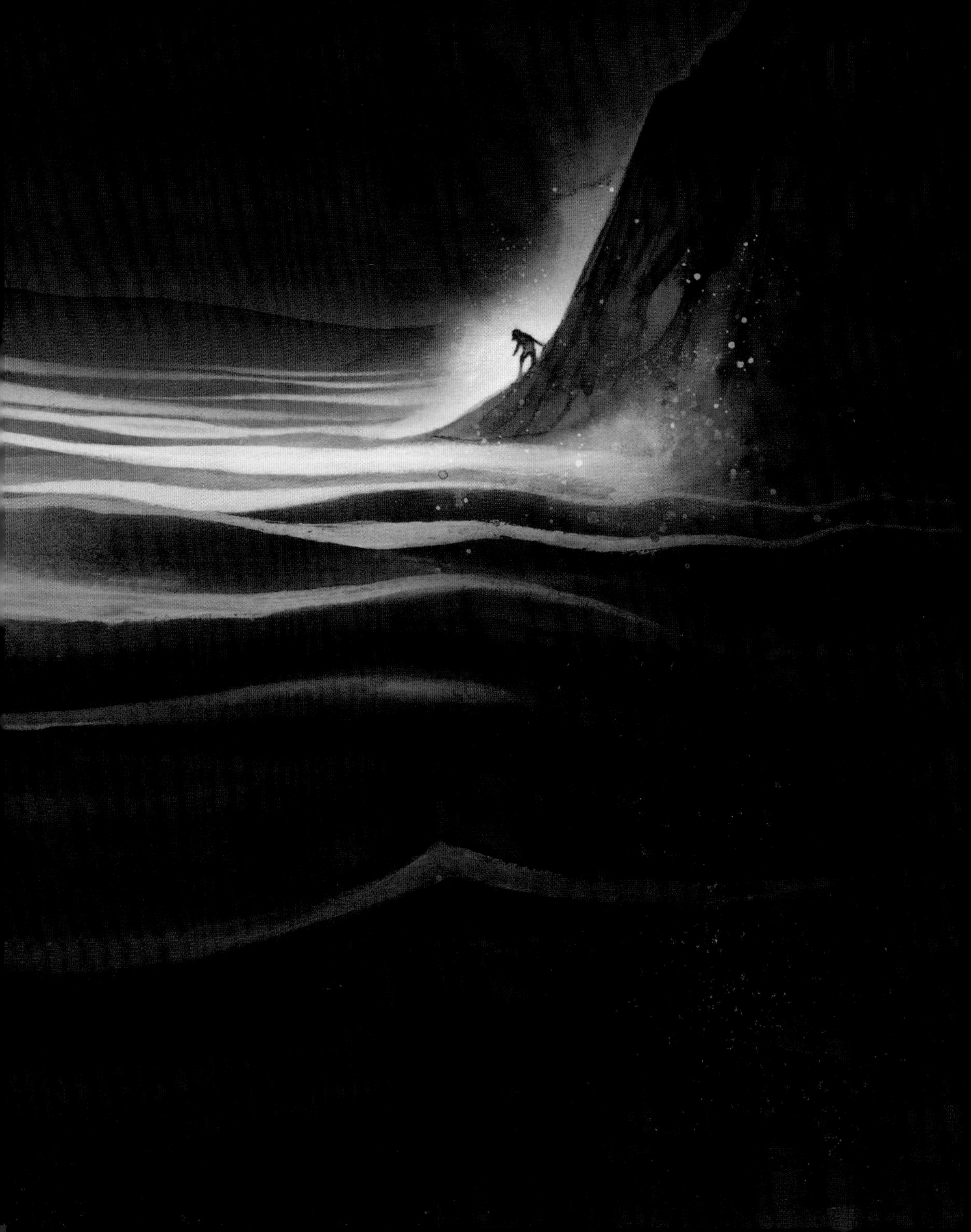

He struggled in the mud and began to sink.

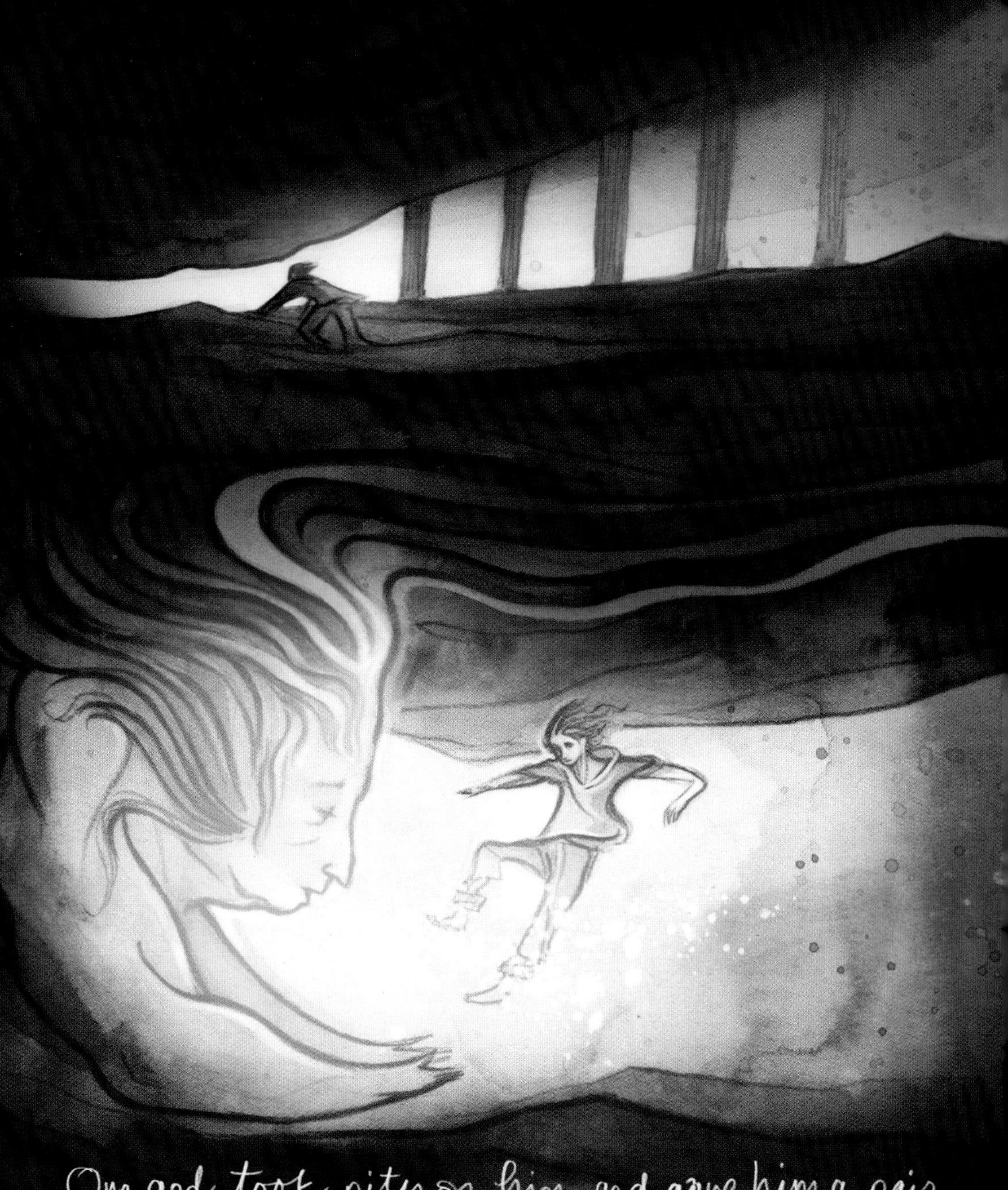

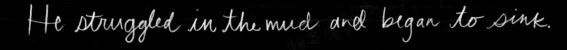

One god took pity on him and gave him a pair of boots that would prevent him from sinking.

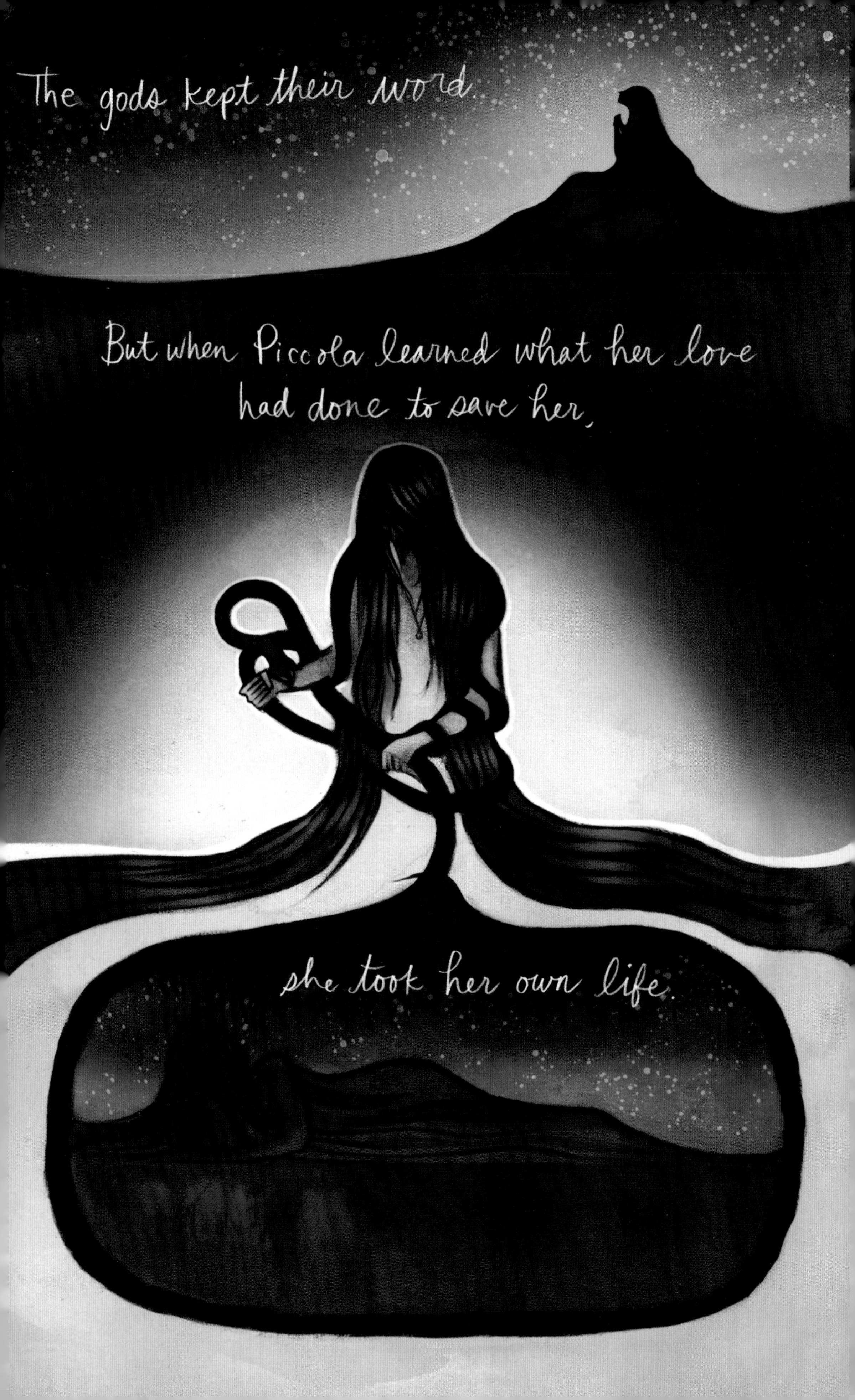
The gods kept their word.
But when Piccola learned what her love had done to save her,
she took her own life.

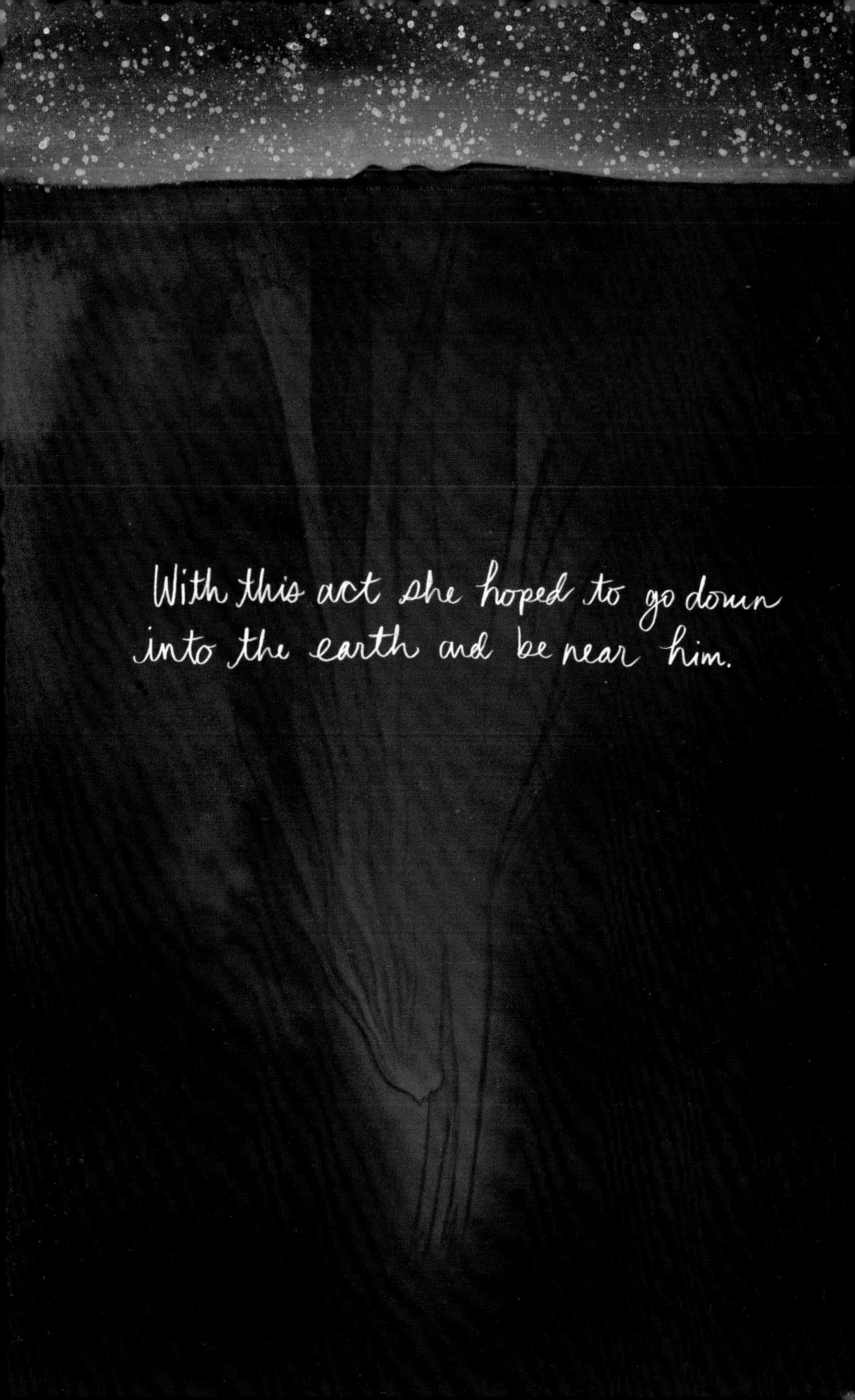
With this act she hoped to go down
into the earth and be near him.

When she arrived beneath the earth's surface, a shadow the gods had appointed to watch over the things that creep under the grass caught her

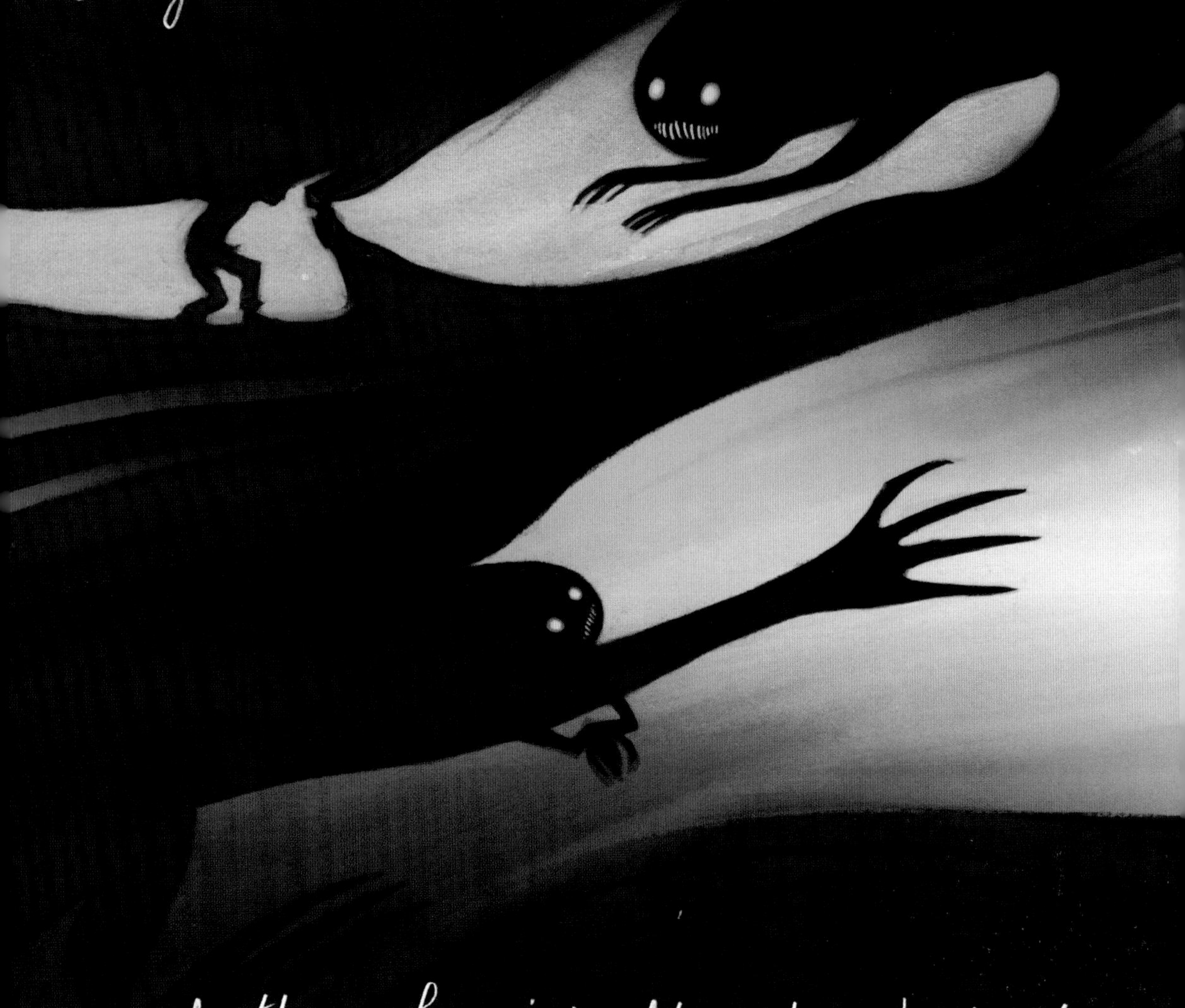

and threw her into the sky, but not before she was able to give Onere a necklace of ruby.

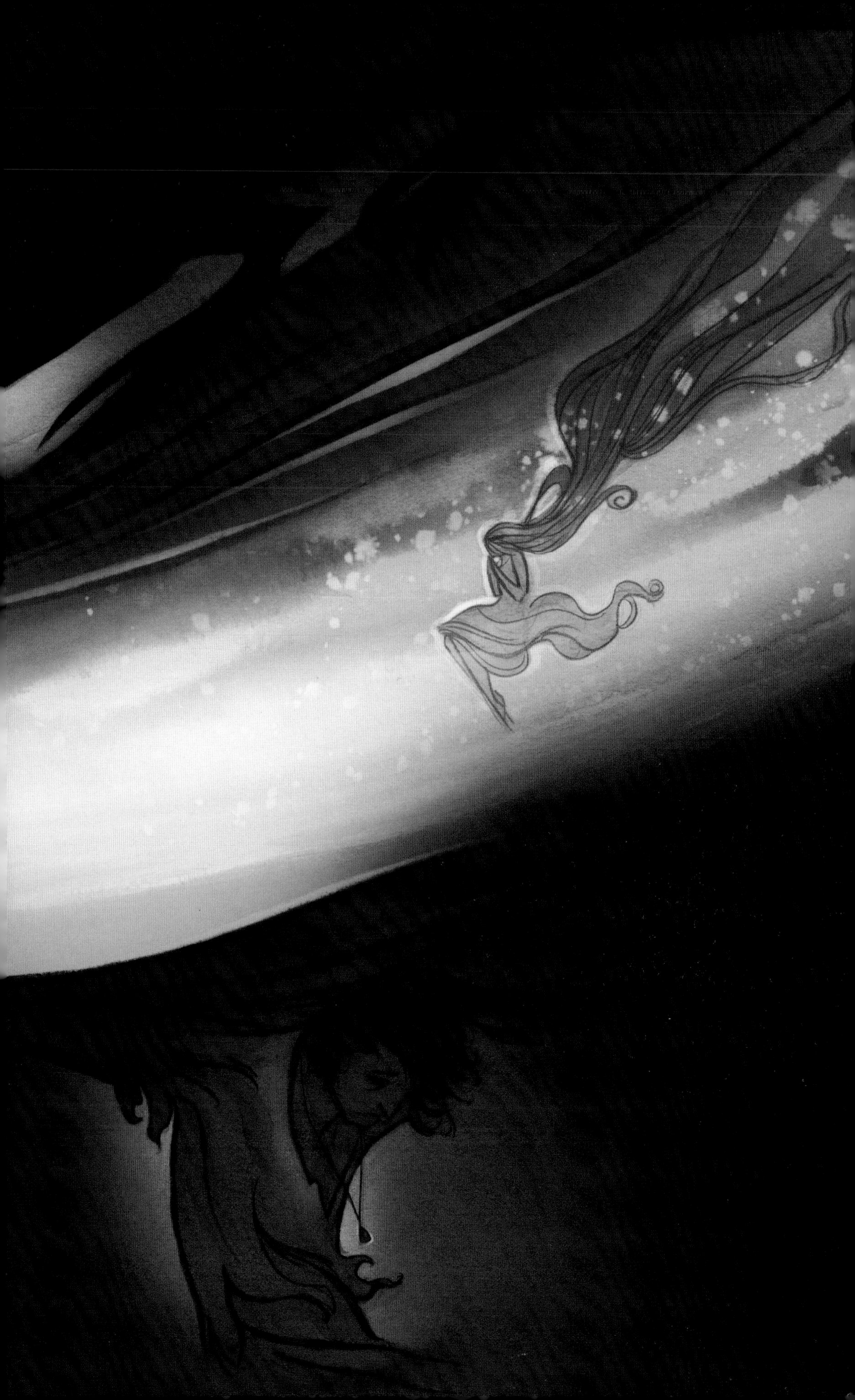

Onere, enraged by the loss of his love a second time, shook the earth so violently that great cracks were opened.

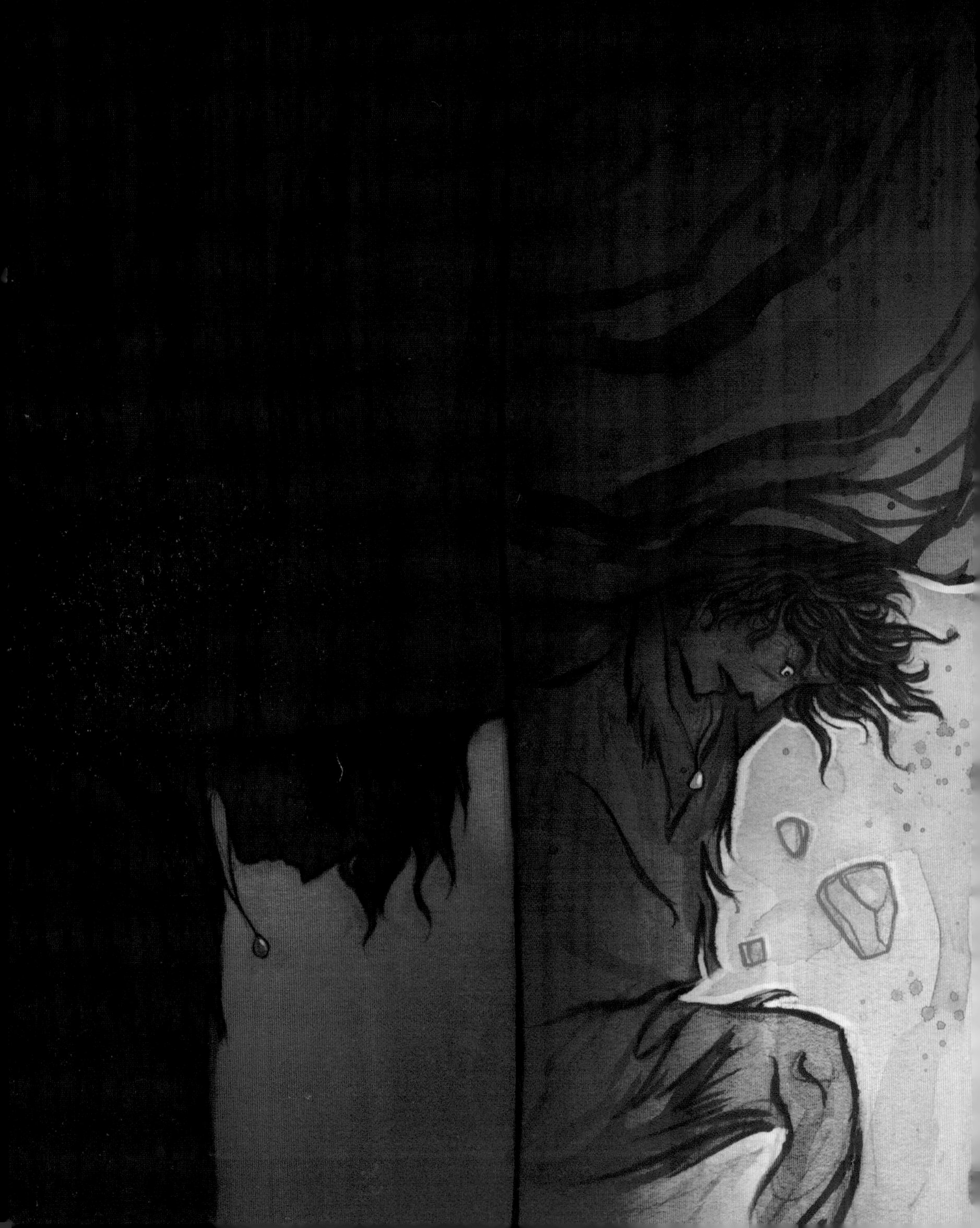

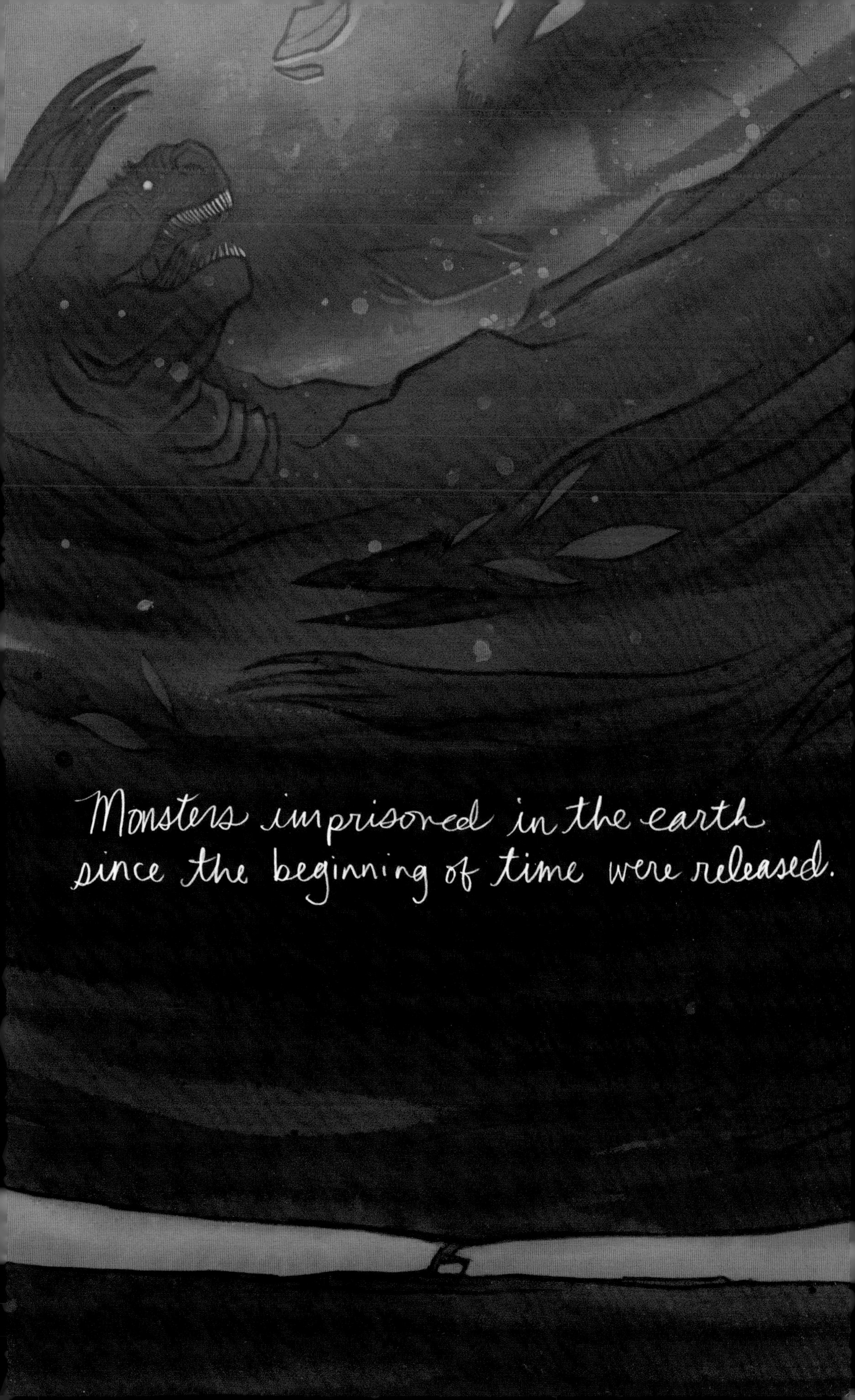
Monsters imprisoned in the earth
since the beginning of time were released.

The great and awful creatures battled with the gods as they had in ages past.

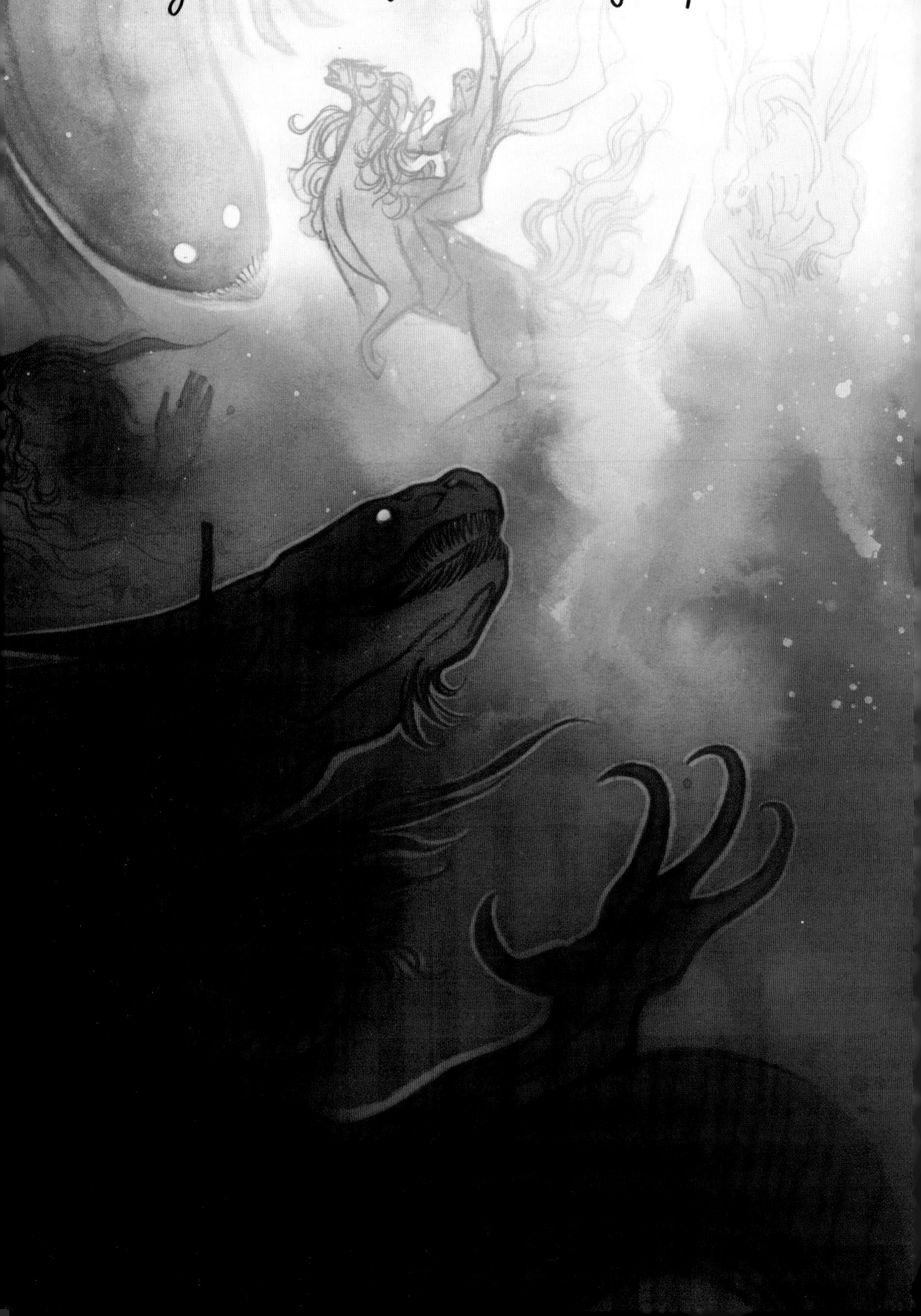

The entire earth quaked and shook.

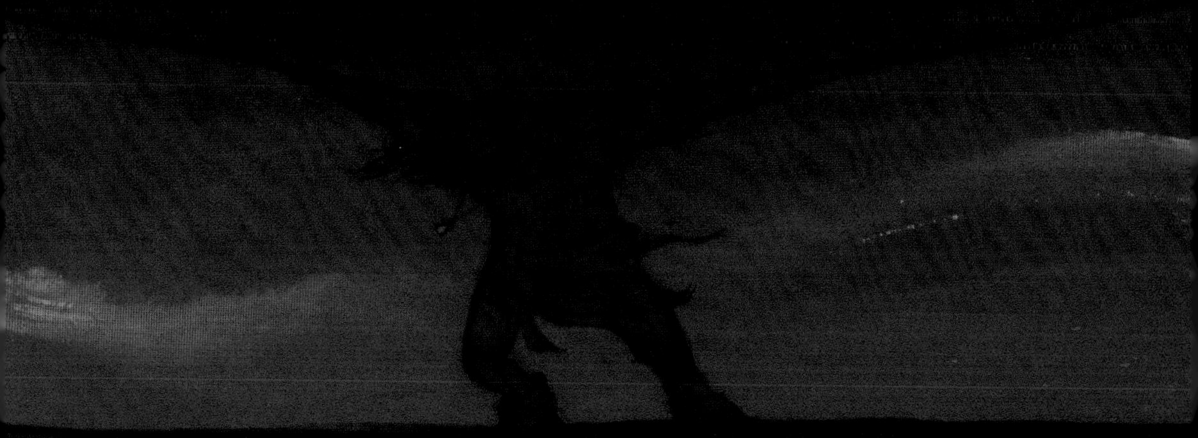

And yet, as the waters increased around him, Onere endured.

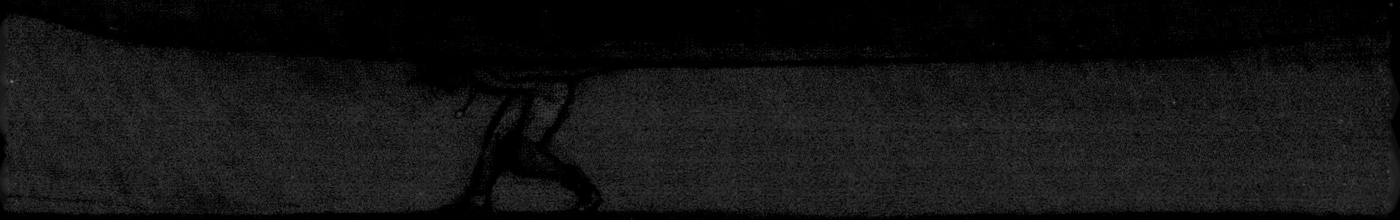

He would not let the earth fall, nor would he permit one more living person to die for the vanity of the gods.

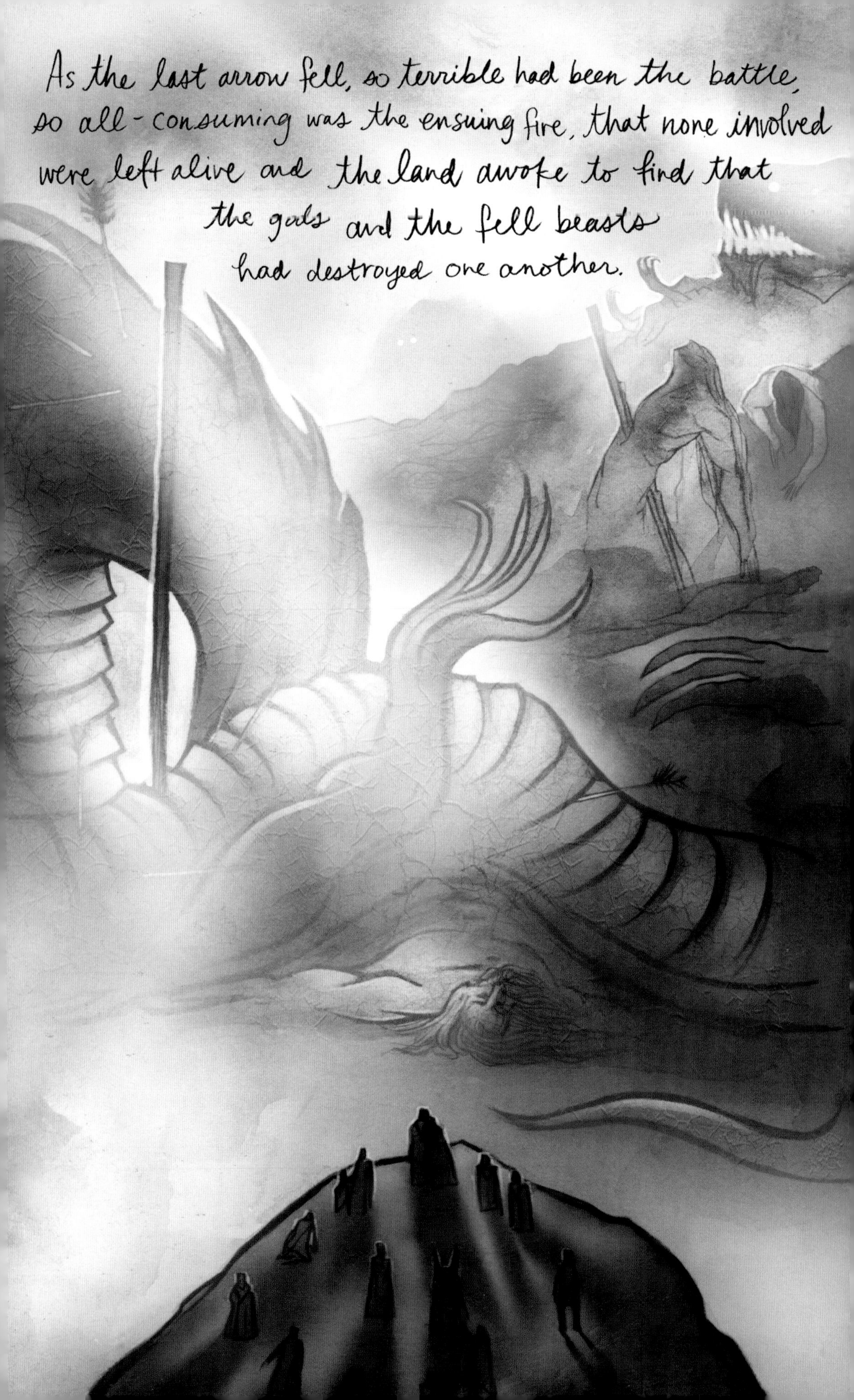
As the last arrow fell, so terrible had been the battle, so all-consuming was the ensuing fire, that none involved were left alive and the land awoke to find that the gods and the fell beasts had destroyed one another.

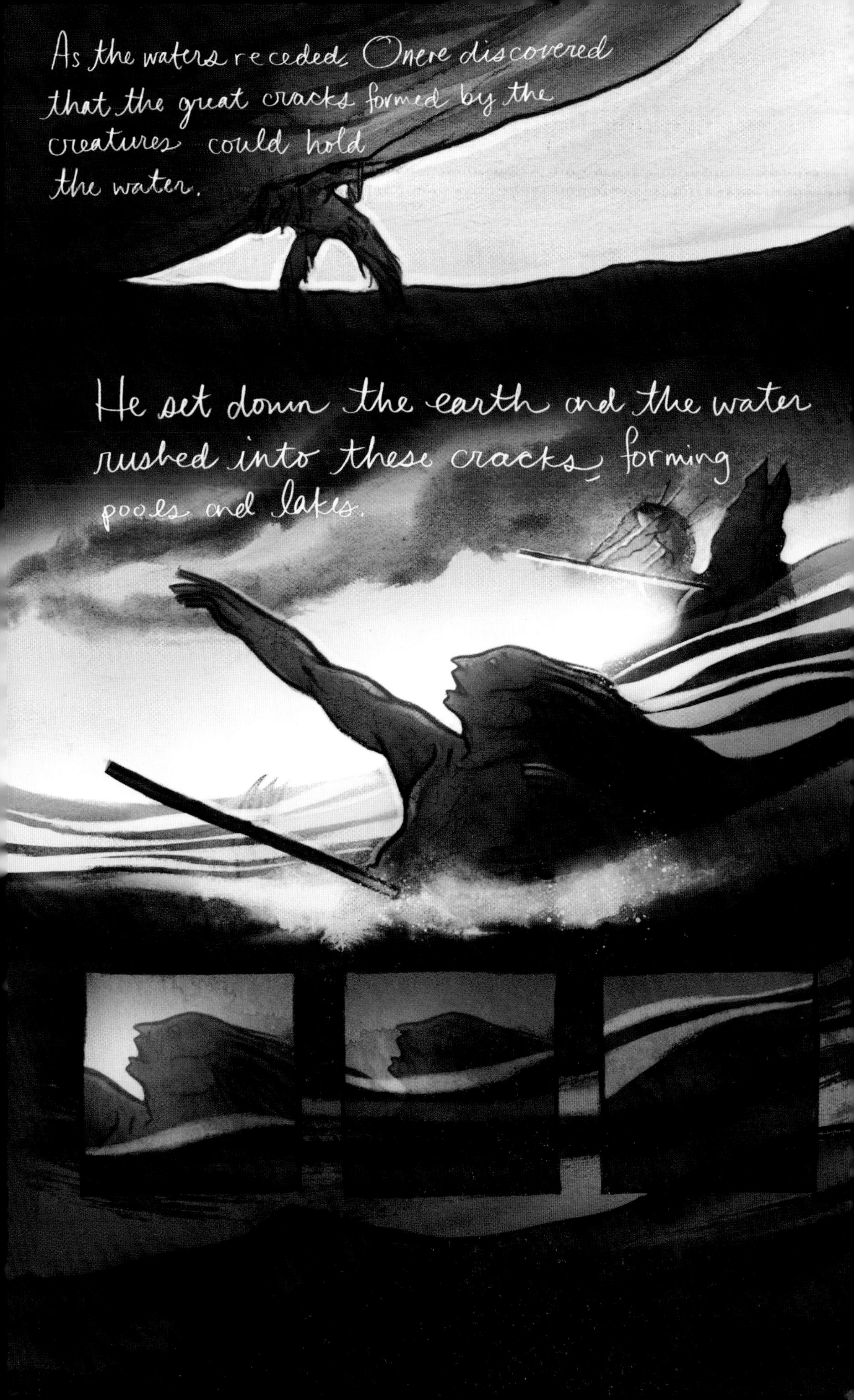
As the waters receded, Onere discovered that the great cracks formed by the creatures could hold the water.
He set down the earth and the water rushed into these cracks, forming pools and lakes.

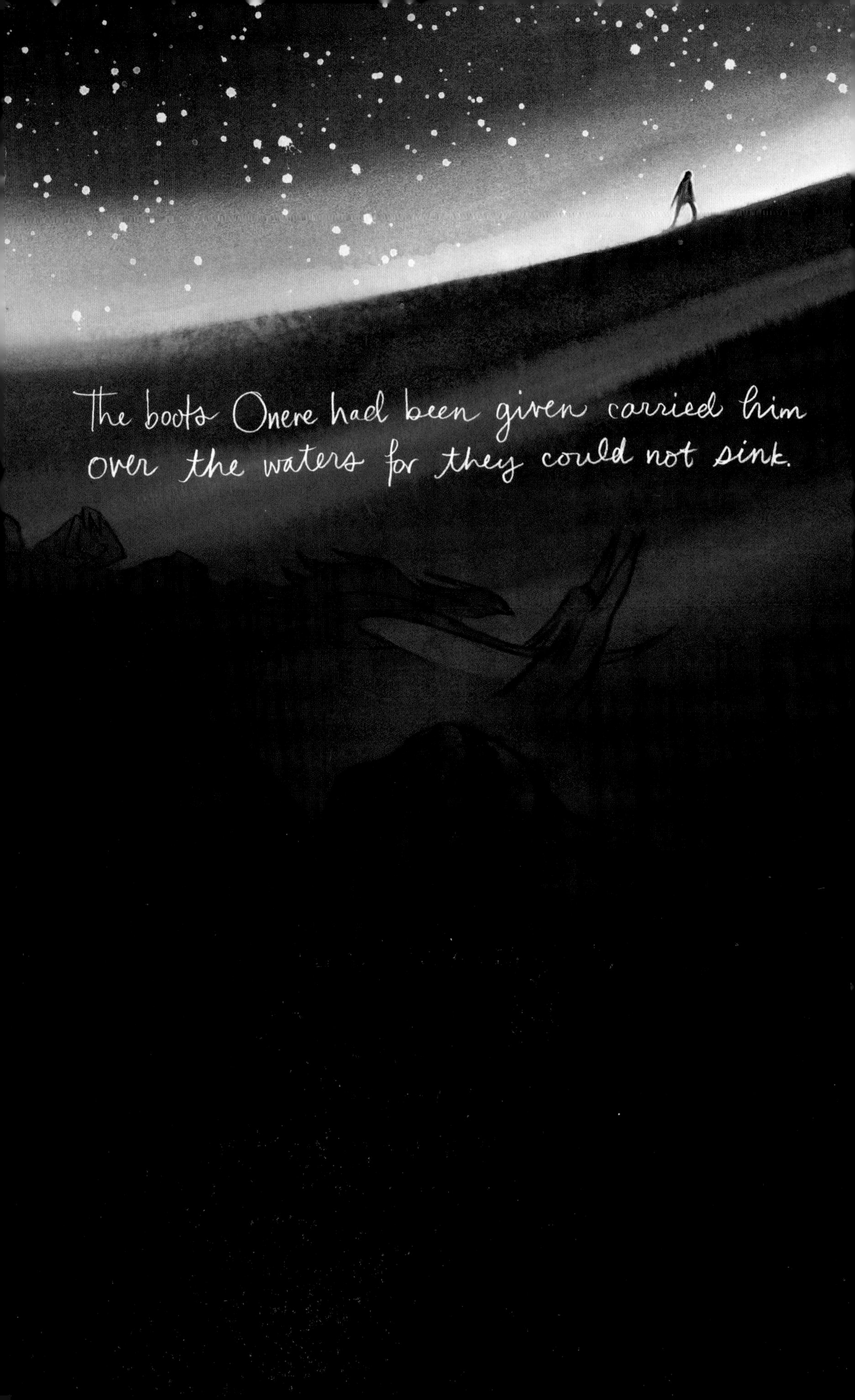
The boots Onere had been given carried him over the waters for they could not sink.

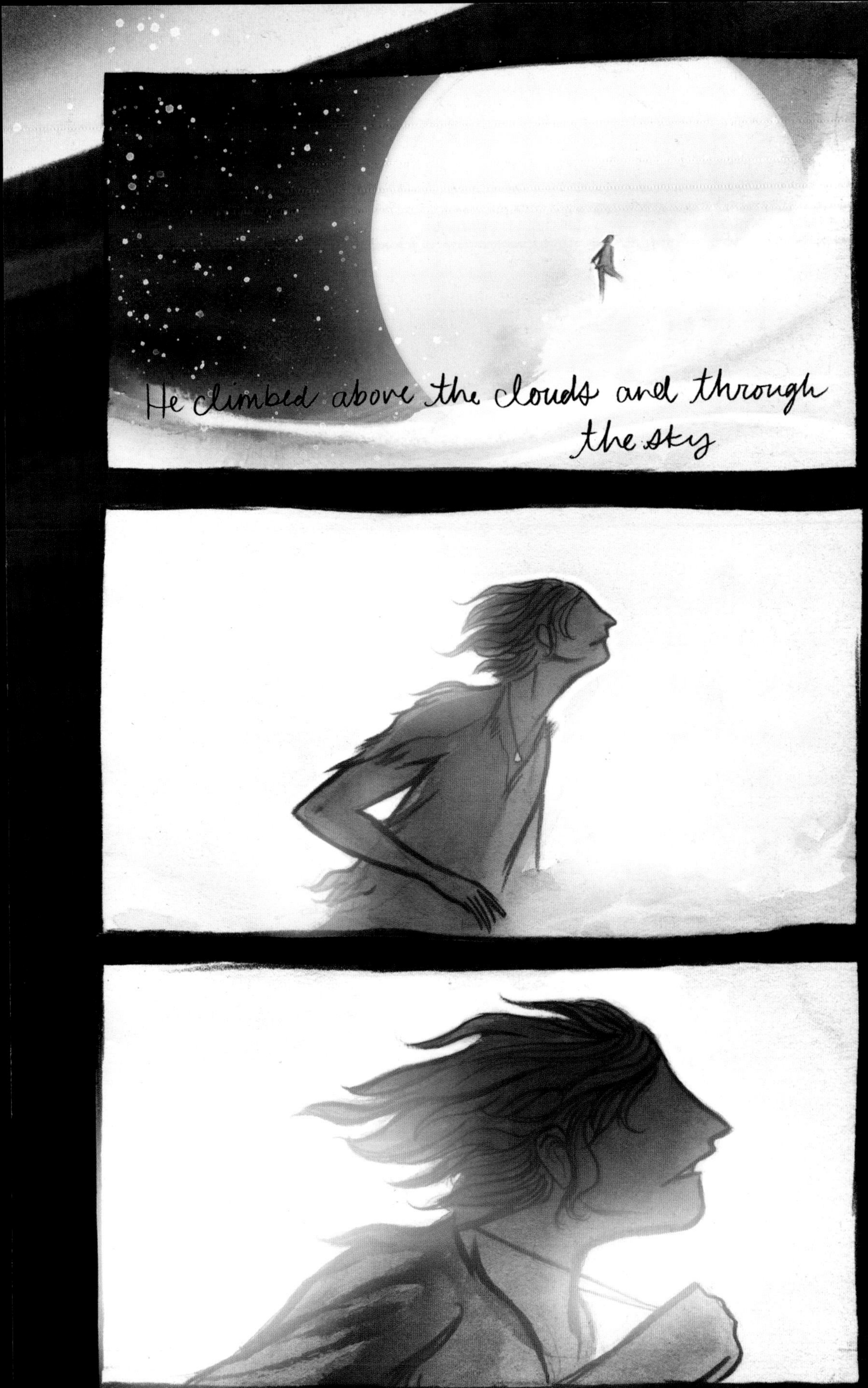
He climbed above the clouds and through the sky

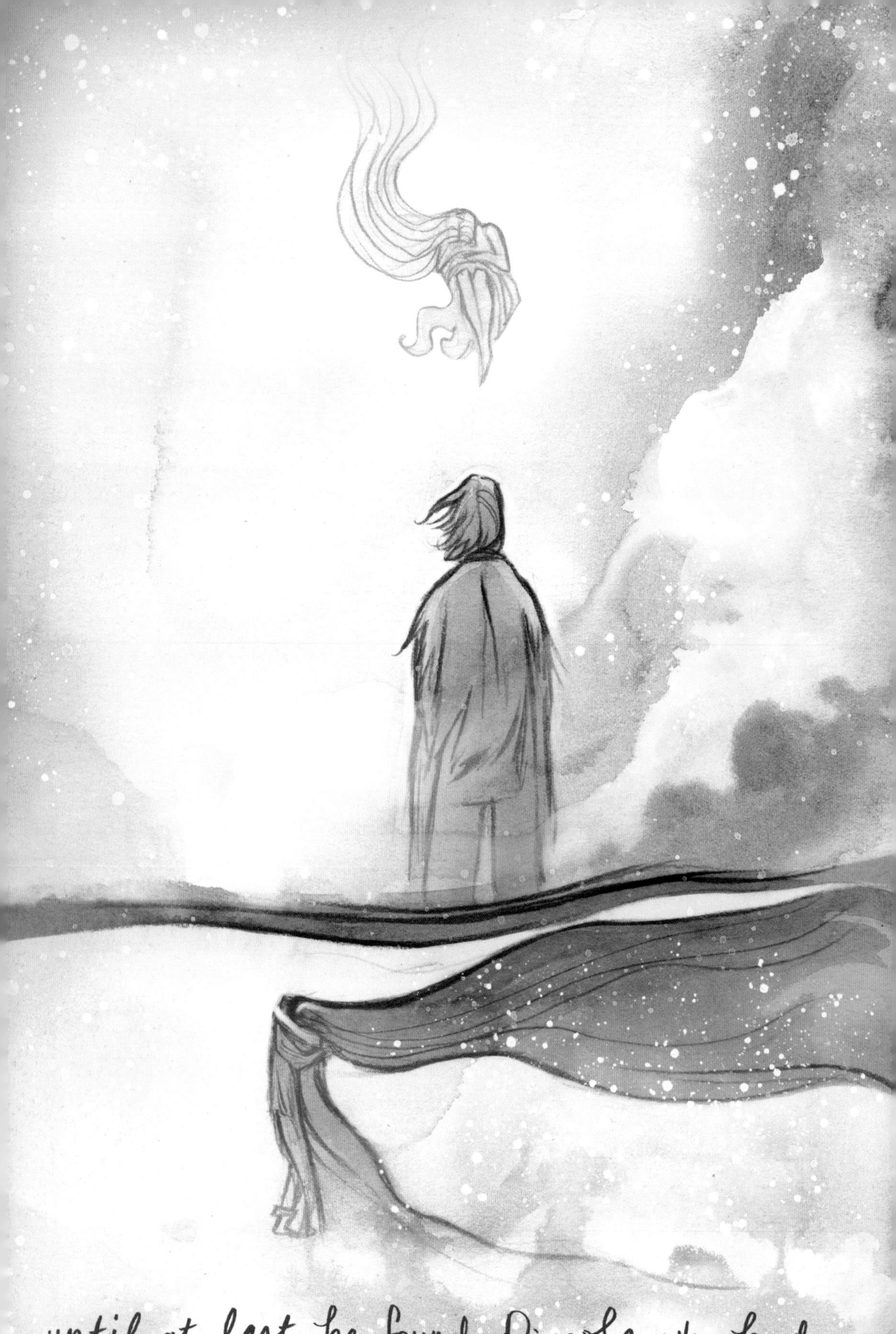

until at last he found Piccola, who had
taken refuge in the stars.

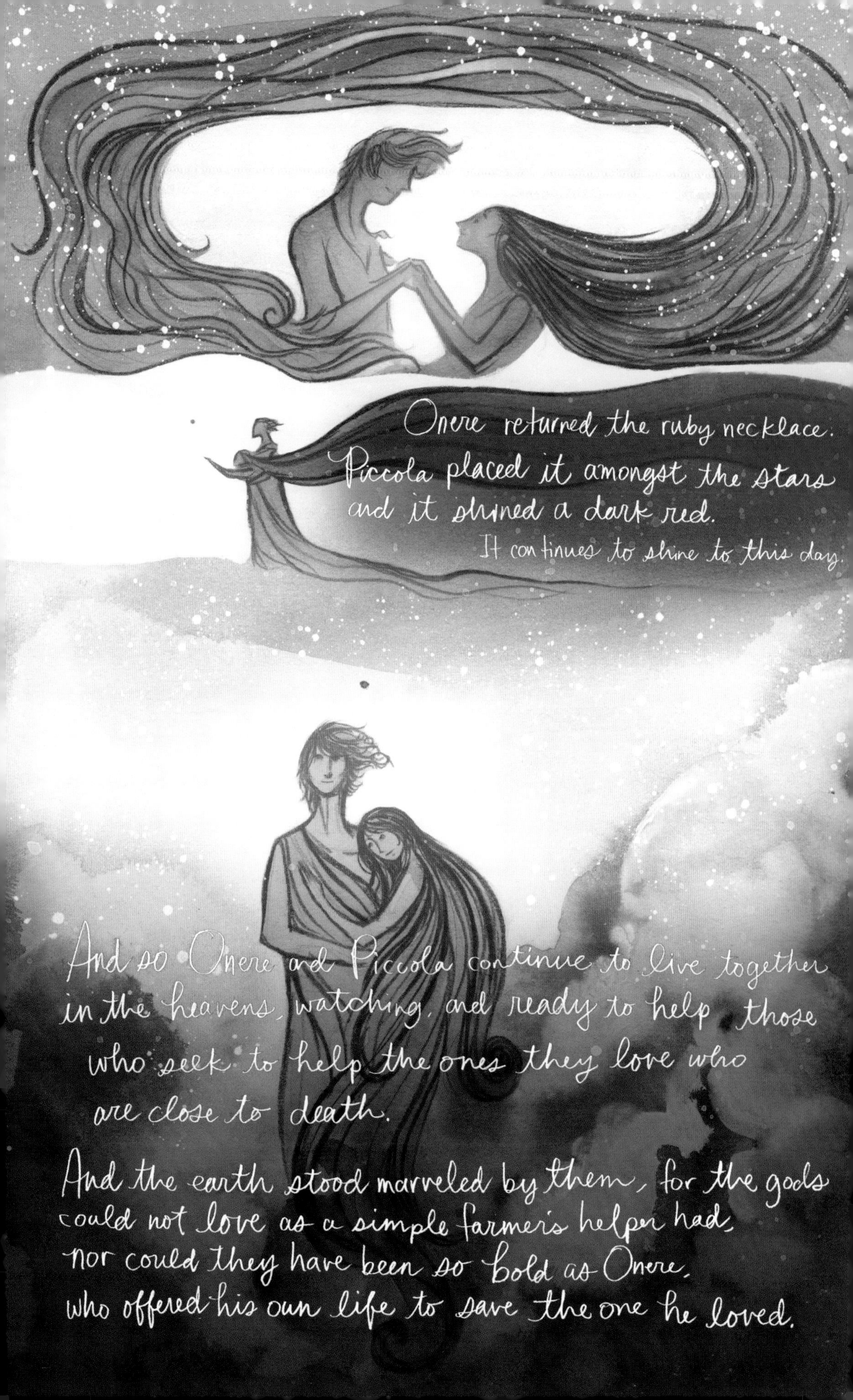
Onere returned the ruby necklace.
Piccola placed it amongst the stars
and it shined a dark red.
It continues to shine to this day.
And so Onere and Piccola continue to live together
in the heavens, watching, and ready to help those
who seek to help the ones they love who
are close to death.
And the earth stood marveled by them, for the gods
could not love as a simple farmer's helper had,
nor could they have been so bold as Onere,
who offered his own life to save the one he loved.

FAIRY *Market*

BY:
KATIE (ART) & **STEVEN** (STORY)
SHANAHAN

INKING ASSISTANCE
(AND MORAL SUPPORT):
GERRY DUCHEMIN

COLOURS:
SELENA DIZAZZO
ADRIANA BLAKE
KATIE SHANAHAN

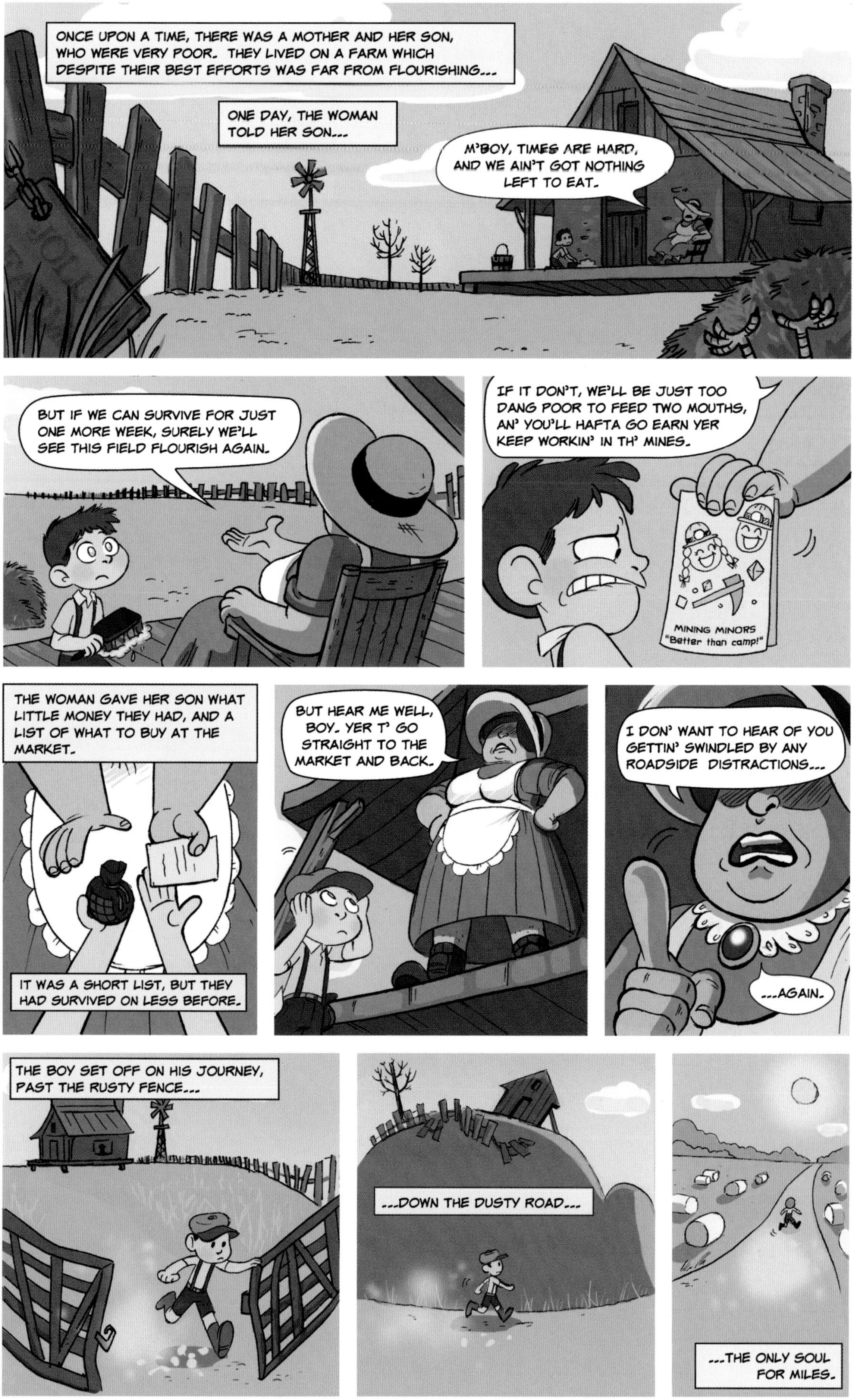
ONCE UPON A TIME, THERE WAS A MOTHER AND HER SON, WHO WERE VERY POOR. THEY LIVED ON A FARM WHICH DESPITE THEIR BEST EFFORTS WAS FAR FROM FLOURISHING...
ONE DAY, THE WOMAN TOLD HER SON...
M'BOY, TIMES ARE HARD, AND WE AIN'T GOT NOTHING LEFT TO EAT.
BUT IF WE CAN SURVIVE FOR JUST ONE MORE WEEK, SURELY WE'LL SEE THIS FIELD FLOURISH AGAIN.
IF IT DON'T, WE'LL BE JUST TOO DANG POOR TO FEED TWO MOUTHS, AN' YOU'LL HAFTA GO EARN YER KEEP WORKIN' IN TH' MINES.
MINING MINORS
"Better than camp!"
THE WOMAN GAVE HER SON WHAT LITTLE MONEY THEY HAD, AND A LIST OF WHAT TO BUY AT THE MARKET.
IT WAS A SHORT LIST, BUT THEY HAD SURVIVED ON LESS BEFORE.
BUT HEAR ME WELL, BOY. YER T' GO STRAIGHT TO THE MARKET AND BACK.
I DON' WANT TO HEAR OF YOU GETTIN' SWINDLED BY ANY ROADSIDE DISTRACTIONS...
...AGAIN.
THE BOY SET OFF ON HIS JOURNEY, PAST THE RUSTY FENCE...
...DOWN THE DUSTY ROAD...
...THE ONLY SOUL FOR MILES.

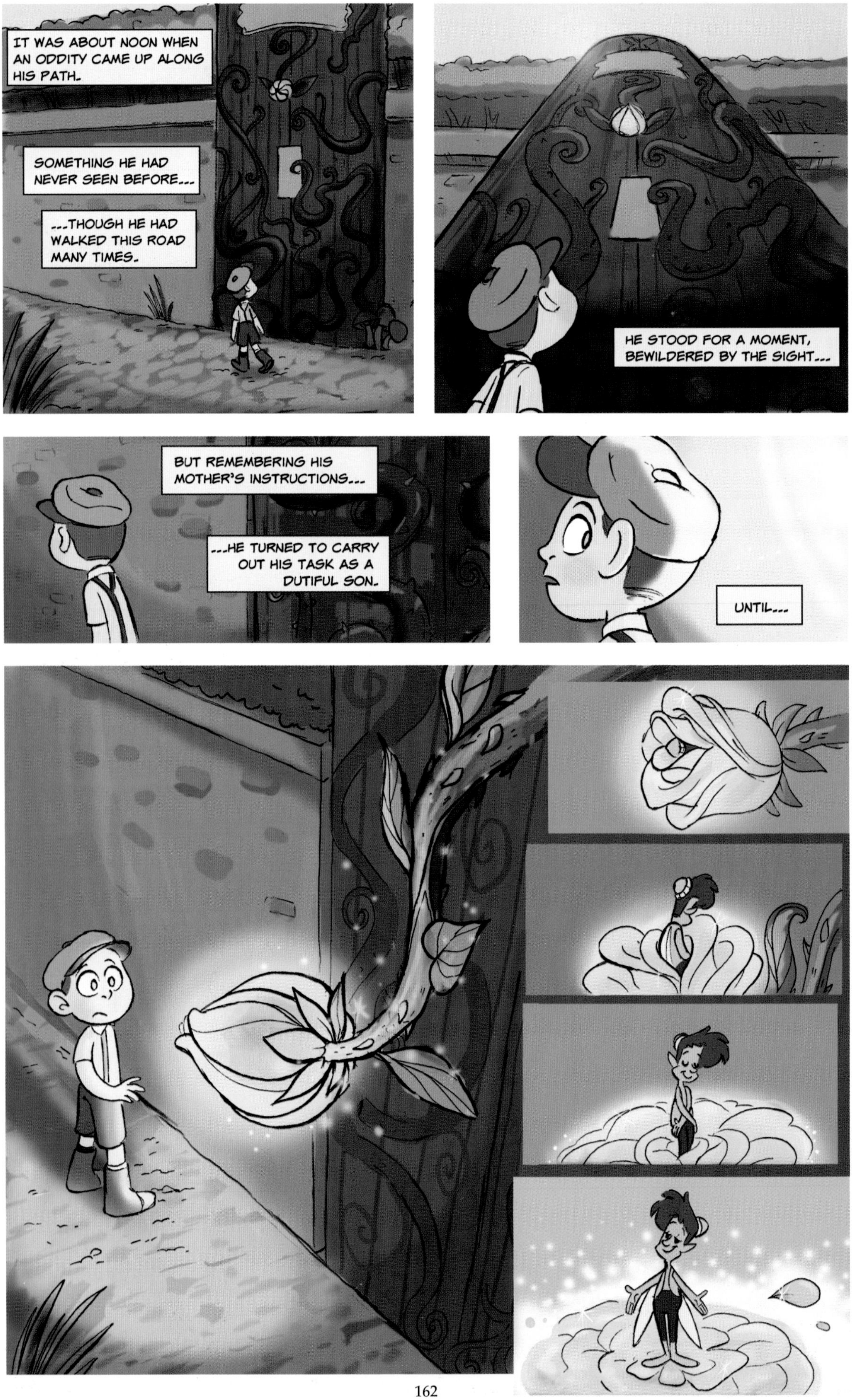
IT WAS ABOUT NOON WHEN AN ODDITY CAME UP ALONG HIS PATH.
SOMETHING HE HAD NEVER SEEN BEFORE...
...THOUGH HE HAD WALKED THIS ROAD MANY TIMES.
HE STOOD FOR A MOMENT, BEWILDERED BY THE SIGHT...
BUT REMEMBERING HIS MOTHER'S INSTRUCTIONS...
...HE TURNED TO CARRY OUT HIS TASK AS A DUTIFUL SON.
UNTIL...

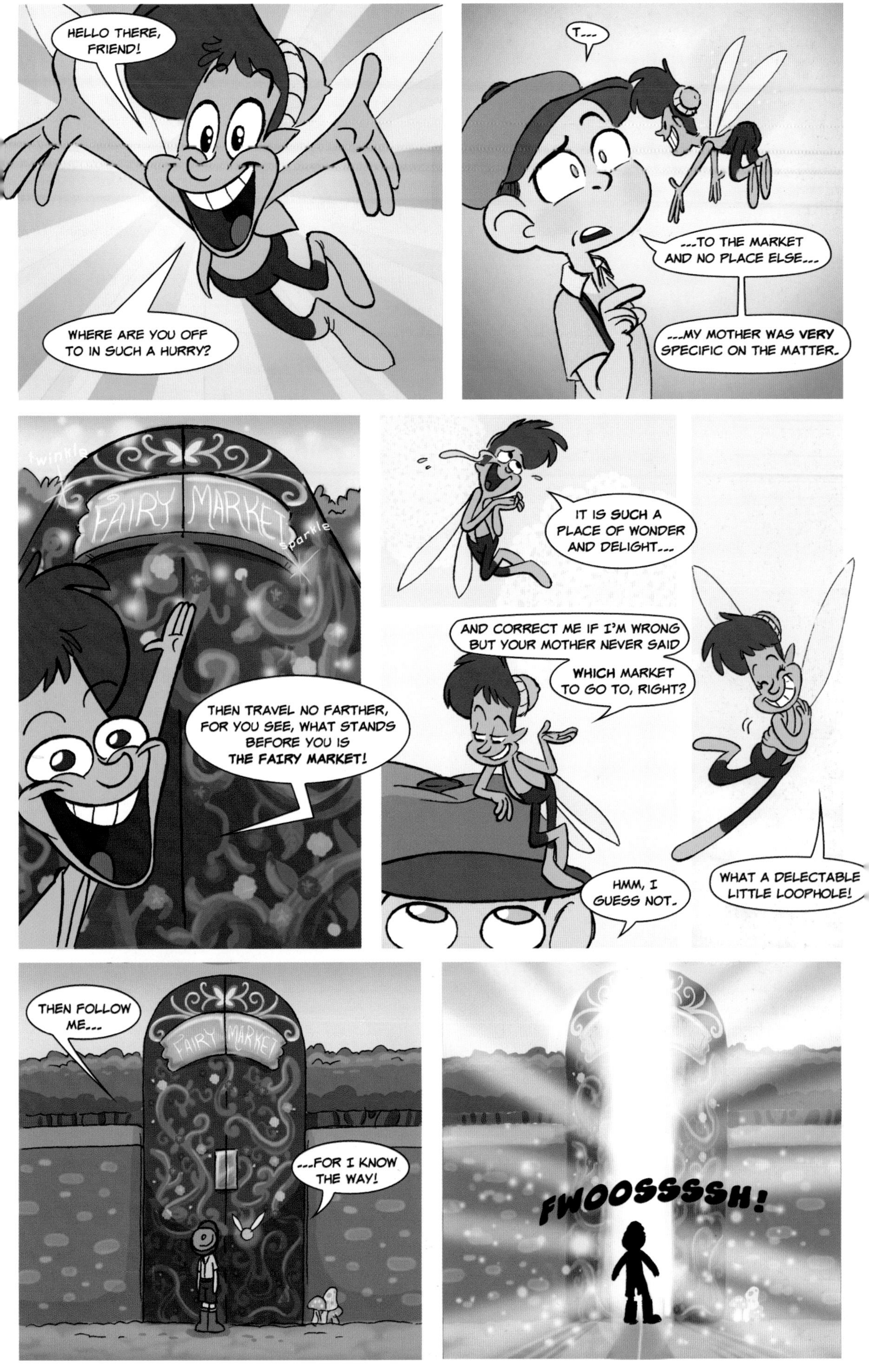
HELLO THERE, FRIEND!
WHERE ARE YOU OFF TO IN SUCH A HURRY?
T...
...TO THE MARKET AND NO PLACE ELSE...
...MY MOTHER WAS VERY SPECIFIC ON THE MATTER.
twinkle
FAIRY MARKET
sparkle
THEN TRAVEL NO FARTHER, FOR YOU SEE, WHAT STANDS BEFORE YOU IS THE FAIRY MARKET!
IT IS SUCH A PLACE OF WONDER AND DELIGHT...
AND CORRECT ME IF I'M WRONG BUT YOUR MOTHER NEVER SAID
WHICH MARKET TO GO TO, RIGHT?
HMM, I GUESS NOT.
WHAT A DELECTABLE LITTLE LOOPHOLE!
THEN FOLLOW ME...
FAIRY MARKET
...FOR I KNOW THE WAY!
FWOOSSSSH!

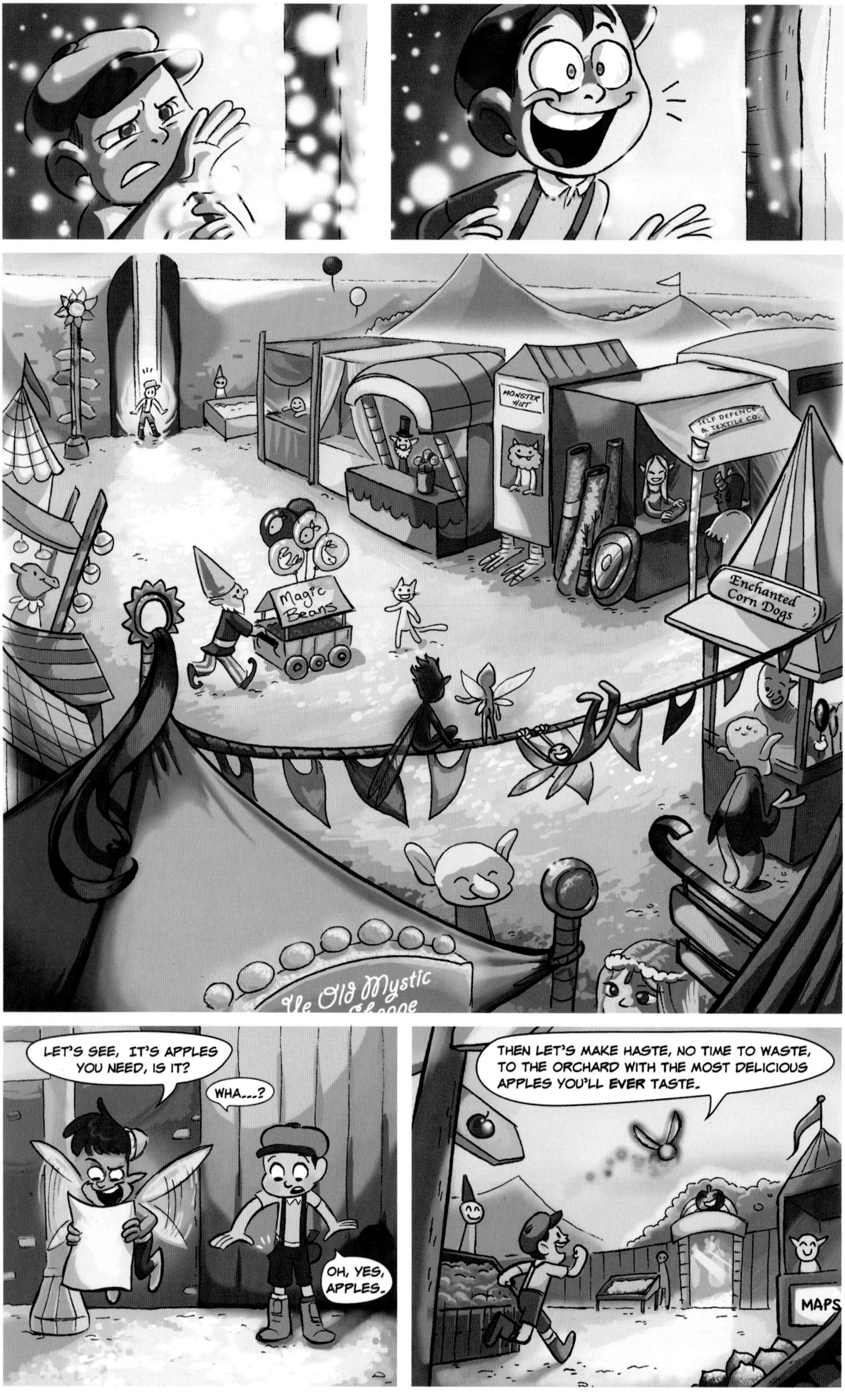
MONSTER HUT
SELF DEFENCE & TEXTILE CO.
Magic Beans
Enchanted Corn Dogs
Ye Old Mystic
LET'S SEE, IT'S APPLES YOU NEED, IS IT?
WHA...?
OH, YES, APPLES.
THEN LET'S MAKE HASTE, NO TIME TO WASTE, TO THE ORCHARD WITH THE MOST DELICIOUS APPLES YOU'LL EVER TASTE.
MAPS

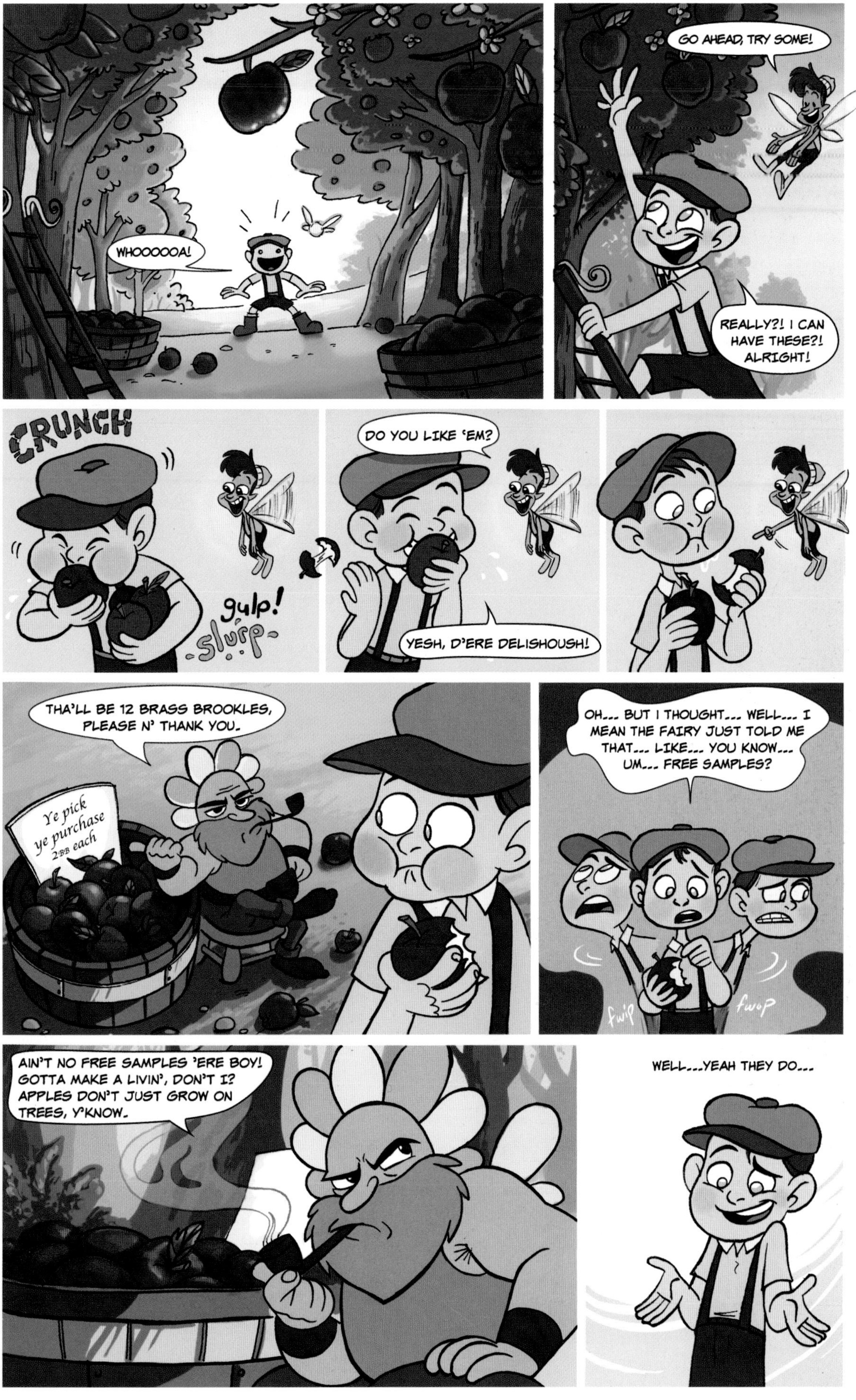
WHOOOOOA!
GO AHEAD, TRY SOME!
REALLY?! I CAN HAVE THESE?! ALRIGHT!
CRUNCH
gulp!
slurp
DO YOU LIKE 'EM?
YESH, D'ERE DELISHOUSH!
THA'LL BE 12 BRASS BROOKLES, PLEASE N' THANK YOU.
Ye pick ye purchase 2BB each
OH... BUT I THOUGHT... WELL... I MEAN THE FAIRY JUST TOLD ME THAT... LIKE... YOU KNOW... UM... FREE SAMPLES?
fwip
fwop
AIN'T NO FREE SAMPLES 'ERE BOY! GOTTA MAKE A LIVIN', DON'T I? APPLES DON'T JUST GROW ON TREES, Y'KNOW.
WELL...YEAH THEY DO...

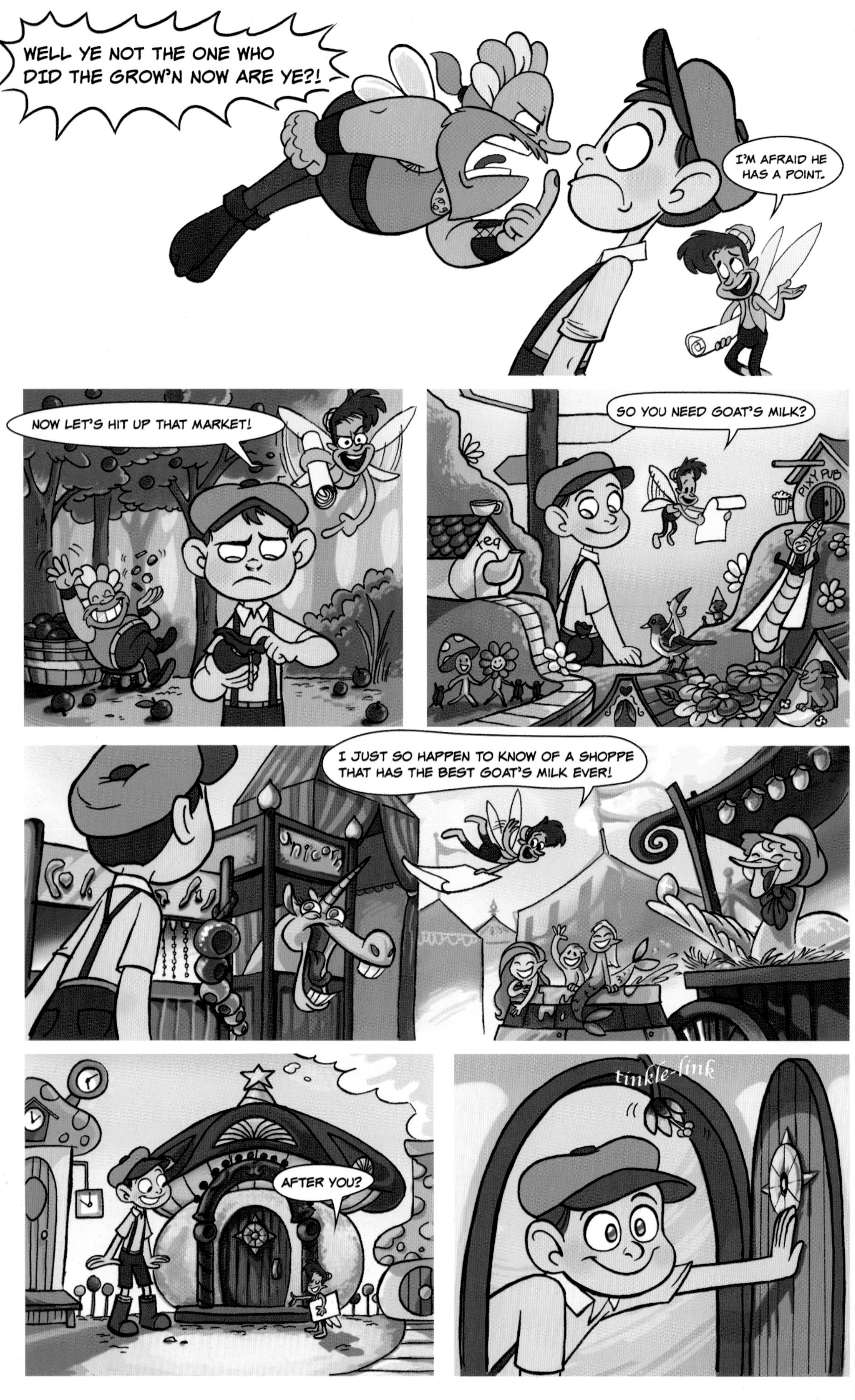
WELL YE NOT THE ONE WHO DID THE GROW'N NOW ARE YE?!
I'M AFRAID HE HAS A POINT.
NOW LET'S HIT UP THAT MARKET!
SO YOU NEED GOAT'S MILK?
PIXY PUB
I JUST SO HAPPEN TO KNOW OF A SHOPPE THAT HAS THE BEST GOAT'S MILK EVER!
Unicorn
AFTER YOU?
tinkle-link

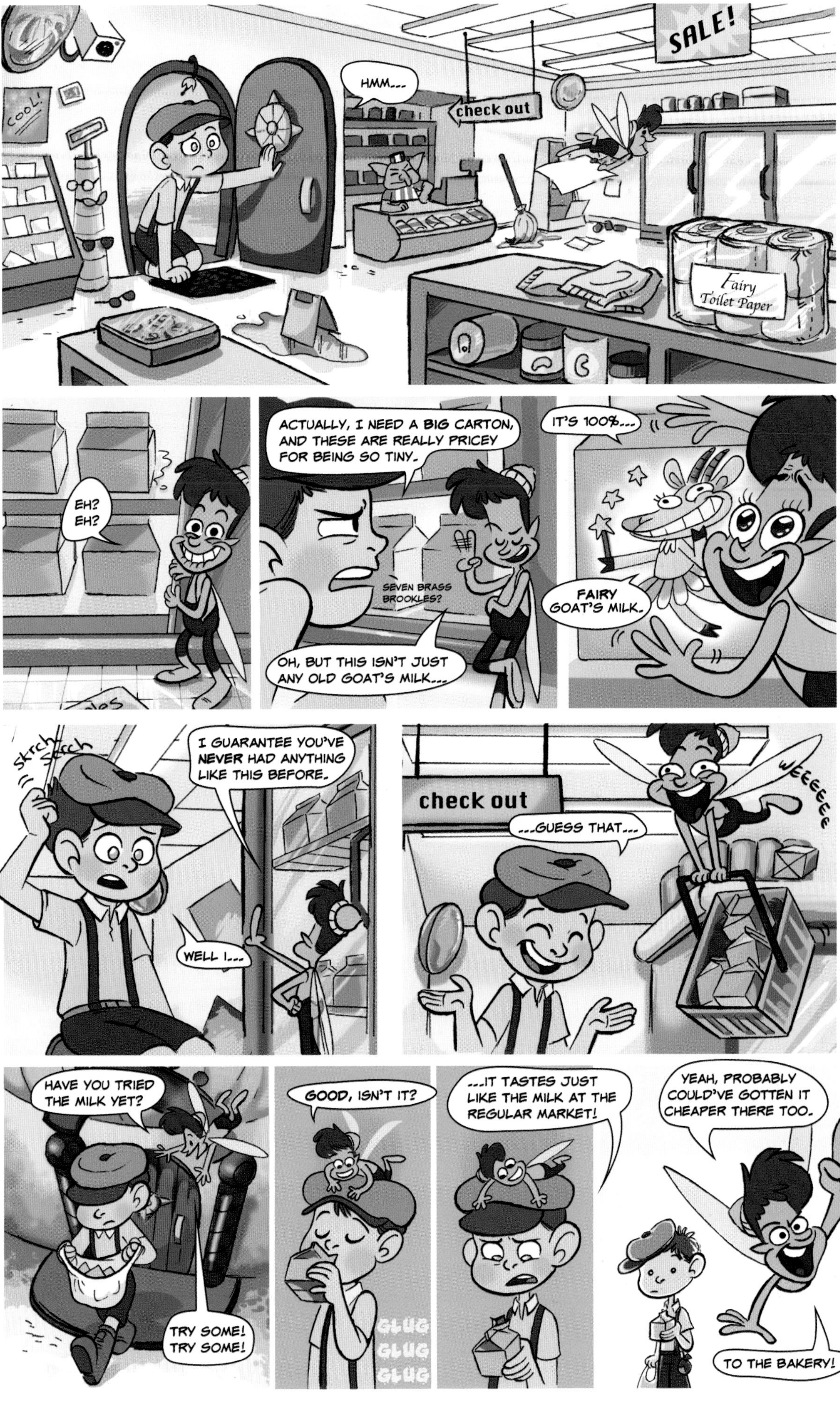

COOL!
HMM...
check out
SALE!
Fairy Toilet Paper
EH? EH?
ACTUALLY, I NEED A BIG CARTON, AND THESE ARE REALLY PRICEY FOR BEING SO TINY.
SEVEN BRASS BROOKLES?
OH, BUT THIS ISN'T JUST ANY OLD GOAT'S MILK...
IT'S 100%...
FAIRY GOAT'S MILK.
skrch skrch
I GUARANTEE YOU'VE NEVER HAD ANYTHING LIKE THIS BEFORE.
WELL I...
check out
...GUESS THAT...
WEEEEEE
HAVE YOU TRIED THE MILK YET?
TRY SOME! TRY SOME!
GOOD, ISN'T IT?
GLUG GLUG GLUG
...IT TASTES JUST LIKE THE MILK AT THE REGULAR MARKET!
YEAH, PROBABLY COULD'VE GOTTEN IT CHEAPER THERE TOO.
TO THE BAKERY!

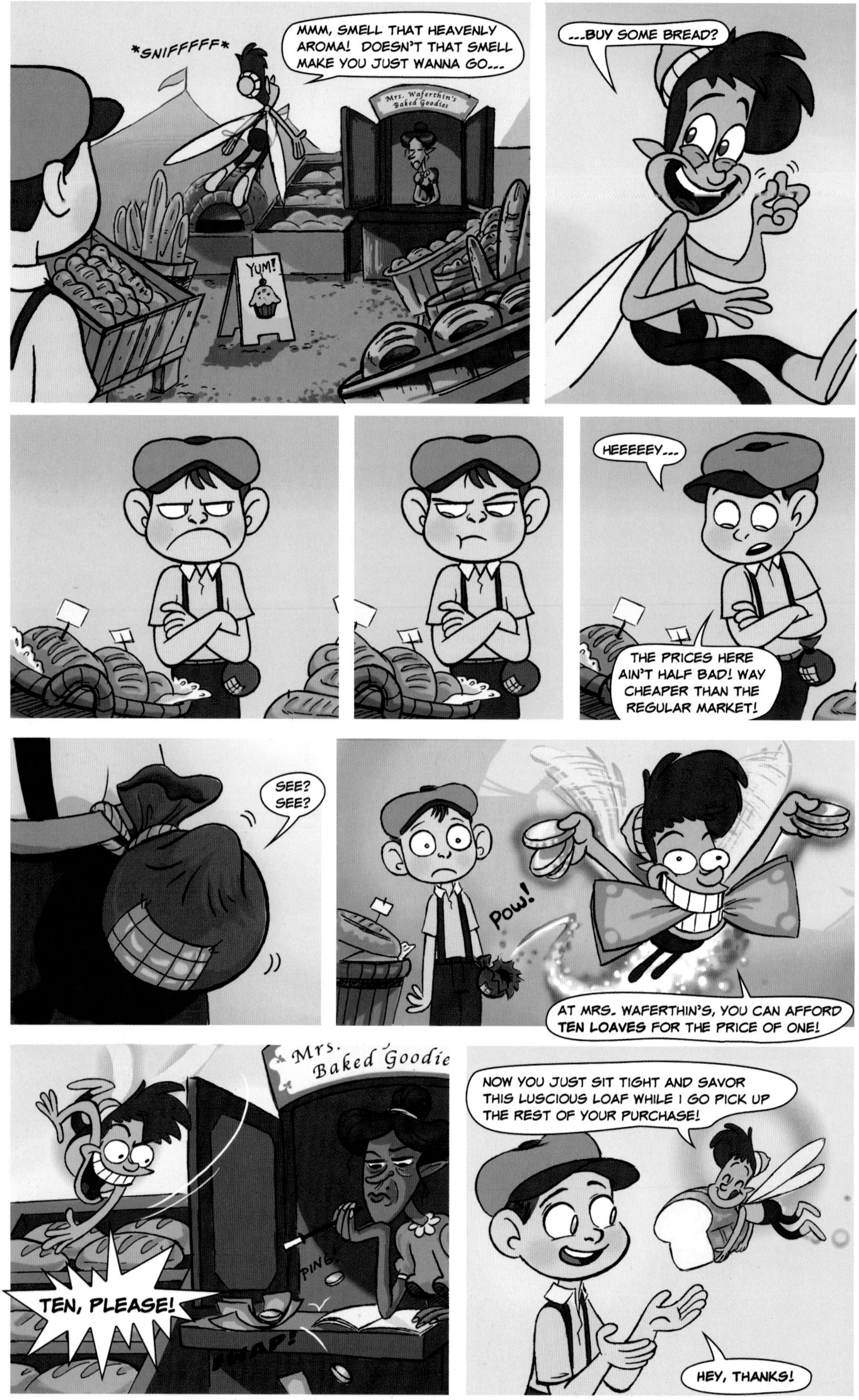
SNIFFFFF
MMM, SMELL THAT HEAVENLY AROMA! DOESN'T THAT SMELL MAKE YOU JUST WANNA GO...
Mrs. Waferthin's Baked Goodies
YUM!
...BUY SOME BREAD?
HEEEEEY...
THE PRICES HERE AIN'T HALF BAD! WAY CHEAPER THAN THE REGULAR MARKET!
SEE? SEE?
POW!
AT MRS. WAFERTHIN'S, YOU CAN AFFORD TEN LOAVES FOR THE PRICE OF ONE!
Mrs.
Baked Goodie
TEN, PLEASE!
PING!
NOW YOU JUST SIT TIGHT AND SAVOR THIS LUSCIOUS LOAF WHILE I GO PICK UP THE REST OF YOUR PURCHASE!
HEY, THANKS!

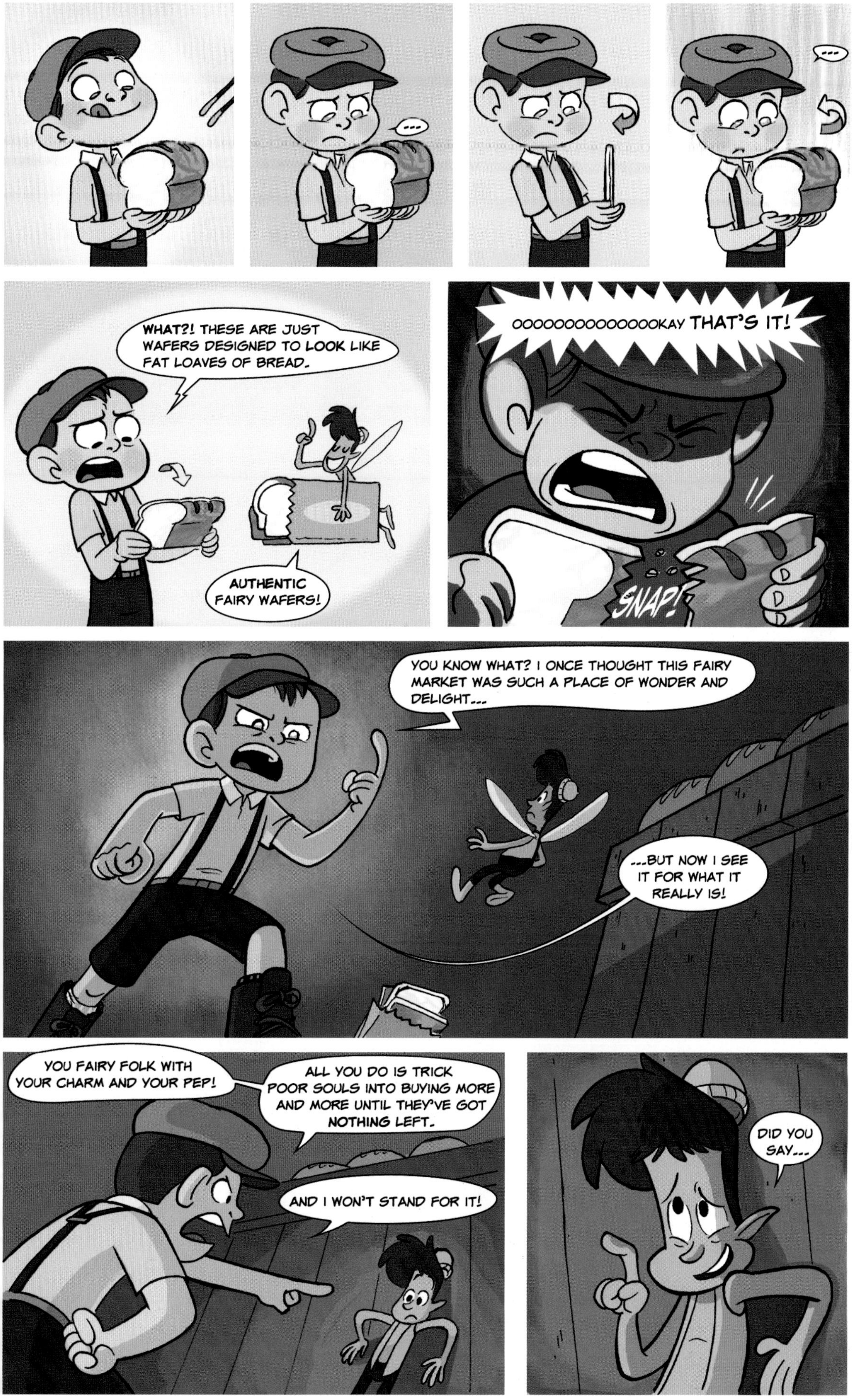
...
...
WHAT?! THESE ARE JUST WAFERS DESIGNED TO LOOK LIKE FAT LOAVES OF BREAD.
AUTHENTIC FAIRY WAFERS!
OOOOOOOOOOOOOOKAY THAT'S IT!
SNAP!
YOU KNOW WHAT? I ONCE THOUGHT THIS FAIRY MARKET WAS SUCH A PLACE OF WONDER AND DELIGHT...
...BUT NOW I SEE IT FOR WHAT IT REALLY IS!
YOU FAIRY FOLK WITH YOUR CHARM AND YOUR PEP!
ALL YOU DO IS TRICK POOR SOULS INTO BUYING MORE AND MORE UNTIL THEY'VE GOT NOTHING LEFT.
AND I WON'T STAND FOR IT!
DID YOU SAY...

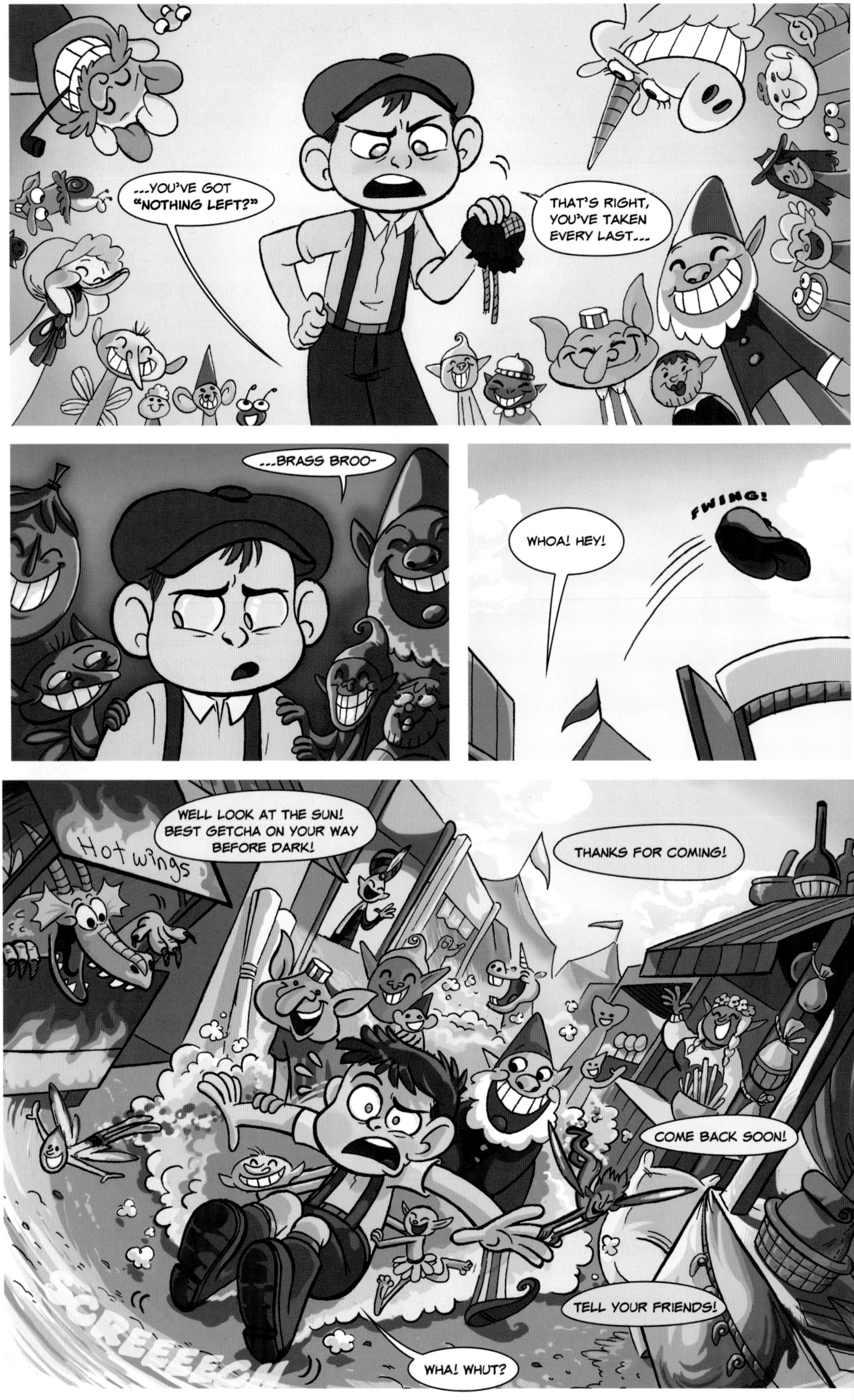
...YOU'VE GOT "NOTHING LEFT?"
THAT'S RIGHT, YOU'VE TAKEN EVERY LAST...
...BRASS BROO-
WHOA! HEY!
FWING!
WELL LOOK AT THE SUN! BEST GETCHA ON YOUR WAY BEFORE DARK!
THANKS FOR COMING!
Hot wings
COME BACK SOON!
TELL YOUR FRIENDS!
WHA! WHUT?
SCREEEECH

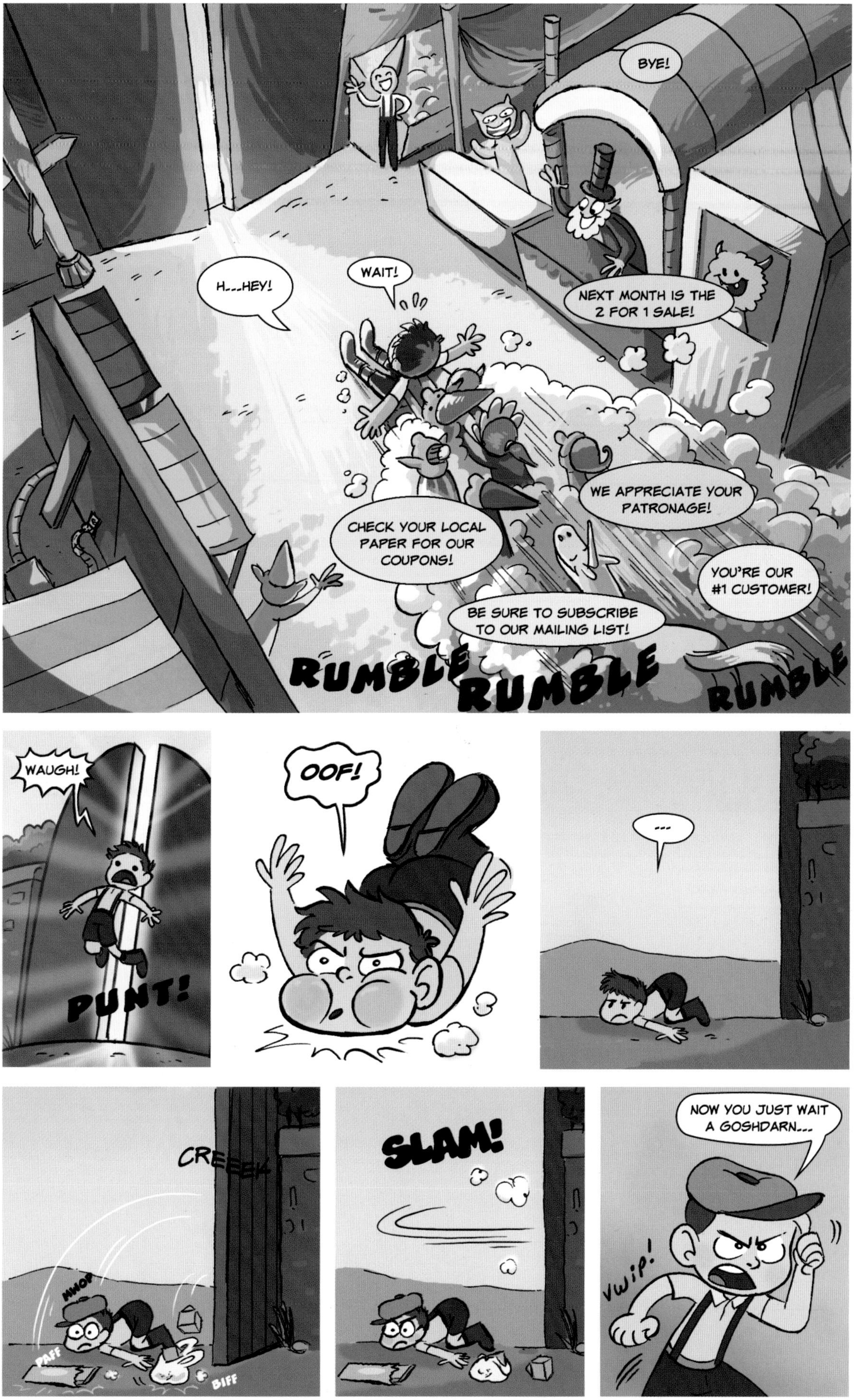
BYE!
H...HEY!
WAIT!
NEXT MONTH IS THE 2 FOR 1 SALE!
WE APPRECIATE YOUR PATRONAGE!
CHECK YOUR LOCAL PAPER FOR OUR COUPONS!
YOU'RE OUR #1 CUSTOMER!
BE SURE TO SUBSCRIBE TO OUR MAILING LIST!
RUMBLE
RUMBLE
RUMBLE
WAUGH!
PUNT!
OOF!
...
CREEEK
MMOF
PAFF
BIFF
SLAM!
NOW YOU JUST WAIT A GOSHDARN...
vwip!

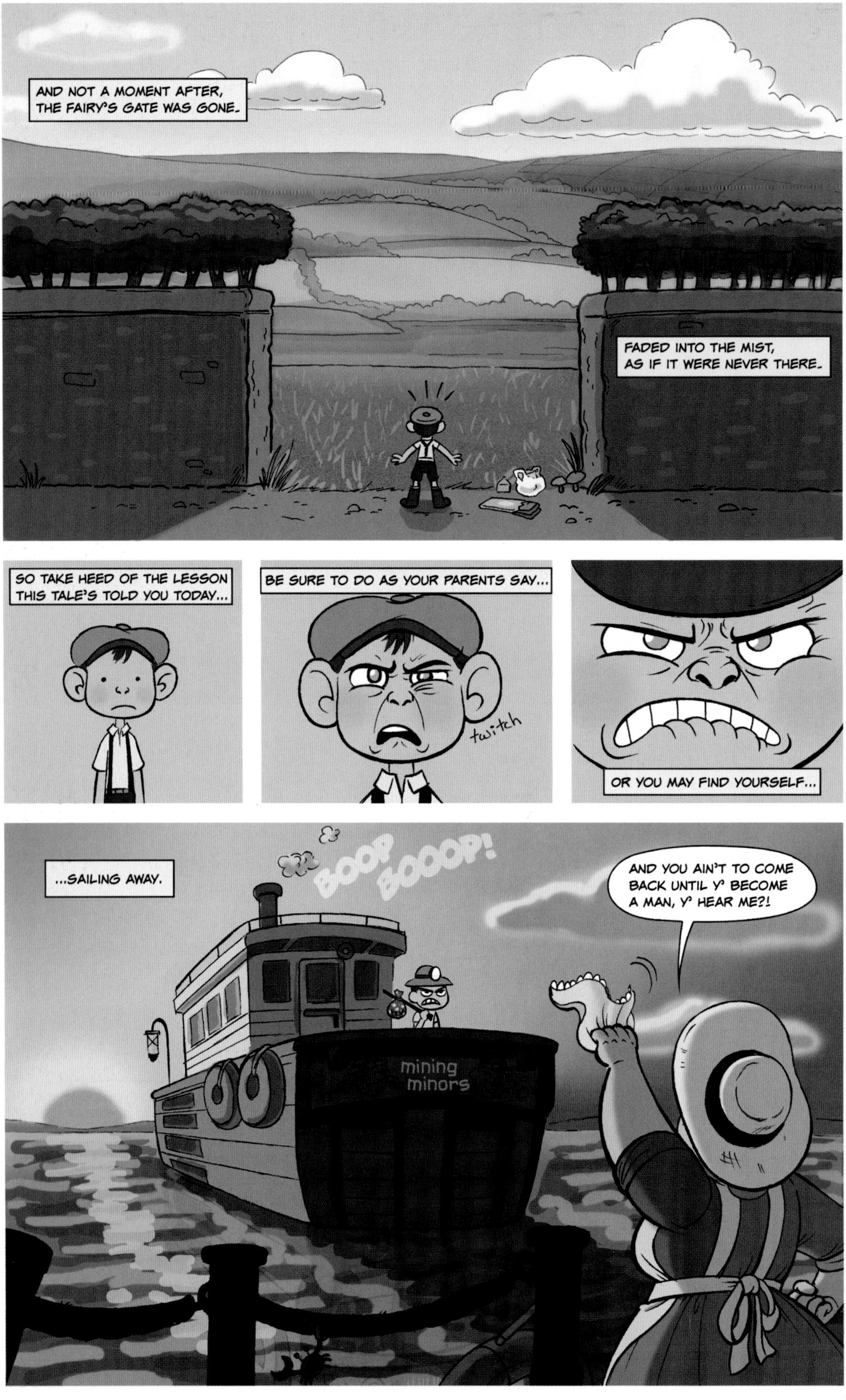
AND NOT A MOMENT AFTER, THE FAIRY'S GATE WAS GONE.
FADED INTO THE MIST, AS IF IT WERE NEVER THERE.
SO TAKE HEED OF THE LESSON THIS TALE'S TOLD YOU TODAY...
BE SURE TO DO AS YOUR PARENTS SAY...
twitch
OR YOU MAY FIND YOURSELF...
...SAILING AWAY.
BOOP BOOOP!
AND YOU AIN'T TO COME BACK UNTIL Y' BECOME A MAN, Y' HEAR ME?!
mining minors

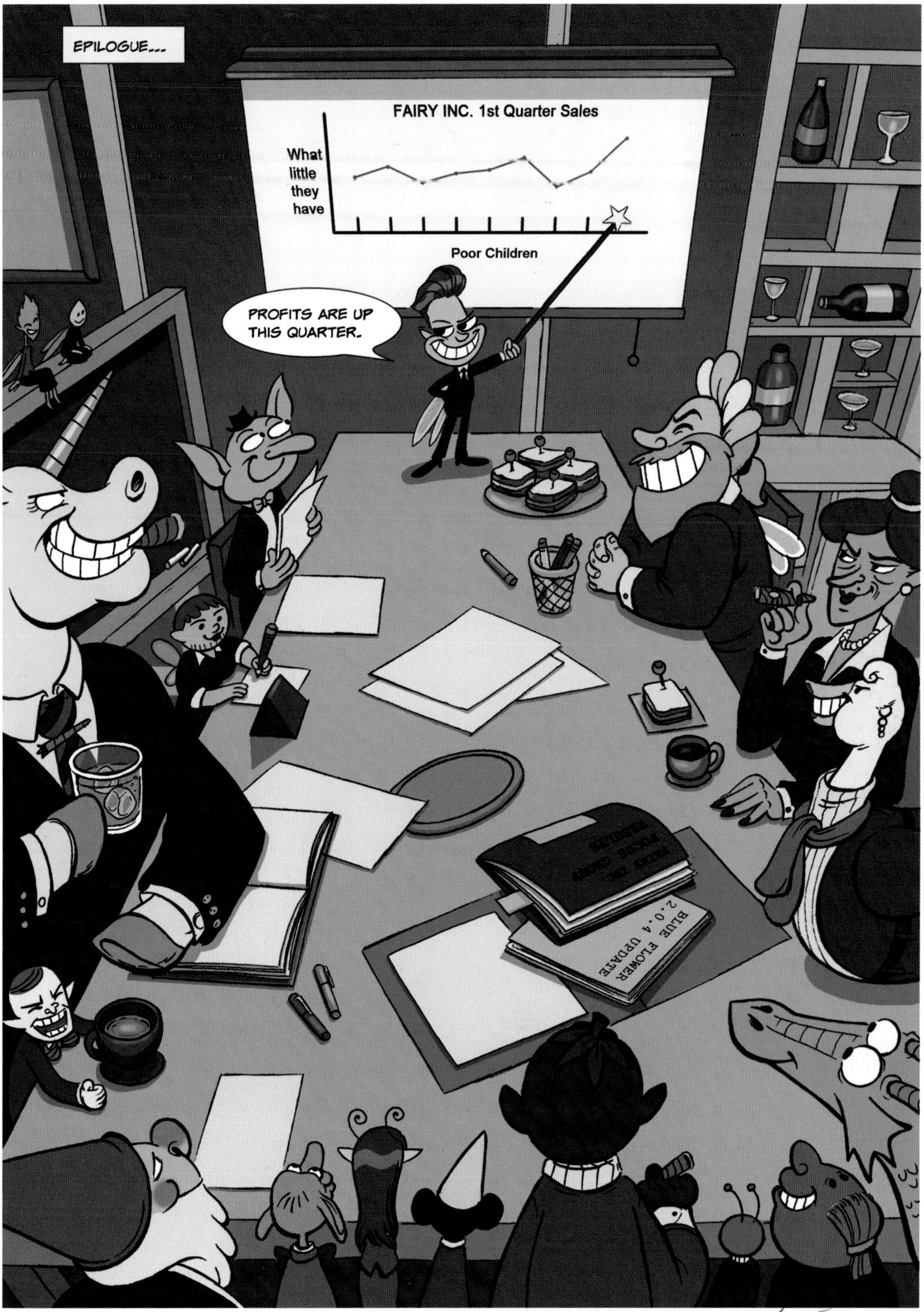
EPILOGUE...
FAIRY INC. 1st Quarter Sales
What little they have
Poor Children
PROFITS ARE UP THIS QUARTER.
FOCUS GROUP RESULTS
BLUE FLOWER 2.0.4 UPDATE

2010

the end

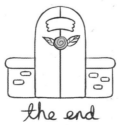

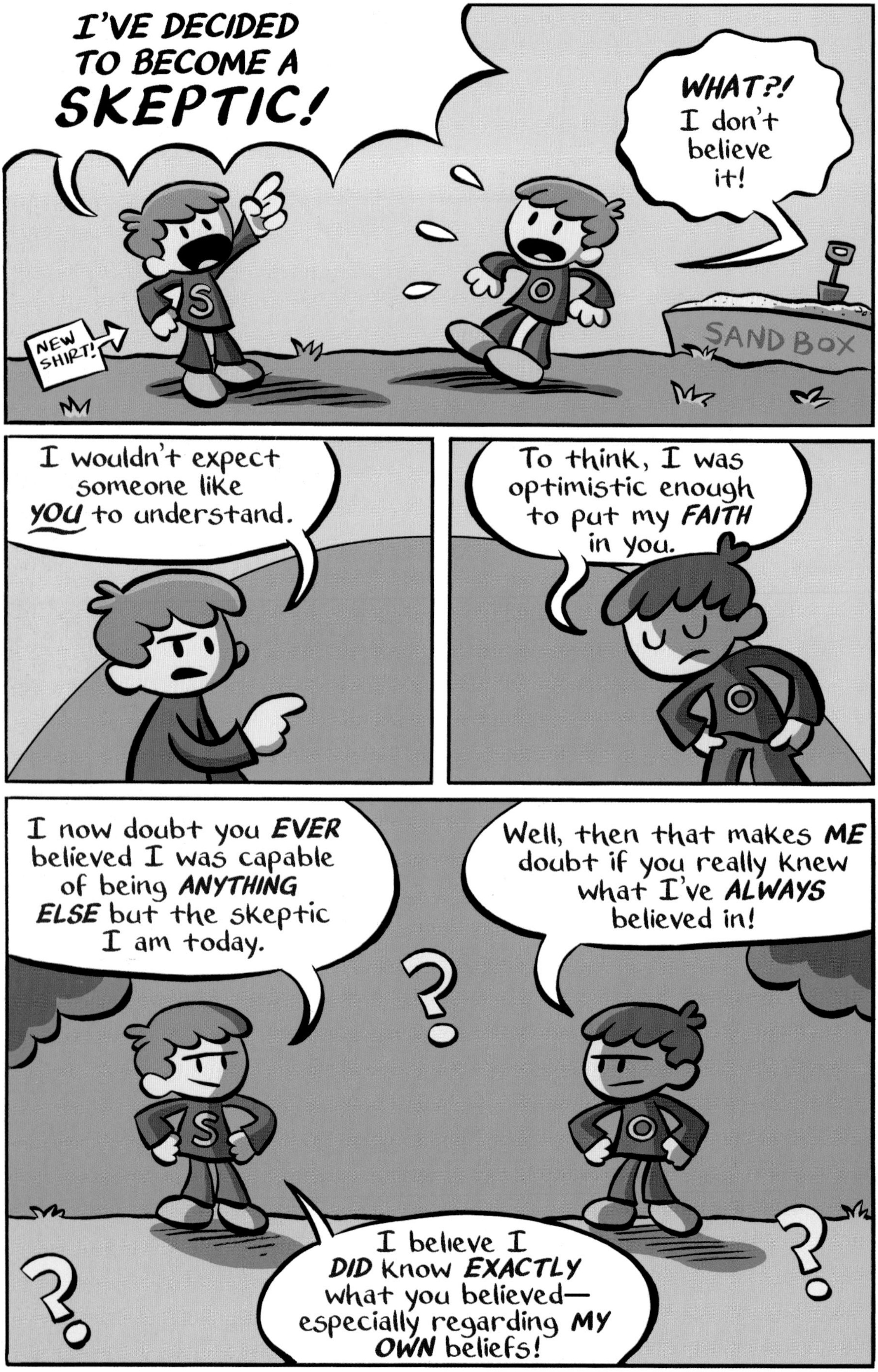
I'VE DECIDED TO BECOME A SKEPTIC!
NEW SHIRT!
WHAT?! I don't believe it!
SAND BOX
I wouldn't expect someone like YOU to understand.
To think, I was optimistic enough to put my FAITH in you.
I now doubt you EVER believed I was capable of being ANYTHING ELSE but the skeptic I am today.
Well, then that makes ME doubt if you really knew what I've ALWAYS believed in!
I believe I DID know EXACTLY what you believed—especially regarding MY OWN beliefs!

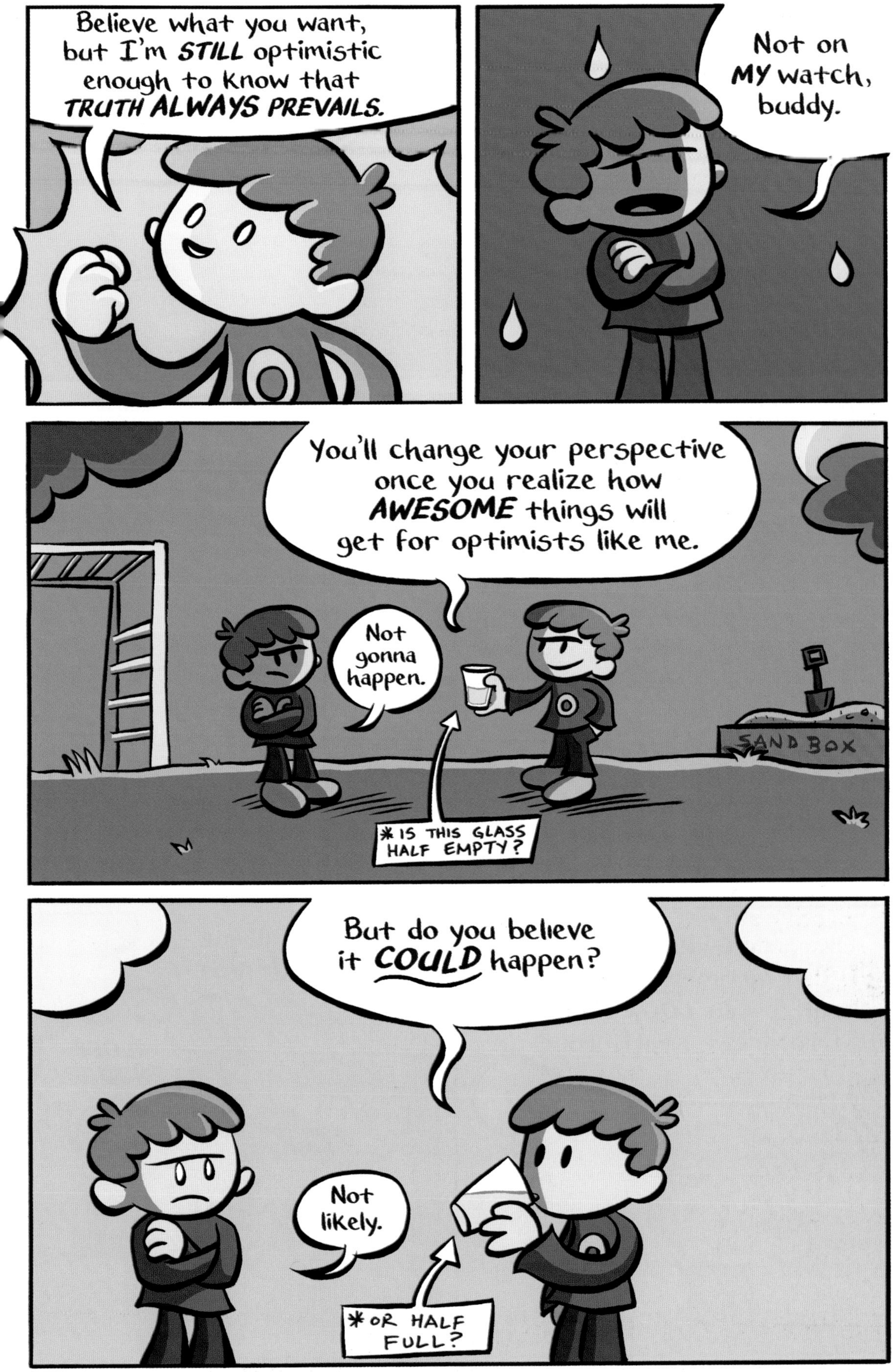

Believe what you want, but I'm STILL optimistic enough to know that TRUTH ALWAYS PREVAILS.
Not on MY watch, buddy.
You'll change your perspective once you realize how AWESOME things will get for optimists like me.
Not gonna happen.
* IS THIS GLASS HALF EMPTY?
SAND BOX
But do you believe it COULD happen?
Not likely.
* OR HALF FULL?

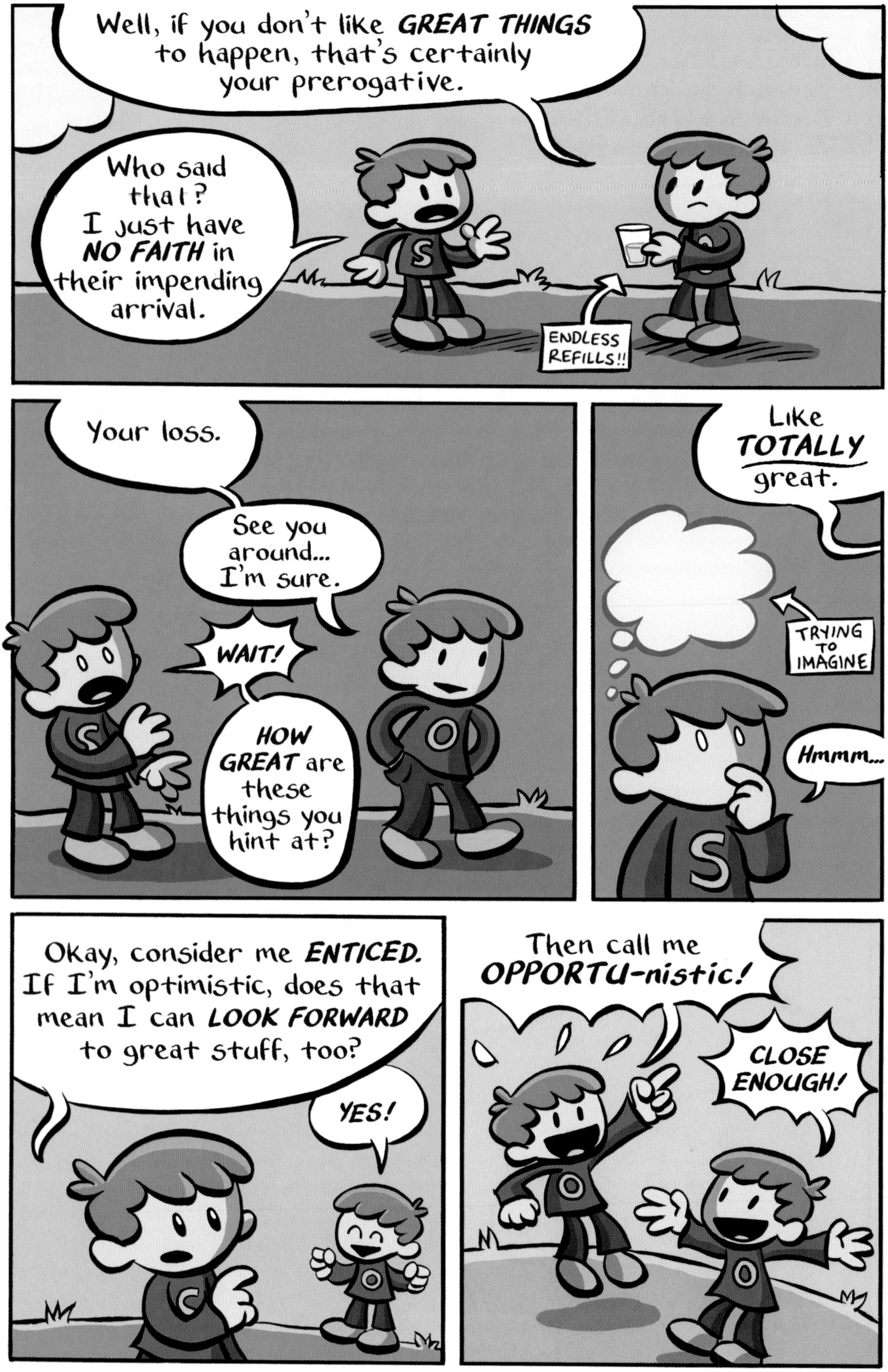
Well, if you don't like GREAT THINGS to happen, that's certainly your prerogative.
Who said that? I just have NO FAITH in their impending arrival.
ENDLESS REFILLS!!
Your loss.
See you around... I'm sure.
WAIT!
HOW GREAT are these things you hint at?
Like TOTALLY great.
TRYING TO IMAGINE
Hmmm...
Okay, consider me ENTICED. If I'm optimistic, does that mean I can LOOK FORWARD to great stuff, too?
YES!
Then call me OPPORTU-nistic!
CLOSE ENOUGH!

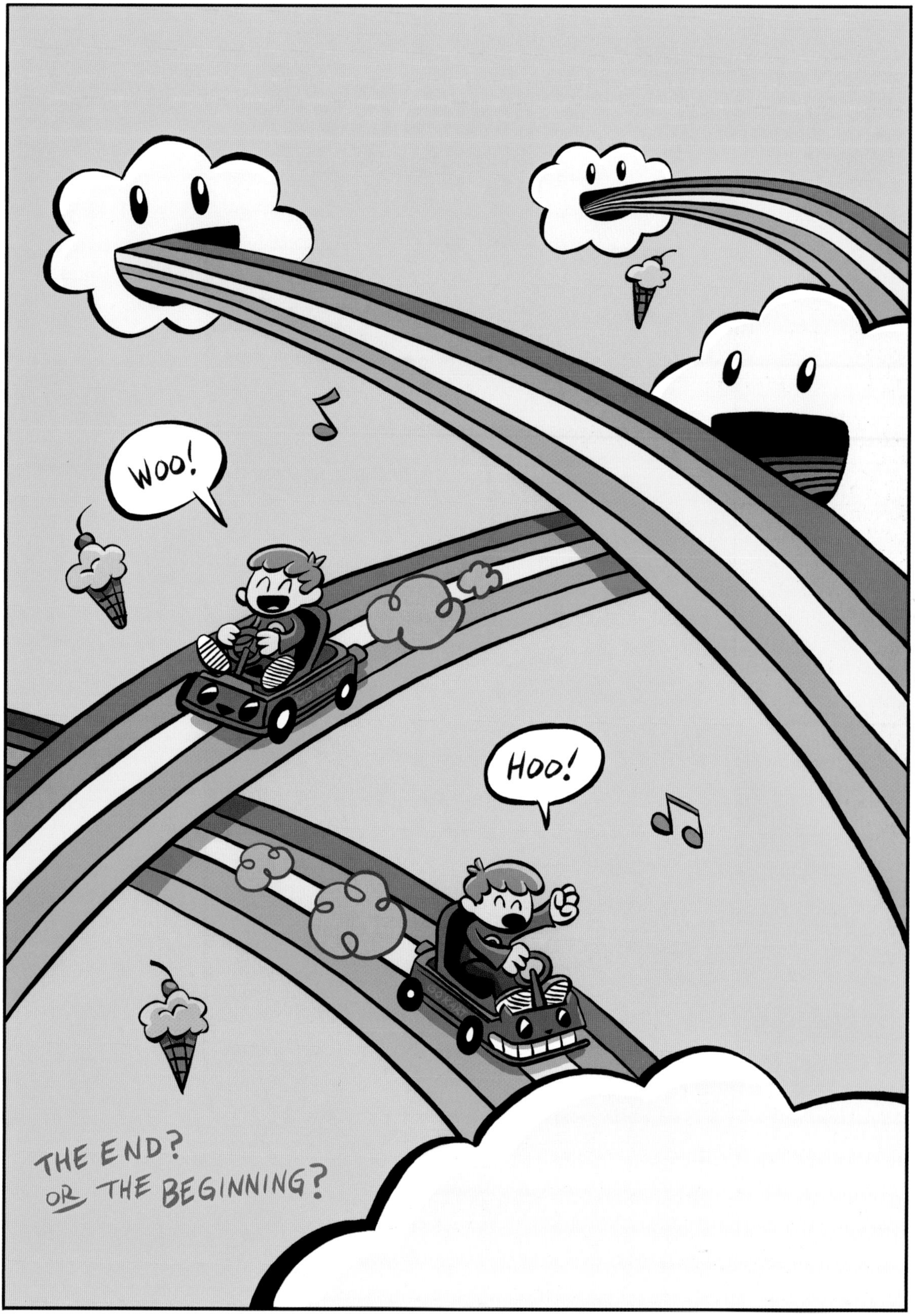
WOO!
HOO!
THE END?
OR THE BEGINNING?

Guardian Angel

Kean Soo

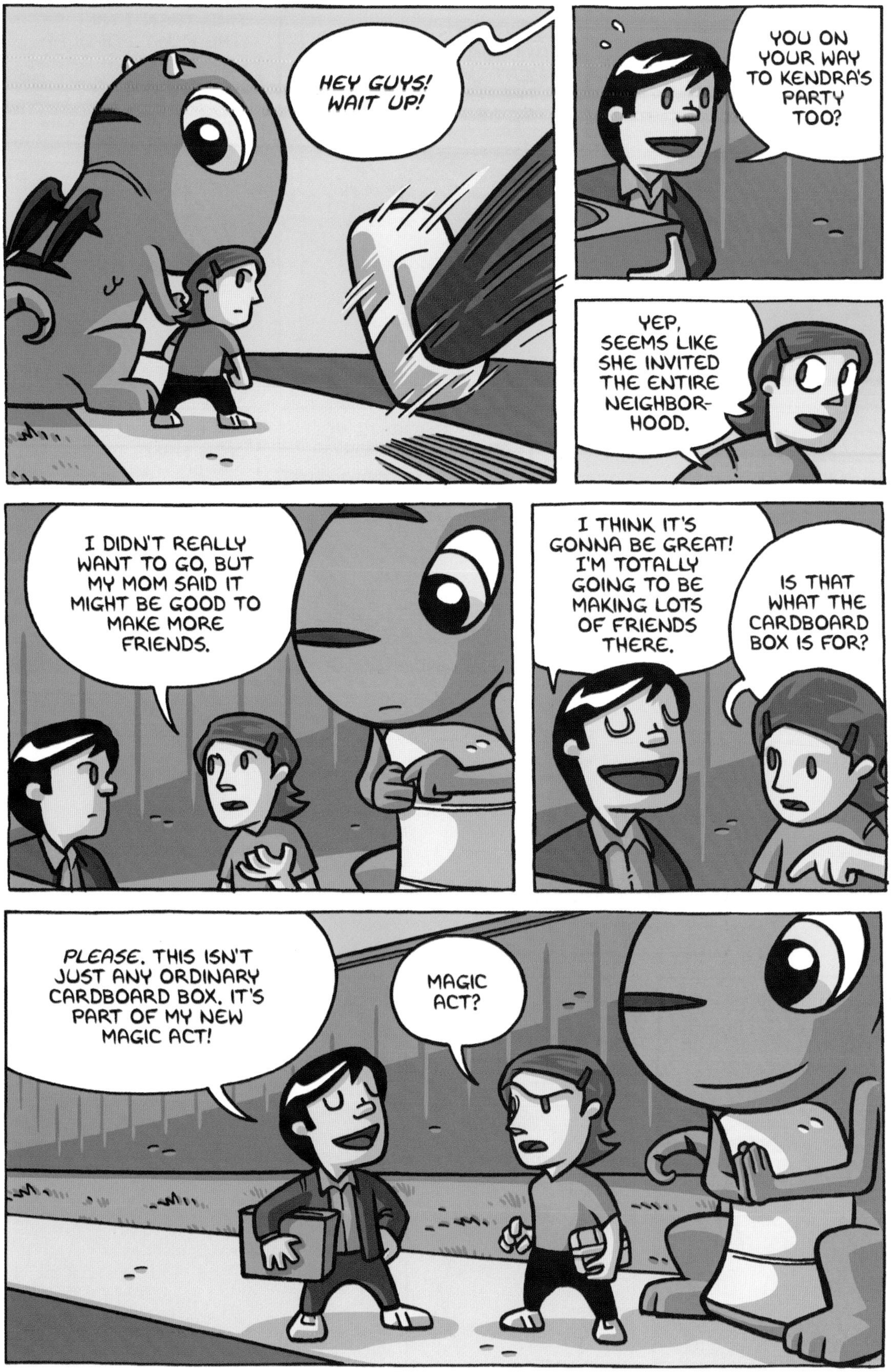
HEY GUYS! WAIT UP!
YOU ON YOUR WAY TO KENDRA'S PARTY TOO?
YEP, SEEMS LIKE SHE INVITED THE ENTIRE NEIGHBOR-HOOD.
I DIDN'T REALLY WANT TO GO, BUT MY MOM SAID IT MIGHT BE GOOD TO MAKE MORE FRIENDS.
I THINK IT'S GONNA BE GREAT! I'M TOTALLY GOING TO BE MAKING LOTS OF FRIENDS THERE.
IS THAT WHAT THE CARDBOARD BOX IS FOR?
PLEASE. THIS ISN'T JUST ANY ORDINARY CARDBOARD BOX. IT'S PART OF MY NEW MAGIC ACT!
MAGIC ACT?

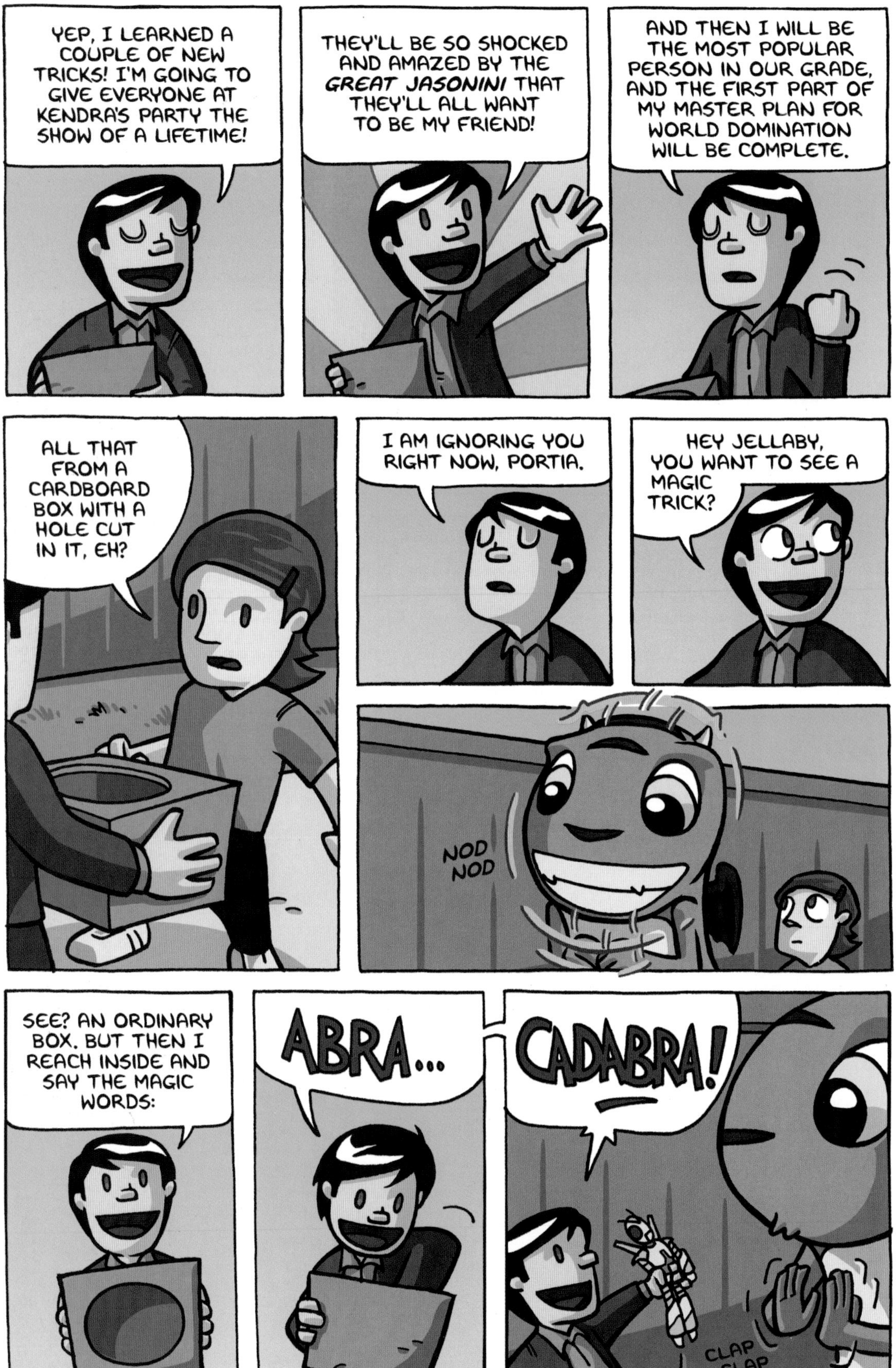
YEP, I LEARNED A COUPLE OF NEW TRICKS! I'M GOING TO GIVE EVERYONE AT KENDRA'S PARTY THE SHOW OF A LIFETIME!
THEY'LL BE SO SHOCKED AND AMAZED BY THE GREAT JASONINI THAT THEY'LL ALL WANT TO BE MY FRIEND!
AND THEN I WILL BE THE MOST POPULAR PERSON IN OUR GRADE, AND THE FIRST PART OF MY MASTER PLAN FOR WORLD DOMINATION WILL BE COMPLETE.
ALL THAT FROM A CARDBOARD BOX WITH A HOLE CUT IN IT, EH?
I AM IGNORING YOU RIGHT NOW, PORTIA.
HEY JELLABY, YOU WANT TO SEE A MAGIC TRICK?
NOD NOD
SEE? AN ORDINARY BOX. BUT THEN I REACH INSIDE AND SAY THE MAGIC WORDS:
ABRA...
CADABRA!
CLAP CLAP

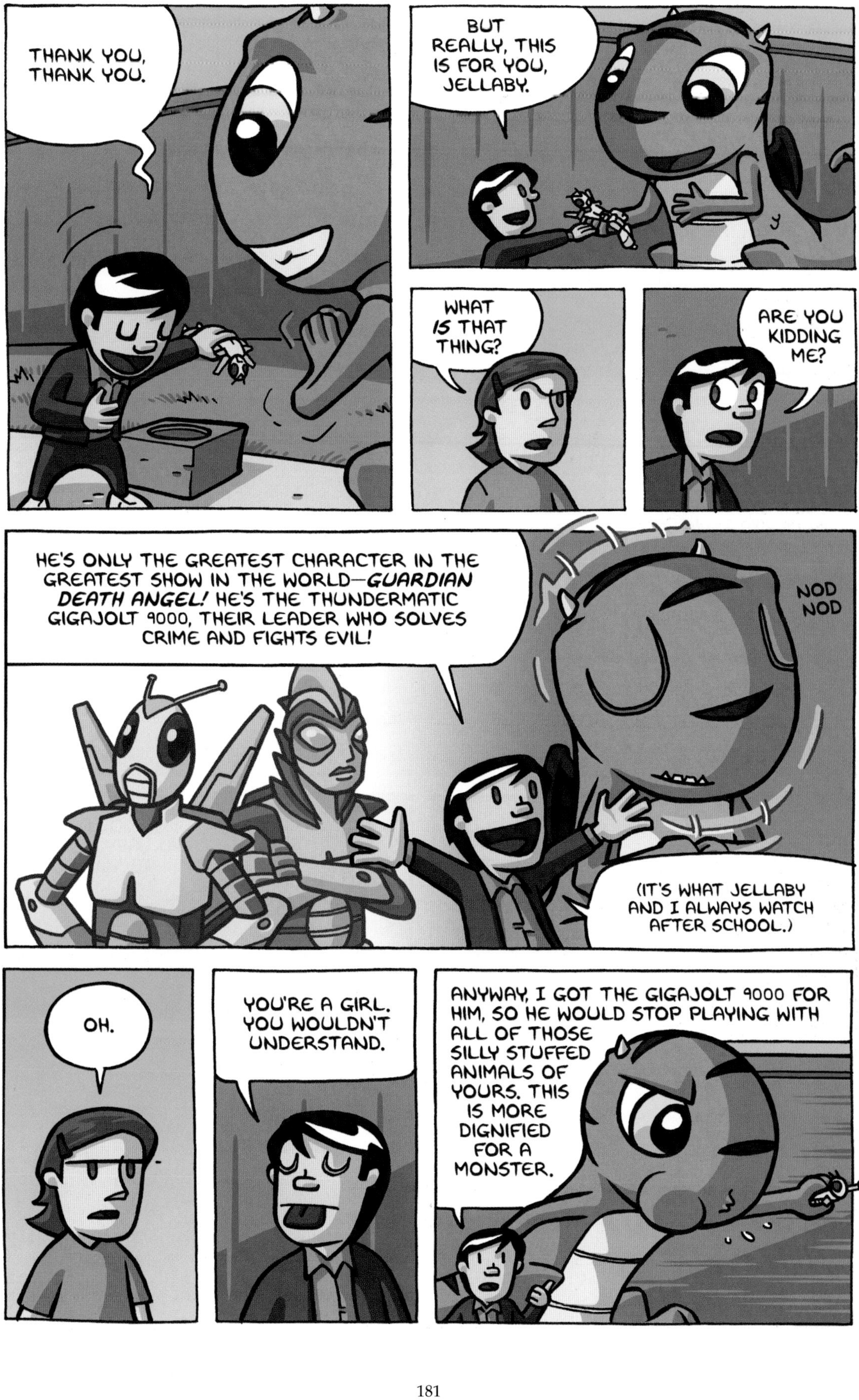
THANK YOU, THANK YOU.
BUT REALLY, THIS IS FOR YOU, JELLABY.
WHAT *IS* THAT THING?
ARE YOU KIDDING ME?
HE'S ONLY THE GREATEST CHARACTER IN THE GREATEST SHOW IN THE WORLD—*GUARDIAN DEATH ANGEL!* HE'S THE THUNDERMATIC GIGAJOLT 9000, THEIR LEADER WHO SOLVES CRIME AND FIGHTS EVIL!
NOD NOD
(IT'S WHAT JELLABY AND I ALWAYS WATCH AFTER SCHOOL.)
OH.
YOU'RE A GIRL. YOU WOULDN'T UNDERSTAND.
ANYWAY, I GOT THE GIGAJOLT 9000 FOR HIM, SO HE WOULD STOP PLAYING WITH ALL OF THOSE SILLY STUFFED ANIMALS OF YOURS. THIS IS MORE DIGNIFIED FOR A MONSTER.

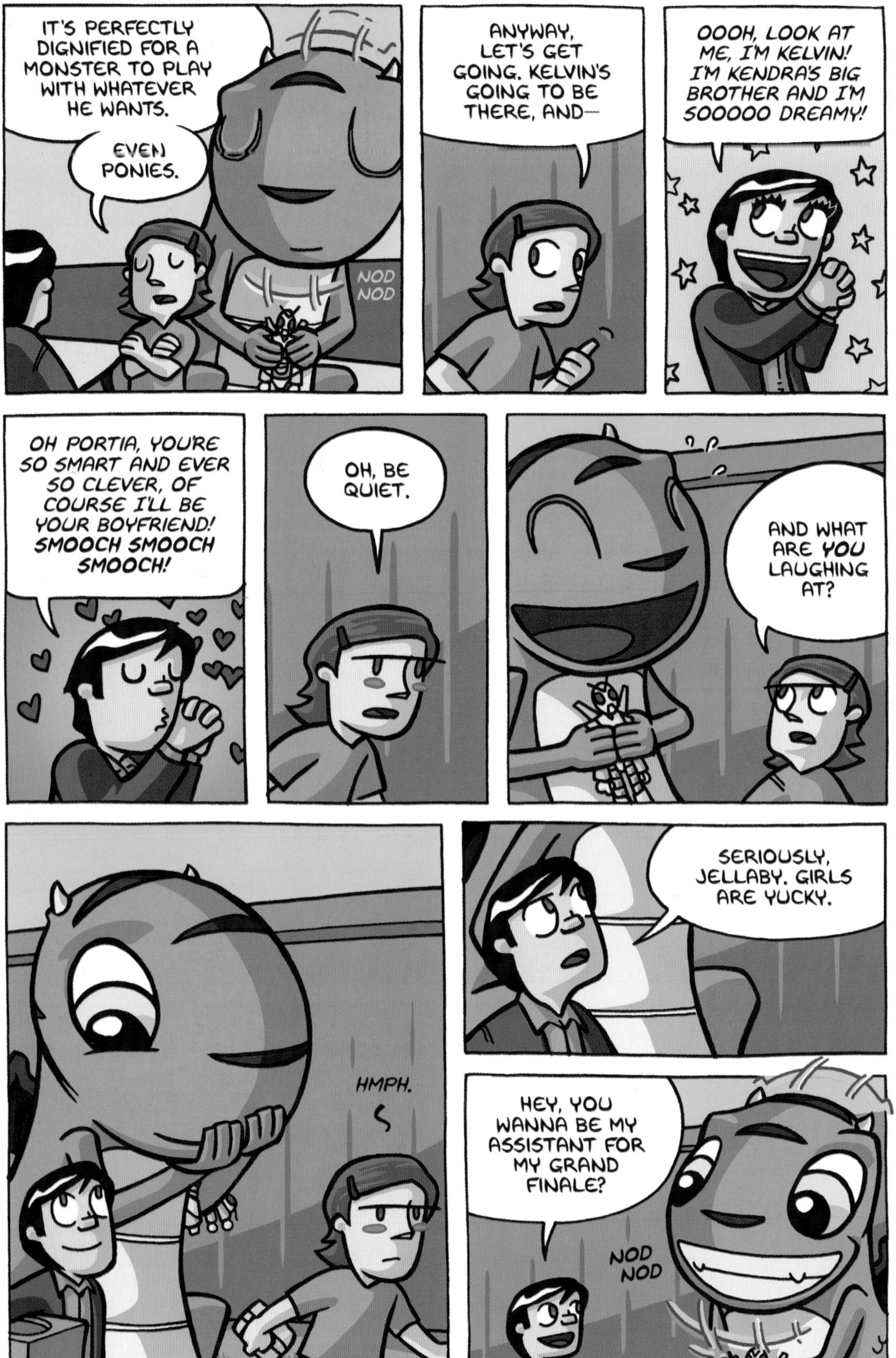
IT'S PERFECTLY DIGNIFIED FOR A MONSTER TO PLAY WITH WHATEVER HE WANTS.
EVEN PONIES.
NOD NOD
ANYWAY, LET'S GET GOING. KELVIN'S GOING TO BE THERE, AND—
OOOH, LOOK AT ME, I'M KELVIN! I'M KENDRA'S BIG BROTHER AND I'M SOOOOO DREAMY!
OH PORTIA, YOU'RE SO SMART AND EVER SO CLEVER, OF COURSE I'LL BE YOUR BOYFRIEND! SMOOCH SMOOCH SMOOCH!
OH, BE QUIET.
AND WHAT ARE YOU LAUGHING AT?
HMPH.
SERIOUSLY, JELLABY. GIRLS ARE YUCKY.
HEY, YOU WANNA BE MY ASSISTANT FOR MY GRAND FINALE?
NOD NOD

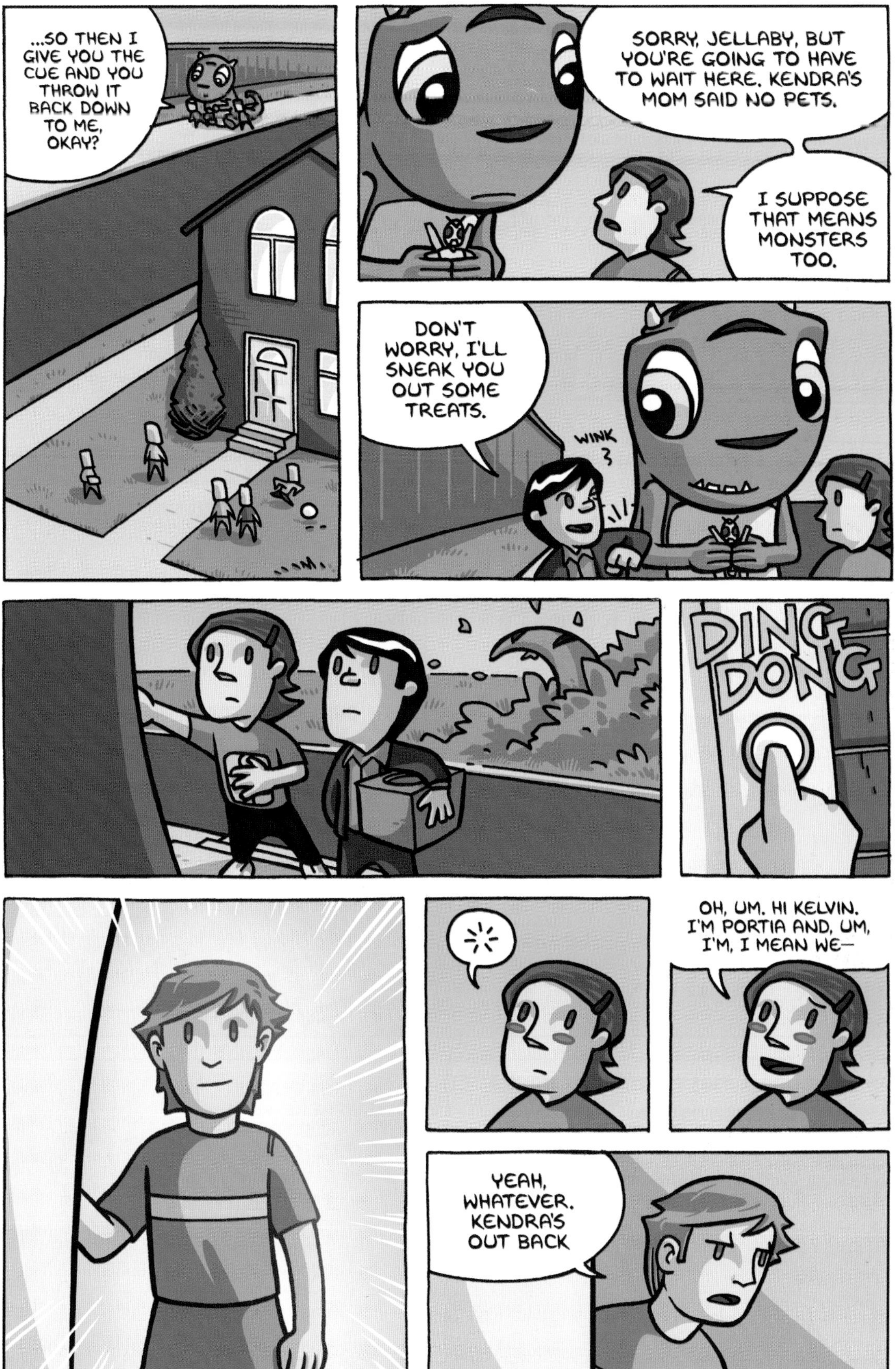
...SO THEN I GIVE YOU THE CUE AND YOU THROW IT BACK DOWN TO ME, OKAY?
SORRY, JELLABY, BUT YOU'RE GOING TO HAVE TO WAIT HERE. KENDRA'S MOM SAID NO PETS.
I SUPPOSE THAT MEANS MONSTERS TOO.
DON'T WORRY, I'LL SNEAK YOU OUT SOME TREATS.
WINK
DING DONG
OH, UM. HI KELVIN. I'M PORTIA AND, UM, I'M, I MEAN WE—
YEAH, WHATEVER. KENDRA'S OUT BACK

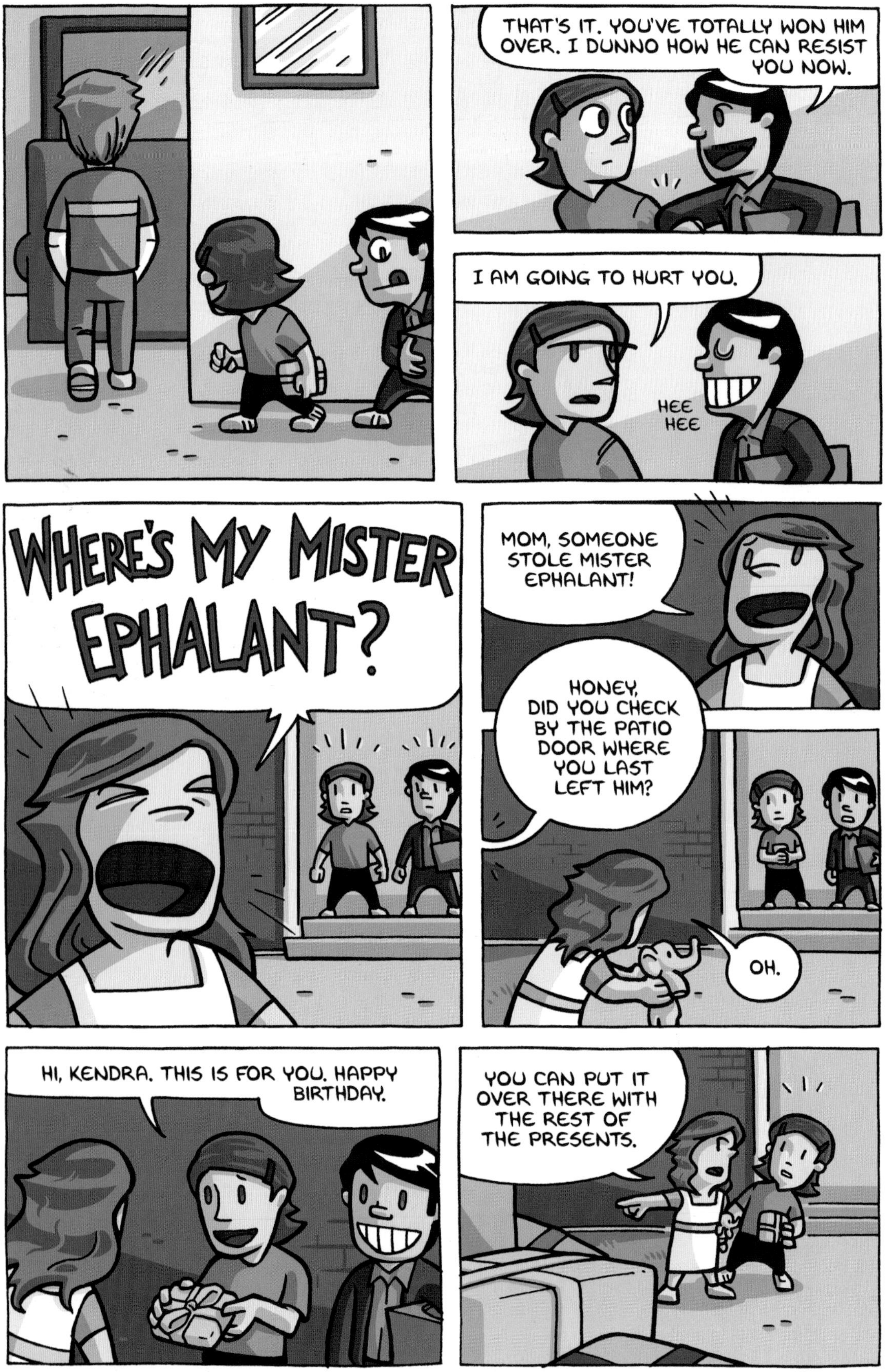
THAT'S IT. YOU'VE TOTALLY WON HIM OVER. I DUNNO HOW HE CAN RESIST YOU NOW.
I AM GOING TO HURT YOU.
HEE HEE
WHERE'S MY MISTER EPHALANT?
MOM, SOMEONE STOLE MISTER EPHALANT!
HONEY, DID YOU CHECK BY THE PATIO DOOR WHERE YOU LAST LEFT HIM?
OH.
HI, KENDRA. THIS IS FOR YOU. HAPPY BIRTHDAY.
YOU CAN PUT IT OVER THERE WITH THE REST OF THE PRESENTS.

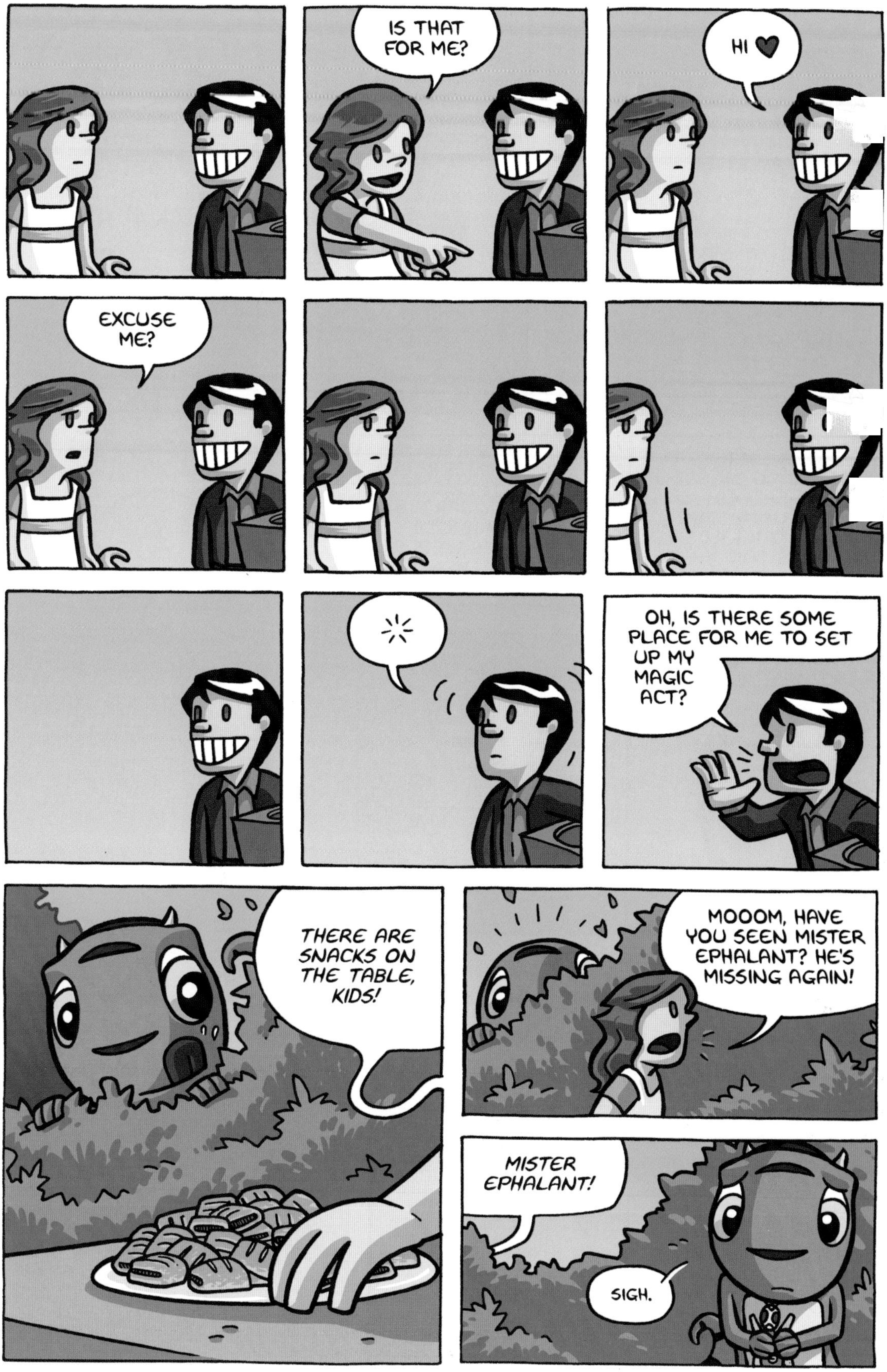
IS THAT FOR ME?
HI ♥
EXCUSE ME?
OH, IS THERE SOME PLACE FOR ME TO SET UP MY MAGIC ACT?
THERE ARE SNACKS ON THE TABLE, KIDS!
MOOOM, HAVE YOU SEEN MISTER EPHALANT? HE'S MISSING AGAIN!
MISTER EPHALANT!
SIGH.

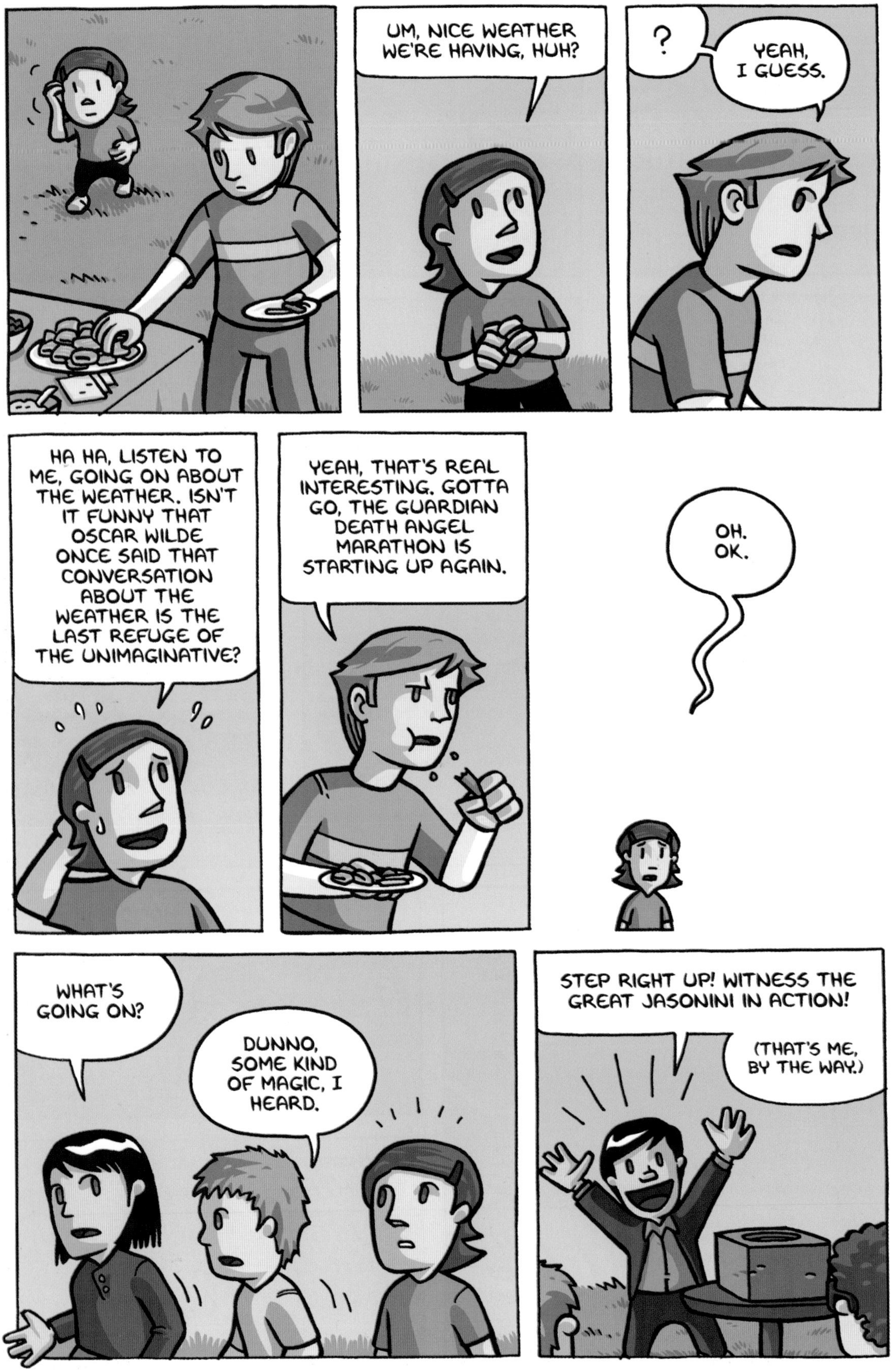
UM, NICE WEATHER WE'RE HAVING, HUH?
?
YEAH, I GUESS.
HA HA, LISTEN TO ME, GOING ON ABOUT THE WEATHER. ISN'T IT FUNNY THAT OSCAR WILDE ONCE SAID THAT CONVERSATION ABOUT THE WEATHER IS THE LAST REFUGE OF THE UNIMAGINATIVE?
YEAH, THAT'S REAL INTERESTING. GOTTA GO, THE GUARDIAN DEATH ANGEL MARATHON IS STARTING UP AGAIN.
OH. OK.
WHAT'S GOING ON?
DUNNO, SOME KIND OF MAGIC, I HEARD.
STEP RIGHT UP! WITNESS THE GREAT JASONINI IN ACTION!
(THAT'S ME, BY THE WAY.)

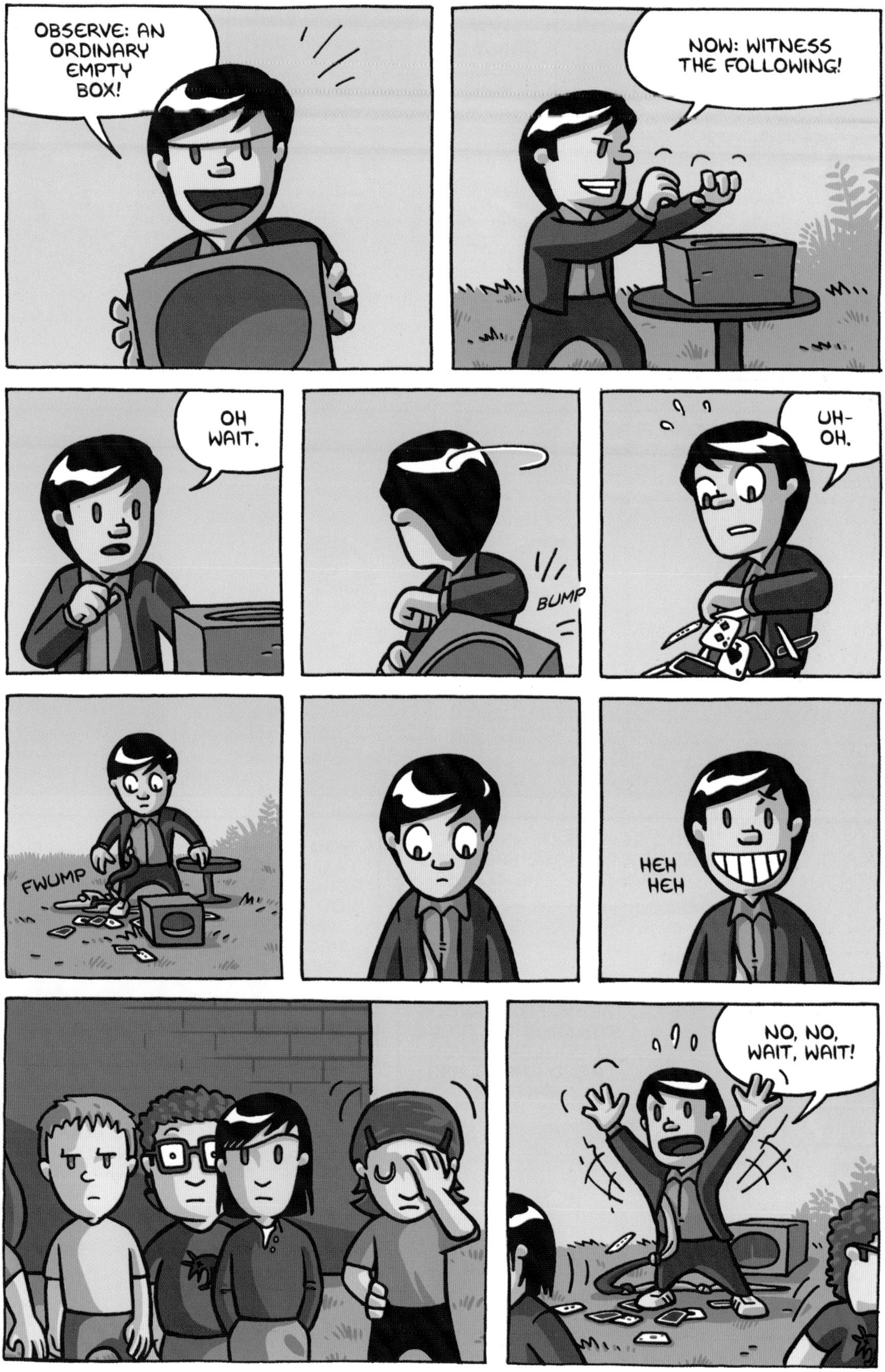
OBSERVE: AN ORDINARY EMPTY BOX!
NOW: WITNESS THE FOLLOWING!
OH WAIT.
BUMP
UH-OH.
FWUMP
HEH HEH
NO, NO, WAIT, WAIT!

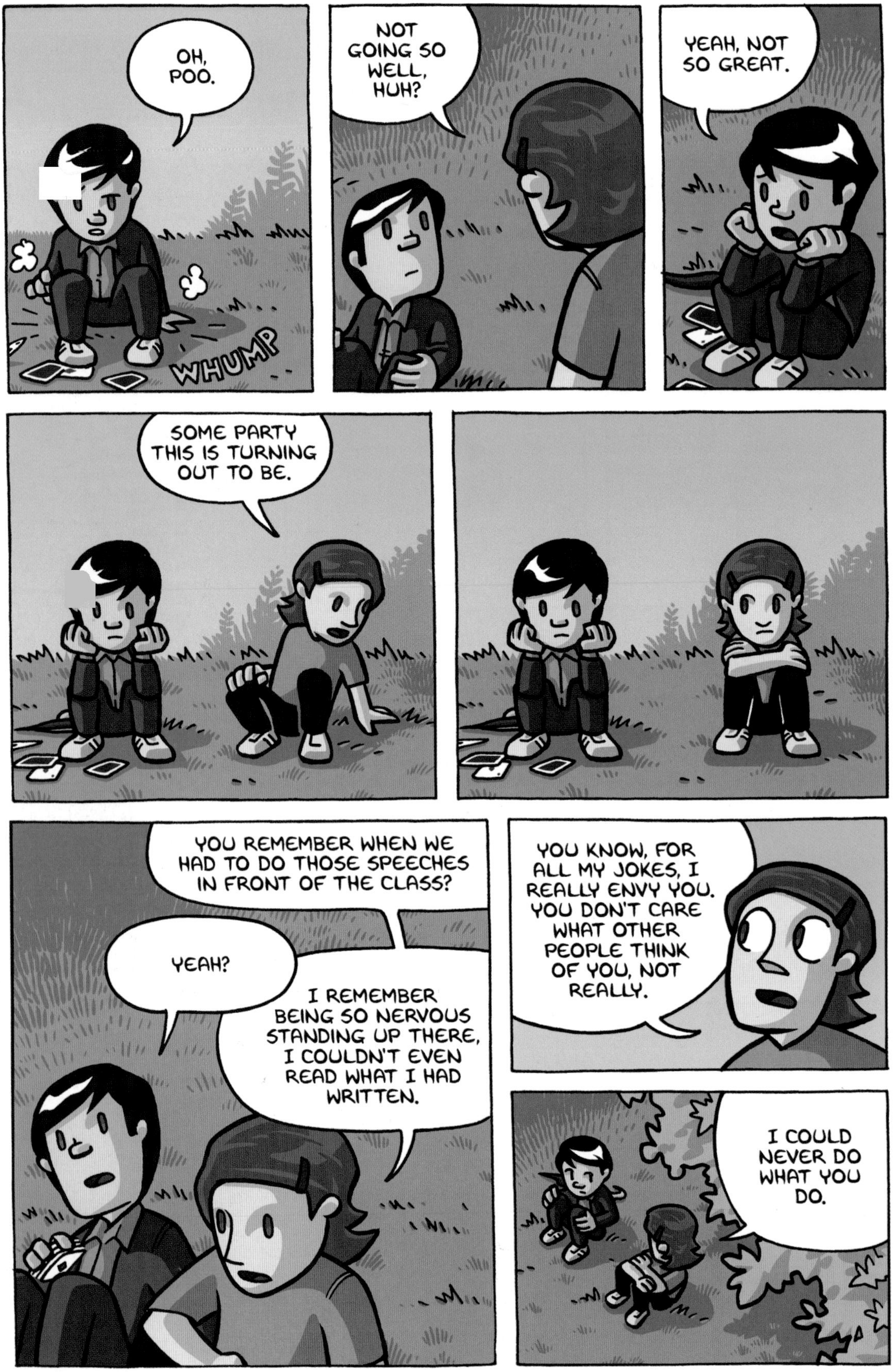
OH, POO.
WHUMP
NOT GOING SO WELL, HUH?
YEAH, NOT SO GREAT.
SOME PARTY THIS IS TURNING OUT TO BE.
YOU REMEMBER WHEN WE HAD TO DO THOSE SPEECHES IN FRONT OF THE CLASS?
YEAH?
I REMEMBER BEING SO NERVOUS STANDING UP THERE, I COULDN'T EVEN READ WHAT I HAD WRITTEN.
YOU KNOW, FOR ALL MY JOKES, I REALLY ENVY YOU. YOU DON'T CARE WHAT OTHER PEOPLE THINK OF YOU, NOT REALLY.
I COULD NEVER DO WHAT YOU DO.

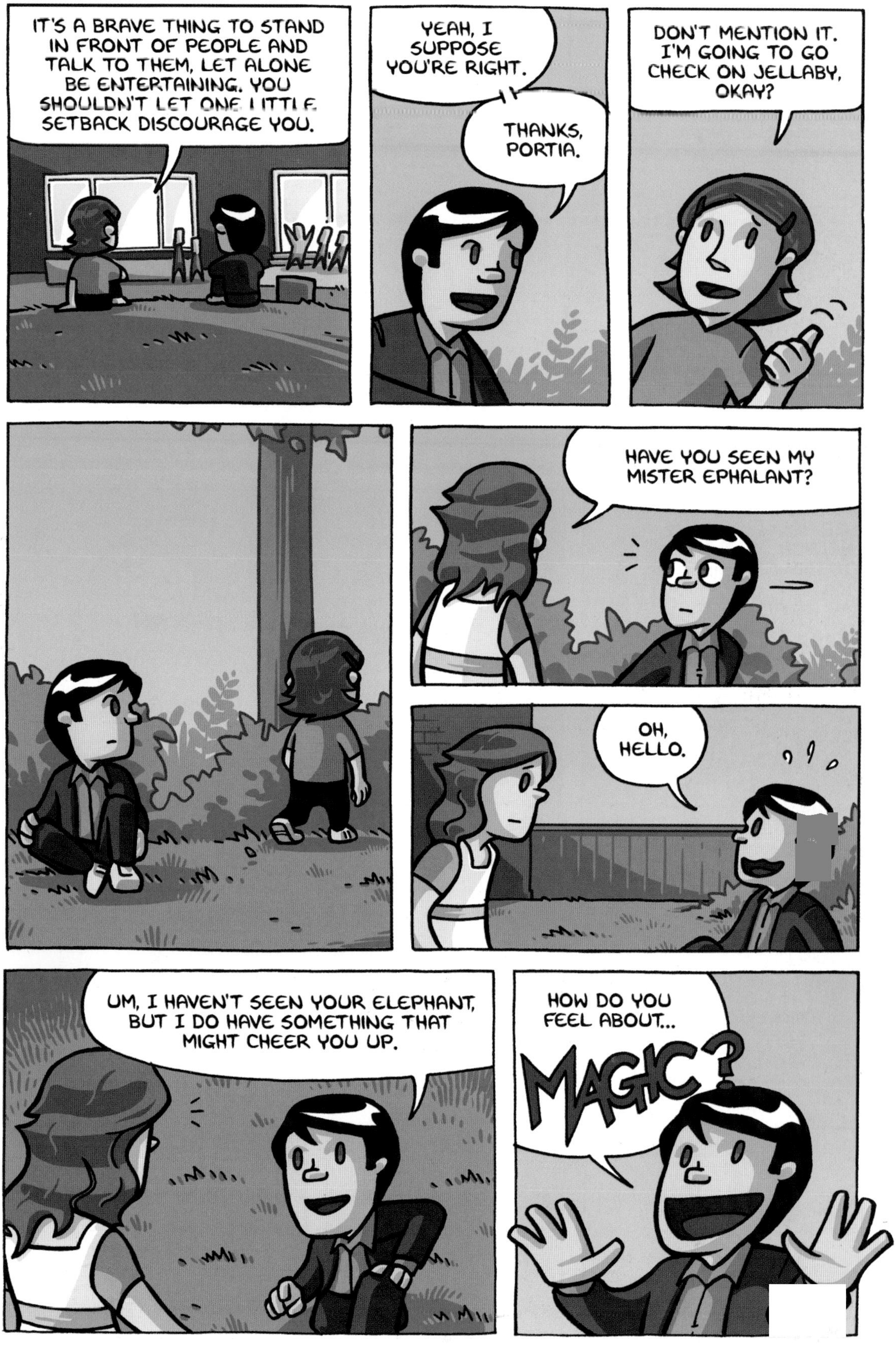
IT'S A BRAVE THING TO STAND IN FRONT OF PEOPLE AND TALK TO THEM, LET ALONE BE ENTERTAINING. YOU SHOULDN'T LET ONE LITTLE SETBACK DISCOURAGE YOU.
YEAH, I SUPPOSE YOU'RE RIGHT.
THANKS, PORTIA.
DON'T MENTION IT. I'M GOING TO GO CHECK ON JELLABY, OKAY?
HAVE YOU SEEN MY MISTER EPHALANT?
OH, HELLO.
UM, I HAVEN'T SEEN YOUR ELEPHANT, BUT I DO HAVE SOMETHING THAT MIGHT CHEER YOU UP.
HOW DO YOU FEEL ABOUT...
MAGIC?

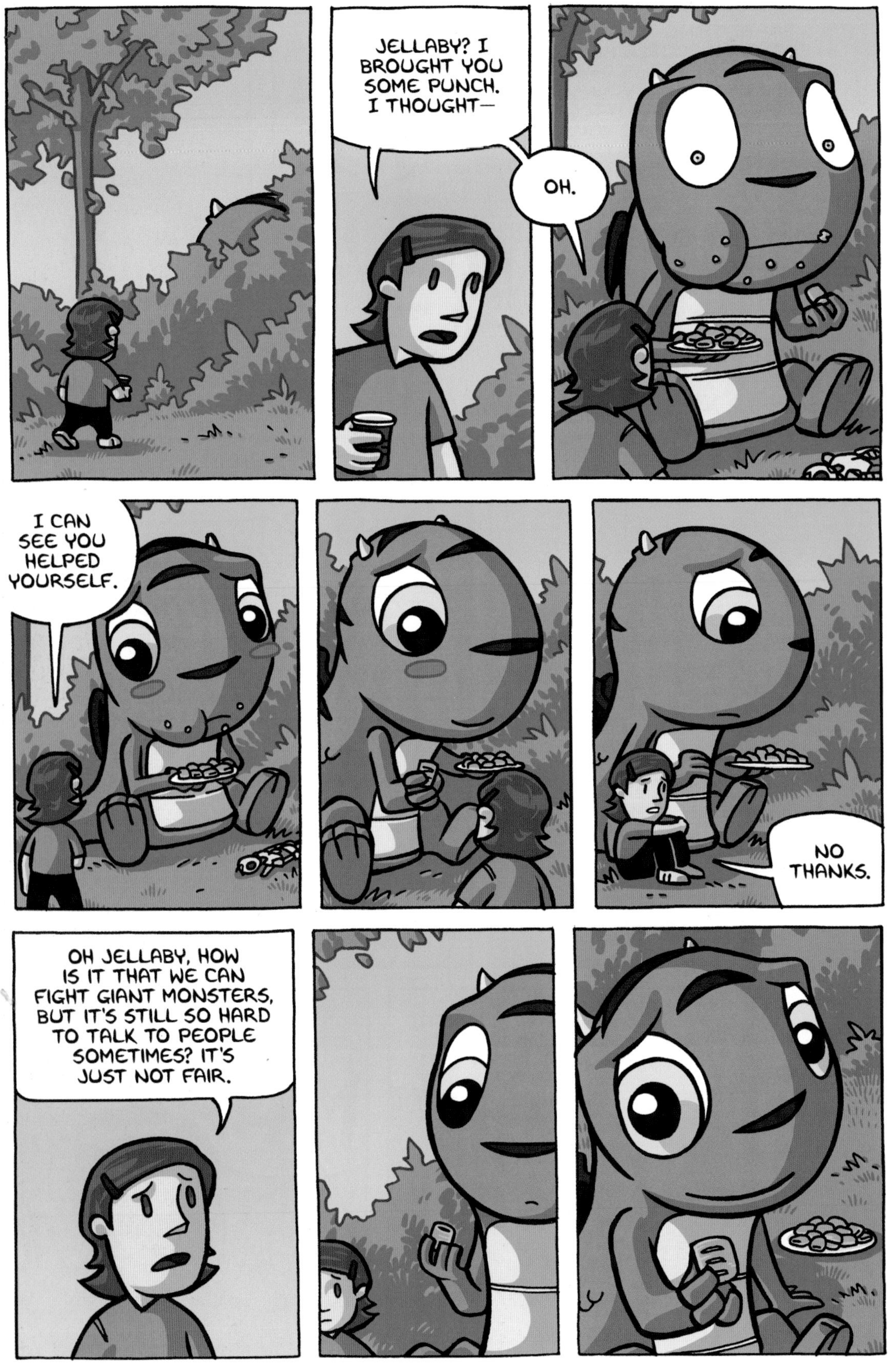

JELLABY? I BROUGHT YOU SOME PUNCH. I THOUGHT—
OH.
I CAN SEE YOU HELPED YOURSELF.
NO THANKS.
OH JELLABY, HOW IS IT THAT WE CAN FIGHT GIANT MONSTERS, BUT IT'S STILL SO HARD TO TALK TO PEOPLE SOMETIMES? IT'S JUST NOT FAIR.

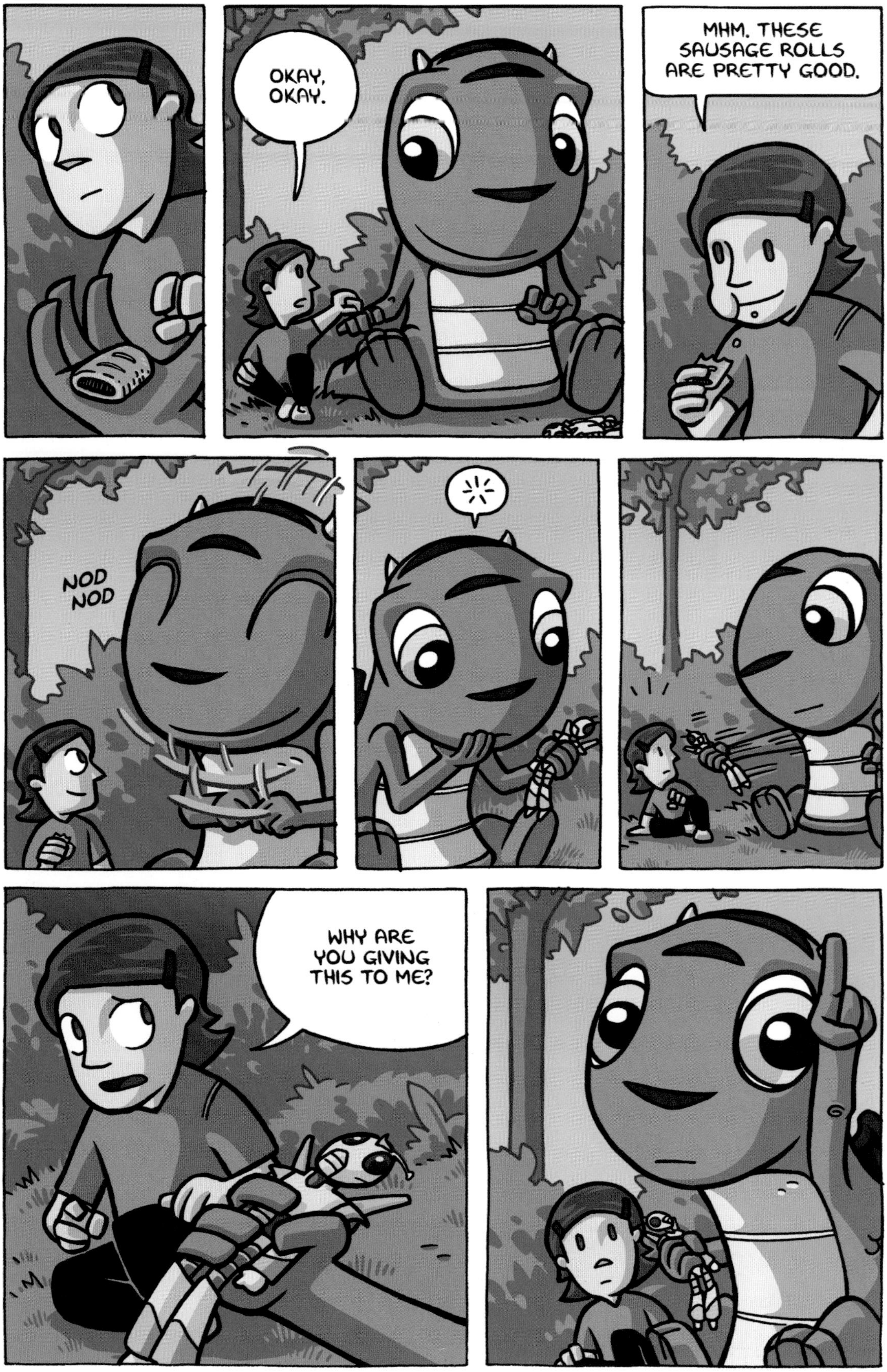
OKAY, OKAY.
MHM. THESE SAUSAGE ROLLS ARE PRETTY GOOD.
NOD NOD
WHY ARE YOU GIVING THIS TO ME?

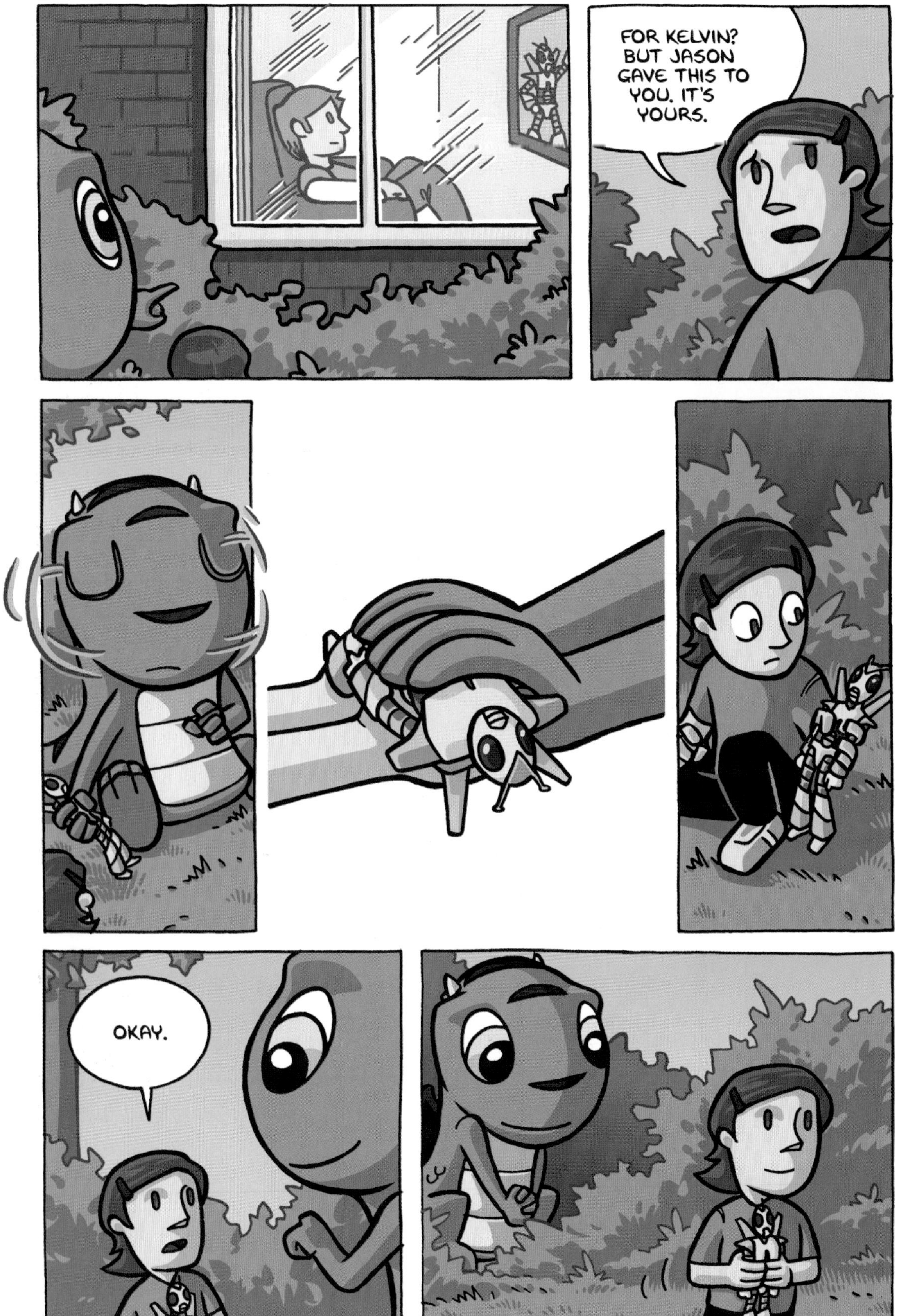
FOR KELVIN? BUT JASON GAVE THIS TO YOU. IT'S YOURS.
OKAY.

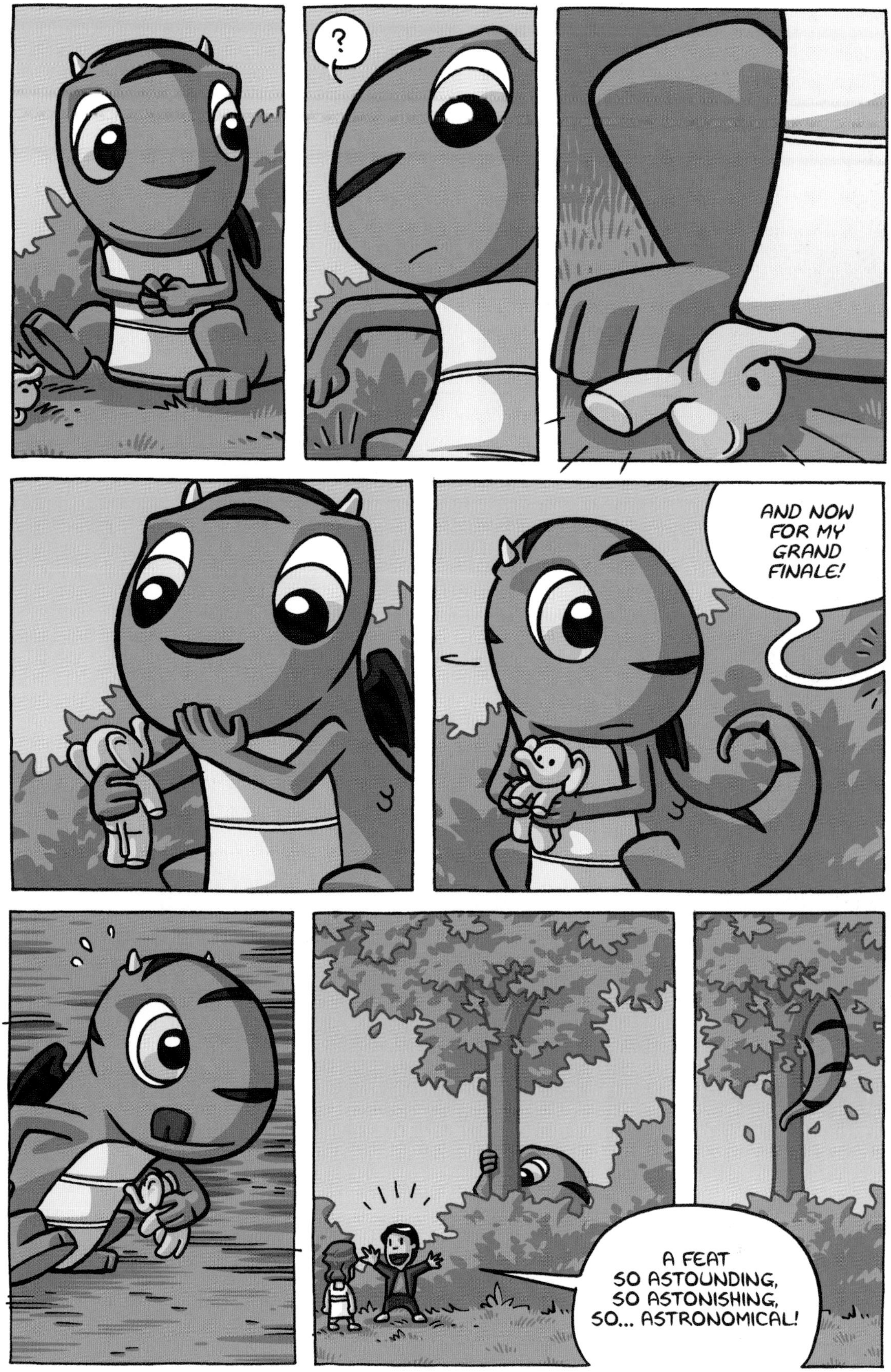

?
AND NOW FOR MY GRAND FINALE!
A FEAT SO ASTOUNDING, SO ASTONISHING, SO... ASTRONOMICAL!

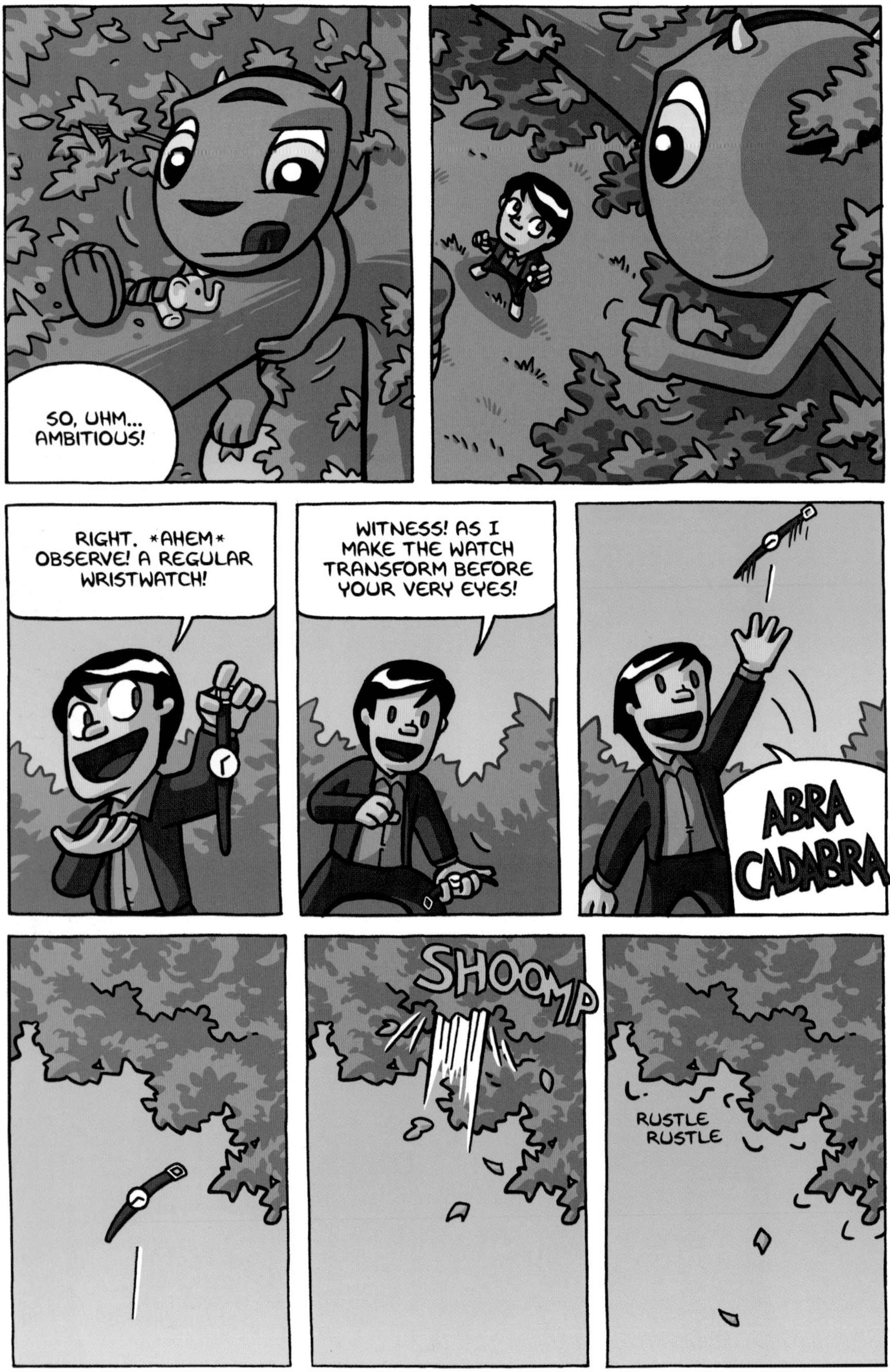
SO, UHM... AMBITIOUS!
RIGHT. *AHEM* OBSERVE! A REGULAR WRISTWATCH!
WITNESS! AS I MAKE THE WATCH TRANSFORM BEFORE YOUR VERY EYES!
ABRA CADABRA!
SHOOMP
RUSTLE RUSTLE

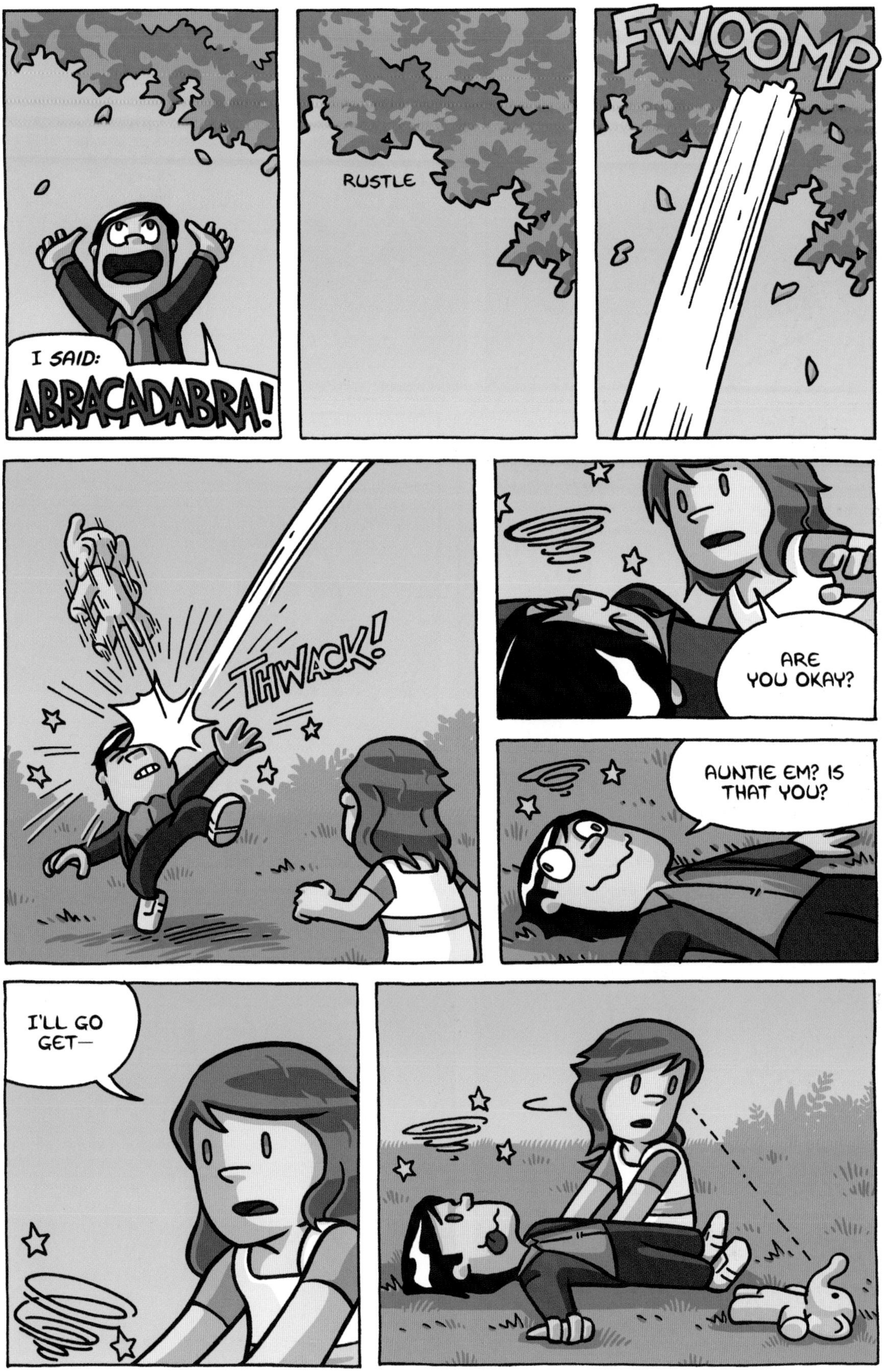
I SAID:
ABRACADABRA!
RUSTLE
FWOOMP
THWACK!
ARE YOU OKAY?
AUNTIE EM? IS THAT YOU?
I'LL GO GET—

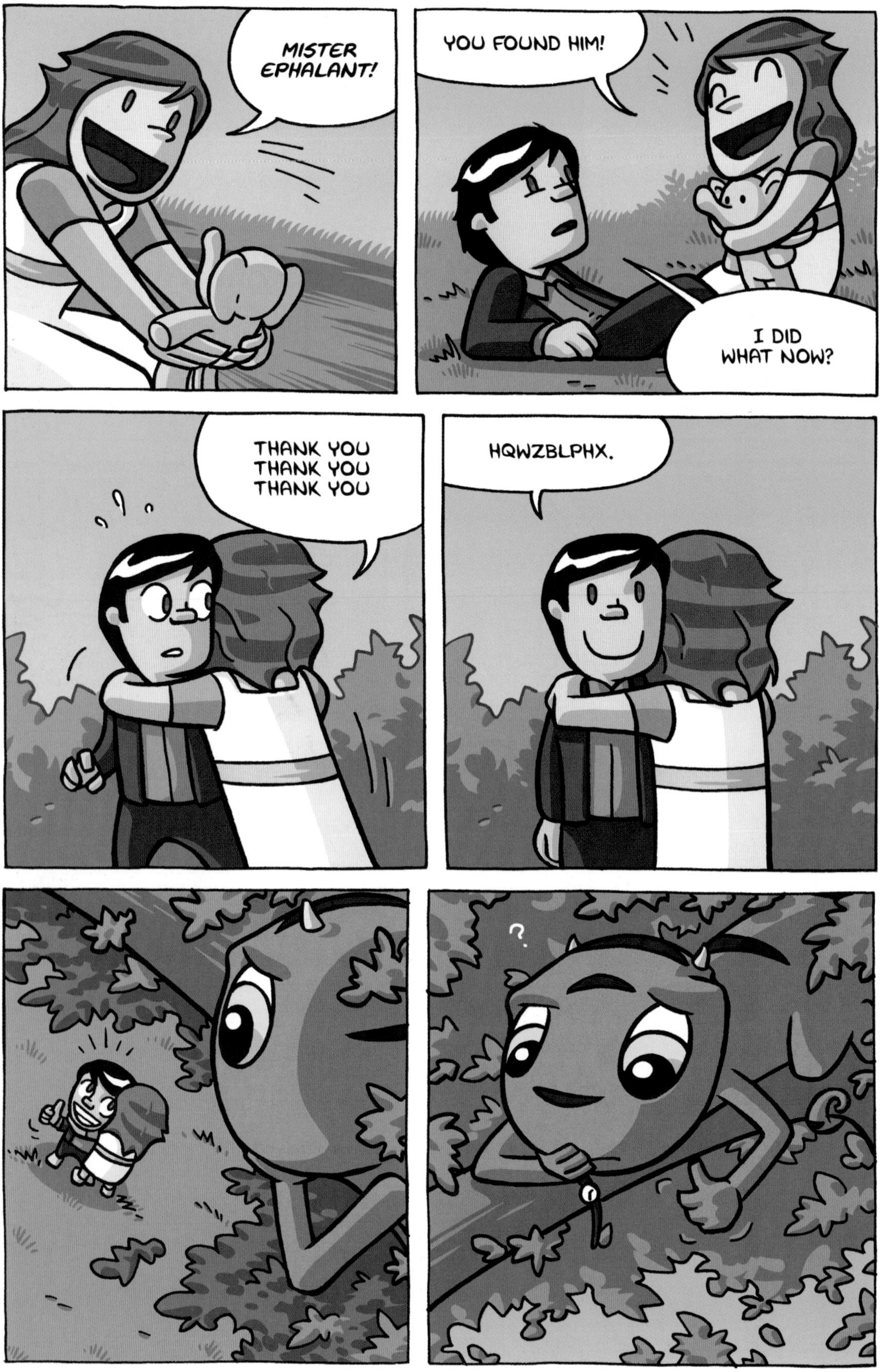
MISTER EPHALANT!
YOU FOUND HIM!
I DID WHAT NOW?
THANK YOU THANK YOU THANK YOU
HQWZBLPHX.

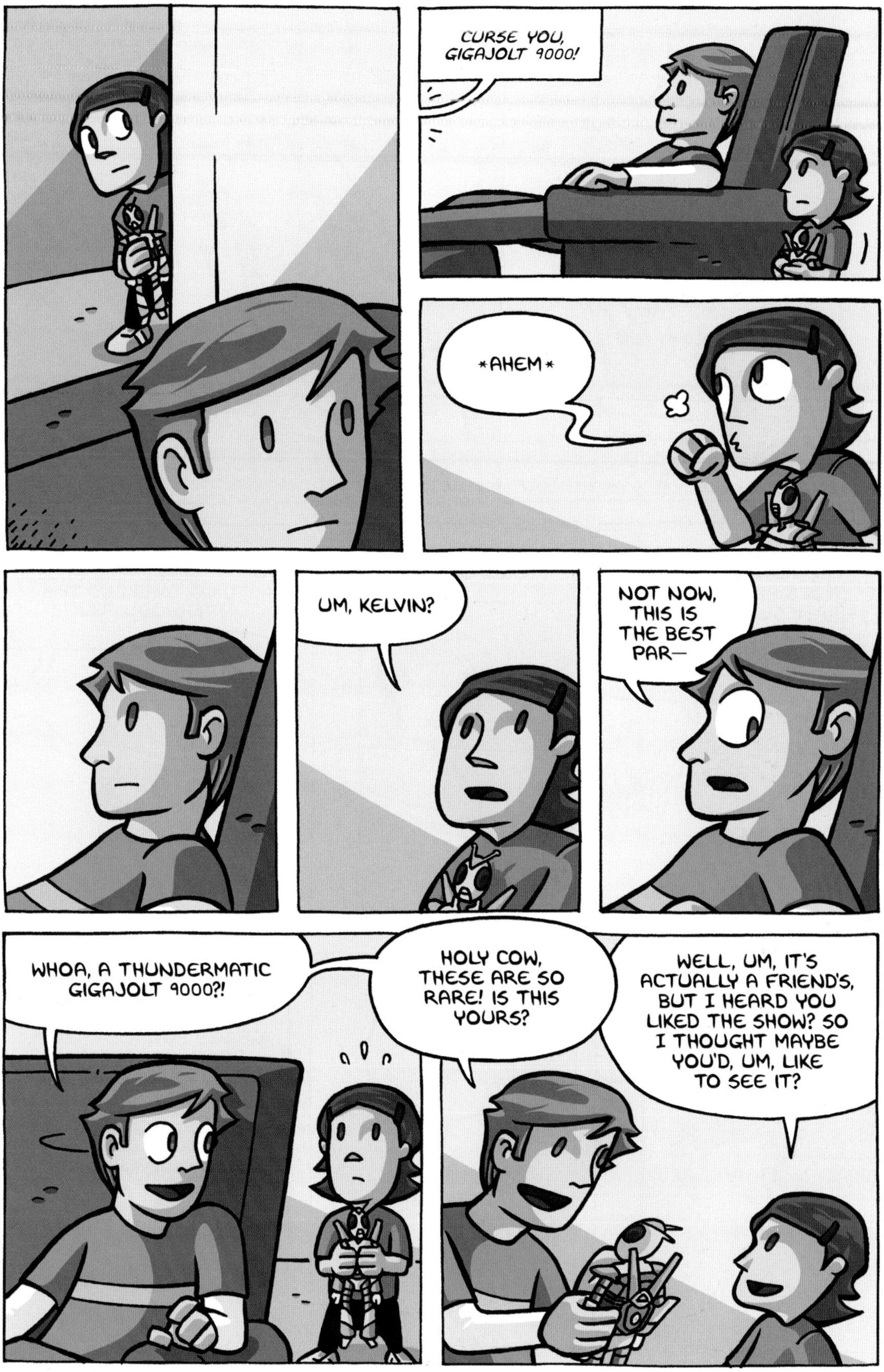
CURSE YOU, GIGAJOLT 9000!
AHEM
UM, KELVIN?
NOT NOW, THIS IS THE BEST PAR—
WHOA, A THUNDERMATIC GIGAJOLT 9000?!
HOLY COW, THESE ARE SO RARE! IS THIS YOURS?
WELL, UM, IT'S ACTUALLY A FRIEND'S, BUT I HEARD YOU LIKED THE SHOW? SO I THOUGHT MAYBE YOU'D, UM, LIKE TO SEE IT?

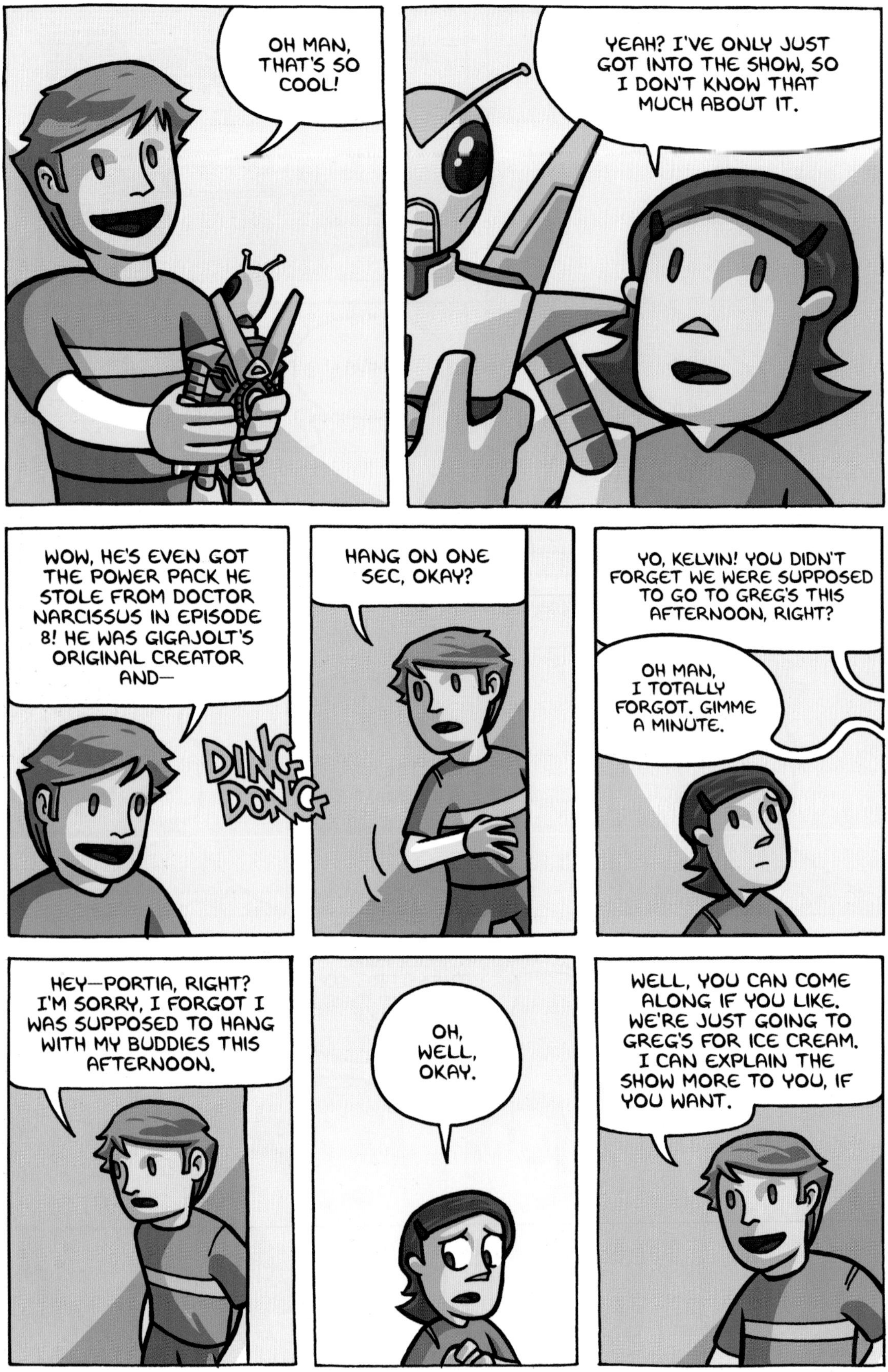
OH MAN, THAT'S SO COOL!
YEAH? I'VE ONLY JUST GOT INTO THE SHOW, SO I DON'T KNOW THAT MUCH ABOUT IT.
WOW, HE'S EVEN GOT THE POWER PACK HE STOLE FROM DOCTOR NARCISSUS IN EPISODE 8! HE WAS GIGAJOLT'S ORIGINAL CREATOR AND—
DING DONG
HANG ON ONE SEC, OKAY?
YO, KELVIN! YOU DIDN'T FORGET WE WERE SUPPOSED TO GO TO GREG'S THIS AFTERNOON, RIGHT?
OH MAN, I TOTALLY FORGOT. GIMME A MINUTE.
HEY—PORTIA, RIGHT? I'M SORRY, I FORGOT I WAS SUPPOSED TO HANG WITH MY BUDDIES THIS AFTERNOON.
OH, WELL, OKAY.
WELL, YOU CAN COME ALONG IF YOU LIKE. WE'RE JUST GOING TO GREG'S FOR ICE CREAM. I CAN EXPLAIN THE SHOW MORE TO YOU, IF YOU WANT.

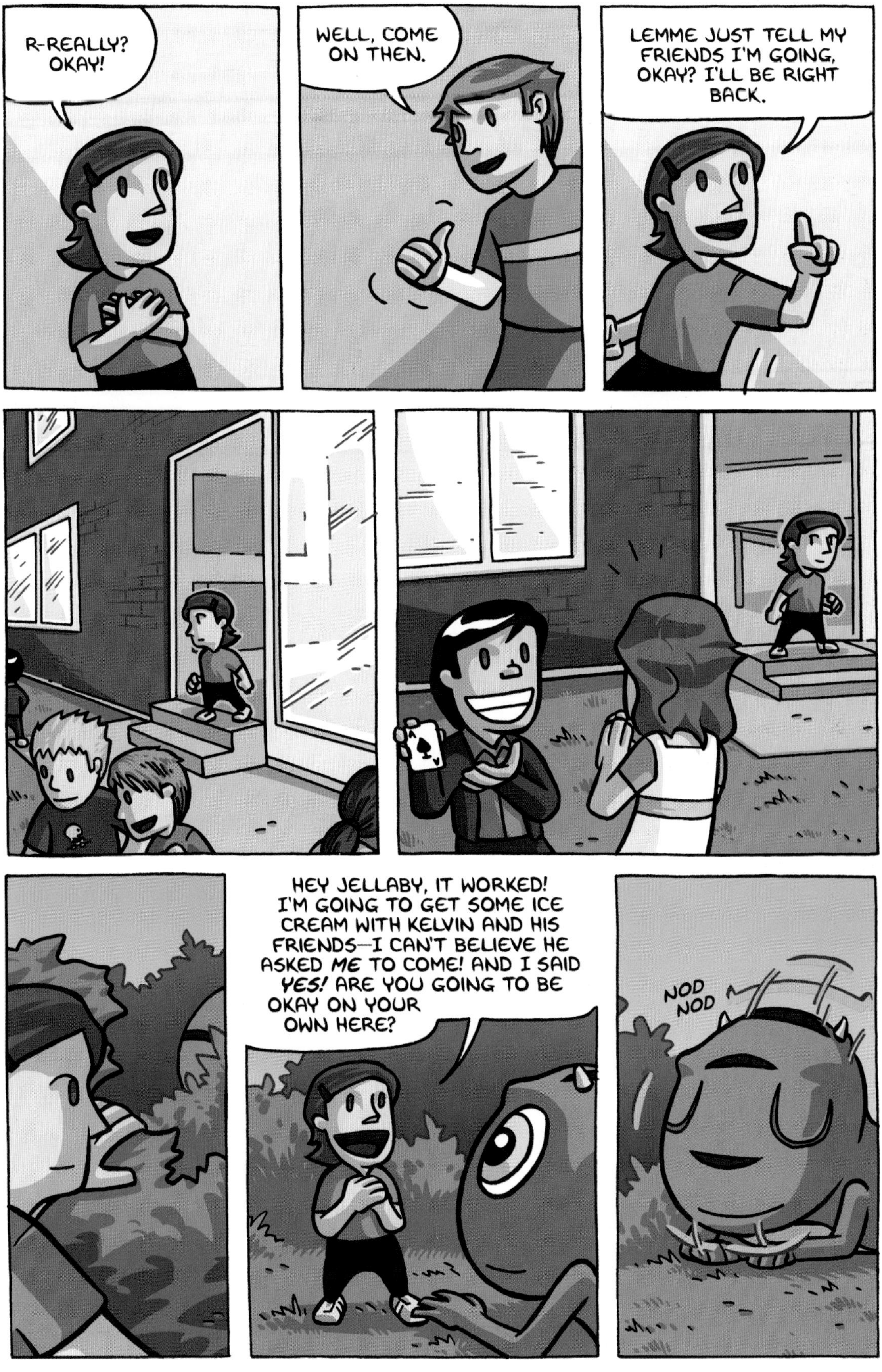
R-REALLY? OKAY!
WELL, COME ON THEN.
LEMME JUST TELL MY FRIENDS I'M GOING, OKAY? I'LL BE RIGHT BACK.
HEY JELLABY, IT WORKED! I'M GOING TO GET SOME ICE CREAM WITH KELVIN AND HIS FRIENDS—I CAN'T BELIEVE HE ASKED *ME* TO COME! AND I SAID *YES!* ARE YOU GOING TO BE OKAY ON YOUR OWN HERE?
NOD NOD

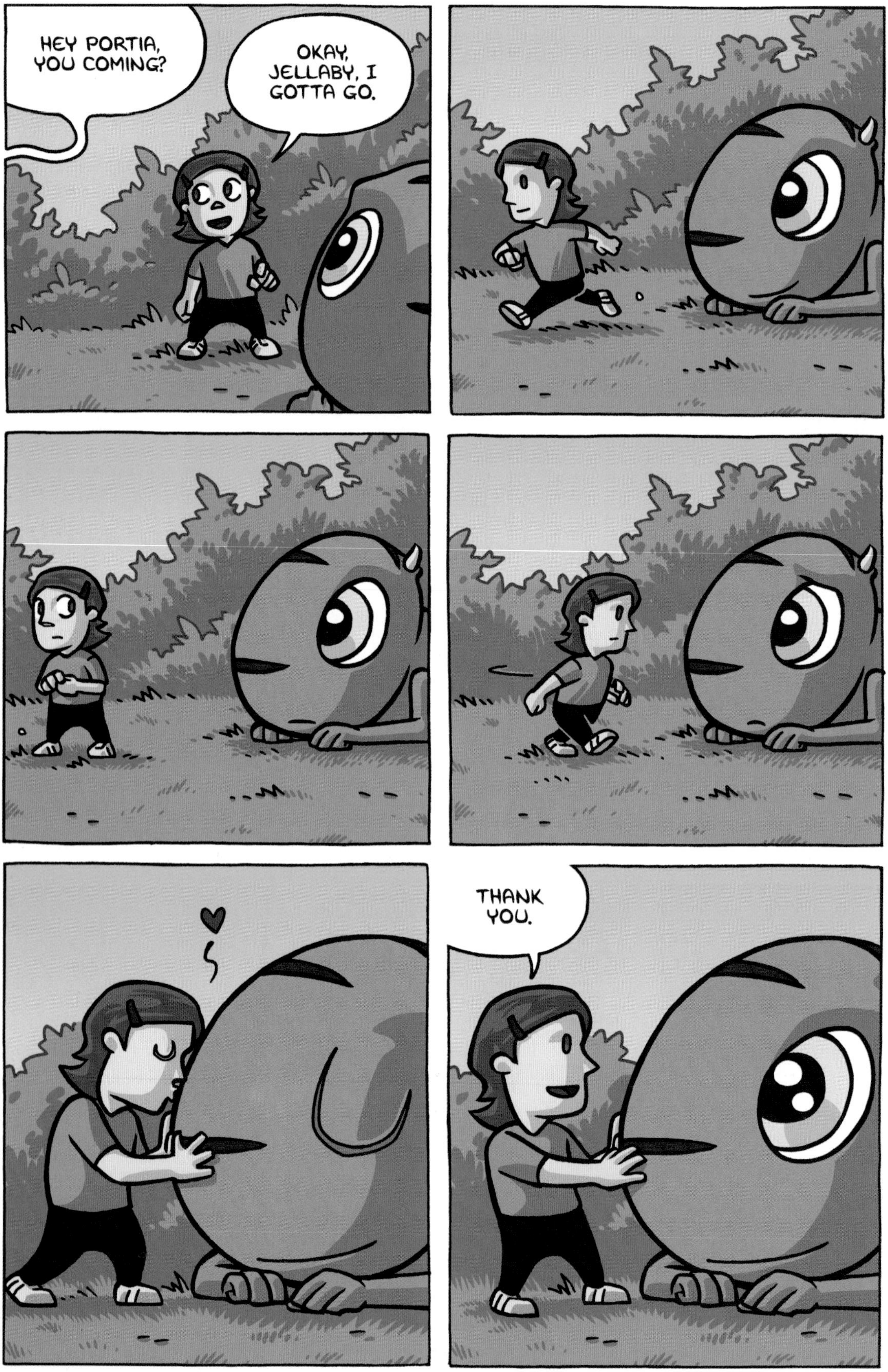
HEY PORTIA, YOU COMING?
OKAY, JELLABY, I GOTTA GO.
THANK YOU.

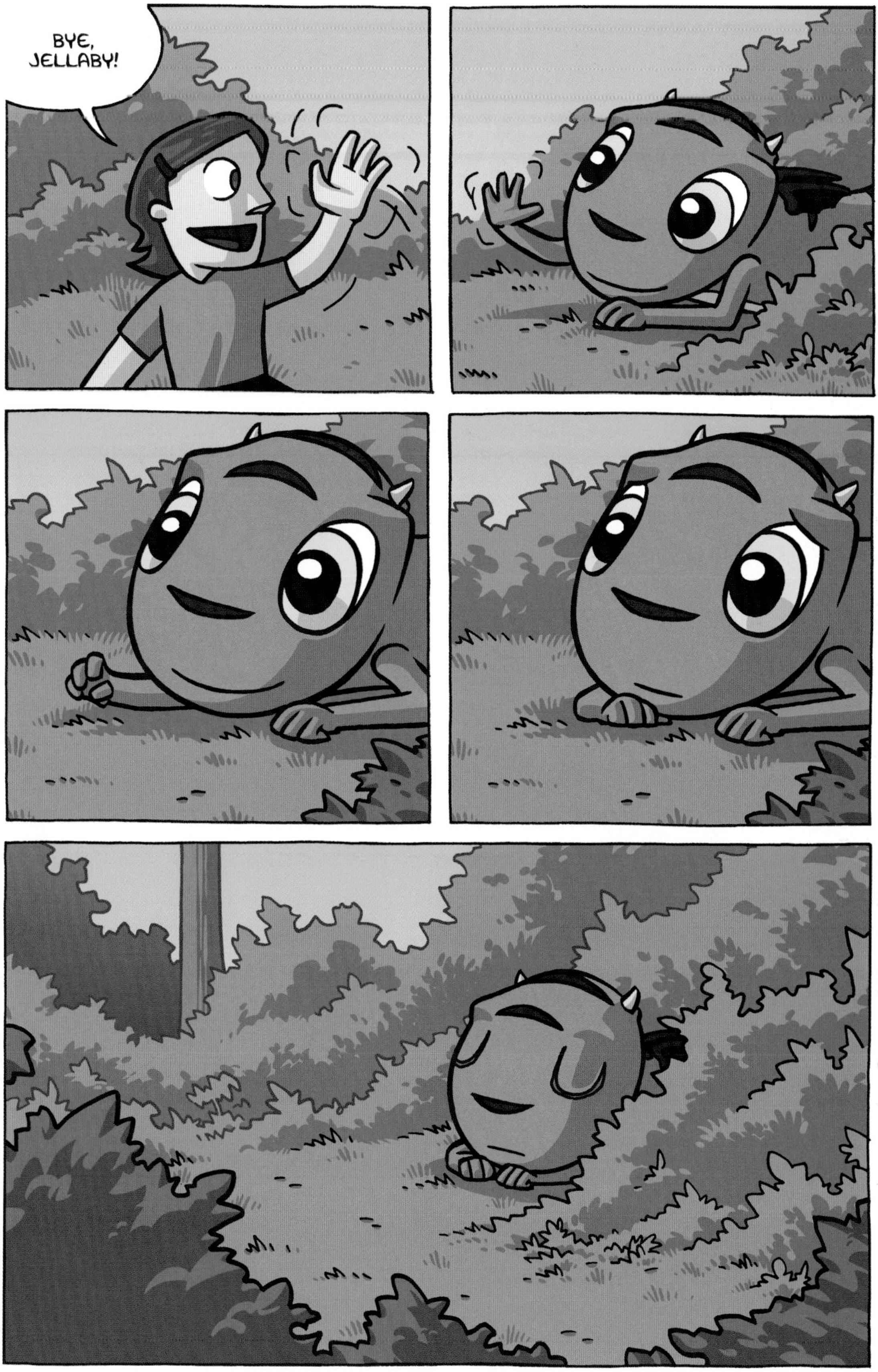
BYE, JELLABY!

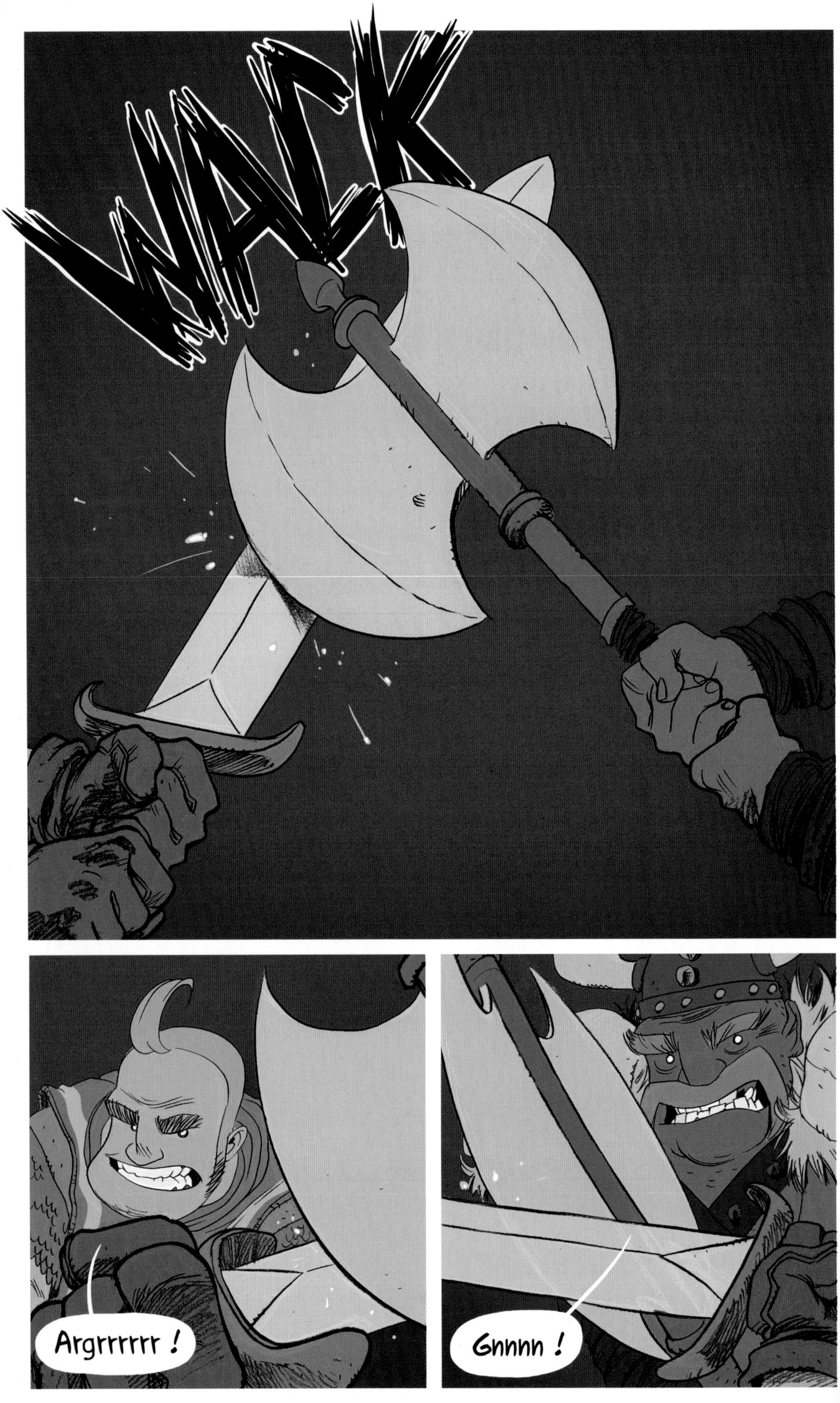
WACK
Argrrrrrr !
Gnnnn !

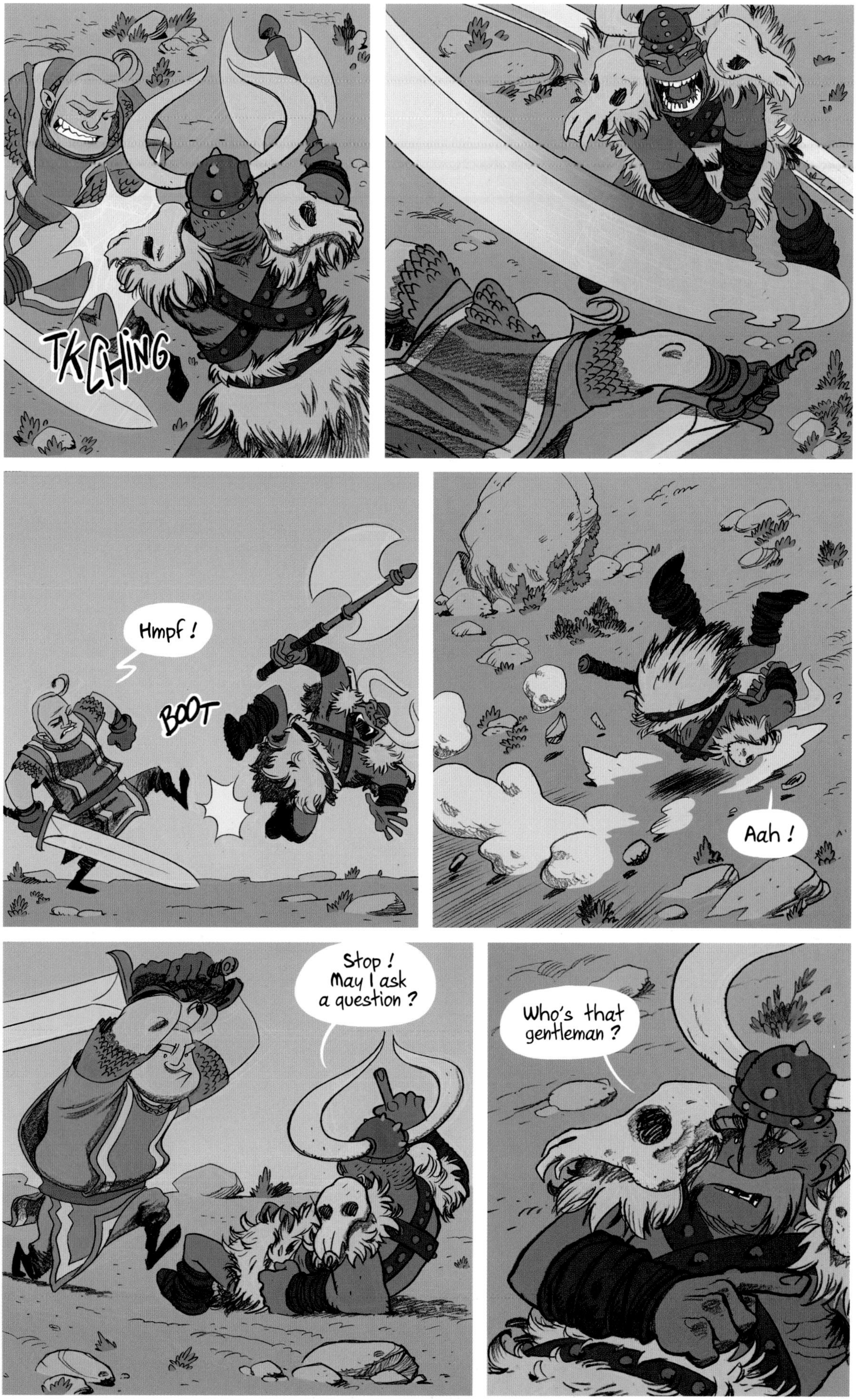
TKCHING
Hmpf!
BOOT
Aah!
Stop! May I ask a question?
Who's that gentleman?

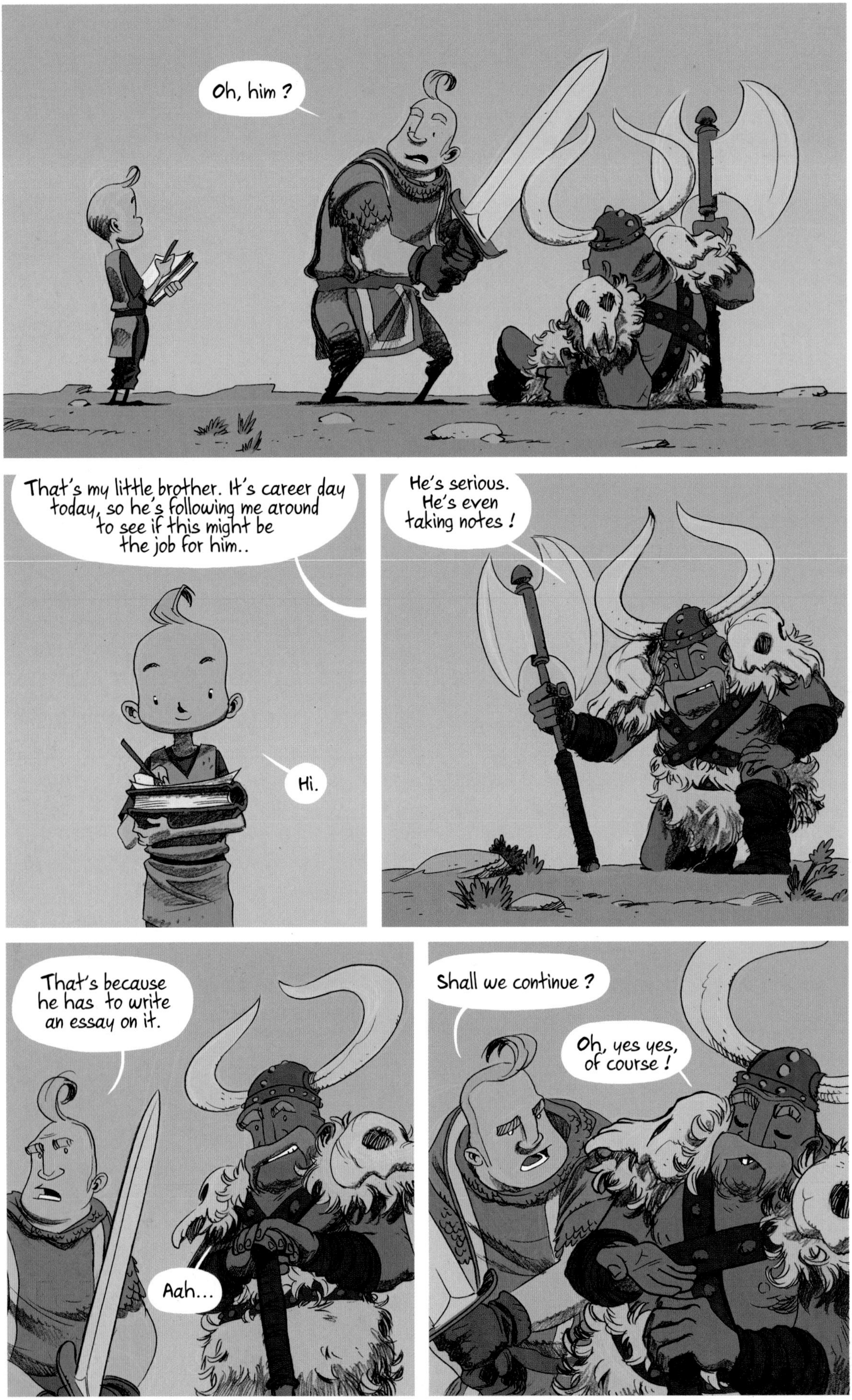
Oh, him ?
That's my little brother. It's career day today, so he's following me around to see if this might be the job for him..
Hi.
He's serious. He's even taking notes !
That's because he has to write an essay on it.
Aah...
Shall we continue ?
Oh, yes yes, of course !

Career Day

by Bannister & Grimaldi

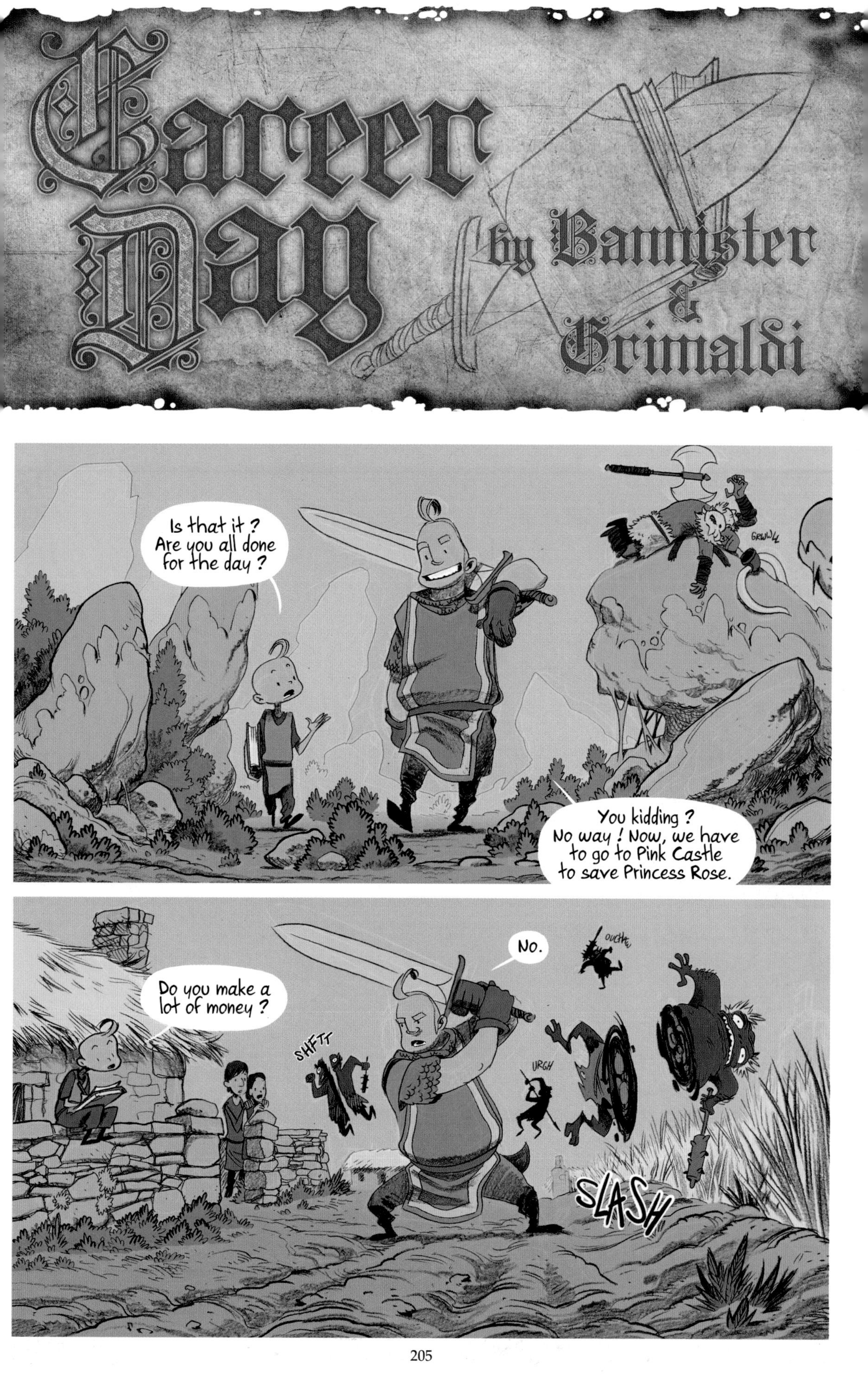
Is that it ? Are you all done for the day ?
GRWWL
You kidding ? No way ! Now, we have to go to Pink Castle to save Princess Rose.
Do you make a lot of money ?
No.
SHFTT
URGH
SLASH

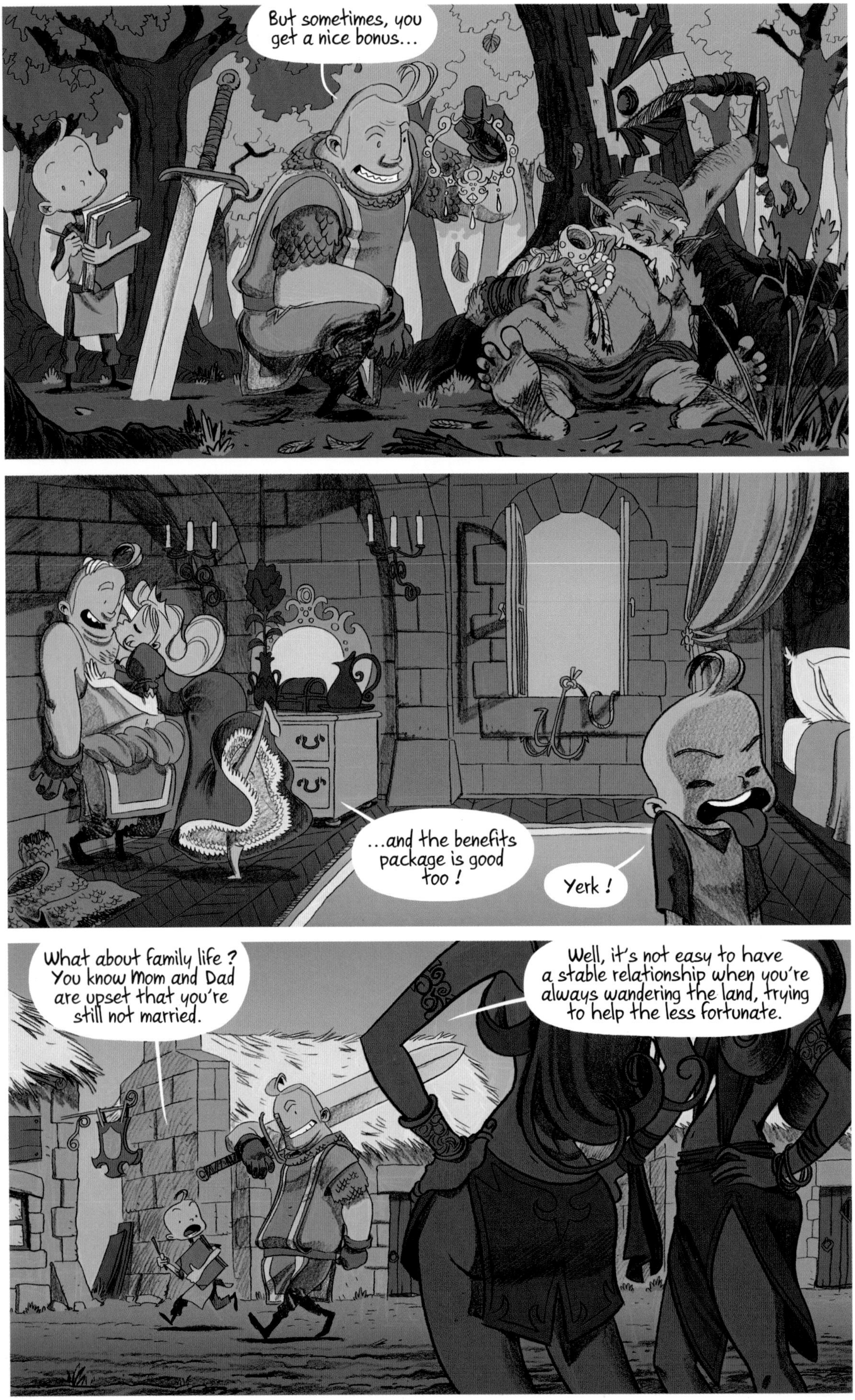
But sometimes, you get a nice bonus...
...and the benefits package is good too !
Yerk !
What about family life ? You know Mom and Dad are upset that you're still not married.
Well, it's not easy to have a stable relationship when you're always wandering the land, trying to help the less fortunate.

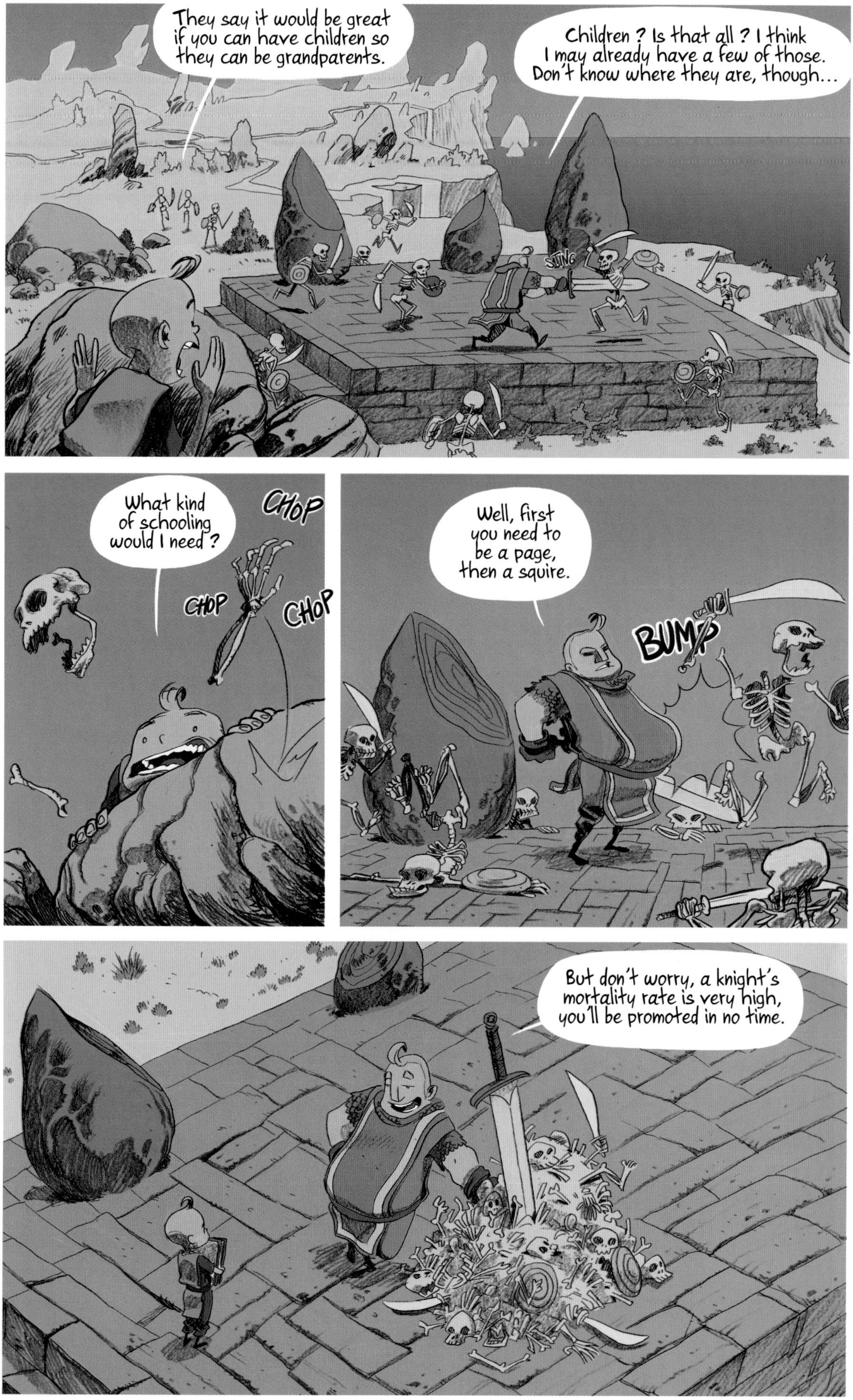
They say it would be great if you can have children so they can be grandparents.
Children ? Is that all ? I think I may already have a few of those. Don't know where they are, though...
SLING
What kind of schooling would I need ?
CHOP
CHOP
CHOP
Well, first you need to be a page, then a squire.
BUMP
But don't worry, a knight's mortality rate is very high, you'll be promoted in no time.

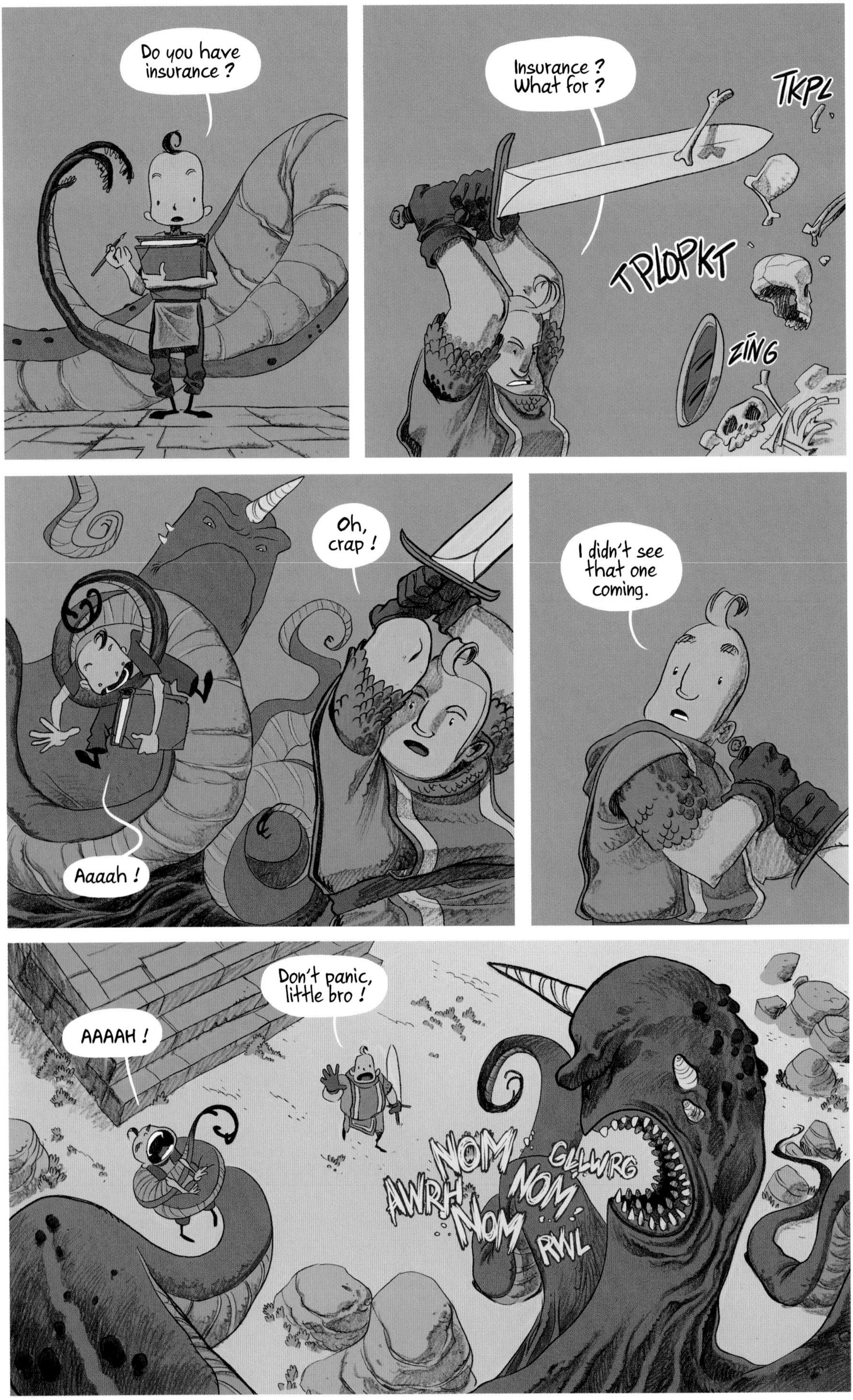
Do you have insurance ?
Insurance ? What for ?
TKPL
TPLOPKT
ZING
Oh, crap !
Aaaah !
I didn't see that one coming.
AAAAH !
Don't panic, little bro !
NOM
GLLWRG
NOM
AWRH
NOM
RWL

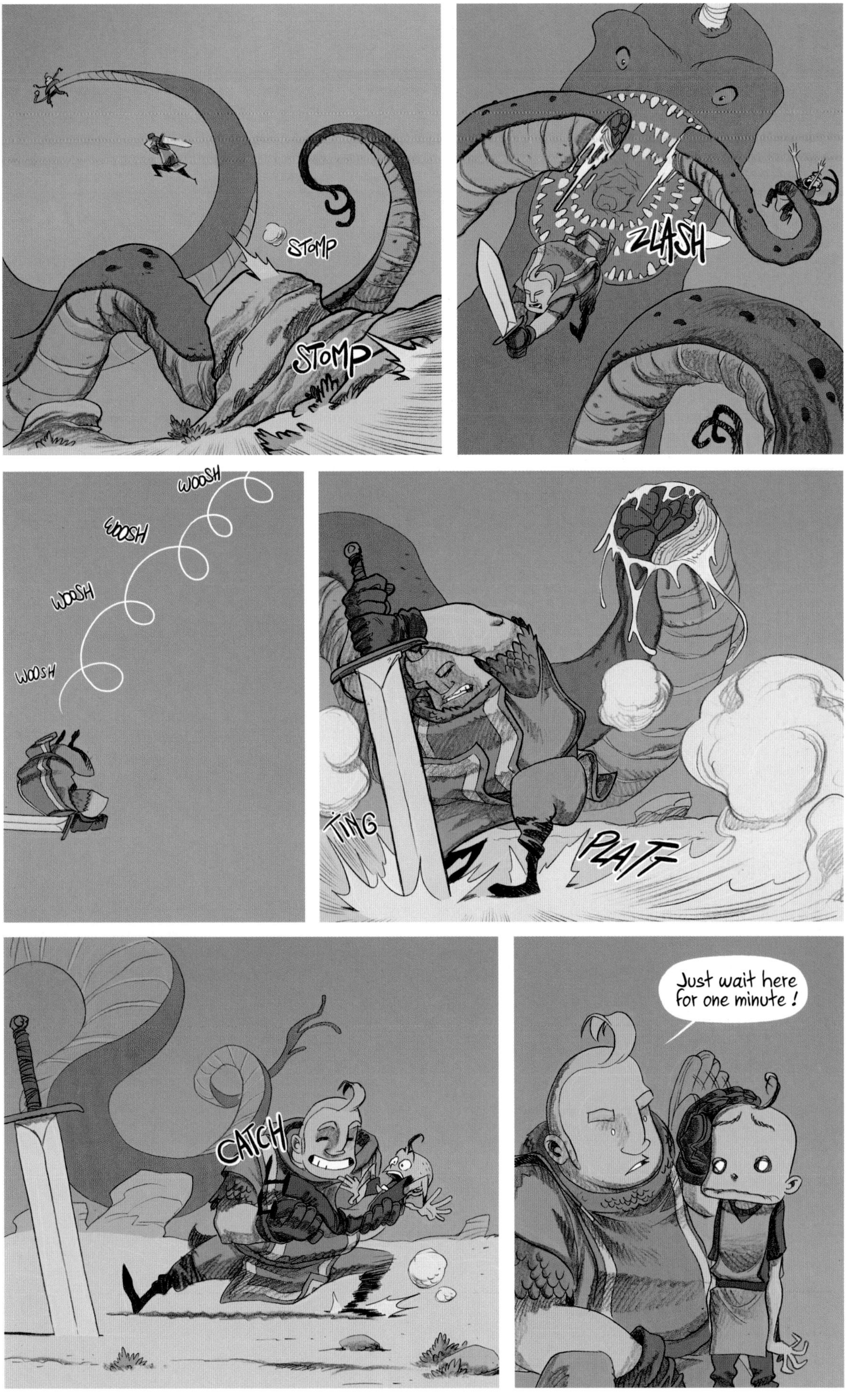
STOMP
STOMP
ZLASH
WOOSH
WOOSH
WOOSH
WOOSH
TING
PLATT
CATCH
Just wait here for one minute !

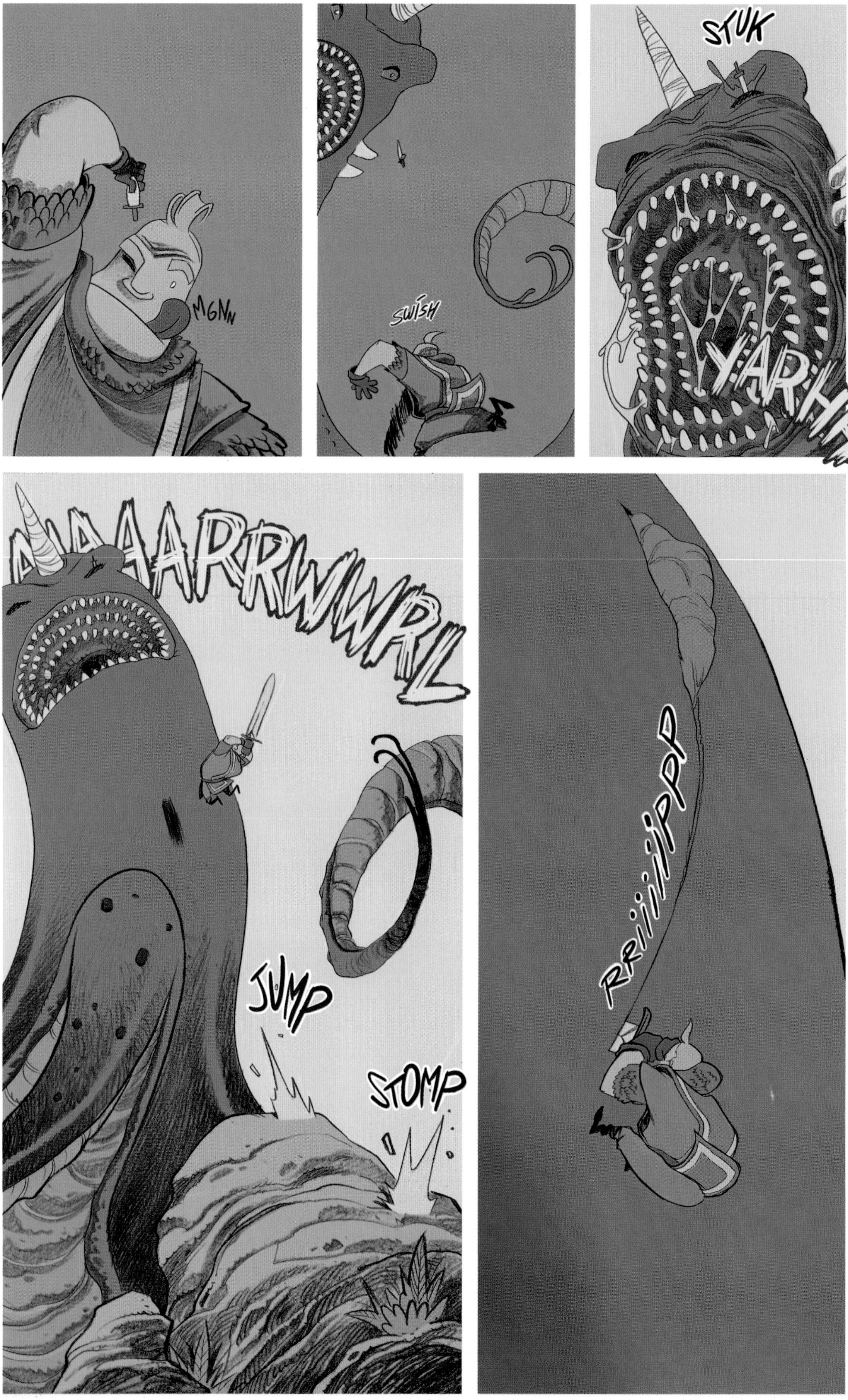
MGNN
SWISH
STUK
YARHH
AAAARRWWRL
JUMP
STOMP
RRIIIIIPPP

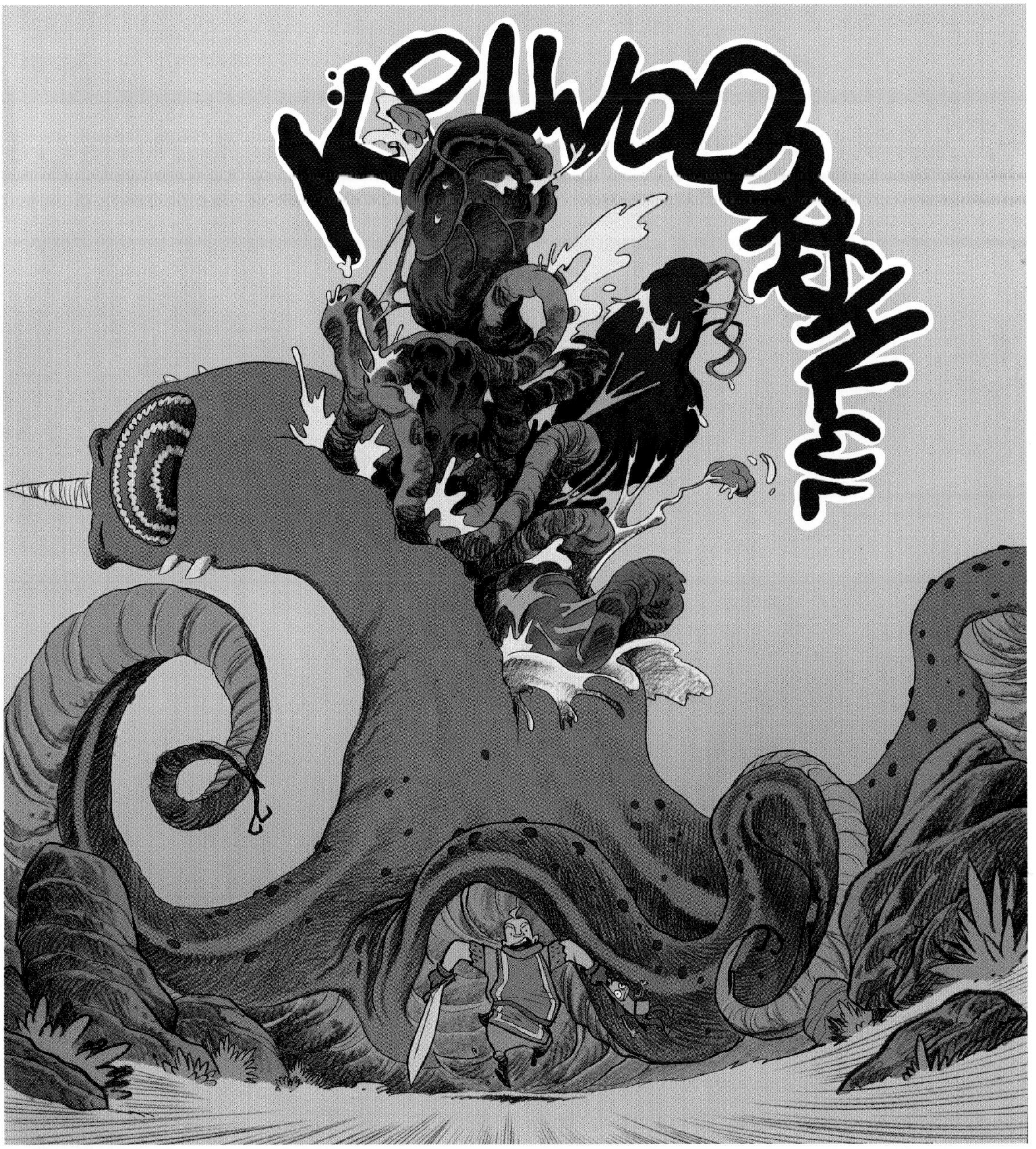

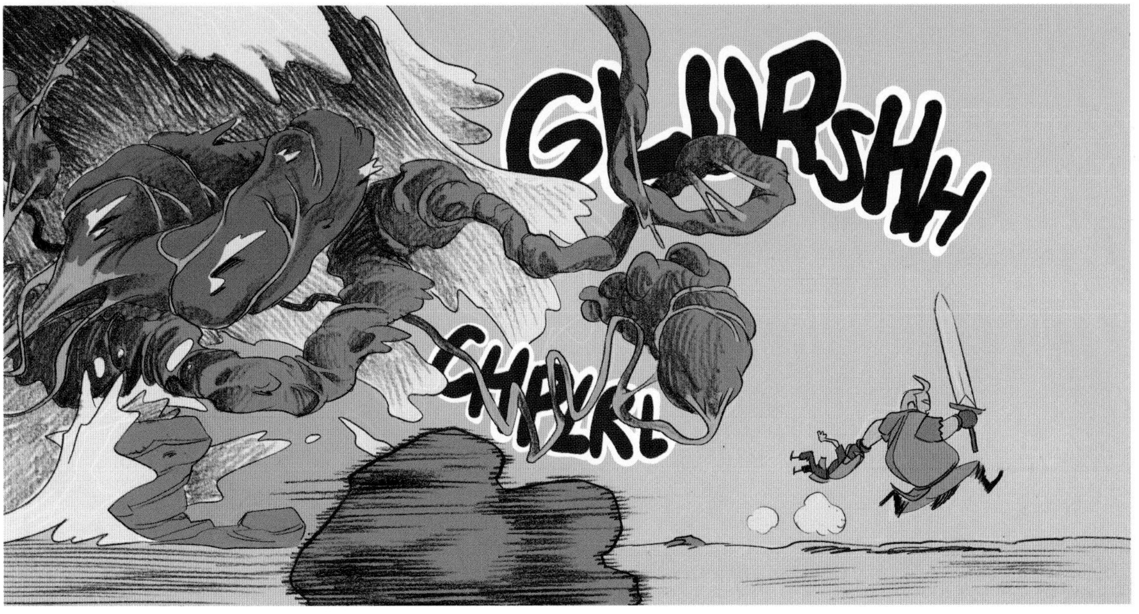
GLURSHH

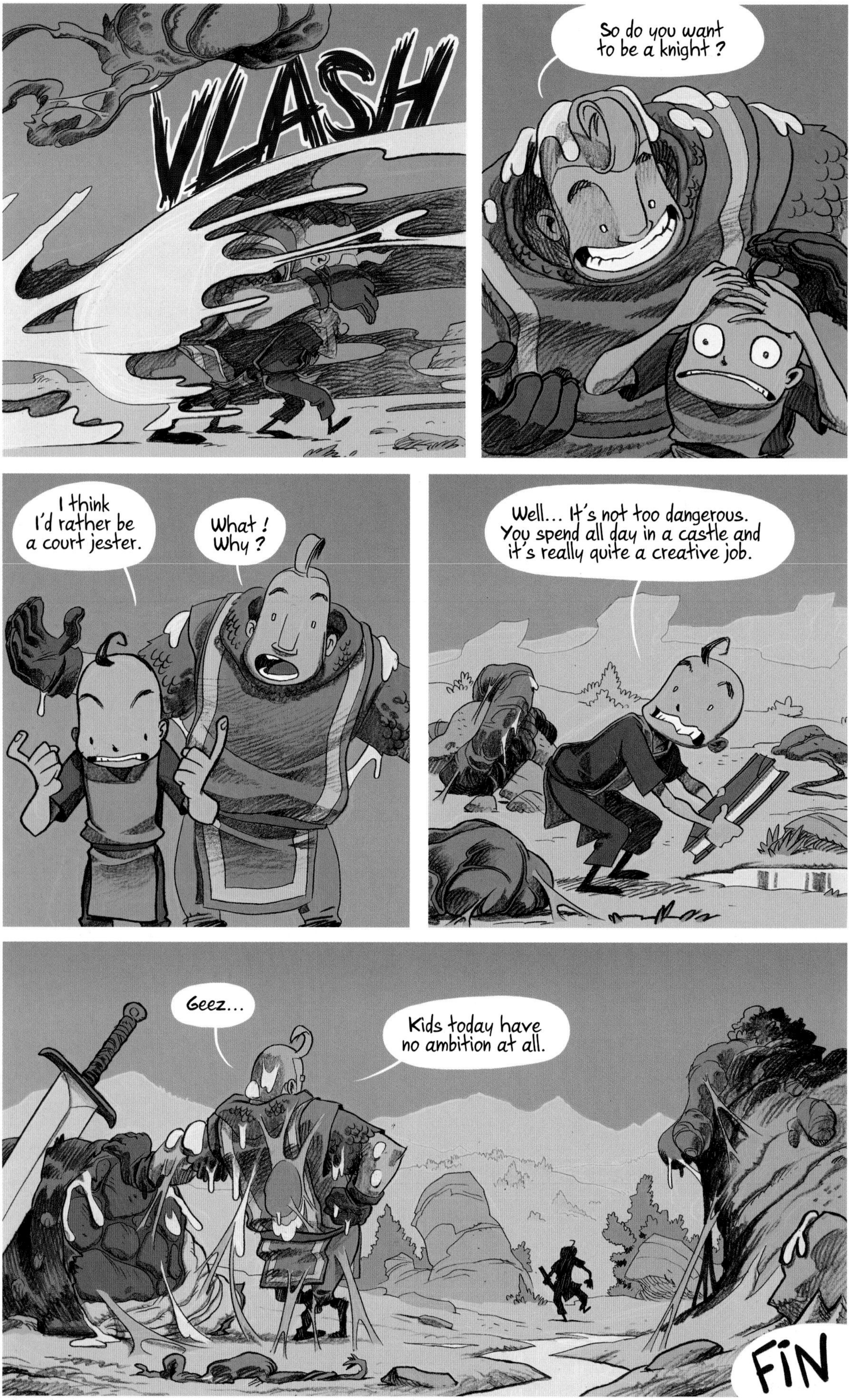
VLASH
So do you want to be a knight ?
I think I'd rather be a court jester.
What ! Why ?
Well… It's not too dangerous. You spend all day in a castle and it's really quite a creative job.
Geez…
Kids today have no ambition at all.
FIN

Bannister + Grimaldi 2010

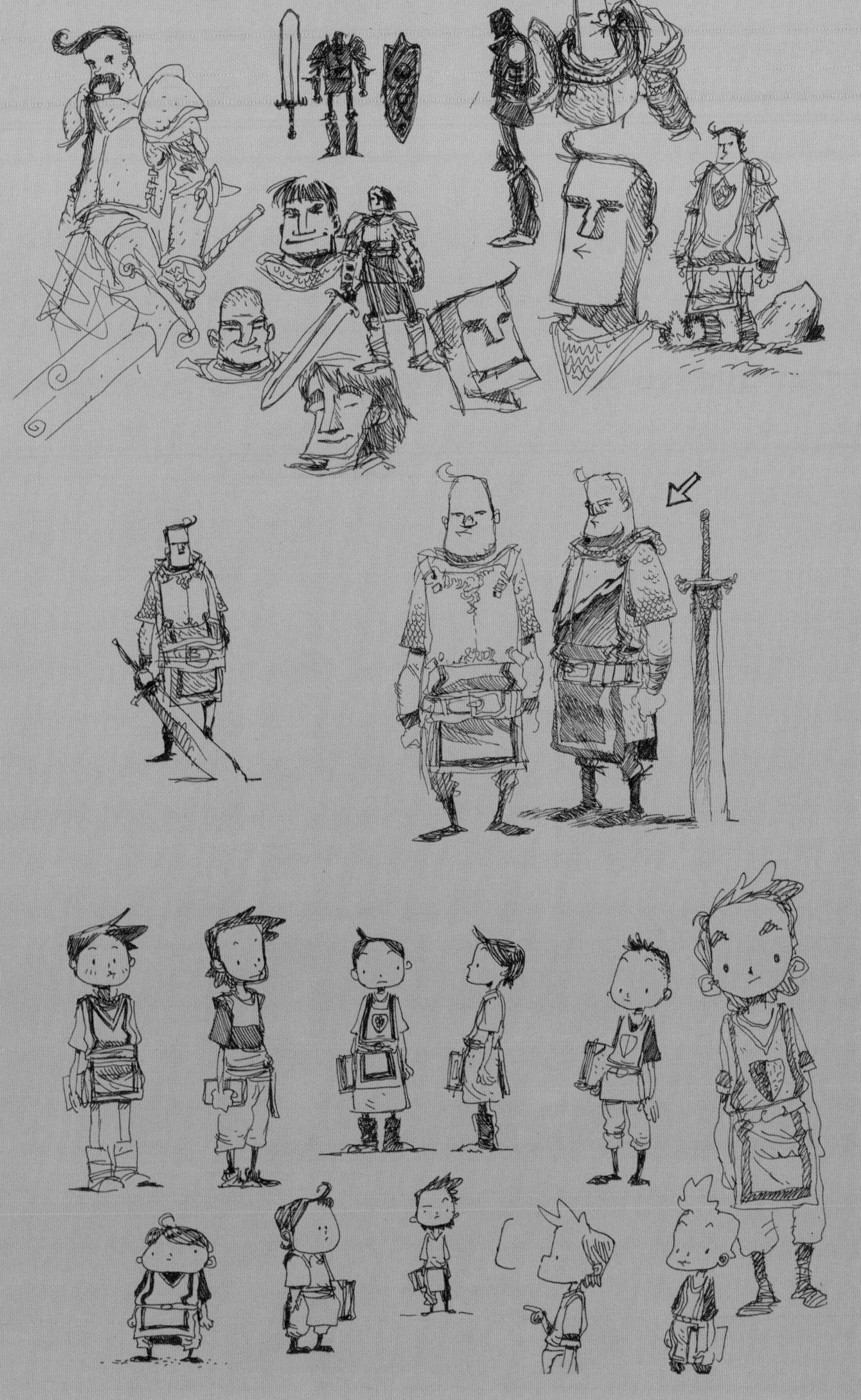

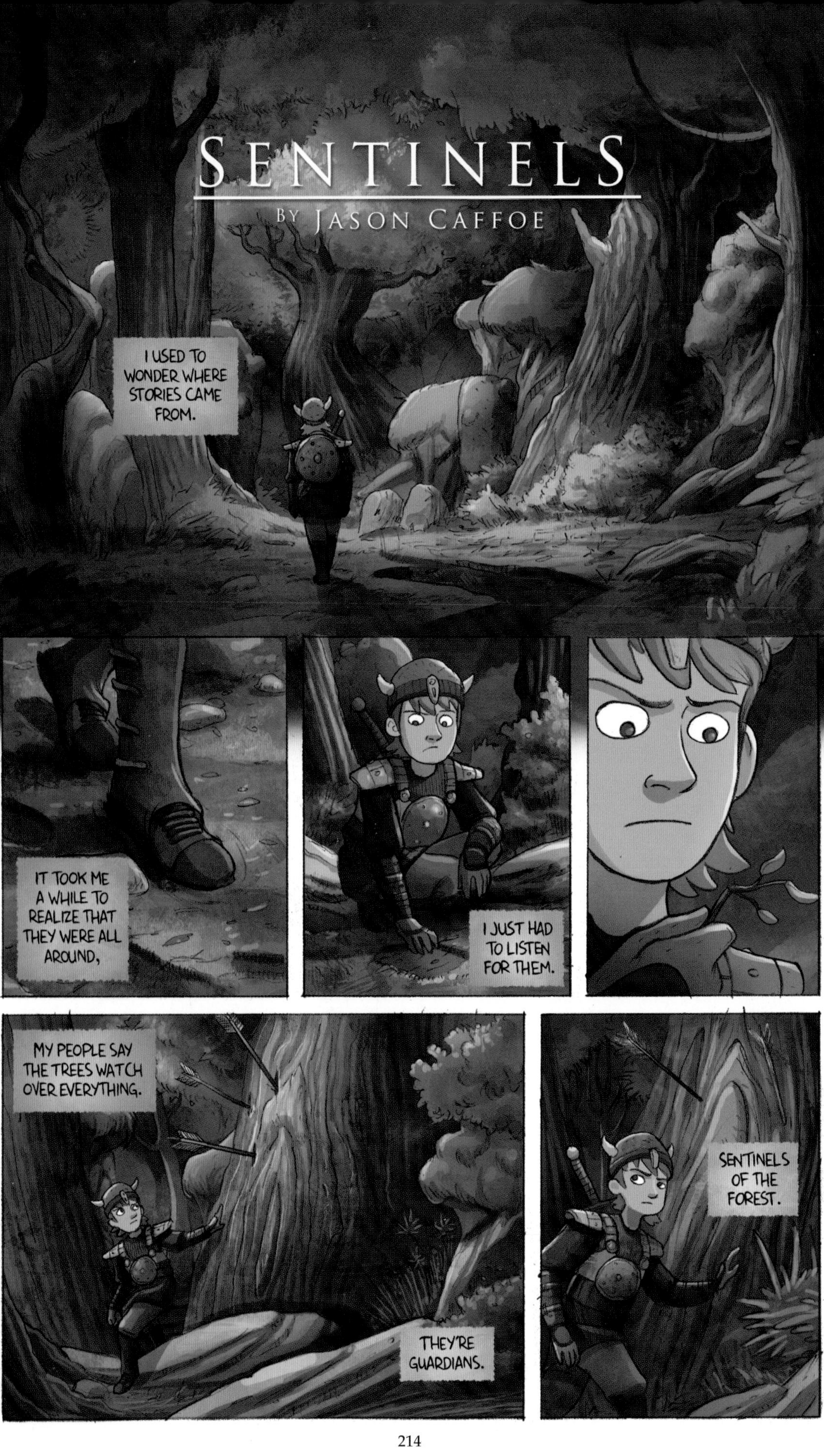
SENTINELS
By JASON CAFFOE
I USED TO WONDER WHERE STORIES CAME FROM.
IT TOOK ME A WHILE TO REALIZE THAT THEY WERE ALL AROUND,
I JUST HAD TO LISTEN FOR THEM.
MY PEOPLE SAY THE TREES WATCH OVER EVERYTHING.
THEY'RE GUARDIANS.
SENTINELS OF THE FOREST.

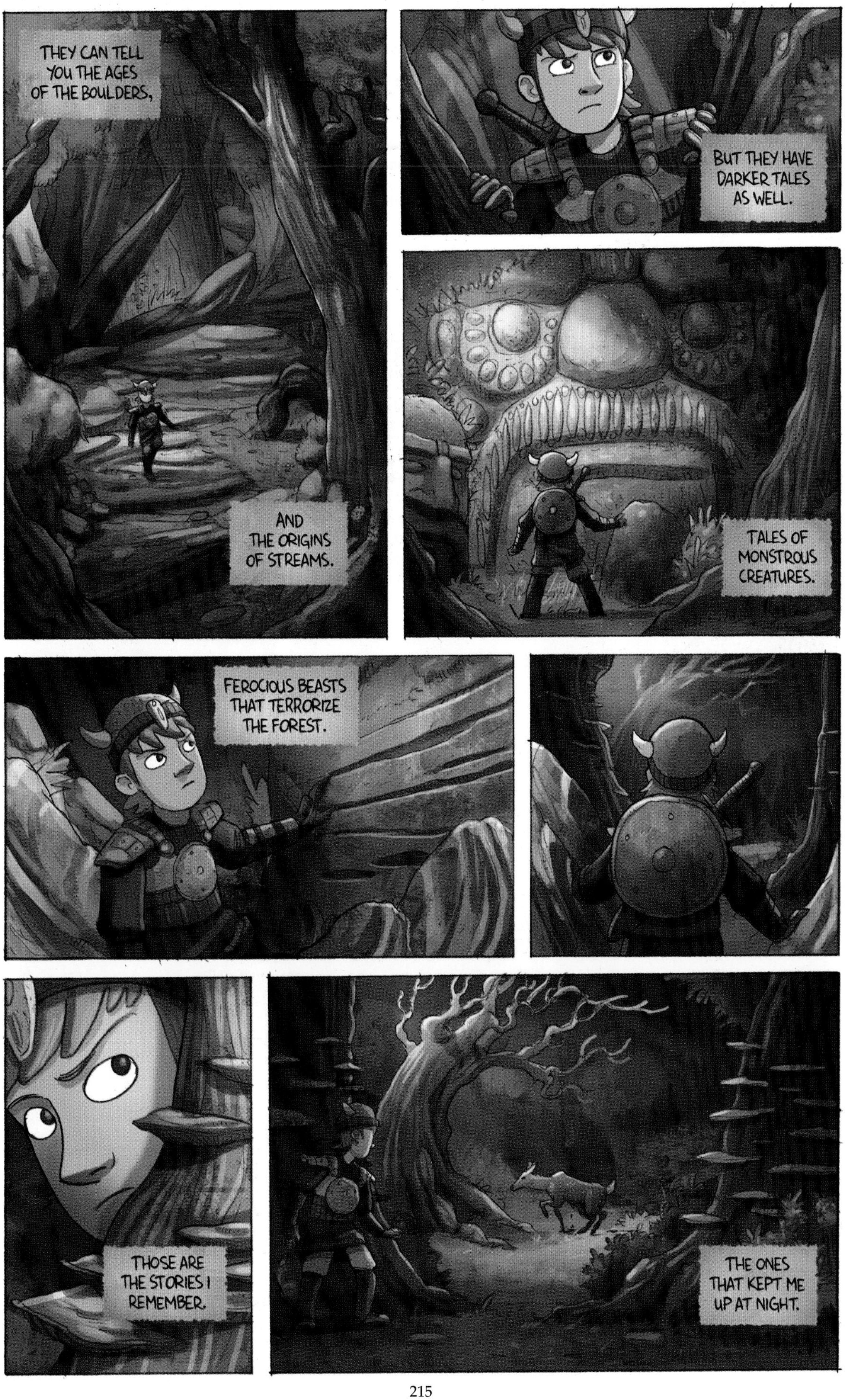
THEY CAN TELL YOU THE AGES OF THE BOULDERS,
BUT THEY HAVE DARKER TALES AS WELL.
AND THE ORIGINS OF STREAMS.
TALES OF MONSTROUS CREATURES.
FEROCIOUS BEASTS THAT TERRORIZE THE FOREST.
THOSE ARE THE STORIES I REMEMBER.
THE ONES THAT KEPT ME UP AT NIGHT.

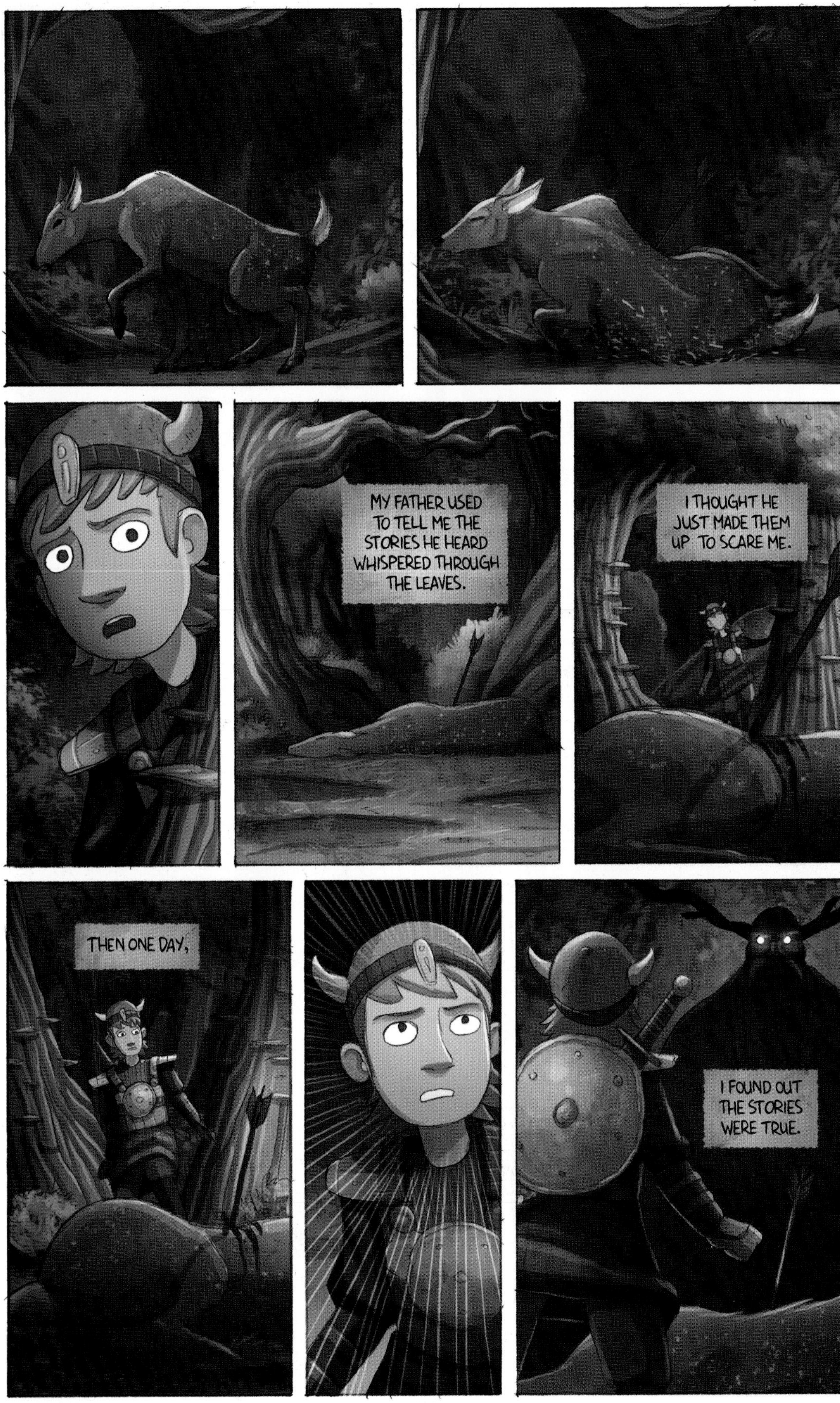
MY FATHER USED TO TELL ME THE STORIES HE HEARD WHISPERED THROUGH THE LEAVES.
I THOUGHT HE JUST MADE THEM UP TO SCARE ME.
THEN ONE DAY,
I FOUND OUT THE STORIES WERE TRUE.

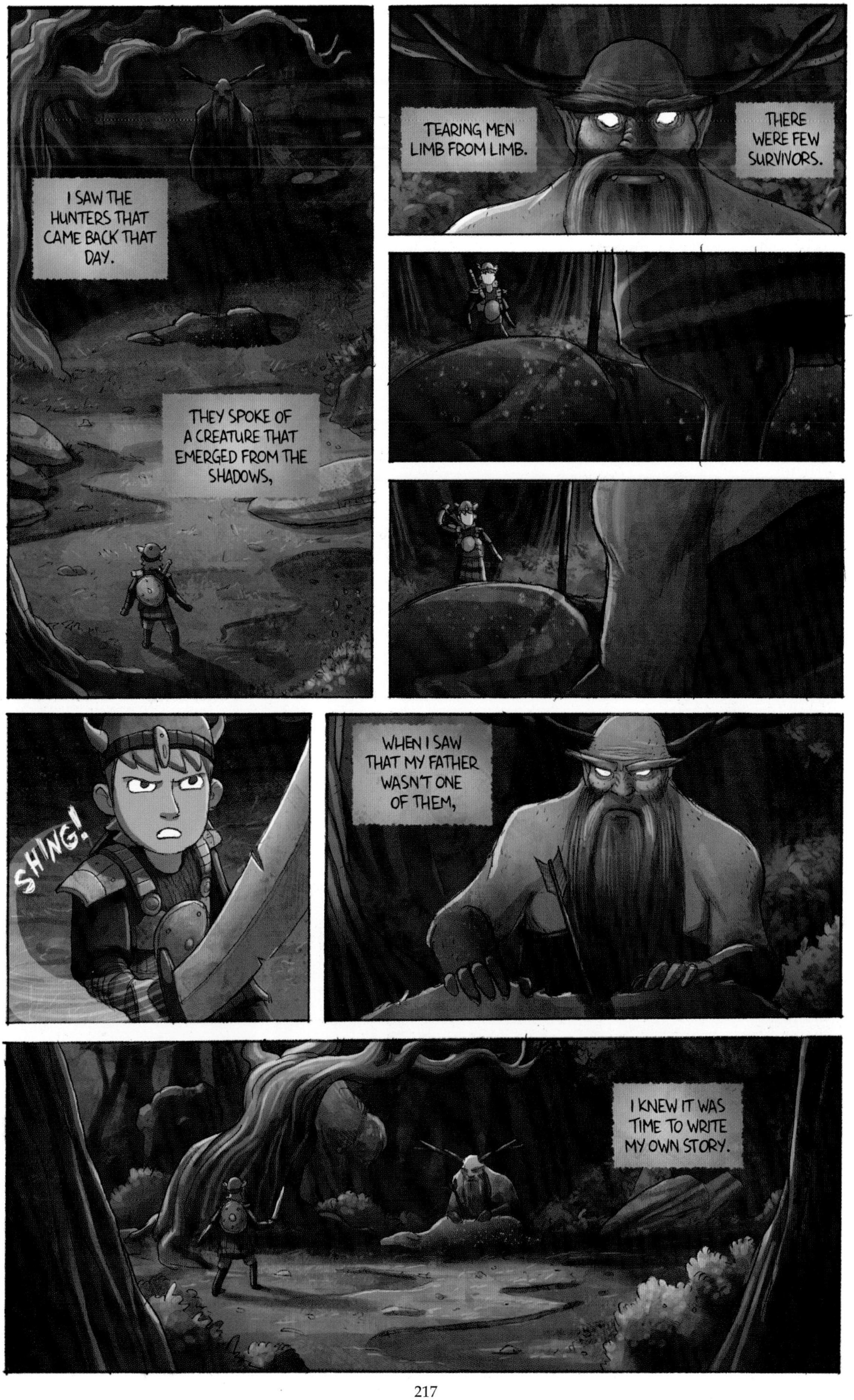
I SAW THE HUNTERS THAT CAME BACK THAT DAY.
THEY SPOKE OF A CREATURE THAT EMERGED FROM THE SHADOWS,
TEARING MEN LIMB FROM LIMB.
THERE WERE FEW SURVIVORS.
SHING!
WHEN I SAW THAT MY FATHER WASN'T ONE OF THEM,
I KNEW IT WAS TIME TO WRITE MY OWN STORY.

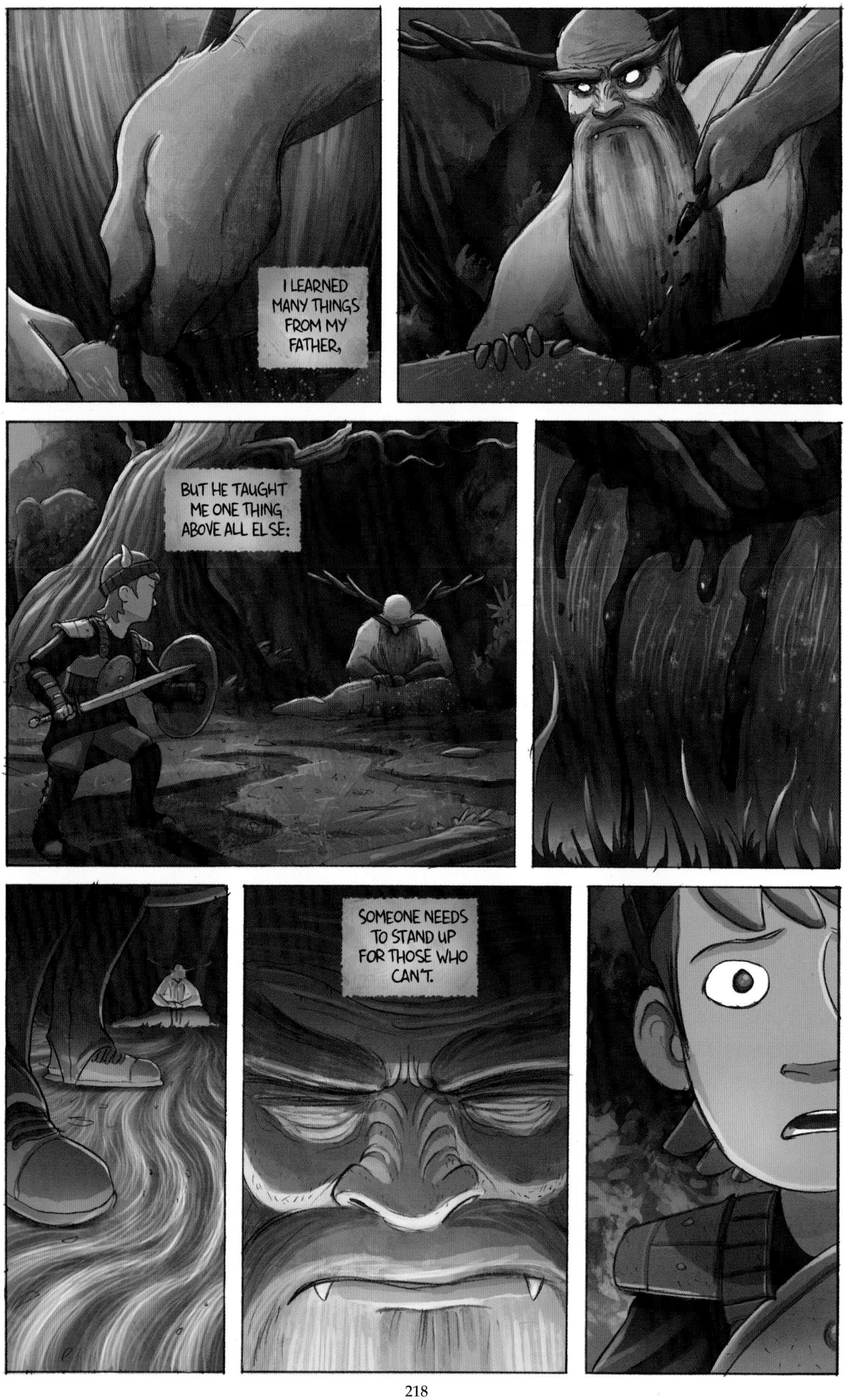
I LEARNED MANY THINGS FROM MY FATHER,
BUT HE TAUGHT ME ONE THING ABOVE ALL ELSE:
SOMEONE NEEDS TO STAND UP FOR THOSE WHO CAN'T.

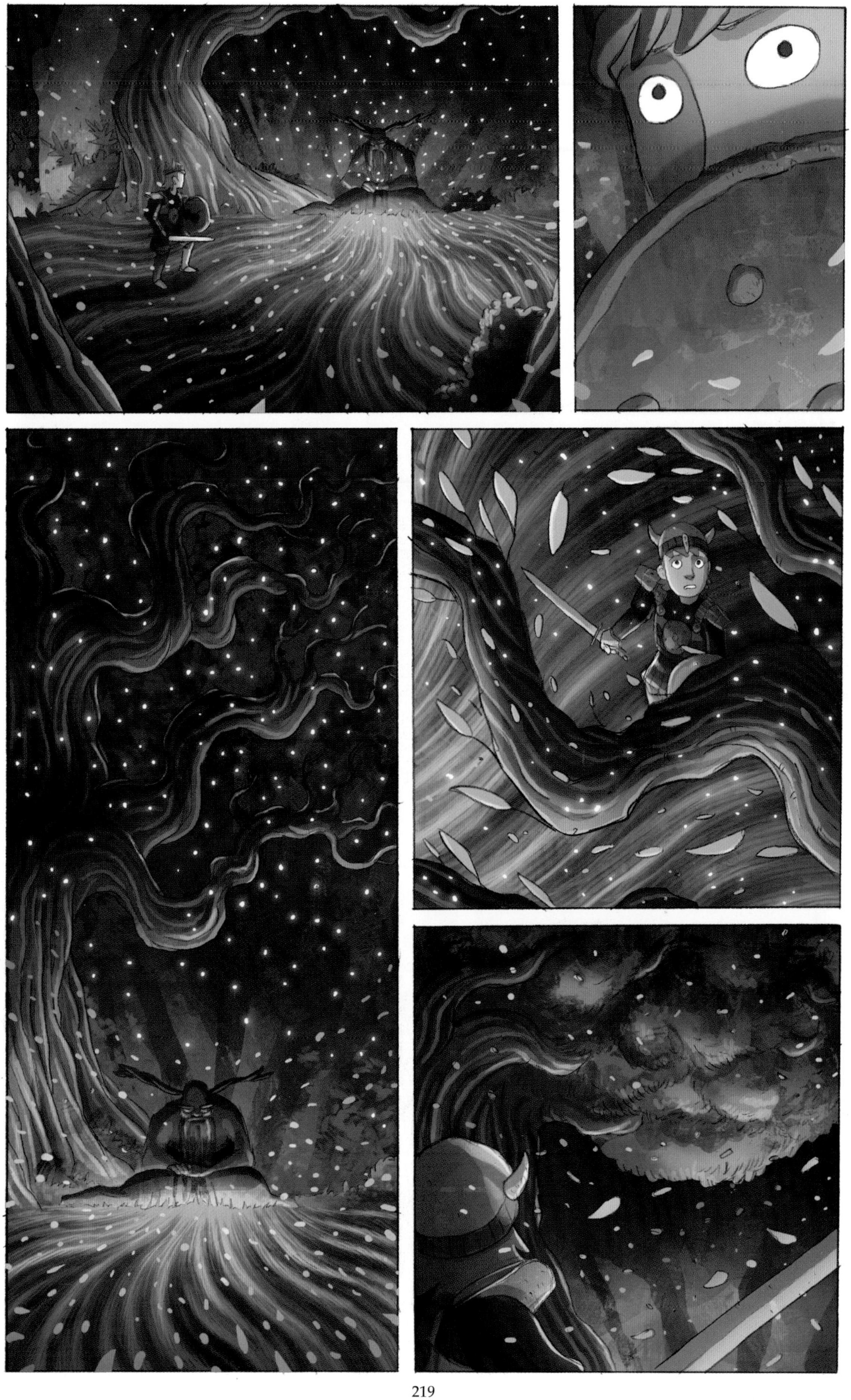

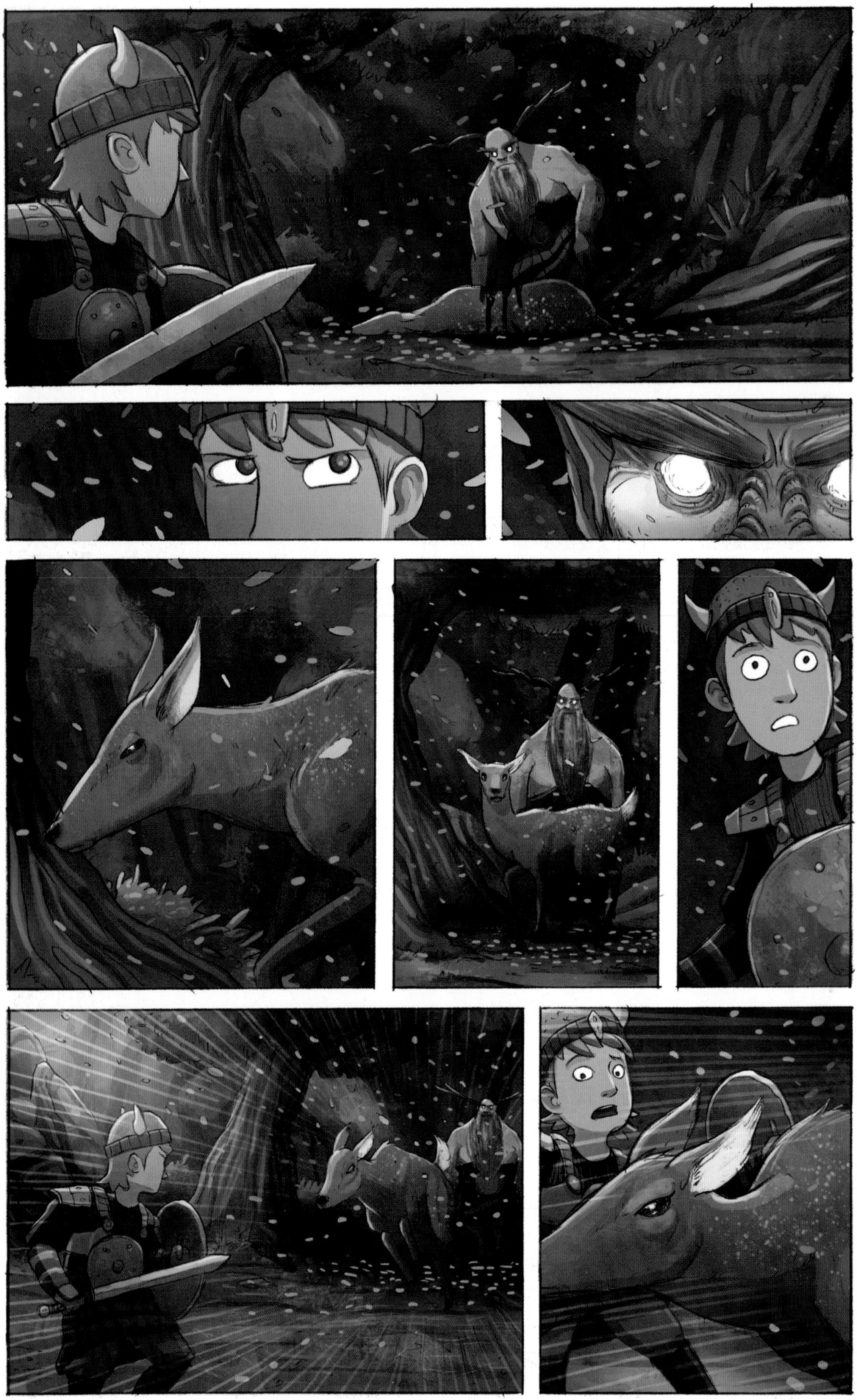

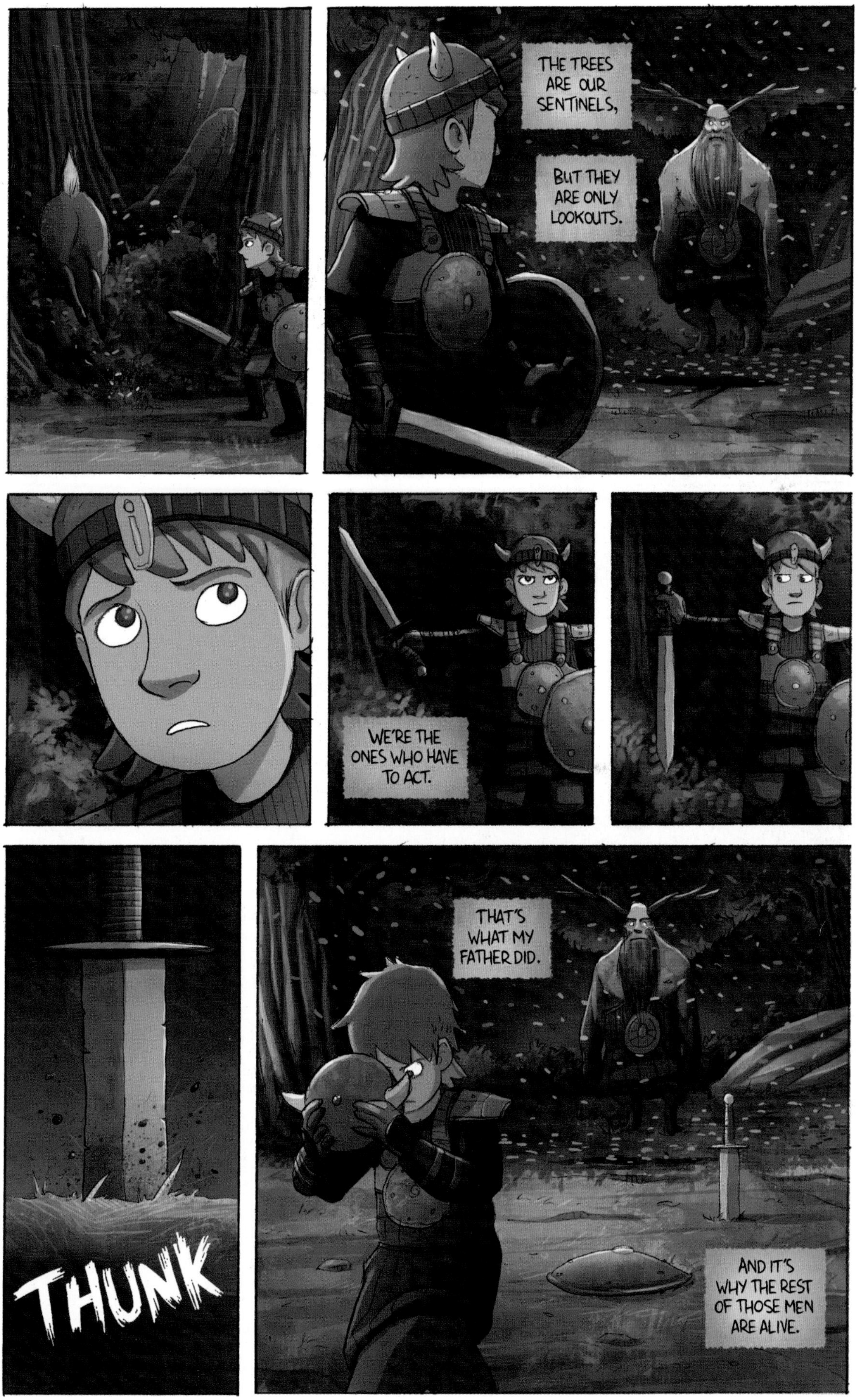
THE TREES ARE OUR SENTINELS,
BUT THEY ARE ONLY LOOKOUTS.
WE'RE THE ONES WHO HAVE TO ACT.
THUNK
THAT'S WHAT MY FATHER DID.
AND IT'S WHY THE REST OF THOSE MEN ARE ALIVE.

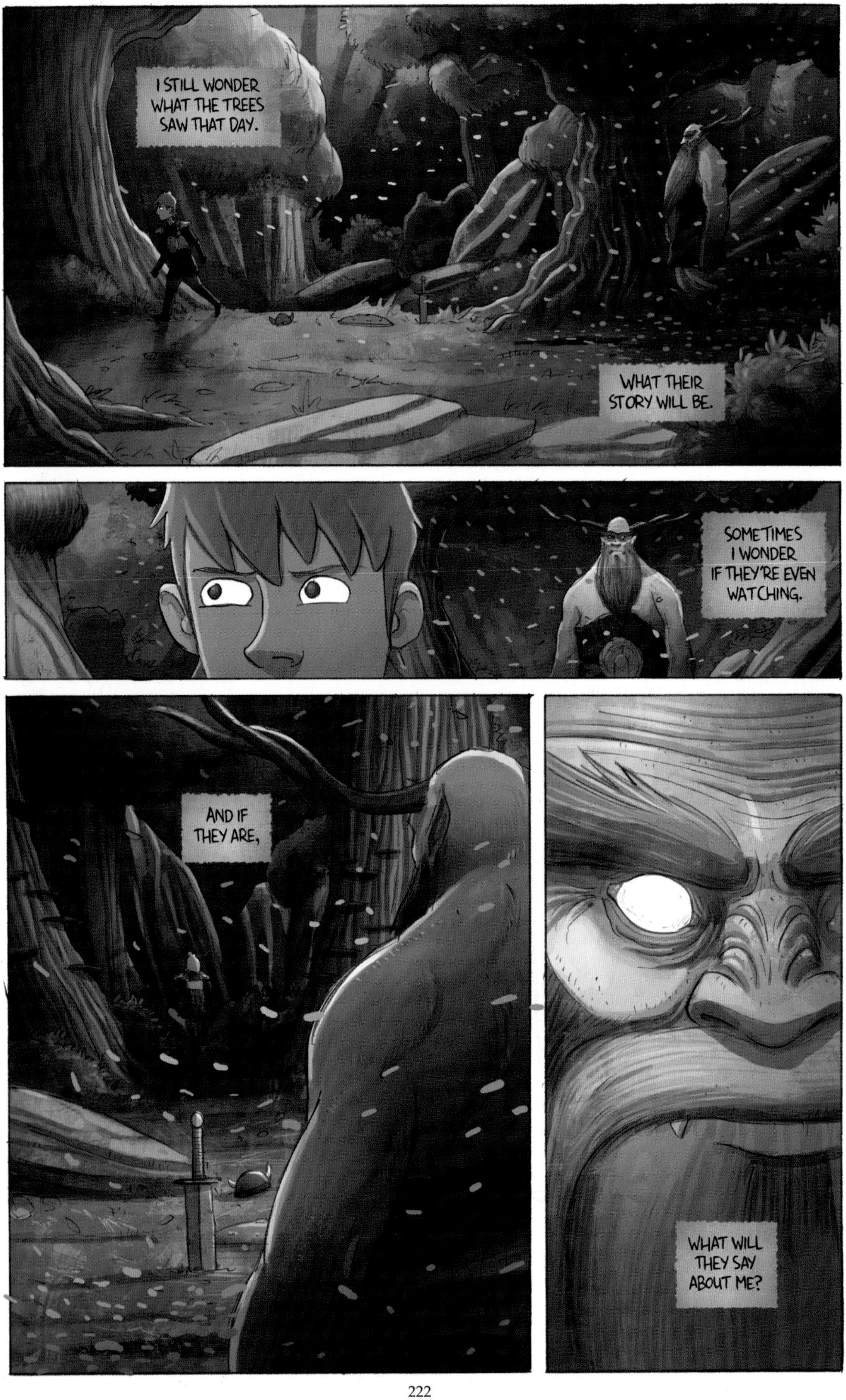
I STILL WONDER WHAT THE TREES SAW THAT DAY.
WHAT THEIR STORY WILL BE.
SOMETIMES I WONDER IF THEY'RE EVEN WATCHING.
AND IF THEY ARE,
WHAT WILL THEY SAY ABOUT ME?

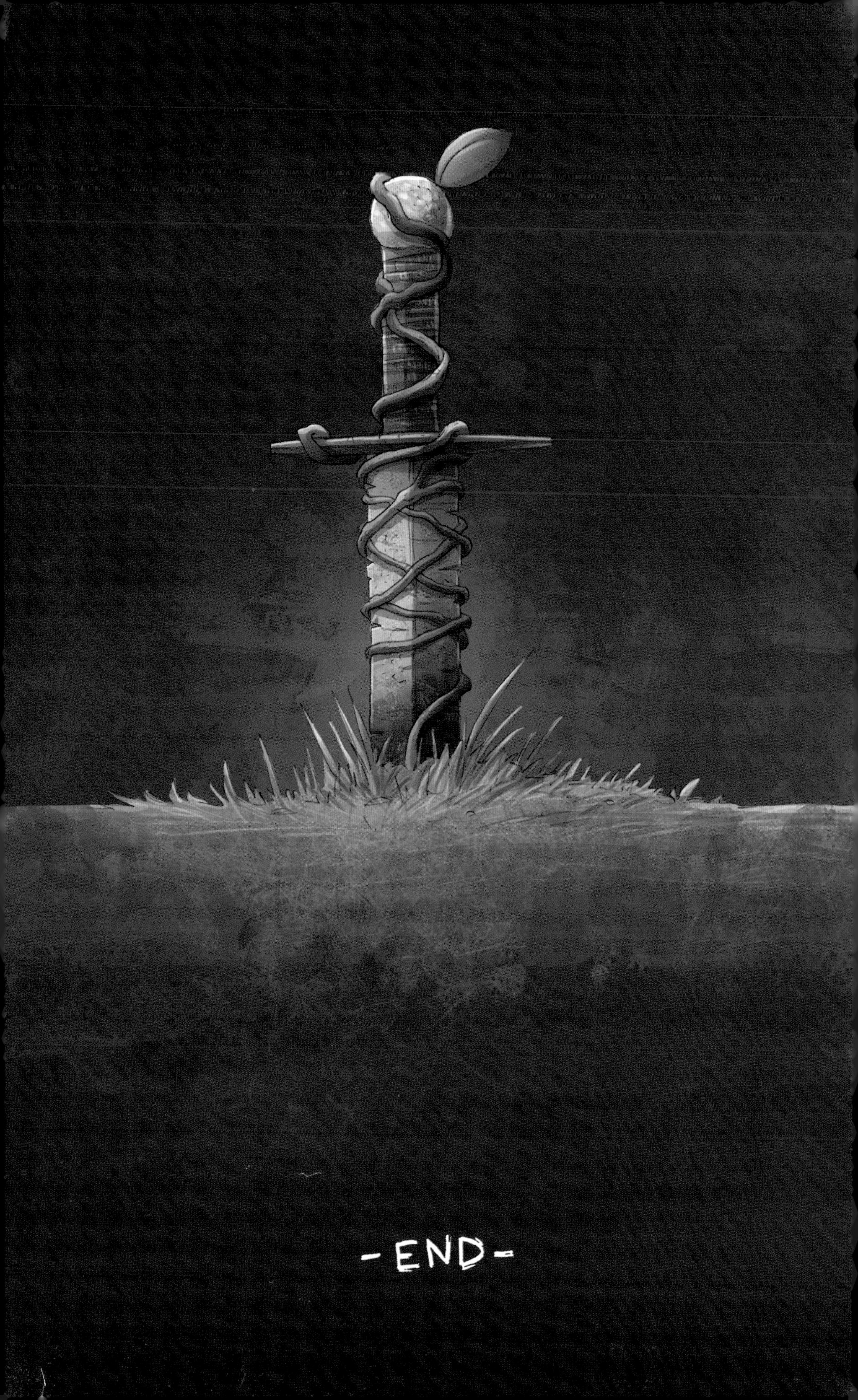
-END-

KING OF BEASTS
WHAT'S YOURS IS MINE!
PAUL HARMON

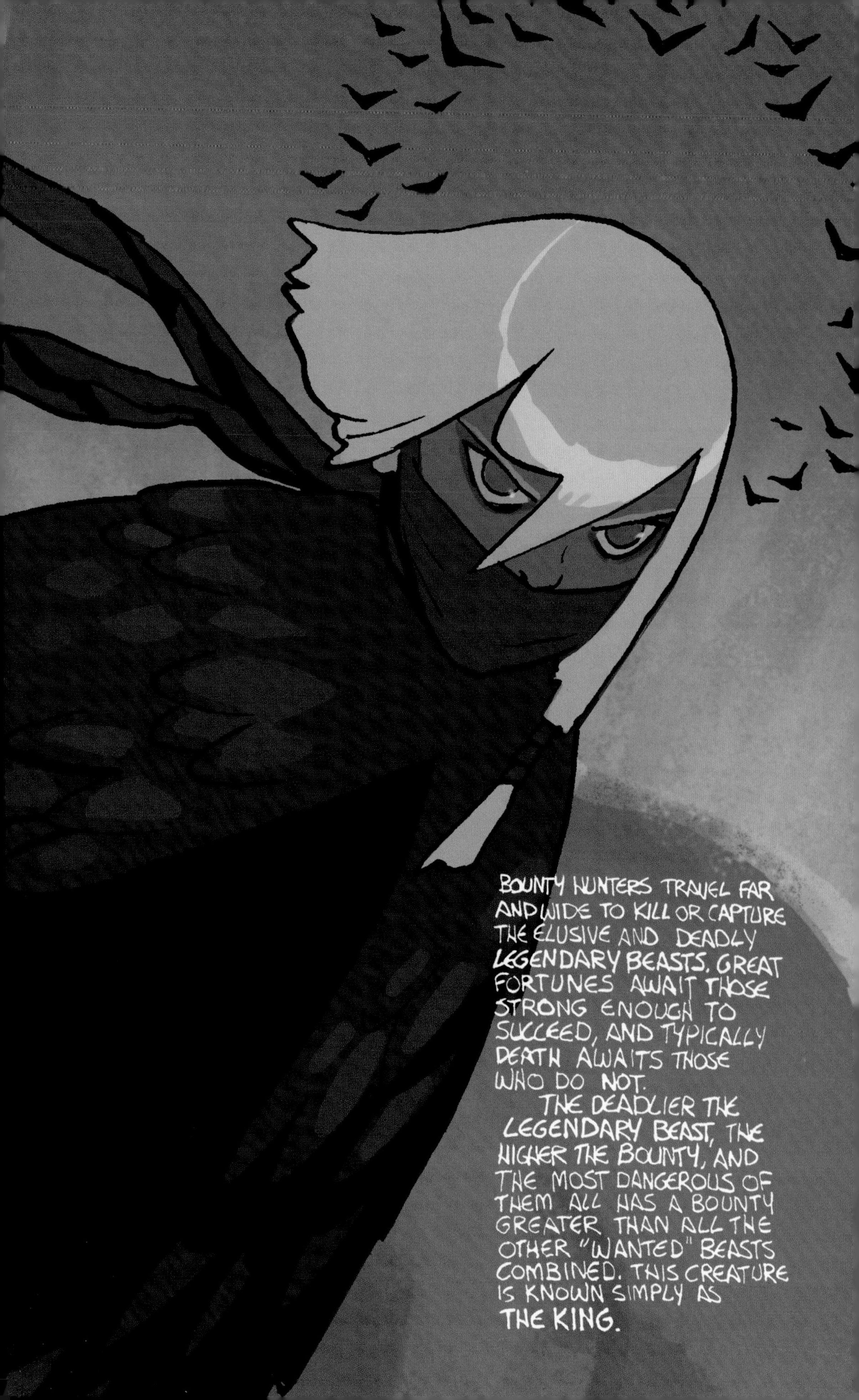
BOUNTY HUNTERS TRAVEL FAR AND WIDE TO KILL OR CAPTURE THE ELUSIVE AND DEADLY LEGENDARY BEASTS. GREAT FORTUNES AWAIT THOSE STRONG ENOUGH TO SUCCEED, AND TYPICALLY DEATH AWAITS THOSE WHO DO NOT.
THE DEADLIER THE LEGENDARY BEAST, THE HIGHER THE BOUNTY, AND THE MOST DANGEROUS OF THEM ALL HAS A BOUNTY GREATER THAN ALL THE OTHER "WANTED" BEASTS COMBINED. THIS CREATURE IS KNOWN SIMPLY AS THE KING.

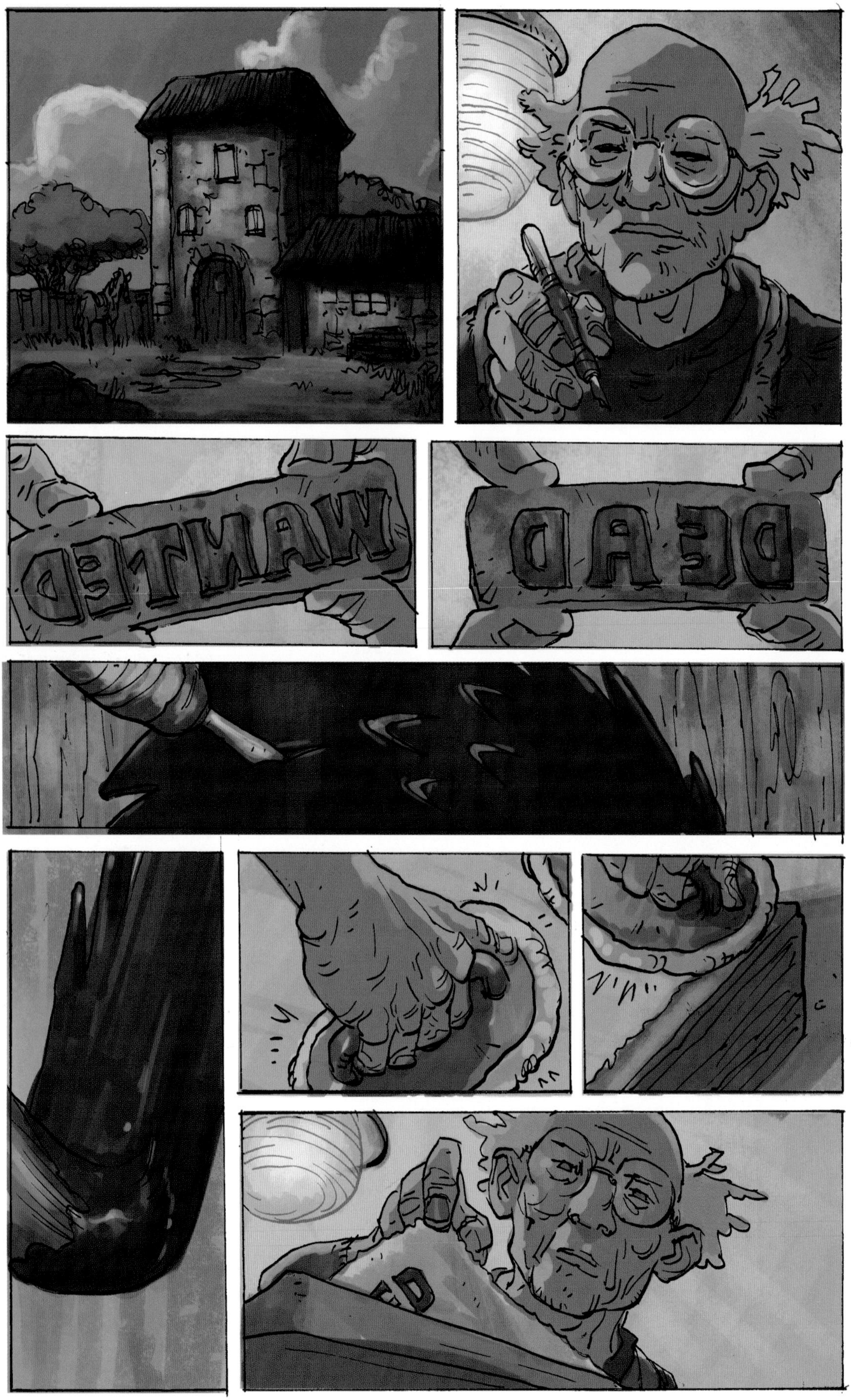
WANTED
DEAD

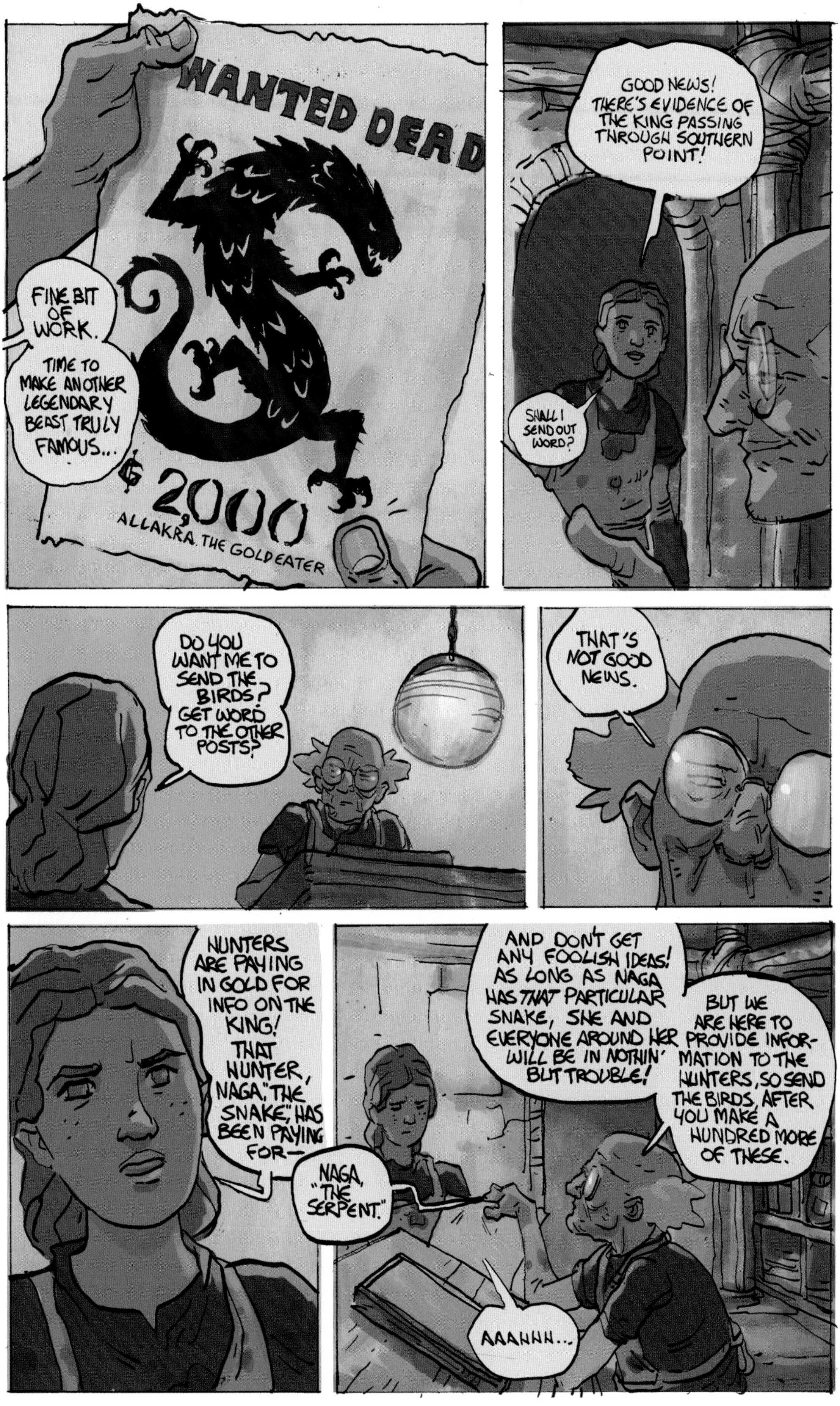
WANTED DEAD
₲ 2,000
ALLAKRA THE GOLDEATER
FINE BIT OF WORK.
TIME TO MAKE ANOTHER LEGENDARY BEAST TRULY FAMOUS...
GOOD NEWS! THERE'S EVIDENCE OF THE KING PASSING THROUGH SOUTHERN POINT!
SHALL I SEND OUT WORD?
DO YOU WANT ME TO SEND THE BIRDS? GET WORD TO THE OTHER POSTS?
THAT'S NOT GOOD NEWS.
HUNTERS ARE PAYING IN GOLD FOR INFO ON THE KING!
THAT HUNTER, NAGA "THE SNAKE," HAS BEEN PAYING FOR—
NAGA, "THE SERPENT."
AND DON'T GET ANY FOOLISH IDEAS! AS LONG AS NAGA HAS THAT PARTICULAR SNAKE, SHE AND EVERYONE AROUND HER WILL BE IN NOTHIN' BUT TROUBLE!
BUT WE ARE HERE TO PROVIDE INFORMATION TO THE HUNTERS, SO SEND THE BIRDS, AFTER YOU MAKE A HUNDRED MORE OF THESE.
AAAHHH...

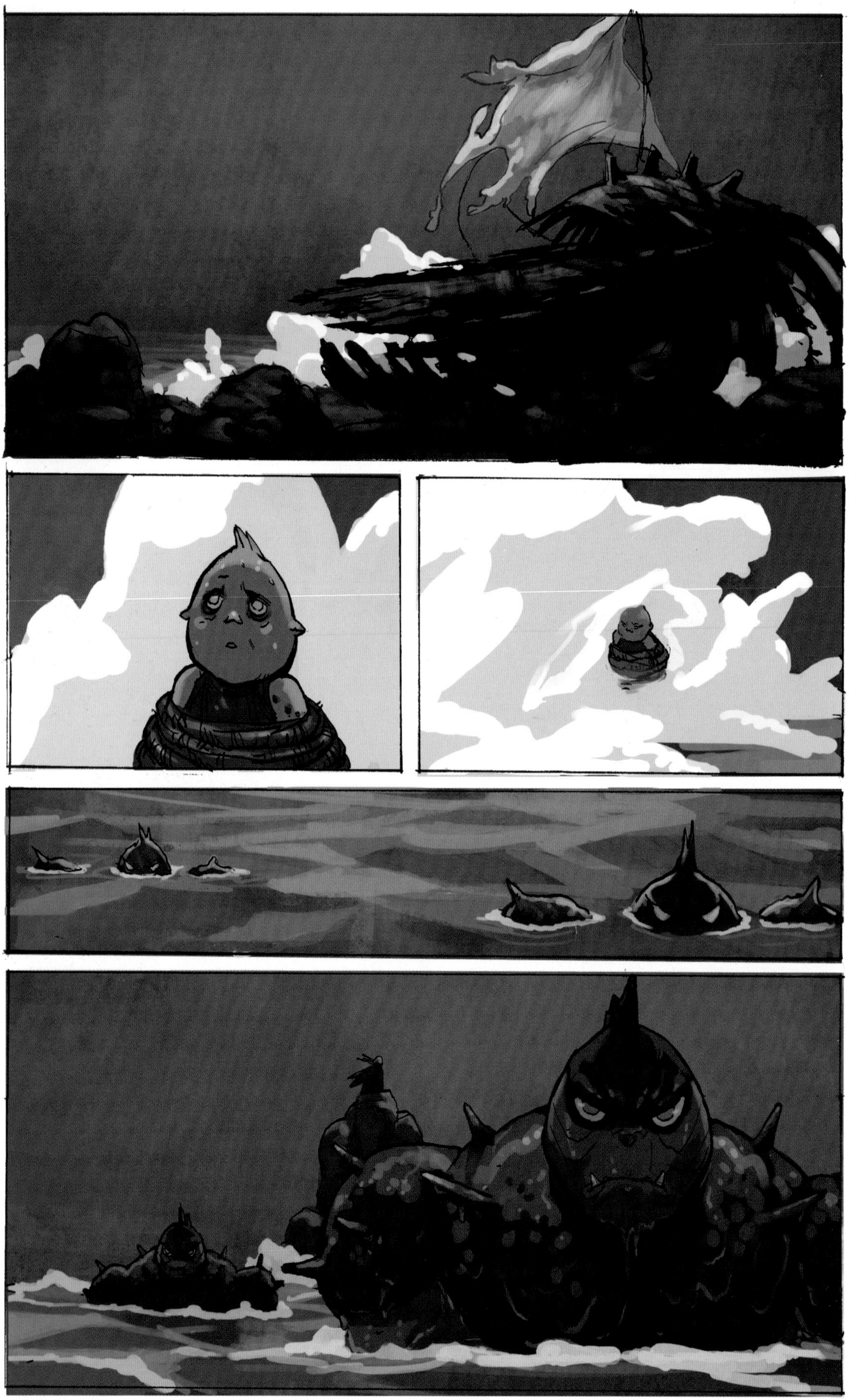

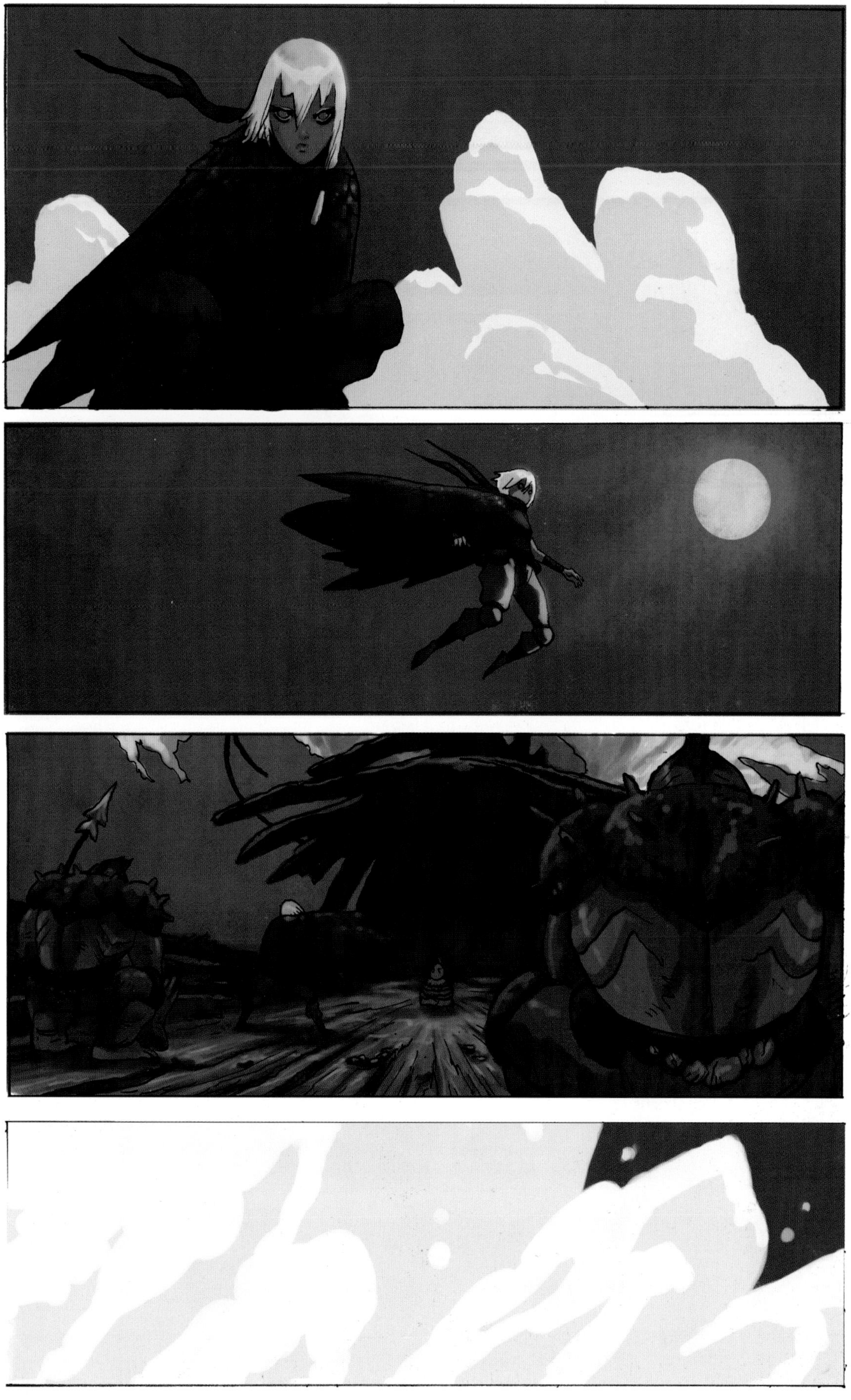

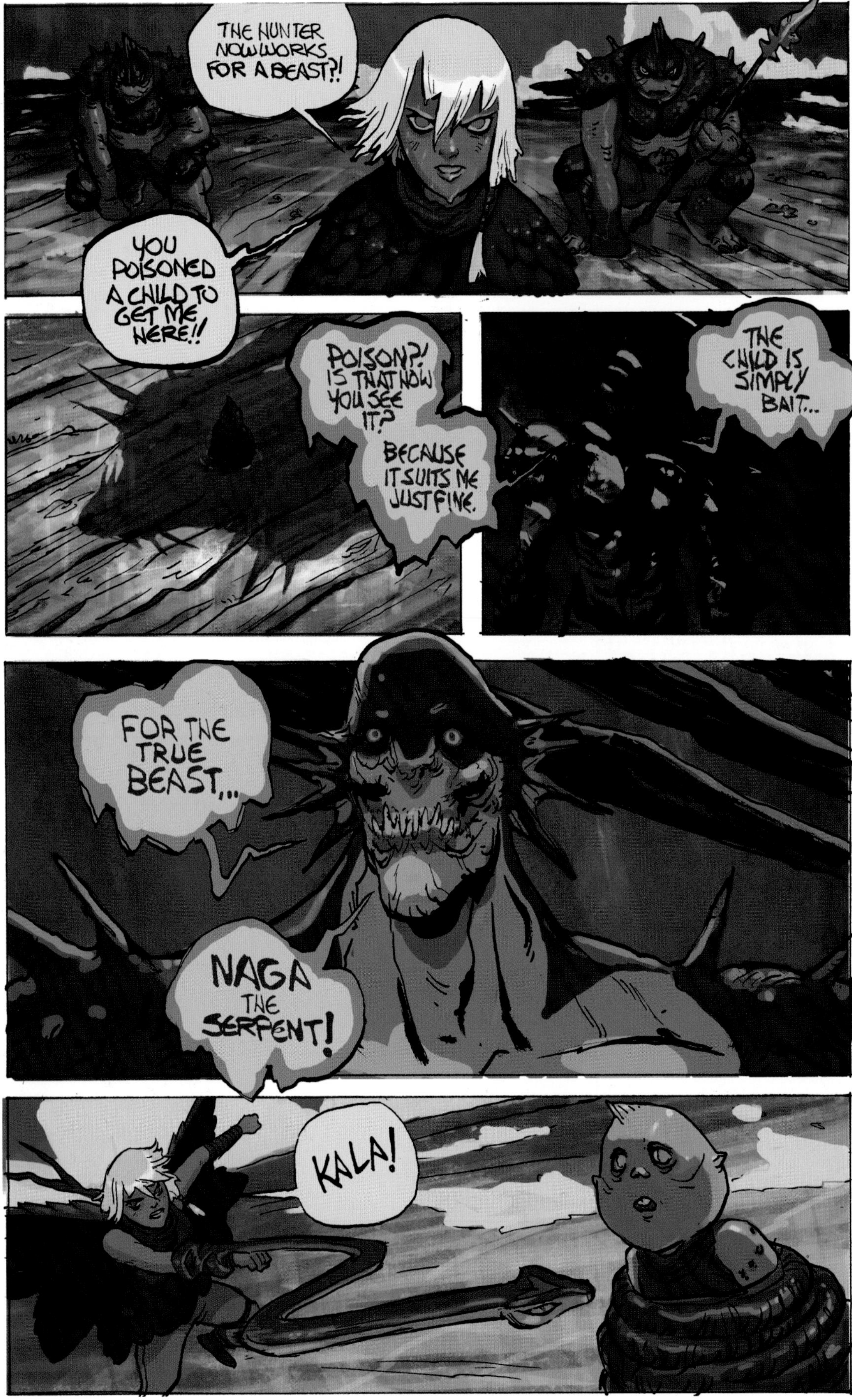
THE HUNTER NOW WORKS FOR A BEAST?!
YOU POISONED A CHILD TO GET ME HERE!!
POISON?! IS THAT HOW YOU SEE IT?
BECAUSE IT SUITS ME JUST FINE.
THE CHILD IS SIMPLY BAIT...
FOR THE TRUE BEAST,...
NAGA THE SERPENT!
KALA!

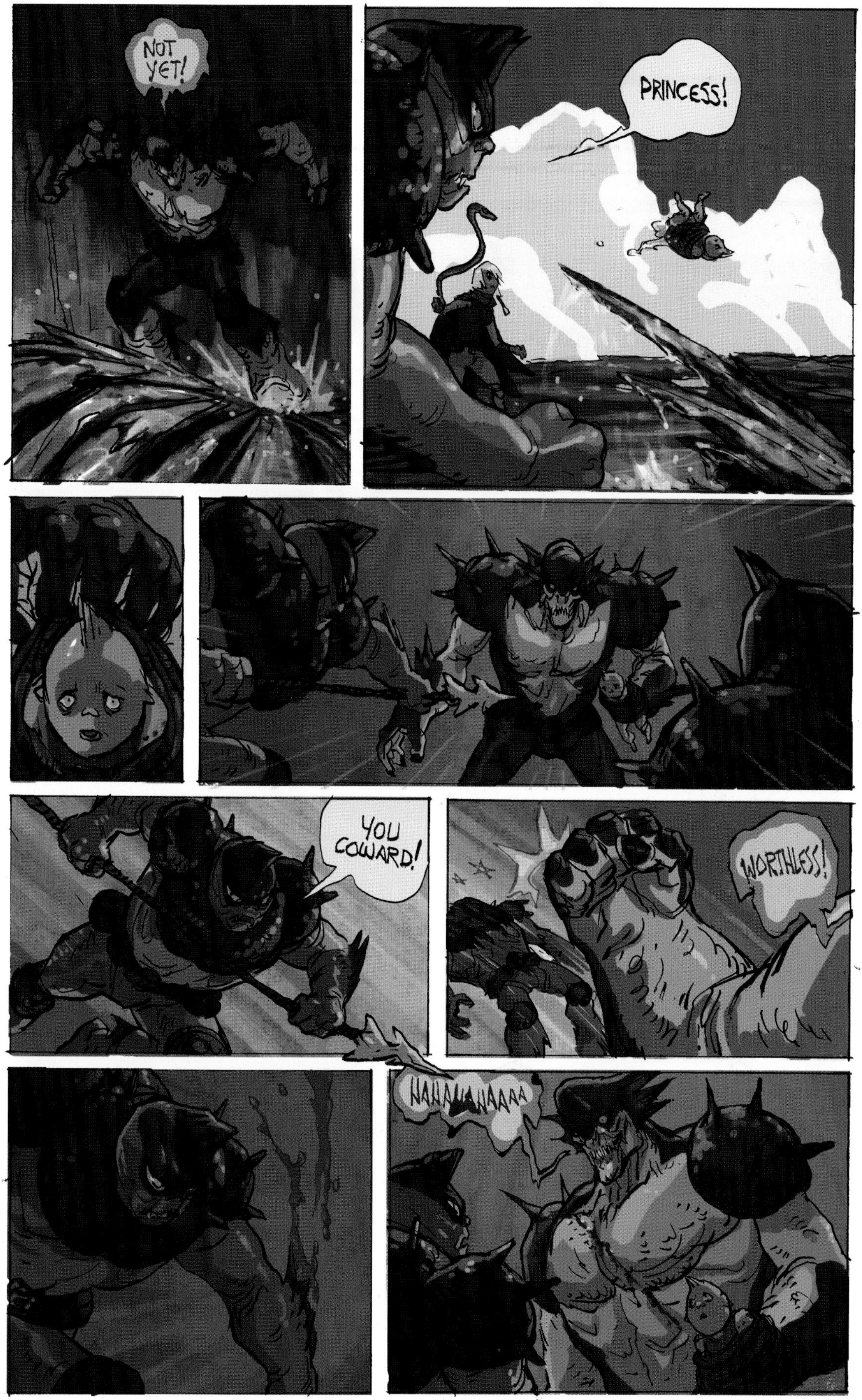
NOT YET!
PRINCESS!
YOU COWARD!
WORTHLESS!
NAHAHAHAAAA

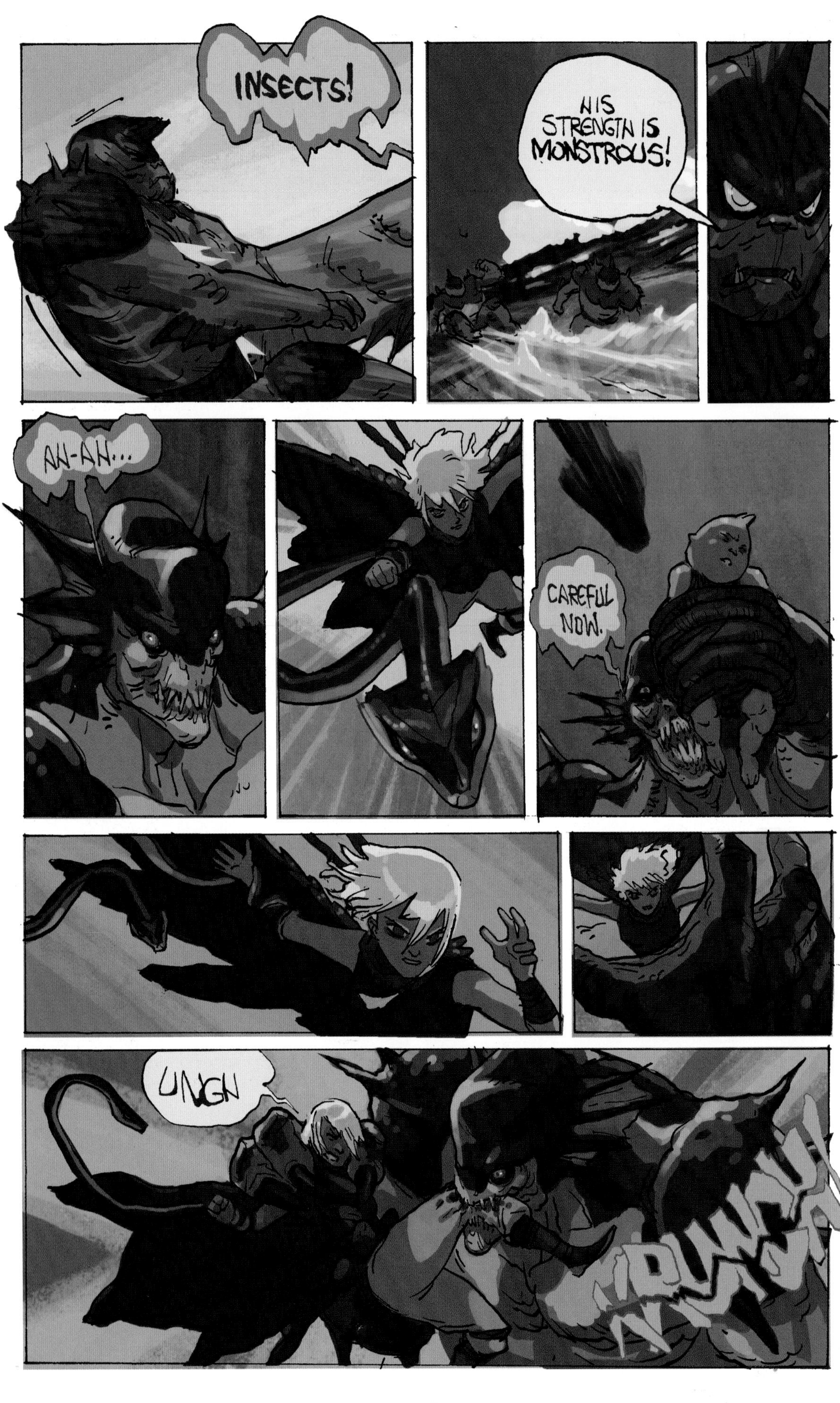
INSECTS!
HIS STRENGTH IS MONSTROUS!
AH-AH...
CAREFUL NOW.
UNGH

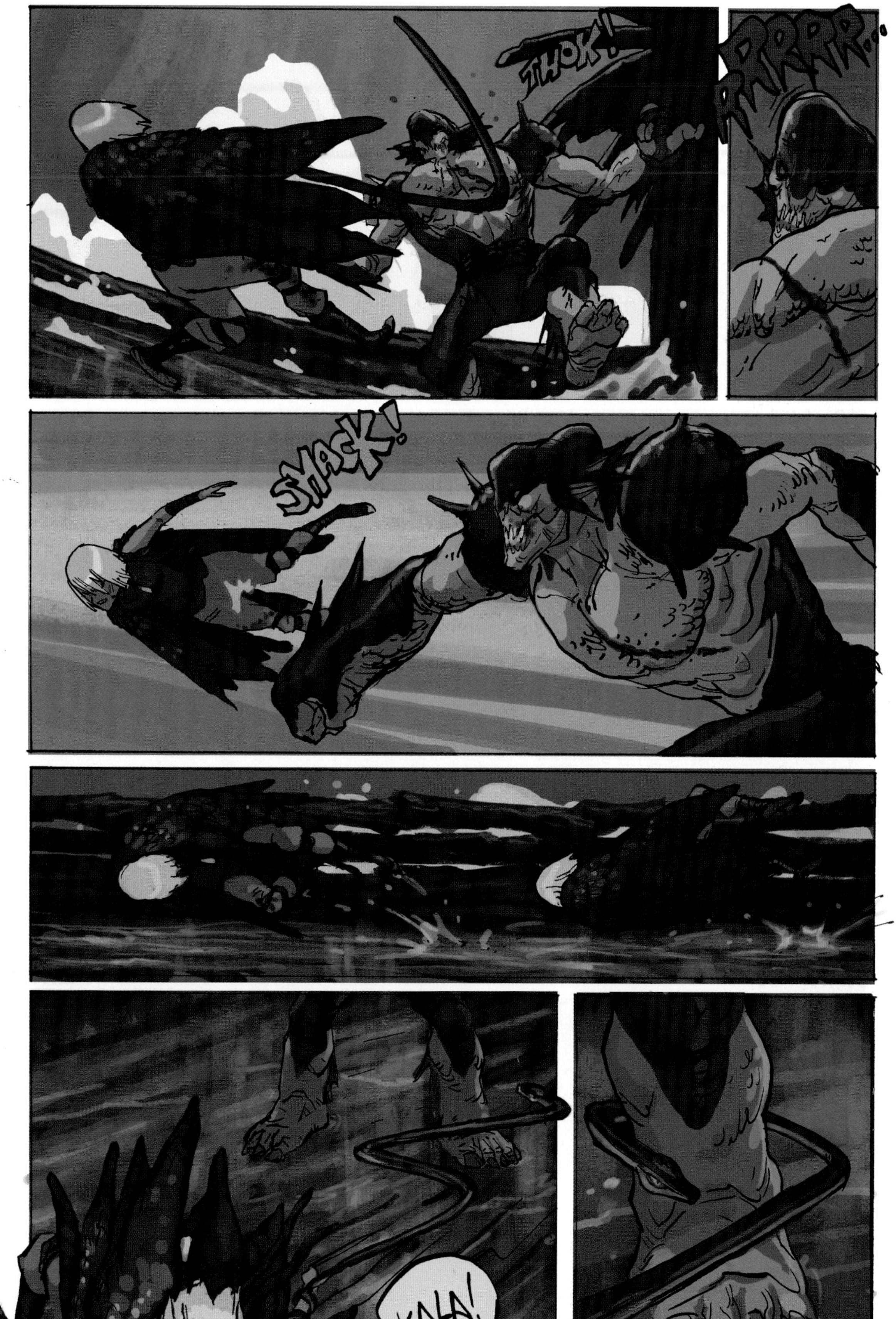
THOK!
RRRR...
SMACK!
KALA!

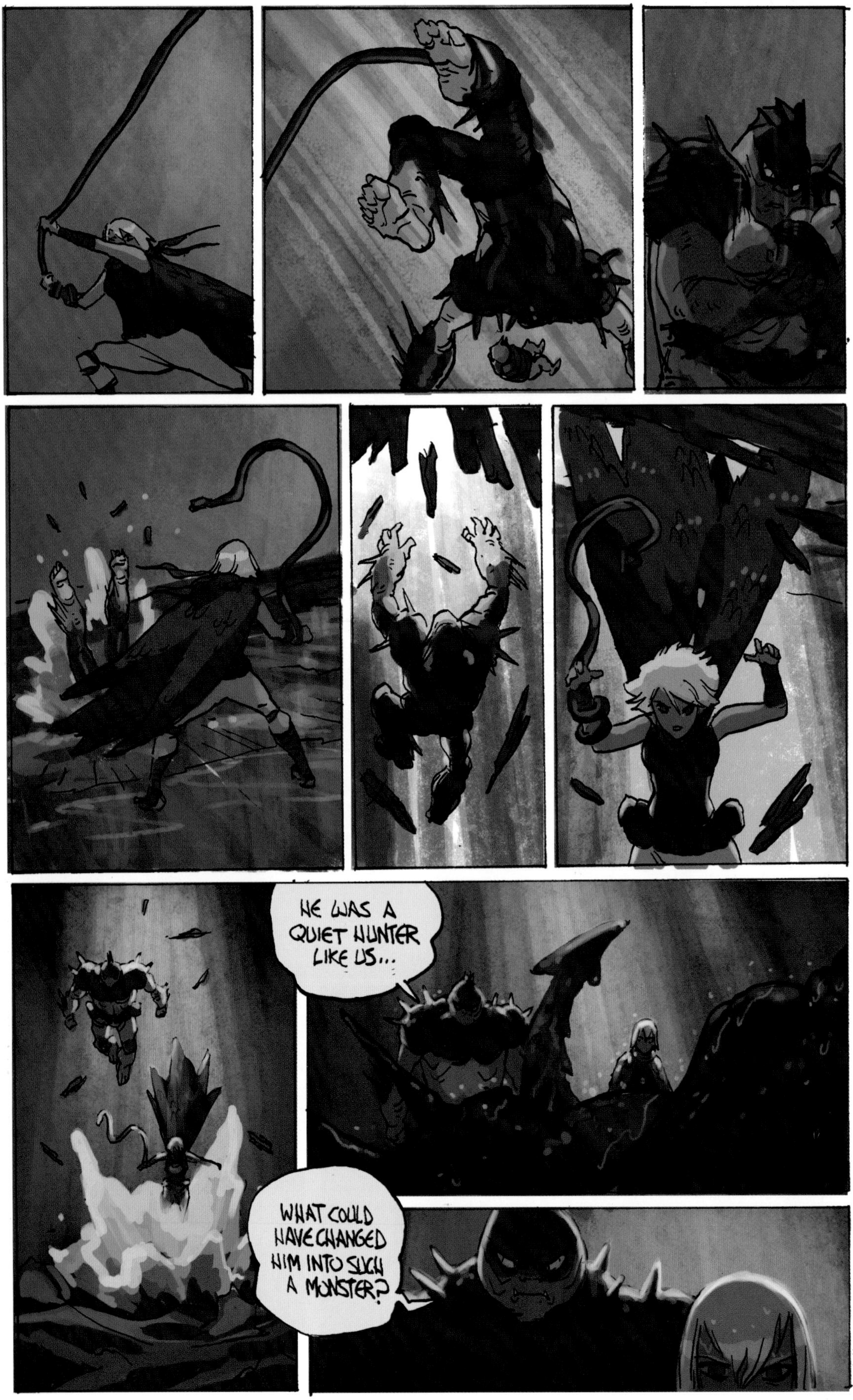
HE WAS A QUIET HUNTER LIKE US...
WHAT COULD HAVE CHANGED HIM INTO SUCH A MONSTER?

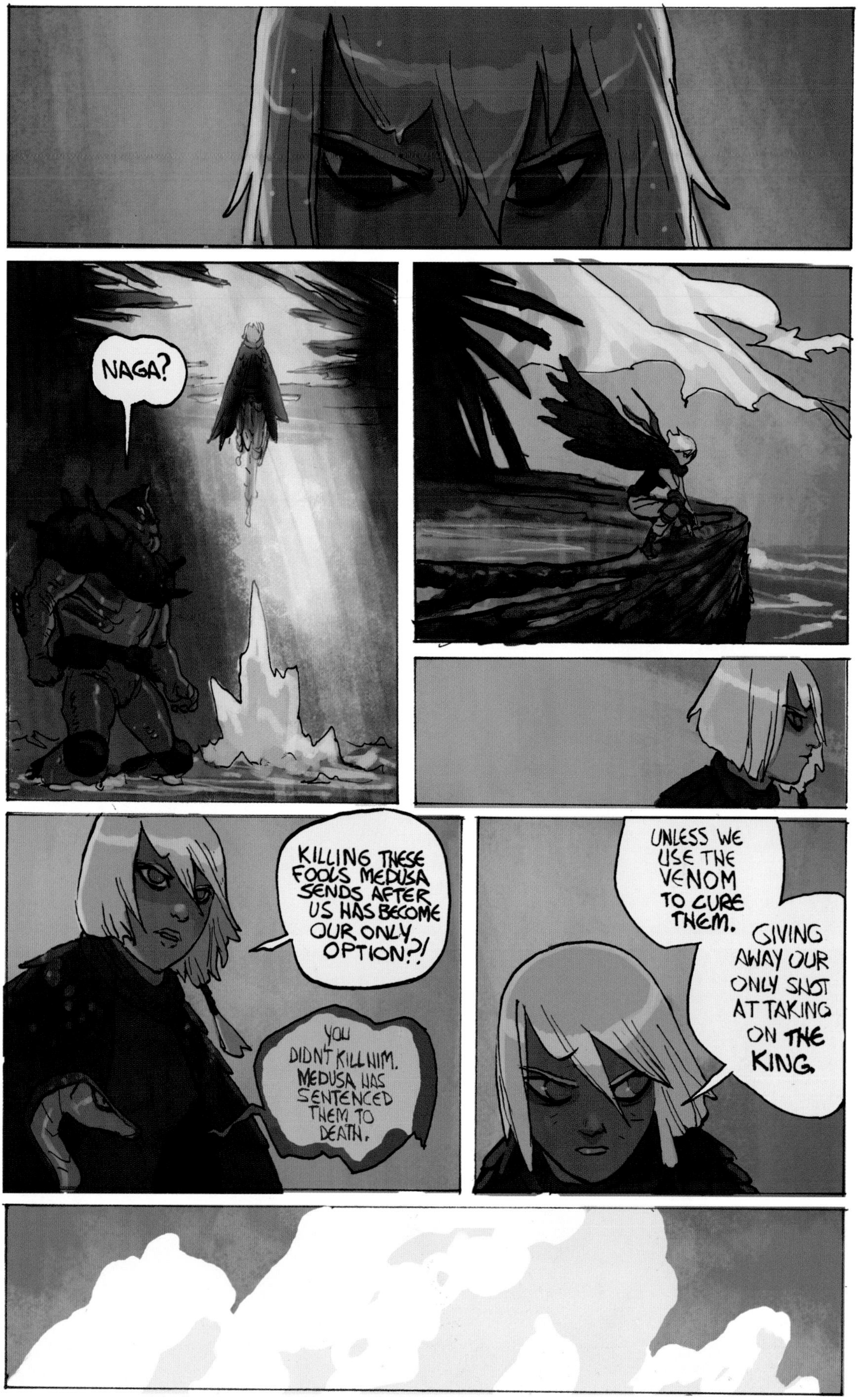
NAGA?
KILLING THESE FOOLS MEDUSA SENDS AFTER US HAS BECOME OUR ONLY OPTION?!
YOU DIDN'T KILL HIM. MEDUSA HAS SENTENCED THEM TO DEATH.
UNLESS WE USE THE VENOM TO CURE THEM.
GIVING AWAY OUR ONLY SHOT AT TAKING ON THE KING.

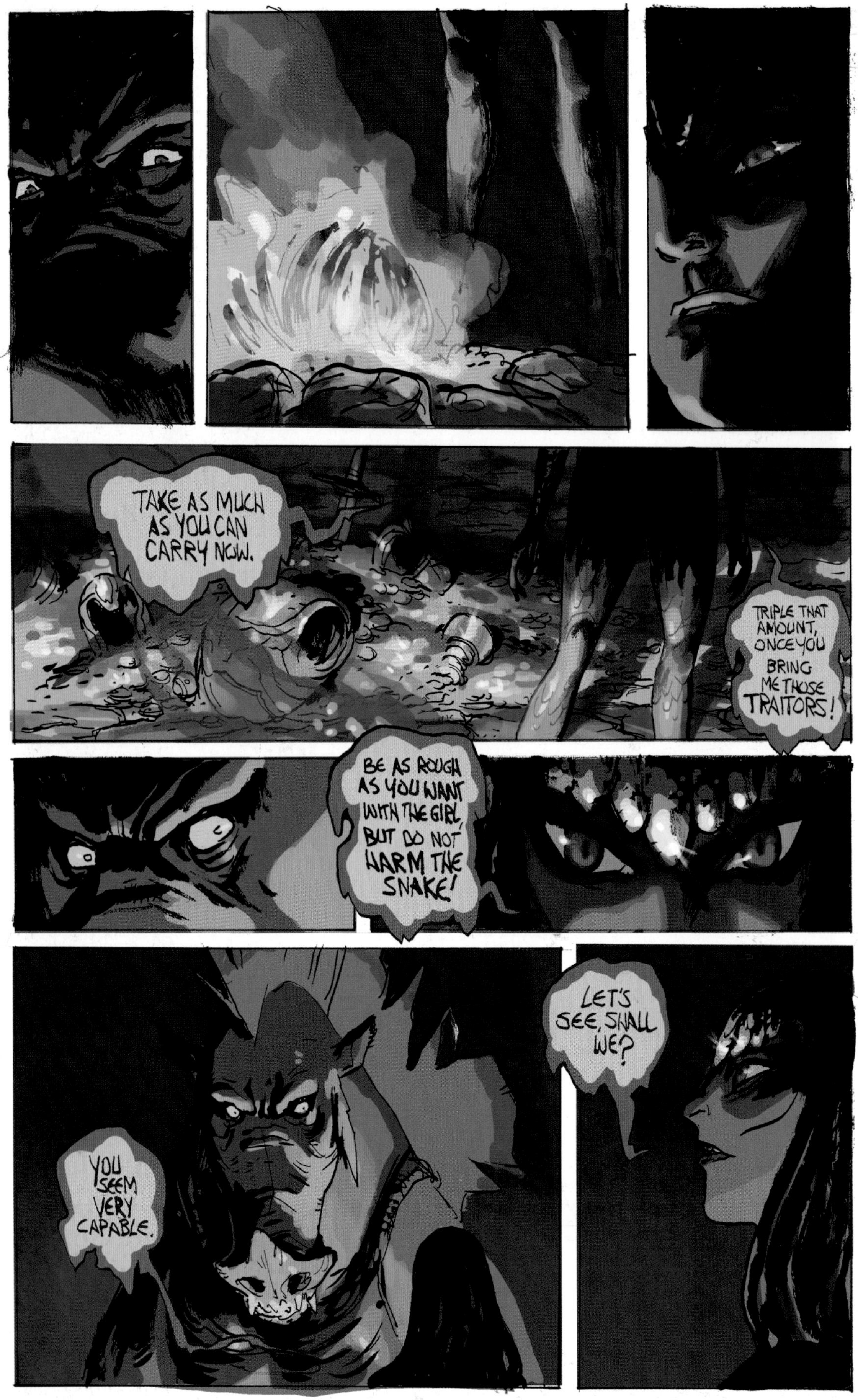
TAKE AS MUCH AS YOU CAN CARRY NOW.
TRIPLE THAT AMOUNT, ONCE YOU BRING ME THOSE TRAITORS!
BE AS ROUGH AS YOU WANT WITH THE GIRL, BUT DO NOT HARM THE SNAKE!
YOU SEEM VERY CAPABLE.
LET'S SEE, SHALL WE?

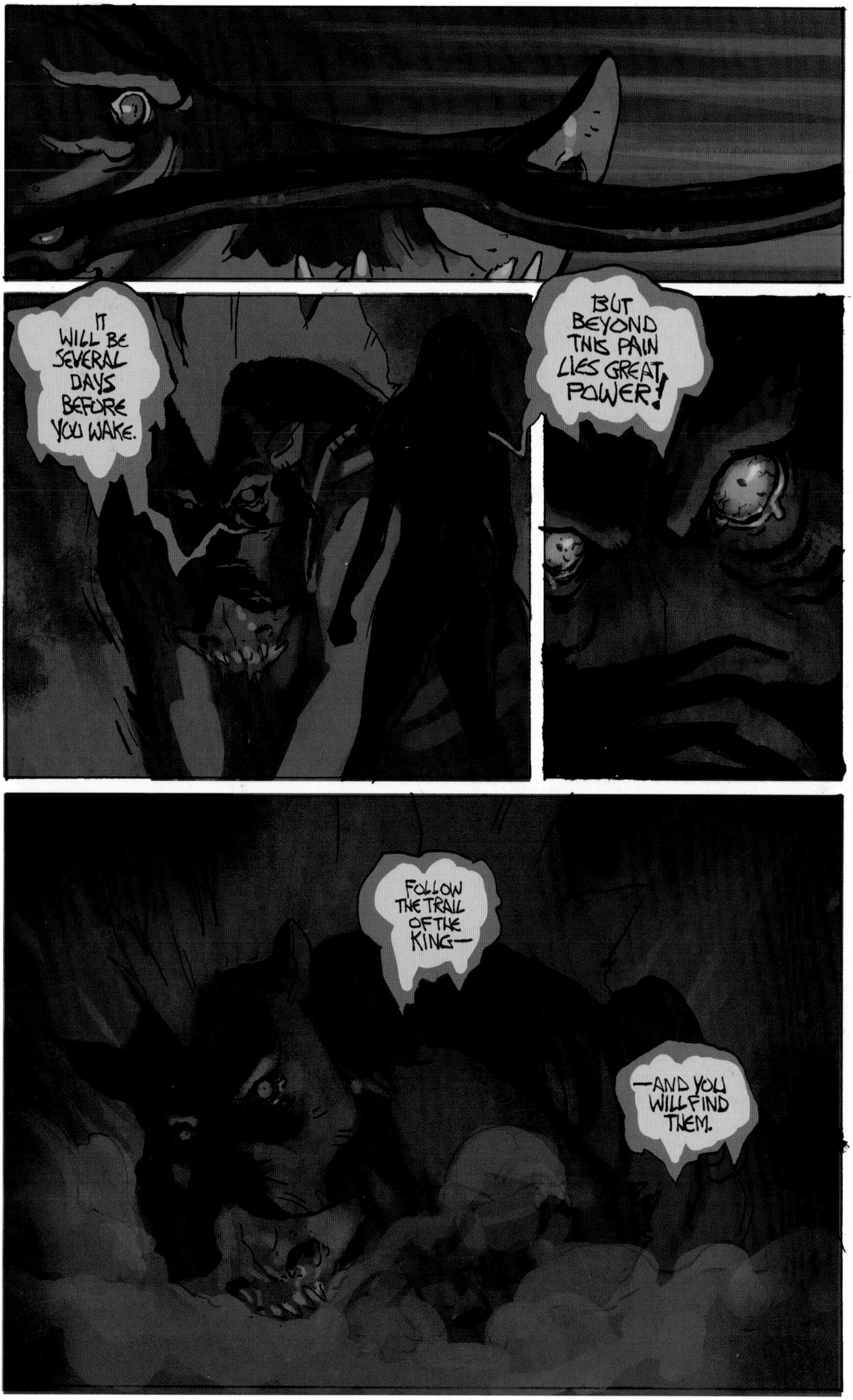
IT WILL BE SEVERAL DAYS BEFORE YOU WAKE.
BUT BEYOND THIS PAIN LIES GREAT POWER!
FOLLOW THE TRAIL OF THE KING—
—AND YOU WILL FIND THEM.

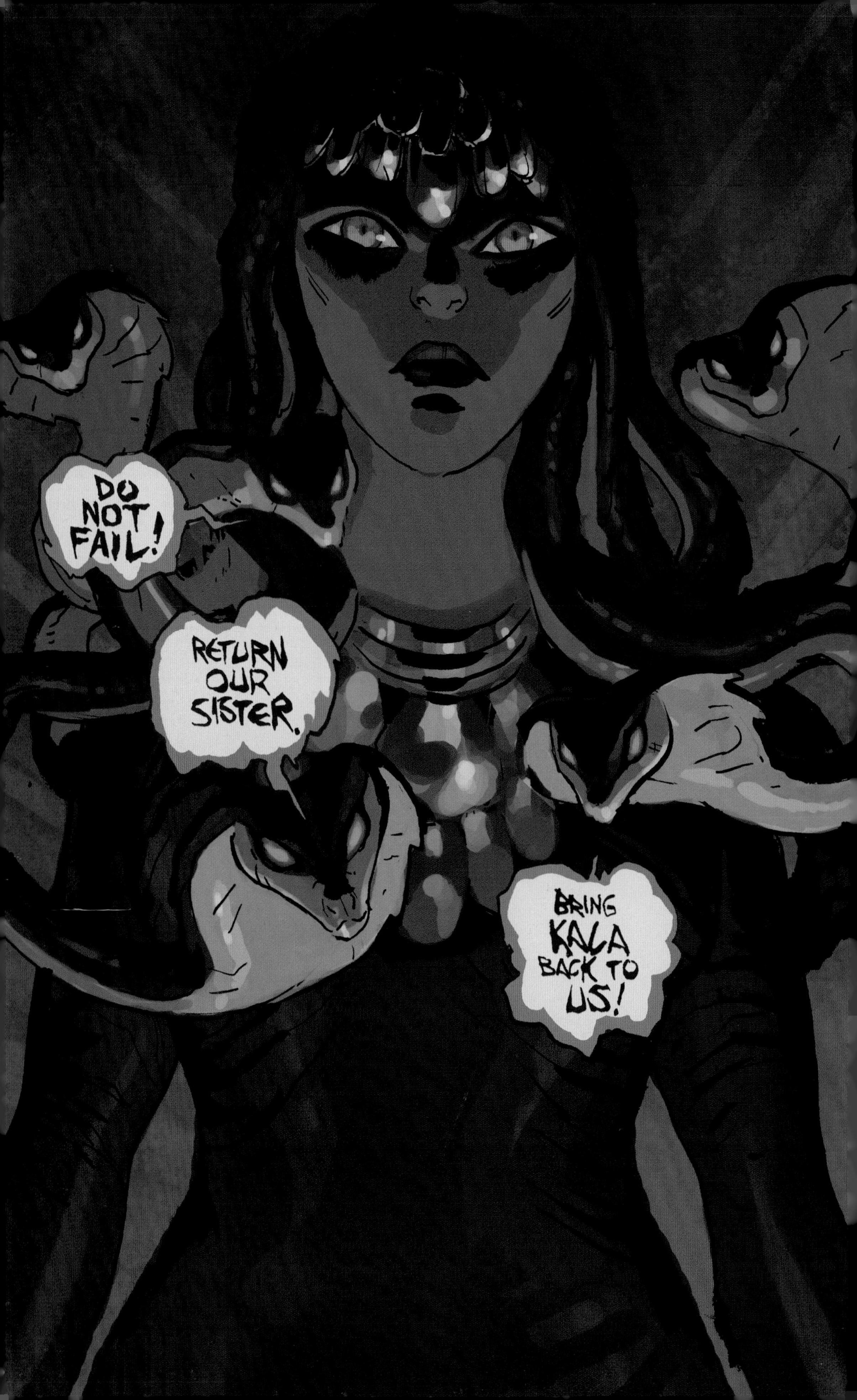
DO NOT FAIL!
RETURN OUR SISTER.
BRING KALA BACK TO US!

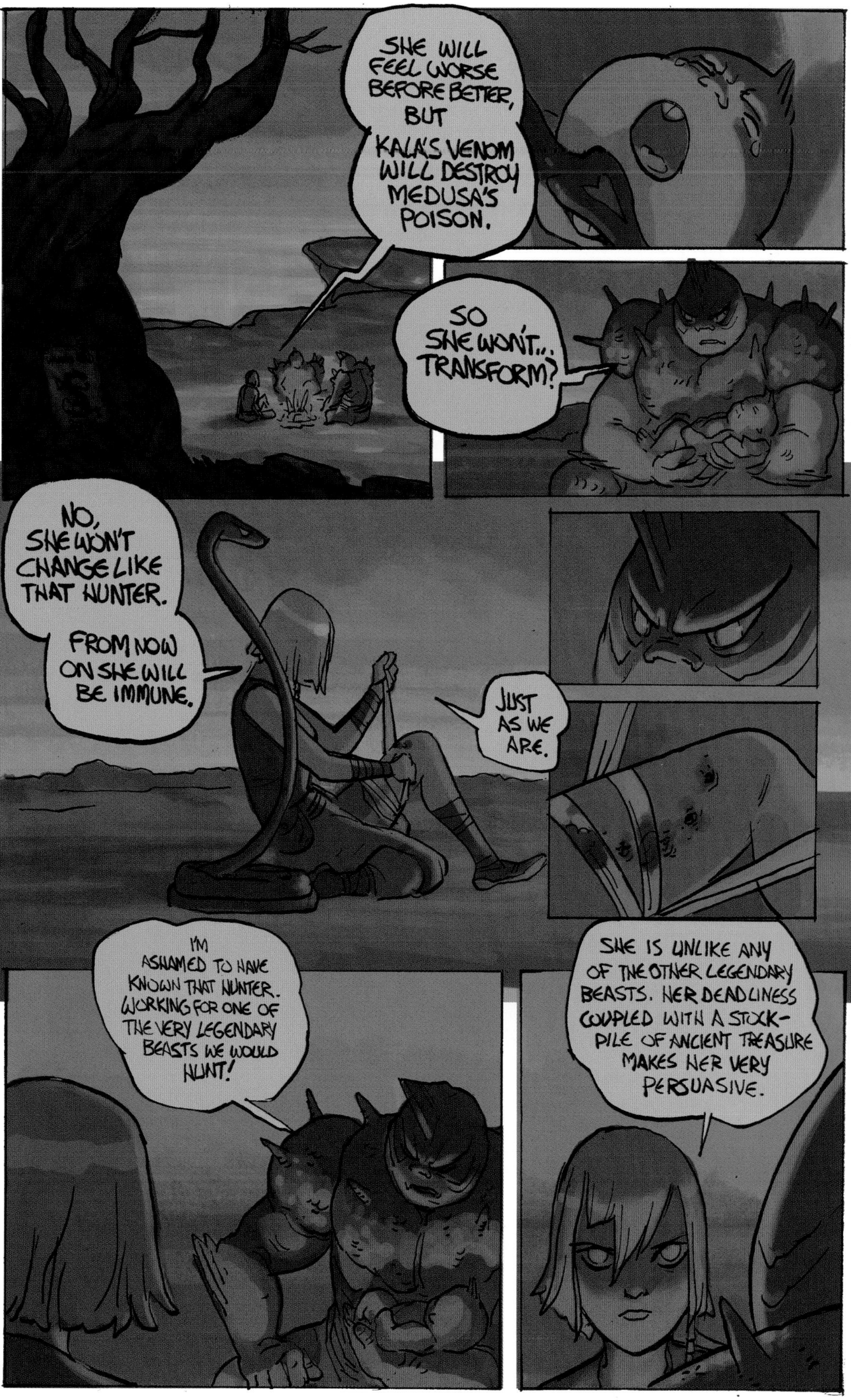
SHE WILL FEEL WORSE BEFORE BETTER, BUT KALA'S VENOM WILL DESTROY MEDUSA'S POISON.
SO SHE WON'T... TRANSFORM?
NO, SHE WON'T CHANGE LIKE THAT HUNTER.
FROM NOW ON SHE WILL BE IMMUNE.
JUST AS WE ARE.
I'M ASHAMED TO HAVE KNOWN THAT HUNTER. WORKING FOR ONE OF THE VERY LEGENDARY BEASTS WE WOULD HUNT!
SHE IS UNLIKE ANY OF THE OTHER LEGENDARY BEASTS. HER DEADLINESS COUPLED WITH A STOCK-PILE OF ANCIENT TREASURE MAKES HER VERY PERSUASIVE.

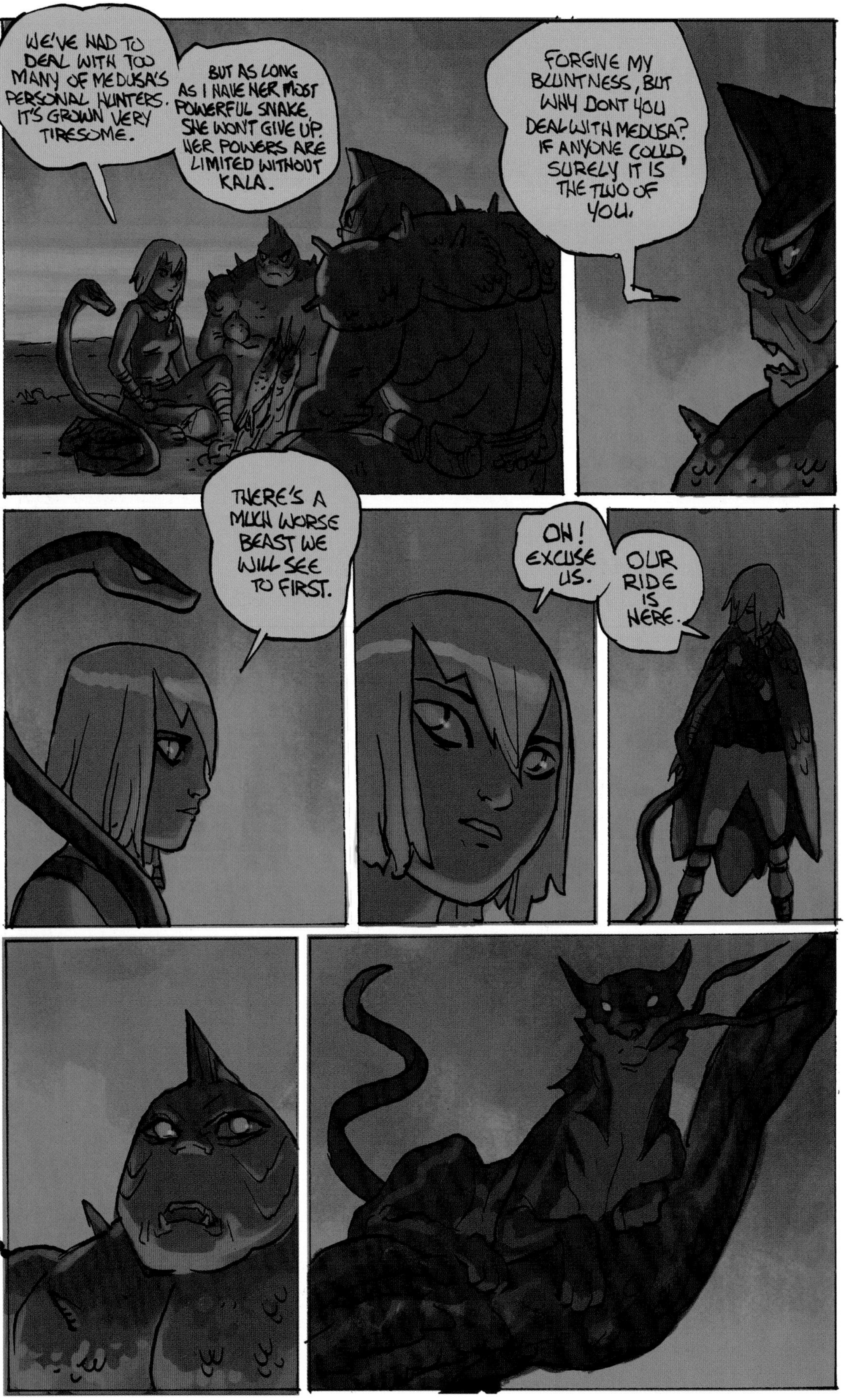
WE'VE HAD TO DEAL WITH TOO MANY OF MEDUSA'S PERSONAL HUNTERS. IT'S GROWN VERY TIRESOME.
BUT AS LONG AS I HAVE HER MOST POWERFUL SNAKE, SHE WON'T GIVE UP. HER POWERS ARE LIMITED WITHOUT KALA.
FORGIVE MY BLUNTNESS, BUT WHY DONT YOU DEAL WITH MEDUSA? IF ANYONE COULD, SURELY IT IS THE TWO OF YOU.
THERE'S A MUCH WORSE BEAST WE WILL SEE TO FIRST.
OH! EXCUSE US.
OUR RIDE IS HERE.

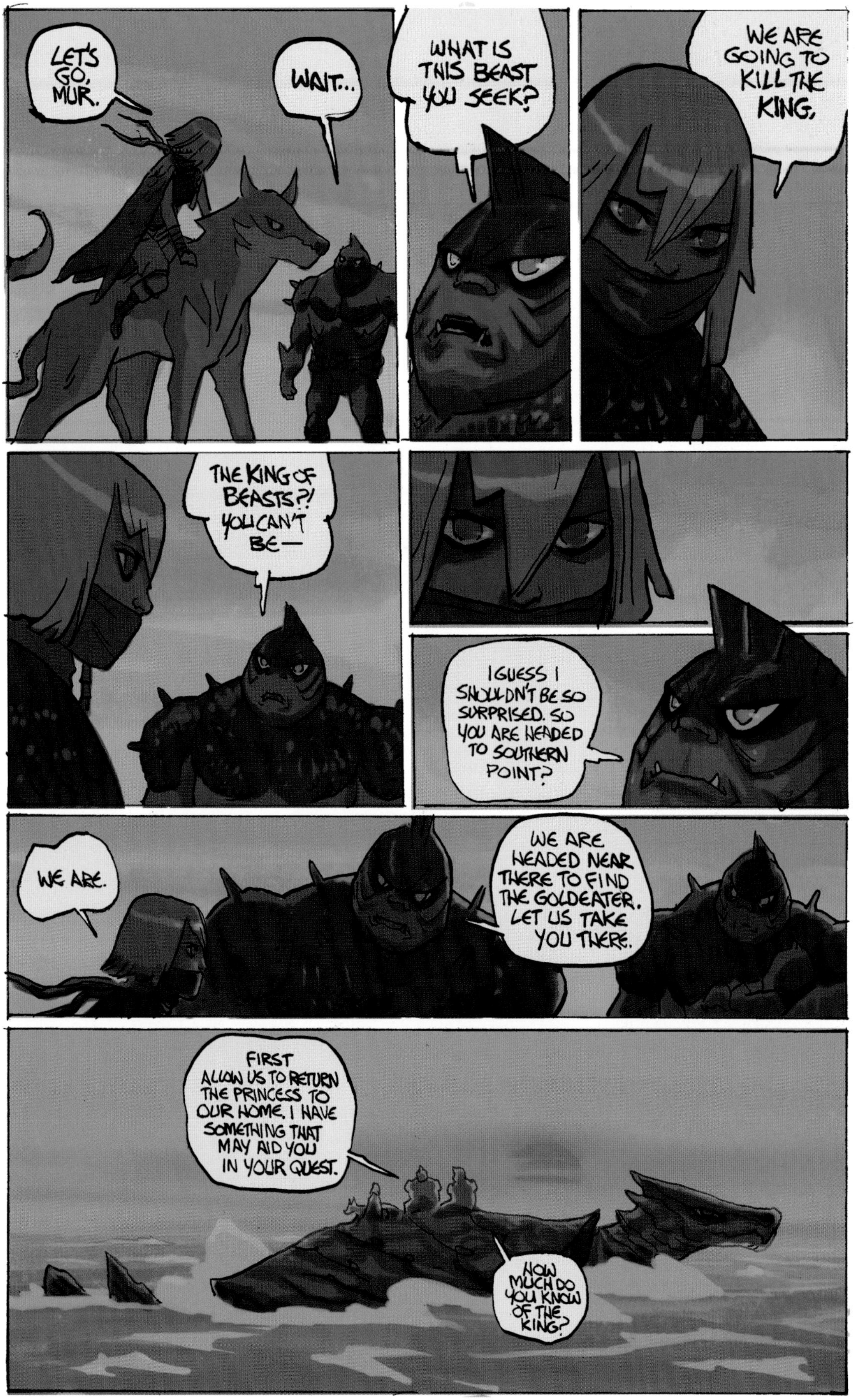
LET'S GO, MUR.
WAIT...
WHAT IS THIS BEAST YOU SEEK?
WE ARE GOING TO KILL THE KING.
THE KING OF BEASTS?! YOU CAN'T BE—
I GUESS I SHOULDN'T BE SO SURPRISED. SO YOU ARE HEADED TO SOUTHERN POINT?
WE ARE.
WE ARE HEADED NEAR THERE TO FIND THE GOLDEATER. LET US TAKE YOU THERE.
FIRST ALLOW US TO RETURN THE PRINCESS TO OUR HOME. I HAVE SOMETHING THAT MAY AID YOU IN YOUR QUEST.
HOW MUCH DO YOU KNOW OF THE KING?

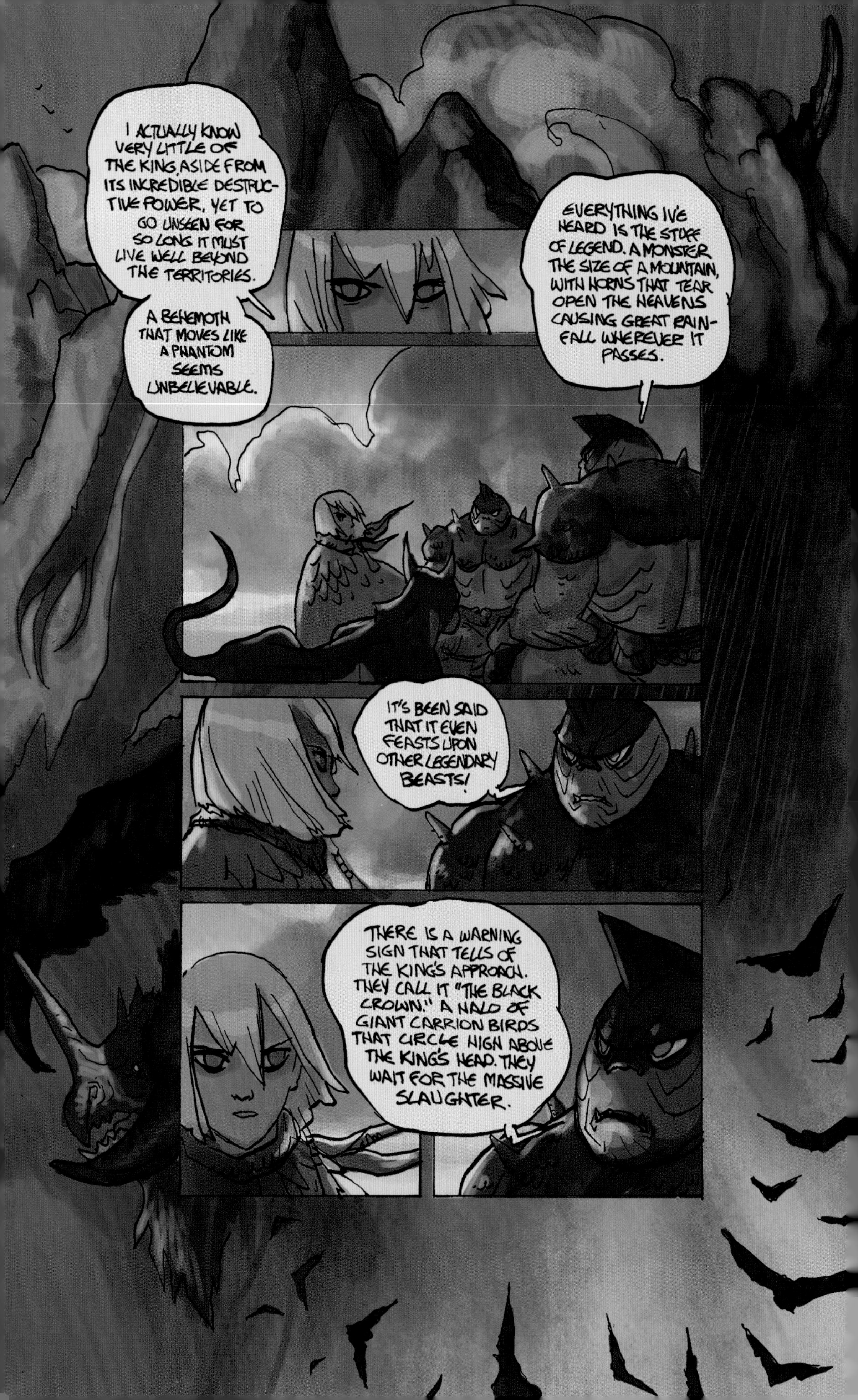
I ACTUALLY KNOW VERY LITTLE OF THE KING, ASIDE FROM ITS INCREDIBLE DESTRUCTIVE POWER. YET TO GO UNSEEN FOR SO LONG IT MUST LIVE WELL BEYOND THE TERRITORIES.
A BEHEMOTH THAT MOVES LIKE A PHANTOM SEEMS UNBELIEVABLE.
EVERYTHING I'VE HEARD IS THE STUFF OF LEGEND. A MONSTER THE SIZE OF A MOUNTAIN, WITH HORNS THAT TEAR OPEN THE HEAVENS CAUSING GREAT RAINFALL WHEREVER IT PASSES.
IT'S BEEN SAID THAT IT EVEN FEASTS UPON OTHER LEGENDARY BEASTS!
THERE IS A WARNING SIGN THAT TELLS OF THE KING'S APPROACH. THEY CALL IT "THE BLACK CROWN." A HALO OF GIANT CARRION BIRDS THAT CIRCLE HIGH ABOVE THE KING'S HEAD. THEY WAIT FOR THE MASSIVE SLAUGHTER.

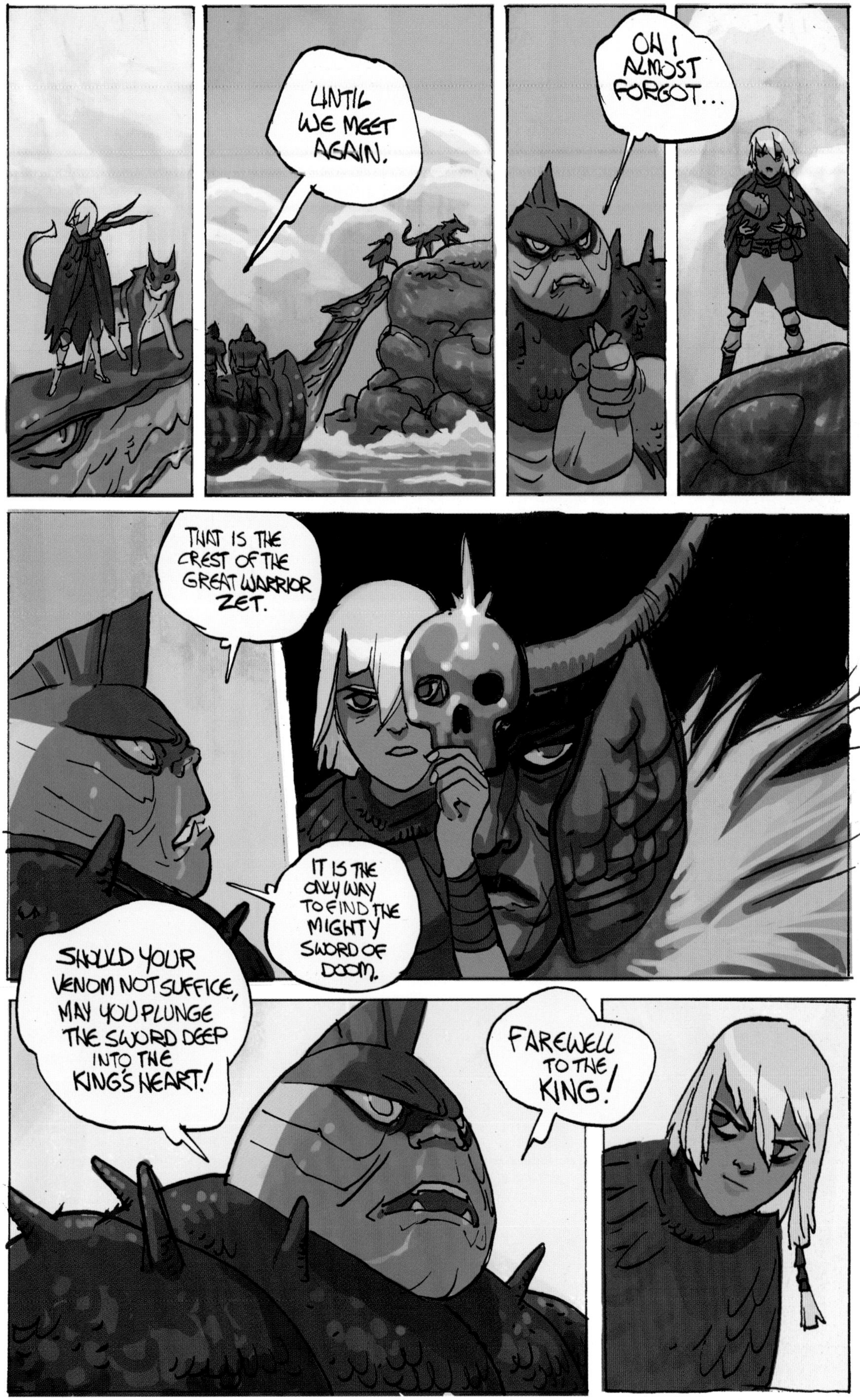
UNTIL WE MEET AGAIN.
OH I ALMOST FORGOT...
THAT IS THE CREST OF THE GREAT WARRIOR ZET.
IT IS THE ONLY WAY TO FIND THE MIGHTY SWORD OF DOOM.
SHOULD YOUR VENOM NOT SUFFICE, MAY YOU PLUNGE THE SWORD DEEP INTO THE KING'S HEART!
FAREWELL TO THE KING!

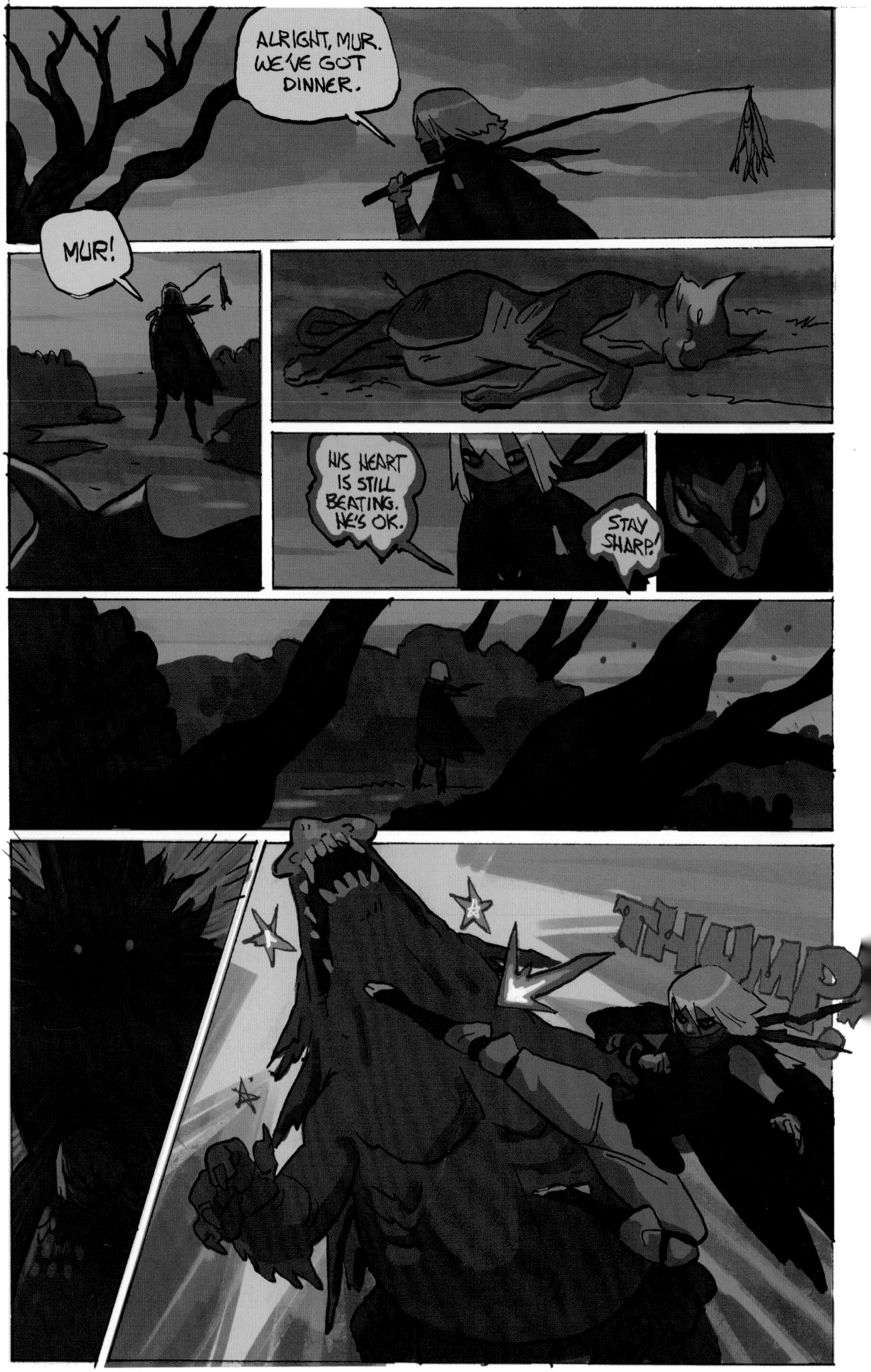
ALRIGHT, MUR.
WE'VE GOT
DINNER.
MUR!
HIS HEART
IS STILL
BEATING.
HE'S OK.
STAY
SHARP!
THUMP

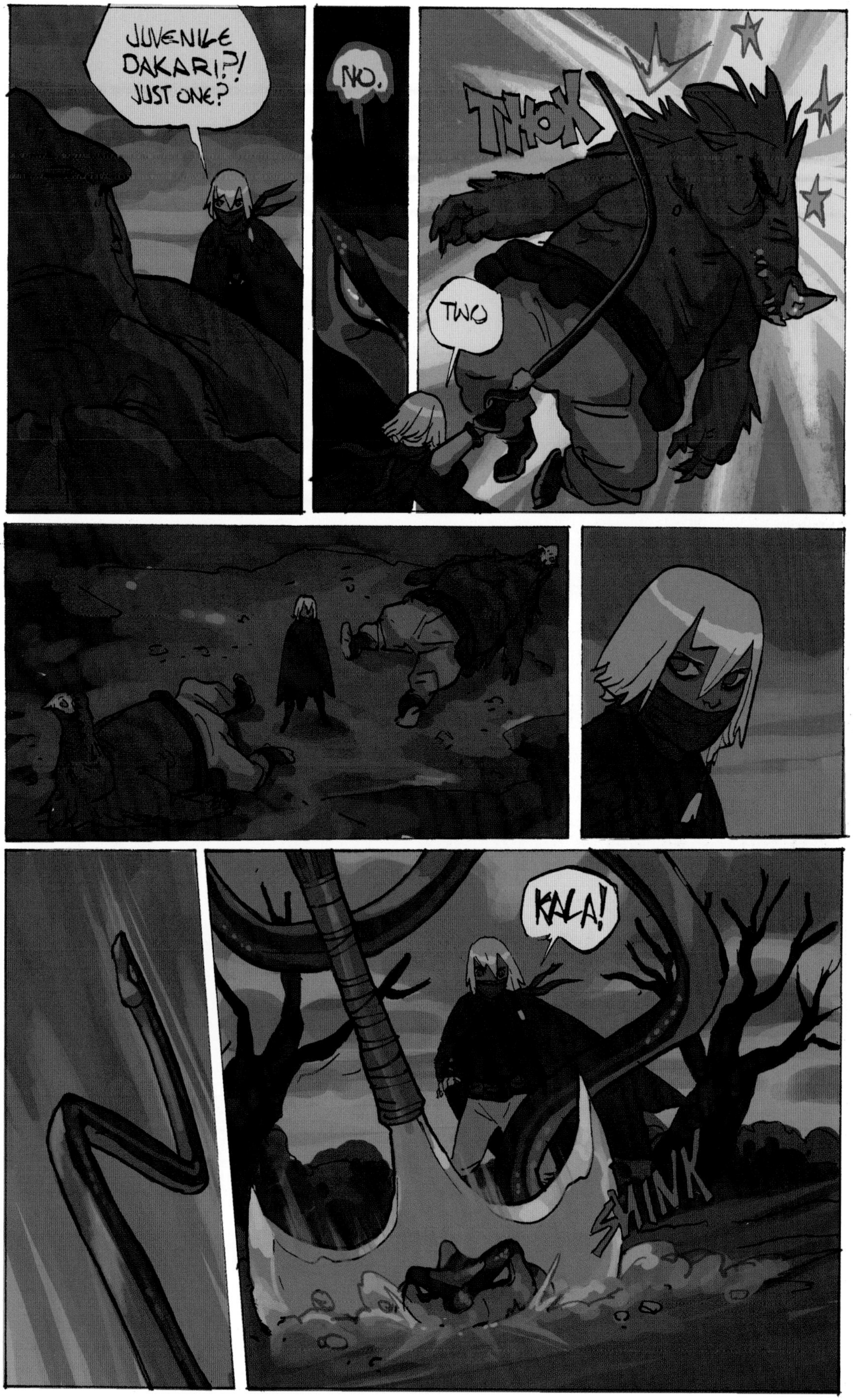

JUVENILE DAKARI!?! JUST ONE?
NO.
THOK
TWO
KALA!
SHINK

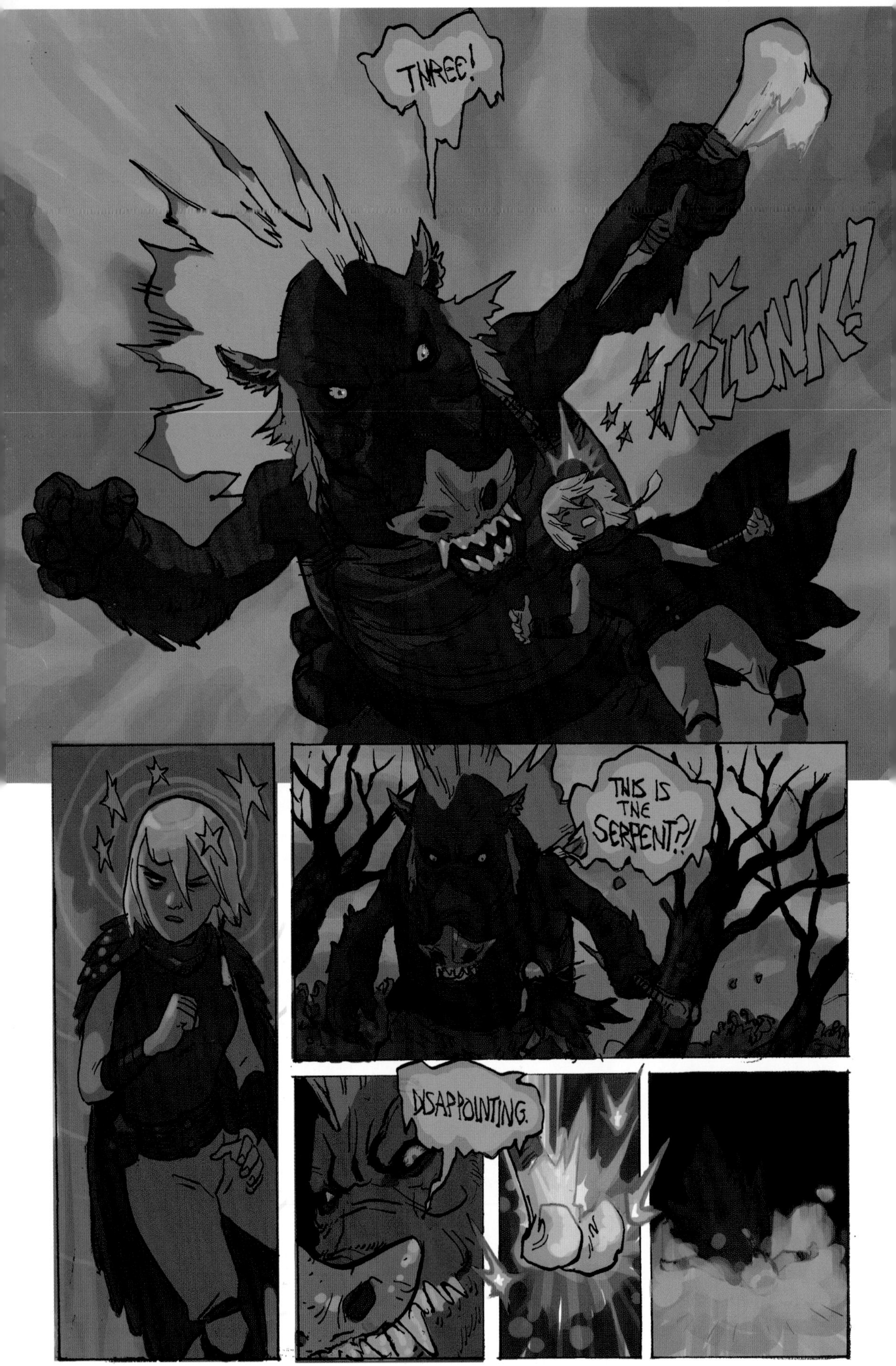
THREE!
KLUNK!
THIS IS THE SERPENT?!
DISAPPOINTING.

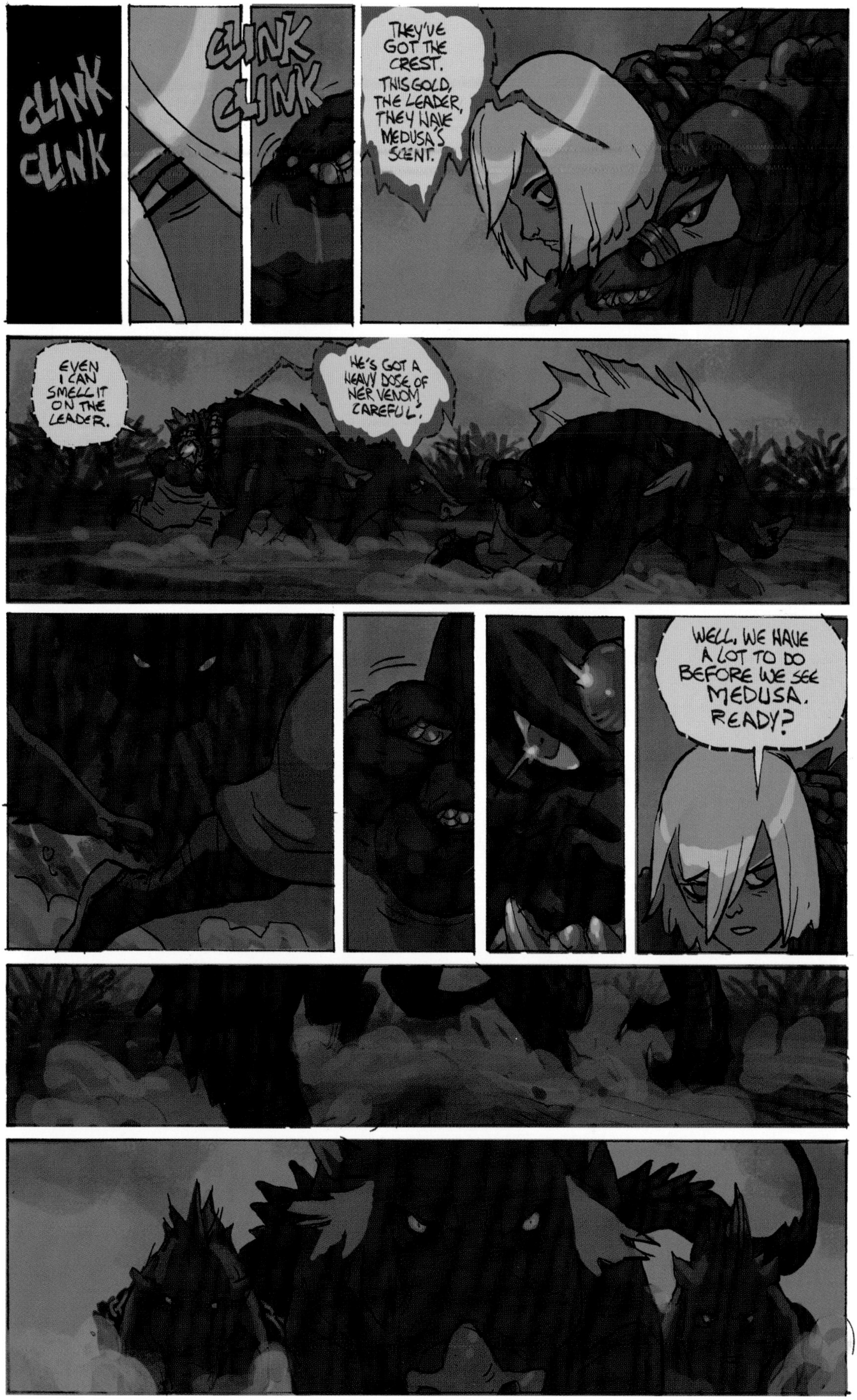
CLINK CLINK
CLINK CLINK
THEY'VE GOT THE CREST. THIS GOLD, THE LEADER, THEY HAVE MEDUSA'S SCENT.
EVEN I CAN SMELL IT ON THE LEADER.
HE'S GOT A HEAVY DOSE OF NER VENOM! CAREFUL!
WELL, WE HAVE A LOT TO DO BEFORE WE SEE MEDUSA. READY?

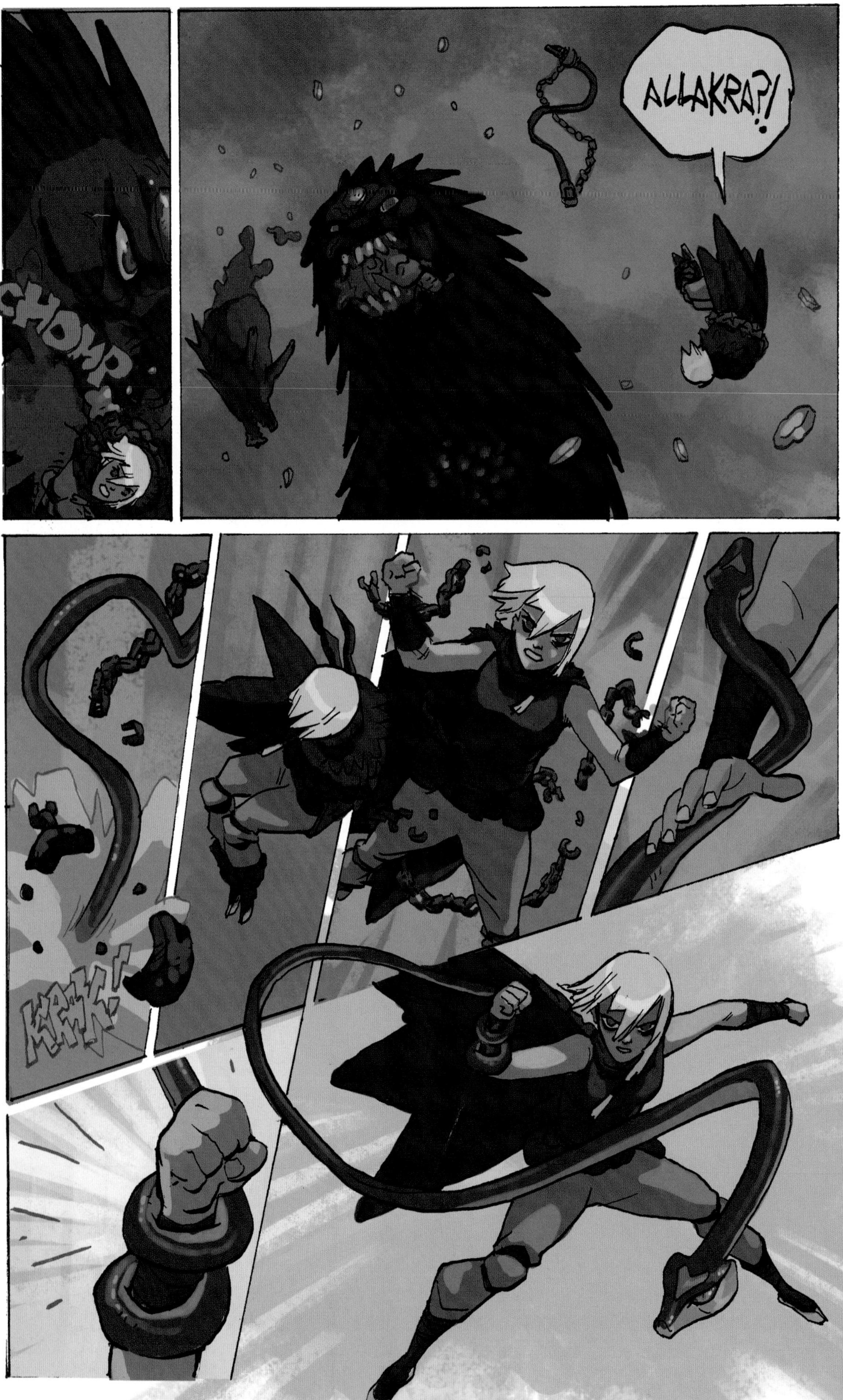
CHOMP
ALLAKRA?!
KRAKK!

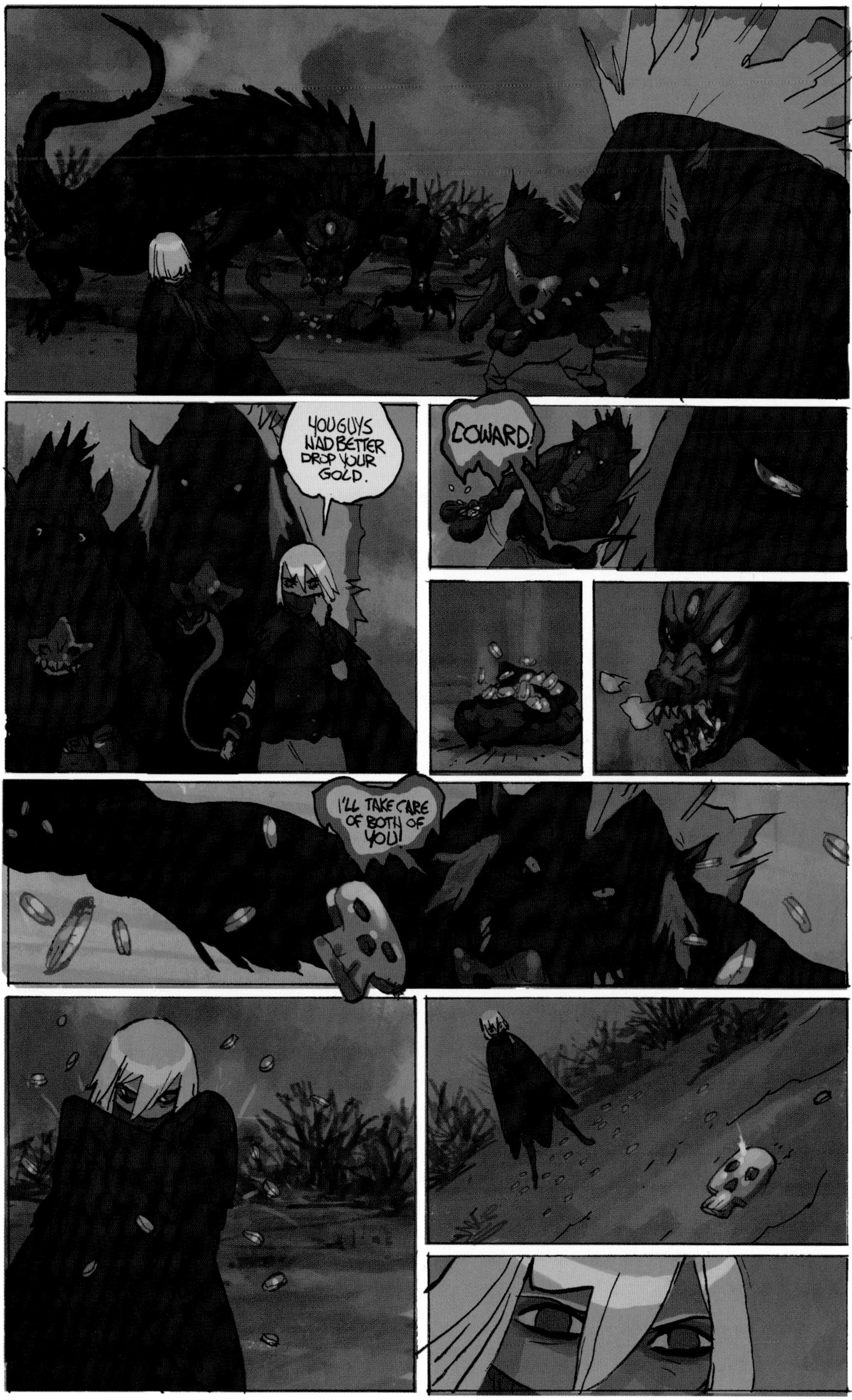
YOU GUYS HAD BETTER DROP YOUR GOLD.
COWARD!
I'LL TAKE CARE OF BOTH OF YOU!

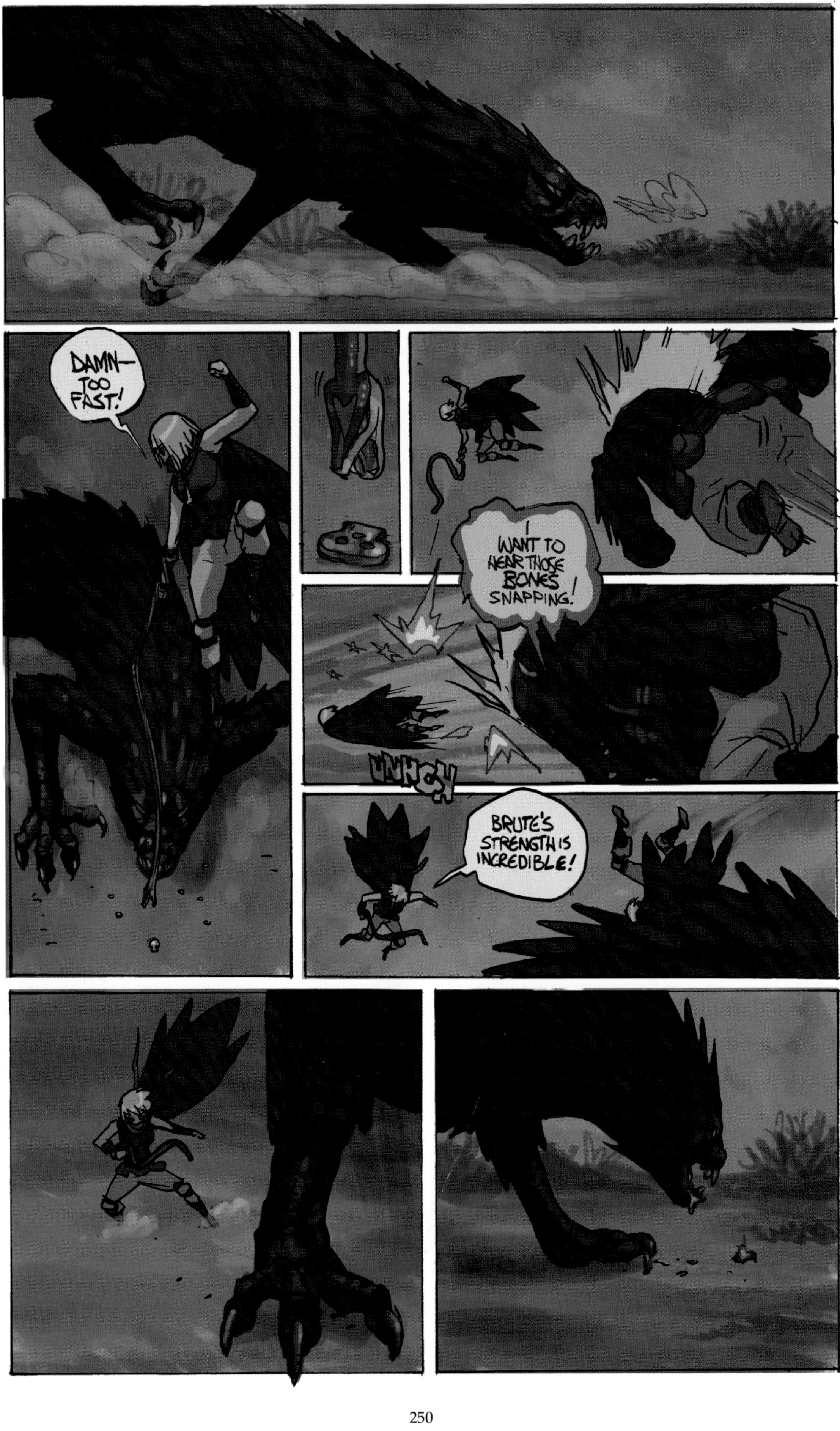
DAMN—TOO FAST!
I WANT TO HEAR THOSE BONES SNAPPING!
UNHCH
BRUTE'S STRENGTH IS INCREDIBLE!

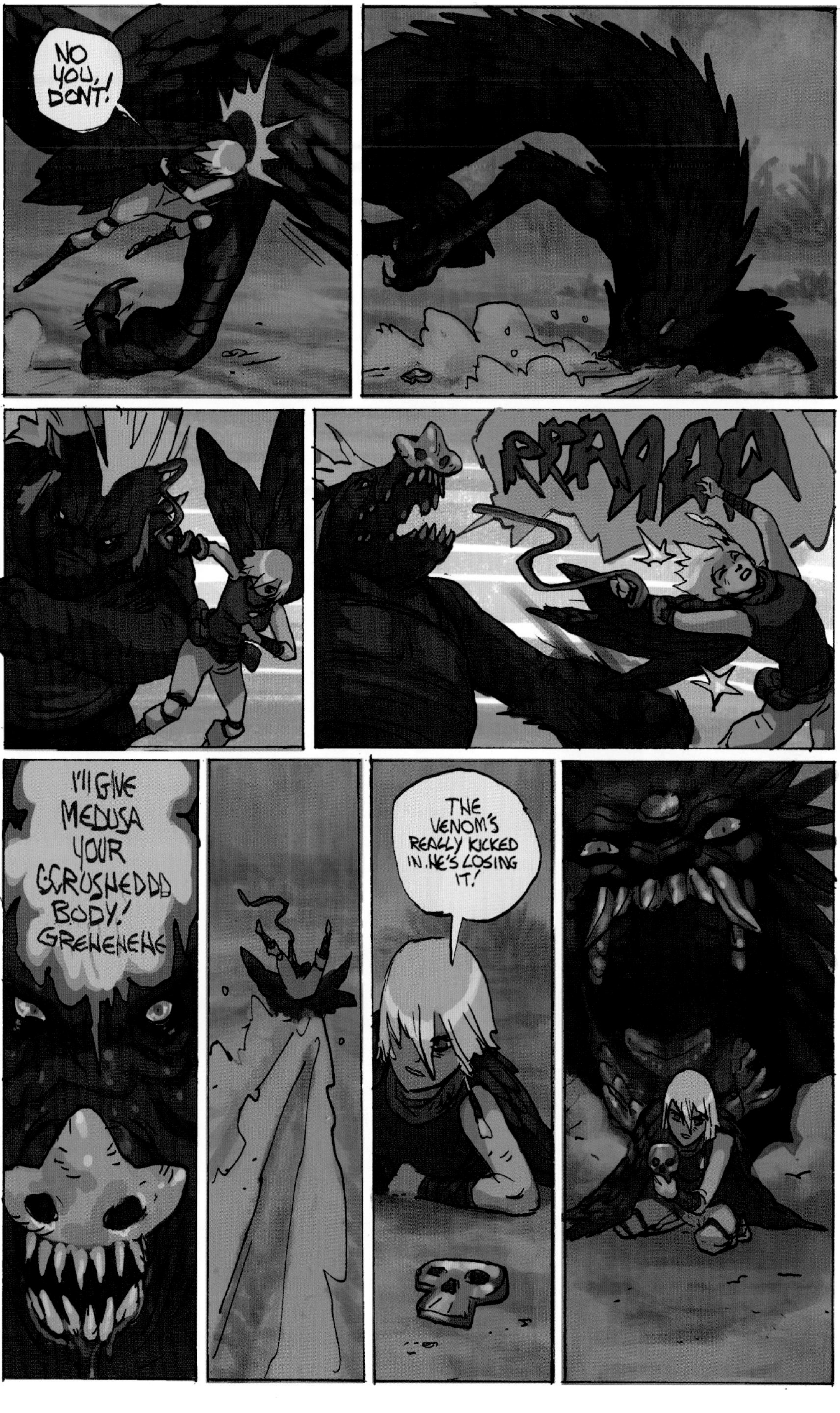
NO YOU, DONT!
RRAAAA
I'll GIVE MEDUSA YOUR CCRUSHEDDD BODY! GREHEHEHE
THE VENOM'S REALLY KICKED IN. HE'S LOSING IT!

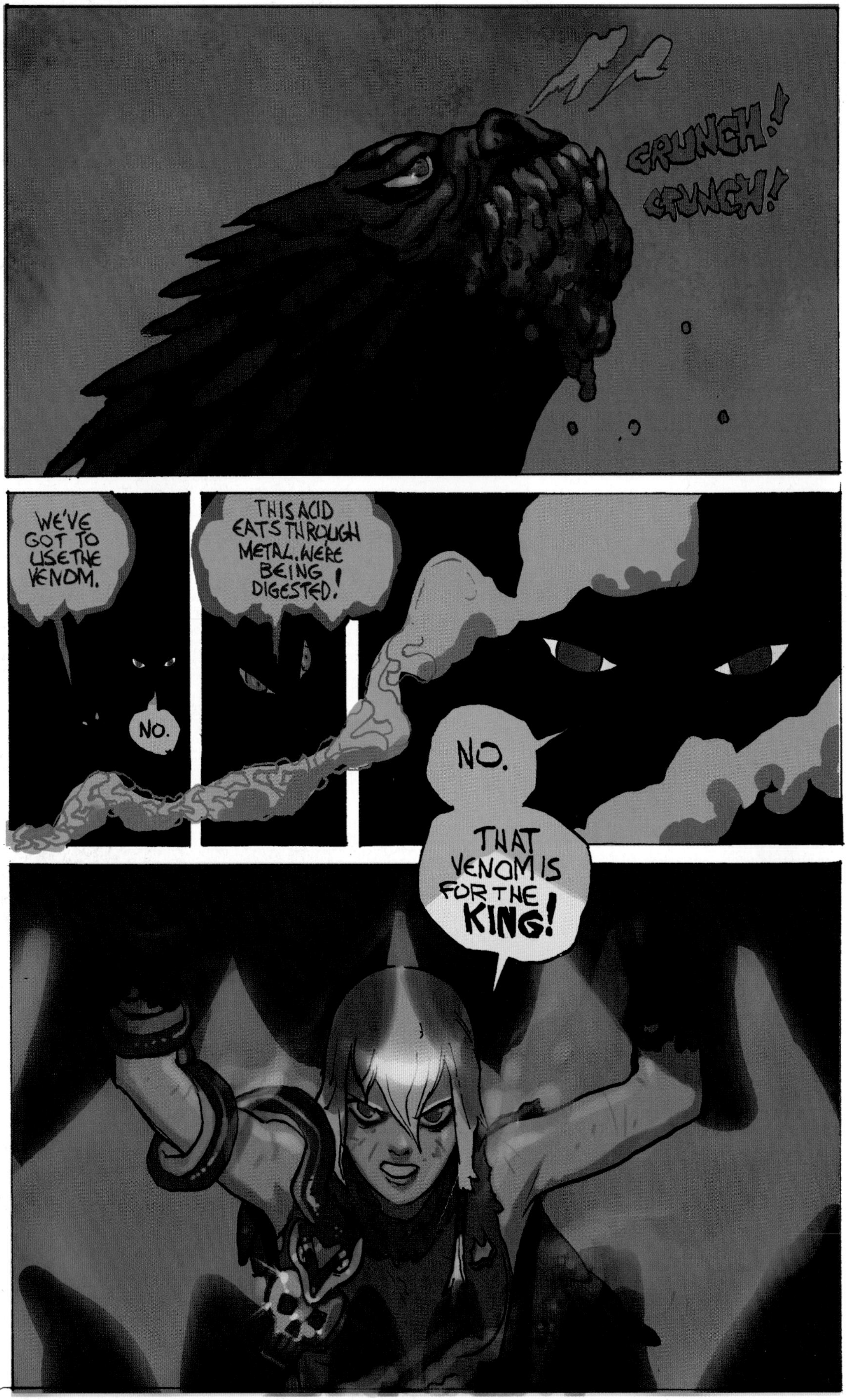
CRUNCH!
CRUNCH!
WE'VE GOT TO USE THE VENOM.
NO.
THIS ACID EATS THROUGH METAL. WE'RE BEING DIGESTED!
NO.
THAT VENOM IS FOR THE KING!

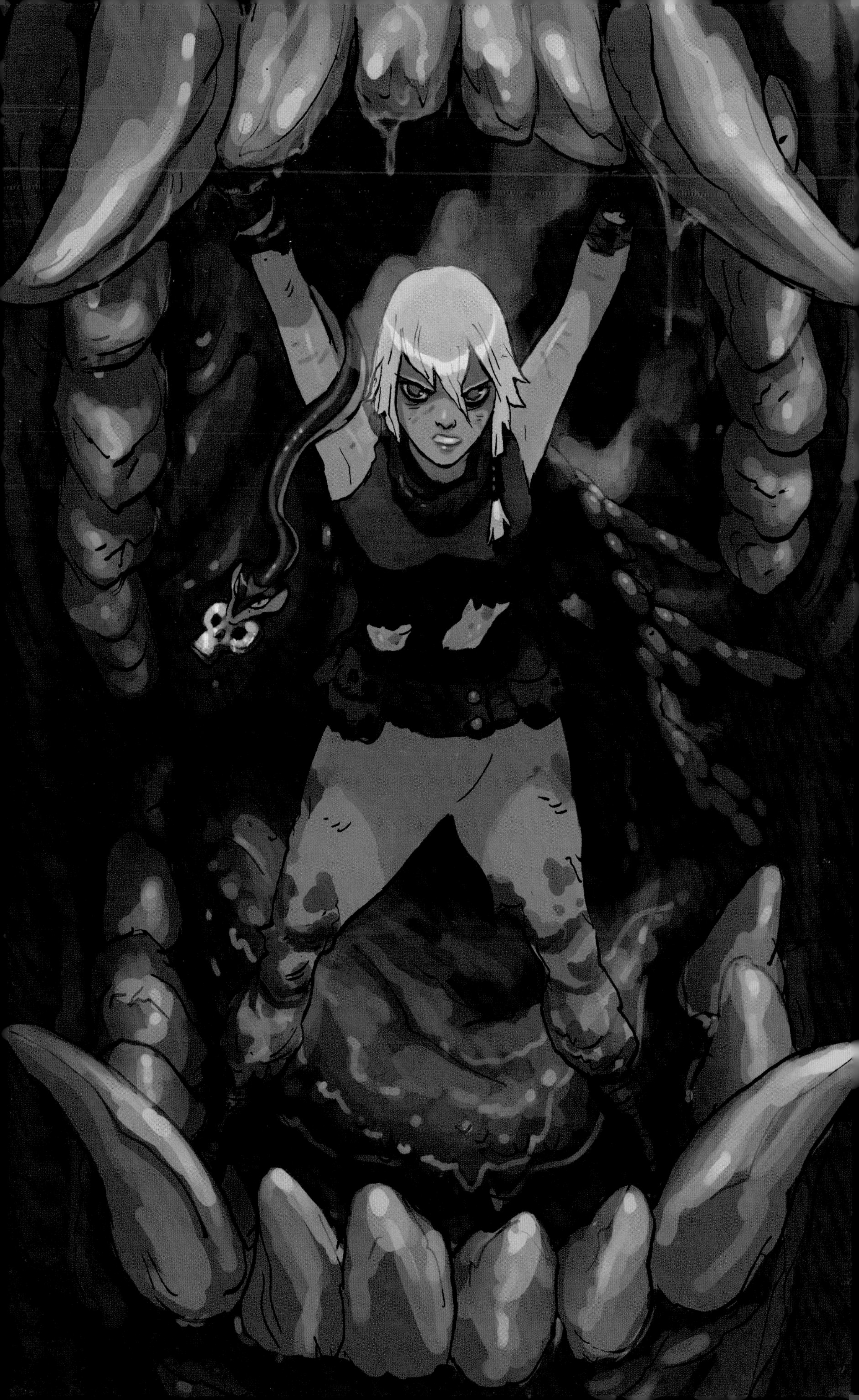

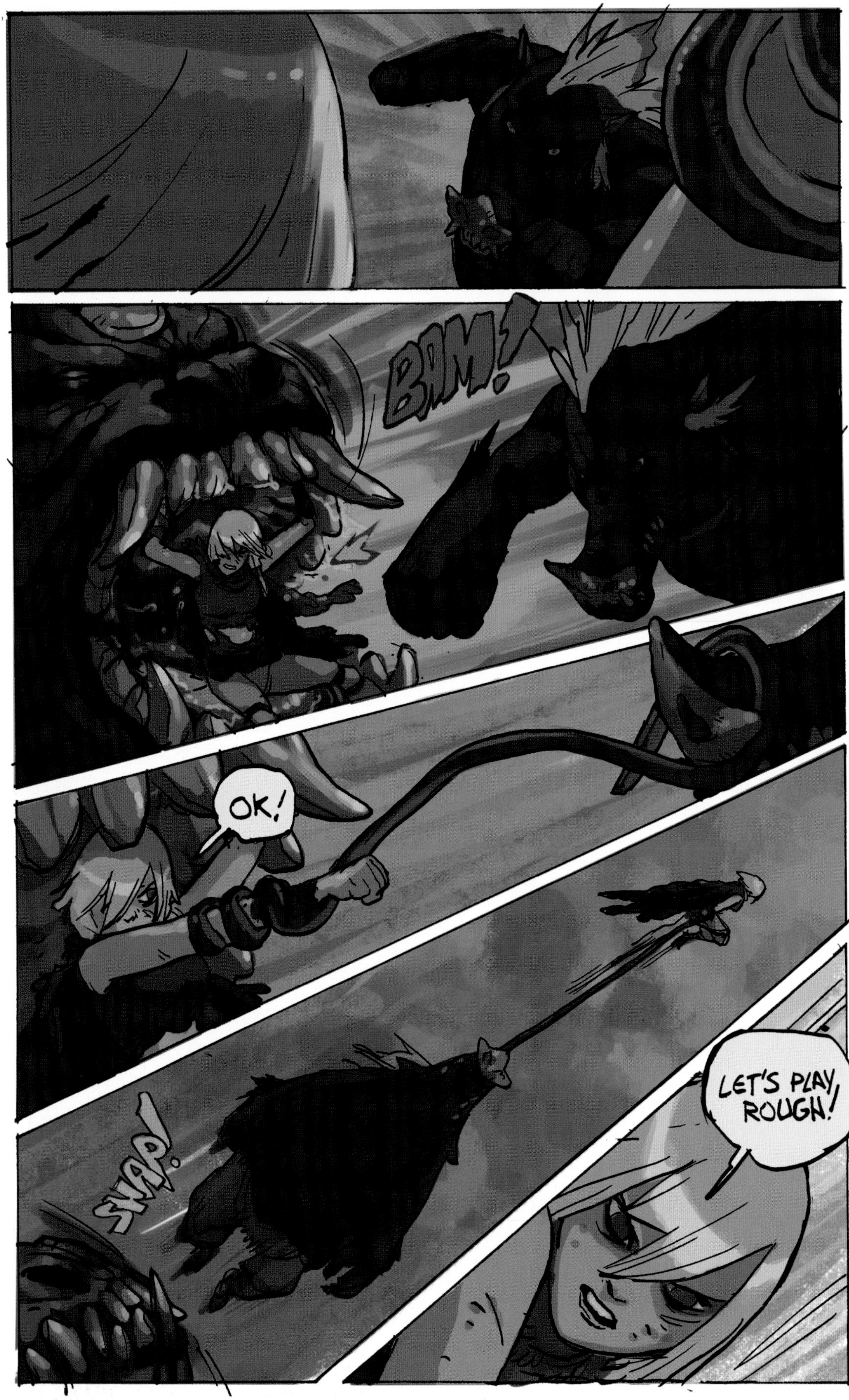
BAM!
OK!
SNAP!
LET'S PLAY ROUGH!

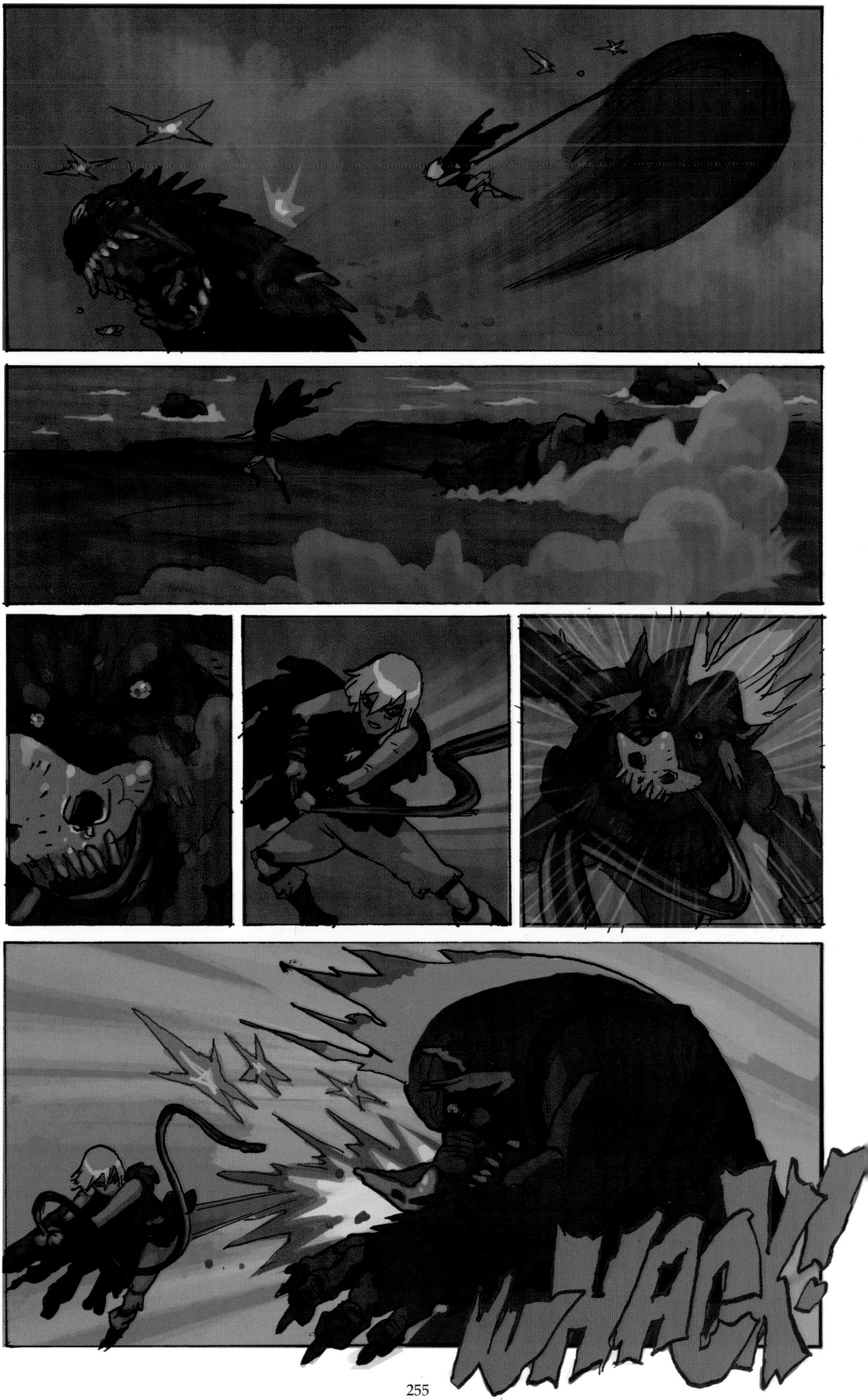
WHACK!

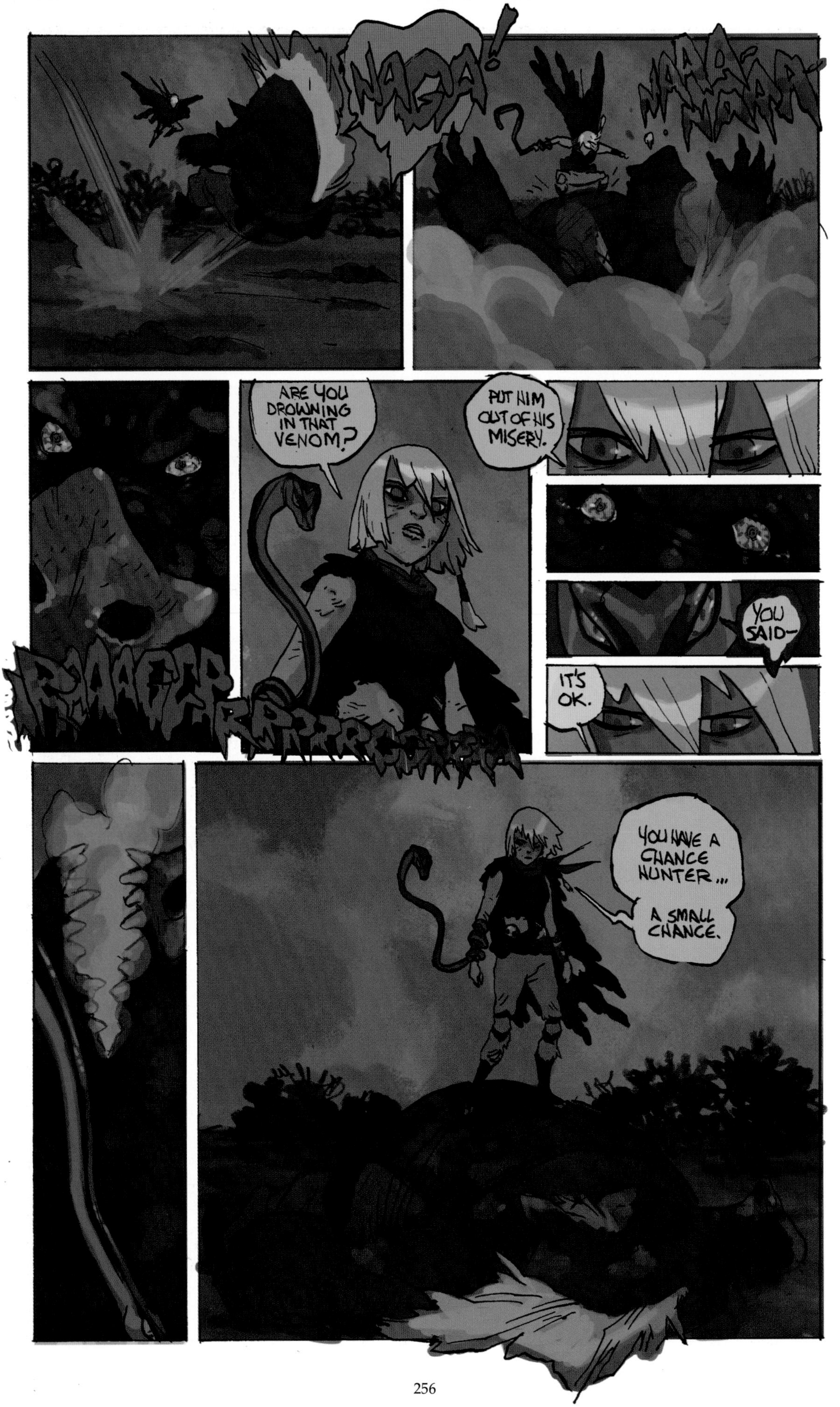
NAGA!
NAA-NAAA
ARE YOU DROWNING IN THAT VENOM?
PUT HIM OUT OF HIS MISERY.
YOU SAID-
IT'S OK.
YOU HAVE A CHANCE HUNTER...
A SMALL CHANCE.

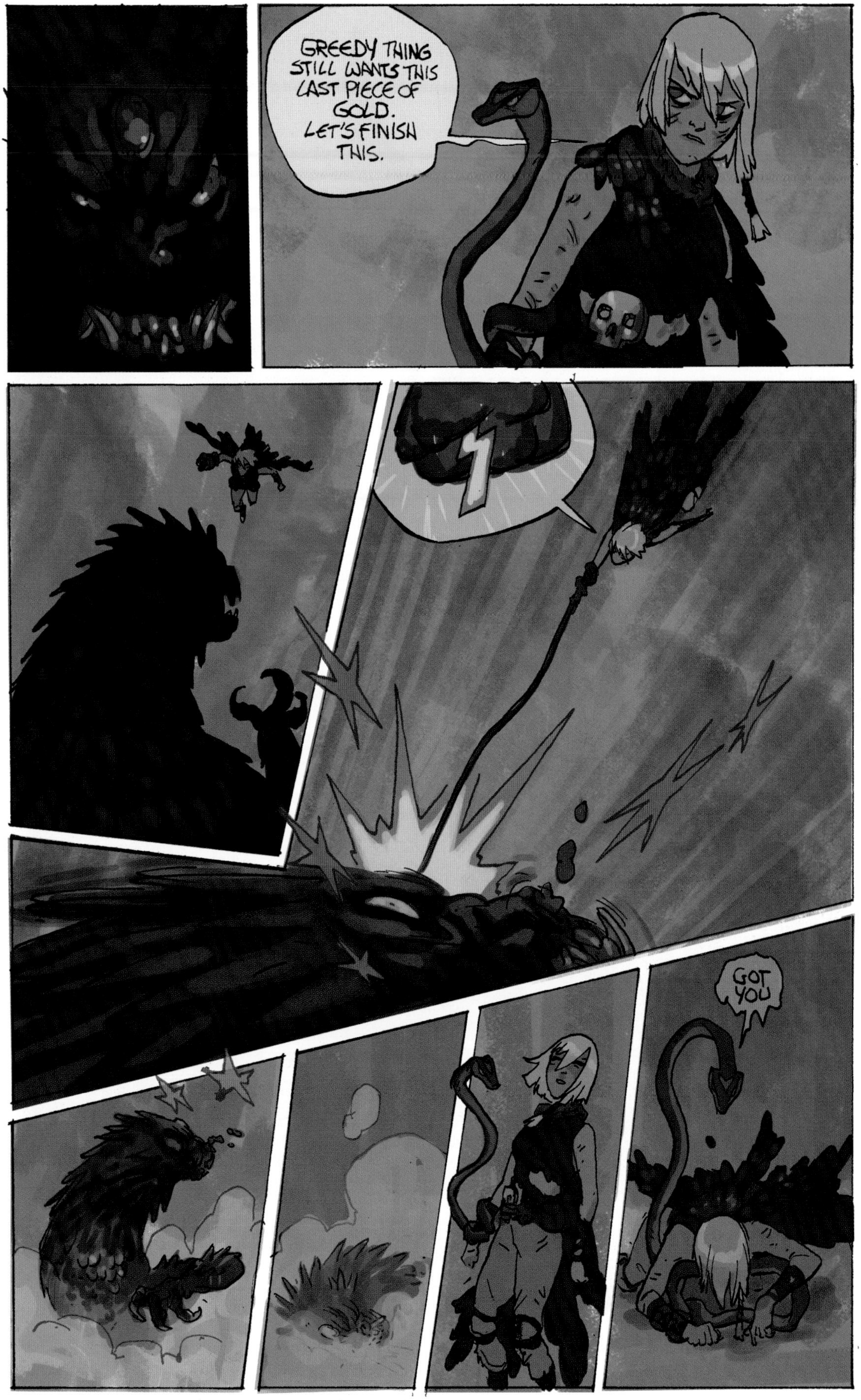
GREEDY THING STILL WANTS THIS LAST PIECE OF GOLD. LET'S FINISH THIS.
GOT YOU

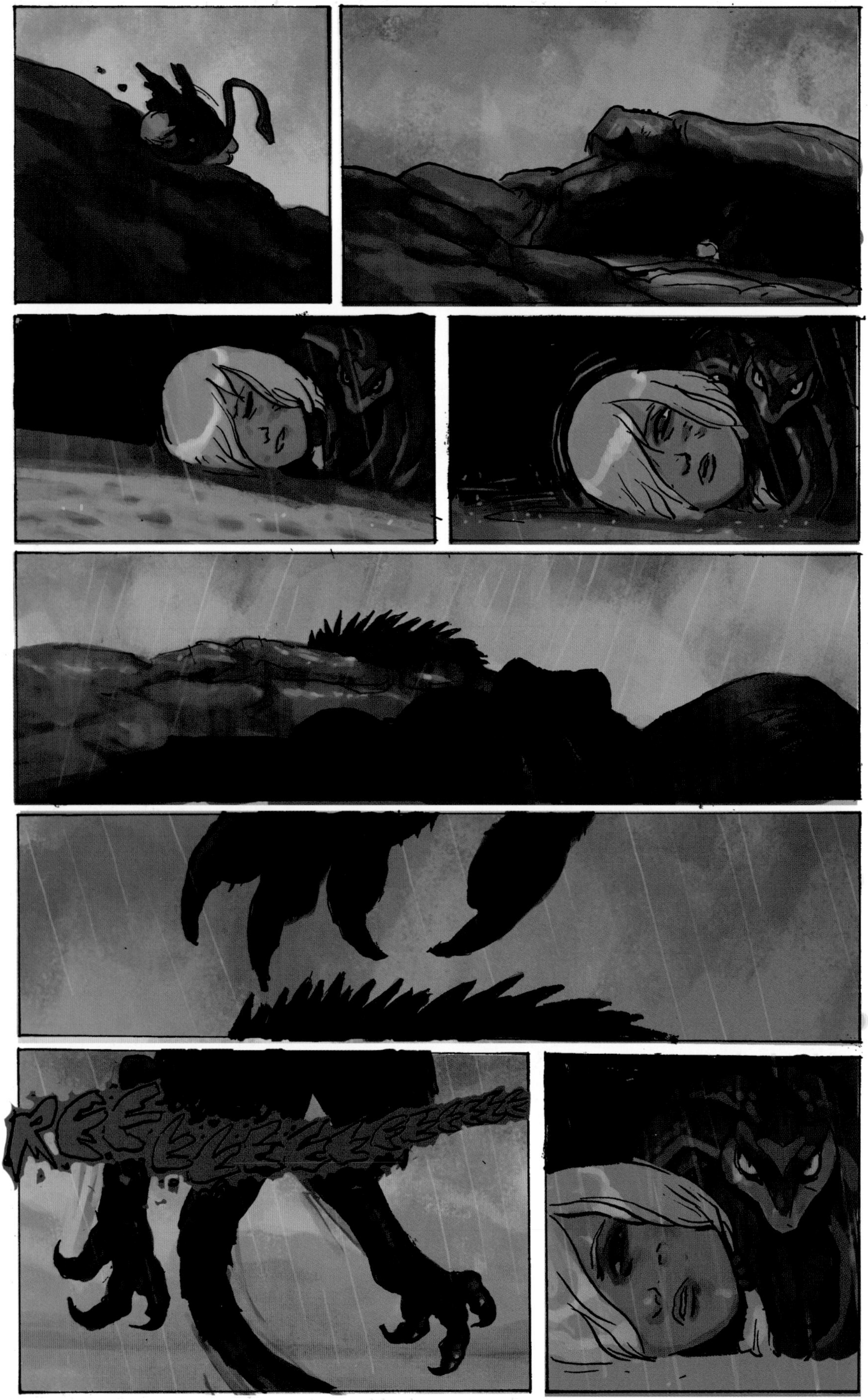
REEEEEEEEEEEEE

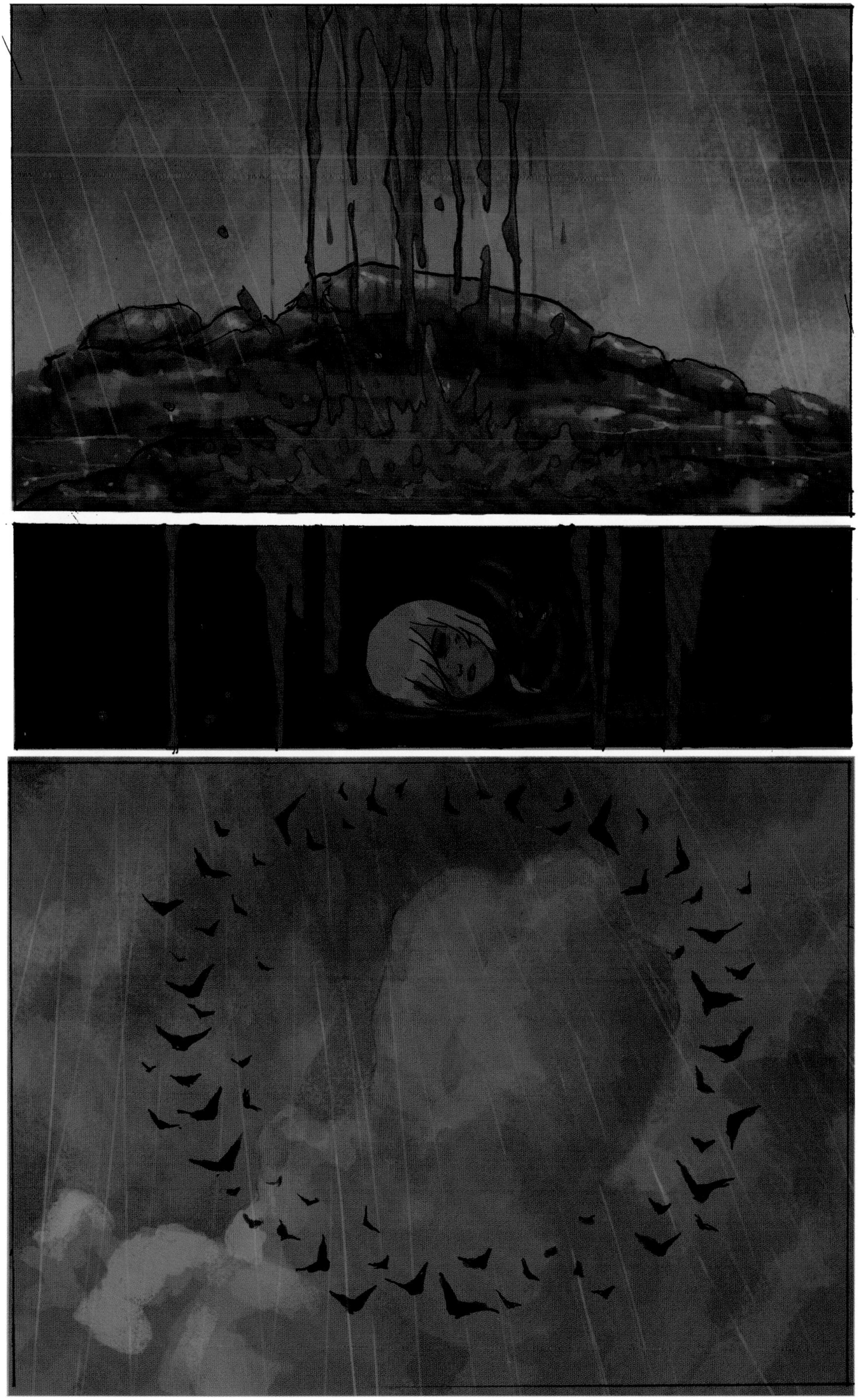

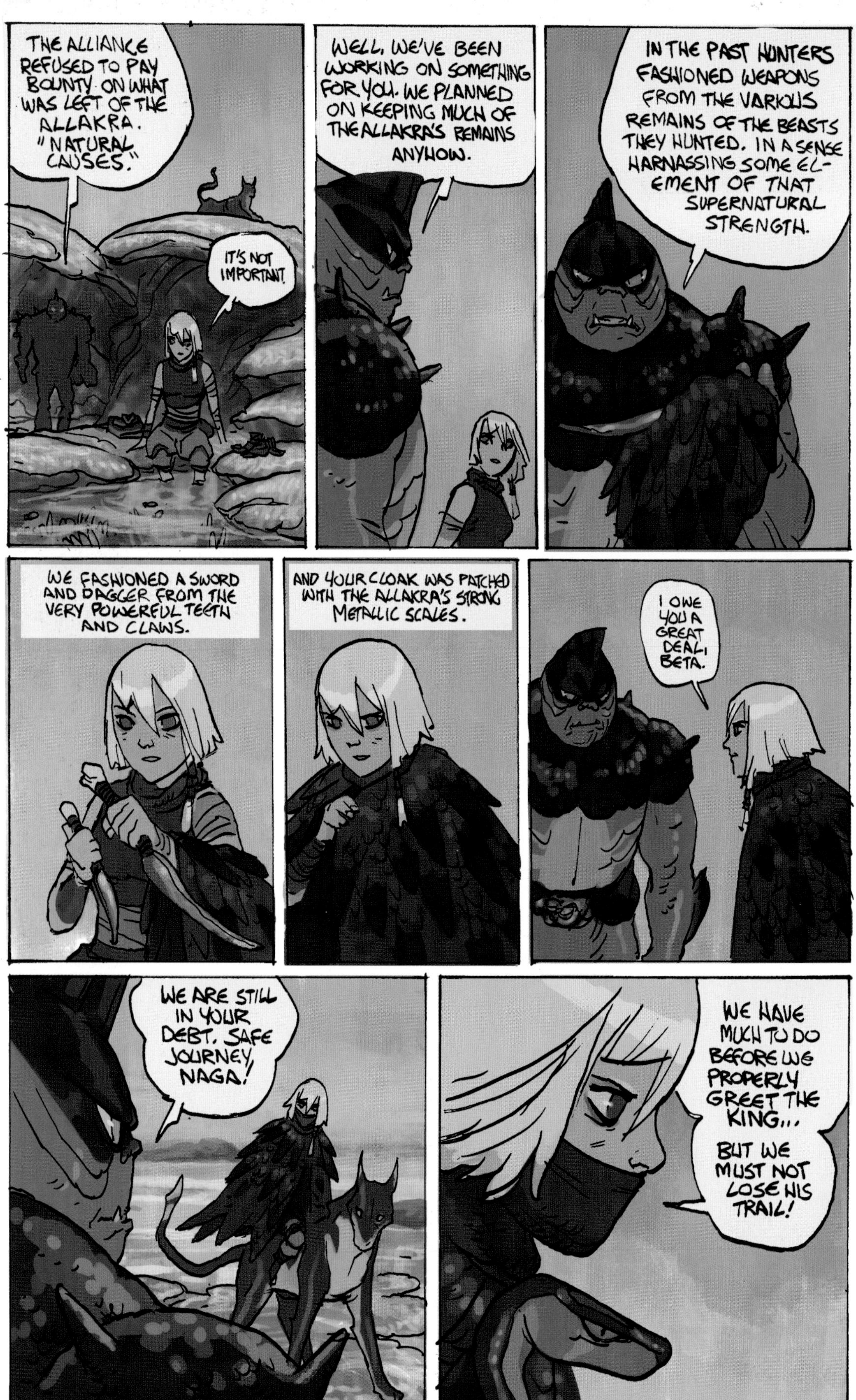
THE ALLIANCE REFUSED TO PAY BOUNTY ON WHAT WAS LEFT OF THE ALLAKRA. "NATURAL CAUSES."
IT'S NOT IMPORTANT.
WELL, WE'VE BEEN WORKING ON SOMETHING FOR YOU. WE PLANNED ON KEEPING MUCH OF THE ALLAKRA'S REMAINS ANYHOW.
IN THE PAST HUNTERS FASHIONED WEAPONS FROM THE VARIOUS REMAINS OF THE BEASTS THEY HUNTED. IN A SENSE HARNASSING SOME ELEMENT OF THAT SUPERNATURAL STRENGTH.
WE FASHIONED A SWORD AND DAGGER FROM THE VERY POWERFUL TEETH AND CLAWS.
AND YOUR CLOAK WAS PATCHED WITH THE ALLAKRA'S STRONG METALLIC SCALES.
I OWE YOU A GREAT DEAL, BETA.
WE ARE STILL IN YOUR DEBT. SAFE JOURNEY, NAGA!
WE HAVE MUCH TO DO BEFORE WE PROPERLY GREET THE KING...
BUT WE MUST NOT LOSE HIS TRAIL!

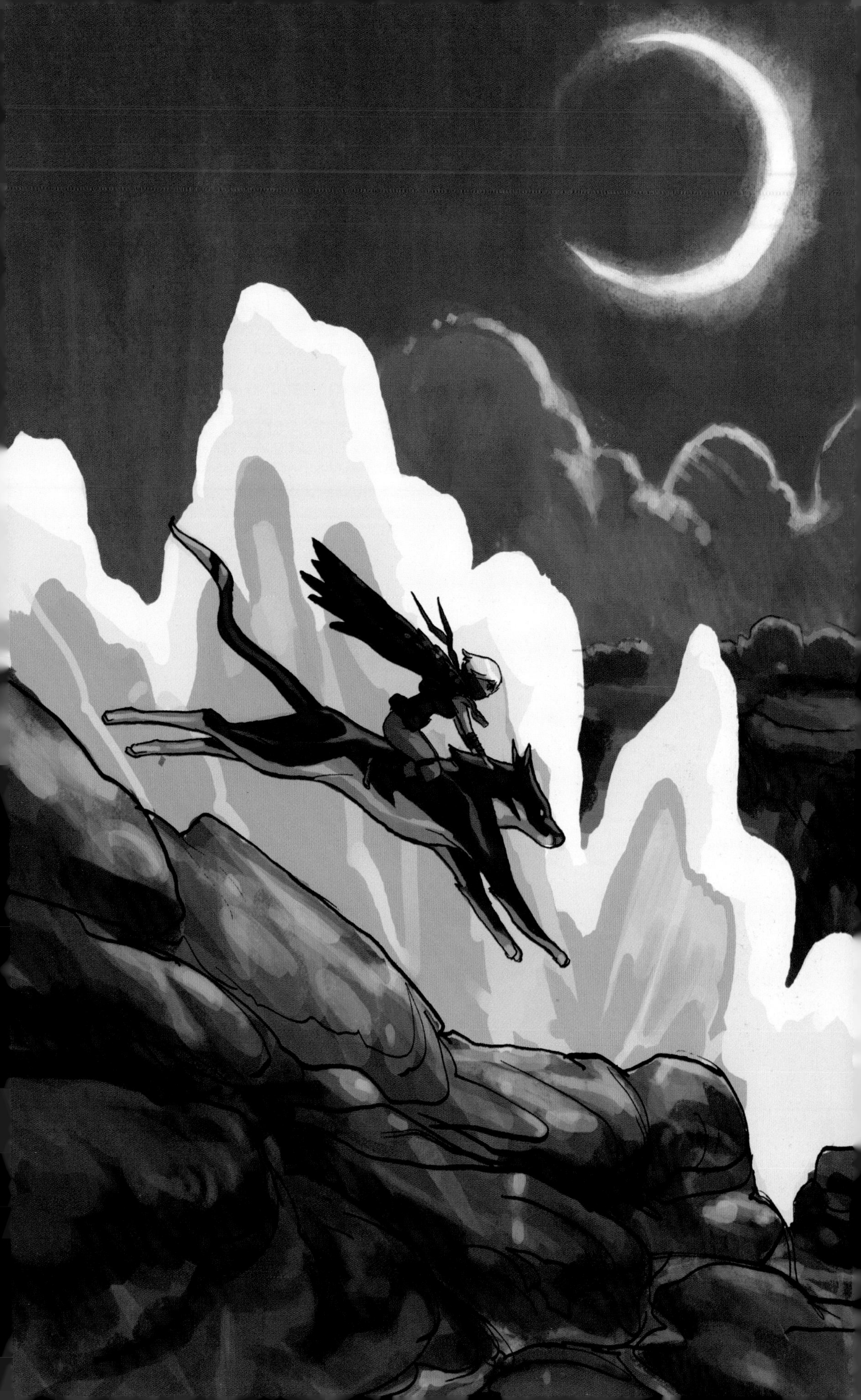

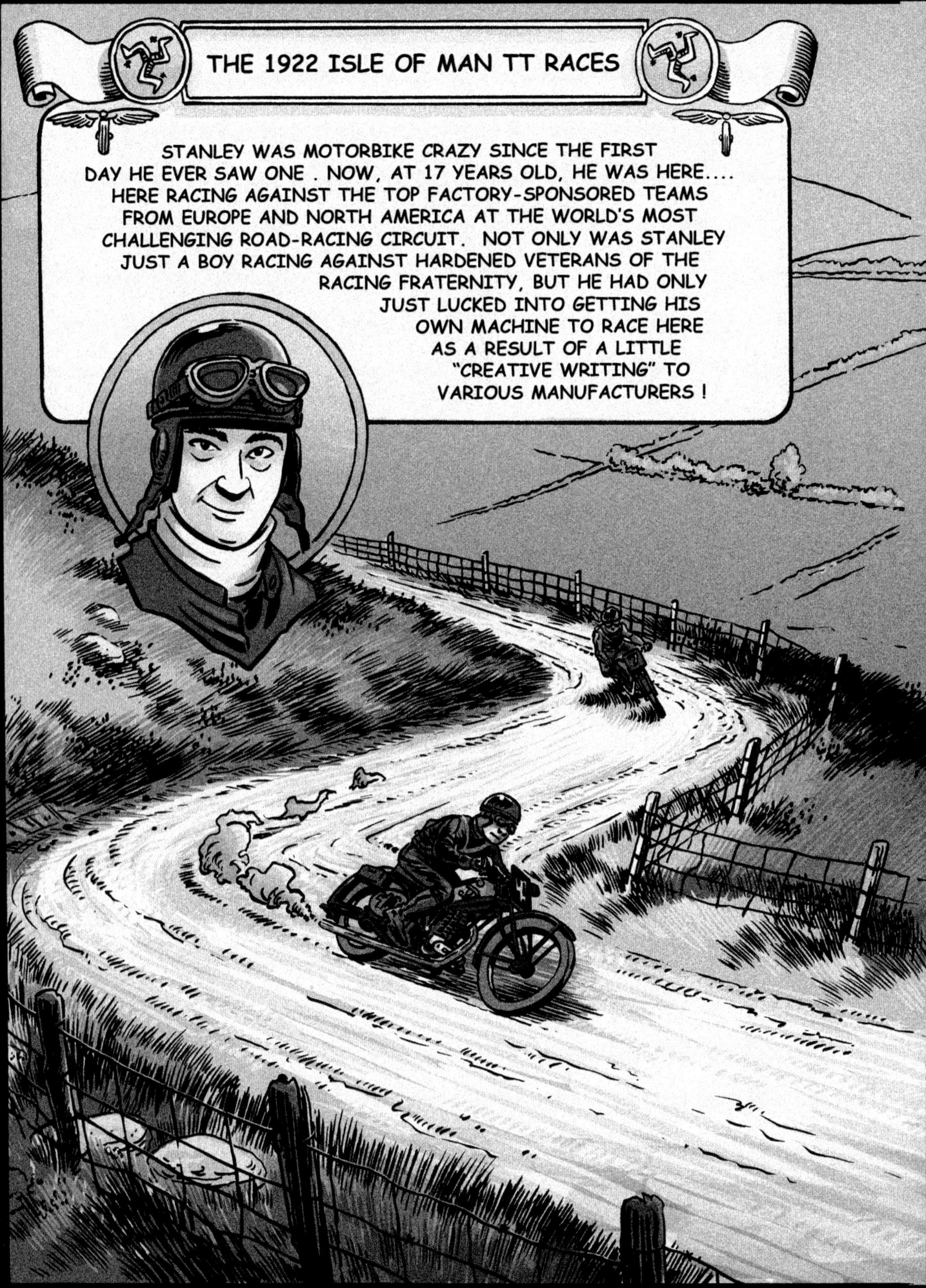
THE 1922 ISLE OF MAN TT RACES
STANLEY WAS MOTORBIKE CRAZY SINCE THE FIRST DAY HE EVER SAW ONE . NOW, AT 17 YEARS OLD, HE WAS HERE.... HERE RACING AGAINST THE TOP FACTORY-SPONSORED TEAMS FROM EUROPE AND NORTH AMERICA AT THE WORLD'S MOST CHALLENGING ROAD-RACING CIRCUIT. NOT ONLY WAS STANLEY JUST A BOY RACING AGAINST HARDENED VETERANS OF THE RACING FRATERNITY, BUT HE HAD ONLY JUST LUCKED INTO GETTING HIS OWN MACHINE TO RACE HERE AS A RESULT OF A LITTLE "CREATIVE WRITING" TO VARIOUS MANUFACTURERS !

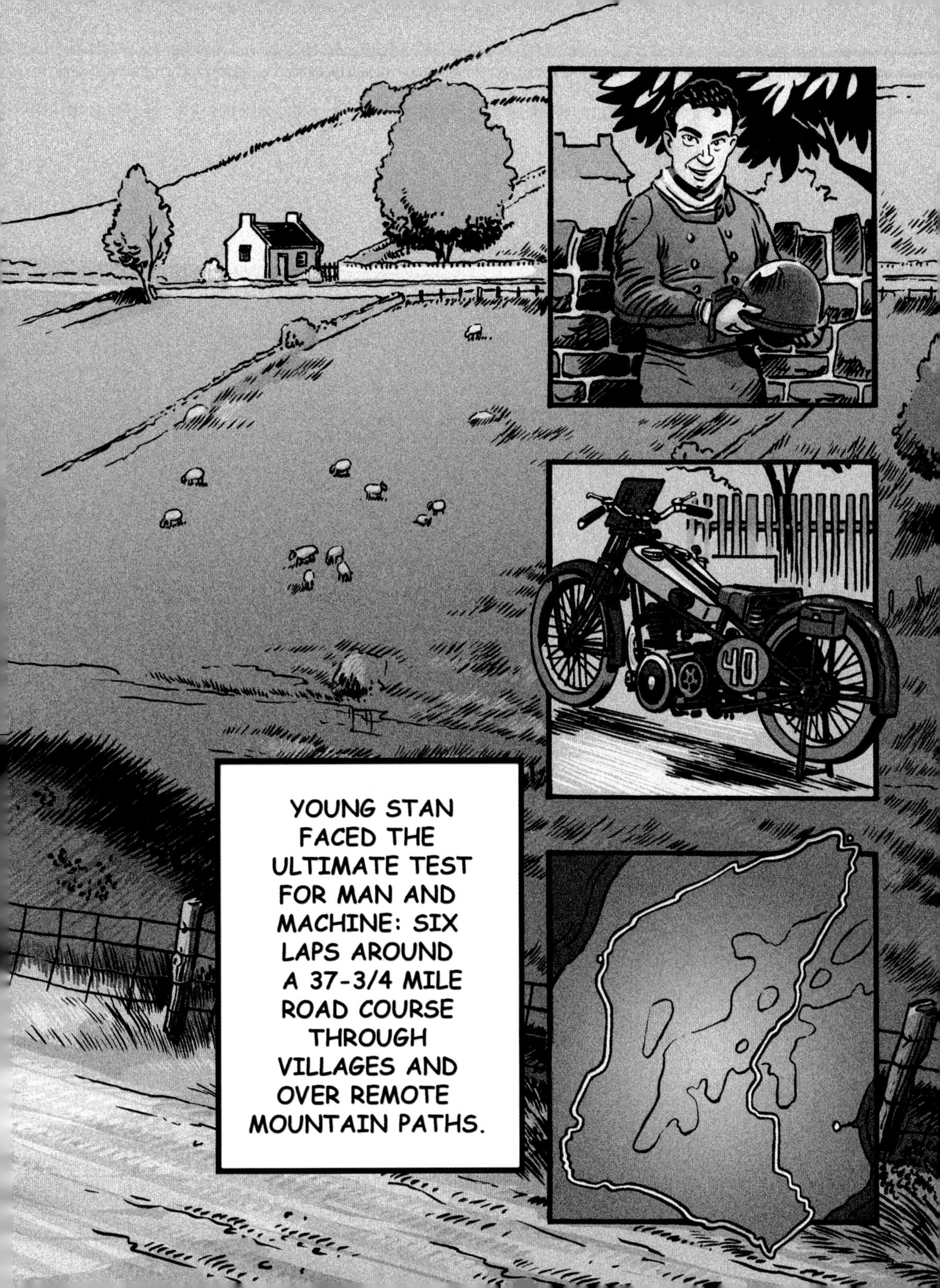

YOUNG STAN FACED THE ULTIMATE TEST FOR MAN AND MACHINE: SIX LAPS AROUND A 37-3/4 MILE ROAD COURSE THROUGH VILLAGES AND OVER REMOTE MOUNTAIN PATHS.

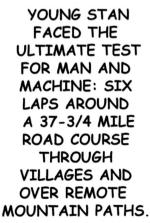

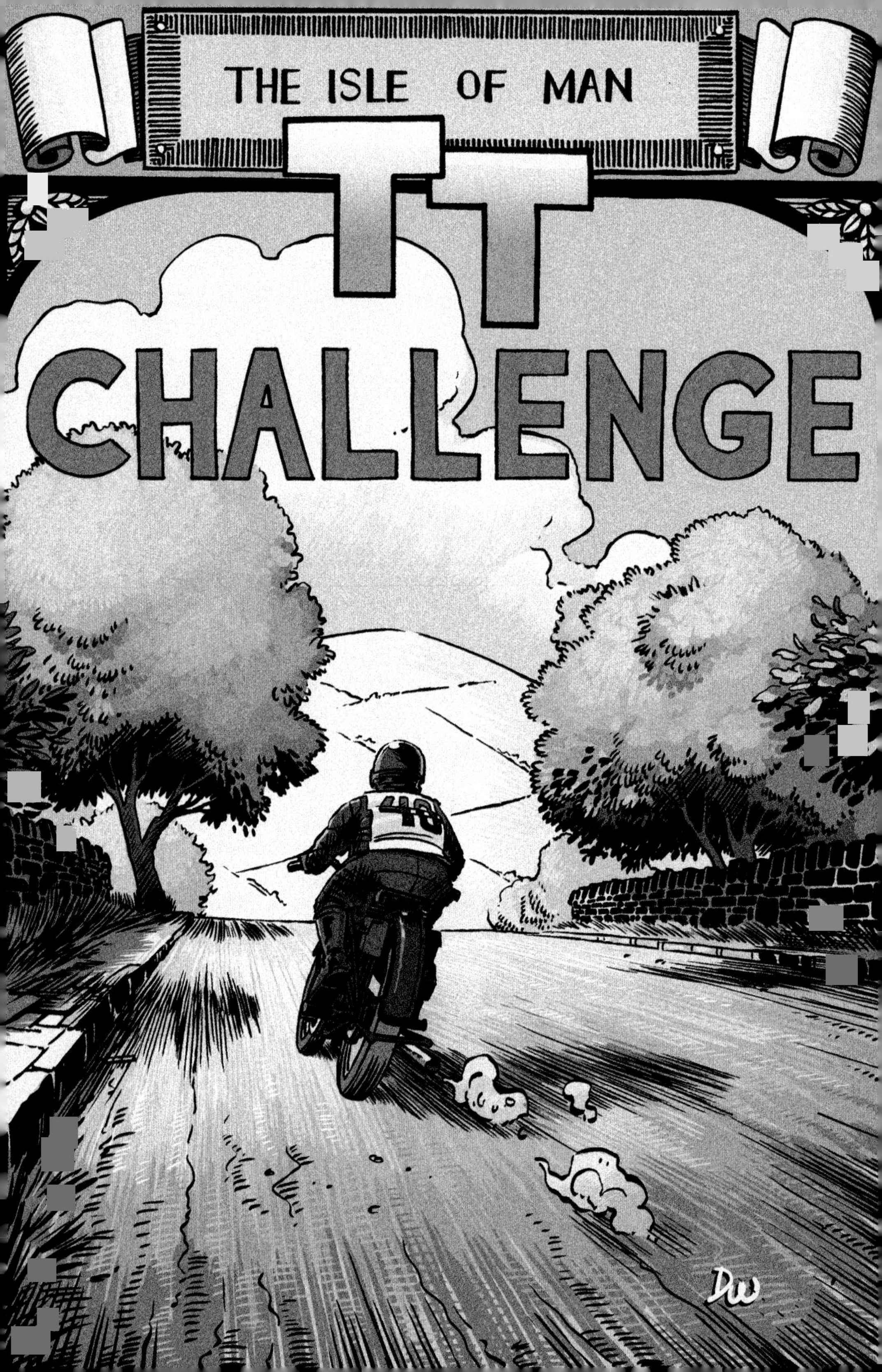
THE ISLE OF MAN
TT
CHALLENGE
DW

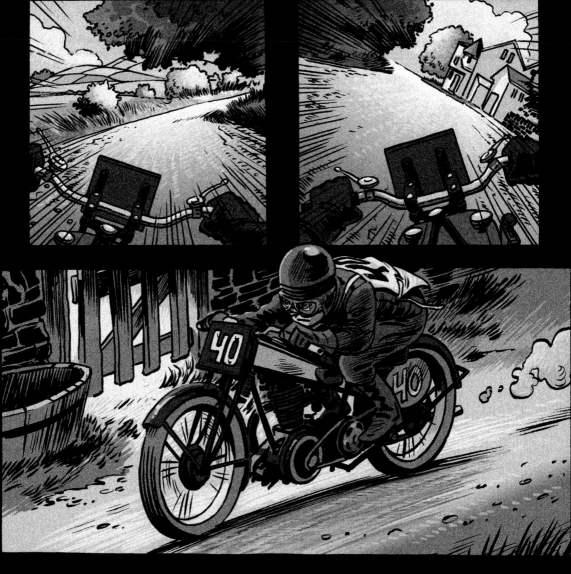

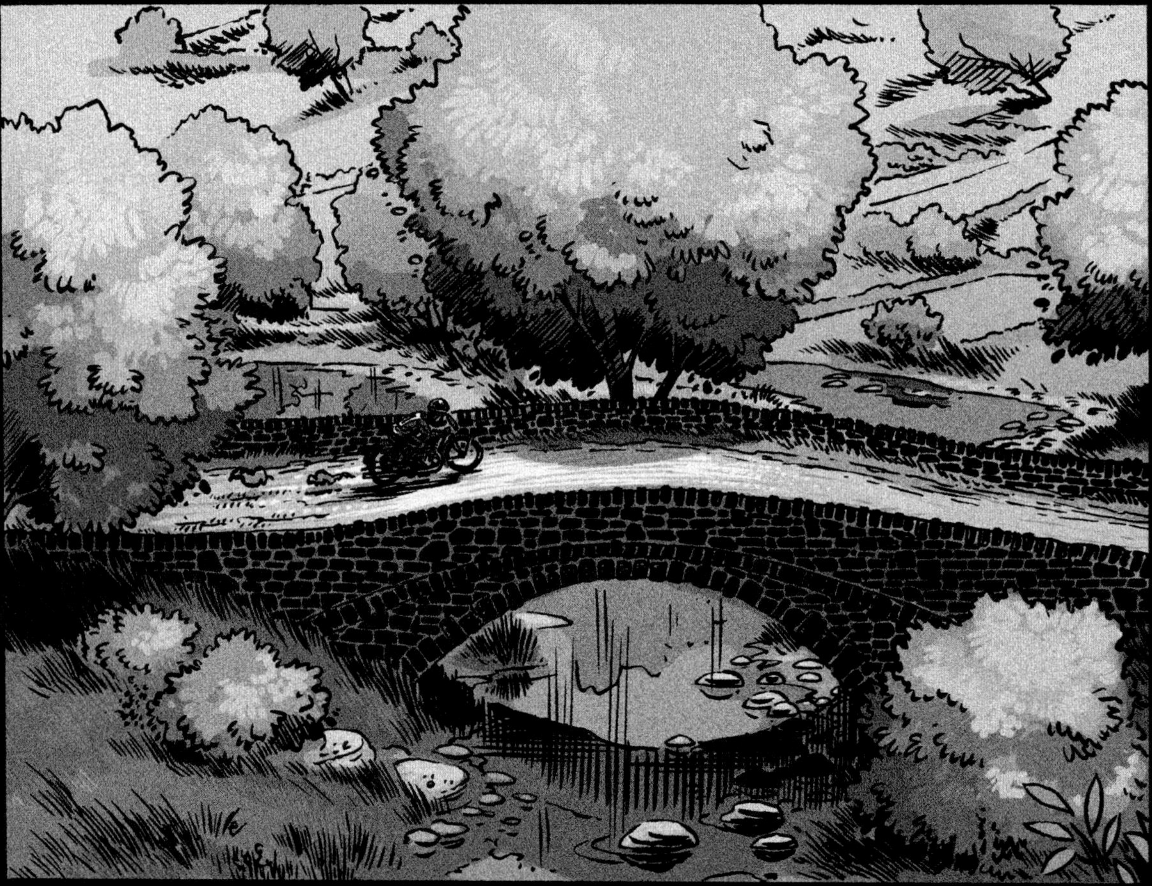

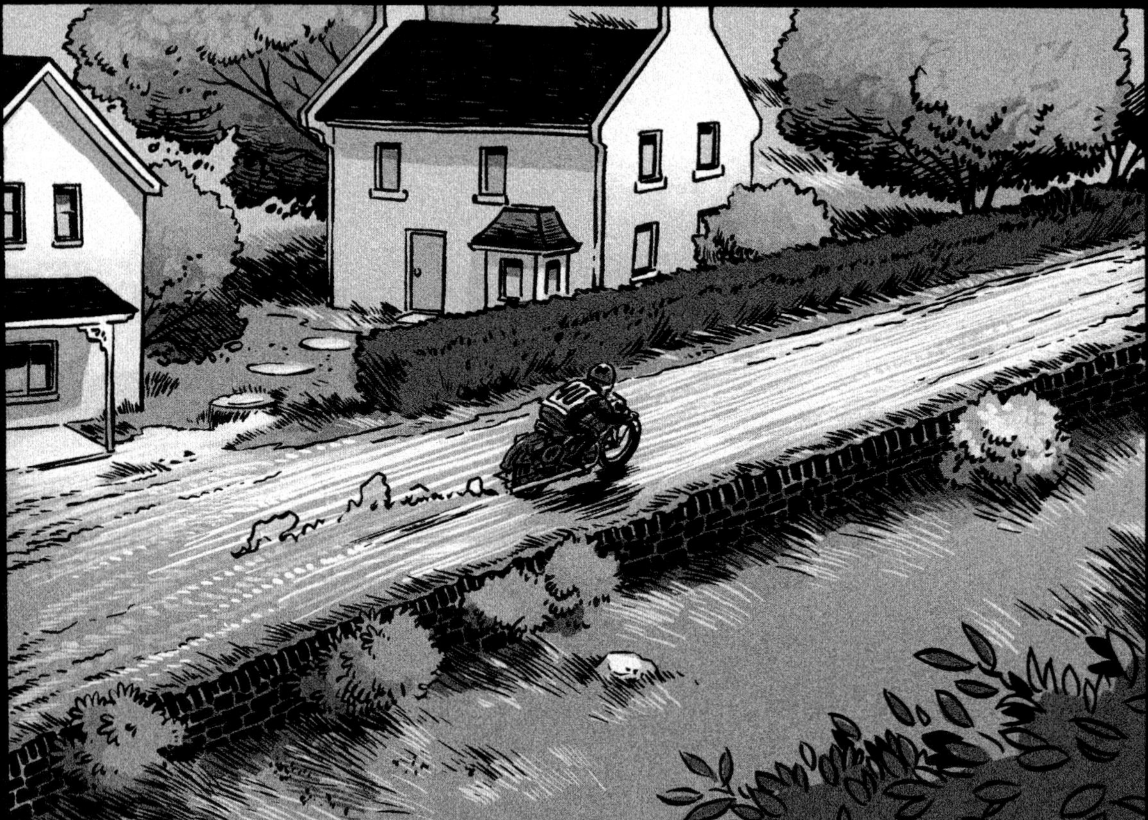

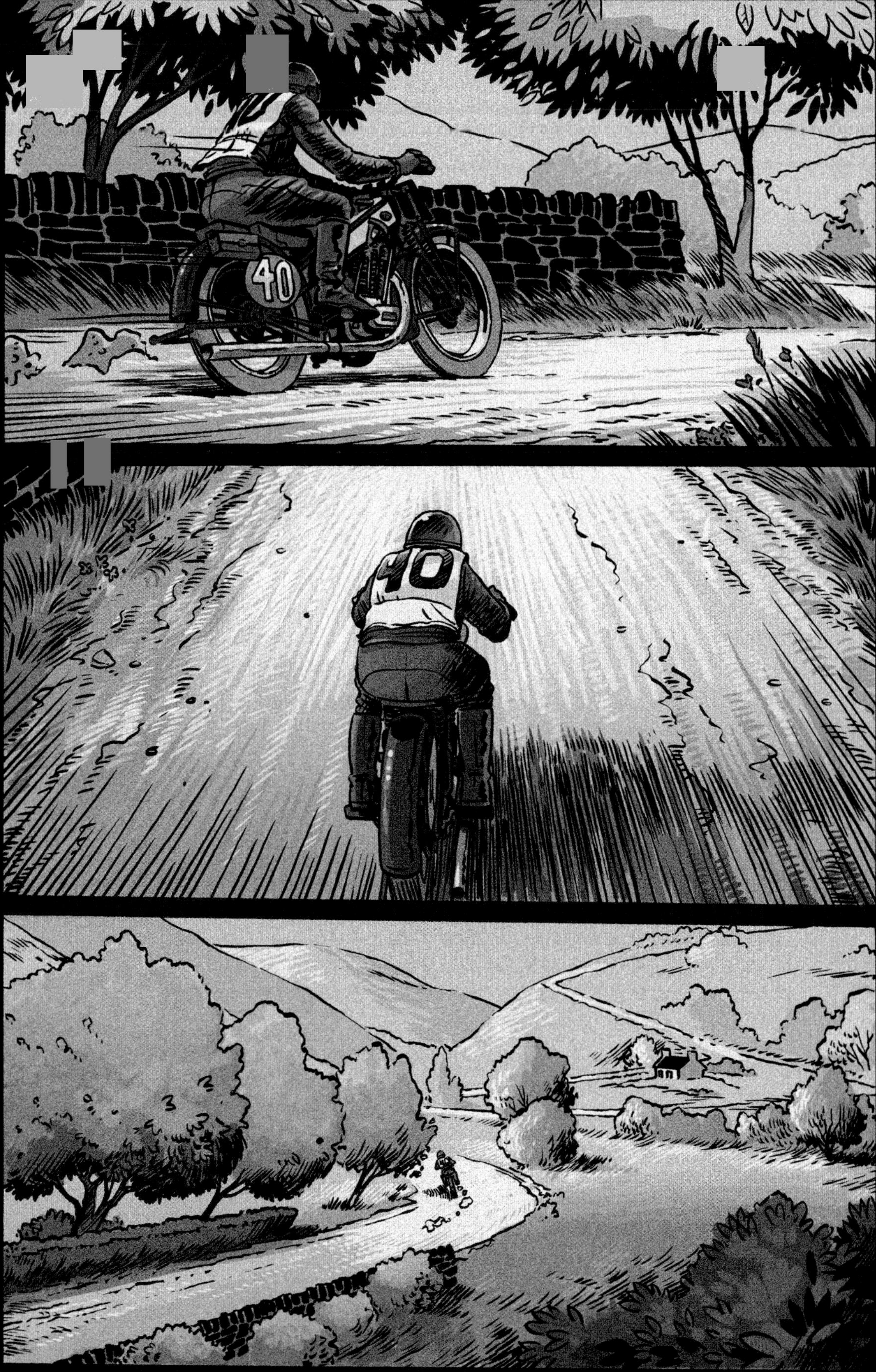
40
40

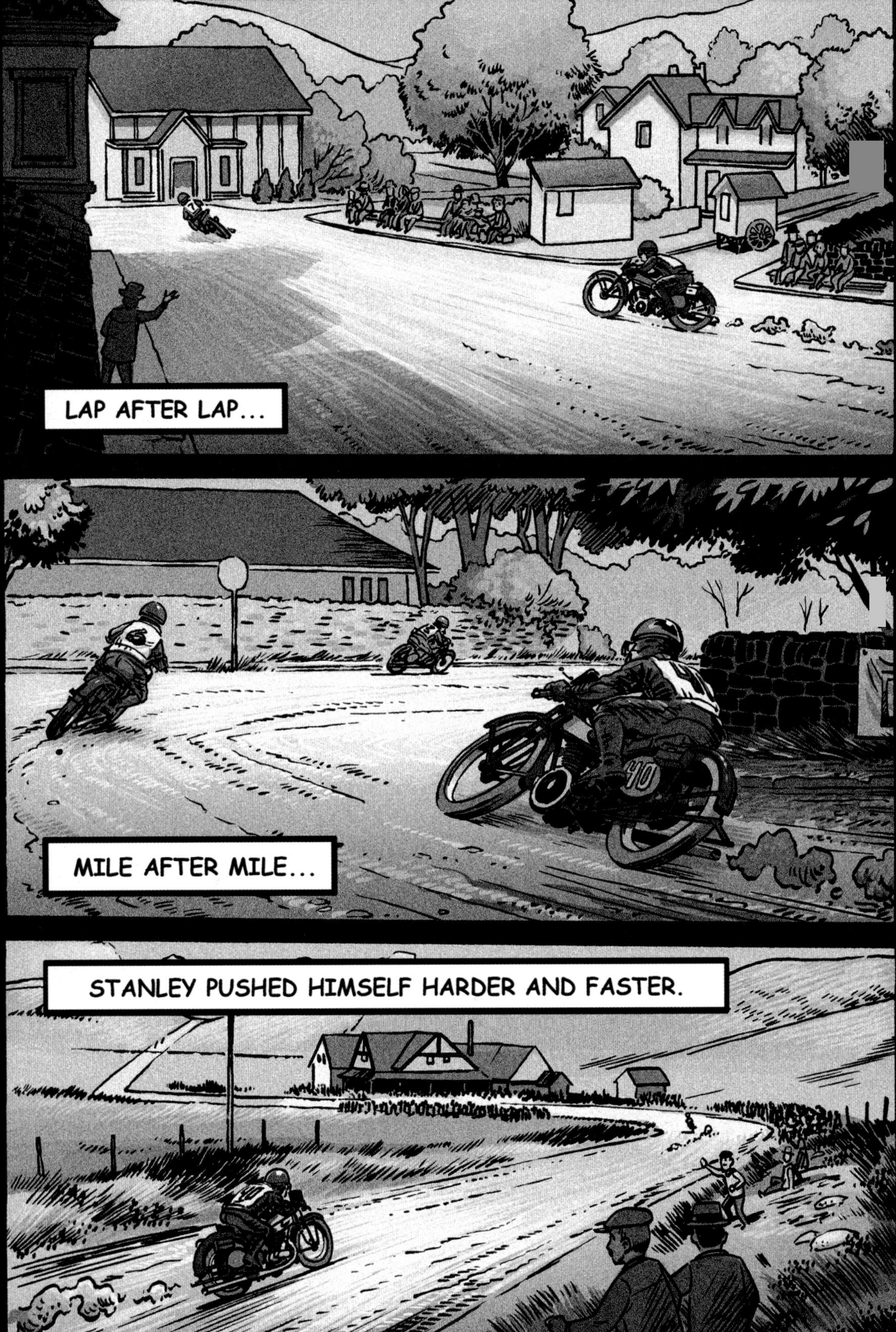
LAP AFTER LAP...
MILE AFTER MILE...
STANLEY PUSHED HIMSELF HARDER AND FASTER.

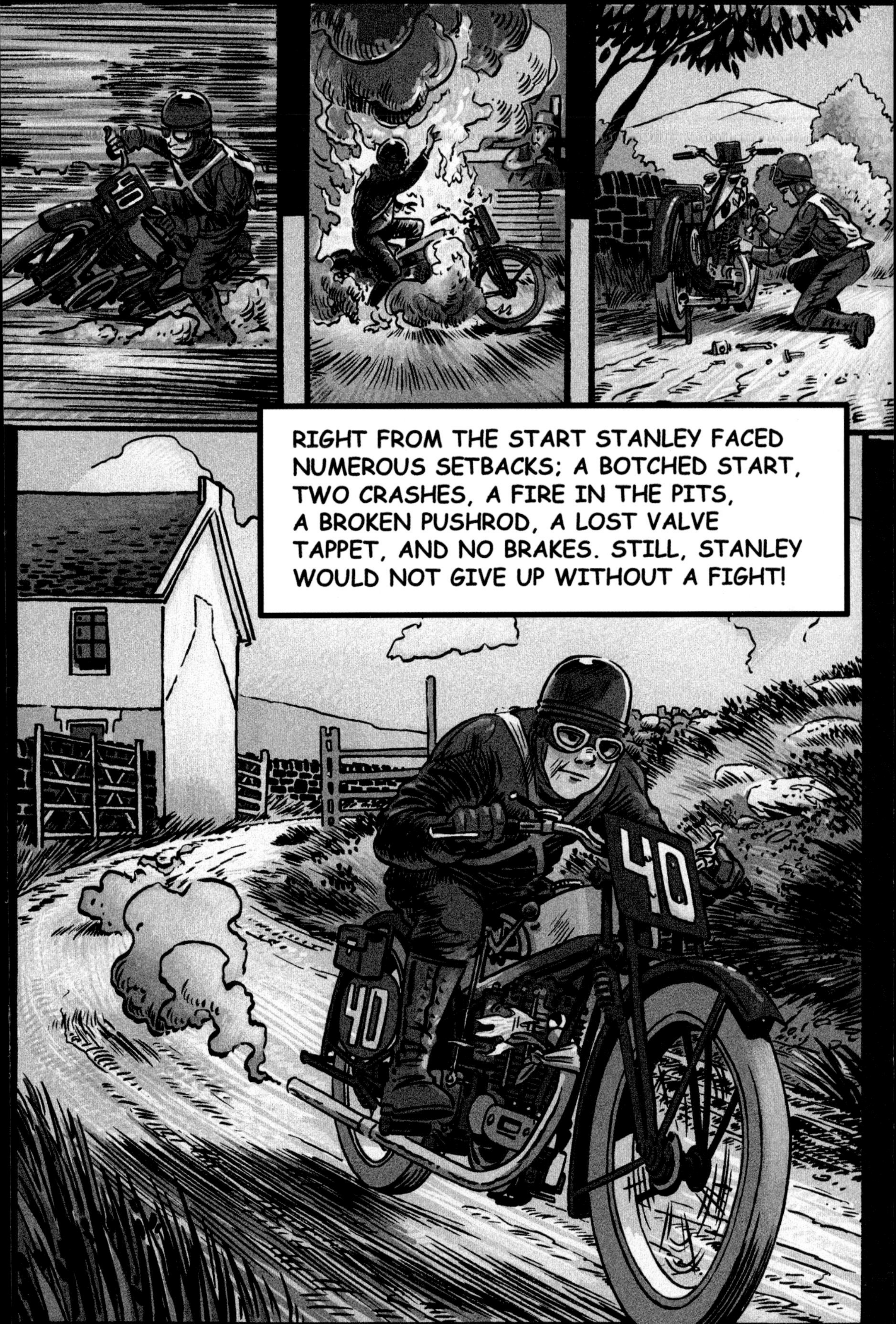
RIGHT FROM THE START STANLEY FACED NUMEROUS SETBACKS; A BOTCHED START, TWO CRASHES, A FIRE IN THE PITS, A BROKEN PUSHROD, A LOST VALVE TAPPET, AND NO BRAKES. STILL, STANLEY WOULD NOT GIVE UP WITHOUT A FIGHT!

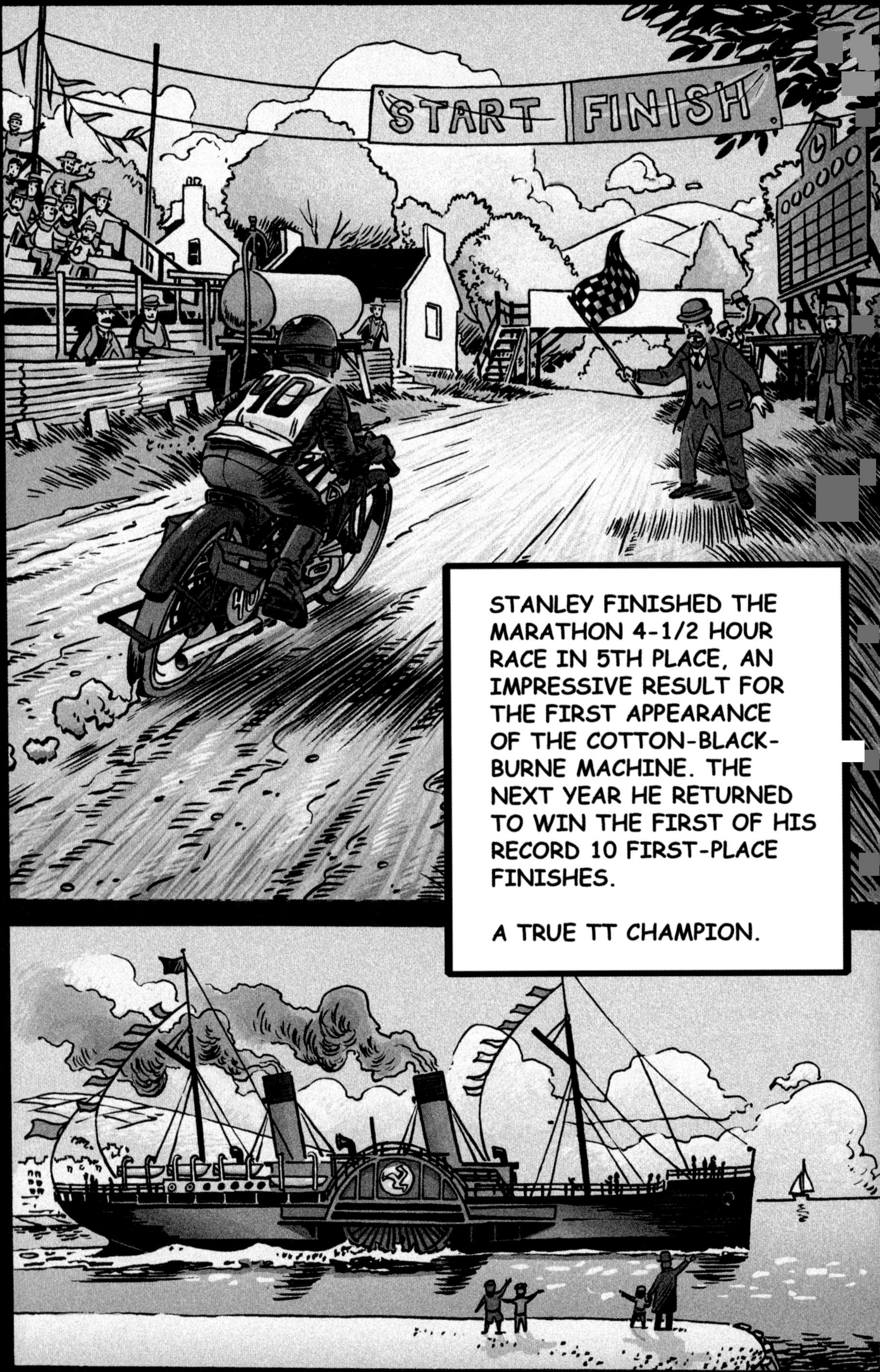
START
FINISH
40
STANLEY FINISHED THE MARATHON 4-1/2 HOUR RACE IN 5TH PLACE, AN IMPRESSIVE RESULT FOR THE FIRST APPEARANCE OF THE COTTON-BLACKBURNE MACHINE. THE NEXT YEAR HE RETURNED TO WIN THE FIRST OF HIS RECORD 10 FIRST-PLACE FINISHES.
A TRUE TT CHAMPION.

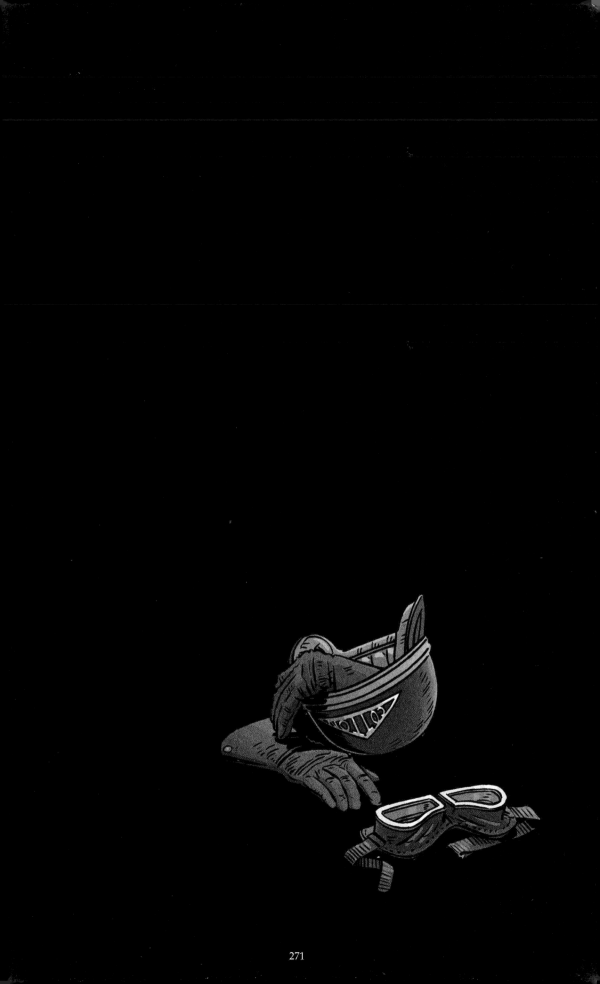

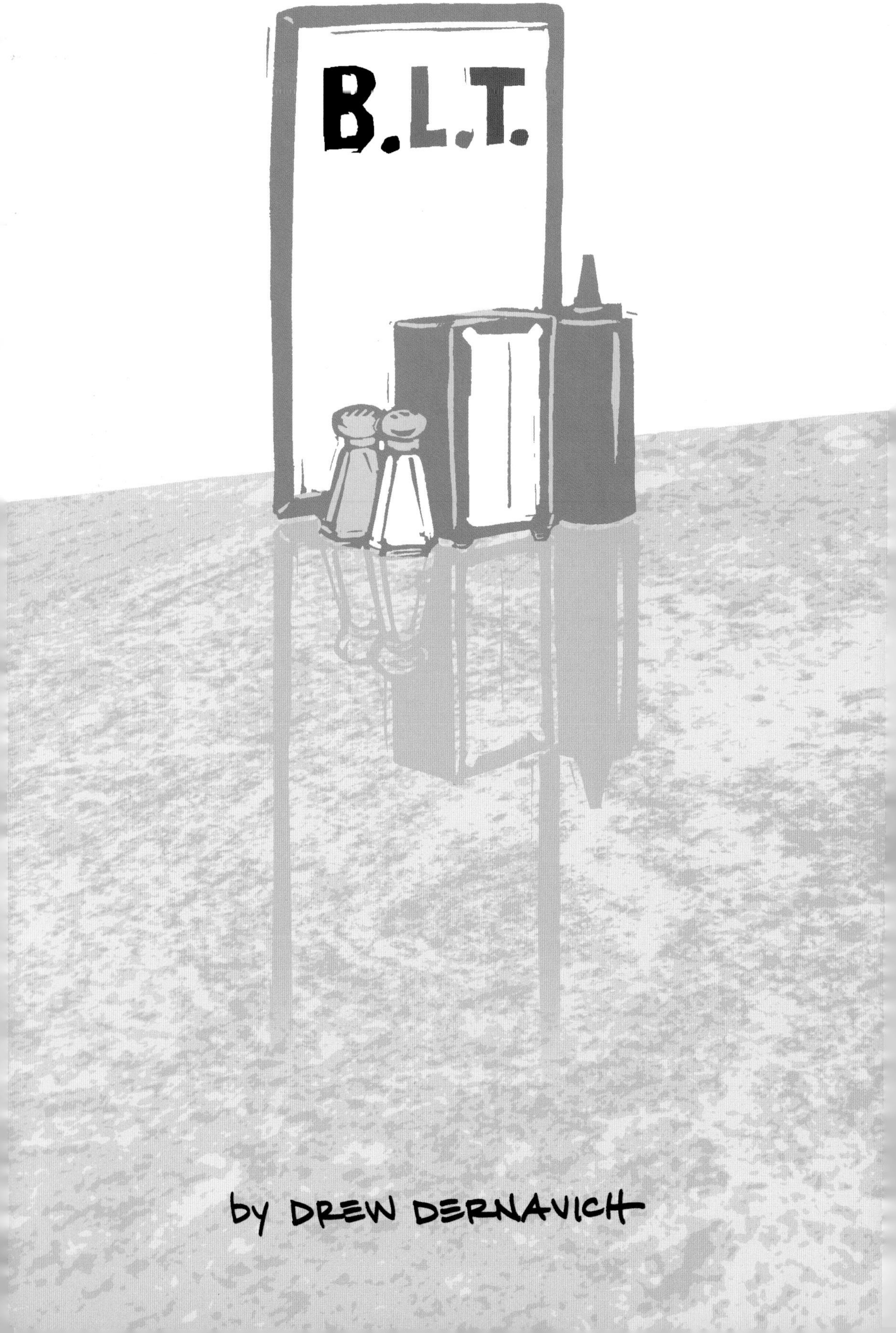
B.L.T.
by DREW DERNAVICH

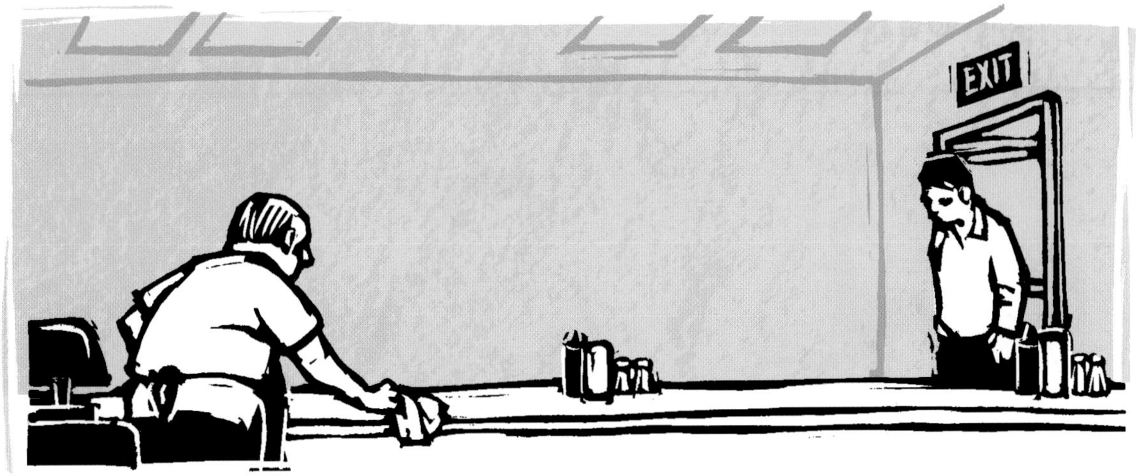
EXIT

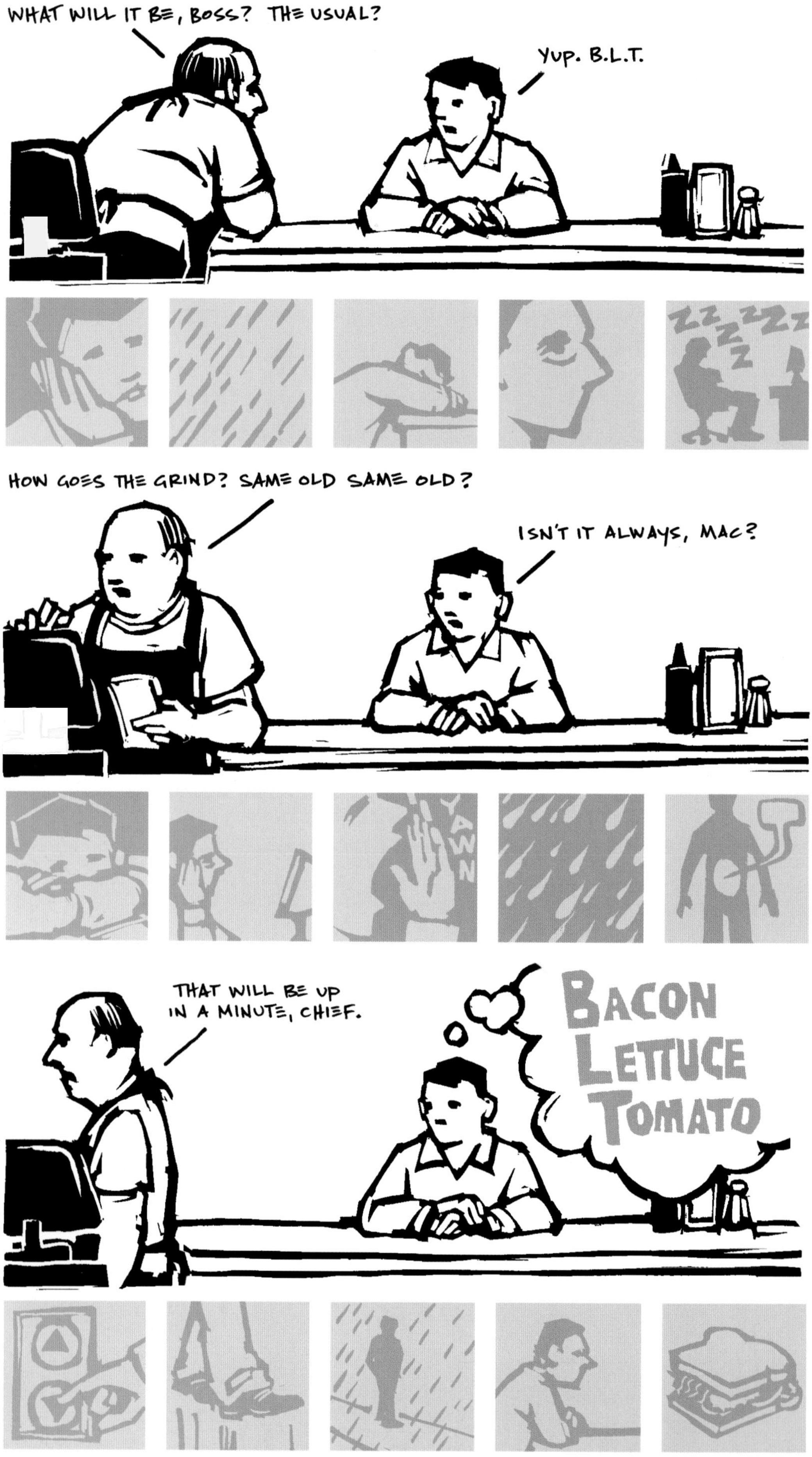
WHAT WILL IT BE, BOSS? THE USUAL?
YUP. B.L.T.
HOW GOES THE GRIND? SAME OLD SAME OLD?
ISN'T IT ALWAYS, MAC?
YAWN
THAT WILL BE UP IN A MINUTE, CHIEF.
BACON LETTUCE TOMATO

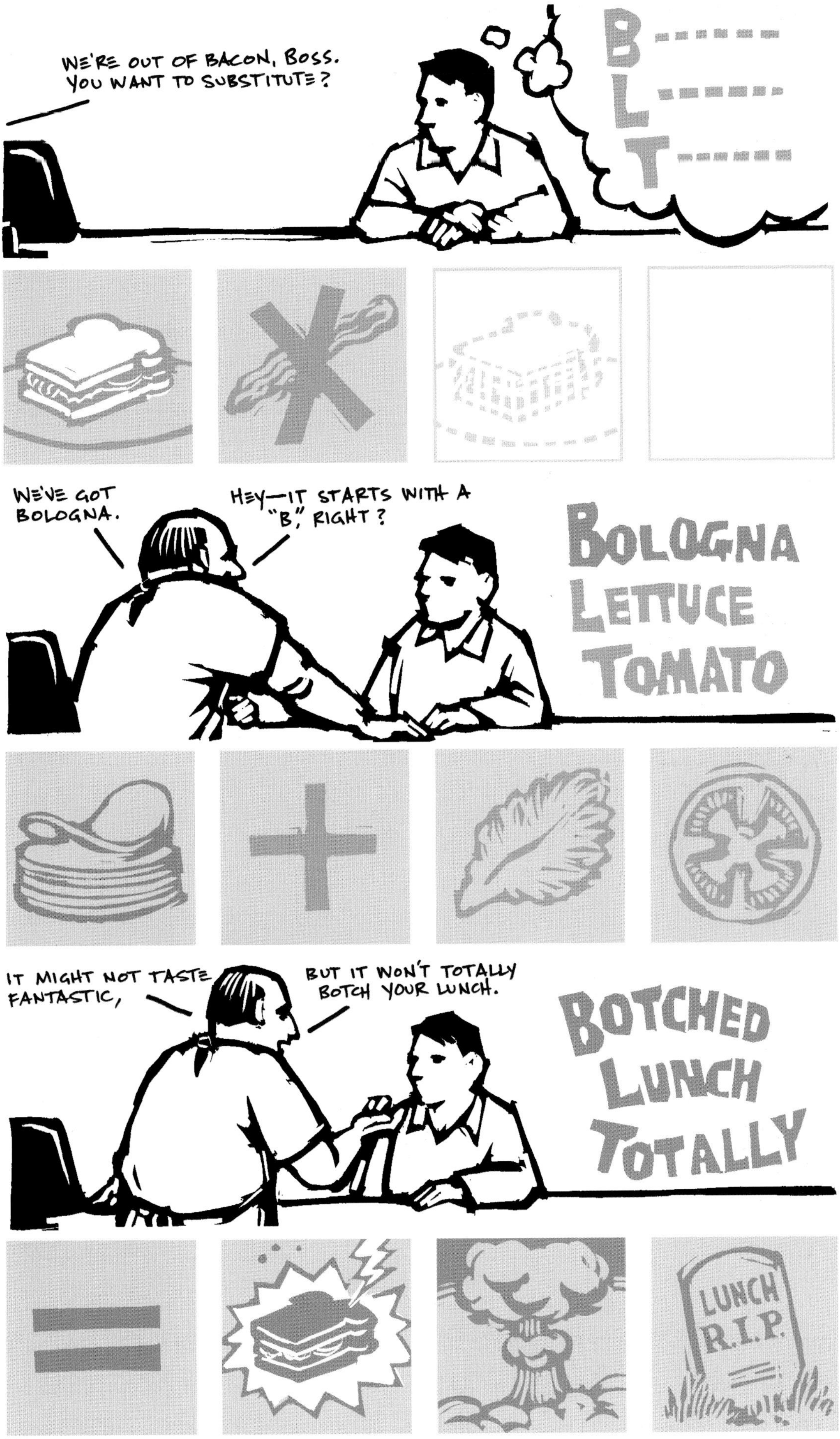

WE'RE OUT OF BACON, BOSS. YOU WANT TO SUBSTITUTE?
B
L
T
WE'VE GOT BOLOGNA.
HEY—IT STARTS WITH A "B," RIGHT?
BOLOGNA
LETTUCE
TOMATO
IT MIGHT NOT TASTE FANTASTIC,
BUT IT WON'T TOTALLY BOTCH YOUR LUNCH.
BOTCHED
LUNCH
TOTALLY
LUNCH
R.I.P.

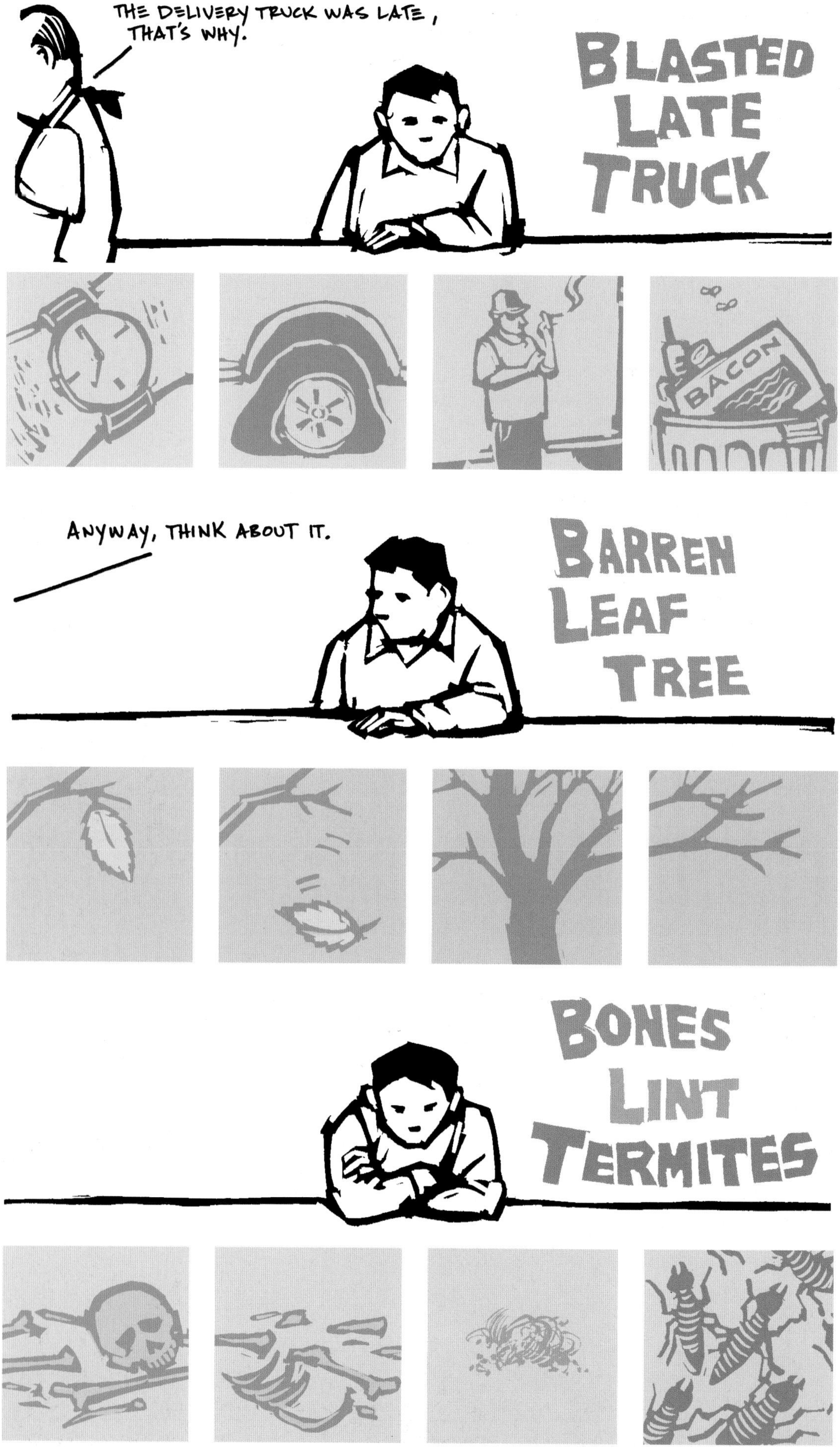
THE DELIVERY TRUCK WAS LATE, THAT'S WHY.
BLASTED LATE TRUCK
BACON
ANYWAY, THINK ABOUT IT.
BARREN LEAF TREE
BONES LINT TERMITES

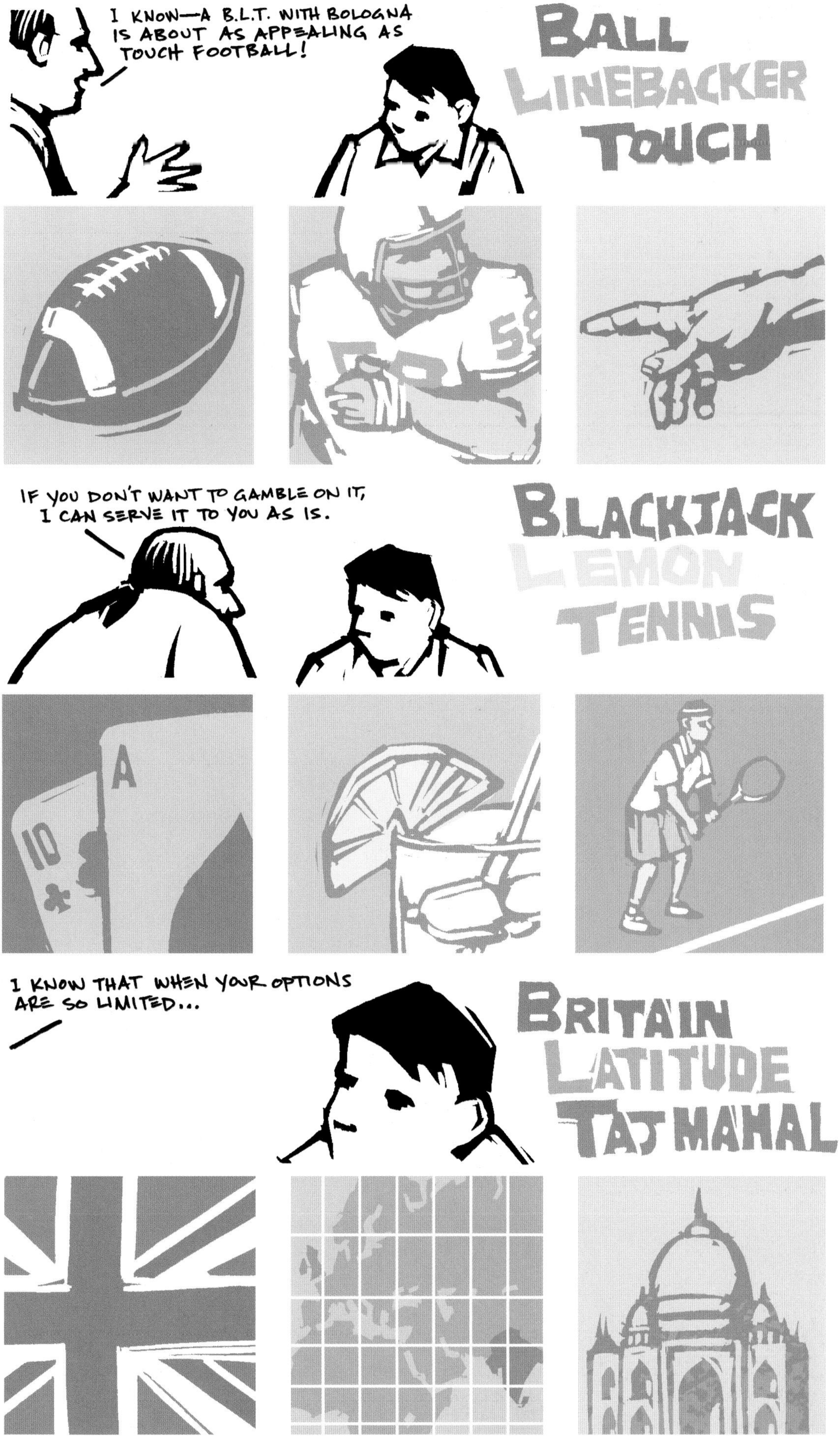

I KNOW—A B.L.T. WITH BOLOGNA IS ABOUT AS APPEALING AS TOUCH FOOTBALL!
BALL
LINEBACKER
TOUCH
IF YOU DON'T WANT TO GAMBLE ON IT, I CAN SERVE IT TO YOU AS IS.
BLACKJACK
LEMON
TENNIS
I KNOW THAT WHEN YOUR OPTIONS ARE SO LIMITED...
BRITAIN
LATITUDE
TAJ MAHAL

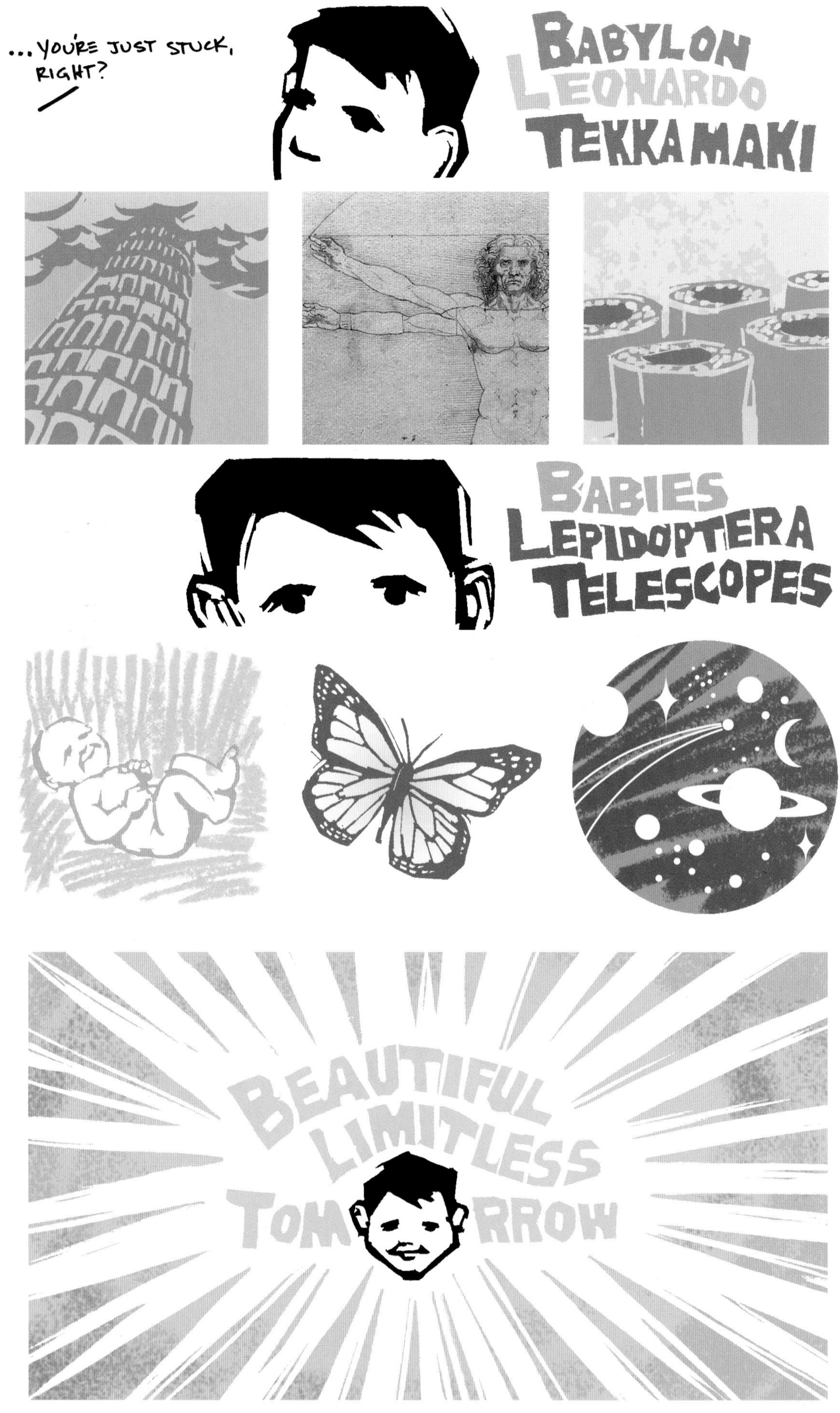
...YOU'RE JUST STUCK, RIGHT?
BABYLON
LEONARDO
TEKKAMAKI
BABIES
LEPIDOPTERA
TELESCOPES
BEAUTIFUL
LIMITLESS
TOMORROW

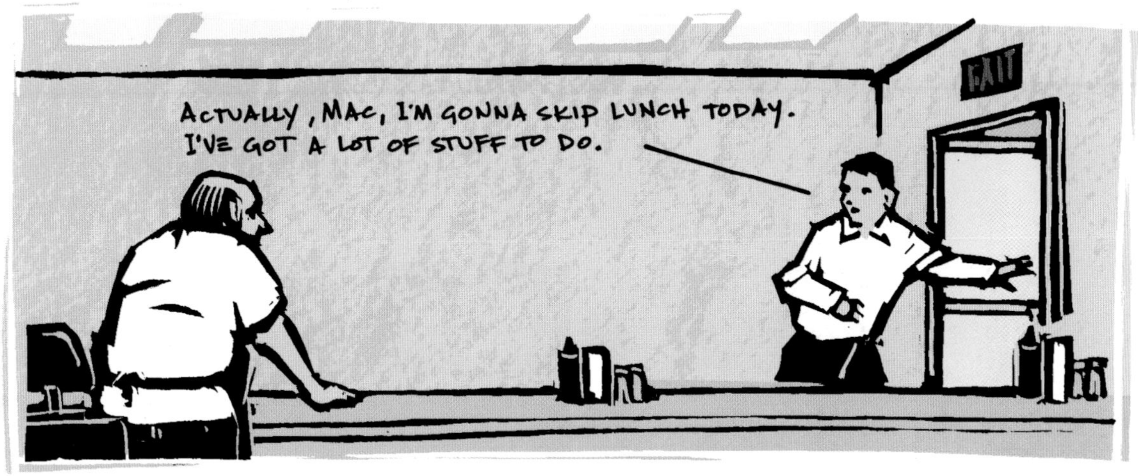
ACTUALLY, MAC, I'M GONNA SKIP LUNCH TODAY. I'VE GOT A LOT OF STUFF TO DO.
EXIT

FLIGHT: VOLUME SEVEN CONTRIBUTORS

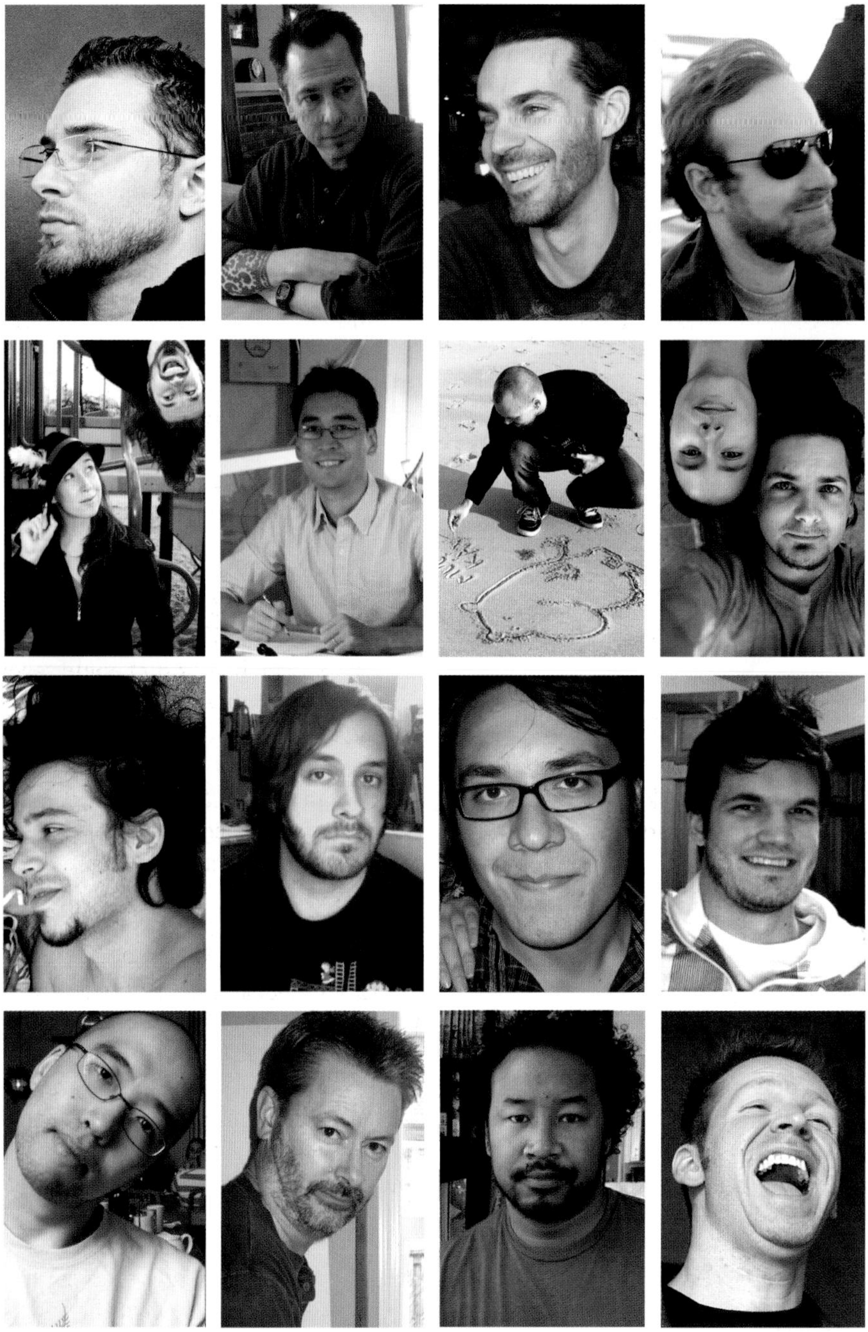

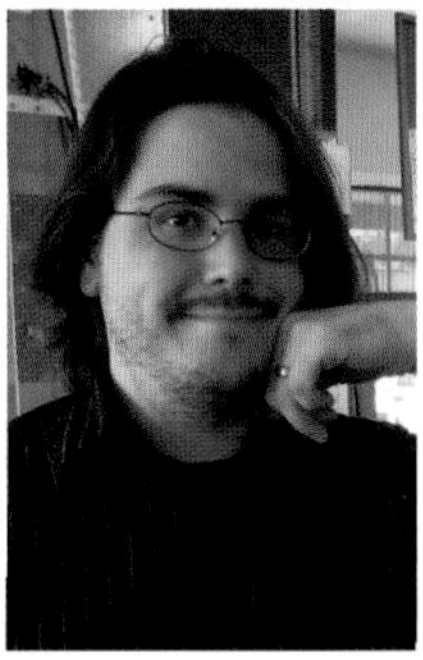

Flight: Volume Seven Contributors

(from left to right)
Top Row: Justin Gerard, Leland Myrick, Phil Craven, Michel Gagné
2nd Row: Katie and Steven Shanahan, Kazu Kibuishi, JP Ahonen, Bannister and Grimaldi
3rd Row: Kostas Kiriakakis, Cory Godbey, Stuart Livingston, Jason Caffoe
4th Row: Kean Soo, Dermot Walshe, Paul Harmon, Drew Dernavich
Bottom Row: Dave Roman

After a failed attempt as a freelance ninja, **JP Ahonen** thought it best to pursue a career in the next best thing—making comics. He wants to thank Dan Taylor and Dean Trippe for their coloring help on this volume's story, and aims to one day pack San Diego Comic-Con to the brim with nerds in Kenneth Shuri costumes. www.jpahonen.com

Bannister and **Grimaldi** live in France and make comics for a living. Bannister is co-author of the award-winning series *Les Enfants d'ailleurs* (published in the United States as *The Elsewhere Chronicles*). Grimaldi is a story-writer and colorist, and she works together with Bannister on their comic series for preschoolers, *Titoss & Ilda.* www.bannister.fr www.elsewherechronicles.com

Adriana Blake is a Venezuelan American living in Canada with her husband and two birds. She is an artist, animator, and author of the web comic *Fall on Me.* She loves books, music, and tea. www.littleteacup.net

Jason Caffoe graduated from the Savannah College of Art and Design with a degree in sequential art. He is currently living in Alhambra, California, where he works full-time as a production assistant and colorist for Kazu Kibuishi. Most of Jason's days are spent coloring pages for the *Amulet* series, but Kazu finds plenty of other things for him to do as well. Terrible, unspeakable things. www.jasoncaffoe.com

Phil Craven studied sequential art at the Savannah College of Art and Design. He now lives in Los Angeles, where he draws storyboards for DreamWorks Animation. He has now drawn more pandas than he has any other critter on Earth.

Drew Dernavich gets that his first name is the past tense of "draw," so please don't bring it up. He is a regular cartoonist for *The New Yorker* magazine, among others, and won the National Cartoonists Society award for magazine cartooning in 2006. His woodcut-style cartoons are drawn on scratchboard, which would be really cool if it was still 1932. He lives in Hoboken, New Jersey, with his wife, Lori. This is his first appearance in *Flight.* www.drewdernavich.com

Selena DiZazzo was born in London, Ontario, and has enjoyed comics and drawing since her kindegarden teacher put her in charge of the crayons. She's since moved away to hover around Toronto, storyboarding by day and racing green ninjas by night. seaofbloo.blogspot.com

Michel Gagné was born in Québec, Canada, and has had a highly successful career drawing characters and special effects for animated and live-action feature films such as *The Iron Giant* and *Osmosis Jones.* His independant short film, *Prelude to Eden,* is a favorite among animation students and teachers, and has played in festivals throughout the world. Michel and his wife created Gagné International Press in 1998, and he has been writing, illustrating, and publishing books and comics ever since. www.gagneint.com

Justin Gerard is an illustrator who has traveled the world in search of the perfect medium to paint in. He has not found it, but along the way he has met some fascinating people, seen some interesting places, and had a chance to paint a lot of great subjects. His work has been featured in *Spectrum Fantastic Arts, Society of Illustrators,* and *Expose.* He enjoys good music, chocolate chip cookies, and tank battles. www.justingerard.com

Cory Godbey is an illustrator, animator, and writer for Portland Studios. He has illustrated picture books and book covers for Oxford University Press, Random House, and Thomas Nelson to name a few, and has worked on several animated shorts and commercials with clients including Prudential Insurance, Microsoft Zune, and Xbox. In 2008, Cory's work was published in the *Society of Illustrators 50th Annual of American Illustration.* In early 2009, Cory founded the popular Maurice Sendak tribute site Terrible Yellow Eyes, where professional artists from all over the world contribute works inspired by *Where the Wild Things Are.* Cory seeks to tell stories with his work. He also likes to draw monsters. www.corygodbey.com

Paul Harmon works full-time as a storyboard artist in animation. His first published comic work was an original series he created, *MORA,* which was published by Image Comics. He has also worked on several issues of *Tales of the Teenage Mutant Ninja Turtles,* and getting to draw the Turtles was, of course, a childhood dream come true. dogmeatsausage.blogspot.com

Kazu Kibuishi is the editor and art director of the *Flight* comics anthology. He is also the writer and artist of the *Amulet* graphic novel series for Scholastic Publishing. His first graphic novel, *Daisy Kutter,* was chosen as a winner of the YALSA Best Books for Young Adults Award. His newest book, *Copper,* collects his long-running web comic into a single volume. He lives and works in Alhambra, California, along with his wife, Amy, and his son, Juni. www.boltcity.com

Kostas Kiriakakis is occasionally drawing pictures the way others tell him to, in exchange for food. Once sated, he falls back into his lifelong habit of drawing as he wishes, until he starves again. He found out fairly recently that drawing a bunch of pictures in a row gives you a whole new game to play with. He'd really like to play some more. www.kiriakakis.net

Stuart Livingston is a story artist and illustrator from Pago Pago, American Samoa. While creating this story, his first for *Flight,* he adopted a clever cat who plays fetch—quite well, in fact! He currently resides in Sherman Oaks, California, with the talented and lovely Stephanie Ramirez, whom he'd like to thank for the hundredth time for her help on his story. www.stuartlivingston.com www.rocketpigeon.net

Leland Myrick is the Ignatz and Harvey Award–nominated author and illustrator of *Missouri Boy, Bright Elegy,* and *The Sweet Collection.* His writing and illustrations have appeared in publications as diverse as First Second Books, Dark Horse Comics, *GQ* Japan, and *Vogue* Russia. He recently finished illustrating *Feynman!* for First Second Books. He lives in Pasadena, California. www.lelandmyrick.com

Dave Roman draws the web comic *Astronaut Elementary* (soon to be published by First Second) and has written several graphic novels, including *Agnes Quill: An Anthology of Mystery* and *Jax Epoch and the Quicken Forbidden.* He recently collaborated with his wife, Raina Telgemeier, on *X-Men: Misfits* and co-wrote *The Last Airbender* manga tie-ins. Dave is a co-founder of Life Meter Comics and was an editor for *Nickelodeon* magazine for eleven years. www.yaytime.com

Katie and **Steven Shanahan** are Toronto-based siblings sitting pretty in their mid-twenties. Katie has worked in TV animation for five years (currently as a storyboard artist), and in her spare time draws the goofy auto-bio web comic *Shrub Monkeys,* which can be read at Girlamatic.com. Steven has spent the past five years as a graphics compositor for television shows and makes YouTube videos on the side, under the guise of ShaggyShan. For more stuff from these two, take a gander at their websites! ktshy.blogspot.com www.youtube.com/user/ShaggyShan

Kean Soo is the author of the award-winning *Jellaby* series of graphic novels, published by Disney-Hyperion. Throughout the making of this particular *Flight* story, Kean was constantly craving sausage rolls. www.secretfriendsociety.com

Daniel Taylor works as an all-purpose pixel pusher at a small video game studio in Southern California, who never imagined he'd be working on both video games *and* comics.

Dean Trippe is the founder and editor of Project: Rooftop. And was a contributing artist to the Eisner and Harvey Award–winning comic book *Tattoo.* He is a former comic shop manager and a lifelong superhero fan, who has an actual degree in comics. www.deantrippe.com

Dermot Walshe has been making ends meet as a freelance artist in animation for over twenty years, and is an accomplished vintage motorcycle racer and a cappella harmony/barbershop singer! He currently lives in Oakville, Ontario, with his wife, Affee, and three wonderful daughters: Sara, Paige, and Lauren. Dermot likes frogs and turtles a lot. zoomfrog.blogspot.com

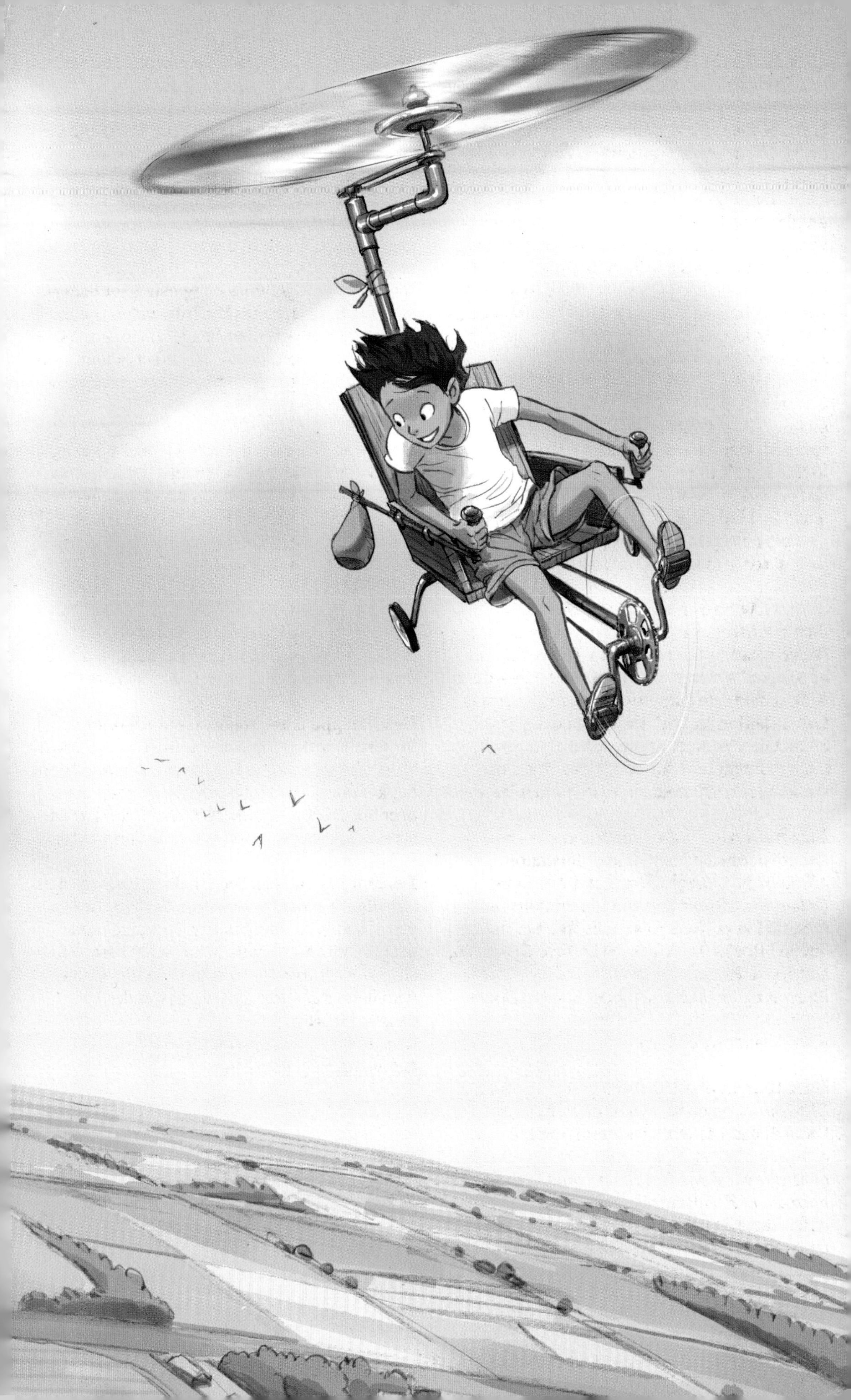

LET YOUR IMAGINATION TAKE FLIGHT!

Savor the work of today's top illustrators—
complete your FLIGHT library today.

Available from Villard Books everywhere books
or comics are sold